Linux System Security

ISBN 0-13-015807-0

Linux System Security

The Administrator's Guide to Open Source Security Tools

Scott Mann and
Ellen L. Mitchell

Prentice Hall PTR
Upper Saddle River, NJ 07458
www.phptr.com

Library of Congress Cataloging-in-Publication Data

Mann, Scott
  Linux system security: the administrator's guide to open source security tools / Scott Mann and
  Ellen L. Mitchell.
    p. cm.
  Includes bibliographical references and index.
  ISBN 0-13-015807-0

  1. Linux. 2. Operating systems (Computers). 3. Computer security. I. Mitchell, Ellen L. II.
  Title.
QA76.76.063 M3515 2000
005.8—dc21

                      99-059100
                        CIP

Editorial/production supervision: *BooksCraft, Inc., Indianapolis, IN*
Acquisitions editor: *Mary Franz*
Editorial assistant: *Noreen Regina*
Marketing manager: *Lisa Konzelmann*
Manufacturing manager: *Maura Goldstaub*
Cover design director: *Jerry Votta*
Cover designer: *Anthony Gemmellaro*
Project coordinator: *Anne Trowbridge*

© 2000 by Prentice Hall PTR
Prentice-Hall, Inc.
Upper Saddle River, NJ 07458

To my wonderful wife, Connie,
and our three beautiful children,
Melissa, Joshua, and Christiana.
—Scott

To my parents, Fred and Beverly Mitchell,
and to my sister, Sara.
—Ellen

Contents

Chapter 5

Been Cracked? Just Put PAM On It!

Chapter 9

Want to Be root?

Chapter 10

Which Doors Are Open?

Chapter 11 The Secure Shell 257

Let 'Em Sniff the Net!

Chapter 16   Packet Filtering with `ipchains` **435**

We Must
Censor!

Figures

Examples

Tables

Preface

This book exists because we need it! In many ways, we (well, Scott, anyway) wish someone else had written it so that we could have just read it. We have found that it is much easier to read than it is to write (unlike disk drives, however, it takes orders of magnitude longer to write than to read!)

This book provides an introduction to installing, configuring, and maintaining Linux systems from a security perspective. In fact, it is really an administrator's guide to implementing security and security tools on Linux (although much of what is discussed can easily apply to other UNIX variants). It isn't a definitive book about security (there aren't any), but we think it provides a reasonable starting point for preparing and maintaining secure systems. If you follow the procedures outlined in this book, you will certainly reduce your overall level of vulnerability, and you will have an early warning system that may be able to prevent the most serious of system and network breaches.

We really tried to avoid discussing topics that are covered well elsewhere. Subjects such as cryptography, security policies, Transmission Control Protocol/Internet Protocol (TCP/IP) networking, firewalls, and so on are well documented in other sources. We've noted resources for these topics at the end of each appropriate chapter and in Appendix A. We've also tried to provide similar resources for the many topics we did not have time to cover (publishers are *so* deadline intensive).

This book will not teach you how to break into systems, although some obvious tricks are described to heighten your awareness. Neither will this document describe the process of system and code auditing for vulnerability assessment—that task is left to people far more industrious than we are. Simply, this book will provide a framework—a foundation if you will—that will allow you to learn more and, hopefully, be as dynamic as the field of computer security itself.

ABOUT THIS BOOK

The intent of this book is to give you a process to follow (with whatever modifications you feel are appropriate) to better secure your computing environment. We also tried to write in such a way that each chapter could stand on its own. For those of you who are unfamiliar with implementing secure computing environments, you may well benefit from reading this book in its entirety and then using it as a reference. If you are *really* new to the subject of security, read *Practical UNIX and Internet Security*[1] or something similar first. Then read this book.

We have included instructions for compiling most of the utilities covered in this book. The reason behind such madness (mad, because those instructions will be out of date very quickly) is that, while there are resources that generically describe the procedure of building software, there are few that provide real-world examples. It has been our experience that very few new or junior system and network administrators have the experience necessary to fetch a publicly available tool, modify it appropriately, and successfully compile it. It is for those readers in particular that we have included these instructions. For those of you who don't need these instructions, just skip over them.

The first four chapters are overviews. We begin in Chapter 1 with a survey of vulnerabilities. Chapter 2 introduces the critical topic of security policies. Chapter 3 covers a wide range of topics from cryptography to networking to give us a framework for what follows. Chapter 4 provides a survey of user accounts, file permissions, and filesystem options as they relate to security.

Chapters 7 and 8 cover the topics of system accounting and system logging, respectively. A book about system security would not be complete without a discussion of these topics, which are very important in securing a system. Chapters 5, 6, and 9–17 are the heart of the book, providing a detailed look at utilizing the security capabilities of Linux and implementing publicly available tools to augment Linux security. Please be sure to learn about and utilize `tiger` (Chapter 13) and Tripwire (Chapter 14) before going live with any of the tools discussed elsewhere in the book. These two utilities will give you a high confidence level regarding the state of security of your systems, if used properly.

Chapter 18 shows how to implement all that is covered in the book. If you are in a hurry, you may want to read through this chapter early on in your study of this topic to get a sense of what needs to be done to provide a secure environment.

We sincerely hope you find this book as useful as we do!

Typographical Conventions

We use `courier` for Linux commands, daemons, flags, options, web sites, etc.

We use *`courier italic`* for variables that are replaced with values; for example, when you see *`hostname`* it means to replace the hostname variable with the actual host name.

---

1. Simson Garfinkel and Gene Spafford, *Practical UNIX and Internet Security*, 2d ed., Sebastopol, Calif., O'Reilly & Associates, Inc., 1996.

We use *courier bold italic* for hidden text such as passwords. For example

```
foghorn login: bjt
Password: foobiebletch
```

Here, *foobiebletch* is the password and will not actually appear on the screen.

Italic is used in the text for titles, such as book, chapter, and section titles. **Bold** and *italic* are used in the text for emphasis. Distinguishing between the use of *italic* is clear from the context.

ERRATA OR, MORE SIMPLY, BUGS

There will be those! While we tested everything presented in this book for accuracy on RedHat 5.2 and almost everything on Red Hat 6.0, there are undoubtedly mistakes in this text. If you find any, please e-mail them or any other comments you might have to us at

```
linux_upat@thekeyboard.com
```

We probably won't always answer, but we will post updates and corrections to

```
http://www.phptr.com/ptrbooks/ptr 0130158070.html
```

Please check the web site once in a while for new information.

ACKNOWLEDGMENTS FROM SCOTT MANN

Writing this book has been a remarkable journey. I have had the pleasure of meeting a number of people who have made a real difference in my life and have received a tremendous amount of support from friends and acquaintances. I would like, therefore, to acknowledge the following people.

Mary Franz is a really wonderful editor (well, senior editor actually, but I don't think she's very old). She put up with all my phone calls and silly questions. She even listened to my technical tangents when she probably had lots of other stuff to do. Thanks, Mary—I hope this book doesn't disappoint you.

Early on in the writing of this book, Mary put me in touch with Camille Trentacoste, a veritable compendium of knowledge relating to editing, writing, FrameMaker, and probably a host of other things. I learned more from Camille about FrameMaker in 10 minutes than I had in my previous 10 years of using that word processing software (OK, so I never read the manual). Thanks, Camille.

My thanks to Noreen Regina for taking care of all the reviews and always being so pleasant. Also, to all the folks at Prentice Hall who supported this project, thank you. I'm sure that there are many of you who I'll never know except through Mary's assurances of your efforts.

Radia Perlman provided a lot of support for this project. Her comments were invaluable and her enthusiasm for the book was tremendous. Radia's sage advice has made this a much better document. Todd O'Boyle provided enthusiastic support for the book as well as extremely useful comments. Todd caught a number of things that I would have easily overlooked. Tom Daniels likewise contributed his support and made a number of very useful comments. Thanks to you all!

Ellen L. Mitchell started out reviewing this book. She tested out many of the examples and pointed out numerous bugs. I roped her into helping me finish the book so that it would get out on time. She did it while working full time and on her Ph.D! Thanks, Ellen! This book wouldn't be what it is without you.

Sue Finnegan said to me one day, "You really ought to write a book." Next thing I know, I get a call from Mary Franz. Thanks, Sue, for getting this started and for all the years of friendship.

If there is one person who gets the credit for the idea of this book, it is Mark Wright. A consummate professional and unbelievably insightful man with an incredible amount of integrity. Thanks, Mark, for all your support and friendship.

A special thanks to Bruce Robb, whose legal advice was almost as valuable as his common sense.

My sincerest appreciation to Mike Cook, whose effusive enthusiasm for this project supported its successful completion. To Sharon Dean, who's support was always there.

I'd also like to thank my family for all their support. My parents Richard and Julie Mann, my sister Lisa, my mother-in-law Susie Cook, and most especially my wife Connie and our children, Melissa, Joshua, and Christiana. I think I can come out and play now, guys.

A special thanks goes to those who responded to my e-mails, newsgroup postings, etc. Particularly, thanks to Tom Dunigan for his tips on compiling CFS Version 1.4.0beta2; to Aniello Del Sorbo for the assistance with TCFS; to Rob Braun for his responses to my questions about `xinetd`. Thanks to Craig Metz for his information regarding OPIE. And a very special thank you to David A. Ranch for all his feedback about `ipchains`.

Last, but far from least, my sincerest appreciation to Anita Booker for her understanding and support in my completing this project while the pressure was on. Anita, I look forward to a long and mutually satisfying relationship.

ACKNOWLEDGMENTS FROM ELLEN L. MITCHELL

First of all, I would like to thank Scott Mann for giving me the opportunity to work on this project. It has been a lot of work, especially for him. I never heard him complain once. Scott, it has been a pleasure working with you.

Thank you to Noreen Regina at Prentice Hall, who worked hard to keep everything moving on time, and to everyone else involved that I never had the opportunity to meet.

E. Todd Atkins quickly answered my questions about `swatch`. Thanks again, Todd.

Special thanks to Douglas Lee Schales and David K. Hess, two of the original authors of `tiger`, who patiently answered my many questions and reviewed some of this material. I am grateful for their input and for their friendship.

Thanks finally to my friends and co-workers for their support and friendship.

How Did *That* Happen?

Vulnerability Survey

Late one night...

"Look! It's world exportable! All I have to do is get a valid user account," aB1_tR3kr (pronounced "able trekker") said aloud.

"What's world exportable?" asked p13b (pronounced "plebe"), between bites of chocolate donut.

"This home directory on windfall.naive.com."

"Windfall?" asked p13b.

"Yeah, it'll be our windfall in a moment!"

"What're ya gonna do?" queried p13b, trying to learn as much as possible.

"Well," smiled aB1_tR3kr, "if they are silly enough to allow NFS over the Internet, they probably aren't using a shadow file either."

"Shadow file?" Now p13b is really perplexed.

"Yeah. See, all I have to do is create a user account on my Linux box that matches one of theirs...yep, there's a user called joe." aB1_tR3kr typed rapidly away on the keyboard as p13b looked over his shoulder. "Now, I'll login here as joe, and whataya know, I've got Joe's home directory from windfall. naive.com!"

"Wow! That was easy!" p13b's thinking that this breaking into UNIX/ Linux systems is simple stuff.

"Now, lemme create the .rhosts file here, and then we'll login remotely." aB1_tR3kr continued with his running commentary as he worked. "OK! We're in as joe over there. Now, let's check the password file...whooooya! No shadow file! I'll just e-mail this password file back to myself, like so. Done!"

"So what good is that file? All the passwords are jumbled up," remarked `pl3b`.

"No problem, my wannabe friend. We'll just use Crack!" `aBl_tR3kr` smiled confidently. And another system fell into his clutches.

NOTE

> While this dialog is for illustrative purposes, it does represent a very serious exploit. It does not necessarily reflect a typical attack nor does it reveal all of the potential exploits associated with gaining unauthorized access to a user account. In particular, there are numerous methods available to gain root access once unprivileged access is obtained. We expressly discourage this type of activity; however, it is important to have a sense of the kinds of things that might occur in order to better prevent them. We do encourage the study of the various vulnerabilities in common use for preventative purposes. Further information about general system and network exploits are available in the references given in Appendix A.

WHAT HAPPENED?

This dialog poses a number of ill-configured services that allowed for unauthorized access to an Internet system. We will see that this is all too often the case as illustrated in Chapter 2.

The first problem with the system `windfall.naive.com` is the fact that user home directories are exported via the Network File System (NFS) to the world. This could have been prevented by setting access restrictions on the NFS resources (discussed in *Some Major Applications* on page 37 in Chapter 3), on the `portmap` utility (discussed in Chapter 10), through `ipchains` (discussed in Chapter 16), or preferably through a combination thereof (see Chapter 18).

Our happy cracker, `aBl_tR3kr`, also took advantage of the trusted host file, `.rhosts` in this case, to gain unauthorized access to the system. The use of the `.rhosts` file in the dialog allowed `aBl_tR3kr` to log in to `windfall.naive.com` as `joe` without a password. We will discuss such files and recommend against their use in Chapter 3. Then we will talk about how to securely replace them in Chapter 11.

The next problem with the system `windfall.naive.com` is that it doesn't use password shadowing (described in *Password Aging and the Shadow File* on page 61 in Chapter 4). In this case, the lack of password shadowing means that a world-readable file (`/etc/passwd`), including each user's hashed (sometimes referred to as "encrypted") password, is available to anyone who can access a valid user account, which `aBl_tR3kr` was able to do. If a shadow file had been in use, he wouldn't have been able to get a list of hashed passwords as easily because the shadow file is readable only by the root user.

While the hashed password cannot be used to log in, the Crack utility (discussed in detail in Chapter 12) may be used to guess the password based on the hashed password. And Crack is pretty good at what it does. You can't prevent the bad-guys from using Crack, but you can make it harder on them by using alternate hashing methods, as we will see in Chapter 5.

Other Cracker Activities

Once an intruder has gained access to an account, there are a variety of things the intruder might do. Among the things that such a malicious user will almost certainly do is create a back door to make returning easier. The intruder will also erase any evidence of his or her activity. There are all sorts of freely available utilities that make these tasks simple.

The purpose of this book is to provide ways to make it difficult to break in initially as well as to detect the evidence of the attack quickly. But you must not use this book, or any other books, as your *only* resource of information for this purpose. New vulnerabilities are identified all the time, and patches and fixes are generated in response. Also, full-disclosure sites (noted in *Full-Disclosure Resources* on page 9), e-mail lists, and newsgroups will provide additional details regarding the ever changing scene of computer security. Appendix A lists resources that will assist you in staying current.

SO, ARE YOU GOING TO SHOW US HOW TO BREAK INTO SYSTEMS?

No.

The purpose of the dialog at the beginning of this chapter is to illustrate the types of activities that occur all too frequently. The intent of this book is to provide you with skills, knowledge, and tools that will allow you to better prepare your systems for use in environments where you do not always know who is accessing what. The techniques and methods discussed are all from the perspective of restricting use to authorized access and making it as difficult as possible for crackers to gain unauthorized access.

This book is how-to oriented. This means that we will discuss the ways in which various utilities may be used to help protect your environment. What you should do in terms of implementing security at your site is largely left to other texts. While we make recommendations throughout this book, nothing can replace a good organizational Security Policy (discussed in Chapter 2). Also, we provide references at the end of each chapter if you wish to further investigate each topic we discuss. You will find that many of these references discuss the particulars of what ought to be done to maintain good security generally.

Before we get into the details of using publicly available tools to help secure your Linux[1] system(s), we will spend the rest of this chapter discussing

---

1. Most of what we discuss in this book is relevant to commercial UNIX platforms as well.

the types of vulnerabilities and attacks that are in common use today. We will not detail how they work; rather we will define their characteristics so that you have an understanding of what they are. You can also find additional information through the references cited in *For Further Reading* on page 7.

A Survey of Vulnerabilities and Attacks

We will consider vulnerabilities in three separate categories—technical, social, and physical. Attackers may attempt to exploit vulnerabilities in one or more of these categories.

Technical

There are many types of attacks against the technology we use in computing. Some of these attacks are perpetrated through a modification of a program or script or data, while others take advantage of the way a particular technology works. The following is a summary of common terms describing attacks that exploit various aspects of computing.

Trojan Horses.   Hidden program or script, usually embedded in an authorized program or script, that causes undesirable or unauthorized behavior when the authorized program or script is executed. A particularly nasty example of embedding a Trojan horse or back door in a C compiler is noted in *Trusting Trust*, pp. 801–802, of *Practical UNIX and Internet Security*. This type of exploit is rather difficult to prevent. Various sections of Chapter 3, describe ways to reduce the likelihood of this type of attack. In particular, verifying checksums and Pretty Good Privacy (PGP) signatures on files that contain them is described in Chapter 3 and revisited throughout this book.

Back Doors.   Hidden program, script, or funtionality embedded in a normal program or script, which ultimately allows unauthorized access to a system. Similar to Trojan horses.

Password Cracking.   Guessing passwords or utilizing a tool such as Crack to guess passwords. Mitigating password-related problems is discussed throughout this book, and particularly in Chapters 4, 5, 6, and 11.

File Permissions and `path` Settings.   Improper settings of either of these can cause systems to be compromised. Further discussion of this topic may be found in Chapter 4.

SUID Scripts and Programs.   Scripts or programs that run with the real or effective user identifier (UID) set to someone other than the user who invoked the script or program. Normally, the concern is with programs that set UID (SUID) to root. A large number of exploits which allow an unprivileged user to become root take advantage of this mechanism. Similar, though fewer exploits take advantage of set group identifier (SGID). We take a look at these issues in Chapter 4.

Trusted Hosts.   The use of trusted host files often permits an exploit of one system to spread throughout an entire network. (These files are discussed in Chapter 3.) We talk about replacement functionality for these files in Chapter 11.

Buffer Overflows.   Failure to bound a read buffer in a program may allow exploitation of the system by writing into the system memory allocated by the read buffer. While writing a program to take advantage of unbounded buffers is difficult and requires special skills, many programs written by such skilled folks are readily available on the Internet. We take a further look at mitigating these types of problems in the section *Software Testing* on page 48 in Chapter 3.

Scanning and Sniffing.   Network scanning may allow an attacker to identify the operating system (OS) running on a particular system as well as the network daemons available. Network sniffing may allow an attacker to obtain confidential information. Network scanning and sniffing is also very useful for security testing and debugging. We discuss some of the tools available for these purposes in Chapters 3 and 16. Ways of reducing the effects of attacks perpetrated with network scanners are discussed in Chapters 10 and 16. Methods to mitigate the effects of attacks using network sniffers are described in Chapters 11 and 15.

Spoofing.   A user pretending to be another user, a host another host, an Internet Protocol (IP) address another IP address,[2] a domain another domain or address—all are examples of spoofing. These types of attacks and reducing their likelihood are detailed in the books, *Hacker Proof* and *Maximum Security*, as cited in *For Further Reading* on page 7. We discuss ways of alleviating these types of attacks in Chapter 16.

TCP/IP Attacks.   Taking advantage of the way that Transmission Control Protocol (TCP) network connections work may lead to a variety of attacks. These types of attacks are quite difficult to prevent and detect. Many of the techniques we discuss in Chapters 10, 11, and 16 temper these attacks. However, you may also wish to consult *Hacker Proof* as cited in *For Further Reading* on page 7 for more details on TCP/IP attacks and what you can do to prevent them.

Session Hijacking.   Whenever a user assumes control of a network session or connection. A special case of TCP/IP desynchronization attacks. See *TCP/IP Attacks* above.

---

2. Well, it is spoofing if the bad-guys do it. We'll have a look at *masquerading* in Chapter 16.

Denial of Service.   Any activity which prevents the normal use of system and network resources is considered a denial of service (DoS). Generally speaking, you can make DoS attacks much more difficult for the perpetrator, but you cannot prevent them. In Chapter 10, we discuss the `xinetd` replacement to `inetd` which has the capability of preventing certain network-related DoS attacks.

Other Vulnerabilities.   There are a variety of vulnerabilities in various network and system applications. Some of them are discussed throughout this book. Your best resource for continuing information about vulnerabilities in many applications is by keeping up to date (see Appendix A). We also note some resources in the section, *For Further Reading* on page 7.

Social

The weakest link in any Security Policy (see Chapter 2) is the people who are authorized to use the computing environment. Those who deliberately attempt to compromise a computer environment by attacking this weakest link are engaged in what is called *social engineering*. Of all of the aspects of security, this one is the hardest to control. While this aspect of security is outside the scope of this book, we note a few of the common types of social engineering attacks and cite additional general security references in the section *Web Sites* on page 8.

Shoulder Surfing.   As its name implies, this is the process of capturing sensitive information, such as a user's password, by looking over someone's shoulder.

Manipulation.   This category of social engineering attacks is often employed to obtain sensitive information. Examples include pretending to be a system administrator or professing to be a high-level official of the organization in order to obtain sensitive information from unwary individuals within the organization.

Physical

It is often said that once physical security is compromised then the game is over. This statement reflects the fact that, if an unauthorized person gains physical access to some part of your computing environment, all the technical security solutions in the world cannot prevent such a person from perpetrating some form of attack. This topic is also not investigated in this book; however, we list a few potential vulnerabilities. A good reference site for this and social engineering security issues may be found at the home page of the International Information Systems Security Certification Consortium, Inc. [(ISC)^2, Inc.] as noted in the section *Web Sites* on page 8.

System Access. Once physical access to a computer has been gained, everything from booting the system in single-user mode (see *A Note about LILO* on page 22 for a discussion of restricting single-user-mode access) to simply taking the system becomes possible. Physically restricting access to your most critical systems is highly encouraged.

Networking Issues. Networks are commonly implemented over electrically based media, such as 10/100 base T, radio frequency (RF) communications, microwave technology, and satellite communications. All of these forms of communication may be intercepted through various tapping techniques.[3] The use of fiber-optic media substantially tempers this issue. See the (ISC)² home page, as referenced in the section *Web Sites* on page 8, for further information about this topic.

Other Physical Access Issues. There are a great many vulnerabilities associated with unauthorized physical access ranging from pulling a fire alarm to looting as a result of a natural disaster. Check out the (ISC)² home page, as referenced in *Web Sites* on page 8, for further information about this topic.

SUMMARY

This chapter provides an overview of a variety of different vulnerabilities and exploits as they relate to computers and networks. While not the focus of this book, this chapter motivates the requirement for securing systems, which *is* the focus of this book. We've provided numerous references for further study.

FOR FURTHER READING

Books

1. Anonymous, *Maximum Security: A Hacker's Guide to Protecting Your Internet Site and Network*, Indianapolis, Indiana, Sams.net Publishing, 1997.

2. Atkins, Derek, et al., *Internet Security: A Professional Reference*, Indianapolis, Indiana, New Riders Publishing, 1996.

3. Barret, Daniel J., *Bandits on the Information Superhighway*, Sebastopol, California, O'Reilly & Associates, Inc., 1996.

4. Chapman, D. Brent, and Elizabeth D. Zwicky, *Building Internet Firewalls*, Sebastopol, California, O'Reilly & Associates, Inc., 1995.

5. Cheswick, William R., and Steven M. Bellovin, *Firewalls and Internet Security: Repelling the Wily Hacker*, Reading, Massachusetts, Addison-Wesley Publishing Company, 1994.

---

3. Newt Gingrich found this out the hard way!

6. Cooper, Frederic J., et al., *Implementing Internet Security*, Indianapolis, Indiana, New Riders Publishing, 1995.

7. Denning, Dorothy E., *Information Warfare and Security*, New York, New York, Addison-Wesley, 1998.

8. Garfinkel, Simson, and Gene Spafford, *Practical UNIX and Internet Security*, 2d ed., Sebastopol, California, O'Reilly & Associates, Inc., 1996.

9. Garfinkel, Simson, and Gene Spafford, *Web Security & Commerce*, Sebastopol, California, O'Reilly & Associates, Inc., 1997.

10. Hughes, Larry Jr., *Actually Useful Internet Security Techniques*, Indianapolis, Indiana, New Riders Publishing, 1995.

11. Icove, David, et al., *Computer Crime: A Crimefighter's Handbook*, Sebastopol, California, O'Reilly & Associates, Inc., 1995.

12. Klander, Lars, *Hacker Proof: The Ultimate Guide to Network Security*, Las Vegas, Nevada, Jamsa Press, 1997.

13. Kyas, Othmar, *Internet Security Risk Analysis, Strategies and Firewalls*, London, England, International Thomson Computer Press, 1997.

14. Pabrai, Uday O., and Vijay K. Gurbani, *Internet and TCP/IP Network Security Securing Protocols and Applications*, New York, New York, McGraw-Hill, 1996.

15. Siyan, Karanjit, Ph.D., and Chris Hare, *Internet Firewalls and Network Security*, Indianapolis, Indiana, New Riders Publishing, 1995.

Interesting Cracker Tales

These references do not provide any technical details but do relate stories about (in)famous attacks.

1. Dreyfus, Suelette, *Underground Tales of Hacking, Madness, and Obsession on the Electronic Frontier*, Kew, Australia, Mandarin, 1997.

2. Littman, Jonathan, *The Watchman*, Boston, Massachusetts, Little, Brown and Company, 1997.

3. Shimomura, Tsutomu, with John Markoff, *Takedown*, New York, New York, Hyperion, 1996.

4. Stoll, Cliff, *The Cuckoo's Egg*, New York, New York, Pocket Books, 1990.

Web Sites

For information related to Domain Name Service (DNS), InterNetNews (INN), and Dynamic Host Configuration Protocol (DHCP), check out the home of the Internet Software Consortium (ISC),

```
http://www.isc.org/
```

The home of `sendmail`, a commonly used mail transfer agent (MTA), has lots of good information about `sendmail` related vulnerabilities:

```
http://www.sendmail.org/
```

For good general security information, links, and references, visit the Information Systems Security Association site,

```
http://www.issa-intl.org/
```

Professional certification in the field of security is available from $(ISC)^2$, Inc. This site also has information about technical, physical, personnel, and many other areas of security. Their home page is

```
http://www.isc2.org/
```

For an excellent collection of security tools and resources, visit the home of the Computer Operations, Audit, and Security Technology (COAST) site at

```
http://www.cs.purdue.edu/coast/
```

which also contains a great many links. Check them out!

Other good security sites include

```
http://www.fish.com/security/
ftp://ftp.porcupine.org/pub/security/index.html
```

Full-Disclosure Resources

The following web sites are considered full-disclosure sites because they publish details of various vulnerabilities and often offer code samples that exploit some of the vulnerabilities. The purpose of listing these sites here is to inform you about what the bad-guys already know.

```
http://www.insecure.org/
http://www.l0pht.com/
http://www.8lgm.org/
http://www.rootshell.com/
http://www.security-focus.com/
```

You will also find a list of underground sites at

```
http://www.cs.purdue.edu/coast/hotlist/
```

## CHAPTER 2

Imagine That! You're Big Brother!

Security Policies

The whole concept of security, from the perspective of the system and network administrator, is often so very foreign. Many of us simply do not think like a cracker or a cop. Our role is to keep the systems up, the applications going, the services networked, and the users happy.[1] Unfortunately, as exciting as technological advances in computing are, they have and will continue to transform the role of the system and network administrator to one that incorporates security concerns to a greater and greater degree.

Central processing units (CPUs) are faster and cheaper than ever, random access memory (RAM) is plentiful, and the Internet continues to grow. Furthermore, connections to the Internet are faster than ever. Connections like aDSL[2] and cable are affordable in many regions of the country; no longer are people limited to 56k modems. With the continuing increase in those who have access to computers and the Internet comes the increase of business and service activities that utilize that infrastructure. On-line stores, banking, and government services reflect just some of those activities. The proliferation of these services implies the potential for greater productivity as well as the potential for greater destruction.

---

1. Said one system administrator to another, "I had no idea that 'Users are Losers' bumper sticker was about drugs!"

2. Asymmetric Digital Subscriber Line. A telecommunications service offering a slow uplink (33–56Kbps, for example) and a high-speed downlink (3–6Mbps, for example).

With each new generation, the level of computer literacy among people increases and at earlier ages. Just think back to what you did when *you* were 16. Now, suppose that you were a fluent programmer and highly computer savvy at that age. Connect the dots.

As we noted in Chapter 1, programming skills aren't required for many exploits. All that is required is access to the Internet, particularly access to Internet sites (some of which are noted in Chapter 1) that post software designed to compromise computers, and basic knowledge of how to compile and install those utilities. The number of computer crackers is thereby increased.

Internet mischievousness is not the only concern. Each year, the Computer Security Institute (CSI), in conjunction with the Federal Bureau of Investigation (FBI), releases the Computer Crime and Security Survey.[3] The 1999 survey reported that, while 31% of the respondents experienced system penetration by outsiders over the course of a year, 97% of the respondents reported abuse of access by insiders and 55% reported unauthorized access by insiders. Furthermore, 86% reported that a likely source of attack came from disgruntled employees as compared to 53% reporting a domestic competitor as a likely source of attack. These statistics serve to remind us that we must be concerned about unauthorized access from the inside as well as the outside and that we must be careful about those whom we inherently trust as well as those we don't.

Given the increase in the number of people accessing the public Internet, the greater speeds at which access is obtained, the availability of cracker tools at large, and the tendency for insiders to abuse the access they have been granted, it is no wonder that the CSI/FBI survey also reports increases in attacks and compromises in their 1999 survey over previous years. And they expect the trend to continue.

In order to address these issues, it is imperative that any company that depends upon computer technology for ongoing business activities have a plan to protect its computing resources and the data contained therein. This plan is normally a part of a *Security Policy.* A Security Policy is a document that stipulates the rules for which a company's assets and data are to be configured, maintained, and used. It also identifies the relative value of the company's assets and data. It is a document that should change as the company's business needs, activities, and assets change.

This chapter does not serve as a thorough study of Security Policy development nor its precursive requirements (such as the *risk analysis*, described in the section *Risk Analysis* on page 14. For a thorough treatment of these topics, refer to the material listed in *For Further Reading* on page 18). Rather, it provides a high-level overview of these topics as they pertain to computing resources. Within that context, it also provides some rules of thumb that may

---

3. For the complete survey, see http://www.gocsi.com/.

be derived from a Security Policy. We begin with an overview of computer and network security.

WHAT IS COMPUTER AND NETWORK SECURITY?

One definition for security is a means to defend oneself. Computer and network security, therefore, may simply be defined as a means to defend computers and networks. This definition raises this question: against what or whom are we defending these resources and when is it necessary? This question does not have a simple answer and depends upon a variety of factors. Let's begin by categorizing what a computing environment is expected to provide.

Elements of a Computing Environment

We use the phrase *computing environment* generally to represent computers, networks, and their collective interaction. The functional requirements of a computing environment may be characterized by

☞ Reliability
☞ Integrity
☞ Confidentiality

A computing environment is considered completely *reliable* if it behaves in the way in which it was configured to behave at all times. Many factors contribute to a reduction in the reliability of a system. Examples include unscheduled downtime (due to hardware problems, power failures, etc.), inadvertent human activity (like accidentally rebooting a system or router), software bugs, and DoS attacks.

The *integrity* element of a computing environment is the correctness of the data in that environment. This concept incorporates application data and configuration data (password files, routing tables, DNS information, and the like). Integrity compromises occur as the result of—among other sources and activities—software bugs, accidental introduction of errors, and deliberate modifications of data.

Confidentiality represents the concept of making computing resources, especially the data contained therein, available only to authorized personnel. Confidentiality may be compromised through inadvertent software misconfiguration or the deliberate exploitation of the components of a computing environment designed to ensure confidentiality.

Thus, we may further define computer and network security as a means of defending the reliability, integrity, and confidentiality of a computing environment. This definition and the identified categories of reliability, integrity, and confidentiality provide a means to perform a series of analyses that generate information that is used to form a Security Policy.

Risk Analysis

A *risk analysis*, specifically as it pertains to computing resources, is a process of determining the potential fiscal cost of having one or more of the three elements (reliability, integrity, and confidentiality) of the computing environment degraded or compromised in comparison with the fiscal cost of implementing preventative measures, often referred to as *countermeasures*, to preclude degradations or compromises. Two major components of a risk analysis are a *vulnerability assessment* and a *threat assessment*.

A vulnerability assessment or *vulnerability analysis* involves identifying what could occur that would negatively affect the reliability, integrity, and/or confidentiality of the computing environment. A threat assessment or *threat analysis* is the process of identifying those who might want to negatively affect the reliability, integrity, and/or confidentiality of the computing environment. These assessments must also incorporate the value of computing resources and the likelihood of those resources being attacked. For example, a database server containing proprietary information is considerably more valuable and much more likely to be attacked than a guest user workstation which has no proprietary data and no access to the company's internal network.

The results of these analyses provide the information used in the first part of a risk analysis: the cost associated with the degradation or compromise of the computing environment and the likelihood or probability that such a loss will occur. Based on this first part of the risk analysis, countermeasures are identified and selected based on a comparison of the cost of a potential loss and the cost of implementing a risk-reducing countermeasure (this comprises the second part of the risk analysis). For example, if we assume, for simplicity, that the vulnerabilities associated with the previously mentioned database server and guest user workstation are identical, the countermeasures we implement for the database server are likely to be extensive, require administrative attention, and cost the company money. On the other hand, if we choose to implement countermeasures on the guest user workstation, they are unlikely to require a lot of attention or incur much cost.

A thorough risk analysis is a lengthy endeavor. Even in small companies, it may take months to complete. The result of the analysis, however, is extremely valuable as it provides the framework for the Security Policy.

The Security Policy

A Security Policy incorporates the results of a risk analysis into a plan that provides procedures for managing a computing environment. In particular, it gives the system administrator operating guidelines for the environment, such as rules for user account management, system installation procedures, communication procedures between system administrators, the use of security tools, procedures for handling unauthorized access, identification of critical systems, and, very important, a procedure for changing the Security Policy.

The effect of properly using the Security Policy is a consistent and predictable environment with the added benefit of making anomalies, such as break-ins or unauthorized access, easier to detect.

Do not underestimate the value of this document. It is the single most critical element to a secure computing environment. Of course, in order for this to be true, it must be well implemented and properly used. *For Further Reading* on page 18 lists very valuable resources that we recommend reading.

NOTE

> A derivative of the Security Policy that details the permitted use of an organization's assets is often called an Acceptable Use Policy (AUP).

SECURING COMPUTERS AND NETWORKS

This book details a variety of publicly available utilities for the express purpose of assisting you in securing your systems and networks. The use of these tools generally becomes less effective in the absence of well-thought-out procedures. Therefore we strongly recommend that, in the absence of a formal Security Policy, you formulate a plan for securing your computing resources as a part of your overall security program. References noted in *For Further Reading* on page 18 will greatly assist you in that process.

The following rules of thumb will serve as the guidelines used throughout this book. It will give us the framework we need for the purposes of describing and implementing the various tools. It may also be useful to you in sketching out a philosophy to live by with respect to your computing environment. If your organization has a Security Policy, be sure to modify these rules in accordance with that policy.

You are not invulnerable!   There is no way to completely secure any system. If it is powered on and connected to a network, regardless of the security precautions taken, it is vulnerable, and it may ultimately make other systems on the network vulnerable. Always assume that you have not identified all the vulnerabilities and threats; then be vigilant and persevere in your efforts to further secure the environment.

People are the weakest link.   If an employee of a company has access to computing resources as part of his or her job, then he or she has information that may be valuable to someone who would like to compromise that computing environment. Here are some simple examples of how information may be compromised.

☞ Hard-to-guess passwords are also often hard to remember, so people write them down.

☞ Casual conversations may reveal valuable information about the computing environment.

☞ Social engineering, or manipulative behavior by attackers, may ultimately lead to the compromise of computing resources. For example, a bad-guy posing as an authority figure of the company may coerce a naive user to disclose sensitive information. Another example might be that a bad-guy, posing as a user, coerces a naive system administrator to give out a password over the telephone.

☞ Unhappy employees represent a significant source of threat. This is a particularly acute threat if the disgruntled employee is an administrator and has root access or is in a position to access sensitive or proprietary information.

An organization's best defense against these types of vulnerabilities and threats is training, awareness activities, and violation enforcement. Through training, users are made aware of the AUP and their responsibilities associated with access to the organization's assets. An organization's security group can heighten security awareness by, for example, posting signs to remind users of the most pertinent elements of the Security Policy and generating regular communications reminding employees of their responsibilities and informing them of Security Policy changes. Violations of the rules specified in the Security Policy must be enforced; otherwise employees may ignore those rules, especially the most inconvenient ones.

The role of the system and network administrator in these efforts is largely supportive, but nonetheless critical. For example, an administrator does have the capability of monitoring user activity and, by being thoroughly familiar with the AUP, can identify unauthorized activity and subsequently report such activity to the appropriate security personnel.

That which is not expressly permitted is forbidden.   Adopting this philosophy as part of your overall security practice makes securing systems easier because you will have a list of services that are permitted—all else is denied. This philosophy also makes the incorporation of an AUP simpler since it will stipulate those activities in which users are permitted to engage. Anything else is not allowed. This approach also makes it easier to detect misuse—such activity will stand out like a sore thumb.

Certain organizations cannot adopt this philosophy because of the nature of their business model (colleges and universities, for example, often have networks of systems that are implemented with the opposite philosophy—that which is not expressly forbidden is permitted). If this is your situation, your role in securing such systems becomes more difficult because you will not be able to close a wide variety of vulnerabilities. In such a scenario, the best approach is to separate those networks that must incorporate more freedom from the ones that contain sensitive data and/or activity. This may be accomplished through the use of firewalls or by completely disconnecting the networks.

Implementing this philosophy technically may be fairly simple, but getting people to adopt it is often not an easy task.

Always assume the bad-guy knows more than you do. In short, don't let your guard down.

It is a full time job to keep up to date with the various *published* exploits (see Appendix A), let alone those that are not yet published. Additionally, information that you may consider secret is often compromised through various means including those identified in the section, *People are the weakest link* on page 15.

Practice vigilance and perseverance. Be ever watchful of the activity in your environment. Whenever something unusual is identified, track down the cause. As vulnerabilities and threats are identified, wherever possible close the vulnerabilities and mitigate the likelihood of threats.

One of the best resources for vigilantly monitoring your environment is your log files. Log files and their management are discussed throughout this book. Reviewing these files will inform you as to what occurred and perhaps who was responsible. It may also identify vulnerabilities and/or threats. Acting on this information to persist in the reduction of vulnerabilities and threats is almost always an entirely human process.

Always thoroughly investigate any publicly available software you decide to use. One of the major benefits of publicly available software is that the source code is *publicly available*. Although you may not be able to audit the code or set up a test environment, many other people will. These folks often report their findings to the software authors, maintainers, and/or e-mail lists such as bugtraq.

So, always check for vulnerabilities and the PGP signature (see Chapter 3 for an overview of PGP) of anything you download. If one or the other or both of these is unavailable, audit the source code (if you can) and/or set it up in a safe environment and use it for a while to see what happens.

With few exceptions, the implementation of any security measure will reduce either system and network performance or user convenience or both. While this statement, in and of itself, does not necessarily directly impact the security of your environment, it may well be that users, especially those who contribute directly to the profitability of the company, have a great deal of influence in the way in which a computing environment is configured. If people view certain security measures as causing them to be less productive, reduced security will be the result.

Plan for change. Your Security Policy must have a mechanism that permits change. The computer industry is very dynamic—hardware changes, software changes, and vulnerabilities change. Make sure that your policy is designed to change with this very active field.

User Privacy and Administrator Ethics

Another aspect to securing computing resources involves the privacy of the users who have access to that environment and the ethics, or moral standards, employed by those controlling the environment. Much of what has been discussed in this chapter revolves around the monitoring of user activity. Indeed, this topic is carried throughout this book. There is a line between reasonable monitoring activity and invasion of user privacy. The monitoring of e-mail or capturing of keystrokes, for example, is normally considered an extreme action. Such activity should be undertaken only when absolutely necessary and with the full consent of management and legal counsel. Even if your organization's policy is such that the company's computing resources are not to be used for private purposes, there are a variety of circumstances under which the computing resources may be used for private communications. For example, managers often write and store employee performance evaluations on computers. These evaluations may be exchanged between employees and managers via e-mail. Excessive monitoring could lead to litigation, ultimately costing the company far more than the assets it seeks to protect.

The Security Policy must address these issues and may even include a code of ethics for system and network administrators. As you embark on the process of securing your computing resources, remember to consider the impact your actions in this regard have on the rights and privacy of those using the resources.

Summary

In this chapter we provided an overview of the preparation of a Security Policy and emphasized its importance. We provided a framework for implementing that policy and closed by noting the very important issue of ethical security administration.

For Further Reading

Books

Both of the reference books below describe risk assessment and Security Policy creation.

1. Neumann, Peter G., *Computer Related Risks,* Reading, Massachusetts, Addison-Wesley Publishing Company, 1995.
2. White, Gregory B., Eric A. Fisch, and Udo W. Pooch, *Computer System and Network Security,* Boca Raton, Florida, CRC Press, 1996.

Web Resources

You will find an excellent collection of Security Policy templates and related information at `http://www.sans.org/newlook/resources/policies/policies.html`—this is an excellent starting point for developing a Security Policy. For related information, also visit

```
http://ciac.llnl.gov/cgi-bin/index/documents/
http://www.cert.org/nav/
```

Other Resources

A very thorough reference and a must read for anyone concerned with the security of computing resources.

1. Fraser, B., *RFC2196: Site Security Handbook*, September 1997. Available at `http://www.faqs.org/rfcs/rfc2196.html`.

This 'n That

Background Information

Before we embark on our journey through the world of publicly available tools, there are a few concepts and utilities that we must discuss initially since we will be referring to them throughout the book. We will cover the following topics in this chapter, each of which has its own section.

- ☞ Basic Input/Output System (BIOS) Passwords
- ☞ Linux Installation and the Linux Loader (LILO)
- ☞ Start-up scripts
- ☞ Red Hat Package Manager (RPM)
- ☞ TCP/IP networking overview
- ☞ Request for Comment (RFC)
- ☞ Cryptography
- ☞ Testing and production environments
- ☞ Public licenses

Each of these topics is presented in various levels of detail, but none definitively. Thus, we provide additional reading material pointers within or at the end of each section.

BIOS PASSWORDS

Many modern PCs support the setting of a password in the BIOS. If your system provides this feature, we recommend that you take advantage of this feature unless your system is physically secure. Check your system documentation for more details about BIOS passwords.

LINUX INSTALLATION AND LILO

With the advent of wizard-like, X Window System driven Linux installation, it is easy to just point and click your way to a running Linux system. However, convenience is often a security impediment. Before installing your Linux system, decide which packages and services you need. In particular, do not run services you do not need. For example, suppose that you access your e-mail through a Post Office Protocol (POP) or Internet Message Access Protocol (IMAP)[1] server (such as through an Independent Service Provider [ISP]), then you do not want to run `sendmail`. By default, `sendmail` will be installed and started at each boot, which is not desirable if you are not using it. After installing, you may disable services manually, as described in the section *Start-Up Scripts* on page 24, or through the Red Hat Control Panel, Run Level Editor.

A Note about LILO

The Linux Loader is a flexible boot loader for Linux and other operating systems (such as DOS, Windows 95/98/NT, and various flavors of UNIX). It does not depend on a particular filesystem and can manage booting from a variety of devices (floppy, hard drive, CD-ROM, etc.). Put simply, LILO's job is to boot the selected operating system. If Linux is selected, it starts the Linux kernel (`/boot/vmlinuz` or similar). There are other boot loaders, but LILO has become the most common one for Intel platforms. By default, LILO will be configured on your system when you install Red Hat.

LILO reads the `/etc/lilo.conf` configuration file at boot time. By default, this file will be world readable. You should set the permissions on this file to read/write by root only. Also, consider setting the immutable bit (see *File Attributes* on page 75 of Chapter 4 for a discussion of `chattr` and the immutable bit) on this file. These two steps are shown in Example 3-1.

Example 3-1 Setting Secure Permissions and Attributes on `/etc/lilo.conf`

```
# chmod 600 /etc/lilo.conf
# chattr +i /etc/lilo.conf
```

There are a variety of things that you can do with this file, many of which are discussed in the resources provided in *Installation and LILO Resources* on

---

1. POP, IMAP, and `sendmail` provide mail services to clients, such as `/bin/mail`.

page 24. One capability provided by /etc/lilo.conf is to require a password whenever you boot into single-user mode. An illustrative /etc/lilo.conf file is provided in Example 3-2.

Example 3-2 Sample /etc/lilo.conf File

```
boot=/dev/hda
map=/boot/map
install=/boot/boot.b
prompt
linear
timeout=50
restricted
password=L3t_m3_1n
image=/boot/vmlinuz-2.0.36-0.7
        label=linux
        root=/dev/hda1
        read-only
image=/boot/vmlinuz.test
        label=test
        root=/dev/hda1
        read-only
```

Note that the password in Example 3-2 is cleartext, hence the steps outlined in Example 3-1. After you have modified /etc/lilo.conf, you **must** execute /sbin/lilo in order for the changes to take effect.

The reason that you want to do this is because booting into single-user mode puts the invoking user into a root shell without requiring a password. Putting the system into single-user mode is accomplished by executing linux single at the LILO: or boot: prompt, as shown in Example 3-3. Notice the password requirement.

Example 3-3 Booting into Single-User Mode

```
LILO: <tab>
linux test
boot: linux single
Password:L3t_m3_1n
Loading linux......
```

In Example 3-3, there are two choices for booting, linux or test. In this case, linux is a stable kernel and test is a kernel under development; thus we could also have entered test single to invoke the development kernel in single-user mode. The argument single is not processed by LILO; rather it is passed to the kernel for processing. For further and extensively detailed information about LILO, see the LILO related references in the section *Installation and LILO Resources* on page 24.

While the steps outlined in the previous paragraphs will impose a password whenever someone boots into single-user mode, it will not prevent someone from rebooting the machine. To restrict such activity, most modern PCs will allow you to specify a password in the BIOS. Also, you may restrict the boot device in most PC BIOSs. Set the boot device to the C drive and the system will not boot from either the floppy or the CD-ROM.

Recovering a Corrupt System

There may be times when you need to recover from a corrupt or misconfigured system. Under circumstances such as when the system boots but you can't log in, you will likely be able to recover by simply booting into single-user mode (remember your password, if you have taken the steps outlined in *A Note about LILO* on page 22) and correcting the problem. In other circumstances, you will need to boot an uncorrupted kernel, which may be on a floppy or series of floppies. The process of creating the necessary floppies for getting the system to a point where you can access the disk (called *rescue mode*) may be found on the Red Hat 5.2/6.0 CD (or image if you use ftp) in /doc/rescue.txt.

Installation and LILO Resources

An excellent resource is the *LILO User's Guide* which may be found in /usr/doc/lilo*. Other lilo documentation includes

```
/usr/doc/HOWTO/mini/LILO
/usr/doc/HOWTO/mini/Multiboot-with-LILO
/usr/doc/HOWTO/BootPrompt-HOWTO
```

If these resources are not on your system, it is likely because the howto-5.2-2.src.rpm (Red Hat 5.2) or howto-6.0-4.src.rpm (Red Hat 6.0) packages (see *Red Hat Package Manager* on page 26 for more information regarding RPM packages) are not loaded. If you cannot or do not wish to load these or other documentation packages, there are some excellent web resources. The latest documentation regarding most of the Linux components may be found at

```
http://metalab.unc.edu/LDP/
```

and documentation specific to the Red Hat distribution may be found at

```
http://www.redhat.com/support/
```

START-UP SCRIPTS

The last step in the kernel boot sequence (invoked by LILO or other boot loader is to start the process /sbin/init. The init process reads the configuration file, /etc/inittab, which informs init as to which processes to start and which *run level* to achieve. A system's run level describes the state of the system based on the processes that are running. Run levels are given as integers ranging from 0 to 9 inclusive and s or S (synonyms for single-user mode). By default, run levels 7, 8, and 9 are not configured. The processes which are started and/or stopped for a particular run level are determined by the directions in the /etc/inittab file and the start-up scripts found in the `/etc/rc.d/rcN.d` directory, where *N* may be any one of the integers 0 through 9 inclusive. Thus it is these start-up (often referred to as start/stop or start/kill) scripts that define a run level.

You may change run levels by executing `init` *N*, where *N* is any one of the integers 0 through 9 inclusive, or s, or S. If the run level is not defined, `init` simply exits. You may determine the system's current run level by executing the `/sbin/runlevel` command.

Additional information about `init` and `runlevel` are available in the `init(8)` and `runlevel(8)` `man` pages. For more complete details related to this topic, check out the books

1. Hein, Jochen, *Linux Companion for System Administrators*, Harlow, England, Addison Wesley Longman Limited, 1999.

2. Komarinski, Mark F., and Cary Collett, *Linux System Administrator's Handbook*, Upper Saddle River, New Jersey, Prentice Hall PTR, 1998.

or other similar resources.

We will refer to start-up scripts at various points in this book. Here, we will provide a brief description of the structure, common use, and manipulation of start-up scripts.

By default, all of the start-up scripts except for `/etc/rc.d/rc.local` are located in the directory `/etc/rc.d/init.d`. The scripts found in the `/etc/rc.d/rcN.d` directories previously mentioned are symbolic links (refer to the `ln(1)` `man` page for information about symbolic links) to the entries in `/etc/rc.d/init.d`. Each script in `/etc/rc.d/init.d` may accept a number of arguments, but minimally will accept the two arguments: `start` and `stop`. When a script is executed with the `start` argument, then the process or processes controlled by that script will be started. Given the `stop` argument, then the process or processes will be terminated.

For example, the script `/etc/rc.d/init.d/lpd`, which controls the `/usr/sbin/lpd` daemon, is symbolically linked to by the scripts shown in Example 3-4. The scripts in Example 3-4 are normally only invoked through `init`. When invoked by `init`, the scripts whose names begin with K will cause `/etc/rc.d/init.d/lpd` to be invoked with the `stop` argument and those beginning with S will cause `/etc/rc.d/init.d/lpd` to be invoked with the `start` argument. The number 60 is used to determine the invocation order with respect to other scripts in the same directory that the `lpd` script is in.

Example 3-4 Symbolic Links to `/usr/sbin/lpd`

```
/etc/rc.d/rc0.d/K60lpd
/etc/rc.d/rc1.d/K60lpd
/etc/rc.d/rc2.d/S60lpd
/etc/rc.d/rc3.d/S60lpd
/etc/rc.d/rc4.d/S60lpd
/etc/rc.d/rc5.d/S60lpd
/etc/rc.d/rc6.d/K60lpd
```

Since all of the start-up scripts invoked by init are symbolic links to those scripts in /etc/rc.d/init.d, when we need to make changes we need to modify only those in /etc/rc.d/init.d. Whenever you wish to add a start-up script, put the script in /etc/rc.d/init.d and then create appropriate s* and κ* symbolic links in the various /etc/rc.d/rcN.d (replace N with the appropriate number) directories. To disable functionality, say sendmail, you may remove or rename the symbolic links pointing to the sendmail start-up script, /etc/rc.d/init.d/sendmail.

The one exception to this structure is /etc/rc.d/rc.local. This file is symbolically linked to by s99local in /etc/rc.d/rc2.d, /etc/rc.d/rc3.d, and /etc/rc.d/rc5.d by default. It is the last script invoked when the system enters run level 2, 3, or 5.

If this is your first look at run levels, it would be well worth your time to read the reference material noted in this section.

RED HAT PACKAGE MANAGER

The Red Hat Package Manager (RPM) is the software that manages the *packages* on your Linux system. A package is a collection of related files that ordinarily provides a functional component of software (we say ordinarily because sometimes a package depends on other packages). RPM allows you to add, remove, build, query, and verify packages. Documentation for RPM is quite extensive, and the primary resources are listed in *RPM Resources* on page 28. In this section, we will discuss a few RPM commands that we will revisit at various points in this book.

Verifying Packages with RPM

RPM allows you to verify your installed packages and files. It can check each file's size (S), permissions or mode (M), the MD5 hash (5—see *Hash Functions and Digital Signatures* on page 44 for more information about MD5), major and minor numbers (D), symbolic link contents (L), owner (U), group (G), and modification time (T). It will also tell you if the file is a configuration file (c). It performs these checks against the originally installed configuration contained in the RPM database (a collection of files in /var/lib/rpm). Files and packages may be verified using the -v option. For example, we can verify /etc/exports and all of the files in the package that contain /etc/exports with

```
# rpm -Vf /etc/exports
S.5....T c /etc/exports
S.5....T c /etc/hosts.allow
S.5....T c /etc/hosts.deny
S.5....T c /etc/printcap
S.5....T c /etc/services
S.5....T c /etc/exports
#
```

Note that the f option specifies that the argument is a file. The output reflects the fact that the verification failed. Each file's size, MD5 hash, and modification time are different than they were originally. This is no big deal, since each of these files is a configuration file (note the "c") and is likely to change.

If a verification passes, there is no output. For example

```
# rpm -Vf /sbin/ifconfig
#
```

indicates that /sbin/ifconfig and all other files in the package containing /sbin/ifconfig have not changed since installation.

You may also verify installed packages against the CD. For example, insert the Red Hat distribution CD into your CD-ROM drive and

```
# mount /mnt/cdrom
# rpm -Vp /mnt/cdrom/RedHat/RPMS/bash-1.14.7-13.i386.rpm
#
```

which verifies that the package, bash-1.14.7-13, loaded on your system matches the one found on the CD.

This capability can assist you in improving your security by verifying the integrity of your packages. See *Maximum RPM* in the section, *RPM Resources* on page 28, for further details.

Checking PGP Signatures with RPM

Some RPM packages will incorporate PGP signatures (PGP is discussed in *An Overview of PGP* on page 45). If you obtain such an RPM, you may verify the signature with the -K flag. For example, we verify the signature on a Secure Shell (SSH) RPM.

```
# rpm -K ssh-1_2_26-1us_i386.rpm
ssh-1_2_26-1us_i386.rpm: size pgp md5 OK
#
```

Note that the MD5 hash is also verified. If we would like more verbose output, we can add the -v option as in

```
# rpm -Kv ssh-1_2_26-1us_i386.rpm
ssh-1_2_26-1us_i386.rpm:
Header+Archive size OK: 172248 bytes
Good signature from user "Jan "Yenya" Kasprzak <kas@fi.muni.cz>".
Signature made 1998/07/11 18:13 GMT using 1024-bit key, key ID
D3498839

WARNING: Because this public key is not certified with a trusted
signature, it is not known with high confidence that this public key
actually belongs to: "Jan "Yenya" Kasprzak <kas@fi.muni.cz>".
MD5 sum OK: ebf641babe96926bd4c9f9d9cfbba171
#
```

If you are missing the public key required to verify a signature, RPM will tell you; for example

```
# rpm -K sudo-1_5_7p4-1_src.rpm
sudo-1_5_7p4-1_src.rpm: size (PGP) md5 OK (MISSING KEYS:
PGP#396D16C1)
#
```

Now you have to go off and find the public key. See *An Overview of PGP* on page 45.

RPM Resources

Unfortunately, at the time of this writing, RPM version 3.0.x is in common use (Red Hat 6.0 incorporates RPM version 3.0.1), but most of the documentation relates to RPM version 2.5.x. Since there are numerous differences, this is somewhat problematic. The RPM 2.5.x documentation is still quite useful, but there are a number of issues which require careful review of the changes. So we have broken out the documentation into two sections, identified by version. Also, join the RPM mailing list, as noted below, for more resources. Despite the fact that it is dated, *Maximum RPM* is the definitive guide to RPM and we highly recommend it.

Version 2.5.x

On-Line:

/usr/doc/HOWTO/RPM-HOWTO

Book:

3. Bailey, Edward C., *Maximum RPM*, Indianapolis, Indiana, redhat press, 1997.

Maximum RPM is also available via the Internet at,

http://www.redhat.com/knowledgebase/rhlinuxdocs.html

Version 3.0.x

You will find a number of documents in the directory on Red Hat 6.0:

/usr/doc/rpm-3.0.1/

RPM Mailing List

You may join the RPM mailing list by sending an e-mail to rpm-list-request@redhat.com with subscribe in the body of the e-mail. Subsequently, you may communicate to the list by sending e-mail to rpm-list@redhat.com. This is an excellent list and we strongly encourage your participation.

TCP/IP NETWORKING OVERVIEW

Let's start with a few definitions. A networking *model* reflects a design or architecture to accomplish communication between different systems. A networking

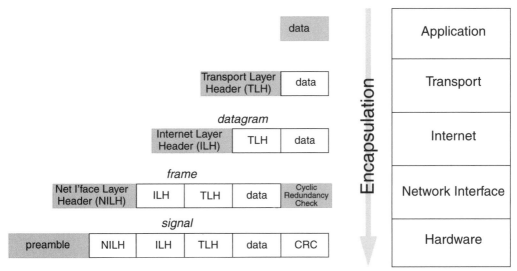

Fig. 3.1 The TCP/IP Model

model usually consists of *layers*. Each layer of a model represents specific functionality. Within the layers of a model, there are usually *protocols* specified to implement specific tasks. You may think of a protocol as a set of rules or a language. A layer is normally a collection of protocols.

The TCP/IP networking model takes its name from two of its protocols, TCP (the Transmission Control Protocol which lives in the Transport layer) and IP (the Internet Protocol which lives in the Internet layer). Figure 3.1 provides a five-layer[2] representation of the TCP/IP model.

The middle three layers of the model represent functionality performed internally by the kernel. The Application layer includes commands and daemons. The Hardware layer is comprised of hardware components.

The process of initiating a network communication, like executing `telnet` `hostname`, causes the initiator (usually the *client*) to *encapsulate* application data, beginning at the top of the model and moving down, for the network transmission. In other words, each layer encapsulates the application data with information used to determine where the packet is supposed to go and which service needs to be invoked to handle the data itself. The receiving system, normally the *server*, performs the same steps except in reverse (bottom to top), *deencapsulating* the data.

On the left-hand side of Figure 3.1, you see an increasing number of rectangles as you scan down the layers. The area in gray represents the information added to the growing *packet* by each layer to the right. In the following

---

2. Many texts will use a four-layer representation, combining the Hardware and Network Interface layers.

sections, we will briefly review the information generated by each layer and its purpose.

The TCP/IP Model Layers

The Hardware Layer   The Hardware layer is responsible for exactly that. Hardware. This includes cables, interface cards, and repeaters. It accepts the data passed to it by the Network Interface layer and prefixes the *preamble*, which is a well-known sequence of 64 bits used for synchronization purposes. After prefixing the preamble, it generates a *signal* to be submitted to the media (electrically based cables in most cases). The Hardware layer also imposes the maximum transfer unit (MTU), which is used by the Internet layer to ensure that the Hardware layer does not get *frames*[3] that are too large or too small. For Ethernet, the MTU for the frame is 1518 octets, and the minimum frame size is 64 octets.

There are two hardware devices that operate at this layer: repeaters and amplifiers. A repeater is a device with a number of ports (usually four or more) that is capable of receiving signals, filtering out noise (phenomena not related to the communication at hand), and repeating the signals to every port except the ingress (incoming) port. Amplifiers perform the same task, except that they do not filter noise. Consequently, we find repeaters in environments using electrical communications and amplifiers in environments using light-based communications. These devices are also often called *hubs* or *concentrators*.

The Network Interface Layer   You may think of the Network Interface layer as a collection of device drivers. Its responsibility is to prepare the data passed to it from the Internet layer for signalling. It does this by prefixing its header (indicated as NILH in Figure 3.1), computing a cyclic redundancy check (CRC—a 32-bit checksum), appending the CRC to the datagram, and passing this information to the device (interface) for signalling in a frame. In particular, this layer understands *physical* addresses (often referred to as media access control [MAC] addresses). When using Ethernet, this is often called an *Ethernet* address. Physical addresses are local and need to be unique only within a *local network* (defined in the section, *The Internet Layer* on page 32). For Ethernet interface chipsets, they are 48-bit addresses permanently written into programmable read only memory (PROM).

The Network Interface layer writes both the destination and source physical address into its header. Consequently, it is at this layer that initial decisions are made about whether or not to continue processing an incoming packet up the stack (deencapsulate). When generating a frame, the Network

---

3. The output of the Network Interface layer is called a *frame* when such output varies in size. More formally, when using Ethernet, it should be called an *Ethernet frame*. Fixed-size output, such as that produced by asynchronous transfer mode (ATM), is called a *cell*.

Interface layer obtains the destination physical address through the Address Resolution Protocol (ARP). This internal kernel function uses special packets to query a remote interface of a host so that it can obtain the physical address associated with that interface. It stores the collection of pairs of remote interface Internet Protocol addresses and physical addresses in the `arp` table. The contents of this table may be viewed with the `arp -a` command. For further information about this command see the `arp man` page and the references cited in *General TCP/IP Networking Resources* on page 39.

NOTE

Ethernet implements a shared media mechanism for communication. This means that all interfaces attached to the same communications medium will read all of the signals. Normally, the decision by a receiving system to process the packet is made by inspecting the destination physical address. If that address is one that the system is configured to process—such as its own physical address, a broadcast physical address, or a multicast address—it will pass the packet up the stack; otherwise it will destroy the packet. However, since the packet is initially read by the interface regardless of the destination, a packet-sniffing program, such as `tcpdump`, `sniffit`, `snoop`, or `etherfind` can capture the packet and record this information to a terminal or file. This is how your root passwords get sniffed! Such tools have enormous debugging value and, as it turns out, security implications. Tools of this type are discussed in *Network Monitoring* on page 38.

There is one device associated with this layer. It is a *bridge* or a *switch* (we'll use the term switch). This device looks very much like a repeater—a piece of hardware with at least two network ports—but it is more intelligent than a repeater. Since it operates at the Network Interface layer, it is able to examine the destination physical address of each packet. Given the destination physical address, the switch will determine a port, based on a table of addresses it associates with each port, to which the packet needs to be forwarded. Figure 3.2 shows the differences between a repeater and a switch when a packet is sent from host A to host D.

There are significant security advantages in using switches rather than repeaters. Since the switch forwards packets only to the destination port, only the systems that share the same port have access to the network packets. In the case of repeaters, all systems have access to all the traffic on the

Fig. 3.2 Difference between a Repeater and a Switch

cables. As described in the note on page 31, packet sniffers may be used to capture all packets received on an interface regardless of the destination address. The value, therefore, of a switch is that it forwards packets only to pertinent ports. Therefore, there is less traffic to sniff. It turns out that less traffic is good for performance as well! Switches are perhaps the only thing that will improve both performance and security. Normally, security enhancements result in performance degradations (or user inconvenience, which most users will assert is identical to a performance degradation). For further information about the Network Interface layer (also referred to as layer 2) technologies, see the references cited in the section, *Layer 2 Related Books* on page 39.

The Internet Layer   The Internet layer is responsible for a variety of tasks. In order to accomplish these tasks it uses three principal protocols: the Internet Protocol (IP), the Internet Control Messaging Protocol (ICMP), and the Internet Group Management Protocol (IGMP). There are currently two versions of IP in use—IPv4 and IPv6. The fundamental difference between the two is that IPv4 implements 32-bit addresses while IPv6 implements 128-bit addresses. Also, IPv4 and IPv6 generate incompatible headers. See *IPv6: The New Internet Protocol* in *General TCP/IP Networking Resources* on page 39 for further details.

The IP is responsible for *routing* and *fragmentation*.[4] Routing is the process of moving packets from one point to another. Fragmentation is the process of breaking up packets so that they do not exceed the MTU. The ICMP generates error messages, assists routing through redirection, may implement rudimentary flow control, supports the `ping` command, supports router discovery, and may generate timestamp and netmask queries and responses. The IGMP supports Internet layer multicasting.

There are many details related to the Internet layer, and you should be comfortable with them. This is particularly true for the discussions in Chapter 16, in which various elements of the Internet layer header, routing, fragmentation, and sub-networking are discussed. Take advantage of the resources listed in *General TCP/IP Networking Resources* on page 39.

The Transport Layer   The Transport layer is responsible for the end-to-end flow of data. There are two distinct protocols used within this layer—the Transmission Control Protocol (TCP) and the User Datagram Protocol (UDP). If you are not familiar with these protocols, please read *TCP/IP Network Administration* and refer to some of the other references cited in *General TCP/IP Networking Resources* on page 39.

---

4. Actually, IPv6 discovers the smallest MTU along a communication path and uses that as the largest packet size in order to avoid fragmentation. Many IPv4 implementations (including that in Linux) attempt to do the same thing, but IPv4 will fragment if necessary.

Source and destination *port numbers* are stored in the Transport layer header. A port number is simply a positive integer that is associated with an application. Many port numbers and their associated services are listed in the `/etc/services` file. Port numbers ranging from 0 to 1023 are called *privileged* ports because only root can invoke a process that uses them. Port numbers below 256 are reserved for *well-known* services like `ftp`, `telnet`, and DNS. Port numbers above 1023 (up to 65535) are unprivileged. Some services, like the X Window System, use port numbers in this range (X uses port 6000 and above).

There are numerous vulnerabilities associated with both TCP and UDP. The references listed in *Network Vulnerability and Security Books* on page 39 provide a good start to understanding them.

The Application Layer   This layer of the TCP/IP stack is where all the network applications reside. Throughout this book we will discuss many of them. A more thorough discourse is left to the resources listed in the section *General TCP/IP Networking Resources* on page 39. Here we will describe the client-server model and examine some of the major server-side daemons.

Most network applications operate under the *client-server* model. The server is the system that makes the resources available, while the client utilizes those resources. Many client-server applications, such as NFS (discussed in *Some Major Applications* on page 37), allow for a system to act as both a client and a server simultaneously.

Since clients access resources, the client initiates the communication over the network to the server by making a request. When the server receives the client's request it will pass the request on to the appropriate daemon process that serves that request. The daemon may either be running at all times or invoked when necessary by another daemon such as `inetd`[5] (see the references in the section, *General TCP/IP Networking Resources* on page 39, for a complete discussion of `inetd`). Daemons that run all the time are normally invoked by a start-up script (described in the section, *Start-Up Scripts* on page 24). Daemons invoked only when requested are commonly invoked by `inetd`, which uses the `/etc/inetd.conf` configuration file to determine which daemons are available. We will generally refer to these server-side daemons as services.

In order to make a service unavailable on your system, you first need to determine whether it runs all the time or is invoked by `inetd`. If the service runs all the time, you can disable the service on a running system by sending a termination signal to the service. For example, if you want to terminate `sendmail`, execute

```
# killall -TERM sendmail
```

To prevent it from running at the next boot, you would need to remove its start-up script as described in the section, *Start-Up Scripts* on page 24.

---

5. We discuss `xinetd`, a replacement for `inetd`, in Chapter 10.

If the service is invoked through `inetd`, you need to comment out or remove the appropriate entry from the file `/etc/inetd.conf` and then inform `inetd` of the changes you've made. For example, suppose that you want to disallow `rlogin` requests from all clients. Edit the `/etc/inetd.conf` file and change the entry

```
login   stream tcp    nowait root    /usr/sbin/tcpd in.rlogind
```

to the following, by simply adding the # comment character at the beginning of the line,

```
#login   stream tcp    nowait root    /usr/sbin/tcpd in.rlogind
```

Then inform `inetd` of the change by executing

```
# killall -HUP inetd
```

Now, `inetd` will refuse all requests for `in.rlogind` which supports the `rlogin` client-side program.

Some services have numerous vulnerabilities. Table 3.1 lists many of the services available and recommends whether or not they should be made available. It also lists the default state (On or Off) and the port number with which it is associated.

Table 3.1 Standard Services and Recommended Usage

Service	State/Port	Description of Function	Recommended Use
chargen	Off/19	Generates ASCII data for debugging purposes.	Leave it off.
daytime	Off/13	Provides day and time in ASCII.	Normally not necessary. Leave it off.
discard	Off/9	Discards any data received. Used for debugging.	Leave it off.
echo	Off/7	Echoes back all data received. Used for debugging.	Leave it off.
ftp	On/21	File Transfer Protocol for transferring files over the network.	Often a required service.
gopher	On/70	Command-line based predecessor to web browsers.	Normally not used. Turn it off.
smtp	Off/25	Simple Mail Transfer Protocol	Required for POP; otherwise leave it off.
nntp	Off/119	Network News Transfer Protocol	Necessary only if the system will be a network news server.
shell	On/514	Supports the remote shell service.	Turn it off. Replace with `sshd`.
login	On/513	Supports the remote login service.	Turn it off. Replace with `sshd`.

Table 3.1 Standard Services and Recommended Usage (Continued)

Service	State/Port	Description of Function	Recommended Use
exec	Off/512	Supports remote command execution through rexec.	Leave it off.
talk ntalk	On/517 On/518	Provides for text based interactive communications.	Turn them off. Use Internet relay chat (IRC) or e-mail.
imap	On/143	Internet Message Access Protocol e-mail services.	Unless the system is an IMAP server, turn it off.
pop-2 pop-3	On/109 On/110	Provides Post Office Protocol (POP) e-mail services.	Unless the system is a POPv2 or POPv3 mail server, turn these off.
uucp	Off/117	UNIX-to-UNIX copy provides batch-oriented and on-demand file transfer service.	Unless the system must provide uucp services, turn it off.
tftp	Off/69	Trivial File Transfer Protocol. A simplified version of ftp that performs no authentication checking.	Used only for systems that will act as install or diskless client servers.
bootps	Off/67	Provides booting service for network clients, such as X-terminals and diskless nodes.	Used only for systems that will act as a boot server.
finger	On/79	Provides user information.	Turn it off unless specially configured for DMZ operations.
systat	Off/11	Provides system information via ps.	Leave it off.
netstat	Off/15	Provides network statistics via netstat.	Leave it off.
time	On/37	Used for time synchronization of hosts through the remote execution of commands such as rdate or ntp.	This may be necessary for host clock synchronization.
auth	On/113	Provides connection ownership information.	Normally this service is turned on for systems attached to the Internet.
linuxconf	On/98	Provides system administrative graphical user interface (GUI) over the network.	Unless absolutely necessary, turn it off.
portmap	On/111	Not controlled through inetd.	Used for remote procedure call (RPC) services. Usually necessary. Discussed further in *Remote Procedure Call Applications* on page 36.
mountd	On/635	Not controlled through inetd.	Necessary for NFS services. Also required by CFS and TCFS discussed in Chapter 15. If you aren't using any of these services, turn it off.

If you are unfamiliar with `inetd`, you really must minimally read *TCP/IP Network Administration* cited in *General TCP/IP Networking Resources* on page 39. For even greater understanding, check out some of the other references noted in that section.

Remote Procedure Call Applications

There are a variety of services, including NFS and Network Information Services (NIS) (see *Some Major Applications* on page 37), that use remote procedure calls (RPC) to manage the communication, including port use. RPC applications are invoked through the `portmap` daemon (discussed in Chapter 10). The `portmap` daemon will supply a port number for the requested service, and that number will be used for the duration of the communication.

As with the other topics in this chapter, RPC is a topic with which you should be familiar. If you are not, check out some of the resources noted in *General TCP/IP Networking Resources* on page 39.

Trusted Host Files and Related Commands

In this section, we will provide an overview description of the behavior of the `$HOME/.rhosts`, `/etc/hosts.equiv`, and `$HOME/.netrc`[6] files, which we collectively refer to as *trusted host* files. These files are server-side files and related to the server-side daemons `in.rlogind`, `in.rshd`, `in.rexecd`, and `in.ftpd`. The related client-side applications are `rlogin`, `rsh`, `rcp`, `ftp`, and `rexec` (often referred to collectively as the r-commands or Berkeley r-commands, as they are derived from the Berkeley System Distribution [BSD]). Table 3.2 provides a list of trusted host files and their application associations.

Table 3.2 Trusted Host Files and Application Associations

Client-Side Application	Server-Side Daemon	Server-Side Trusted Host Files
rlogin	in.rlogind	/etc/hosts.equiv $HOME/.rhosts
rsh	in.rshd	/etc/hosts.equiv $HOME/.rhosts
rcp	in.rshd	/etc/hosts.equiv $HOME/.rhosts
ftp	in.ftpd	$HOME/.netrc
rexec	in.rexecd	$HOME/.netrc

---

6. The shell environment variable HOME contains the home directory of the user.

The `/etc/hosts.equiv` file provides an authentication database for non-root users. The `$HOME/.rhosts` and `$HOME/.netrc` files provide authentication databases for the users in whose home directory they reside. The purpose of these files is to provide user authentication without requiring a password.

The syntax of the `$HOME/.netrc` file is documented in the `ftp(1)` man page. The syntax of the `/etc/hosts.equiv` and `$HOME/.rhosts` files are documented in such resources as *TCP/IP Network Administration*, cited in *General TCP/IP Networking Resources* on page 39. Additional configuration information is provided in the `in.rlogind(8)` and `in.rshd(8)` man pages.

Since the trusted hosts files permit user login without a password, their use is strongly discouraged. If you configure trusted hosts in your network, then a compromise of one system will lead to a compromise of all systems that trust it. Hence, the r-commands are often referred to as the evil r-commands. All of the functionality of the r-commands can and should be securely replaced with SSH (discussed in Chapter 11).

Some Major Applications

Throughout this book we will discuss the Network File System (NFS), Samba, the Network Information Services (NIS), and the Domain Name Service (DNS) as they relate to the various utilities we describe.

The NFS is a remote filesystem developed by Sun Microsystems, Inc. It allows for transparent local access to remote directories over TCP/IP. Unfortunately authentication has not been implemented for NFS in Linux as of the kernel version 2.2.x. Access control lists may be specified by the server in `/etc/exports`, and access by identified UID may be squashed (disallowed). You should *always* use access restrictions on *every* NFS resource. See the `exports(5)`, `nfs(5)`, and `mount(8)` man pages for more details. It is best from a security perspective to allow NFS access only within your organization's network and not to allow incoming NFS requests from the Internet (or other public network). This may be accomplished with `ipchains` (discussed in Chapter 16) or similar utility. For more information, additional references are cited at the end of this section.

Samba is conceptually similar to NFS except that it is implemented over the Microsoft Networking Protocol. Samba versions 1.9.17p2 and later are considered reasonably secure. Samba allows for password-based authentication and may be configured to pass hashed passwords instead of cleartext passwords over the network. It may also be configured with access control lists. Samba servers can be made to run in a `chroot` environment. Make sure that you take advantage of these security features.

NIS provides a mechanism to centrally administrate a collection of systems that are networked together. NIS was not designed with security in mind; rather it was designed for convenience. Do not allow access to your NIS database from networks other than those specifically involved in your NIS management. Implement access control through `portmap` (see Chapter 10).

Restrict access to all NIS servers, especially the master server. For further details, see the references cited below.

DNS is a decentralized naming service for hostname-to-IP-address and IP-address-to-hostname translations. There are a large number of security issues associated with DNS; see the references below for further details.

You can learn more about all of these applications as well as the security ramifications of their use, by reading the resources cited in *NFS, Samba, NIS, and DNS Resources* on page 40 and *Network Vulnerability and Security Books* on page 39.

Network Monitoring

The Linux distribution incorporates the utility `tcpdump`, which captures packets on the network by placing a local interface in *promiscuous* mode. Normally your network interface will ignore any packets that are not addressed to your system. By placing your interface in promiscuous mode, `tcpdump` captures all packets regardless of address and allows you to examine the headers contained in those packets. This is quite useful for debugging. It is also quite useful for bad-guys who are attempting to gather information about your environment. Unless you are using applications that employ encryption, such as SSH (see Chapter 11), CFS, or TCFS (see Chapter 15), all network communications are passed in the clear.

A more user-friendly utility, `sniffit` (available from `http://sniffit.rug.ac.be/~coder/sniffit/sniffit.html`), allows for the inspection of network packets as does `tcpdump`, but it is also capable of displaying the data portion of the packets. Note that this will include all cleartext passwords, e-mail, file transfers, and so on. It is quite useful for debugging and for verifying that your connections are encrypted. Once again, it is also useful to those who would exploit the information obtained through `sniffit`.

There are many similar programs for monitoring your networks. Collectively they are often referred to as *network sniffers*.

If you are concerned about the use and abuse of utilities like `tcpdump` and `sniffit`, there are a couple of things you can do.

Consider using switches instead of repeaters (see the section, *The Network Interface Layer* on page 30). This will isolate network traffic so that a system running a sniffer will see only the traffic sent by the switch and not all of the traffic in the local network.

There are also promiscuous mode detectors that you may run to determine if someone has put an interface in promiscuous mode. One such utility is `neped`, available from `http://www.apostols.org/projectz/neped/`. Another is AntiSniff, available from `http://www.10pht.com/antisniff/overview.html`.

You may also be able to remove all network monitoring software from those systems that you control. Unfortunately, this does not prevent sniffing on systems outside your control. The best defense against network sniffing is to utilize encryption solutions.

General TCP/IP Networking Resources

Application-Oriented Books

1. Graham, Buck, *TCP/IP Addressing: Designing and Optimizing Your IP Addressing Scheme*, Boston, Massachusetts, AP Professional, 1997.
2. Hunt, Craig, *TCP/IP Network Administration*, 2d ed., Sebastopol, California, O'Reilly & Associates, Inc., 1998.
3. Miller, C. Kenneth, *Multicast Networking and Applications*, Reading, Massachusetts, Addison-Wesley, 1999.
4. Miller, C. Kenneth, *Troubleshooting TCP/IP*, 2d ed., New York, New York, M&T Books, 1996.

Theory-Oriented Books

1. Comer, Douglas E., *Internetworking With TCP/IP, Vol I: Principles, Protocols, Architecture*, 3d ed., Englewood Cliffs, New Jersey, Prentice Hall, 1995.
2. Huitema, Christian, *IPv6: The New Internet Protocol*, Upper Saddle River, New Jersey, Prentice Hall PTR, 1996.
3. Huitema, Christian, *Routing in the Internet*, Englewood Cliffs, New Jersey, Prentice Hall PTR, 1995.
4. Perlman, Radia, *Interconnections: Bridges, Routers, Switches, and Internetworking Protocols*, 2d ed., New York, New York, Addison-Wesley, 2000.
5. Stevens, W. Richard, *TCP/IP Illustrated, Volume 1: The Protocols*, Reading, Massachusetts, Addison-Wesley, 1994.

Layer 2 Related Books

1. Held, Gilbert, *High-Speed Networking with LAN Switches*, New York, New York, John Wiley & Sons, Inc., 1997.
2. Held, Gilbert, *Virtual LANs: Construction, Implementation, and Management*, New York, New York, John Wiley & Sons, Inc., 1997.
3. Kercheval, Barry, *TCP/IP Over ATM: A No-Nonsense Internetworking Guide*, Upper Saddle River, New Jersey, Prentice Hall PTR, 1997.

Network Vulnerability and Security Books

1. Anonymous, *Maximum Security: A Hacker's Guide to Protecting Your Internet Site and Network*, Indianapolis, Indiana, Sams.net Publishing, 1997.
2. Atkins, Derek, et al., *Internet Security Professional Reference*, Indianapolis, Indiana, New Riders Publishing, 1996.
3. Klander, Lars, *Hacker Proof: The Ultimate Guide to Network Security*, Las Vegas, Nevada, Jamsa Press, 1997.

NFS, Samba, NIS, and DNS Resources

NFS On-Line Documents

```
/usr/doc/HOWTO/NFS-HOWTO
/usr/doc/HOWTO/mini/NFS-Root
/usr/doc/HOWTO/mini/NFS-Root-Client
```

NIS On-Line Documents

```
/usr/doc/HOWTO/NIS-HOWTO
```

NFS and NIS Books

1. Hunt, Craig, *TCP/IP Network Administration*, 2d ed., Sebastopol, California, O'Reilly & Associates, Inc., 1998.
2. Stern, Hal, *Managing NFS and NIS*, Sebastopol, California, O'Reilly & Associates, Inc., 1991.

Samba Resources

You'll find extensive documentation in the on-line directory,

```
/usr/doc/samba-1.9.18p10/docs/
```

with numerous examples in the directory,

```
/usr/doc/samba-1.9.18p10/examples/
```

Also, check out the book,

1. Blair, John D., *Samba: Integrating UNIX and Windows*, Seattle, Washington, Specialized Systems Consultants, Inc. (SSC), 1998.

DNS Resources

On-line:

```
/usr/doc/HOWTO/DNS-HOWTO
```

Book:

1. Albitz, Paul, and Cricket Liu, *DNS and BIND*, 2d ed., Sebastopol, California, O'Reilly & Associates, Inc., 1997.

REQUEST FOR COMMENT

Request for comments (RFCs) specify a standard or protocol. There are two major sources of RFCs—the Internet Engineering Task Force (IETF), which maintains and issues RFCs largely relating to the Internet, and the Open Group, which maintains and issues RFCs mostly relating to the Distributed Computing Environment (DCE).

For more information about IETF RFCs, please see

`http://www.ietf.org/rfc.html`

For further information regarding the Open Group RFCs, please visit

`http://www.opengroup.org/rfc/`

CRYPTOGRAPHY

Cryptography is the art, or science, of secret writing. It has been widely used as a way to provide private conversations very early in human history. In the context of modern computing, it is associated with private electronic communications. It may be used to protect files, e-mail, and various types of network connections like `ftp`, `telnet`, and `http`.

First let's define some terms.

An electronic communication or, more generically, a *message* that is not disguised is called *plaintext* or *cleartext*. The process of disguising a message is known as *encryption* or *encipherment*; this process transforms the cleartext into *ciphertext*. Reversal of the process is called *decryption* or *decipherment*. A cleartext message, therefore, may be encrypted or enciphered into ciphertext; a ciphertext message may then be decrypted or deciphered back into its original cleartext form.[7] An algorithm that implements encryption and decryption is also known as a *cryptographic* algorithm. Such an algorithm is also often called a *cipher*. A *key* is normally a large numeric value (sometimes supplied in the form of a password or passphrase) used in conjunction with a cryptographic algorithm to either encrypt cleartext and/or decrypt ciphertext. Figure 3.3 provides an overview of converting cleartext into ciphertext through the use of an encryption algorithm.

Cryptanalysis is the study of decrypting ciphertext without the benefit of knowing the keys. There are many algorithms for this purpose and they are generally referred to as *cryptanalytic* algorithms. The cryptanalytic process is also often referred to as cracking or breaking the encryption. *Cryptology* is the study of the mathematics associated with cryptography and cryptanalysis.

The Purpose of Cryptography

Cryptography is used for a variety of purposes. Our discussion of cryptography in this chapter, and throughout this book, will focus on using cryptographic algorithms for

---

7. The International Standards Organization (ISO) 7498-2 specification prefers the terms encipher and decipher over encrypt and decrypt. We will use these terms synonymously.

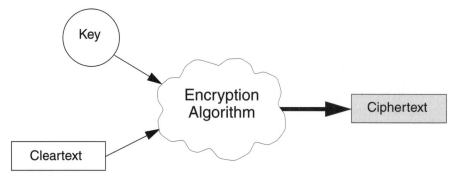

Fig. 3.3 Converting Cleartext into Ciphertext through Encryption

☞ *Confidentiality*. Allowing information to be made available only to those who are participants in a particular communication. Historically, confidentiality is the predominant use of cryptography.

☞ *Authentication*. The process of verifying a particular individual's identity. This is often accomplished through the use of some form of verification such as a picture identification or a fingerprint. Authentication through cryptographic means is used predominantly to validate a user's identity when other means are not available. Digital signatures offer one such cryptographic method and are very valuable in assuring that the author is in fact who he or she claims to be.

☞ *Integrity*. Within the context of data, an assessment of the completeness and correctness of information. In a computing environment, data integrity validation is used to ensure that the original data has not been corrupted or changed. Cryptographic one-way hash functions are commonly used to provide this functionality.

The following sections will generally describe the use of cryptography, which provides confidentiality, authentication, and integrity in computing environments.

Algorithm Types

Symmetric Encryption   A *symmetric* encryption algorithm is one that requires a key to encipher and to decipher messages. This is also often called a *shared-key* algorithm, because all users of such an algorithm involved in the communication must have the same key. We will refer to the shared key as a *secret* key.[8]

There are a number of symmetric algorithms in common use today. Among them are the Data Encryption Standard (DES), the International Data

---

8. Some texts refer to this key as a *private* key.

Encryption Algorithm (IDEA, patented algorithm) which is incorporated in PGP, and Blowfish (an unpatented algorithm written by Bruce Schneier and incorporated in, among other tools, SSH—see Chapter 11).

One of the concerns about available symmetric algorithms is their cryptographic *strength*. The strength of a cryptographic algorithm is a measure of its resistance to cryptanalytic attacks. A thorough treatment of this topic may be found in the references cited in the section *Cryptography References* on page 47. In part, an algorithm's strength is measured by the size of its key. IDEA uses a 128-bit key. Blowfish offers a user configurable key size ranging from 32 bits to 448 bits. The longer the key, the greater the cryptographic strength. DES uses a 56-bit key. It is considered a relatively weak algorithm for this and other reasons (see *Cracking DES* in the section, *Cryptography References* on page 47).

One way to increase the strength of symmetric encryption is to use multiple keys and execute the algorithm multiple times. An example implementation is that of Triple-DES (incorporated into some publicly available tools), wherein the data is first encrypted with one key, then the encrypted data is decrypted with a second key, and finally that data is encrypted with yet a third key.[9]

The fundamental problem with the use of symmetric algorithms is the shared-key requirement. In order to successfully enter into an encrypted communication, we must first make sure that all parties to the communication have the necessary keys. There are many ways to ensure this, such as sending the key to the other parties by FAX, postal service, or courier. These methods are cumbersome at best and each has its own set of vulnerabilities. A more convenient approach, although not without vulnerabilities itself, is to use asymmetric encryption to encrypt the secret key or keys and send them electronically through the same network used to carry the encrypted communication.

Asymmetric Encryption An *asymmetric* encryption algorithm is one that requires one key to encrypt and a different but related key to decrypt. This type of algorithm is also often called a *public-key* or *two-key* algorithm. One of the two keys will be disclosed to anyone requesting it. This key is called the *public* key. The other key should never be disclosed to anyone except the owner and is known as the *private* key.[10]

The motivation for the development of asymmetric encryption algorithms came from the need to pass secret keys over insecure channels. The first such system was developed by Ralph Merkle in 1974.[11] The first asymmetric algorithm to gain popular use was the Diffie-Hellman algorithm, which was created

---

9. This is one way to implement Triple-DES. There are others.

10. Some texts refer to this key as the *secret* key.

11. Ralph Merkle, *Secure Communication Over Insecure Channels*, Communications of the ACM 21, no. 4, 1978, pp. 294–299.

by Whitfield Diffie and Martin Hellman in 1976. In 1977, Ron Rivest, Adi Shamir, and Len Adleman developed a similar algorithm called RSA.

Generally, asymmetric encryption algorithms can perform general data encryption (confidentiality) and can be used to generate digital signatures (authentication). It turns out that asymmetric algorithms are poor performers relative to symmetric algorithms. Consequently, asymmetric algorithms are most commonly used to encrypt secret keys for transmission over insecure channels and to generate digital signatures.

Hash Functions and Digital Signatures

One-Way Cryptographic Hash Functions   A *hash function* (also known as a *message digest*), as it generally relates to computer science, is a mathematical function that takes data as input and produces a storage address as output. The output of any hash function is simply called the *hash*. A *cryptographic one-way hash* function, or simply a *one-way hash* function, is a mathematical transformation having the following properties:

☞ It accepts variable sized data and produces a value that is fixed in size (e.g., 160 bits).

☞ Computation of the hash from the data is easy.

☞ It is computationally impractical to compute the original data given the hash.

☞ It is computationally unfeasible to find two similar data sets that when transformed by the function, result in the same hash (this is called *collision resistance*).

The whole idea behind this type of algorithm is to come up with an identifier for any given file or message that will change if someone changes the file. In this way we can use these functions to *fingerprint* files.

Unfortunately, since most such hash algorithms are readily available, it is possible that someone could change both the file and the hash, making it impossible to detect the change. There are a number of ways to combat this potential vulnerability. One way is to compute the hash on important files in their pristine state and store them off-line. Such is the approach of Tripwire (discussed in Chapter 14) and `tiger` (Chapter 13). Another method is to compute, then encrypt the hash. For example, include the hash in a digital signature (see *Digital Signatures* on page 45). This can also be done with RPM (see *RPM Resources* on page 28).

One purpose of such functions is to verify the integrity of data. We explore the application of hashing for integrity purposes in our discussions of `tiger` and Tripwire. Another purpose of hashing is for authentication. We examine this purpose in our discussions of pluggable authentication modules (PAM—see Chapter 5) and one-time passwords (OTP—see Chapter 6).

There are a number of hash algorithms available. Among them are the RSA Data Security, Inc., MD4 Message Digest Algorithm (simply known as MD4); the RSA Data Security, Inc., MD5 Message Digest Algorithm (simply known as MD5); the Secure Hash Algorithm (SHA-1), which is part of the larger specification known as the Digital Signature Algorithm[12] (DSA); and the Research and Development in Advanced Communication Technologies in Europe Integrity Primitives Evaluation Message Digest (RIPEMD).

Passwords Aren't Encrypted, They're Hashed!

Another hashing algorithm is the Linux crypt(3) function. It implements a modified DES algorithm which accepts a maximum 64-bit input (8 characters) and produces a 104-bit hash value (13 characters, the first 2 of which are not part of the hash [see man 3 crypt]). This is the function used as the standard password hashing function. Each user's 13-character hashed password is stored in /etc/shadow (or, in its absence, /etc/passwd). Quite often, the hashed password is referred to as the *encrypted* password. The use of the term *encrypted* implies that the encrypted data may be decrypted. While it may be possible to decrypt a hashed password, it is computationally difficult (perhaps impossible when MD5 is used) and it is not done. Instead, when a user enters his or her password, the password is hashed by crypt(3) and the resulting hash is compared to what is stored in /etc/shadow. For this reason, we will use the phrase *hashed password* instead of *encrypted password* throughout the book.

Digital Signatures   A *digital signature* is an authentication mechanism designed to verify the author or sender of electronic information. Digital signatures are commonly generated using asymmetric algorithms. Very frequently, digital signatures include the hash value of the signed file to verify not only the author but also the integrity of the file.

An Overview of PGP

Pretty Good Privacy (PGP) was written by Phil Zimmerman. It is a software package that utilizes asymmetric algorithms (RSA only in PGP version 2.6.x; RSA and Diffie-Hellman are available in PGP version 5.0 and later) for general data encryption (generally e-mail and secret keys) and for the generation and validation of digital signatures. PGP also uses IDEA for symmetric encryption of files.

---

12. DSA is an algorithm that incorporates El Gamal for encryption and SHA-1 for hash computations. It was adopted by the National Institute of Standards and Technology (NIST) in 1991.

Many of the utilities discussed in this book are available with PGP signatures. We strongly recommend that you obtain and install a copy of PGP minimally for the purpose of verifying these PGP signatures. At various points throughout this text we will provide examples of PGP usage.

You may obtain PGP in the United States and Canada at

```
http://www.pgp.com/
```

An international version of PGP is available at

```
http://www.pgpi.com/
```

for folks outside the United States (Canadians have a choice!). You may also obtain PGP, both international and U.S. versions, in RPM format (RPM is discussed in the section, *Red Hat Package Manager* on page 26) from,

```
http://www.replay.com/redhat/pgp.html
```

These versions of PGP are free for personal use, but require a license for commercial use.

The Free Software Foundation (FSF) has an OpenPGP (RFC 2440—see *Request for Comment* on page 40 for a discussion of RFC) project in the works. It is called GNU Privacy Guard (GNUPG) and is compatible with PGP version 5.0 and later. It is distributed under the GNU Public License (GPL—see the section *Licenses* on page 50 for a discussion of GPL); it is completely free for all users. At the time of this writing, GNUPG is in beta. You may obtain a copy at

```
http://www.gnupg.org/gnupg.html
```

and find further details about the GNUPG project.

For further implementation and usage information, read the documentation that comes with PGP. A very good book, *PGP: Pretty Good Privacy* (see *Cryptography References* on page 47), is also available.

A Note on Obtaining PGP Public Keys   Most PGP-signed files are signed by authors who make their public keys available at the same site as the signed files. This is not a secure way of distributing public keys because we do not know whether the site is really the author's site or whether it is spoofed or has been compromised. Despite this weakness, most public keys are distributed in this way. See the references listed in the section, *Cryptography References* on page 47, for some things you can do to mitigate this problem.

Additionally, there are no conventions regarding the storage of public keys on `ftp` or `http` sites. Some public keys will be found in a file with the suffix, `.asc` or `.pgp`. Other public keys are stored in a README file. Still others are obtainable by using the `finger` command with the author's e-mail address as the argument. In some cases, you must e-mail the author and request his or her public key. Whatever the case, obtaining the public key for a particular signed document often takes some research. The location of the public keys for the tools used in this book will be noted, where appropriate.

Cryptography References

General

1. Electronic Frontier Foundation, *Cracking DES*, Sebastopol, California, O'Reilly & Associates, Inc., 1998.
2. Kaufman, Charlie, Radia Perlman, and Mike Speciner, *Network Security: Private Communication in a Public World*, Englewood Cliffs, New Jersey, Prentice Hall, 1995.
3. Schneier, Bruce, *Applied Cryptography*, 2d ed., New York, New York, John Wiley and Sons, 1996.

PGP Specific

1. Garfinkel, Simson, *PGP: Pretty Good Privacy*, Sebastopol, California, O'Reilly & Associates, Inc., 1995.

TESTING AND PRODUCTION ENVIRONMENTS

All of the publicly available utilities discussed in this text are available over the Internet. In fact, we identify the sites from which you may obtain these tools. Unfortunately, most of the tools you obtain in this way are not guaranteed to be without Trojan horses, back doors, or other sources of trouble (see Chapter 1 for a survey of vulnerabilities). Even though many of these tools will include a PGP signature most signers do not distribute their public keys securely.

There are some things that you can do to reduce the likelihood of many of these vulnerabilities. We list them here and discuss them below.

☞ Search the security archives for vulnerabilities.
☞ Test the software in a *safe* environment.
☞ Audit the source code.
☞ Maintain *pristine* backups for recovery.

Security Archives

Whenever you download any utility from the Internet, including those discussed in this book, it is a good idea to research the available security archives for known vulnerabilities before you use the utility. One of the best resources for such research is the bugtraq archive. You will find a searchable bugtraq archive at http://www.securityfocus.com/. You may also subscribe to the bugtraq mailing list by sending an e-mail message to listserv@securityfocus.com with

```
subscribe bugtraq your_e-mail_address
```

in the body of the message. Substitute your e-mail address. If you subscribe to this list, be prepared to receive a lot of e-mail (as many as 50 messages per day)!

There are a number of other security mailing lists, newsgroups, and archives. See Appendix A for more information.

Software Testing

You should also test the software you download in a safe environment. *Safe* means that the system or network that you use for testing does not contain invaluable data and is **not** connected to your production environment (where the real work is performed). If a system becomes corrupt in this safe environment, for whatever reason, it is recoverable from a simple reinstallation of all software from source. If resources permit, you should build a test environment for the purpose of testing all publicly available software.

When you install new software from an untrusted source (such as the Internet) in your testing environment, the purpose is to thoroughly familiarize yourself with the behavior of the software. Read all of the associated documentation and test as much of the software's functionality as possible. Work with the software until you have become proficient with it.

In particular, you will want to pay close attention to

☞ All files created by the software

☞ Any e-mail generated by the software

☞ Any subprocesses spawned by the software

☞ Any network connections generated by the software

For each of these items, you will want to understand completely the purpose of each activity. If you observe one of these activities, determine whether any sensitive data (such as usernames and passwords) is being written or passed. Set all files to the least permissive setting possible. Find out if the activity is required for some functional purpose; if you don't need it, configure it off whenever possible. If you notice any activity that is not documented, utilize all available resources to determine why. Most utilities will either have a mailing list or will be discussed in a newsgroup such as comp.security.unix.

Even all of this testing will not inform you if there is a back door in the software. Detecting back doors requires source code auditing.

Source Code Auditing

Another precautionary step is to perform a source code audit of any software you intend to use. Unfortunately, source code audits require special skills and a substantial investment in time. You can learn more about code auditing and secure programming by reading the Secure Programming FAQ

```
http://www.whitefang.com/sup/
```

Also, both software testing and secure programming is covered in *Practical UNIX and Internet Security* as cited in *Security Resources* on page 49.

Not even this can prevent a back door if you are using a compiler that puts one into the resulting executable! For a description of this phenomenon see *Trusting Trust*, pp. 801–802, of *Practical UNIX and Internet Security*.

Pristine Backups

Always be prepared to recover from tainted software by having a *pristine* backup. A pristine backup is a complete backup of your system from when it was known to be in a secure state. For example, the first time you install your system and before you attach it to a network, the system is considered to be pristine (even though it may contain bugs, vulnerabilities, etc.). In other words it is in a known and recoverable state.

There will be various other points at which you may consider your system to be in a pristine state. For example, after you have run `tiger` (discussed in Chapter 13) and Tripwire (discussed in Chapter 14) successfully, your system will be at a known, recoverable state.

The idea is that you want to make your backups in conjunction with these pristine states, so that when you need to recover your system you can do so from a pristine backup. This approach is discussed further in Chapter 18.

Security Resources

Be sure to read the following, very excellent book.

1. Garfinkel, Simson, and Gene Spafford, *Practical UNIX and Internet Security*, 2d., Sebastopol, California, O'Reilly & Associates, Inc., 1996.

The URL below is the home page of TrinityOS written by David A. Ranch. The TrinityOS document is an outstanding resource for system, network, and security administration of Linux systems.

```
http://www.ecst.csuchico.edu/~dranch/TrinityOS.wri
```

Another good security resource is *Securing Linux: Step by Step* by Lee Brotzman and David A. Ranch. This book is published by System Administration, Networking, and Security (SANS) and is available at

```
http://www.sans.org/
```

LICENSES

All of the tools discussed in this book are, at a minimum, free for noncommercial use. The basic terms of the license for each tool is noted when that tool is discussed. A reference is made to the file in which the complete license is disclosed. Be sure to read each license because it may contain restrictions that apply to you.

Many of the tools discussed throughout this book are distributed with the GNU (GNU's Not UNIX) Public License (GPL). Essentially, this license permits unrestricted use and modification of the software it pertains to as long as you do not restrict the use or source code access of the software in any way. It reflects the quintessential philosophy of open source. The terms of the GPL are provided in Example 3-5.

Example 3-5 The GPL

```
    GNU GENERAL PUBLIC LICENSE
       Version 2, June 1991

Copyright (C) 1989, 1991 Free Software Foundation, Inc.
59 Temple Place, Suite 330, Boston, MA 02111-1307 USA
Everyone is permitted to copy and distribute verbatim copies
of this license document, but changing it is not allowed.

    Preamble

  The licenses for most software are designed to take away your
freedom to share and change it. By contrast, the GNU General Public
License is intended to guarantee your freedom to share and change free
software--to make sure the software is free for all its users. This
General Public License applies to most of the Free Software
Foundation's software and to any other program whose authors commit to
using it. (Some other Free Software Foundation software is covered by
the GNU Library General Public License instead.) You can apply it to
your programs, too.

  When we speak of free software, we are referring to freedom, not
price. Our General Public Licenses are designed to make sure that you
have the freedom to distribute copies of free software (and charge for
this service if you wish), that you receive source code or can get it
if you want it, that you can change the software or use pieces of it
in new free programs; and that you know you can do these things.

  To protect your rights, we need to make restrictions that forbid
anyone to deny you these rights or to ask you to surrender the rights.
These restrictions translate to certain responsibilities for you if you
distribute copies of the software, or if you modify it.

  For example, if you distribute copies of such a program, whether
gratis or for a fee, you must give the recipients all the rights that
you have. You must make sure that they, too, receive or can get the
source code. And you must show them these terms so they know their
rights.

  We protect your rights with two steps: (1) copyright the software, and
(2) offer you this license which gives you legal permission to copy,
distribute and/or modify the software.

  Also, for each author's protection and ours, we want to make certain
that everyone understands that there is no warranty for this free
software. If the software is modified by someone else and passed on, we
want its recipients to know that what they have is not the original, so
that any problems introduced by others will not reflect on the original
```

Example 3-5 The GPL (Continued)

authors' reputations.

Finally, any free program is threatened constantly by software patents. We wish to avoid the danger that redistributors of a free program will individually obtain patent licenses, in effect making the program proprietary. To prevent this, we have made it clear that any patent must be licensed for everyone's free use or not licensed at all.

The precise terms and conditions for copying, distribution and modification follow.

    GNU GENERAL PUBLIC LICENSE
  TERMS AND CONDITIONS FOR COPYING, DISTRIBUTION AND MODIFICATION

0. This License applies to any program or other work which contains a notice placed by the copyright holder saying it may be distributed under the terms of this General Public License. The "Program", below, refers to any such program or work, and a "work based on the Program" means either the Program or any derivative work under copyright law: that is to say, a work containing the Program or a portion of it, either verbatim or with modifications and/or translated into another language. (Hereinafter, translation is included without limitation in the term "modification".) Each licensee is addressed as "you".

Activities other than copying, distribution and modification are not covered by this License; they are outside its scope. The act of running the Program is not restricted, and the output from the Program is covered only if its contents constitute a work based on the Program (independent of having been made by running the Program). Whether that is true depends on what the Program does.

1. You may copy and distribute verbatim copies of the Program's source code as you receive it, in any medium, provided that you conspicuously and appropriately publish on each copy an appropriate copyright notice and disclaimer of warranty; keep intact all the notices that refer to this License and to the absence of any warranty; and give any other recipients of the Program a copy of this License along with the Program.

You may charge a fee for the physical act of transferring a copy, and you may at your option offer warranty protection in exchange for a fee.

2. You may modify your copy or copies of the Program or any portion of it, thus forming a work based on the Program, and copy and distribute such modifications or work under the terms of Section 1 above, provided that you also meet all of these conditions:

    a) You must cause the modified files to carry prominent notices stating that you changed the files and the date of any change.

    b) You must cause any work that you distribute or publish, that in whole or in part contains or is derived from the Program or any part thereof, to be licensed as a whole at no charge to all third parties under the terms of this License.

    c) If the modified program normally reads commands interactively when run, you must cause it, when started running for such interactive use in the most ordinary way, to print or display an announcement including an appropriate copyright notice and a notice that there is no warranty (or else, saying that you provide a warranty) and that users may redistribute the program under these conditions, and telling the user how to view a copy of this License. (Exception: if the Program itself is interactive but does not normally print such an announcement, your work based on the Program is not required to print an announcement.)

These requirements apply to the modified work as a whole. If identifiable sections of that work are not derived from the Program, and can be reasonably considered independent and separate works in themselves, then this License, and its terms, do not apply to those

Example 3-5 The GPL (Continued)

sections when you distribute them as separate works. But when you distribute the same sections as part of a whole which is a work based on the Program, the distribution of the whole must be on the terms of this License, whose permissions for other licensees extend to the entire whole, and thus to each and every part regardless of who wrote it.

Thus, it is not the intent of this section to claim rights or contest your rights to work written entirely by you; rather, the intent is to exercise the right to control the distribution of derivative or collective works based on the Program.

In addition, mere aggregation of another work not based on the Program with the Program (or with a work based on the Program) on a volume of a storage or distribution medium does not bring the other work under the scope of this License.

   3. You may copy and distribute the Program (or a work based on it, under Section 2) in object code or executable form under the terms of Sections 1 and 2 above provided that you also do one of the following:

   a) Accompany it with the complete corresponding machine-readable source code, which must be distributed under the terms of Sections 1 and 2 above on a medium customarily used for software interchange; or,

   b) Accompany it with a written offer, valid for at least three years, to give any third party, for a charge no more than your cost of physically performing source distribution, a complete machine-readable copy of the corresponding source code, to be distributed under the terms of Sections 1 and 2 above on a medium customarily used for software interchange; or,

   c) Accompany it with the information you received as to the offer to distribute corresponding source code. (This alternative is allowed only for noncommercial distribution and only if you received the program in object code or executable form with such an offer, in accord with Subsection b above.)

The source code for a work means the preferred form of the work for making modifications to it. For an executable work, complete source code means all the source code for all modules it contains, plus any associated interface definition files, plus the scripts used to control compilation and installation of the executable. However, as a special exception, the source code distributed need not include anything that is normally distributed (in either source or binary form) with the major components (compiler, kernel, and so on) of the operating system on which the executable runs, unless that component itself accompanies the executable.

If distribution of executable or object code is made by offering access to copy from a designated place, then offering equivalent access to copy the source code from the same place counts as distribution of the source code, even though third parties are not compelled to copy the source along with the object code.

   4. You may not copy, modify, sublicense, or distribute the Program except as expressly provided under this License. Any attempt otherwise to copy, modify, sublicense or distribute the Program is void, and will automatically terminate your rights under this License. However, parties who have received copies, or rights, from you under this License will not have their licenses terminated so long as such parties remain in full compliance.

   5. You are not required to accept this License, since you have not signed it. However, nothing else grants you permission to modify or distribute the Program or its derivative works. These actions are prohibited by law if you do not accept this License. Therefore, by modifying or distributing the Program (or any work based on the Program), you indicate your acceptance of this License to do so, and all its terms and conditions for copying, distributing or modifying

Example 3-5 The GPL (Continued)

the Program or works based on it.

6. Each time you redistribute the Program (or any work based on the Program), the recipient automatically receives a license from the original licensor to copy, distribute or modify the Program subject to these terms and conditions. You may not impose any further restrictions on the recipients' exercise of the rights granted herein. You are not responsible for enforcing compliance by third parties to this License.

7. If, as a consequence of a court judgment or allegation of patent infringement or for any other reason (not limited to patent issues), conditions are imposed on you (whether by court order, agreement or otherwise) that contradict the conditions of this License, they do not excuse you from the conditions of this License. If you cannot distribute so as to satisfy simultaneously your obligations under this License and any other pertinent obligations, then as a consequence you may not distribute the Program at all. For example, if a patent license would not permit royalty-free redistribution of the Program by all those who receive copies directly or indirectly through you, then the only way you could satisfy both it and this License would be to refrain entirely from distribution of the Program.

If any portion of this section is held invalid or unenforceable under any particular circumstance, the balance of the section is intended to apply and the section as a whole is intended to apply in other circumstances.

It is not the purpose of this section to induce you to infringe any patents or other property right claims or to contest validity of any such claims; this section has the sole purpose of protecting the integrity of the free software distribution system, which is implemented by public license practices. Many people have made generous contributions to the wide range of software distributed through that system in reliance on consistent application of that system; it is up to the author/donor to decide if he or she is willing to distribute software through any other system and a licensee cannot impose that choice.

This section is intended to make thoroughly clear what is believed to be a consequence of the rest of this License.

8. If the distribution and/or use of the Program is restricted in certain countries either by patents or by copyrighted interfaces, the original copyright holder who places the Program under this License may add an explicit geographical distribution limitation excluding those countries, so that distribution is permitted only in or among countries not thus excluded. In such case, this License incorporates the limitation as if written in the body of this License.

9. The Free Software Foundation may publish revised and/or new versions of the General Public License from time to time. Such new versions will be similar in spirit to the present version, but may differ in detail to address new problems or concerns.

Each version is given a distinguishing version number. If the Program specifies a version number of this License which applies to it and "any later version", you have the option of following the terms and conditions either of that version or of any later version published by the Free Software Foundation. If the Program does not specify a version number of this License, you may choose any version ever published by the Free Software Foundation.

10. If you wish to incorporate parts of the Program into other free programs whose distribution conditions are different, write to the author to ask for permission. For software which is copyrighted by the Free Software Foundation, write to the Free Software Foundation; we sometimes make exceptions for this. Our decision will be guided by the two goals of preserving the free status of all derivatives of our free software and

Example 3-5 The GPL (Continued)

```
of promoting the sharing and reuse of software generally.

    NO WARRANTY

    11. BECAUSE THE PROGRAM IS LICENSED FREE OF CHARGE, THERE IS NO WARRANTY
FOR THE PROGRAM, TO THE EXTENT PERMITTED BY APPLICABLE LAW. EXCEPT WHEN
OTHERWISE STATED IN WRITING THE COPYRIGHT HOLDERS AND/OR OTHER PARTIES
PROVIDE THE PROGRAM "AS IS" WITHOUT WARRANTY OF ANY KIND, EITHER EXPRESSED
OR IMPLIED, INCLUDING, BUT NOT LIMITED TO, THE IMPLIED WARRANTIES OF
MERCHANTABILITY AND FITNESS FOR A PARTICULAR PURPOSE. THE ENTIRE RISK AS
TO THE QUALITY AND PERFORMANCE OF THE PROGRAM IS WITH YOU. SHOULD THE
PROGRAM PROVE DEFECTIVE, YOU ASSUME THE COST OF ALL NECESSARY SERVICING,
REPAIR OR CORRECTION.

    12. IN NO EVENT UNLESS REQUIRED BY APPLICABLE LAW OR AGREED TO IN WRITING
WILL ANY COPYRIGHT HOLDER, OR ANY OTHER PARTY WHO MAY MODIFY AND/OR
REDISTRIBUTE THE PROGRAM AS PERMITTED ABOVE, BE LIABLE TO YOU FOR DAMAGES,
INCLUDING ANY GENERAL, SPECIAL, INCIDENTAL OR CONSEQUENTIAL DAMAGES ARISING
OUT OF THE USE OR INABILITY TO USE THE PROGRAM (INCLUDING BUT NOT LIMITED
TO LOSS OF DATA OR DATA BEING RENDERED INACCURATE OR LOSSES SUSTAINED BY
YOU OR THIRD PARTIES OR A FAILURE OF THE PROGRAM TO OPERATE WITH ANY OTHER
PROGRAMS), EVEN IF SUCH HOLDER OR OTHER PARTY HAS BEEN ADVISED OF THE
POSSIBILITY OF SUCH DAMAGES.

    END OF TERMS AND CONDITIONS


    How to Apply These Terms to Your New Programs

    If you develop a new program, and you want it to be of the greatest
possible use to the public, the best way to achieve this is to make it
free software which everyone can redistribute and change under these terms.

    To do so, attach the following notices to the program. It is safest
to attach them to the start of each source file to most effectively
convey the exclusion of warranty; and each file should have at least
the "copyright" line and a pointer to where the full notice is found.

 <one line to give the program's name and a brief idea of what it does.>
    Copyright (C) 19yy <name of author>

    This program is free software; you can redistribute it and/or modify
    it under the terms of the GNU General Public License as published by
    the Free Software Foundation; either version 2 of the License, or
    (at your option) any later version.

    This program is distributed in the hope that it will be useful,
    but WITHOUT ANY WARRANTY; without even the implied warranty of
    MERCHANTABILITY or FITNESS FOR A PARTICULAR PURPOSE. See the
    GNU General Public License for more details.

    You should have received a copy of the GNU General Public License
    along with this program; if not, write to the Free Software
    Foundation, Inc., 59 Temple Place, Suite 330, Boston, MA 02111-1307 USA

Also add information on how to contact you by electronic and paper mail.

If the program is interactive, make it output a short notice like this
when it starts in an interactive mode:

    Gnomovision version 69, Copyright (C) 19yy name of author
    Gnomovision comes with ABSOLUTELY NO WARRANTY; for details type 'show w'.
    This is free software, and you are welcome to redistribute it
    under certain conditions; type 'show c' for details.

The hypothetical commands 'show w' and 'show c' should show the appropriate
parts of the General Public License. Of course, the commands you use may
be called something other than 'show w' and 'show c'; they could even be
mouse-clicks or menu items--whatever suits your program.

You should also get your employer (if you work as a programmer) or your
school, if any, to sign a "copyright disclaimer" for the program, if
necessary. Here is a sample; alter the names:
```

Example 3-5 The GPL (Continued)

> Yoyodyne, Inc., hereby disclaims all copyright interest in the program
> 'Gnomovision' (which makes passes at compilers) written by James Hacker.
>
> <signature of Ty Coon>, 1 April 1989
> Ty Coon, President of Vice

This General Public License does not permit incorporating your program into
proprietary programs. If your program is a subroutine library, you may
consider it more useful to permit linking proprietary applications with the
library. If this is what you want to do, use the GNU Library General
Public License instead of this License.

Of Course, I Trust My Users!

Users, Permissions, and Filesystems

The very first step in securing any Linux system (or any UNIX system, for that matter) is to secure the user and group accounts of that system. This includes encouraging good password selection; restricting user access to only those files, directories, and shells that are absolutely necessary; and properly managing the root account. Linux provides a variety of tools to assist you in managing your users and groups from a security perspective. This chapter will describe the fundamental elements of user and group account management, file and directory permissions, and filesystem management as it relates to user and group access. The primary purpose of this chapter is to cover the necessary basics. For a more thorough coverage of the material presented here, please read *Practical UNIX and Internet Security* as referenced in the section, *System Security* on page 80.

USER ACCOUNT MANAGEMENT

Linux provides a multiuser environment.[1] This means that many users have the opportunity of accessing and utilizing the same Linux computer. Some systems will have many user accounts, while others will have few. Each user

---

1. For further information regarding creating and maintaining user and group accounts, from an administrative perspective, see *For Further Reading* on page 80.

account on a Linux system represents a potential vulnerability (see Chapter 1). Here are some tips for creating and maintaining user accounts with security in mind.

- ☞ Choose good passwords.
- ☞ Ensure that all user accounts either have passwords or are locked.
- ☞ Use password aging and the shadow file.
- ☞ Maintain restrictive file permissions.
- ☞ Use pluggable authentication modules (PAM—discussed in Chapter 5).
- ☞ Use `xlock` or `xscreensaver`.

Additional user and group security management practices include accounting (discussed in Chapter 7), logging (discussed in Chapter 8 and Chapter 17), and auditing (such as with `tiger`, discussed in Chapter 13).

Good Passwords

Choosing good passwords is a double-edged sword. You want users to pick passwords that are difficult to guess, yet easy to remember. Difficult to guess means that the password should not be something associated with the user, such as names of siblings, children, dogs, car license plates, or something that the user enjoys doing. If this type of password is chosen, anyone who even casually knows the user may be able to guess the user's password.

Good password choices should also not include dictionary words. Programs such as Crack (detailed in Chapter 12) will easily guess dictionary words and passwords based on dictionary words. For example, using `g1zm0s` as a password is a poor choice because it is based on the dictionary word *gizmos*. Even more complex variations make poor choices. For instance, `18rd00dz`, is based upon *later dudes*.

One way to select a difficult-to-guess password is to remember a sentence, such as:

The two foxes jumped over the brown fence.

From this sentence, there are a number of ways to derive passwords; we give two examples. The first, *T2fjotbf*, comes simply by taking the first letter from each word, except for the word *two*, which is replaced with the number 2. The second, *h2ouvhre*, is obtained by taking the second letter of each word, except again for the word *two*. Use your imagination to come up with other more sophisticated schemes. The point of this discussion is to encourage choosing difficult-to-guess, but easy-to-remember passwords.

Another approach to selecting good user passwords is to assign them. You could write or use an existing password-generating program or manually select passwords, such as *i%8TQ#1r*. In this way, you, the administrator, have complete control over user passwords. Unfortunately, your user probably won't be able to remember such a password. So what will the user do? Write it down, of course! At this point, you can only hope that the user doesn't write it on a sticky note and paste it on the corner of his or her monitor! This problem gets worse if you enforce password aging. See *Password Aging and the Shadow File* on page 61.

In spite of all your efforts, even a difficult-to-guess password becomes essentially worthless with the advent of fast, cheap computers, utilities like Crack, and network sniffers.[2] If a bad-guy obtains a list of your usernames and hashed passwords,[3] he can run Crack against the list until Crack succeeds in matching a hashed password. If the user is logging in over a network, both username and password are sent in the clear (unless the session is encrypted). This makes it even easier for a bad-guy. All he needs is a network sniffer to capture all the passing packets in the clear! No need for Crack now! There are many things discussed throughout this book that you can do to mitigate these types of attacks, most of which revolve around the rule, *practice perseverance and vigilance* (see Chapter 2).

The attacks outlined above work in good part because Linux login passwords, by default, are static. That is, the same password is used repeatedly until the user or administrator changes it. Instead of using static passwords, you may wish to explore the use of one-time passwords (OTP). Utilities providing OTP functionality will be discussed in Chapter 6. Generally speaking, however, it is the unusual environment that uses OTP inside an organization's computing environment (as opposed to external or outside or passing through a public network). So, choose good passwords!

All Accounts Must Have Passwords! Or Be Locked!

Never allow an account without a password! Never! If you have such an account, it is simply a matter of time before a bad-guy compromises your system. If you need to grant access to a guest user on a system, do so for the minimum amount of time necessary and give her or him a password during that time. Give any such transient user a restricted shell (see *Restricted Accounts* on page 64). You may also set a password expiration date using chage discussed in the section *Password Aging and the Shadow File* on page 61.

There are many accounts on a Linux system that are locked; that is, they do not have a valid password and therefore cannot be logged into directly.

---

2. Network sniffer is a general term describing a utility capable of capturing network packets passing through the network interface. The tcpdump and sniffit utilities, discussed in the section, *Network Monitoring* on page 38, are examples.

3. The password entry contained in /etc/passwd or /etc/shadow is often referred to as *encrypted*. For the reasons cited in *One-Way Cryptographic Hash Functions* on page 44 we will use the term *hashed* instead.

Example 4-1 below shows a few sample entries in a Linux password file (which is **not** using /etc/shadow). Notice that a number of accounts have an asterisk (*) in the password field instead of a hashed password. These accounts cannot be logged into except by root through the use of su (or sudo—see Chapter 9 for a discussion of sudo). Each line in this file represents a record. Each record is a series of colon (:) separated fields. The fields are, from left to right, username, hashed password, UID, GID, comment field, home directory, and shell.

Example 4-1 Truncated Sample /etc/passwd File

```
root:otlYOTgV5e.Bk:0:0:root:/root:/bin/bash
bin:*:1:1:bin:/bin:
daemon:*:2:2:daemon:/sbin:
adm:*:3:4:adm:/var/adm:
lp:*:4:7:lp:/var/spool/lpd:
sync:*:5:0:sync:/sbin:/bin/sync
shutdown:*:6:0:shutdown:/sbin:/sbin/shutdown
halt:*:7:0:halt:/sbin:/sbin/halt
mary:.Ql7yU3a8bNrK:103:103:Mary Smith:/home/mary:/bin/bash
```

The accounts with no valid passwords (* in the second field) exist to allow programs to be run as the UID associated with that account. They are not direct login accounts. If you must create such an account, remember to disable direct access in this way.

OH, BY THE WAY...

Using an asterisk (*) in the password field is not the only way to disable user authentication. Any entry that does not represent a valid hashed password will suffice. Generally, this means that any entry in the second field of the /etc/passwd (or /etc/shadow, if you are using the shadow file [discussed in *Password Aging and the Shadow File* on page 61]) that is less than 13 characters will suffice. Using a single character like * makes it visually simpler to identify locked accounts.

There is another use for locked accounts. When users leave your organization, if you need to retain their environments, lock their account. In this way, those accounts won't easily be compromised but, as root, you will still be able to access them. One of the most common ways that systems are compromised is through the use of dormant accounts. Always either lock or remove all such accounts as soon as possible.

Unfortunately, simply locking the account by disabling the password, as described in this section, is not sufficient to prohibit access to the locked account. Whenever you lock a user account, you must also remove all .rhosts, .netrc, and .forward files (the functionality of these files is described in Chapter 3) in the user's home directory to prevent access as that user. You should also change the user's shell in /etc/passwd to an invalid shell such as /dev/null or /bin/false, the latter being a shell script that executes exit. That way, even if someone is able to log in as that user, an immediate exit will be the result.

Password Aging and the Shadow File

Password aging is the process of limiting the length of time for which a user's password is valid. Password aging may be implemented on a systemwide basis as described in the section *The /etc/login.defs File* on page 63. It may also be implemented on a per-user basis by using the /etc/shadow file. This file, often referred to as simply the shadow file, contains the hashed password and password aging information for each user. It does not exist, by default. Let's take a look at creating and using the shadow file.

The Red Hat 5.2/6.0 distribution of Linux makes it easy to create a shadow file. If your distribution of Linux supports the shadow file, you should use it. Here's why. The shadow file contains the hashed password of each user, together with password aging information. Further, its permissions are set to read-only by root. Thus, by creating the shadow file, you significantly restrict access to the system's hashed passwords, and you get additional password aging capabilities. Since the permissions of the /etc/passwd file include world readability by default, any user is able to read and, therefore, copy it. If you don't use a shadow file, this means that all hashed passwords are retained in /etc/passwd. Enter Crack (see Chapter 12) and your system is compromised.

To create the shadow file on Red Hat 5.2/6.0, simply execute the pwconv command as root. It will automatically create the /etc/shadow file and move all of the hashed passwords into it. It also removes all password entries (hashed passwords or *) from /etc/passwd and puts an x in the second field of each user account. If for some reason you need to reverse this process, it is very simple; just execute pwunconv as root. Of course, you will lose all password aging information contained in /etc/shadow after executing pwunconv.

Password aging, on a per-user basis, becomes functional only with the existence of the /etc/shadow file. Once created, you can use the chage command to generate password aging entries for each user. Example 4-2 shows a sample incomplete shadow file (**not** related to Example 4-1 on page 60).

Example 4-2 Truncated Sample /etc/shadow File

```
root:otlY/YgV5e.Bk:10640:0:99999:7:::
bin:*:10640:0:99999:7:::
daemon:*:10640:0:99999:7:::
adm:*:10640:0:99999:7:::
lp:*:10640:0:99999:7:::
sync:*:10640:0:99999:7:::
joe:E/ulR7fLAQO6o:10640:0:99999:7:::
mary:VBtHXaJk3IPD6:10640:7:30:3:45::
guest1:xdbt9JIxfCUvo:10640:0:99999:7::10640:
```

Much like the password file, the shadow file contains a record (one line) for each user. Each record contains a colon-separated list of fields. There are nine fields per record. The meaning of each field is described in Table 4.1.

There is no requirement to use any or all password aging parameters listed in Table 4.1. You may use those options that are appropriate for your users and environment.

Table 4.1 Fields within `/etc/shadow`

Field Number	Field Name	Command to Modify Field	Description
1	username	useradd, usermod, and userdel	The user account name. It must match identically an entry in /etc/passwd and each name must appear in the same order.
2	password	passwd	The hashed password. A 13- to 34-character entry using any of the ASCII characters a–z, A–Z, 0–9, ., $, and /.
3	last change	passwd or chage -d	The number of days since the epoch* that the password was changed.
4	minimum change	chage -m	The number of days that must pass after the password has been changed before it can be changed again.
5	maximum change	chage -M	The number of days after which the password must be changed.
6	warn	chage -W	The number of days before the password expires that the user is warned.
7	failed expire	chage -I	The number of days after a password expires that the account is locked.
8	expiration date	chage -E	The number of days since the epoch that this account will expire. At midnight on that date the account will be locked.
9	reserved	N/A	Reserved for future use.

*The Linux epoch is January 1, 1970.

Using `chage`   The `chage` command requires root privilege except for the `-l` option. All other options are defined in Table 4.1. Let's look at some examples.

Give the user `joe` a minimum of 14 days before he can change his password and a maximum of 30 days before he must change his password.

```
# chage -m 14 -M 30 joe
```

Expire `guest` on April 4, 1999.

```
# chage -E 04/04/99 guest
```

Here's how an ordinary user can examine when her password will expire.

```
$ chage -l mary
Minimum:           7
Maximum:           30
Warning:           3
Inactive:          45
Last Change:       Feb 18, 1999
Password Expires:  Mar 20, 1999
```

```
Password Inactive: May 04, 1999
Account Expires:   Never
```

The /etc/login.defs File   It turns out that using the /etc/shadow file isn't the only way to enforce password aging. The Red Hat 5.2/6.0 distribution includes the systemwide file /etc/login.defs. It has the ability to set password aging for all users (except root). This file also contains a number of other entries. Let's take a look at them.

The first part of the file contains directives that determine the location of each user's mailbox (see the comments in /etc/login.defs for more details).

The next part of the file, shown in Example 4-3, deals with systemwide password aging. The PASS_MAX_DAYS, PASS_MIN_DAYS, and PASS_WARN_AGE operate exactly like the maximum change, minimum change, and warn fields, respectively, in the /etc/shadow file (see Table 4.1 on page 62). If these entries and /etc/shadow entries exist for a particular user, the entries in /etc/shadow take precedence. If no entries exist in /etc/shadow for a user, the entries in /etc/login.defs will apply.

Example 4-3 Password Aging Directives in /etc/login.defs

```
PASS_MAX_DAYS    30
PASS_MIN_DAYS    10
PASS_MIN_LEN     5
PASS_WARN_AGE    7
```

The PASS_MIN_LEN directive dictates the minimum password length in characters for all users, except root. If you have implemented PAM, the PAM settings will take precedence (see Chapter 5).

Remember, /etc/shadow entries are per user, so, if the entries are set in /etc/login.defs and if there are not entries for every user, then for those users without /etc/shadow entries, password aging will behave in accordance with the directives listed here. This means that you may use this file to set standard password aging parameters and then fine-tune them for specific users.

The remainder of the file contains the entries shown in Example 4-4. The CHFN_AUTH and CHFN_RESTRICT directives may be set to either yes or no. If CHFN_AUTH is yes, whenever users execute the chfn or chsh commands,[4] the system will prompt them for their password. If you change this value to no, it will allow a user to change his or her *finger* information without supplying a password. Only root may change another user's *finger* information. If CHFN_RESTRICT is set to yes, the system will disallow the user from changing his or her "real" names with chfn -f.

The remaining entries are associated with the useradd and userdel commands. The useradd, usermod, and userdel commands are command-line utilities for managing user accounts. In the Red Hat 5.2/6.0 distribution, the

---

4. The chfn command allows users to change their finger information. The chsh command allows users to change their default shell in /etc/passwd.

Example 4-4 Remaining Directives in `/etc/login.defs`

```
UID_MIN                       500
UID_MAX                     60000
GID_MIN                       500
GID_MAX                     60000
#
CHFN_AUTH                   yes
#
CHFN_RESTRICT              yes
#
#USERDEL_CMD      /usr/sbin/userdel_local
#
CREATE_HOME       yes
```

UID_MIN, UID_MAX, and CREATE_HOME directives in the `/etc/login.defs` file set default behavior for the useradd command, while USERDEL_CMD is an optional enhancement directive for the userdel command.

With these settings, if you use the useradd command without specifying the UID, useradd will assign a UID of 500 to the first user you create, a UID of 501 to the second user, and so on up to the maximum UID of 60000. The CREATE_HOME directive may take on the value of yes or no. If set to yes, when useradd is invoked it will automatically create a home directory for the user in `/home`. If set to no, you must specify the -m flag with useradd in order to have it create the user's home directory. Additional defaults for useradd are specified in `/etc/default/useradd`. Where redundancy exists, the `/etc/login.defs` file prevails. For further information about useradd(8) on your system, refer to its man page.

The USERDEL_CMD directive specifies a script or program (absolutely qualified pathname) that is invoked prior to deleting a user account. By default, no script or program exists. The userdel command will not delete a user if that user is logged in and/or there are any running processes owned by the user. An administrator could use this directive to specify a custom script or program that would check for, and perhaps act on, anything that would prevent the deletion of the user account.

The GID_MIN and GID_MAX directives operate similarly to their UID counterparts except that they apply to GIDs. Groups, as well as the purpose of these directives, are discussed in more detail in the section *Group Account Management* on page 69.

The Red Hat 5.2/6.0 distribution, as well as other Linux variants, offer GUI tools that perform most or all of the actions described in this section. On Red Hat 5.2/6.0, if you prefer a GUI, look into linuxconf and/or the Red Hat Control Panel.

Restricted Accounts

If you need to set up a guest account, the best way to do so is to specify the restricted shell as the guest user's default shell. The Red Hat 5.2/6.0 distribution provides a restricted Korn shell. This shell imposes the following limitations.

☞ The cd command is disabled.

☞ The SHELL, ENV, and PATH shell environment variables cannot be changed.

☞ Only commands found in the directories listed in the PATH environment variable may be executed.

☞ Redirections that create files cannot be used.

Unfortunately, the only way to invoke the restricted shell (Red Hat 5.2/6.0) is with the /bin/ksh -r command. The reason this is unfortunate is because you can't specify a flag in the /etc/passwd file. So, we have to write a program that invokes the restricted shell. Example 4-5 serves this purpose. To compile this program, put it in a file called rksh.c and execute

```
$ gcc -o rksh rksh.c
```

and copy it to /bin/rksh and set it up to be owned by root with the permissions 755.

Example 4-5 Restricted Shell Program

```
/*        *******************************
                Restricted ksh
          *******************************
*/
#include <unistd.h>
#include <stdlib.h>
#include <errno.h>
int main()
{
        extern int errno;
        char *const rksh_argv[] = {"ksh", "-r", 0};
        int retval=0;
/*      Set up the environment   */
        putenv("PATH=/restrict/bin:/usr/local/rbin");
        putenv("IFS= \t\n");
        putenv("SHELL=/bin/rksh");
        putenv("ENV=/restrict/etc/profile");
/*      Invoke the restricted ksh       */
        retval=execv("/bin/ksh", rksh_argv);
        if (retval < 0)
                exit(errno);
        else
                exit(0);
}
```

Notice that this program specifies certain environment variables (with putenv). If you want to override any other shell environment variables, do so here. One of the variables set is the PATH environment variable. Given the PATH setting in Example 4-5, the user will not be able to execute any commands until you put them in /restrict/bin or /usr/local/rbin (in this example). Note that neither /restrict/bin nor /usr/local/rbin exists by default; they are shown here as examples. Make sure that there aren't any executables in the user's PATH that will allow access to an unrestricted shell, such as shells themselves (bash, ksh, csh, etc.), the chsh command, and editors like vi and emacs that permit shell escapes. Other applications or commands that permit access to an unrestricted shell should also not appear in any directory in the restricted PATH.

Also, you may wish to disallow this user write access to his or her home directory. To accomplish this, set the owner and group owner of the restricted user's home directory to a special user, like noaccess, who cannot login (no valid password; no valid shell; no .rhosts, .netrc, or .forward files). You should create the noaccess account specifically for this purpose and use it for nothing else. Set the permissions on the restricted user's home directory to 755 and the user will have a read-only home directory and a restricted shell.

There are other ways to implement restricted accounts. One such method is to use chroot (change root directory). Use of this utility will put a user into a directory that appears to be the root directory. See the man pages for chroot(1) (command line interface) and chroot(2) (programmatic interface). Whichever approach you take, whether from this book or elsewhere, be very careful setting up restricted accounts and test, test, test!

Shell History

An often overlooked resource of information is the shell history. The history built-in function of the bash shell, for example, maintains a list of commands executed by each user. This information is found in the $HOME/.bash_history by default. The contents of this file may be quite useful for troubleshooting and for auditing purposes. See the bash(1) man page or the man page of the shell you prefer for further details.

THE ROOT ACCOUNT

Root! The ultimate source of power on Linux! This one account grants God-like power over the entire system. It is very convenient and useful. The problem is that, if you are responsible for the system, you likely don't want unauthorized people to have this capability. Meanwhile, there are those who have tasted the power and want more!

The topic of most of this book surrounds making root access difficult, both through preparation and maintenance. Here we just make some simple suggestions for configuring and using the root account.

Using the Root Account

There are four very important rules to live by regarding the use of the account.

1. Allow root access only through su or sudo (sudo is discussed in Chapter 9).
2. Become root only when absolutely necessary.
3. Execute every command as root with caution.
4. Whenever you must remotely administer a system as root, use SSH (discussed in Chapter 11) and sudo.

Running as root all the time is not a good idea. Consider the root account to be a very special account (which it is!) for use under very special circumstances. Become root only to perform tasks that must be performed as root. In Chapter 9, we discuss the use of sudo to assist in restricting root access and generating a root audit trail. Restricting root access through su or sudo is discussed in the section, *Configuring /etc/securetty* on page 68.

When you do become root, be careful! For example, before you issue the shutdown command, verify that you are logged in to the system that you want to shut down by executing uname -n or hostname first. Before you execute rm -r *, make sure that you are in the right directory! Red Hat 5.2/6.0 helps out here by aliasing rm to rm -i (which causes rm to ask you if you want to delete each file before it actually deletes the file). In general, think twice before you perform some action as root.

Here are some tips for configuring the root account more restrictively.

1. Set up your PATH environment variable so that it contains a minimum number of entries.

   ✗ Do not put user writable directories in root's PATH. A more naive administrator may be coerced into executing a Trojan horse (see Chapter 1).

   ✗ For the same reason do not put "." (hard link to the current directory) in root's PATH.

2. Use absolute pathnames when invoking commands.
3. Do not specify / as root's home directory (Red Hat 5.2/6.0 uses /root).

SSH (which we explore thoroughly in Chapter 11) is capable of performing authentication beyond simple Linux passwords. It also builds an encryption tunnel between two systems, securing all aspects of the communication. Always use this utility (or something similar) when you must become root on a remote system.

Multiple root Users

On major systems, it is not uncommon for administration needs to require more than one person to be root. Sometimes multiple root accounts are configured for this purpose. Suppose, for example, that Mary and Bill are responsible for maintaining a particular system. One way to track the root activities of Mary and Bill is to set up two accounts, say rootm for Mary and rootb for Bill, each with a unique password and each with a UID of 0. Whenever Mary needs to gain privileged access, she would log in or `su` as `rootm`. Bill would do so as `rootb`.

The advantage of doing this is that it provides an audit trail (audit trails in the form of process accounting are described in Chapter 7 and in the form of system logging and `auditd` are described in Chapter 8) for each administrator and avoids the necessity of sharing a single password. The disadvantage is that each duplicated UID 0 account is another potential vulnerability. A better approach to maintaining an audit trail of administrator activity is to use `sudo` (discussed in Chapter 9).

Adding another UID 0 account is also a common cracker activity. Review your `/etc/passwd` file regularly (`tiger`, discussed in Chapter 13, can do this automatically for you) to detect any unauthorized entries, particularly unauthorized duplicate root accounts.

Minimizing the Impact of root Compromise

For all intents and purposes, after a bad-guy gains root access on one of your systems, the bad-guy owns that system. There are two things you can do to minimize the impact of root compromise. They are

1. Encrypt all sensitive files with such tools as CFS (described in Chapter 15) and PGP (discussed in Chapter 3).
2. Make pristine backups (discussed in Chapter 3) frequently. Pristine backups are based on Tripwire (discussed in Chapter 14), `tiger` (discussed in Chapter 13), and perhaps other similar utilities having been run.

If implemented properly, the use of encryption will make it quite difficult for the bad-guy to get to your sensitive data. And pristine backups ensure that you can recover to a known state after a compromise occurs.

Configuring `/etc/securetty`

The `/etc/securetty` file controls from where root may log in. By default on most Linux distributions, this file is set up so that root may log in only at the console (the monitor directly attached to the system or virtual console[s], accessed through the device `/dev/tty1`) and any virtual consoles (normally, `/dev/tty2` through `/dev/tty8`). If you are attempting to log in as root from any device not listed in `/etc/securetty`, it will be disallowed, forcing you to log in as an ordinary user and then to execute `su` to become root. Here is the default file from Red Hat 5.2/6.0:

```
# cat /etc/securetty
tty1
tty2
```

```
tty3
tty4
tty5
tty6
tty7
tty8
#
```

In particular, no entries of the form pts* are in this file, meaning that logging in over the network as root is prohibited. You may restrict this further by removing any unnecessary entries. You may also add additional entries, but you should do so with caution. Unless you use virtual consoles, you will want to allow root access only at the console which means that the /etc/securetty file should contain only tty1.[5]

If the /etc/securetty file exists, but is empty, then root may **not** log in from any device. This will force root access through su or sudo (sudo is discussed in Chapter 9) and represents a much more secure approach.

WARNING!

If the /etc/securetty does not exist at all, then root may log in from anywhere! The absence of this file should therefore always be avoided.

GROUP ACCOUNT MANAGEMENT

As discussed in *The /etc/login.defs File* on page 63, whenever a new user account is created in the Red Hat 5.2/6.0 distribution with the useradd command (or one of the GUIs), the GID is automatically selected by default. It turns out that, when it is automatically selected in this way, the GID is identical to the UID. This procedure is called user-private groups (UPG).

The advantage of using UPG is that each user will have his or her own group. In this way you could set the umask to 007 instead of 027 (see *User File and Directory Permissions* on page 71 for a discussion of umask). You may subsequently set up groups for collections of users separately.

Another feature of the Red Hat 5.2/6.0 distribution is that you may configure passwords for your groups and set up a group shadow file. You may execute grpconv, which is analogous to pwconv, to create an /etc/gshadow file to hold the hashed group passwords. When a group password is created with gpasswd (must be executed by root, or root may assign one of the group members to be the group administrator), members of the group are unaffected and may still use newgrp to assume the GID of that group. Nonmembers of the group may assume a GID if they know the group password. This is less secure

---

5. Note that serial devices in Linux are referenced through /dev/ttyS*. If you wish to allow root access over a serial connection, you would need to add for example ttyS0 to /etc/securetty.

than having no group passwords—when there are no group passwords, the newgrp command will disallow a user from assuming a GID of a group to which the user does not belong. Fear not however, if you still want to use group passwords, root may execute the gpasswd -R command on all system (or other sensitive) groups—this has the effect of disallowing newgrp to those groups (except for the root user, of course) altogether.

Exercise caution when creating groups of users. Make sure that they are always nonsystem groups (GID greater than 100 but less than 60001) and that they are assigned to files and directories in nonsystem filesystems (e.g., not /, /usr, /var, etc.). If you choose to enable group passwords, it would be wise to disable newgrp access (with gpasswd -R) minimally on all system groups.

FILE AND DIRECTORY PERMISSIONS

Establishing good file and directory permission standards for your system is a very important element of securing your computing environment. Many vulnerabilities arise simply because a file or directory has unsecure permissions.

In this section, we will briefly review file and directory permissions and their meanings. For a more thorough treatment of this topic, please refer to your system documentation and *For Further Reading* on page 80. We will also cover the special file attributes associated with the Linux second extended filesystem (ext2) in detail.

The command ls -l will display, among other things, the file type and permission settings of a file. Figure 4.1 shows an example of such a listing and identifies the permission applicability.

File permissions are displayed in triplets. The first triplet belongs to the user (u) who owns the file, the second triplet belongs to the group (g) that owns the file, and the third triplet belongs to every other (o) user. This last triplet is also referred to as the *world triplet*. Each triplet contains three fields. Recall that the octal representation of the permissions shown in Figure 4.1 is 755. The definitions of each of the fields is listed in Table 4.2.

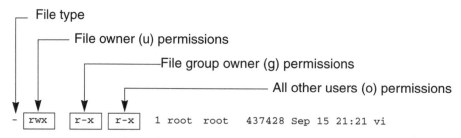

Fig. 4.1 File Type and Permissions

Table 4.2 File Permission Description

Permission	Description
r = read	On a file, this means that the file is readable. On a directory, it means that the contents of the directory may be viewed. It is located in the first position of a triplet.
w = write	On a file, this means that a file may be changed. On a directory, it means that files contained in the directory may be deleted or added. It is located in the second position of a triplet.
x = execute	On a file, this means that the file is executable. On a directory, it means that commands may be executed on the directory. It is located in the third position of a triplet.
s = set UID (SUID) or set GID (SGID)	This symbol is found only in the third position of the owner triplet or group triplet. If in the owner triplet, it means that, when executed, this file will execute with the UID of the owner of the file instead of the UID of the user executing the program. If in the group triplet, the executed file will assume the GID of the group owner instead of the primary GID of the user executing the program. If the SGID bit is set on a directory, then all files and subdirectories inherit the GID of the SGID directory instead of the GID of the process. Note that this flag has other meanings in other contexts. See the references cited in *System Administration* on page 80 for further details.
t = sticky	This symbol is found in the third position of the other triplet for some directories such as /var/tmp. Ordinarily, if the execute and write permissions are specified in the other triplet on a directory, then any user may, for example, delete any file in that directory regardless of ownership and permissions. The use of this setting prevents users other than the owner (or root) from removing or modifying a file in such a directory. See the references cited in *System Administration* on page 80 for further details.
- = no permission	If this symbol appears in any position, it means that no permissions are assigned in that position.

User File and Directory Permissions

When a user creates a file or directory, the final permissions assigned to that file or directory are controlled by the umask. The umask is a built-in shell function that removes (masks out) certain permission bits set by a program.

OH, BY THE WAY...

The way a file or directory ends up with its permission settings at creation time is as follows: The program that creates the file or directory sets the permissions a certain way. For example, the touch command sets file permissions to 666. Before the file permissions are set, however, the umask value is applied. So, if the umask value is 022, then the final file permission setting is 644. It is often stated that this is as a result of subtracting the umask from the programmatic permission setting. While this may be an easy way to remember the process, it is not exactly correct.

Oh, By the Way... (Continued)

What actually occurs is that the requested permissions (by `touch` in our example) are logically ANDed with the 1's complement of the `umask` value. This sounds complex, but it really isn't. So let's go through it. Each of the logical operations—AND (`&&`) and 1's complement (′)—are binary operations. We define the logical AND operation in Table 4.3.

Table 4.3 Definition of Logical AND

&&	0	1
0	0	0
1	0	1

The 1's complement means to flip the bit. That is:

```
(1)′ = 0
(0)′ = 1
```

So now that we know the definitions of `&&` and ′, let's try an example. Suppose that the permission settings of the file are 666 (that's octal) and the `umask` is 022 (also octal). First, convert the octal values to binary. That's easy—

```
666 in octal is 110110110 in binary
022 in octal is 000010010 in binary
```

Next take the 1's complement of the `umask` value,

```
(022)′ = (000010010)′ = 111101101
```

Now, apply the logical AND

```
    110110110
 && 111101101
   ──────────
    110100100
```

and we arrive at the result—110100100 in binary or 644 in octal. Which we knew all along. And if we think of it as subtraction, it works because 666 − 022 = 644. OK, but what if the `umask` value is 027, just how do you go about subtracting 027 from 666? (All right, it's easy to figure out, but we'll do it "right" anyway, OK?) If you use the definition, it works out right.

```
    110110110
 && (000010111)′
   ──────────
    110100000
```

Therefore, starting off with permissions 666 (110110110) and a `umask` value of 027 (000010111), the final permissions are 640 (110100000). Think how useful this will be on the Linux Trivia Game Show!

The default setting of the `umask` in Red Hat 5.2/6.0 is normally controlled by the `/etc/profile` file. In that file you will find that users with UPGs (see *Group Account Management* on page 69 for a discussion of UPGs) have their `umask` set to 002, while all other users have their `umask` set to 022. If we use the latter setting, it means that, for programs like `mkdir` and `vi`, directory permissions are set to 755 (`rwxr-xr-x`) and file permissions are set to 644 (`rw-r--r--`) when they are created. The problem with this default setting is that the world triplet retains permissions, meaning any user can read (and therefore copy) the directory or file. Your users are probably not going to pay a lot of attention to what should and should not be world readable. If you sincerely adopt the philosophy of *that which is not expressly permitted is forbidden*, then minimally you would change the `umask` to 027. Such a `umask` setting would eliminate all permissions from the world triplet on all newly created directories and files. Of course, whenever necessary, you may always change permission settings with `chmod`.

Unfortunately, from a security perspective, any user or process may set the `umask` for its shell. As a system administrator, you can put a more restrictive `umask` entry, like `umask 027`, in a global shell initialization file such as is described above, but any user can override this simply by executing

```
$ umask 022
```

or by placing this same statement in a local shell start-up file such as `$HOME/.profile`. Since `umask` is a shell built-in function, it is not an easy task to restrict it from general use. The only way to prevent this activity is to convince your users that the more restrictive setting is in everybody's best interest.

Most complaints about world permissions are likely to go away if groups (discussed in the section *Group Account Management* on page 69) are configured appropriately. If nothing else, a restrictive `umask` will force your users to think about it every time they want to grant world permissions.

System File and Directory Permissions

For the most part, system file and directory permissions should be static; that is, the operating system software that you install should be configured appropriately. Unless you have a good reason such as closing an identified vulnerability (see Appendix A), don't change it.

Maintaining proper ownership and permission settings on your system files and directories requires a fair amount of effort. The good news is that there are tools available to assist you in this regard, many of which will be discussed throughout this book. Of particular interest are the tools covered in Chapter 13 where we discuss `tiger`. Unfortunately, using such tools and maintaining what you believe to be the appropriate ownership and permission settings isn't enough. You must keep up-to-date on the latest vulnerabilities. Very often an exploit will be uncovered that takes advantage of system files and directories having certain ownership or permission settings by default. By keeping up-to-date, you will remain aware of any newly identified vulnerabilities shortly after they are published. See Appendix A for further details.

SUID and SGID

There are many programs and scripts on Linux that have the SUID and/or SGID permission setting. Many of these are necessary. However, each of them is a potential vulnerability. The most dangerous SUID programs and scripts are those owned by root.

In Chapter 1 we saw how dangerous an SUID root program can be. In *Filesystem Restrictions* on page 78, we look at some ways to mitigate SUID problems by disabling SUID on a filesystem basis.

In general, SUID or SGID system programs and scripts are there to support system functionality. You must determine whether or not all such functionality should be permitted on a given system (many resources for this activity are provided in Appendix A). If you determine that one or more SUID files are unnecessary, disable them with chmod and, most important, record what you have done. You may need to recover the functionality at some future date.

Monitor the SUID and SGID programs closely. It is quite common for a bad-guy to exploit some vulnerability and then leave an SUID root program or script in place as a back door. The key here is to use Tripwire (see Chapter 14) and tiger and keep up to date! Tripwire and tiger are two major weapons against system compromise. While they will not tell you the instant a compromise occurs, if you use them regularly and properly, they will identify system modifications and back doors when you do run them.

Keeping up-to-date is imperative. By paying attention to security advisories from organizations like CERT and bugtraq,[6] you will be empowered to plug security holes—hopefully before they are exploited.

SUID scripts are generally more dangerous than SUID programs. This is largely due to the fact that running a script first invokes a shell. If the script is SUID root, then the invoked shell will run as root. It is possible, after the shell is invoked but before the script runs, to interrupt the kernel and replace the file that the shell is going to execute. The replaced file could be any executable shell script, including another shell (which, in this case, would be a root shell). Unfortunately, there are numerous programs freely available on the Internet which exploit this type of vulnerability, so eradicate those SUID root scripts wherever possible.

If you *must* create a SUID root utility, write a C program or use Perl with the tainted (-T in Perl5) option. And practice secure programing techniques.[7]

---

6. See Appendix A for further information on these and other security tracking and reporting web sites and lists.

7. For an excellent discourse on this topic, see Simson Garfinkel and Gene Spafford, "Writing Secure SUID and Network Programs," *Practical UNIX and Internet Security*, 2d Ed., Sebastopol, California, O'Reilly & Associates, Inc., 1996, Chapter 23.

File Attributes

One of the really nice features of the Linux ext2 filesystem is the attribute capability. You may view a file's attributes with the `lsattr` command and change them with the `chattr` command. For example

```
# lsattr /bin/login
lsattr 1.12, 9-Jul-98 for EXT2 FS 0.5b, 95/08/09
----i--- /bin/login
```

In this example, the program `/bin/login` has the immutable (`i`) bit set. The immutable bit means that the file cannot be changed, no link may be created to this file, and the file cannot be renamed or deleted. Only root can remove this attribute. Table 4.4 summarizes the attributes. Note that not all Linux versions will support all attributes. The Red Hat 5.2 (kernel version 2.0.x) release does not support `A`, `c`, or `u`. The `s`, `i`, and `a` bits are the most significant with respect to security. Let's look at how `chattr` is used to set these attributes.

Let's suppose that you (or the organization for which you work) have some files with extremely sensitive data in them. At some point you may need to delete these files. Normally, when a file is deleted, the reference pointers to that file are dereferenced and made available for use by other files. The actual

Table 4.4 File Attributes

Symbol	Attribute Name	Description
s	secure deletion	If this attribute is set, when the file is deleted all of the blocks allocated for that file are zeroed out and written back to disk.
u	undelete	This attribute causes the file to be saved on deletion so that it may be undeleted.
c	compress	The file with this attribute set causes the kernel to compress the file.
S	synchronous	When a file with this attribute set is modified, all changes are written synchronously to the disk. Normally, this is done asynchronously.
i	immutable	If this attribute is set, the file cannot be modified, no link may be created to it, and it may not be removed or renamed. Only root can change this setting.
a	append only	A file with this attribute may be modified only in append mode. Only root can set or unset this attribute.
d	no dump	The file is not a candidate for the `dump` backup utility.
A	no atime	This attribute suppresses the updating of `atime`, the access timestamp of the file.

data is still out on the disk. Someone may access that data, either inadvertently or deliberately. To avoid this, set the secure deletion attribute on the file. When the file is deleted, all data blocks will be set to 0 and written to disk.[8] For example, we can set this attribute on the file really_private:

```
$ chattr -V +s really_private
chattr 1.12, 9-Jul-98 for EXT2 FS 0.5b, 95/08/09
Flags of really_private set as s-------
$
```

The -V flag of chattr is for verbose output, essentially saving the step of executing lsattr to confirm the setting. Notice that you need not be root to set the secure delete attribute. The only attributes requiring root privilege are the immutable (i) and append-only (a) attributes.

The a attribute is useful for log or similar files to which data is appended but not overwritten. When the a attribute is set, the only way to modify the file is by appending data to it. Once this bit is set, even root cannot remove the file. You can set the append-only attribute, for example, on /var/log/secure.

```
# chattr -V +a /var/log/secure
chattr 1.12, 9-Jul-98 for EXT2 FS 0.5b, 95/08/09
Flags of /var/log/secure set as -----a--
#
```

Let's verify that this file cannot be removed:

```
# rm /var/log/secure
rm: /var/log/secure: Operation not permitted
#
```

You may also set multiple flags using the = operator instead of the + operator:

```
# chattr -V =Aa /var/log/secure
chattr 1.12, 9-Jul-98 for EXT2 FS 0.5b, 95/08/09
Flags of /var/log/secure set as -----a-A
#
```

Here we are also setting the A attribute (no atime—see Table 4.4 on page 75), which suppresses access timestamp updating.

At some point you may need to unset an attribute. For example, to unset the a attribute on /var/log/secure:

```
# chattr -V -a /var/log/secure
chattr 1.12, 9-Jul-98 for EXT2 FS 0.5b, 95/08/09
Flags of /var/log/secure set as -------A
#
```

---

8. This does not guarantee complete erasure of the data. There are techniques to reconstruct the data on media even after the blocks are overwritten numerous times. See Chapter 15 for a more secure file deletion solution.

Of course, bear in mind that the bad-guys are reading this book, too! Always assume they know more than you do! Nothing discussed in this section will help if the root account is compromised. However, if you follow the guidelines laid out here, it will make the bad-guy execute more commands and take more time. That might just give you enough of an edge. In any event, using file attributes such as i and a will certainly prevent inadvertent actions by root on those files so protected.

USING xlock AND xscreensaver

One of the easiest things to do is to walk away from your system while you are still logged in. Maybe you want to get another cup of coffee, but instead of returning right away you end up speaking with a colleague for a time. Meanwhile, Murphy is at work.[9] You left your system logged in as root and Jack the Cracker wanders by. You know the rest.

To avoid this problem, use xlock. The xlock program will disable X Window System access to your computer until you enter your password. For example

```
# xlock -mode random
```

This invocation of xlock will select one of the 60 or so screensavers that come with the standard X11R6 release of X and lock your X Server (the display device, normally your monitor). You may accomplish the same thing by selecting Lock Screen from your background menu (choices may vary depending upon your window manager and/or desktop).

The problem with xlock is that you still have to remember to run it. So, you are effectively back to where you were at the beginning of this section. Fortunately, help is available in the form of xscreensaver.

The xscreensaver utility provides for the automatic locking of your X server. Simply place

```
xscreensaver.timeout: 2
```

in your $HOME/.Xdefaults file. This particular entry will cause your X server to automatically lock after two minutes of no mouse or keyboard activity. After you have changed the $HOME/.Xdefaults file, you will need to update your X server with

```
$ xrdb < $HOME/.Xdefaults
```

Note that these instructions will vary depending upon your choice of desktop (KDE, Gnome, etc.) and window manager (twm, fvwm, etc.). Check the appropriate documentation for details.

---

9. Murphy's Law: If something can go wrong, it will. O'Toole's comment about Murphy: He was an optimist.

FILESYSTEM RESTRICTIONS

Another element to assist in securing your system relates to the options specified when mounting local filesystems. Normally a Linux system will have a number of filesystems; however, it is possible to configure a Linux system with only one or very few filesystems. One reason why you may want to create multiple filesystems is to control access on them through the use of `mount` options specified in `/etc/fstab`.

In Example 4-6, we see an `/etc/fstab` file that was created, by default, at installation. For complete details on the syntax of this file and the definitions of each field, reference your system documentation or one of the System Administration references in *For Further Reading* on page 80. Our focus will be on the options field (fourth from left).

Example 4-6 The `/etc/fstab` File

```
/dev/hda1          /                    ext2      defaults      1 1
/dev/hda5          /usr                 ext2      defaults      1 2
/dev/hdb1          /home                ext2      defaults      1 2
/dev/hda6          /var                 ext2      defaults      1 2
/dev/hda7          swap                 swap      defaults      0 0
/dev/fd0           /mnt/floppy          ext2      noauto        0 0
/dev/cdrom         /mnt/cdrom           iso9660   noauto,ro     0 0
none               /proc                proc      defaults      0 0
```

Table 4.5 lists some of the options available to be placed in the fourth field (or as arguments of the `-o` flag to `mount` at the command line) of each record shown in Example 4-6. The table lists those options that are of interest from a security perspective.

Table 4.5 Security Related `mount` Options

Option	Description
defaults	Sets the mount options to `rw` (read/write), `suid` (allow SUID and SGID executions), `dev` (allow character or block special devices), `exec` (allow execution of binaries), `auto` (allow `mount -a`), `nouser` (only root can mount the filesystem), and `async` (asynchronous I/O).
nodev	Do not interpret or allow the creation of character or block special files (device files) on this filesystem.
noexec	Do not allow the execution of binaries or scripts on this filesystem.
nosuid	Do not allow SUID or SGID to take effect on this filesystem.
noatime	Suppresses the updating of the access time on all files and directories in this filesystem. This option is available in kernel version 2.2.x (Red Hat 6.0) and not in kernel version 2.0.x (Red Hat 5.2).
ro	Set this filesystem to read-only.
user	Allow users other than root to mount this filesystem. This automatically sets the options `noexec`, `nosuid`, and `nodev` unless explicitly overridden.

Prior to installing your system consider carefully the types of access required by your users. This may well dictate the filesystems you create. Consider these `mount` option guidelines for local filesystems:

1. Users' home directories should not be a breeding ground for SUID scripts and programs, and should never have character and block special files.

2. Any filesystem that has directories writable by other than root should minimally use the `nosuid` option. The `/var` filesystem is one such filesystem and is critical to your system.

3. Any filesystem that does not need to be written to except occasionally should be mounted read only.

Consider Example 4-6 on page 78. We ought to apply guideline 2 to the `/var` filesystem and guideline 1 to the `/home` filesystem. For user convenience, we may also wish to add the `user` option to `/mnt/cdrom`. This will allow nonroot users to mount CDs without root intervention. The additional restrictions associated with the `user` option—namely `nosuid`, `noexec`, and `nodev`—should offer sufficient security in exchange for this amenity.

Suppose that in the `/usr` filesystem you have a `/usr/local/bin` subdirectory that contains executables used by many users. If these executables don't change very often, you may wish to create a separate filesystem and to mount `/usr/local/bin` with the `ro` option. We'll show both this filesystem and `/usr/local/lib` (containing libraries or executables that may be invoked by other programs) with the `ro` option in Example 4-7. Unfortunately, if you do this, whenever you need to change something in `/usr/local/bin` or `/usr/local/lib`, you will need to remount it `rw` (preferably in single-user mode). With few exceptions, enhancing system and network security will have an impact on performance or convenience or both.

Example 4-7 shows our revised `/etc/fstab` table.

Example 4-7 A More Secure `/etc/fstab`

```
/dev/hda1            /                ext2      defaults               1 1
/dev/hdb4            /usr/local/bin   ext2      ro,nosuid              1 2
/dev/hdb9            /usr/local/lib   ext2      ro,nosuid              1 2
/dev/hda5            /usr             ext2      defaults               1 2
/dev/hdb1            /home            ext2      noexec,nodev,nosuid    1 2
/dev/hda6            /var             ext2      nosuid                 1 2
/dev/hda7            swap             swap      defaults               0 0
/dev/fd0             /mnt/floppy      ext2      noauto                 0 0
/dev/cdrom           /mnt/cdrom       iso9660   noauto,ro,user         0 0
none                 /proc            proc      defaults               0 0
```

SUMMARY

In this chapter, we took a cursory look at security issues surrounding user and group account management, file and directory permissions, and filesystems. We also pointed to some reference material that covers the topics discussed in greater detail.

FOR FURTHER READING

System Administration

1. Hein, Jochen, *Linux Companion for System Administrators*, Harlow, England, Addison-Wesley, 1999.
2. Komarinski, Mark F., and Cary Collett, *Linux System Administrator's Handbook*, Upper Saddle River, New Jersey, Prentice Hall PTR, 1998.
3. Nemeth, Evi, et al., *UNIX System Administration Handbook*, 2d ed., Englewood Cliffs, New Jersey, Prentice Hall PTR, 1995.

System Security

The following book is outstanding.

1. Garfinkel, Simson, and Gene Spafford, *Practical UNIX and Internet Security*, 2d ed., Sebastopol, California, O'Reilly & Associates, Inc., 1996.

An excellent general security resource for Linux is TrinityOS written by David A. Ranch. You can find his document at

```
http://www.ecst.csuchico.edu/~dranch/TrinityOS.wri
```

Been Cracked? Just Put PAM On It!

Pluggable Authentication Modules

Although pluggable authentication modules (PAM) cannot protect your system after it has been compromised, it can certainly help prevent the compromise to begin with. It does this through a highly configurable authentication scheme. For example, conventionally UNIX users authenticate themselves by supplying a password at the password prompt after they have typed in their username at the `login` prompt. In many circumstances, such as internal access to workstations, this simple form of authentication is considered sufficient. In other cases, more information is warranted. If a user wants to log in to an internal system from an external source, like the Internet, more or alternative information may be required—perhaps a one-time password. PAM provides this type of capability and much more. Most important, PAM modules allow you to configure your environment with the necessary level of security.

This chapter describes the use of pluggable authentication modules for Linux (Linux-PAM or just PAM[1]), as distributed with Red Hat 5.2/6.0, which provides a lot of authentication, logging, and session management flexibility. We generally describe PAM and its configuration, take a look at many of the available PAM modules,[2] and consider a number of examples.

---

1. Pluggable authentication modules were originally developed by Sun Microsystems, Inc.
2. Pluggable authentication modules modules (PAM modules) is brought to you by the department of redundancy department.

Most recent Linux distributions include PAM. If your version does not, check out the web site:

    http://www.kernel.org/linux/libs/pam/

There you will find source code and documentation. It is well worth the effort to download, compile, and integrate PAM into your system.

PAM provides a centralized mechanism for authenticating all services. It applies to `login`, remote logins (`telnet` and `rlogin` or `rsh`), `ftp`, Point-to-Point Protocol (PPP), and `su`, among others. It allows for limits on access of applications, limits of user access to specific time periods, alternate authentication methods, additional logging, and much more. In fact, PAM may be used for any Linux application! Cool! Let's see how it works.

PAM OVERVIEW

In this section, we will describe the way in which PAM operates, generally how to configure PAM, and the keywords and options associated with the PAM configuration files. Figure 5.1 presents an overview diagram of the Linux-PAM interaction with Linux applications. This diagram depicts the major components of a PAM implementation—applications, such as `login`, `ftp`, `su`, etc.; the Linux-PAM engine (the PAM libraries, found in `/lib`), which is

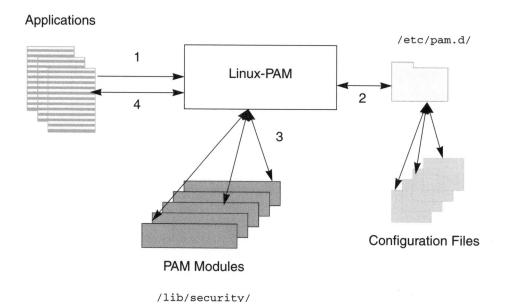

Fig. 5.1 Linux-PAM Overview

responsible for loading the necessary PAM modules based on the configuration files. The general flow of execution follows:

1. The application—for example `login`—makes an initial call to Linux-PAM.

2. Linux-PAM locates the appropriate configuration file in `/etc/pam.d` (or, alternatively, `/etc/pam.conf`) to obtain the list of modules necessary for servicing this request.

3. Linux-PAM then loads each module in the order given in the configuration file for processing. Depending upon configuration parameters, not all modules listed in the configuration file will necessarily be invoked.

4. Some, or all, of the modules may need to have a *conversation* with the user through the calling application. This conversation normally includes prompting the user for some sort of information, like a password or challenge, and receiving a response. If the user's response satisfies the particular PAM module, or if the PAM module is satisfied in some other way, control is passed back to Linux-PAM for processing of the next module (steps 3 and 4 being repeated for each module in the configuration file associated with the application in question). Ultimately, the processing completes with either success or failure. In the case of failure, it is generally true that the error message displayed to the user will not be indicative of the cause of failure. This generic error messaging approach is a security feature since it limits information that could be used in compromise efforts. Fortunately, most PAM modules offer varying levels of logging, allowing system administrators to track down problems and identify security violations.

PAM Configuration

There are two different PAM configuration compile-time options. The first causes PAM either to use a single `/etc/pam.conf` file as its configuration file or to look for a collection of configuration files in `/etc/pam.d`, but not both. The second option uses both mechanisms and entries in `/etc/pam.d` directory override those in `/etc/pam.conf`. The first option is recommended and reflects the implementation used by the Red Hat 5.2/6.0 distributions.

There is little difference between using a single `/etc/pam.conf` and a collection of files in `/etc/pam.d`. Essentially, if you are using `/etc/pam.conf`, each entry in `/etc/pam.conf` contains a leading service-type field that specifies the PAM-aware application to which this entry pertains. If you use `/etc/pam.d`, you will find a file in that directory whose name matches a PAM-aware application. Consequently, the service-type field is dropped from each of these files. We will discuss the configuration options under the assumption of the use of `/etc/pam.d`. For those of you who use `/etc/pam.conf`, just add the service type to the entries described here.

Let's begin by taking a look at the contents of `/etc/pam.d`, shown in Example 5-1. This effectively lists the PAM-aware applications that ship with the Red Hat 5.2 distribution (6.0 is similar). Each of the files listed has a PAM-aware application associated with it. In all of these configuration files, lines beginning with # are comment lines and are ignored by PAM.

Example 5-1 Contents of `/etc/pam.d`

```
# ls /etc/pam.d
chfn           linuxconf-pair   ppp        su
chsh           login            rexec      vlock
ftp            mcserv           rlogin     xdm
imap           other            rsh        xlock
linuxconf      passwd           samba
```

Each of the PAM configuration files contains the entry types shown in Example 5-2. The `module-type` field specifies the type of PAM module. Currently there are four module types, `auth`, `account`, `session`, and `password`. They are described in Table 5.1.

Example 5-2 PAM Configuration File Entry Fields

```
module-type    control-flag    module-path    arguments
```

The `control-flag` field specifies the action to be taken depending on the result of the PAM module. More than one PAM module may be specified for a given application (this is called *stacking*). The `control-flag` also determines the relative importance of modules in a stack. As we will see, stack order and `control-flags` are very significant. The four possible values for this field are `required`, `requisite`, `optional`, and `sufficient`. They are summarized in Table 5.2.

The `module-path` field indicates the absolute pathname location of the PAM module. Red Hat 5.2/6.0 places all PAM modules in `/lib/security`. (Table 5.15 on page 110 provides an overview of many of the available PAM modules, both from the Red Hat distribution and the public domain.)

Table 5.1 PAM Module Types

Module Type	Description
auth	The `auth` module instructs the application to prompt the user for identification such as a password. It may set credentials and may also grant privileges.
account	The `account` module checks on various aspects of the user's account such as password aging, limit access to particular time periods or from particular locations. It also may be used to limit system access based on system resources.
session	The `session` module type is used to provide functions before and after session establishment. This includes setting up an environment, logging, etc.
password	The `password` module type is normally stacked with an `auth` module. It is responsible for updating the user authentication token, often a password.

Table 5.2 PAM Control Flags

Control Flag	Description
required	This module must return success for the service to be granted. If this module is one in a series of stacked modules, all other modules are still executed. The application will not be informed as to which module or modules failed.
requisite	As above, except that failure here terminates execution of all modules and immediately returns a failure status to the application.
optional	As the name implies, this module is not required. If it is the only module, however, its return status to an application may cause failure.
sufficient	If this module succeeds, all remaining modules in the stack are ignored and success is returned to the application. In particular, if the module succeeds, this means that no subsequent modules in the stack are executed, regardless of the control flags associated with the subsequent modules. If this module fails it does not necessarily cause failure of the stack, unless it is the only module in the stack.

The arguments field is used for specifying flags or options that are passed to the module. Specifying arguments is optional. There are certain general arguments available for most modules which are listed in Table 5.3. Other arguments are available on a per-module basis and will be discussed appropriately with each module.

In summary, each file in /etc/pam.d is associated with the service or application after which the file is named and contains a list of records, each of which contains a module type, control flag, module name and location, and optional arguments. If the modules are of the same type, they are considered to be stacked and will be executed in the order in which they appear, unless control flags terminate execution earlier. The entire stack, not just one module,

Table 5.3 PAM Standard Arguments

Standard Arguments	Description
debug	Generates additional output to the syslog* utility. Most PAM modules support this argument. Its exact definition depends on the module to which this argument is supplied.
no_warn	Do not pass warning messages to the application.
use_first_pass	This module will use the password from the previous module. If it fails, no attempt is made to obtain another entry from the user. This argument is intended for auth and password modules only.
try_first_pass	As above, except that, if the password fails, it will prompt the user for another entry. This argument is intended for auth and password modules only.

*The syslog utility is discussed in detail in Chapter 8.

controls behavior for the given service and module type. Arguments are optionally used to further control the behavior of the module.

Now let's see how this mechanism is actually implemented.

PAM ADMINISTRATION

One of the joys of working with freely available software is that it is often
poorly or incorrectly documented or it doesn't work quite right (or at all!).
There are various news groups to which you may post queries (see Appendix
A), and some vendors (such as Red Hat and S.u.S.E.) maintain their own mailing lists which are helpful from time to time. Often, however, you will find
yourself having to figure it all out on your own. This section will go beyond the
currently available documentation and hopefully will give you a good start on
using PAM.

PAM and Passwords

We begin by taking a look at how PAM may be used to control password
choices and password aging. Example 5-3 shows the /etc/pam.d/passwd configuration file. Notice that there are two entries with the password module type.
This is an example of stacked entries. Let's go through these entries in detail.
It gets a little complicated, but once we get through it, the rest of this chapter
should be easier to understand.

Example 5-3 The /etc/pam.d/passwd Configuration File

```
auth       required     /lib/security/pam_pwdb.so
account    required     /lib/security/pam_pwdb.so
password   required     /lib/security/pam_cracklib.so retry=3
password   required     /lib/security/pam_pwdb.so use_authtok
```

NOTE

Throughout this chapter, we will often refer to the PAM modules without the trail-
ing .so. For example, we will refer to /lib/security/pam_pwdb.so as simply
pam_pwdb in the text but /lib/security/pam_pwdb.so will be used in all examples, as required.

The Password Database Library   The /lib/security/pam_pwdb module interacts with and requires the password database library (pwdb library, libpwdb,
found in /lib). The purpose of the pwdb library is to provide a centralized database for lookups of information associated with users and groups. Specifically,
it provides the source of passwords for pam_pwdb.

The pwdb library requires an /etc/pwdb.conf configuration file. Example
5-4 shows a sample file. The file contains two distinct sections—the first, preceded by the user: keyword, pertains to information associated with users.

Example 5-4 The /etc/pwdb.conf File

```
# This is the configuration file for the pwdb library
    #
user:
 unix+shadow
 nis+unix+shadow
group:
 unix+shadow
 nis+unix+shadow
```

The second, preceded by the group: keyword, pertains to information associated with groups. After the section header, you see keywords concatenated with + symbols, called *lists*. Each list represents the collection of databases that are merged to form the records for each user or group. For example, the unix+shadow list under the user: section is a list consisting of the contents of the /etc/passwd and /etc/shadow files. The nis+unix+shadow entry specifies the list containing NIS[3] (formerly yp) records as well as the contents of the /etc/passwd and /etc/shadow files. The entries for groups are entirely similar.

When the pam_pwdb module is invoked, it in turn invokes the pwdb library. The pwdb library will find the first entry that matches the user or group passed to it by pam_pwdb, based on the entries in /etc/pwdb.conf. Thus order is important in that file. The lists that appear first are searched first and pwdb stops at the first match.

The pam_pwdb Module   The pam_pwdb module is capable of operating in support of all four module types.

Module type auth.   When the auth type is specified, it functions to authenticate the user by prompting the user for a password and querying pwdb with the username/password pair. It can take the following arguments: debug, use_first_pass, try_first_pass, nullok, and nodelay. All other arguments supported by pam_pwdb but not by the auth module type are silently ignored. Any other arguments will be logged as errors through syslog, but will not affect the function of the module. The first three arguments are described in Table 5.3 on page 85.

The nullok argument *allows accounts with no passwords*. Of course, you would never specify this argument, right? The default behavior, therefore, is that this module treats accounts with no passwords as if they were locked accounts. This is good!

The nodelay argument causes this module to return immediately on failure. Normally this module will delay prior to reporting an authentication failure, making it slower for an attacker to try to guess passwords.

So what is the purpose of the line:

```
    auth        required        /lib/security/pam_pwdb.so
```

3. See Chapter 3 for further details about NIS. NIS was formerly known as Yellow Pages (YP).

Table 5.4 Arguments for `pam_pwdb` Module Type `password`

Argument	Description
nullok	Allows for the changing of a null (nonexistent) password. For the reasons outlined earlier, use of this argument is not recommended.
not_set_pass	Causes this module to ignore passwords from previous modules and disallows this module from passing new passwords to subsequent modules.
use_authtok	This argument forces the module to set the new password to the one received from the previously stacked module.
md5, bigcrypt	Instead of using the conventional UNIX password hashing algorithm (invoked through the `crypt` function call), you may choose one or the other of these.
shadow, radius, unix	Allows for the transfer of passwords from one database to another through the `pwdb` library.

in Example 5-3 on page 86? It causes users to be prompted for their old password prior to being prompted (by `pam_cracklib`) for their new password! Cool, huh? The root user is excepted from this requirement.

Module type password.   When the `pam_pwdb` module is used as module type `password`, it performs the task of updating the password. This means that, when a user invokes the `passwd` command, upon successfully entering a new password (as determined by `pam_cracklib`), `pam_pwdb` will update the new password with the `pwdb` library. The acceptable argument types are `debug`; `nullok`; `not_set_pass`; `use_authtok`; `try_first_pass`; `use_first_pass`; `md5`;[4] `bigcrypt`; `shadow`; `radius`; `unix`. Those arguments not already discussed are summarized in Table 5.4.

Notice in Example 5-3 on page 86, the `use_authtok` argument is specified. This means that `pam_pwdb` will use the new password it receives from `pam_cracklib`. Essentially, `pam_cracklib` controls the choice of the new password, but `pam_pwdb` actually does the updating.

NOTE

> The use of `md5` (MD5 is discussed in Chapter 3) or `bigcrypt` (a modified `crypt(3)` that allows for up to a 16-character password) arguments instead of the default, traditional UNIX `crypt(3)` for hashing is highly recommended. It allows for longer passwords that may be harder to guess by programs such as Crack (discussed in Chapter 12). In Red Hat 6.0, choosing MD5 is an install time option.

---

4. RSA Data Security, Inc., MD5 Message-Digest Algorithm.

Module type account.   When using `pam_pwdb` as module type `account`, its purpose is to verify account information of the user. This includes validating that the user has an account, what password aging parameters, if any, are associated with the user, and whether or not the user needs to be warned about a pending password expiration or offered advice on the choice of a new password. As this module type, `pam_pwdb` recognizes only the `debug` argument.

Module type session.   When using `pam_pwdb` as module type `session`, its sole purpose is to log the username and service type to `syslog`, once at login and then subsequently at logout. It recognizes no arguments.

The `pam_cracklib` Module   The `pam_cracklib` module is intended to work only with the `password` module type. It's purpose is to check a password for strength and for length, both elements being configurable with arguments described below. This module functions only in a stack, since it has no updating capabilities. It requires the `libcrack` library and the `cracklib_dict` Crack dictionary, both of which are found in `/usr/lib` of the Red Hat 5.2/6.0 distribution. As you can see, this module depends heavily on elements of the Crack utility, which is discussed in Chapter 12.

The flexibility of PAM is evidenced by the fact that this is not the only password strength checking PAM module. Another is `pam_passwd+`, which is available at

> `http://www.us.kernel.org/pub/linux/libs/pam/modules.html`

The arguments available to `pam_cracklib` are described in Table 5.5.

Table 5.5 Arguments for `pam_cracklib`

Argument	Description
`debug`	This argument writes additional module behavior information to `syslog`, but **does not** log passwords.
`type=STRING`	This argument replaces the string `UNIX` with `STRING` in the messages it generates, such as `New UNIX password:`.
`retry=n`	This is the number of retries this module allows a user when changing a password. The default is 1.
`difok=n`	This represents the number of characters in the new password that must be different from the old password. The default is 10. Regardless of this limit, however, any new password that has at least half the characters different from the old will be accepted.
`minlen=n`	This argument specifies the minimum password length + 1. By default it is set to 9 which means the minimum password length is actually 10. To further confuse the issue, this minimum length may actually be reduced depending upon the values specified for the `*credit` parameters listed below.

Table 5.5 Arguments for `pam_cracklib` (Continued)

Argument	Description
lcredit=*n*	The value specified here is the number of characters by which the `minlen` value is *reduced* by virtue of having at least one lowercase character in the new password. The default is 1. Can be set to 0 to eliminate the credit.
ucredit=*n*	The value specified here is the number of characters by which the `minlen` value is *reduced* by virtue of having at least one uppercase character in the new password. The default is 1. Can be set to 0 to eliminate the credit.
dcredit=*n*	The value specified here is the number of characters by which the `minlen` value is *reduced* by virtue of having at least one numeric character in the new password. The default is 1. Can be set to 0 to eliminate the credit.
ocredit=*n*	The value specified here is the number of characters by which the `minlen` value is *reduced* by virtue of having at least one nonalpha-numeric character in the new password. The default is 1. Can be set to 0 to eliminate the credit.

In addition to the configurable options in Table 5.5, the `pam_cracklib` checks the new password for strength by

1. Verifying that the new password is not the reverse of the old password.
2. Verifying that the new password is not a simple case change of some characters of the old password.
3. Checking if the new password is in the `cracklib_dict`. If it is, it warns the user but does not force another password choice.

The Effect of Stacking `pam_pwdb` and `pam_cracklib` For Module Type `password`   In this section, we will take a look at how `pam_cracklib` interacts with `pam_pwdb` in the stack shown in Example 5-3 on page 86.

Recall that in Example 5-3 the two stacked entries appeared in `/etc/pam.d/passwd`.

```
password    required    /lib/security/pam_cracklib.so retry=3
password    required    /lib/security/pam_pwdb.so use_authtok
```

The first entry invokes `pam_cracklib` and prompts the user for his or her new password (remember that the `auth` module type `pam_pwdb` entry is responsible for prompting the user for his or her *old* password, for authentication). After the user has supplied the new password, `pam_cracklib` requests that it be repeated for verification. Once completed, `pam_cracklib` performs its checks to see if the password is acceptable. If so, it passes the new password to `pam_pwdb` which has the `use_authtok` argument meaning it will accept this new password and request the `pwdb` library to update the appropriate database.

Let's take a look at the power and flexibility of these modules by considering an example. Suppose that we would like to use md5 instead of the standard UNIX crypt(3) mechanism for hashing purposes. This is a good idea, because popular password-guessing tools like Crack require significantly more CPU resources to guess passwords (see *The White Hat Use of Crack* on page 337). The major benefit of using md5 is that you can require longer passwords—20, 30, or even more characters. Let's look at an example requiring 20-character passwords. We'll also set the type argument to see if our users are paying attention. Example 5-5 shows what the stack might look like if we impose these changes in /etc/pam.d/passwd.

Example 5-5 Using md5 and minlen in /etc/pam.d/passwd

```
password    required      /lib/security/pam_cracklib.so minlen=20\
       retry=3 type=SECRET
password    required      /lib/security/pam_pwdb.so md5 use_authtok
```

WARNING

If you make changes similar to what is shown in Example 5-5, you must also change all equivalent instances of pam_pwdb and pam_cracklib using module type password. In Red Hat 5.2, this would minimally include the files chfn, chsh, login, rlogin, su, and xdm in /etc/pam.d.

Now that we have made these changes, let's see what happens to the user, mary, when she tries to change her password in Example 5-6. She is offered three opportunities to select a password. This is due to the retry=3 argument to pam_cracklib (see Example 5-5 on page 91). Actually, it appears that Mary is attempting to make good password choices. Unfortunately she doesn't know about the changes to PAM and therefore doesn't know that she needs to choose a longer password. So you, being the responsive administrator, inform her that she needs to use a 20-character password. "What?!" she replies. And you gently tell her that she can use a passphrase. Happy now, she goes about her task (Example 5-7).

Example 5-6 Unsuccessful Password Change

```
$ passwd
Changing password for mary
(current) UNIX password: j3n#Ky
New SECRET password: Rt!72g
BAD PASSWORD: is too simple
New SECRET password: 8x@$iI
BAD PASSWORD: is too simple
New SECRET password: P5-+yh
BAD PASSWORD: is too simple
New SECRET password: 8x@$iI
passwd: Authentication token manipulation error
$
```

Example 5-7 Successful Password Change

```
$ passwd
Changing password for mary
(current) UNIX password: j3n#Ky
New SECRET password: I need a #%$3+ raise
Retype new SECRET password: I need a #%$3+ raise
passwd: all authentication tokens updated successfully
$
```

Notice that the message displayed by `pam_cracklib` contains our type entry, `New SECRET password:`. This change does not appear in the message from `pam_pwdb`—`(current) UNIX password:`—because `pam_pwdb` does not support the `type` argument.

NOTE

> Normally, the passwords displayed in Example 5-6 and Example 5-7 are not visible. They are shown here for clarifying the examples.

While she chose a password of 20 characters (spaces count!), she wouldn't have been required to, because the default values of `dcredit`, `ucredit`, `lcredit`, and `ocredit` (see Table 5.5 on page 89) are 1 each. Because of her password choice, she would have a credit of 4, which would have allowed her to choose a password as short as 16 characters in length.

PAM and Passwords Summary

Figure 5.2 reviews Example 5-3 on page 86 in its entirety. When Mary executes the `passwd` command, Linux-PAM is invoked. Linux-PAM reads the `/etc/pam.d/passwd` file and executes each module listed in order. First

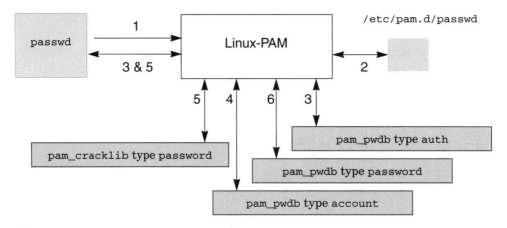

Fig. 5.2 PAM-Controlled Password Change

Mary is authenticated with her old password; this occurs due to the pam_pwdb entry with module type auth. Second, pam_pwdb is invoked with module type account to verify Mary's account (and to check, for example, if password aging permits her to change it now). Third, Mary is prompted for the new password by the pam_cracklib entry with module type password. Fourth, and finally, after Mary has successfully entered a new password, pam_pwdb with module type password updates the pwdb library. Now she has a new password.

NOTE

> The root user is not subject to any of these constraints and may set any password for any user.

Notice that all four entries in /etc/pam.d/passwd use the control flag required, which means that all four modules must be satisfied in order for the password change to be successful.

Now that we have a fundamental understanding of PAM, let's go on and look at some of the other services it manages.

PAM and login

The /etc/pam.d/login configuration file is read by Linux-PAM whenever the login (/bin/login) program is executed. Example 5-8 is a sample of this file. From the previous section, we have a good idea of what is going on here. Let's examine the details of the action of each module type.

Example 5-8 Sample /etc/pam.d/login File

```
auth        required     /lib/security/pam_securetty.so
auth        required     /lib/security/pam_pwdb.so
auth        required     /lib/security/pam_nologin.so
account     required     /lib/security/pam_pwdb.so
password    required     /lib/security/pam_cracklib.so minlen=20\
            retry=3 type=SECRET
password    required     /lib/security/pam_pwdb.so md5 use_authtok
session     required     /lib/security/pam_pwdb.so
```

Module Type auth   There are three modules stacked for type auth. The first is pam_securetty. This is an auth module type only. It accepts no arguments. Its sole purpose is to check /etc/securetty against the device of the login attempt, if the user logging in is root. It will fail only if someone is trying to log in as root from a device not in /etc/securetty. Since this module is required, a failure here would cause the login to fail. Recall, however, that the control flag, required, will still allow subsequent modules to be executed, and therefore the user will not be refused access until after all three modules in this stack are executed.

The second module is pam_pwdb. As discussed in *PAM and Passwords* on page 86, its role here is to authenticate the user.

The third module in the stack is `pam_nologin`. This is also an `auth`-only module type that accepts no arguments. Its purpose is to check for the existence of `/etc/nologin`. If `/etc/nologin` exists, then no users, except root, are allowed to log in; if `/etc/nologin` contains a message, it is displayed. For example, if the `/etc/nologin` is

```
System down for maintenance until 2/28/99 at 4pm
```

then Example 5-9 exhibits the system's behavior when the user `joe` attempts to `telnet` to the system.

Example 5-9 Attempted Login with the Presence of `/etc/nologin`

```
$ telnet livfreeordie
Trying 10.1.1.1...
Connected to livfreeordie.
Escape character is '^]'.

Red Hat Linux release 5.2 (Apollo)
Kernel 2.0.36 on an i686
login: joe
Password:
System down for maintenance until 2/28/99 at 4pm

Login incorrect

login:
```

OH, BY THE WAY...

Did you ever wonder about how to get rid of the message that appears when you connect to a system? In Example 5-9, it is the two-line message beginning with "Red Hat Linux." This message gives away information about your system, which does not reflect good security practice. On Red Hat 5.2/6.0, the message displayed reflects the contents of `/etc/issue.net` for remote connections and `/etc/issue` for local connections. At this point, you may be tempted to rush off and modify these files to suit your needs. Don't. The files are rewritten at every reboot! In order to modify these files, you must modify `/etc/rc.d/rc.local`. `/etc/rc.d/rc2.d/S99local` is a symbolic link to `/etc/rc.d/rc.local`, which is executed upon entering run level 2. Be sure to replace this message with something appropriate, maybe something like "This is a restricted system. All activities are logged." But whatever you do, don't reveal the operating system, hardware, or other information that may be used against you. And don't use words like "Welcome"! There are many other ways to replace this message, some of which will be discussed at various points in this text.

By default, Joe will actually be able to attempt to log in three more times, but of course the result will be the same. Existing login sessions are not affected by the `/etc/nologin` file.

This file is normally used for purposes of system maintenance, but it also is beneficial in case of a system breach. This topic is discussed in Chapter 3.

Normally, the `/etc/nologin` file does not exist and the user, once authenticated, will be granted access. The subsequent modules in `/etc/pam.d/login` are then invoked.

Module Types account, password, and session The pam_pwdb entry for the account module type, as previously described, performs the task of checking the user's account. If the user's password has expired, for example, the entries with module type password will be invoked and the events described in *PAM and Passwords* on page 86 will occur. The session entry is for the exclusive purpose of logging connection information to syslog.

Many other PAM configuration files besides /etc/pam.d/login incorporate the use of these modules and module types. Since each configuration file represents an application, it follows that any application that requires authentication by password will incorporate some or all of the modules and module types in /etc/pam.d/login. Included among these are rsh, rlogin, su, ppp, chfn, chsh, and ftp. Bear this in mind whenever you decide to make changes to one of these configuration files. For continuity, and for security, you will ordinarily make changes across the board. Think carefully if you decide not to change a particular configuration file whenever you change others.

Next let's take a look at some additional restrictions that may be imposed through PAM.

Time and Resource Limits

You may also wish to impose access time restrictions and resource limitations on your users. PAM affords the opportunity to impose such limitations through the modules pam_time and pam_limits, respectively.

Using pam_time This module is used with module type account only. Although it accepts no arguments, it does expect a configuration file, /etc/security/time.conf (Red Hat 5.2/6.0; other distributions may vary), to supply it with login location and time limitations. The absence of this file has the effect of not restricting access in any way. The limitations apply to *all* users, including root.

Suppose that you'd like to impose some limits on user access to a particular system. Take a look at the account module type entries in Example 5-10. The pam_time and the pam_pwdb entries both use the control flag required. This has the effect of causing the account verification step to proceed. For example, if Mary's password has expired, when she attempts to log in, she will be so informed and refused access regardless of the limitations imposed by pam_time. Let's assume that Mary's password has expired and that she is attempting to connect to the system livfreeordie outside the limits imposed by /etc/security/time.conf (see *The /etc/security/time.conf File* on page 96). Example 5-11 shows what happens if Mary attempts to log in under these assumptions and /etc/pam.d/login is configured as shown in Example 5-10. Even though Mary is logging in outside of her approved time, the only information she gets is that her password has expired.

Example 5-10 Partial Configuration File Using `pam_time required`

```
account      required      /lib/security/pam_pwdb.so
account      required      /lib/security/pam_time.so
```

Example 5-11 Login Attempt with Expired Password and Outside of Permitted Times 1

```
$ telnet livfreeordie
Trying 10.1.1.1...
Escape character is '^]'.

Red Hat Linux release 5.2 (Apollo)
Kernel 2.0.36 on an i686

login: mary
Password:
Your account has expired; please contact your system administrator

User account has expired
Connection closed by foreign host.
$
```

If you reverse the entries and set the control flag to `requisite` for `pam_time`, the behavior is quite different. Example 5-12 shows the new configuration. Example 5-13 shows what happens with the new configuration when Mary attempts to log in.

Example 5-12 Partial Configuration File Using `pam_time.so requisite`

```
account      requisite      /lib/security/pam_time.so
account      required       /lib/security/pam_pwdb.so
```

Example 5-13 Login Attempt with Expired Password and Outside of Permitted Times 2

```
$ telnet livfreeordie
Trying 10.1.1.1...
Escape character is '^]'.

Red Hat Linux release 5.2 (Apollo)
Kernel 2.0.36 on an i686

login: mary
Password:

Permission denied
Connection closed by foreign host.
$
```

The moral of these examples is: watch your order and control flag settings. Experiment before you implement! Make sure the configuration settings provide the functionality you expect.

Next we turn our attention to the `time.conf` file.

The /etc/security/time.conf File.   This file controls access time and login location by device when using the `pam_time` module. Each line in the file is a record, called a rule, except lines beginning with # which are comments. Each record has the following syntax:

```
services;ttys;users;times
```

This syntax is further detailed in Table 5.6.

The phrase *logical list* referenced in Table 5.6 means that the special characters, described in Table 5.7, are used as conditional operators.

Logical operators may be mixed. For example, `tty* & !ttyp*` means that any serial device is allowed for this rule, but all pseudo-devices are not.

The syntax used to specify days in `timed.conf` is summarized in Table 5.8. These codes are then used with time ranges, all times being specified by the 24-hour clock. For example, `Wd0800-1600` means weekends between

Table 5.6 Description of `/etc/security/time.conf` Entries

Parameter	Description
services	A logical list of the services associated with PAM. Multiple records with the same service are acceptable. Examples include `login`, `rsh`, and `su`.
ttys	A logical list of device(s). The login device is stored in PAM_TTY. Normally this includes such devices as `tty1` and `tty2` for the console, `ttyS0` and `ttyS1` for serial ports, and `ttyp1` and `ttyp2` for pseudo-devices normally associated with network and X Window connections.
users	A logical list of (valid) users. May include root.
times	A logical list of times at which this rule applies.

Table 5.7 Conditional Operators Used in `/etc/security/time.conf`

Operator	Function	Examples
&	logical AND	`user1 & user2`—means this rule applies to both `user1` and `user2`.
|	logical OR	`tty1 | tty2`—means this rule applies to either `tty1` or `tty2`.
!	logical NOT	`! login`—this rule does not apply to the login service.
*	wildcard	Matches any value, its meaning depending on its location in a field.

Table 5.8 Day Codes in `/etc/security/timed.conf`

Day Code	Description
Mo, Tu, We, Th, Fr, Sa, Su	Each code individually applies to the day of the week it indicates. These codes may be concatenated; for example, `MoTuWe` means Monday, Tuesday, and Wednesday.
Wk and Wd	`Wk` means weekdays while `Wd` means weekends (Saturday and Sunday). Note that, for example, `MoWk` means all weekdays except Monday.
Al	All seven days. Note that, for example, `AlSu` means all days except Sunday.

the hours of 8 A.M. and 4 P.M.. Notice that there are no spaces between the day code and the time.

Example 5-14 shows a series of entries in a sample /etc/security/ time.conf file. In this example, the root user has access to all services all of the time so long as root logs in from tty1. The users—joe, bill, and jane— have access every day of the week between 8 A.M. and 6 P.M. from any device so long as they connect via login or rsh. The user guest may log in from anywhere, Monday through Friday between the hours of 9 A.M. and 4 P.M., except between 12 noon and 1 P.M. Finally, any user may access the system using ftp from any source Monday through Friday between the hours of 9 A.M. and 4 P.M. All other users are unrestricted.

Example 5-14 Sample /etc/security/time.conf File

```
*;tty1;root;Al0000-2400
login & rsh;*;joe|bill|jane;Al0800-1800
login;*;guest;Wk0900-1600&!Wk1200-1300
ftp;*;*;Wk0900-1600
```

This file is not order dependent. If there are entries that overlap, the least permissive (actually, the intersection of all entries) is used. Remember, you must place a pam_time entry in each file in /etc/pam.d for those services for which you want to restrict access. If you are going to limit access using pam_time, consider placing entries in at least the following files (and hence the associated services will be limited) in /etc/pam.d: ftp, login, ppp, rexec, rlogin, rsh, su, and xdm.

WARNING!

If you use an entry of the form

```
*;*;*;!AL0000-24000
```

in the /etc/security/time.conf file, you will lock out all users, including root, from the system! Should you find yourself locked out of the system, see the section *Recovering a Corrupt System* on page 24 in Chapter 3 for recovery procedures.

Using pam_limits   You may additionally restrict user accounts by imposing limits on the system resources available to each user login session. This may be useful in limiting system-based DoS attacks. The pam_limits module operates as a session module type only. It supports two arguments—debug and conf=/path/to/config_file (the default configuration file is /etc/security/ limits.conf). It does not impose any limits on the root account.

The /etc/security/limits.conf file is used to impose limits on a per-user or per-group basis. All limits specified apply to a single session. Each line in the file is a record, except for those beginning with #. The syntax of a record is

```
username|@groupname type resource limit
```

where `username|@groupname` specifies that either a username or a groupname preceded with @ may be used. The wildcard character * is acceptable and represents all users (hence all groups). The `type` field is either the `hard` or `soft` parameter; `hard` imposes a fixed limit and `soft` specifies a default limit. The `resource` parameter is one of the items described in Table 5.9. The `limit` parameter is the limit itself on the associated `resource`.

It is important to note that the limits imposed are on a per-session basis. The total limitation may be controlled with the `maxlogins` parameter. Limits may be completely disabled for particular users with the special character, -, an instance of which is shown in Example 5-15 . In this example, all users are limited to a resident set size of approximately 10 megabytes (MB) per session. All users may also have a maximum of only four simultaneous logins. It is this value that sets the overall maximum per user. The user, `bin`, has all limits disabled, including the previous entries in the file. The remaining limitations in the file are additional limitations for the users and groups indicated. The user `ftp` is allowed only 10 logins (this is an excellent limit to impose on anonymous `ftp` accounts since it limits the number of simultaneous logins). All users in the group `managers` have a process limitation of 40 and all users in the group `developers` have a `memlock` limit of approximately 64 MB.

Example 5-15 Sample `/etc/security/limits.conf` File

```
*               hard    rss             10000
*               hard    maxlogins       4
bin             -
ftp             hard    maxlogins       10
@managers       hard    nproc           40
@developers     hard    memlock         64000
```

Table 5.9 Limitable Resources in `/etc/security/limits.conf`

Resource	Description
core	Limits the size of a core file (KB[*])
data	Maximum data size (KB)
fsize	Maximum file size (KB)
memlock	Maximum locked-in memory address space (KB)
nofile	Maximum number of open files
rss	Maximum resident set size (KB)
stack	Maximum stack size (KB)
cpu	Maximum CPU time in minutes
nproc	Maximum number of processes
as	Address space limit
maxlogins	Maximum number of logins allowed for this user

[*]kilobytes

Of course, you must determine the limits necessary for each system at your site. Make sure you place the entry

```
session     required    /lib/security/pam_limits.so
```

in each appropriate file in /etc/pam.d.

Access Control with pam_listfile

Any PAM-aware application may be given an access control list with pam_listfile. This is an authentication-only module that takes a number of arguments, as displayed in Table 5.10. In order to clarify Table 5.10, we'll look at two examples.

Suppose that we have a guest account on our system and we would like to disable chsh for guest. The chsh command allows a user to change his or her default shell in /etc/passwd to any shell listed in /etc/shells. Since chsh is a PAM-aware application, we can use pam_listfile to implement this restriction (no problem!). Add the pam_listfile entry to the existing /etc/pam.d/chsh configuration file as shown in Example 5-16. By now, everything in this file should be familiar except the pam_rootok entry (and of course the pam_listfile entry, which we haven't finished talking about). Actually, the pam_rootok entry is quite simple. Notice that it uses the control flag sufficient meaning that, if this module is satisfied, none of the other auth module types needs to be executed. The pam_rootok module does what you'd expect. If it's root, it's OK! So, in this case, if root wants to change any user's shell, root will not be authenticated (not prompted for a password).

Example 5-16 The chsh Configuration File with a pam_listfile Entry

```
auth        sufficient   /lib/security/pam_rootok.so
auth        required     /lib/security/pam_listfile.so onerr=fail\
            item=user    sense=deny   file=/etc/security/nochsh
auth        required     /lib/security/pam_pwdb.so
account     required     /lib/security/pam_pwdb.so
password    required     /lib/security/pam_cracklib.so minlen=20 retry=3
password    required     /lib/security/pam_pwdb.so md5 use_authtok
session     required     /lib/security/pam_pwdb.so
```

Now back to pam_listfile. In Example 5-16, the argument onerr=fail is set. This means that, if there are *any* error conditions generated by the execution of this module, the module will fail. Since it is a required module, this further implies that authentication will fail and the user will not be allowed to change his or her shell. Errors will be logged to syslog, so you may view them in /var/log/messages. Unless you are debugging in a safe environment (i.e., not connected to a production environment), this is the recommended setting for this argument.

The remaining arguments deal with the access control file, which in this case is /etc/security/nochsh. The item=user argument tells pam_listfile

Table 5.10 Arguments to `pam_listfile`

Argument	Description
onerr	Takes either `succeed` or `fail`. If an error occurs, such as an unreadable configuration file, should this module return success or failure?
sense	Takes either `allow` or `deny`. This tells the module whether the list is an allow or deny list.
file	Requires the absolute pathname to the configuration file.
item	One of `user`, `tty`, `rhost`, `ruser`, `group`, or `shell`. It tells the module what to look for in the configuration file.
apply	Takes a username or a groupname preceded by @. It is only meaningful if `item` is set to `tty`, `rhost`, or `shell`.

that it should expect to find usernames—one per line—in /etc/security/ nochsh. The `sense=deny` argument tells `pam_listfile` that /etc/security/ nochsh is a deny list; that is, any user listed in that file will cause `pam_listfile` to fail and therefore (because of the `required` control flag) cause authentication to fail and disallow the user from changing the shell.

All that remains is to create /etc/security/nochsh and list the users to whom we wish to deny `chsh` capability. Here is an example file:

```
guest
joe
```

The two users, `guest` and `joe` (we don't trust him anymore), will not be able to successfully execute `chsh`, as the user `guest` demonstrates in Example 5-17. Hopefully, the flow of events is becoming clear. When guest executes `chsh`, a PAM-aware application, Linux-PAM is invoked and the `auth` stack in /etc/ pam.d/chsh is executed. Referring back to Example 5-16 on page 100, the first `auth` module invoked is `pam_rootok`. Since `guest` is not `root`, that module fails and `pam_pwdb` is invoked and causes the password prompt. The user `guest` successfully enters the correct password (you'll have to trust me here) and execution is passed to `pam_listfile`, which checks its deny list and finds `guest` in it, causing authentication to fail (hence the generic `Password error` message).

Example 5-17 Failed `chsh` Attempt Due to `pam_listfile`

```
$ telnet livfreeordie
Trying 10.1.1.1...
Escape character is '^]'.
This is a restricted system. All activity is logged.
login: guest
Password:
livfreeordie$ chsh -s /bin/bash
Changing shell for guest.
Password:
Password error.
livfreeordie$
```

Consider another example. Suppose that we want to limit the users to which others may su—we want to restrict su use generally (not just su to root) to a specific set of users. We add a pam_listfile entry to /etc/pam.d/su as displayed in Example 5-18. This time we are using an allow list. Just place each allowed username, one per line, in the /etc/security/suok file. For example, if our /etc/security/suok contains the users:

```
root
mary
bill
jane
efram
```

then these are the only users that will be accepted as a user argument to su. Anyone may execute su, but only to become one of the users in this list. Example 5-19 shows what happens when paul tries to su to guest and then to root. The su attempt to guest fails because guest is not in the /etc/security/suok file. The su to root, however, succeeds because root is in the /etc/security/suok file and Paul knows the root password.

Example 5-18 The su Configuration File with pam_listfile

```
auth          required        /lib/security/pam_listfile.so onerr=fail \
         item=user  sense=allow  file=/etc/security/suok
auth          required        /lib/security/pam_pwdb.so
account       required        /lib/security/pam_pwdb.so
password      required        /lib/security/pam_cracklib.so minlen=20 retry=3
password      required        /lib/security/pam_pwdb.so md5 use_authtok
session       required        /lib/security/pam_pwdb.so
```

Example 5-19 Failed su Attempts Due to pam_listfile

```
$ whoami
joe
$ su - guest
Password:
su: incorrect password
$ su -
Password:
#
```

Notice that the error message is not indicative of the actual failure. If you review the previous failure messages from other PAM modules, you'll see that this is a feature of PAM. The idea is to not reveal any information to the user through error messages. As an administrator with root access, you may always check out the log files. By default, you will find PAM-generated log messages in /var/log/messages (these files and syslog, in general, will be discussed in Chapter 8).

Note that when sense=allow changes to sense=deny in Example 5-18, the /etc/security/suok file becomes a deny list, meaning that a user would not be able to su to any of the users in the list. This is particularly useful if you wish to implement sudo (sudo is discussed in Chapter 9) and completely disallow su to root.

PAM and `su`

Unlike the last `pam_listfile` example, which restricts the users that may be switched to with `su`, `pam_wheel` is used to specifically restrict the successful execution of `su` to the root user. It does so by utilizing a special group called `wheel` with the GID of 0. Its default behavior is to allow only members of the `wheel` group to `su` to root when this module is in force. This is another authentication-only module. Its arguments are described in Table 5.11. This module has some arguments that you really don't want to use. The `use_id` argument causes the `pam_wheel` to use the effective UID of the user. In this way a non-`wheel` group member could `su` to a `wheel` group member and then `su` to root. This is probably not the behavior you seek.

The `trust` argument could cause `wheel` members to be able to `su` to root without a password, depending on the way in which modules are stacked. Avoid these two arguments, unless you are debugging or are otherwise prepared for their consequences.

On many releases of Linux, there is a GID 0, the `root` group. You may wish, therefore, to create a `wheel` group with a different GID—for example GID=10 (Red Hat 5.2/6.0 does this for you)—then use the `group` argument to `pam_wheel`. Example 5-20 displays a representative `/etc/pam.d/su` file. Make sure that you have a group called `wheel` in `/etc/group`. Any member of that group will be allowed to `su` to root. All other users will get a `Password incorrect` error message, even if they know the correct password.

Example 5-20 The `/etc/pam.d/su` File with `pam_wheel`

```
auth        required     /lib/security/pam_wheel.so group=wheel
auth        required     /lib/security/pam_pwdb.so
account     required     /lib/security/pam_pwdb.so
password    required     /lib/security/pam_cracklib.so minlen=20 retry=3
password    required     /lib/security/pam_pwdb.so md5 use_authtok
session     required     /lib/security/pam_pwdb.so
```

Table 5.11 Arguments of `pam_wheel`

Argument	Description
`debug`	Generates additional output to `syslog`.
`use_id`	Uses the current process UID and not that returned by `getlogin`. This may result in the use of an effective UID and is not recommended for production use.
`trust`	Causes this module to succeed if the user is a member of the `wheel` group. This option may cause members of `wheel` to become root without a password. Be *very* careful when using this argument.
`deny`	Reverse the logic of this module.
`group=`*groupname*	Instead of allowing users in the group wheel, allow the users in *groupname*.

Using `pam_access`

The `pam_access` module is another access control module. It is similar to `pam_listfile` in that it is a generic access control mechanism. It differs from `pam_listfile`, however, in two ways. First, it supports only module type `account`. Essentially, this difference means that we have similar access control functionality available to use for module type `auth` (`pam_listfile`) and module type `account` (`pam_access`). This allows us to control applications that do not support one or the other module type. An example of such a situation is given in the section *Further Restricting Access with PAM* on page 304 in Chapter 11.

Second, it requires the configuration file, `/etc/security/access.conf`. Entries in this file are of the form

```
permission : users : origins
```

Each of the fields in `/etc/security/access.conf` are described in Table 5.12. When the `pam_access` module is invoked, the `/etc/security/access.conf` file is searched for the first entry that matches the `username` and `tty` or `hostname` pair. If no match is found, then access is granted.

For example, suppose that you wish to restrict login access to certain users from certain hosts on a particular system; let's call the local host `pyramid`. Example 5-21 illustrates a sample `/etc/security/access.conf` file that provides access restrictions on `pyramid`. The line numbers in Example 5-21 are provided for clarity and are not part of the file. In this case, line 2 disallows all access from the domains, `evil.com` and `spam.org`. Line 3 disallows all access at the console except by root. Line 4 grants access to all users except root if the connection is arriving from the 172.17.0.0 network. Line 5 grants access to all members of the `wheel` group and to the user `paul` from the host `leghorn`. Line 6 denies all other access.

Table 5.12 Fields in `/etc/security/access.conf`

Field	Description
permission	Either + indicating access is allowed or − indicating access is denied.
users	A space-separated list of usernames, groupnames, or netgroups. All netgroup names must be preceded by @. The special wildcard ALL may also be used to always match in this field. You may also use the special keyword EXCEPT to conditionalize a list.
origins	A space-separated list of ttynames, hostnames, domainnames (any name beginning with a "."), or network addresses (the network portion of the IP address ending in a "."). The wildcards ALL (which always matches) and LOCAL (which matches any name not ending with a ".") may also be used. You may also use the special keyword EXCEPT to conditionalize a list.

Example 5-21 Sample `/etc/security/access.conf` File

```
1.   # access.conf file
2.   -:ALL:.evil.com .spam.org
3.   -:ALL EXCEPT root: tty1
4.   +:ALL EXCEPT root:172.17.
5.   +:wheel paul:leghorn
6.   -:ALL:ALL
```

Now, simply add the line

```
account      required      /lib/security/pam_access.so
```

as desired to any of the configuration files in the `/etc/pam.d` directory. Example 5-22 shows this entry in **bold** in the `/etc/pam.d/login` file.

Example 5-22 Adding `pam_access` to the `/etc/pam.d/login` File

```
auth       required      /lib/security/pam_securetty.so
auth       required      /lib/security/pam_pwdb.so
auth       required      /lib/security/pam_nologin.so
account    required      /lib/security/pam_pwdb.so
account    required      /lib/security/pam_access.so
password   required      /lib/security/pam_cracklib.so minlen=20\
           retry=3 type=SECRET
password   required      /lib/security/pam_pwdb.so md5 use_authtok
session    required      /lib/security/pam_pwdb.so
```

Any attempted access from a denied location will result in a `Permission denied` error message, as shown in Example 5-23, where Paul attempts to log in at the console.

Example 5-23 Failed Login Attempt Due to `pam_access`

```
pyramid login: paul
Password:
Permission denied
pyramid login:
```

All failed attempts due to `pam_access` are logged in `/var/log/messages` by default. See Chapter 8 for further information about log files.

Using `pam_lastlog`

This module provides the capability of displaying the last time-logged-in message and the `You have new mail` message as module type `auth` and `session`, respectively. The former is of greater concern than the latter, as it gives away information about the computing environment. Fortunately, `pam_lastlog` gives you control over what is displayed.

The `pam_lastlog` module may operate in either module type `auth` or `session`. As an `auth` module it serves the purpose of controlling `lastlog` (see *One Other Command* on page 153 of Chapter 7 for more details) displays after a

Table 5.13 Arguments of `pam_lastlog` as Module Type `auth`

Argument	Description
debug	Provides verbose output to `syslog`.
nodate	Suppresses the display of the date of last login by this user.
noterm	Suppresses the display of the terminal name used in the last login of this user.
nohost	Suppresses the display of the host from which this user last logged in. By utilizing this argument, hostnames in your environment are not disclosed.
silent	Suppresses the entire `lastlog` message.
never	If the user has never logged in before, this will cause a welcome message to be displayed.

user login. In this mode it takes the arguments listed in Table 5.13. To use this module, simply put a record similar to the following line in all appropriate `/etc/pam.d` configuration files (e.g., `login`, `rlogin`, `rsh`).

```
auth    optional    /lib/security/pam_lastlog.so nohost
```

Notice the `optional` control flag. If you use `required` instead, no one will be able to log in! You also probably want to put this line last in your `auth` stack. In this example, the `lastlog` message will be displayed, but no previous host information will be shown.

As a `session` module, `pam_lastlog` informs the user about electronic mail. It takes no arguments and once again must use the `optional` control flag. Here is a sample entry:

```
session    optional    /lib/security/pam_lastlog.so
```

Once again, make sure that this entry appears in each appropriate `/etc/pam.d` configuration file.

NOTE

Another application may display `lastlog` or e-mail information after the PAM authentication steps are complete. Any such applications would obviate the configuration of `pam_lastlog`.

Using `pam_rhosts_auth`

The evils of the Berkeley r-commands were extolled in Chapter 1, where we looked at some of the vulnerabilities associated with these utilities. In Chapter 11, we will look at completely replacing the Berkeley r-commands.

Table 5.14 Arguments to `pam_rhosts_auth`

Arguments	Description
debug	Generates more output to `syslog`.
no_hosts_equiv	Disables `/etc/hosts.equiv` functionality.
no_rhosts	Ignores `$HOME/.rhosts` files.
no_warn	Suppresses warning messages to the user. As of this writing, the module generates no warning messages anyway!
privategroup	Normally, if a `$HOME/.rhosts` file is writable by other than the owner, this module will assume the file has been compromised and return a failure. This argument will allow the `$HOME/.rhosts` file to be writable by the owner and the owner's group if the owner's group is a UPG.* This will be true if the UID and GID are identical and greater than 500.
promiscuous	The default behavior of this module is to ignore + wildcards in `$HOME/.rhosts` and `/etc/hosts.equiv` files. This argument will allow such wildcards. Use of this argument cannot be advised. See Chapter 3.
suppress	Suppresses error messaging to `syslog`.

*See *Group Account Management* on page 69 of Chapter 4 for a discussion of UPGs.

Here we will look at using `pam_rhosts_auth` to limit or altogether eliminate trusted hosts.

This module is an `auth`-type module only. It accepts the arguments listed in Table 5.14. Configuration of this module is highly system specific and site dependent. Allowing this functionality internally may be acceptable and, in the eyes of your users, necessary. On certain systems, such as restricted servers, systems within perimeter networks,[5] and firewalls, `$HOME/.rhosts` and `/etc/hosts.equiv` files should be strictly regulated if not completely forbidden.

You will want to place entries for this module in `/etc/pam.d/rsh` and `/etc/pam.d/rlogin` and any other PAM-aware service that uses these files. To affect the traditional implementation (allow trusted hosts), use an entry such as

```
auth     sufficient    /lib/security/pam_rhosts_auth.so
```

at the top of the `auth` stack (minimally, this module must appear before the module in the stack that prompts the user for his or her password) in `/etc/`

---

5. Perimeter networks (or DMZs) typically consist of systems that are available to external access. See the references listed in *General Firewall References* on page 488 of Chapter 16 for further information.

`pam.d/rsh` and `/etc/pam.d/rlogin`. A more restrictive entry could be placed in these same files on sensitive systems. For example, an entry of the form

```
auth     required     /lib/security/pam_rhosts_auth.so no_rhosts
```

at the top of the `auth` stack (or, again, before a module generating a password prompt) would completely disable the use of `$HOME/.rhosts` files, but would preserve the use of `/etc/hosts.equiv` (which does not apply to root).

One-Time Password Support

Both `pam_opie` and `pam_skey` support OTP. These are discussed in Chapter 6.

PAM and the `other` Configuration File

So far we have discussed discrete PAM-aware applications and how to grant or limit access through PAM by those applications. It turns out that, if a PAM-aware application has no configuration file of its own, Linux-PAM will supply a special set of modules from the `/etc/pam.d/other` file. This file is normally used to reject all other requests and, by default, will likely appear as in Example 5-24. For example, if you download a PAM-aware application, such as `ssh` 1.2.27 (see Chapter 11), and fail to provide an `ssh` configuration file in `/etc/pam.d`, then the `other` file is used, and, if it is as in Example 5-24, then `ssh` connections will always fail. Furthermore, `pam_deny` generates no messages whatsoever! Unfortunately this means that you may end up spending a lot of time trying to figure out why something doesn't work. All `pam_deny` does, as its name suggests, is deny all requests for any available module type.

Example 5-24 A Common `/etc/pam.d/other` File

```
auth       required     /lib/security/pam_deny.so
account    required     /lib/security/pam_deny.so
password   required     /lib/security/pam_deny.so
session    required     /lib/security/pam_deny.so
```

But there is good news! There is another module, the `pam_warn` module, that logs to `syslog` informational messages, including the service requested, the terminal name, the username, the remote username, and the remote hostname. The `pam_warn` module operates only for module type `auth` and `password`. So you may want to modify your `/etc/pam.d/other` file as in Example 5-25. In this way, all other services that make `auth` or `password` requests will have log entries generated. The `pam_warn` module is not limited to use with `pam_deny`. It may be used in any `auth` or `password` stack to generate additional log messages.

Example 5-25 Administrator Friendly `/etc/pam.d/other` File

```
auth       required     /lib/security/pam_warn.so
auth       required     /lib/security/pam_deny.so
```

Example 5-25 Administrator Friendly `/etc/pam.d/other` File (Continued)

```
account  required    /lib/security/pam_deny.so
password required    /lib/security/pam_warn.so
password required    /lib/security/pam_deny.so
session  required    /lib/security/pam_deny.so
```

This additional logging capability of `pam_warn` has obvious debugging advantages, but it also has advantages from the security perspective. For example, if you have identified some suspicious activity, you may want to add `pam_warn` in the `auth` stacks surrounding the services in question. You may also want to use the `debug` argument on those modules that support it for more detailed auditing information. Pay close attention when you do this because your log files will get large quickly. And, if the bad-guys are already in, they're reading the log files, too!

There is one other module in this category. It is the antithesis of `pam_deny`. It is called `pam_permit` and—you guessed it—it categorically allows access. It operates for all module types and should be used with great caution, if ever.

Additional PAM Options

There are many other PAM modules, some of which are discussed throughout this book. In *Available PAM Modules* on page 109, many of the modules, both currently available and under development, are listed; in *PAM-Aware Applications* on page 112, many available applications are described.

PAM LOGS

PAM modules log to facility `auth` in `syslog`. What this means is that, in your log, messages will end up in the file specified by the `auth` facility entry in `syslog`. On Red Hat 5.2/6.0, the default location is `/var/log/messages`. We discuss `syslog` in Chapter 8.

AVAILABLE PAM MODULES

Table 5.15 provides a list and brief description of many available PAM modules. Some come with the Red Hat (or other) distributions, while others require downloading. Those that come with Red Hat 5.2/6.0 are so noted (and may be found at `http://www.redhat.com/`); for all others, a web site is specified and an author, if known, is provided. If your system already supports these modules, they will be found in either `/lib/security` or `/usr/lib/security`. If you download and add one, make sure that you put it in the correct directory.

Table 5.15 Overview of PAM Modules

Module	Availability	Description
pam_access	Red Hat 5.2/6.0	Reads the file /etc/security/access.conf to determine whether the user/tty or user/host pair is to be granted or denied access.
pam_console	Red Hat 6.0 or publicly available	Sets up permissions and device ownership when logging in at a physical console device. Expects the /etc/security/console.perms file for permission and ownership parameters; expects the /etc/security/console.apps/ directory for services. Supports auth required and session optional module type/control flag pairs.
pam_cracklib	Red Hat 5.2/6.0	Supports only password module type. Used for checking password choices against the cracklib and disallows any choices found there.
pam_deny	Red Hat 5.2/6.0	Supports all module types. Always returns a failure.
pam_env	Red Hat 5.2/6.0	Supports auth module type only. Uses the /etc/security/pam_env.conf file to set shell environment variables.
pam_filter	Red Hat 5.2/6.0	Supports all module types. This module offers the capability of capturing as much as every keystroke of a session. Requires a filter program, not included.
pam_ftp	Red Hat 5.2/6.0	Supports module type auth only. Implements anonymous ftp.
pam_group	Red Hat 5.2/6.0	Supports module type auth only. Sets GID based upon /etc/security/group.conf file (syntax nearly identical to /etc/security/time.conf, which is discussed in *The /etc/security/time.conf File* on page 96).
pam_if	Publicly available	Supports all module types. A simple conditional used to manage stack execution behavior. Available from http://www.dcit.cz/~kan/pam/. This module is discussed in *OPIE and PAM* on page 143.
pam_lastlog	Red Hat 5.2/6.0	Supports module type auth only. Used to control the display of last login information.
pam_limits	Red Hat 5.2/6.0	Supports module type session only. Uses the /etc/security/limits.conf file to determine whether or not users may log in based on available system resources.
pam_listfile	Red Hat 5.2/6.0	Supports module type auth only. Allows for the use of access control lists based on users, ttys, remote hosts, groups, and shells.
pam_mail	Red Hat 5.2/6.0	Supports module type auth only. Provides the You have new mail service.

Table 5.15 Overview of PAM Modules (Continued)

Module	Availability	Description
pam_nologin	Red Hat 5.2/6.0	Supports module type auth only. Provides the check for the existence of the /etc/nologin file, which, if it exists, will display the contents of the file and fail auth.
pam_opie	Publicly available	Supports module type auth only. Presents an OPIE challenge and requires an OPIE one-time password. Available from http://www.tho.org/~andy/pam-opie.html. This module is discussed in *OPIE and PAM* on page 143.
pam_permit	Red Hat 5.2/6.0	Supports all module types. Always returns success.
pam_pwdb	Red Hat 5.2/6.0	Supports all module types. Replaces the pam_unix_* modules. Colocates authentication databases depending upon the /etc/pwdb.conf file.
pam_pwdfile	Publicly available	This module was announced as this book was in its final stages. It is an authentication-only module that allows for the specification of alternate password files. In this way you can configure separate passwords for various services. For example, you could have one set of usernames and passwords for IMAP and an entirely different set for everything else. You will find this module at http://espresso.ee.sun.ac.za/~cabotha/pam_pwdfile.html.
pam_radius	Red Hat 5.2/6.0	Supports module type session only. Provides the session service for users authenticated through RADIUS.
pam_rhosts_auth	Red Hat 5.2/6.0	Supports module type auth only. Provides for authentication through $HOME/.rhosts files. May be configured to allow or deny such authentication.
pam_rootok	Red Hat 5.2/6.0	Supports module type auth only. Allows the root user access without requiring a password. Makes sense only when used with the sufficient control flag.
pam_securetty	Red Hat 5.2/6.0	Supports module type auth only. Applies only to root. Checks to see if root is logging in from one of the devices listed in /etc/securetty. If so, it returns success; otherwise it fails.
pam_shells	Red Hat 5.2/6.0	Supports module type auth only. Authenticates users if their default shell is listed in /etc/shells.
pam_stress	Red Hat 5.2/6.0	This module is used for debugging and stress testing PAM-aware applications.
pam_tally	Red Hat 5.2/6.0	Supports module type auth only. Keeps track of the number of login attempts made and can deny access based upon a specified number of failed attempts.

Table 5.15 Overview of PAM Modules (Continued)

Module	Availability	Description
pam_time	Red Hat 5.2/6.0	Supports module type account only. Restricts access based on user, tty, service, and time as specified in /etc/security/time.conf.
pam_tcpd	Publicly available	Supports module type auth only. Implements TCP_wrappers-style access control, logging, and functionality through /etc/hosts.allow and /etc/hosts.deny. TCP_wrappers is discussed in Chapter 10. The module is available from http://web.tis.calinet.it/macchese/pam/pam_tcpd.html.
pam_unix_acct pam_unix_auth pam_unix_passwd pam_unix_session	Red Hat 5.2/6.0	These modules provide similar functionality to pam_pwdb except that the authentication database is either /etc/passwd or NIS.
pam_unix-new	Publicly available	Incorporates the above four modules into one and implements many of the features of pam_pwdb. Available at ftp://hunter.mimuw.edu.pl/pub/users/baggins/PAM/.
pam_warn	Red Hat 5.2/6.0	Supports module types auth and password only. This module generates a log message including the remote user and remote host (if available) through the syslog utility.
pam_wheel	Red Hat 5.2/6.0	Supports module type auth only. Provides a way to restrict access to root to those users who are members of the wheel group.
pam_xauth	Red Hat 6.0 or publicly available	Supports module type session with control flag optional only. This module automatically passes X Window System magic cookies to other users (for example, through su), thus allowing effective UIDs to open X applications without requiring the use of the xhost command.

PAM-AWARE APPLICATIONS

Table 5.16 is a list of many of the applications that are PAM-aware, meaning that the application has the necessary calls to invoke PAM. As in Table 5.15, those available in the Red Hat 5.2/6.0 distribution are so noted.

IMPORTANT NOTES ABOUT CONFIGURING PAM

This chapter provides an introductory look at PAM. Many examples are described and some usage tips are provided. Doubtless, however, many of you will have configuration ideas of your own. This section provides some simple, but important, notes about configuring PAM for your environment.

Table 5.16 Overview of PAM-Aware Applications

Application	Availability
chfn	Red Hat 5.2/6.0
chsh	Red Hat 5.2/6.0
ftp	Red Hat 5.2/6.0
imap	Red Hat 5.2/6.0
linuxconf	Red Hat 5.2/6.0
linuxconf-pair	Red Hat 5.2/6.0
login	Red Hat 5.2/6.0
mcserv	Red Hat 5.2/6.0
other	Red Hat 5.2/6.0
passwd	Red Hat 5.2/6.0
ppp	Red Hat 5.2/6.0
rexec	Red Hat 5.2/6.0
rlogin	Red Hat 5.2/6.0
rsh	Red Hat 5.2/6.0
samba	Red Hat 5.2/6.0
su	Red Hat 5.2/6.0
sudo[*]	Publicly Available
vlock	Red Hat 5.2/6.0
xdm	Red Hat 5.2/6.0
xlock	Red Hat 5.2/6.0

[*]Discussed in Chapter 9.

First, and foremost, *always* copy your existing, functioning /etc/pam.d configuration files before making any changes. It is entirely possible to lock out all users, including root, through PAM misconfiguration. By retaining working copies, you will always be able to boot into single-user mode (see *A Note about LILO* on page 22 in Chapter 3 for information about booting into single-user mode), correct the configuration, and bring the system back up.

Second, configure your /etc/pam.d directory with the permissions read/ write/execute by root only, and configure its contents read/write by root only. No one else needs to read the contents of this directory. You may accomplish this with

```
# chmod u=rwx /etc/pam.d
# cd /etc/pam.d
# chmod u=rw *
```

Third, test your configuration ideas in a safe, preferably nonproduction environment. Try as many possible variations as you can think of before going live. Remember, the order of PAM modules in a stack is significant. Different orders will produce different behavior. Normally you will want pam_pwdb last in the auth stack. Don't forget the control flag settings either. The use of different control flags will cause radically different behavior in many cases. The same holds true for any arguments associated with the different modules. Remember, different module types for the same PAM module will support different arguments.

Fourth, and last, Linux is publicly available software. So are the PAM modules. There aren't any exacting quality assurance programs before release and distribution. In fact, quite frequently, you are the quality assurance mechanism! In short, your success with PAM will vary depending upon the release you obtained, the version of Linux you are running, your hardware platform, and perhaps other factors. Use the resources in Appendix A and any other support mechanisms available to you.

THE FUTURE OF PAM

From the contents of this chapter, it is hopefully clear that a lot of work has been done with PAM. The future is actually quite bright. The Open Software Foundation (OSF) released RFC 86.0 (RFCs are defined in *Request for Comment* on page 40 of Chapter 3) in October 1995 specifically for PAM. Additional work is being done to enhance the control flag option to allow system administrators to specify actions based on return codes from each module. Many of the modules noted in Table 5.15 on page 110 are under development, as is true of many of the applications listed in Table 5.16 on page 113. Given its inherent flexibility, there is no doubt that PAM will be with us for a while.

SUMMARY

This chapter described pluggable authentication modules. We looked at a number of examples for configuring and using PAM. We also reviewed many of the available PAM modules and applications. We noted the flexibility and security features provided by PAM.

FOR FURTHER READING

The best documentation available for PAM is the Linux-PAM System Administrator's Guide, which may be found at

```
http://www.kernel.org/pub/linux/libs/pam/
```

or one of its mirrors. The guide is available in numerous formats including postscript and html.

On-Line Documentation

```
/usr/doc/pwdb-0.55/pwdb.txt
/usr/doc/pam-0.64/ps/pam.ps
/usr/doc/pam-0.64/rfc86.0.txt
```

Just Once, Only Once!

One-Time Passwords

O ne-time passwords (OTP) can really make a difference in securing your computing environment. The vulnerabilities associated with static passwords were noted in Chapter 1 and in *Good Passwords* on page 58 of Chapter 4. We looked at implementing static passwords using either MD5 or bigcrypt in Chapter 5. Nonetheless, it remains that static passwords are inherently vulnerable because they are used repeatedly. Using a password scheme that changes with every login has obvious advantages. Unfortunately, there are vulnerabilities associated with using OTP schemes as well, although it is generally true that OTP will make exploitation of its vulnerabilities more difficult. In this chapter we will explore using one-time passwords and the situations in which it makes sense.

There are at least two publicly available OTP programs—S/Key and One-Time Passwords In Everything (OPIE). These are the two programs that will be detailed on these pages. Also, we will discuss some of the vulnerabilities associated with OTP and how to mitigate them.

Since we will be discussing two different OTP programs, you may want to read the entire chapter before installing an OTP program. If you already know which program you want to use—and this may be dictated by another software package you have decided to use—you may want to skip ahead to the appropriate section, but in any event read the section, *S/Key OTP Overview* on page 119, because it describes the process by which both utilities function.

THE PURPOSE OF ONE-TIME PASSWORDS

An interloper can capture a static password and use it to compromise an account on a system. Using one-time passwords helps avoid this problem. Since, by default, usernames and passwords traverse the network in the clear, anyone snooping the network (using a network sniffer) can easily capture the username and static password. If, instead, an interloper captures a one-time password, that in and of itself will do the interloper no good because once the OTP is used it cannot be used again. Hence, the rationale for enforcing OTP use over the network. You may also decide to require one-time password use at the console of each internal system. Your users will likely find this to be a nuisance; however, it will have the effect of rendering Trojan horses (perhaps unknown to system administrators), which capture usernames and passwords, less effective. Depending upon the needs of your site, you probably will not want to impose one-time passwords everywhere. For example, you may not want to require one-time passwords when users log in at their console, but you do want to require them whenever they log in over either an internal (approximately 75% of all data compromises are internal) or external network.

While the use of one-time passwords does make it more difficult for badguys to compromise an account, it does not completely eradicate the problem, as we will see in *S/Key and OPIE Vulnerabilities* on page 147.

In spite of their vulnerabilities, one-time passwords make for a good alternative to static passwords, especially when used in conjunction with network connections. The benefit of OTP can be significantly enhanced when used with encryption tunnels such as those produced by SSH (discussed in Chapter 11).

S/KEY

The S/Key OTP program was originally written by Neil M. Haller, Philip R. Karn, John S. Walden, and Scott Chasin. Telcordia Technologies (formerly Bell Communications Research or Bellcore) holds the trademark for S/Key. It was based upon the paper, "Password Authentication with Insecure Communication," by Leslie Lamport, which appeared in *Communications of the ACM* (24.11, November 1981, pp. 770–772).

As of this writing, there are a number of versions available, including some that are embedded within other programs (such as logdaemon[1]). The principal sites for S/Key Version 1.1b are

---

1. logdaemon is available from ftp://ftp.porcupine.org/pub/security/index.html#software. It is a replacement for rlogin and rsh and is quite similar to TCP_wrappers and the secure portmap, both of which are discussed in Chapter 10.

```
ftp://ftp.telcordia.com/pub/nmh/
ftp://crimelab.com/pub/skey/
```

Unfortunately, neither of these sites contains a ready-made `Makefile` for Linux. To obtain S/Key 1.1b with a Linux `Makefile`,[2] check the site

```
http://www.jumbo.com/pages/business/linux/
```

for a number of links, one of which is

```
ftp://ftp.cc.gatech.edu/ac121/linux/system/network/sunacm/Other/skey/
```

You may obtain a copy of S/Key 2.2 with a Linux `Makefile` from

```
http://metalab.unc.edu/pub/Linux/system/security/
```

If you obtain the files from `ftp.telcordia.com`, you will also be able to obtain PGP-generated[3] digital signatures, which may be used to verify the sources. Unfortunately, the sites with ready-made Linux `make` files do not supply any digital signatures. The `metalab.unc.edu` (formerly `sunsite.unc.edu`) site will often include an MD5 checksum in the `*.lsm` (for example, you will find `skey-2.2.tar.gz` and `skey-2.2.lsm` in the same directory) file associated with the source. On Linux you could use `md5sum` to compute the MD5 checksum of the file you pull down and compare the result with that found in the `*.lsm` file. Unfortunately, without a digital signature there is no way to be certain that the file on which you are running `md5sum` and the MD5 checksum found in the `*.lsm` file haven't both been changed. Once again, when you download files from the Internet, which are not verifiable, you should research the program for known vulnerabilities from such resources as the `bugtraq` archive (see Appendix A) and apply all recommended patches. Also, if possible, run the program on a test system and watch for unusual behavior.

S/Key OTP Overview

S/Key is a client/server-based application that provides for users on the client-side to generate a list of one-time passwords, by first specifying a secret password on the server-side. The initial setup may be performed by the user or by root on the server. The list of one-time passwords is finite (100 by default with S/Key and 500 by default with OPIE), so when the list is exhausted a new list must be generated by the user (or root) on the server. As with many client/server programs, it is entirely possible that the client-side and server-side operations occur on the same system.

---

2. Well, sortof. It's closer to working for Linux than the ones you'll find at `ftp.telcordia.com`. Don't worry, though, we'll go through all the necessary changes.

3. Pretty Good Privacy is discussed in Chapter 3.

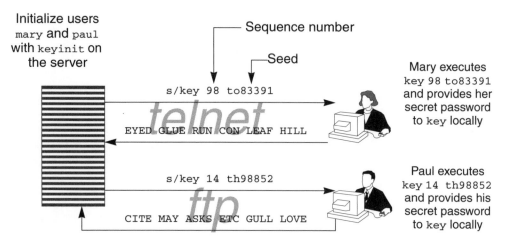

Fig. 6.1 S/Key OTP System

Figure 6.1 provides an overview of the flow of events with respect to the S/Key OTP system. Initially, either the user or root establishes each user on the server as an S/Key client with the `keyinit` command. When `keyinit` is executed, it will prompt for a secret password. The secret password must be known to and remembered by the user, as it is required when the user subsequently wishes to access the server. Once executed, `keyinit` establishes the user in the `/etc/skeykeys` file. This file maintains the information necessary for the server to compute the OTP hash[4] value for the next OTP. In Version 1.1b, the server computes this hash using the RSA Data Security, Inc., MD4 Message-Digest Algorithm (simply known as MD4).

When a user wants to connect to the server—via `telnet`, `rlogin`, or `ftp`, for example—the server will challenge the user with the S/Key sequence number and seed. The sequence number specifies which password in the list of one-time passwords is required and the seed specifies which list to generate. In order for the user to satisfy the challenge of the server, the user will either have a printed list (which must be secured) of one-time passwords, printed when `keyinit` was run, or the user may calculate the appropriate OTP by executing the `key` command and providing it with the sequence number, seed, and—when prompted—the same secret password used with `keyinit`. The output of `key` will be the OTP necessary to respond to the server's challenge. The execution of `key` should always be done locally; otherwise the secret password will traverse the network and may be captured by evildoers and then used to generate the same list that is valid for that particular user. Of course, this defeats the entire purpose of the S/Key system. So, either print out the list or run `key` locally!

---

4. Hash functions are described in Chapter 3.

By default, `keyinit` will generate 99 one-time passwords for each initialized user, and they will be requested in descending order. Each OTP is a collection of six 3- or 4-character, space-separated words. When a user exhausts the list, `keyinit` must be run again on the server, preferably using a different password.

S/Key Version 1.1b

We will discuss installing and configuring S/Key Version 1.1b as if it had been obtained from

```
ftp://ftp.cc.gatech.edu/ac121/linux/system/network/sunacm/Other/skey/
```

or a similar site that includes the ready-made Linux `Makefile`. The file you obtain will be called `skey-linux-1.1b.tar.gz` or something similar. Put this file in a work directory such as `/usr/src`. The first step is to use `gunzip`[5] to uncompress the `tar` file

```
# gunzip skey-linux-1.1b.tar.gz
```

The next step is to extract the archive with `tar`,[6] as shown in Example 6-1. Notice that the `tar` extraction causes the subdirectory, `skey` in this case, to be created. Underneath the `skey` subdirectory, you will find the subdirectories and a README file shown in Example 6-2.

Example 6-1 Extraction of the Files in `skey-linux-1.1b.tar`

```
# cd /usr/src
# tar xvf skey-linux-1.1b.tar
skey/
skey/src/
skey/src/Makefile
skey/src/md4.c
skey/src/put.c
skey/src/skey.c
skey/src/skeyinit.c
skey/src/skeylogin.c
skey/src/skeysubr.c
...
<lots of output snipped>
...
skey/man/
skey/man/key.1
skey/man/keyinit.1
skey/man/skey.1
skey/man/keysh.1
skey/README
skey/tools/
skey/tools/keyinfo
skey/tools/keyaudit
#
```

---

5. The `gzip` and `gunzip` utilities are the GNU compression and uncompression tools, respectively. The are shipped with most (if not all) Linux distributions.

6. Subsequent to this example, we will not normally show `tar` extraction.

Example 6-2 Subdirectories and File of `/usr/src/skey`

```
# ls -F /usr/src/skey
README   man/     misc/    src/     tools/
#
```

The README file means what it says, so read it! It provides information about the S/Key system and how to use it. The man subdirectory contains man pages for the various programs contained in the S/Key distribution. The misc subdirectory contains source code for S/Key-aware replacements of ftpd, su, and login as well as associated Makefile and README files (these will be discussed in *Using the Version 1.1b Replacement Programs* on page 131). The tools subdirectory contains two executable shell scripts, keyinfo and keyaudit. The keyinfo script is used to determine the seed and sequence number of a given user's list. The keyaudit script is used to determine when a user's OTP list is near exhaustion; it should be run out of cron regularly. The src subdirectory contains the source code and Makefile for the S/Key utilities.

After the files have been extracted, you will want to compile some or all of the included programs. To accomplish this you will use the make utility.[7] This utility expects a file called Makefile to be in the same directory as the source code. The Makefile provides make with the necessary instructions for converting (compiling and linking) source code into executable binary files.

Let's look at compiling the S/Key utilities in the src subdirectory. In this case, the Makefile requires an operating-system-type argument. Normally, when a Makefile requires arguments, you can simply execute make and it will return a usage message. Example 6-3 shows the case for the S/Key Version 1.1b Makefile. This tells us that we need to execute make linux. Unfortunately, not all make files are this friendly; very often you will simply get an error message, at which point you will need to examine the Makefile itself to determine its needs. Example 6-4 displays the output of make linux for the src subdirectory.

Example 6-3 Usage Output from make

```
# cd /usr/src/skey/src
# make
Please specify the type of system you are compiling on:
 bsd            Berkeley 4.x, 386BSD, Aviion DG/UX
 linux          Linux
 sunos4         Sun SunOS 4.x
 sunos5         Sun SunOS 5.x (Solaris 2.x)
 ultrix         Dec Ultrix 4.1.x
 sysv           AT&T System V and clones
 irix           Silicon Graphic's IRIX
 next           NeXTStep 2.0
 hpux           HP/UX Hewlett-Packard Unix v9.x

Example: make sunos4
#
```

---

7. For more information on the make utility, reference your system documentation or see Andrew Oram and Steve Talbot, *Managing Projects with make*, 2d ed., Sebastopol, California, O'Reilly & Associates, Inc., 1991.

Example 6-4 Creating the S/Key Version 1.1b Executables

```
# make linux
make all SYS=sysv RANLIB="echo" CFLAGS="-g  -DSYSV -DPOSIX"
make[1]: Entering directory '/usr/src/skey/src'
cc -g  -DSYSV -DPOSIX    -c skeylogin.c -o skeylogin.o
cc -g  -DSYSV -DPOSIX    -c skeysubr.c -o skeysubr.o
cc -g  -DSYSV -DPOSIX    -c md4.c -o md4.o
cc -g  -DSYSV -DPOSIX    -c put.c -o put.o
ar rv libskey.a skeylogin.o skeysubr.o md4.o put.o
a - skeylogin.o
a - skeysubr.o
a - md4.o
a - put.o
echo libskey.a
libskey.a
cc -o key -g  -DSYSV -DPOSIX skey.c libskey.a
cc -o keyinit -g  -DSYSV -DPOSIX skeyinit.c libskey.a  -lcrypt
cc -o keysh -g  -DSYSV -DPOSIX skeysh.c libskey.a
Make completed.
make[1]: Leaving directory '/usr/src/skey/src'
#
```

NOTE

You may get an error message of the form

```
/usr/src/skey/src/skeyinit.c:108: undefined reference to `crypt'
```

when you run make linux as shown in Example 6-4. This indicates that the library containing the crypt system call was not found. To remedy this situation, edit the Makefile in /usr/src/skey/src (or wherever you put it) and change

```
keyinit: skeyinit.c $(LIB)
        $(CC) -o $@ $(CFLAGS) skeyinit.c $(LIB) $(SYSLIBS)
```

to

```
keyinit: skeyinit.c $(LIB)
        $(CC) -o $@ $(CFLAGS) skeyinit.c $(LIB) $(SYSLIBS) -lcrypt
```

and try the make linux command again.

Now you have the binaries associated with S/Key Version 1.1b. They are

```
key
keyinit
keysh
```

The keyinit and key programs were described earlier in association with Figure 6.1 on page 120. The keysh program is a replacement login shell. If you specify it instead of the normal /bin/bash or /bin/ksh or other shell, then the user will always get the S/Key challenge. In a PAM environment, this will occur after any of the PAM requirements are met. This is the ubiquitous approach and, again, may or may not be suitable for your environment. More flexible approaches will be outlined later in this chapter.

At this point, you are ready to install the utilities. Example 6-5 shows the execution of make install. The install argument happens to be supported in this Makefile, and it is quite common, but it will not necessarily be in all make files. Notice that both keyinit and keysh are SUID root; this is necessary to allow for updating the /etc/skeykeys file which is also owned by root. Now that we've got the basic utilities installed, we need to address the keyinfo script next. Then we can look at some examples.

Example 6-5 Installing S/Key Utilities

```
# make install
chmod u+s keyinit keysh
mv key /usr/local/bin
mv keyinit /usr/local/bin
mv keysh /usr/local/bin
#
```

The keyinfo script is a very simple Korn shell script that searches the /etc/skeykeys file for a user's sequence number and seed. Once this information is obtained, the user may execute the key command to obtain the next OTP. The problem with the keyinfo script is that it will not work on Linux as it is written because it references commands using incorrect absolute pathnames. To fix this problem, edit the script (it is in /usr/src/skey/tools in our examples) and make sure that the paths to grep and whoami are correct. The correct paths for these two commands on Red Hat 5.2/6.0 are

```
/bin/grep
/usr/bin/whoami
```

After making these corrections, you may also want to copy the script to a standard location on your system. For our examples we will use /usr/local/etc.

```
# cp /usr/src/skey/tools/keyinit /usr/local/etc/keyinit
# chmod 755 /usr/local/etc/keyinit
```

Finally, before you start using the S/Key programs, you probably want to install the man pages. Since this is add-on software, we'll use /usr/local/man and since they are end-user commands, we'll put them in the man1 subdirectory.

```
# cd /usr/src/skey/man
# cp key.1 /usr/local/man/man1/key.1
# cp keyinit.1 /usr/local/man/man1/keyinit.1
# cp keysh.1 /usr/local/man/man1/keysh.1
# cp skey.1 /usr/local/man/man1/skey.1
```

NOTE

In order to make use of the commands and man pages you've just installed, make sure that all users include /usr/local/bin and /usr/local/etc in their PATH environment variable and /usr/local/man in their MANPATH environment variable.

Using S/Key Version 1.1b   Given the tools we've compiled (and corrected), we may now implement the S/Key system using `keysh`. To begin, we'll establish the user `mary` with S/Key. In the following series of examples, the server system will be called `topcat`. We will perform the following steps as an example:

- ☞ Initialize `mary` with `keyinit`
- ☞ Provide Mary with a printed list of one-time passwords
- ☞ Change the default shell in `/etc/passwd` to `/usr/local/bin/keysh` for `mary`
- ☞ Verify that `mary` can successfully login

Initialize mary with keyinit.   Example 6-6 shows the system administrator, as `root`, executing the `keyinit` command, on behalf of the user, `mary`, to initialize her OTP list with the S/Key system. This step must be executed prior to Mary using the S/Key system. Take note that this command is executed locally on the server. This prevents the secret password from being sent over the network. The execution of `keyinit` has caused the `/etc/skeykeys` file to be updated with a hexadecimal representation of the 99th OTP generated using the given secret password and seed. This is the information required by the server `topcat` to verify the 98th password in the list, which is the password that Mary will be prompted for when she first uses S/Key through `keysh`. The record for `mary` in the `/etc/skeykeys` file as a result of Example 6-6 is

```
    mary 0099 to25065          be9406d891ac86fb  Mar 06,1999 05:25:43
```

The fields in this record are—from left to right—the username, the sequence number of the most recently used OTP, the seed, the 99th OTP in hexadecimal notation, and the date and timestamp reflecting when the record was entered. The pertinent information relating to this record may be viewed with the `key-info` script, as shown in Example 6-7. Note that the output of `keyinfo mary` displays the sequence number of the *next* required password in the OTP list,

Example 6-6 Initializing a User with `keyinit`

```
[root@topcat]# keyinit mary
[Adding mary]
Enter secret password:

Again secret password:

ID mary s/key is 99 to25065
Next login password: MOON JADE MAIN LAW OMIT FANG*
[root@topcat]#
```

*Even though the system claims that this is the next login password, it is actually the 99th OTP and will never be requested; see Example 6-8.

Example 6-7 The `keyinfo` Command

```
# keyinfo mary
98 to25065
#
```

which is one less (remember, S/Key one-time passwords are used in descending order) than that which is recorded in /etc/skeykeys. It also displays the seed.

OH, BY THE WAY...

It turns out that the S/Key algorithm is able to compute OTP number N + 1 of a list whenever it processes OTP number N from the same list. Thus, in our example, topcat maintains the 99th OTP from Mary's list in the /etc/skeykeys file. When Mary first logs in to topcat, it asks her for OTP number 98. The S/Key algorithm on topcat then uses OTP 98 to compute OTP 99. If it matches what is stored in /etc/skeykeys, then Mary is granted access. Otherwise she is denied access. After Mary has used an OTP, the server records the last one used in /etc/skeykeys and decrements the sequence number.

Provide Mary with a Printed List of One-Time Passwords. Since the system administrator (let's call him Bill), as root, executed keyinit on behalf of Mary, Bill has two choices. He must either inform Mary of the secret password used to initialize her account or print out the list of one-time passwords generated in Example 6-6. Let's consider the latter case. Bill needs to generate the OTP list for Mary; to do this he needs to use the key command, and he will also need to know the seed (to25065, in this case) and the secret password used to initialize the user, mary. Example 6-8 shows root generating Mary's list. Example 6-8 illustrates the listing of the OTP list to the screen or window in which Bill is working (default standard output in the shell). In order to print this out, Bill will need to cut and paste the output into a file and then submit it to the printer. If you take this approach, **make sure** that you delete the file containing the OTP list after you have printed it. In the alternative, you may redirect the output to lpr as shown in Example 6-9. In this example, the message ***enter secret password here*** will not actually be displayed—in fact, nothing will be displayed because all output has been sent to lpr. So, where it says ***enter secret password here*** you will see nothing, but you need to enter the secret password so that the OTP list can be generated and sent to the printer. The very first line of the printed output will be Enter secret password:, but the secret password itself will not appear on the printout.

Example 6-8 S/Key List Generated by System Administrator for Another User

```
[root@topcat]# key -n 100 99 to25065
Enter secret password:

0: SEAL LEAD TALK REID SEND NIT
1: MOLT LEN AMMO DOUG GUY MARE
2: BON LO NERO CRUD CELL DIET
3: GOAD RIO EM LEAR HISS SOY
4: LAWN GAD ALSO WAVY IF HOLM
5: THIN INK CUBA BLEW DREW BARD
6: WAG LINK LUND GEE DARK ACE
7: ROWS GINA GIL ANEW LAIN BEAN
...
<lots of output snipped>
...
```

Example 6-8 S/Key List Generated by System Administrator for Another User (Continued)

```
93: RUBE CHEW HUH BANG WISH BUG
94: WEAK FEE RAFT GAM TOLD WACK
95: SEES QUIT CADY SUNK GEAR NEST
96: ROSY NAGY DART GELD ABLE LOSS
97: COON FLOG ORE BILK SARA TEEM
98: WACK DOLT CAKE ROWS BLED ROAD
99: MOON JADE MAIN LAW OMIT FANG
[root@topcat]#
```

Example 6-9 Sending the Output of `key` to `lpr`

```
[root@topcat]# key -n 100 99 to25065 | lpr
enter secret password here
#
```

The alternative to printing out a list, in this case, is for Bill to give the secret password to Mary. Mary would then be able to generate her own list locally on her system.

WARNING!

> Whenever you use the `key` program to generate an OTP list, if you inadvertently enter an incorrect secret password, a list will still be generated. However, none of the passwords in the list will work.

Change the Default Shell in `/etc/passwd` to `/usr/local/bin/keysh` for mary. Next, Bill needs to update `/etc/passwd` by specifying `/usr/local/bin/keysh` as the user `mary`'s default shell. This may be done either by using `chsh` or by editing the `/etc/passwd` file directly. Either way, the final entry will look something like

```
mary:x:103:103:Mary Smith:/home/mary:/usr/local/bin/keysh
```

OH, BY THE WAY...

> The `keysh` program is written to invoke the c-shell. If this is not to your liking you may modify `keysh` to invoke a different shell, say `/bin/bash`. To accomplish this, simply change the line
>
> ```
> char *shell = "/bin/csh";
> ```
>
> in `skeysh.c` to
>
> ```
> char *shell = "/bin/bash";
> ```
>
> and recompile. If you have a large number of users, some of whom have distinct shell preferences, you could simply create multiple executables, each invoking the desired shell. Make sure that you give the executables appropriate names, like `keycsh` for the c-shell, `keybash` for the bourne-again shell, and so on. For untrusted users, you could even create an executable for the restricted shell as it was described in *Restricted Accounts* on page 64 of Chapter 4.

Verify that mary Can Successfully Log In.   Now we can give Mary her OTP list and let her try out the system. Example 6-10 shows the sequence of events when Mary logs in. Now, you may be wondering why Mary first gets a Password: prompt. This is a result of PAM! We haven't modified PAM, so it still expects the standard Linux password to be entered; therefore, in order for Mary to be able to log in, she must now supply both her Linux password and the specified S/Key password, which in this case is number 98 from the list shown in Example 6-8 on page 126.

Example 6-10 Login Requiring S/Key OTP

```
Red Hat Linux release 5.2 (Apollo)
Kernel 2.0.36 on an i686
topcat login: mary
Password: I need a #%$3+ raise
[s/key 98 to25065]
Response: WACK DOLT CAKE ROWS BLED ROAD

[mary@topcat]$
```

Mary may not be too happy with Bill at this point. Having to type in a 20-character password (due to our PAM requirements; see *PAM and login* on page 93) *and* a long OTP is a bit much. You could, at this point, disable PAM authentication by using pam_permit in the appropriate /etc/pam.d/ files (see *PAM and the other Configuration File* on page 108), but this is not the best approach as we will see in *OPIE and PAM* on page 143.

Allowing Users More Freedom   Ha! Never! This is a draconian environment and *I* am in charge! (Sorry, the power of root does this to me sometimes.)

The sequence of examples covered in the sections *Initialize mary with keyinit* on page 125 and *Provide Mary with a Printed List of One-Time Passwords* on page 126 need not be performed by root. Mary could execute these steps herself. She can do this on the server topcat because the keyinit program is SUID to root. For greater security, you may wish to disable this feature by removing the SUID permission on keyinit. Doing so means that only root will be able to initialize users originally and generate new lists subsequently.

WARNING!

While it is true that keyinit may be executed by nonroot users, the keyinit program will prompt nonroot users for their Linux passwords before allowing them to initialize or generate a new list. Since keyinit is not PAM-aware, if you are using MD5 or bigcrypt instead of the standard UNIX hashing mechanism for your Linux passwords, keyinit will never successfully resolve a user-supplied Linux password. In short, nonroot users will be unable to generate their own S/Key lists. Do not despair, however, as we will discuss the integration of OPIE in PAM in *OPIE and PAM* on page 143.

Mary could also execute the step *Change the Default Shell in* `/etc/`
`passwd` *to* `/usr/local/bin/keysh` *for* `mary` on page 127, by using the `chsh` command if, and only if, `/usr/local/bin/keysh` is in `/etc/shells`.

NOTE

> The `root` user can execute `chsh` for any user and specify any executable as the new
> default shell. All other users can successfully change their default shell only to one
> of the shells listed in `/etc/shells`.

Running `key` Locally   You may or may not want to use paper copies of OTP
lists exclusively. It may make sense when a user is on the road and will be
accessing various systems in order to log in on their office systems over various networks. But normally it isn't advisable since such a list is easily compromised or lost. The solution to this problem is the `key` program.

The `key` program is small enough to fit on a floppy disk, and you need to
compile only one version for each operating system/hardware platform in your
environment. Whenever users log in to an S/Key system, they will be
prompted for their OTP passwords in a fashion similar to that of Example 6-
10 on page 128. The S/Key system will provide the sequence number and seed
required by the `key` program. The user must know the secret password. So, if
the system administrator Bill has previously assigned it, then Bill must disclose the secret password to the user, say Paul. Once Paul has the secret password used to generate the list, then he may log in using one window as shown
in Example 6-11. And in another window Paul computes the OTP with `key` as
exhibited in Example 6-12. Paul can cut the result from Example 6-12 and
paste it in Example 6-11 to satisfy the S/Key challenge.

Example 6-11 Logging in to an S/Key-Enabled System

```
[paul@minnie]$ telnet topcat
Trying 172.19.31.104...
Connected to topcat.
Escape character is '^]'.

Red Hat Linux release 5.2 (Apollo)
Kernel 2.0.36 on an i686
login: paul
[s/key 97 to54065]
Response: AYE ROAR HAST KAY HIKE OMAN

[paul@topcat]$
```

Example 6-12 Running `key`

```
[paul@minnie]$ /usr/local/bin/key 97 to54065
Enter secret password:

AYE ROAR HAST KAY HIKE OMAN
[paul@minnie]$
```

It turns out that there are a number of OTP-generating programs that
generate S/Key and OPIE OTP lists using either MD4 or MD5 (both S/Key

Version 2.2 and OPIE are capable of using MD5 instead of MD4). Some are available from

```
http://www.jumbo.com/pages/business/linux/
```

which run on various flavors of UNIX and Microsoft operating systems.

Generating New OTP Lists   As users consume their one-time passwords, new lists need to be generated. This is done with the `keyinit` program. It may be executed by the user (except when using PAM with MD5 or bigcrypt; see Warning on page 128) or by the administrator as root on behalf of the user. It turns out that the `keyinit` program, when invoked with the `-s` flag, may be used securely over the network if the user can run `key` or equivalent locally. Here's how it works.

The user `mary` needs to generate a new list of S/Key passwords. After she logs in to the server `topcat`, she runs `keyinit -s` as shown in Example 6-13. In another window on her local system—`roadrunner`, as shown in Example 6-14—she runs `key` in order to generate the 99th OTP so that she may supply it to the `keyinit` program on `topcat` as shown in Example 6-13. Once again, the server needs to record OTP number 99 in order to subsequently verify OTP number 98. It does this by storing the last OTP in hexadecimal and the sequence number as well as the seed in `/etc/skeykeys`. This procedure provides it with the necessary information.

Example 6-13 Using `keyinit -s` to Remotely Update S/Key OTP Lists

```
[mary@topcat]$ keyinit -s
[Updating mary]
Old key: to31809
You need the 6 english words generated from the "key" command.
Enter sequence count from 1 to 10000: 99
Enter new key [default to31810]:
s/key 99 to54066
s/key access password: FAWN LO DOCK HAAS DUMB WALT

ID mary s/key is 99 to31810
Next login password: FAWN LO DOCK HAAS DUMB WALT
[mary@topcat]$
```

Example 6-14 Using `key` to Obtain an OTP for `keyinit -s`

```
roadrunner$ key 99 to31810
Enter secret password:
FAWN LO DOCK HAAS DUMB WALT
roadrunner$
```

Notice in Example 6-13 that `keyinit -s` affords the opportunity to specify longer or shorter OTP lists and alternate seed numbers. It is probably a good idea to specify your own seed number since S/Key Version 1.1b does no randomizing of the seed. Version 2.2 and OPIE both do a better job of this as we will see in the sections *S/Key Version 2.2* and *OPIE* on page 132, respectively.

If `keyinit` is to be run **without** the `-s` flag (see Example 6-6 on page
125), it must be executed locally on the server because it requires the secret
password (and, once again, you don't want the secret password passing over
the network).

The `keyaudit` Script   The `keyaudit` script, found in `/usr/src/skey/tools`, is
a bourne shell script that checks on the remaining number of OTP passwords
for each user found in `/etc/skeykeys`. If a user has 11 or fewer remaining one-
time passwords, then `keyaudit` will send an e-mail message to the administrator reminding him or her to generate a new list for the user or users whose
lists are growing short. You will need to modify the `keyaudit` script in order to
get it to work on Linux. Change the line

```
HOST='/usr/ucb/hostname'
```

to

```
HOST='/bin/hostname'
```

You will also need to change the ADMIN variable in the script to someone who
reads their mail and will act upon a message from `keyaudit`. For example, if
the user `bill` is the administrator, we would change the line

```
ADMIN=chasin
```

to

```
ADMIN=bill
```

and the `keyaudit` script will work. The `keyaudit` script will also accept a
numeric argument for the number of OTPs remaining. For example, you could
execute `keyaudit 15`, and it will then look through `/etc/skeykeys` for all users
with a sequence number of 14 or less in the `/etc/skeykeys` file. Remember, the
sequence number in the `/etc/skeykeys` file is one greater than the actual
number of remaining one-time passwords in the user's list. If the sequence
number found is strictly less than three, the subject line in the e-mail will
reflect the important nature of the message. You should set `keyaudit` up in
`cron` to run regularly.

Using the Version 1.1b Replacement Programs   Up to this point we have
looked at using `keysh` only to ubiquitously invoke the S/Key system. This is a
valid approach in many cases. It is also a valid approach for all users who are
not allowed to log in at the console.

   You may instead or additionally want to use one of the S/Key-aware
replacement programs found in the `/usr/src/skey/misc` directory. As previously noted, they are `su`, `login`, and `ftpd`. If you are using PAM (and you
should be), you probably don't want to use these programs. However, if you
choose or need to use one or more of them, you may compile them and replace
the original binaries. We will not detail this procedure for S/Key Version 1.1b;

rather we will discuss replacement programs in more detail for OPIE (see *OPIE* on page 132), and suggest that you seriously consider using OPIE as opposed to S/Key Version 1.1b in that case. OPIE offers a number of improvements over S/Key Version 1.1b. Also, much of what we have discussed so far also applies to OPIE.

S/Key Version 2.2

S/Key Version 2.2 differs from Version 1.1b in a number of ways:

1. Version 2.2 pseudorandomizes the seed selection.
2. It incorporates an access control list.
3. It incorporates both MD4 and MD5 algorithms.
4. The `keyinit` utility does not prompt users for their Linux password.
5. It supplies only the `login` replacement program; there is no `keysh`, `su`, nor `ftpd`.

The major advantages of Version 2.2 are the first three items in the list. Item 4 provides for a modest convenience gain for a reduction in security. Item 5 limits overall flexibility. All of the advantages in items 1 through 3 are incorporated into OPIE without the limitation of item 5. Consequently, our discussion will move on to OPIE.

OPIE

The OPIE program was created at the Naval Research Laboratory (NRL) by Randall Atkinson, Dan McDonald, and Craig Metz. The source code and binaries are publicly available subject to the terms of the license included with the software. Be sure that you read and comply with all licenses and copyright notices. The required acknowledgments are displayed in Example 6-15.

Example 6-15 OPIE Acknowledgments

```
This product includes software developed by the University of
California, Berkeley and its contributors.

This product includes software developed at the Information
Technology Division, US Naval Research Laboratory.

This product includes software developed by Craig Metz, The
Inner Net, and other contributors.
```

OPIE is quite similar to S/Key and in fact is derived therefrom. The key generating algorithm for OPIE is nearly identical to that of S/Key Version 1.1b and differs only in that it provides support for MD5. If you are currently using MD4 S/Key, you may upgrade to OPIE and preserve your existing OTP lists. Table 6.1 equates the commands in OPIE to those in S/Key. Both S/Key

Table 6.1 S/Key and OPIE Command and File Comparison

S/Key Commands and Files	OPIE Commands and Files
keyinit	opiepasswd
key	opiekey
keyinfo	opieinfo
/etc/skeykeys	/etc/opiekeys
/etc/skey.access (v2.2)	/etc/opieaccess

Version 1.1b and OPIE offer replacement programs for su, login, and ftpd. OPIE does not provide an equivalent to keysh nor to keyaudit.

OH, BY THE WAY...

It is very simple to modify the keyaudit script to work with OPIE, and it is well worth the effort. Change the following lines in keyaudit (in addition to those already mentioned in *The keyaudit Script* on page 131) from

```
KEYDB=/etc/skeykeys
$ECHO "Type \"keyinit-s\" to reinitialize your sequence number."
```

to

```
KEYDB=/etc/opiekeys
$ECHO "Type \"opiepasswd\" to reinitialize your sequence number."
```

and change all references of S/Key to OPIE. You may also want to rename the script to opieaudit. For the tightest security, set the permissions on the script to 500 and make it owned by root. Don't forget to put it in cron!

Obtaining and Installing OPIE

As of this writing, the current version of OPIE is 2.32. It may be obtained from

```
ftp://ftp.inner.net.pub/opie/
```

Unfortunately, once again, there is no digital signature associated with the gzipped tar file. The file you obtain will be named something like opie-2.32.tar.gz. The first step is to apply gunzip, then use tar to extract the files. This will create a subdirectory, opie-2.32. For our examples, we'll assume that the OPIE files are in /usr/src/opie-2.32.

The OPIE Version 2.32 distribution uses the GNU autoconfiguration utility configure which is used to automatically configure a Makefile for your system. For more information about this utility, check your system documentation and the references noted in *For Further Reading* on page 148.

The steps necessary to successfully configure, compile, and install OPIE are

☞ Execute `configure` in `/usr/src/opie-2.32`.

☞ Execute `make` in `/usr/src/opie-2.32`.

☞ Execute `make install` in `/usr/src/opie-2.32`.

Each of these steps may require one or more optional arguments to implement OPIE in the way that meets your site's needs. The most common options are discussed in the following sections, but be sure to read the supporting documentation including the files README and INSTALL found in the `opie-2.32` subdirectory.

Execute `configure` in `/usr/src/opie-2.32`.   There are numerous options to the OPIE implementation of `configure`. You may take a look at the options by executing `configure --help` as partially shown in Example 6-16.

Example 6-16 Using `configure` with the `--help` Option

```
# ./configure --help
Usage: configure [options] [host]
Options: [defaults in brackets after descriptions]
Configuration:
  --cache-file=FILE       cache test results in FILE
  --help                  print this message
  --no-create             do not create output files
  --quiet, --silent       do not print 'checking...' messages
...
<lots of output snipped>
...
Features and packages:
  --disable-FEATURE       do not include FEATURE (same as --enable-FEATURE=no)
  --enable-FEATURE[=ARG]  include FEATURE [ARG=yes]
  --with-PACKAGE[=ARG]    use PACKAGE [ARG=yes]
  --without-PACKAGE       do not use PACKAGE (same as --with-PACKAGE=no)
  --x-includes=DIR        X include files are in DIR
  --x-libraries=DIR       X library files are in DIR
--enable and --with options recognized:
  --enable-access-file=FILENAME
                          Enable the OPIE access file FILENAME
  --enable-server-md4     Use MD4 instead of MD5 for the server
  --disable-user-locking  Disable user locking
  --enable-user-locking[=DIR]
                          Put user lock files in DIR [/etc/opielocks]
  --enable-retype         Ask users to re-type their secret pass phrases
  --enable-su-star-check  Refuse to switch to disabled accounts
  --disable-new-prompts   Use more compatible (but less informative) prompts
  --enable-insecure-override
                          Allow users to override insecure checks
  --enable-anonymous-ftp  Enable anonymous FTP support
  --disable-utmp          Disable utmp logging
  --disable-wtmp          Disable wtmp logging
#
```

As is readily apparent, there are a lot of options to OPIE `configure`. Unfortunately, this output does not always clearly inform you as to the default values of the various options if you do not specify them at the command line. In many cases it is obvious what the default will be; for example, if `--enable-`

something exclusively exists, then the default must be disable. In other cases such as the two options, --disable-user-locking and --enable-user-locking[=DIR], it is unclear as to what will occur. The simplest way to determine what the defaults are is to run configure with no options. This will create a number of files, including the files shown in Example 6-17. The files config.log and config.status contain debugging information for configure. Look there if you are having problems getting configure to work or if configure is not identifying some component of your system. The config.cache file contains information that is used to build the Makefile. If you determine that configure found libraries that it will use for linking, for example, and you want other libraries used, you may make corrections to config.cache and then execute configure --recheck to rebuild the Makefile. The config.h file contains definitions of various variables that are subsequently used in the compilation process. It is here that you will find the defaults to the various options shown in Example 6-16. You may make corrections to the config.h file itself, but, to avoid mistakes, you are better served by executing make realclean, which removes all files generated by configure; then rerun configure with the desired arguments. This may seem to be a tedious process at first, but with practice you will become more proficient in dealing with configure. It is definitely worth the effort because many publicly available utilities are built using configure.

Example 6-17 Files Created by configure

```
Makefile
config.cache
config.h
config.log
config.status
```

Table 6.2 describes a few of the more important arguments associated with configure for OPIE. This is clearly not a definitive list, and you should examine all of the arguments to determine your needs. It is a good idea to configure and compile OPIE in a test environment first, then re-configure and recompile until you obtain an implementation that works for you.

After determining which options you wish to use with the OPIE configure utility, you are ready to execute it. Example 6-18 shows the output of such an execution (line wraps due to formatting constraints). In our example, we will use the --enable-access-file so that we may explore the associated functionality. We do not recommend the use of the --enable-access-file option unless absolutely necessary.

The entire output of configure will be found in config.log. Notice that configure warns us about the use of the access file, /etc/opieaccess, which will be discussed in *Using /etc/opieaccess* on page 142. It also tells us that the binaries will be installed in /usr/local/bin. This will occur when we run make install (or one of its variants); it is discussed later in this section. Be advised that this location for binaries does not apply to the replacement programs su, login, and ftpd.

Table 6.2 Description of Important OPIE `configuration` Options

OPIE `configure` Option	Description
`--enable-user-locking[=DIR]`	Allows for the specification of an alternate location for lock file directory. Default is `/etc/opielocks`. The purpose of these lock files is to mitigate race attacks and are implemented as required by RFC2289.
`--disable-user-locking`	Disables the use of lock files.
`--enable-access-file=`*FILENAME*	Enable the use of an access control list. *FILENAME* is replaced with the absolute pathname of the file. By default this option is disabled and is not recommended.
`--enable-su-star-check`	Causes all `su` attempts to users with no valid password (* in the password field) to fail. This **does** apply to root. Only meaningful if you use the replacement `su` program.
`--enable-insecure-override`	Ordinarily, OPIE will disallow the disclosure of the secret password over the network. Setting this configuration option allows the use of the `-f` flags with `opie-passwd` and `opiekey` to override the security checks. Use of this option is not recommended.
`--enable-server-md4`	Causes the server-side applications to use MD4 instead of MD5. MD5 is the default and is recommended.

Example 6-18 Running `configure` for OPIE

```
# ./configure --enable-access-file=/etc/opieaccess
creating cache ./config.cache
Using the access file in /etc/opieaccess -- don't say we didn't warn you!
checking for gcc... gcc
checking whether the C compiler (gcc  ) works... yes
checking whether the C compiler (gcc  ) is a cross-compiler... no
checking whether we are using GNU C... yes
...
<lots of output snipped>
...
checking for nonstandard gettimeofday... no
updating cache ./config.cache
creating ./config.status
creating configure.munger
creating libmissing/Makefile
creating libopie/Makefile
creating Makefile.munge
creating config.h

Binaries are going to be installed into /usr/local/bin,
Manual pages are going to be installed into /usr/local/man.

creating Makefile

Have you read the README file?
#
```

Table 6.3 Arguments Supported by the OPIE `Makefile`

Argument	Description
client	Compiles and links the client programs `opiekey` and `opiegen`.[*]
server	Compiles and links the server programs `opiepasswd`, `opieserv`,[†] `su`, `login`, and `ftpd`.
client-install	Installs the client programs.
server-install	Installs the server programs.
install	Installs all programs (client and server).
clean	Removes all binaries and object files.
realclean	Removes all binaries, object files, and files created by `configure` including all `make` files.
no arguments	Compiles and links all programs (client and server).

[*]`opiegen` is a program example provided for developers; it is functionally similar to `opiekey`.
[†]`opieserv` is a program example provided for developers; it is functionally similar to `opiepasswd`.

The OPIE `Makefile` generated by `configure` offers us a few options. It will accept the arguments described in Table 6.3.

For purposes of our examples, we will use `make` with no arguments to compile OPIE and then use `make install` to install OPIE. As described in Table 6.3, this will create the necessary binaries for both client and server activity and then will install all compiled binaries into the appropriate locations. Example 6-19 displays partial output from the execution of `make`. Notice that OPIE executes a series of tests after compiling the utilities. If your `Makefile` has problems, this is one place that it will almost certainly show up.

Example 6-19 OPIE `make`

```
# make
(cd libopie ; make libopie.a CFL='-O -DKEY_FILE='/etc/opiekeys'')
make[1]: Entering directory '/usr/src/opie/opie-2.32/libopie'
gcc -O -DKEY_FILE='/etc/opiekeys' -I..    -c md4c.c -o md4c.o
gcc -O -DKEY_FILE='/etc/opiekeys' -I..    -c md5c.c -o md5c.o
gcc -O -DKEY_FILE='/etc/opiekeys' -I..    -c atob8.c -o atob8.o
gcc -O -DKEY_FILE='/etc/opiekeys' -I..    -c btoa8.c -o btoa8.o
...
<lots of output snipped>
...
opietest: executing 13 tests
( 1/13) testing opieatob8... passed
( 2/13) testing opiebtoa8... passed
( 3/13) testing opiebtoe... passed
( 4/13) testing opieetob... passed
( 5/13) testing opiegenerator... passed
( 6/13) testing opiegetsequence... passed
( 7/13) testing opiehash(MD4)... passed
```

Example 6-19 OPIE `make` (Continued)

```
( 8/13) testing opiehash(MD5)... passed
( 9/13) testing opieinsecure... passed
(10/13) testing opiekeycrunch... passed
(11/13) testing opielock... passed
(12/13) testing opierandomchallenge... passed
(13/13) testing opieunlock... passed
opietest: completed 13 tests. 13 tests passed, 0 tests skipped, 0 tests
failed.
...
<lots more ouput snipped>
...
gcc -O opieftpd.o glob.o popen.o y.tab.o -Llibopie -Llibmissing -lopie
-lposix -lnsl -lcrypt  -lmissing -lopie -o opieftpd
gcc -O   -c opieserv.c -o opieserv.o
gcc -O opieserv.o -Llibopie -Llibmissing -lopie -lposix -lnsl -lcrypt
-lmissing -lopie -o opieserv
#
```

Now that OPIE is compiled, you are ready to install it and start using it. Before you do so, however, read the warning.

WARNING!

When you run `make install` or `make server-install` for OPIE, the replacement programs, `su`, `login`, and `ftpd` will automatically be copied to the appropriate locations. Fortunately, this `Makefile` will copy your existing binaries to *name*`.opie.old` (for example, `/bin/login` becomes `/bin/login.opie.old`). It also clears the permissions on all `*.opie.old` files.

There may be many reasons why you might not want to use these replacement programs, in particular if you are using PAM with OPIE as discussed in *OPIE and PAM* on page 143. To overcome this aspect of installing OPIE, you may either modify the `Makefile` to suit your needs or copy the original files back after OPIE install completes. If you choose the latter approach, be sure to make a note of the file permissions and ownerships on `su`, `login`, and `ftpd` *prior* to installing OPIE.

Another problem with the fact that the replacement programs are automatically installed is that any user who attempts to log in after installation will be unable to do so until an OPIE OTP list is generated for them with `opiepasswd` and `opiekey`. This is a particular problem if the administrator logs out before generating an OTP list for root. You could lock yourself out of the system!

Also, the replacement `ftpd` does not use the same flags as the original; therefore, if you use the replacement `ftpd`, you will need to modify `/etc/inetd.conf` accordingly. After you modify `/etc/inetd.conf`, make sure to execute `killall -HUP inetd`.

Example 6-20 displays the output of `make install`.
We are now ready to implement and use OPIE.

Example 6-20 Output of `make install` for OPIE

```
# make install
Installing OPIE server software...
Copying OPIE user programs
Changing ownership
Changing file permissions
Installing OPIE system programs...
Renaming existing /bin/login to /bin/login.opie.old
Clearing permissions on old /bin/login
Copying opielogin to /bin/login
Changing ownership of /bin/login
Changing file permissions of /bin/login
Renaming existing su to su.opie.old
Clearing permissions on old su
Copying opiesu to su
Changing ownership of su
Changing file permissions of su
Copying OPIE ftp daemon
Changing ownership of ftpd
Changing file permissions of ftpd
Making sure OPIE database file exists
Changing permissions of OPIE database file
Changing ownership of OPIE database file
Creating OPIE lock directory
Installing manual pages
REMEMBER to run opiepasswd on your users immediately.
#
```

NOTE

We could have skipped the `make` in Example 6-19 on page 137 and simply executed `make install` as shown in Example 6-20 to perform both steps.

Implementing and Using OPIE

In this section we will look at the OPIE OTP programs `opiepasswd` and `opiekey`. Then we will take a look at examples that parallel those found in *S/Key Version 1.1b* on page 121.

The procedure used to initialize users and manage OTP lists with OPIE is quite similar to S/Key. With OPIE, the server-side program is `opiepasswd` instead of `keyinit`. The client-side program is `opiekey` instead of `key`.

As noted at the bottom of Example 6-20, the first thing we need to do is use `opiepasswd` to initialize our users. Unlike `keyinit`, which offers only the `-s` option (see Example 6-13), `opiepasswd` provides a number of options, described in Table 6.4.

The `opiekey` program is the OTP generating program. Unlike its S/Key counterpart `key`, there are a number of options available for `opiekey`, which are described in Table 6.5.

Now that we have described the two basic commands, let's take a look at some examples. Once again, we'll call the system administrator `bill` and our example user will be `mary`. Our server system will be `topcat`. As before, either Mary or Bill can use the `opiepasswd` command to initialize or reinitialize

Table 6.4 Options to `opiepasswd`

Option	Description
-v	Displays version and compile-time options.
-h	Displays help message.
-c	Sets console mode. Requests the secret passphrase instead of forcing the use of a local OTP generator. Will automatically fail if requested over an unsecure connection unless compile time option `--enable-insecure-override` included.
-d	Disables OTP logins to specified account. Any user may disable his or her own account. Only root can disable others. This option simply enters an invalid string for the user's last OTP in `/etc/opiekeys`. This option is particularly useful when a user determines that his or her passphrase has been compromised.
-f	Forces `opiepasswd` to continue over an unsecure channel. Only functions if compiled with `--enable-insecure-override`. Not recommended.
-n *sequence number*	Manually specifies the initial sequence number. Default is 499.
-s *seed*	Manually specifies the seed. Ordinarily the seed is pseudorandomly generated. Not recommended.
username	Optionally specifies the user. Only root can successfully use this option.

Table 6.5 Options to `opiekey`

Option	Description
-4 | -5	Generates either an MD4 or MD5 list. The MD4 list is compatible with S/Key Version 1.1b. Note: `opiekey -4` is equivalent to `otp-md4` and `opiekey -5` is equivalent to `otp-md5`.
-v	Displays version and compile-time options.
-h	Displays help message.
-f	Forces `opiekey` to continue over an unsecure channel. Only functions if compiled with `--enable-insecure-override`. Not recommended.
-n *count*	Specifies the number of one-time passwords to print. Default is one.
-x	Outputs OTP in hexadecimal notation.
-t type	Uses extended response types as defined in RFC2243.
-a	Allows for arbitrary secret passphrases (no checks). **Not** implemented, yet.
sequence number	Required argument. The sequence number requested, often obtained from the OTP challenge. This is the number of the OTP in the list that will be displayed.
seed	Required argument. The seed associated with the list you are computing. Often obtained from the OTP challenge.

Mary's OTP list. Bill, as root, initializes the user `mary` at the `topcat` system console in Example 6-21. Of course, Bill will have to tell Mary what secret passphrase he used so that she can generate a list using `opiekey`. OPIE secret passphrases must be between 10 and 127 characters in length. Assuming that Bill told Mary what the passphrase was, she can now login to `topcat` by executing `telnet`, `rlogin`, or `ftp` in one window and using `opiekey` to compute the OTP in another window. These two steps are shown in Example 6-22 and Example 6-23, respectively. Very much like Examples 6-11 and 6-12 on page 129, Mary first executes `telnet` in one window as shown in Example 6-22. After she enters her username at the login prompt, OPIE asks for OTP sequence number `498` and seed `to0967`. In another window, as shown in Example 6-23, she uses `opiekey` with the sequence number and seed as arguments, then supplies her secret password when prompted. This causes `opiekey` to compute the appropriate OTP which she then cuts from Example 6-23 and pastes into Example 6-22 at the `Response:` prompt. Now she is logged in to `topcat`.

Example 6-21 Administrator Initializes an OPIE User at the Console

```
# opiepasswd -c mary
Adding mary:
Only use this method from the console; NEVER from remote. If you are
using telnet, xterm, or a dial-in, type ^C now or exit with no password.
Then run opiepasswd without the -c parameter.
Using MD5 to compute responses.
Enter new secret pass phrase:
Again new secret pass phrase:

ID mary OTP key is 499 to0967
HOWE BOHR COIN HUM BUFF PAT
```

Example 6-22 Mary `telnet`'s from `roadrunner` to `topcat`

```
roadrunner$ telnet topcat
Trying 172.19.31.104...
Connected to topcat.
Escape character is '^]'.

Red Hat Linux release 5.2 (Apollo)
Kernel 2.0.36 on an i686
login: mary
otp-md5 498 to0967 ext
Response: USES LUGE BALM PAN KANE NUT

[mary@topcat]$
```

Example 6-23 Mary Computes the OTP with `opiekey`

```
roadrunner$ opiekey 498 to0967
Using the MD5 algorithm to compute response.
Reminder: Don't use opiekey from telnet or dial-in sessions.
Enter secret pass phrase:
USES LUGE BALM PAN KANE NUT
roadrunner$
```

NOTE

> Unless compiled with the `--enable-override` option, neither `opiekey` nor `opie-passwd` will successfully execute over the network, even if you use the `-f` flag. This may be inconvenient, but it provides substantial additional security by disallowing secret passphrases to be submitted over the network. Consider this feature carefully before you compile with the `--enable-override` option. And don't expect your users not to know about the `-f` flag—they can read man pages, too!

Recall that both `su` and `ftp` are replaced with OPIE versions when OPIE is installed. Thus, those utilities will behave similarly with respect to requiring OTP when invoked.

The biggest problem with using OPIE is that it imposes OTP everywhere, including at the console. This may be desirable, but it also means that, in order to log in at the console, either you will need a printed list of one-time passwords or you will need to have access to another system that can run `opiekey`. One way to work around this issue is to utilize the `/etc/opieaccess` file.

Using /etc/opieaccess   This is a very simple access control list that contains rules using the syntax displayed in Example 6-24. In this file, the keyword `permit` or `deny` is followed by one or more spaces and then the *network/netmask* entry. Both the *network* and *netmask* entries must be in dot decimal notation. The same goes for the host entry, which uses a netmask value of `255.255.255.255` to inform OPIE that it is a rule for a host and not for a network.

Example 6-24 `/etc/opieaccess` Syntax

```
permit network/netmask
permit host/255.255.255.255
deny network/netmask
deny host/255.255.255.255
```

The `deny` keyword indicates that any host coming from the network indicated must respond to an OPIE challenge. The same is true for a single host if the target of `deny` is a host-only entry.

The `permit` keyword means that the *network/netmask* entry to its right will not be required to supply an OPIE OTP; instead the user will be given the option of supplying the OTP password or the Linux password. Consider Example 6-25, which reflects a sample `/etc/opieaccess` file on `topcat`. In this case, the users logging in from host `172.17.31.104` (which is `topcat` itself) will be allowed to supply either an OPIE OTP or a Linux password. The same is true for any user from any host on the subnetwork `172.17.1.0` except for the host `172.17.1.5`. All other access will be required to use OPIE OTP.

Example 6-25 Sample `/etc/opieaccess` File

```
permit 172.17.31.104/255.255.255.255
permit 172.17.1.0/255.255.255.0
deny 172.17.1.5/255.255.255.255
```

Given the `/etc/opieaccess` file as shown in Example 6-25, when Bill logs in at the console, Example 6-26 shows the course of events. Remember, this will work only if OPIE has been compiled with the `--enable-access-file=/etc/opieaccess` option.

Example 6-26 Optional Password Prompt Due to `/etc/opieaccess`

```
topcat login: bill
otp-md5 309 1i0766
Response or Password:
[bill@topcat]$
```

Recall that both `su` and `ftp` are, by default, replaced when you install OPIE. This means that the `/etc/opieaccess` file applies to them as well.

It should be clear that the use of this file could open a large security hole. If someone were to be able to compromise the file or find out which hosts are listed in the file, they would merely need to compromise a static password.

There is another approach that offers a bit more security—using `pam_opie` and `pam_if`.

OPIE AND PAM

PAM[8] is so wonderful! You really should use it! Centralized configuration (and control, control and power, control and power and ... oh, sorry!), finely grained management of authentication mechanisms, and a future that promises many great things (see *The Future of PAM* on page 114).

Among the benefits of implementing OPIE through PAM are that the configuration files are centralized in a single directory (or `/etc/pam.conf` file). Restrictive permissions may be (and should be) imposed on the files in the `/etc/pam.d` directory. PAM offers the further ability to specify which services require which set of procedures. All the features and administrative requirements associated with OPIE still apply; we just don't need to use modified versions of `su`, `login`, and `ftpd`.

We will look at implementing two PAM modules—`pam_opie` and `pam_if`. The `pam_opie` module supports OPIE authentication, while the `pam_if` module provides a way of introducing a conditional operation in a PAM stack. For a thorough discussion of PAM, see Chapter 5.

Obtaining and Installing `pam_opie`

The `pam_opie` module was written by Andy Berkheimer. He distributes it under the GPL (see Chapter 3 for GPL details). It currently supports only

---

8. There is a `pam_skey` module ,but it is unfortunately dated and requires modification to run under current Linux-PAM. See *Available PAM Modules* on page 109.

module type `auth`, but Andy plans to include module type `password` support soon (we hope!) to allow for updating OTP lists. This module is available from

```
http://www.tho.org/~andy/pam-opie.html
```

There you will find `pam_opie-0.21.tar.gz` (as of this writing, Version 0.21). As usual, you need to uncompress the file with `gunzip` and then extract the archive with `tar`.

It does not use `configure`, but it does come with a `Makefile` that works flawlessly under Red Hat 5.2/6.0. You can put the source code in a directory of your choosing or in the standard PAM source tree. In either case, when you execute `make install`, it properly puts `pam_opie.so` in `/lib/security`.

Obtaining and Installing `pam_if`

The `pam_if` module was written by Pavel Kankovsky and is also available under the GPL. It is available from

```
http://www.dcit.cz/~kan/pam/
```

Once again, there is no signature file. The file you will find is `pam_if.tar.gz`.

After you uncompress and extract the files (either in a directory of your choosing or the PAM source tree), you will be able to run `make` with no problems (Red Hat 5.2/6.0, anyway!). However, you will need to modify the `Makefile` in order to properly install the module. The simplest way to accomplish this is to add the following definitions near the top of the file:

```
INSTALL=/usr/bin/install
SECUREDIR=/lib/security
```

Once done, `make install` will work fine.

Implementing `pam_opie` and `pam_if`

Once you have installed these two modules and installed OPIE (but you don't need the replacement programs, `su`, `login`, or `ftpd`), you are ready to implement OPIE through PAM. You will still need to maintain your OTP lists outside of PAM, but using this approach you will have more flexibility in controlling which services require OPIE and under what circumstances OPIE is required. We will first look at implementing `pam_opie` and `pam_if`; then we will describe the parameters to `pam_if`.

In Example 6-27, we see the `/etc/pam.d/login` file with `pam_if` and `pam_opie` implemented. Using this implementation, when a user logs in, the first module invoked is `pam_securetty` which checks the valid login devices for root. Then `pam_nologin` is executed to check for the existence of `/etc/nologin`. Next the `pam_if` module is invoked. If the conditions of the `pam_if`

Example 6-27 `/etc/pam.d/login` File Using `pam_if` and `pam_opie`

```
auth       required     /lib/security/pam_securetty.so
auth       required     /lib/security/pam_nologin.so
auth       sufficient   /lib/security/pam_if.so tty=tty[0-8] -- \
                           pam_pwdb.so
auth       required     /lib/security/pam_opie.so
auth       required     /lib/security/pam_pwdb.so
account    requisite    /lib/security/pam_time.so
account    required     /lib/security/pam_pwdb.so
password   required     /lib/security/pam_cracklib.so
password   required     /lib/security/pam_pwdb.so shadow use_authtok \
                           minlen=20 md5
session    required     /lib/security/pam_pwdb.so
```

module are true, then `pam_pwdb` is invoked as a `sufficient` module (see Chapter 5). Otherwise `pam_opie` and subsequently `pam_pwdb` are invoked (paranoid administrator).

In this example, the `pam_if` module will be satisfied if the `tty` is one of `tty0`, `tty1`, ..., `tty8`. So, if you log in at the console or one of the virtual consoles, you will have to supply only your Linux password. If you log in from anywhere else, you are required to supply first the OPIE OTP and then the Linux password.

These types of entries may be placed in any `/etc/pam.d` configuration file, including `su`, `ftp`, `rlogin`, `chsh`, and any other PAM-aware application. This gives you the ability to control which services require what authentication method or methods. Also, `pam_opie` does not require `pam_if`. Example 6-28 shows the use of `pam_opie` in `/etc/pam.d/ftp`. In this example, any user executing `ftp` to the system containing this `/etc/pam.d/ftp` file must successfully provide an OPIE OTP.

Example 6-28 `/etc/pam.d/ftp` File Using `pam_opie`

```
auth       required     /lib/security/pam_listfile.so item=user \
           sense=deny file=/etc/ftpusers onerr=succeed
auth       required     /lib/security/pam_opie.so
auth       required     /lib/security/pam_shells.so
account    required     /lib/security/pam_pwdb.so
session    required     /lib/security/pam_pwdb.so
```

Similarly, `pam_if` may be used for other purposes.

The `pam_if` Module   The `pam_if` conditional module may be used with any module type. You will likely use it with control flag `sufficient`. The arguments it may take are described in Table 6.6. The first three arguments in Table 6.6 represent the conditions that must be met. Only one argument of the first three may be present; however, you may stack `pam_if` multiple times. The last argument specifies the module that will be invoked if the condition specified matches. Normally, you will use control flag `sufficient`—this means that, if the condition matches, `pam_if` succeeds and passes control to the module specified; if the module specified succeeds it will be sufficient for the given stack. If `pam_if` is used with the `required` control flag, then, if the condition of `pam_if` is met, the module invoked by `pam_if` will be required in addition to

Table 6.6 `pam_if` Arguments

Argument	Description
`user=`*username*	Specifies the username to match.
`tty=`*terminal*	Specifies the terminal to match. Accepts standard metacharacter wildcards.
`rhost=`*hostname*	Specifies the remote hostname to match. Note that there is no reverse lookup capability and thus the hostname may be spoofed.
`debug`	Logs mismatch information to `syslogd` selector `auth.debug`.
`-- pam_*.so`	The PAM module to invoke, if the condition is met.

any other required modules in the stack. The following two examples (6-29 and 6-30) should help clarify this functionality.

In Example 6-29, we see a simple implementation of `pam_if` that allows Mary to change her shell without a password. It requires an OPIE OTP if Joe wants to change his shell. All other users except root must supply their Linux passwords in order to change their shells. Notice that in this example we have stacked two `pam_if` modules to handle two different conditionals, each of which has a different result. In this case the control flag `sufficient` is used, which means that we simply invoke the module passed to `pam_if` as an argument (`pam_permit` for Mary and `pam_opie` for Joe; see what happens when you cross the administrator!).

Example 6-29 An `/etc/pam.d/chsh` File with `pam_if`

```
auth        sufficient   /lib/security/pam_rootok.so
auth        sufficient   /lib/security/pam_if.so user=mary \
                           -- pam_permit.so
auth        sufficient   /lib/security/pam_if.so user=joe \
                           -- pam_opie.so
auth        required     /lib/security/pam_pwdb.so shadow
```

In Example 6-30, we see the use of the `required` control flag to *add* a module to the stack. Here, if Joe `ftps` to the system, additional entries are placed in the log file by `pam_warn`. As far as Joe is concerned, everything is as it always was, but his access via `ftp` will generate a number of additional log entries. So, for Joe we add another module.

Example 6-30 `/etc/pam.d/ftp` File with `pam_if required`

```
auth        required      /lib/security/pam_listfile.so item=user \
              sense=deny file=/etc/ftpusers onerr=succeed
auth        required      /lib/security/pam_if.so user=joe -- pam_warn.so
auth        required      /lib/security/pam_pwdb.so shadow
auth        required      /lib/security/pam_shells.so
```

There is *so* much that you can do with PAM! Have fun with it!

WHICH OTP SYSTEM SHOULD I USE?

There are advantages and disadvantages to both S/Key and OPIE. We will outline some of them here.

Advantages and Disadvantages of S/Key

☞ Incorporates keysh and su allowing for ubiquitous implementation of OTP

☞ Offers OTP replacements for login and ftp

☞ Requires Linux password before OTP list may be (re)initiated by users other than root.

☞ PAM module dated

☞ Uses MD4 hash algorithm which is considered to be less secure than MD5

☞ Only warns the user if a secret key is about to be sent over the network

Advantages and Disadvantages of OPIE

☞ Uses MD5 or MD4

☞ Offers OTP replacements for su, login, and ftp

☞ By default, disallows any user from passing the secret passphrase over the network

☞ Has a working PAM module

☞ Has no equivalent to keysh

☞ Does not require authentication to (re)initiate OTP list

S/KEY AND OPIE VULNERABILITIES

The major vulnerability with S/Key and OPIE is the choice of secret key, password, or passphrase (we will refer to as passphrases here), respectively. Choosing good passphrases will make it more difficult for a bad-guy to guess them. Also, choosing passphrases that are not simple sentences will prevent them from being easily guessed by utilities such as Crack (discussed in Chapter 12), which could be configured to guess passphrases for S/Key or OPIE.

As added protection, consider further protecting /etc/opiekeys and/or /etc/skeykeys by setting their permissions to read/write by root only. This will disallow users other than root from using opieinfo and keyinfo, but it will also make it more difficult for bad-guys to glean information that could be used in guessing attacks.

If you need to implement access control, avoid using `/etc/opieaccess` or `/etc/skey/access` and instead use other access control mechanisms such as TCP_wrappers and various PAM modules like `pam_listfile`.

SUMMARY

In this chapter, we looked at two publicly available one-time password programs, S/Key and OPIE. Each of these programs can substantially reduce the risks associated with system access by utilizing a password only once. This eliminates the capturing of static passwords via a network sniffer.

FOR FURTHER READING

Programming

1. Loukides, Mike, and Andy Oram, *Programming with GNU Software*, Sebastopol, California, O'Reilly & Associates, Inc., 1997.
2. Oram, Andrew, and Steve Talbott, *Managing Projects with `make`*, Sebastopol, California, O'Reilly & Associates, Inc., 1991.

E-Mail Lists

You may subscribe to the `skey-users` mailing list by sending an e-mail message with the keyword `subscribe` in the body of the message to

    skey-users-request@research.telcordia.com

Subsequently, you may post messages to `skey-users@research.telcordia.com`. Both S/Key and OPIE are discussed on this list.

Bean Counting

System Accounting

Although originally not designed for security purposes, Linux system accounting can provide valuable information about various activities taking place on your system. After a brief overview, this chapter discusses the appropriate security elements of system accounting and some situations for using it.

GENERAL SYSTEM ACCOUNTING

Originally system accounting was developed for the purpose of keeping track of user resource consumption so that charges could be made against that user's account. In the days of mainframes and minicomputers, this was, in part, the way that Management Information Systems (MIS) departments got their funding. With the advent of personal workstations, the use of system accounting for that purpose has declined.

The Linux implementation of system accounting does not include many of the postprocessing scripts and configuration files (such as `chargefee` and the `/var/adm/fee` found on Solaris, IRIX, and other commercial UNIX systems) for fiscal accounting purposes, but it does include much (if not all) of the data required for such computations. Instead, Linux focuses on providing connection and process accounting information, each of which is described in detail in this chapter.

This is not the only source of information relating to activity on a Linux system. We saw in *PAM Logs* on page 109 of Chapter 5 that a great deal of connection and user activity information is maintained by PAM through `syslog`. We will explore many other mechanisms that provide such information throughout this book. Here we discuss connection and process accounting as it relates to enhancing overall system security.

CONNECTION ACCOUNTING

Connection accounting is the tracking of current user sessions and user logins and logouts. It is handled in Linux through the `utmp` (for active user sessions) and `wtmp` (for login/logout records) facilities. The `wtmp` utility also maintains rebooting and system state change (via `init`) information. Various programs participate in the updating and maintenance of these utilities, so there is no specific daemon or program that must be run; however, the files for `utmp` and `wtmp` output must exist. The absence of these files effectively turns off connection accounting. All data associated with `utmp` and `wtmp` are collected in the files `/var/run/utmp` and `/var/log/wtmp`, respectively. These files are owned by root and the permissions are set to `644` (`rw-r--r--`). The data in these files are not in human-readable form. There are various utilities to convert the raw `utmp` and `wtmp` data into legible formats, among these are those listed in Table 7.1. As mentioned in the table, `dump-utmp` converts raw connection accounting data into ASCII formatted data. It is parsable because it separates each field in a record with the | character, and it separates each record (or line of data) with a newline (carriage return) character. If you need to process the available data in these files beyond the capabilities of the other commands listed in the table, this command may be of use.

Table 7.1 Connection Accounting Utilities

Command	Description
dump-utmp	Converts the raw data from `/var/run/utmp` or `/var/log/wtmp` into ASCII-parsable format. Good for use with custom scripts.
ac	Prints out the connect time in hours. By default it generates a summary for all users. Various flags cause this command to output connect times on a per-user basis or daily basis or a combination thereof. This command reads `/var/log/wtmp`.
last	Shows a listing of last logged-in users, including login time, logout time (or still logged-in message), device associated with the connection, and hostname of the connection, if not local. Also records reboots and run-level changes through `init`. It reads `/var/log/wtmp`.
who	Shows a listing of currently logged-in users. It reads `/var/run/utmp`.

The `ac` command provides summary statistics regarding user connections. Example 7-1 shows truncated output from `ac` with the `d` and `p` flags. The `d` flag shows the daily total, and the `p` flag breaks up the total connection time in hours on a per-user basis. This type of statistical information may be useful in user profiling and other activities related to intrusion detection (see *Intrusion Detection* on page 172 in Chapter 8 for further references regarding intrusion detection). The `last` and `who` commands are the most likely commands that you will use on a regular, security-perspective basis.

Example 7-1 Connection Summary Using `ac`

```
# ac -dp
 mary                              8.10
 joe                             135.87
 root                             72.00
Feb 24   total       215.97
 joe                              64.80
 jane                             50.20
 root                             24.00
 guest                             0.40
 mary                             34.48
Feb 25   total       172.88
#
```

The `last` Command

As noted in Table 7.1 on page 150, the `last` command provides per-user login times, logout times, and locations as well as system reboot and run-level change information. Example 7-2 shows the execution of `last` with the `-10` option. The `-10` option is used here simply to limit the output of `last` to the most recent 10 entries. By default `last` will list every connection and run-level change recorded in `/var/log/wtmp`. In Example 7-2, we see that Mary has logged in from a system called roadrunner numerous times. The final entry shows that she logged in on Wednesday, February 24, at 3:53 P.M. and remained connected for 1 day, 20 hours, and 22 minutes. The record with no hostname indicates a local login (`tty1`, in this case).

Example 7-2 Output of `last`

```
# last -10
mary     ttyp3     roadrunner     Fri Feb 26 09:14 - 11:46  (02:32)
mary     ttyp2     roadrunner     Fri Feb 26 08:27 - 09:57  (01:30)
mary     ttyp3     roadrunner     Thu Feb 25 18:55 - 18:58  (00:02)
bill     ttyp4     underdog       Thu Feb 25 18:54 - 18:55  (00:00)
mary     tty1                     Thu Feb 25 18:27 - 18:33  (00:05)
joe      ttyp3     roadrunner     Thu Feb 25 13:45 - 13:45  (00:00)
guest    ttyp3     roadrunner     Thu Feb 25 13:44 - 13:45  (00:01)
guest    ttyp3     roadrunner     Thu Feb 25 09:53 - 10:15  (00:22)
mary     ttyp1     roadrunner     Wed Feb 24 15:53 - 12:16  (1+20:22)
```

The value of the `last` command from a security viewpoint is that it provides a way to quickly review connection activity on a given system. Glancing through the output on a daily basis is a good habit to get into and will allow you to catch unusual entries as you become accustomed to reading this output. Unless you are using intrusion detection software, your log files and any automated alert mechanism you may have implemented will not necessarily catch such things as the user `bill` logging in from `underdog` after 6 P.M. (Why did he do that? Was it really Bill?)

The `-x` option of the `last` command can also tell you about run-level changes on your system. Example 7-3 displays representative output of `last -x`. This output will give you a good summary of when the system has changed run states. In Example 7-3 we see that run-level changes were made on February 17 and 18. A clean shutdown was performed on February 18, and the system was down for 7 minutes. Notice the entries for the users `joe` and `root`. These entries appear here because, when the system went down, they were still logged in and therefore a logout was never recorded (because it never occurred).

Example 7-3 The Output of `last -x`

```
# last -x
reboot     system boot                  Thu Feb 18 08:36
shutdown   system down                  Thu Feb 18 08:29 - 08:36   (00:07)
runlevel (to lvl 0)                     Thu Feb 18 08:29 - 08:29   (00:00)
runlevel (to lvl 3)                     Thu Feb 18 08:21 - 08:29   (00:07)
runlevel (to lvl 5)                     Wed Feb 17 15:44 - 08:21   (16:37)
joe        ttyp1        roadrunner      Tue Feb 16 15:36 - down    (1+16:53)
reboot     system boot                  Sat Feb 13 04:31
root       tty1                         Wed Feb 10 12:52 - crash   (2+15:38)
shutdown   system down                  Wed Feb 10 12:42 - 12:51   (00:08)
runlevel (to lvl 0)                     Wed Feb 10 12:42 - 12:42   (00:00)
#
```

The keyword `crash` appears because the system went down uncleanly 2 days, 15 hours, and 38 minutes after Wednesday, February 10, at 12:52 P.M. or more simply on Saturday, February 13, at 04:30. This unclean shutdown could have been caused by many things, such as a power outage or someone switching the power off. If you don't know why this occurred, you should investigate the cause. Investigate all suspicious activity! These are the types of entries that afford clues relating to system break-ins. And that is why you want to examine this type of output regularly.

The `who` Command

As noted in Table 7.1, the primary purpose of `who` is to report which users are currently logged in. It also can tell us which device they are logged in at, when the login was initiated, the hostname if remote or X display value if X Windows is being used, how long the session has been idle, and whether or not the session will accept `write` or `talk` messages.[1] Example 7-4 exhibits the output of `who -iwH`. The `i` flag causes idle time to be displayed, the `w` flag gives us write or talk status, and the `H` flag prints a header.

---

1. The `write` and `talk` utilities allow for interactive communications between logged-in users.

Example 7-4 Sample `who -iwH` Output

```
# who -iwH
USER      MESG LINE      LOGIN-TIME    IDLE  FROM
mary       -    tty1     Feb 18 08:42  old
mary       +    ttyp0    Feb 18 08:43  old   (:0.0)
jane       +    ttyp1    Feb 20 15:33 00:02  (roadrunner)
joe        -    ttyp2    Feb 20 21:01   .    (roadrunner)
bill       +    ttyp3    Feb 20 18:54   .    (roadrunner)
#
```

The output in Example 7-4 shows each currently logged-in user, followed by his or her `write` status (+ means will accept, - means will not accept `write` or `talk` messages). Next is the line (device), followed by the login time, and then idle time expressed in hours:minutes (`old` means idle for more than 24 hours; . means idle for less than 1 minute). The final column of output contains the X-display or hostname (blank for local system) from which the login originated. The security value of this command is that it provides a snapshot of user connection. It is an opportunity to note any suspicious activity.

One Other Command

Another command associated with connection accounting is the `lastlog` command. This command reports data maintained in `/var/log/lastlog`, which is a record of the last time a user logged in. Example 7-5 shows sample output of the `lastlog` command. While of limited use, this command may offer a quick way of checking on user activity. For example, why did `bill` log in at 2:23 A.M., Friday, February 26? If this is not unusual behavior for Bill, it is safe to ignore. On the other hand, it may be worth checking with Bill to find out if he really did log in at that time. If not, someone may have compromised his account!

Example 7-5 Sample Truncated `lastlog` Output

```
# lastlog
Username        Port      From          Latest
root            tty1                     Thu Feb 18 08:42:38 1999
bin                                      **Never logged in**
daemon                                   **Never logged in**
adm                                      **Never logged in**
...
joe             ttyp3     roadrunner     Sat Feb 20 21:42:50 1999
mary            ttyp3     roadrunner     Fri Feb 26 09:14:18 1999
guest           ttyp3     roadrunner     Thu Feb 25 13:44:07 1999
bill            ttyp2     roadrunner     Fri Feb 26 02:23:01 1999
#
```

PROCESS ACCOUNTING

Process accounting is the bookkeeping of process activity. The raw data is maintained in `/var/log/pacct`, which is owned by root and the permissions of which are `600` (`rw-------`). This file must exist in order for process accounting to function. Unlike connection accounting, process accounting must be turned on. This is accomplished with the command

```
# accton /var/log/pacct
```

You may replace /var/log/pacct with the file of your choice; just remember to create it and set the permissions appropriately. This command must be executed at each reboot, so you need to place the following script

```
# Initiate process accounting
if [ -x /sbin/accton ] # verify file exists and is executable
then
        /sbin/accton /var/log/pacct
        echo "Process accounting initiated."
fi
```

or something like it in /etc/rc.d/rc.local or some other system start-up script. You probably want to have accounting start at run level 2, meaning that you will need to create a special script in /etc/rc.d/rc2.d. To turn off process accounting, simply remove this script and execute accton with no arguments.

Once process accounting is configured on your system, you will have three commands at your disposal for interpreting the raw (not human-readable) data in /var/log/pacct. These commands are dump-acct, which is entirely similar to dump-utmp (and therefore good for scripts, but not so good for people); sa, which summarizes process accounting; and lastcomm, which lists out the commands executed on the system.

The sa Command

Like the ac command, the sa command is a statistical command. It allows you to obtain a summary of process usage either on a per-user or per-command basis. It also provides system resource consumption information. For the most part this command is an accounting command. However, it may be useful in identifying suspicious command use by a particular user. It is most useful when we already have a user in mind; otherwise the volume of information is overwhelming and requires postprocessing scripts or programs (at which point you will want to take a look at dump-acct) to sort things out.

Example 7-6 demonstrates the use of sa -u, which sorts command usage by user. In this example, we take a look at the user joe, whom we suspect of misdeeds. Each line of output shows the username followed by the number of CPU seconds consumed followed by the command (maximum 16 characters). Only the command is reported—no flags or arguments—and the pathname (if used) is stripped. Unfortunately, these limitations of the sa output are reflections of the raw data found in /var/log/pacct, which significantly restricts the usefulness of process accounting as a fine-grained auditing tool. A tool that captures considerably more detail of this type is auditd, which is discussed in *The auditd Utility* on page 171.

Example 7-6 Sorting Command Use by User

```
# sa -u|grep joe
joe         0.00 cpu bash              *
joe         0.00 cpu hostname
joe         0.01 cpu ls
joe         0.01 cpu ls
joe         0.00 cpu lastcomm
joe         0.01 cpu ls
joe         0.00 cpu tcpdump
joe         0.01 cpu ls
joe         0.00 cpu tcpdump
joe         0.01 cpu reboot
#
```

It does appear as if our concerns about joe were well founded, but don't expect your attacker to be this easy to spot!

The lastcomm Command

Unlike sa, the lastcomm command produces output on a per-command basis. It also prints a date stamp associated with the execution of each command. In this way, it becomes a more useful interactive security tool than sa.

The lastcomm command can take a command name, username, or terminal name (such as tty1 or ttyp4) as arguments. This allows for reasonably fine-grained searches of the process accounting database. Example 7-7 displays the output of lastcomm joe. Each line of output reflects the command executed, the user (joe in this case), the device (ttyp1), the number of CPU seconds consumed, and the date and time of execution.

Example 7-7 Output of lastcomm joe

```
# lastcomm joe
reboot              joe      ttyp1      0.01 secs Fri Feb 26 18:40
tcpdump             joe      ttyp1      0.00 secs Fri Feb 26 18:39
ls                  joe      ttyp1      0.00 secs Fri Feb 26 18:32
tcpdump             joe      ttyp1      0.00 secs Fri Feb 26 18:32
ls                  joe      ttyp1      0.00 secs Fri Feb 26 18:32
lastcomm            joe      ttyp1      0.00 secs Fri Feb 26 18:31
ls                  joe      ttyp1      0.00 secs Fri Feb 26 18:30
ls                  joe      ttyp1      0.00 secs Fri Feb 26 18:30
hostname            joe      ttyp1      0.00 secs Fri Feb 26 18:29
bash                joe      ttyp1      0.00 secs Fri Feb 26 18:28
#
```

WARNING!

If you know that your system has been compromised, do not trust (but do not ignore) the information in lastlog, utmp, wtmp, and pacct because this data may have been modified by the attacker. Additionally, if your system is currently under attack, it may be that the attacker has replaced programs like who to mask his or her presence. See *Other Cracker Activities* on page 3 in Chapter 1.

In general, the usefulness of process accounting comes into play after you have identified some form of suspicious behavior. Using lastcomm can be very valuable in isolating user activity or command execution at certain times. But in order for it to be available, you must turn it on! (See *Process Accounting* on page 153.)

ACCOUNTING FILES

Essentially, the files `/var/run/utmp`, `/var/log/wtmp`, and `/var/log/pacct` are dynamic database files. Of them, `/var/log/pacct` and `/var/log/wtmp` grow by having entries appended and modified. The problem is that since these files grow dynamically, at some point they become large. The general issue of managing log files is discussed in detail in Chapter 17. However, we provide the following to get you started and to address the immediate problem of managing your growing `/var/log/pacct` and `/var/log/wtmp` files.

There is a really cool program available in the Red Hat 5.2/6.0 Linux distribution called `logrotate`. It reads a configuration file called `/etc/logrotate.conf`, which among other things tells it to read all of the files in the `/etc/logrotate.d` directory.Consequently, whenever you need to manage a file that grows dynamically, all you have to do is put a `logrotate` conforming script in `/etc/logrotate.d`. The script in Example 7-8 is one way to manage the `/var/log/wtmp` accounting files.

Example 7-8 Log Rotation Script for Accounting Files

```
/var/log/wtmp {
    rotate 5
    weekly
    errors root@topcat
    mail root@topcat
    copytruncate
    compress
    size 100k
}
```

Put this script into a file—call it `accounting`, for example—in the `/etc/logrotate.d` directory and your accounting files will be rotated every week. For complete details on how this works see Chapter 17.

While you may be tempted to do something similar with `/var/log/pacct`, don't! Remember that it accumulates data about process activity and, as long as the system is up and running, it will be maintaining that information dynamically. If this file gets too large, archive it while in single-user mode. If the system cannot be brought down on a regular basis, you may turn off process accounting by executing `accton` as root, then archive the file. This latter approach will cause some data loss, so the best solution is to turn off process accounting when the system is most quiescent. You can automate this process with `logrotate` as described in `logrotate` on page 492 in Chapter 17.

SUMMARY

This chapter provides an overview of connection and process accounting. We described the commands that allow us to view the information collected by system accounting and noted the security value of this data.

FOR FURTHER READING

Books

For a good, general, but non-Linux specific, discussion of UNIX system accounting, check out the following two books.

1. Frisch, Aeleen, *Essential System Administration*, 2d ed., Sebastopol, California, O'Reilly & Associates, Inc., 1995.
2. Nemeth, Evi, et al., *UNIX System Administration Handbook*, 2d ed., Englewood Cliffs, New Jersey, Prentice Hall PTR, 1995.

On-Line Documentation

The man pages associated with system accounting are

```
ac(1)
accton(8)
last(1)
lastcomm(1)
lastlog(8)
sa(8)
who(1)
```

And You Thought Wiretapping Was for the Feds!

System Logging

Linux utilizes a variety of log files. Some are used for specific utilities—for example, the `/var/log/xferlog` file is used exclusively to record File Transfer Protocol (FTP) transfers. Other log files, such as the `/var/log/messages` file, usually contain entries from many system and kernel utilities. These log files provide you with information about the state of security on your system. Read them.

This chapter focuses on the two major logging daemons—`syslogd` and `klogd`—and briefly describes many of the other log files generated by the Linux operating system. The purpose of the discussion here is to provide a basic configuration overview. Throughout the remainder of this book, we will suggest modifications to this basic configuration. In Chapter 17 we describe maintaining the log files and managing the information they contain.

THE `syslog` SYSTEM LOGGING UTILITY

The `syslog` facility is available on most UNIX systems with varying levels of flexibility and functionality. Fortunately, the Linux `syslog` implementation is quite flexible, giving us many opportunities to cause the system to take various actions based on different log entries as they occur. There are a great many programs and scripts that also take advantage of the capabilities of `syslog`, not an insignificant number of which are described throughout the remainder of this book.

We begin our discourse by detailing the way in which `syslog` works and how to configure it through the configuration file, `/etc/syslog.conf`. Then we take a look at ways to exploit the flexibility and capability of `syslog` to our benefit.

Overview

Very simply, the `syslog` utility consists of a daemon that accepts incoming log messages and deals with them in accordance with the instructions found in the `/etc/syslog.conf` configuration file. Programs, daemons, and the kernel provide the incoming log messages. Thus, any program that wishes to generate messages may do so through calls to the `syslog` interface. Most internal system utilities such as the mail and printing systems do this, and many add-on programs, such as TCP_wrappers and SSH, also generate such messages. Figure 8.1 illustrates the general flow of events with respect to `syslogd` and its companion daemon `klogd` (`klogd` is described in *The klogd Daemon* on page 170). It should be noted that, unlike some UNIX implementations, the Red Hat 5.2/6.0 `syslog` facility cannot directly invoke a script or a program, but it may pass the log entries through a first-in, first-out (FIFO) file as Figure 8.1 depicts. In this way, an executable like `swatch` or `logcheck` may read the log files directly through the FIFO file.

In general, `syslogd` accepts messages from various *facilities* on the system. Each message will also include a *level* of importance. The `/etc/syslog.conf` file tells `syslogd` how to report messages based on the facility and level of the message—write it to a file, send it to another system, send it to a user, or send it to a program.

The `/etc/syslog.conf` File

The `/etc/syslog.conf` file accepts syntax of the following form:

```
facility.level              action
```

Blank lines and lines beginning with # are ignored. The `facility.level` field, also collectively known as the *selector*, should be separated from the `action` field with one or more tabs. Spaces may be used as separators with most Linux releases; however, other implementations of UNIX do not recognize spaces as separators, so it is a good idea to avoid them in mixed environments. Let's go through each of the three elements (`facility`, `level`, and `action`) of an `/etc/syslog.conf` record. The available facilities are described in Table 8.1. Each daemon, utility, or program on the system that generates `syslog` messages will use one of the facilities in Table 8.1. For example, `inetd`, `telnetd`, and `ftpd` use the daemon facility. The default facility is `user`, so, if a program does not specify a facility, `user` will be used. Multiple facilities may be specified using "," as the separator. For example, an entry of the

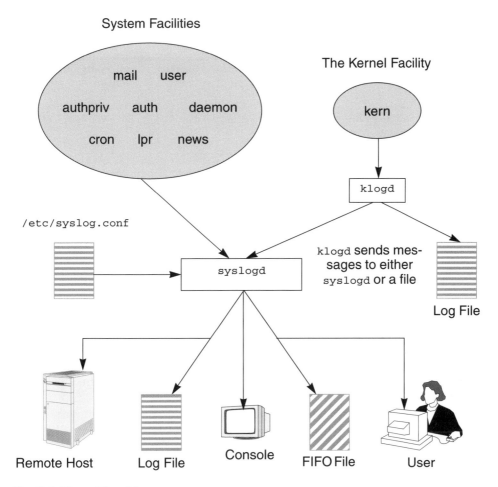

Fig. 8.1 Flow of Log Messages

form daemon, lpr, mail.crit means all crit-level (and higher) messages for the facilities daemon, lpr, and mail. Notice that auth has been deprecated in favor of authpriv. Unfortunately, there currently is no real consistency as to which log entries go to auth and which go to authpriv. For example, TCP_wrappers generates connection messages to authpriv, while most PAM modules generate auth messages. Ironically, the PAM messages contain more sensitive information! In *Configuring /etc/syslog.conf* on page 164, we look at a number of configuration examples and give consideration as to where syslog messages should go.

The various levels or priorities associated with each facility are described in descending order in Table 8.2; that is, level emerg is the highest level, alert the second highest, and so on. By default, the level specified in an /etc/syslog.conf record is treated as that level and above. For example, if user.info is

Table 8.1 The syslog Facilities

Facility	Description
auth	Authentication activity, such as that reported by pam_pwdb. This facility has been deprecated* in favor of authpriv, but continues to be used.
authpriv	Authentication activity that may include privileged information, such as usernames. Normally, private information like passwords are not logged.
cron	Messages associated with cron and at.
daemon	Messages associated with daemons, like inetd.
kern	Kernel messages. These messages normally pass through klogd first.
lpr	Messages related to printing services.
mail	Messages related to electronic mail.
mark	A syslog internal facility used to generate timestamps.
news	Messages from the Internet news server.
syslog	Messages generated by syslog.
user	Any message generated by a user program. Programmatic default.
uucp	Messages generated by uucp.
local0–local7	These facilities are for use with customized programs. For example, we will use local5 as the facility for SSH (see Chapter 11).
*	Wildcard representing all facilities except mark.

*A really fancy way of saying that its use is no longer recommended.

specified as a selector, it means all messages logged to facility user at level info, notice, warning, err, crit, alert, and emerg. If you wish to be more specific, there are two logical operators that will help. They are, ! and =. If you specify

        user.=info

this tells syslog to capture all user facility messages, but only at level info. If you specify

        *.info;mail.!=info;user.none

this informs syslog that you want all facilities at level info and above, except for mail and user. For mail, you are requesting all messages at level notice and above. For user, you are suppressing all messages. Notice also that multiple selectors may appear on one line; use a ; to separate them.

The acceptable action fields are detailed in Table 8.3. As you can see, the Linux-supported actions provide a lot of flexibility. In particular, the ability to use named pipes allows for the postprocessing of messages generated by

Table 8.2 The syslog Levels

Level	Description
emerg or panic	The system is unusable; panic has been deprecated.
alert	A condition exists that needs to be rectified immediately.
crit	An error condition that precludes the functionality of some utility or subsystem.
err	An error condition that precludes the functionality of a component of a utility or subsystem.
warning	A warning message.
notice	A normal condition that has significance.
info	Informational message.
debug	Additional messages that do not reflect functional conditions or problems.
none	No level. Ordinarily used to except a facility when using the wildcard.
*	All levels, except none.

Table 8.3 The syslog Actions

Action	Description
file	The absolute path specification of a log file, like /var/log/messages. The message will be written to this file.
terminal or printer	The fully qualified serial or parallel device specifier, such as /dev/console, /dev/tty1, or /dev/lp1. The message will be written to the specified device.
@hostname	A resolvable remote hostname preceded by @. The remote host must be running syslogd and have a configuration file that accommodates the incoming facility.level selector. This option is useful for centralized logging, but the destination host had better have lots of disk space!
username	Sends the message to the specified user, using write. If the user is not logged in, no message is written. Multiple users may be specified in a comma-separated list, such as root,joe,mary. All users are specified with *.
named pipe	A fully qualified path specification to a FIFO file, created with the mkfifo command, preceded by a |, like |/path/to/fifo. This informs syslog to write the message to the identified FIFO file, which then may be read from by a script or program.

syslogd. This mechanism provides a way of capturing items of particular interest and acting on them in ways not supported directly by syslog, such as generating e-mail or generating a page through a modem. We will look at managing the log messages and log files in detail in Chapter 17.

Invoking the syslogd Daemon

The syslogd daemon is invoked by the script /etc/rc.d/init.d/syslog at run level 2. By default, it is invoked with no options. There are two options that are of interest and may be necessary for the proper configuration of your environment—the -r and -h flags.

If you are going to use a log server, then you must invoke syslogd -r. By default, syslogd will not accept log messages from remote systems. By specifying the -r option, syslogd will listen to incoming UDP packets on port 514. Whenever a log message is received from another host, /etc/syslog.conf will direct syslogd as to how to handle the message. The hostname of the remote system will be prefixed to the log message before it is written. If /etc/syslog.conf does not contain a selector and action for the incoming message, then the message is dropped. The topic of a centralized log server is further discussed in *Logging to a Central Server* on page 167.

If you additionally want the log server to forward log messages, then you must use the -h flag. By default, syslogd will ignore /etc/syslog.conf entries that would cause it to forward a log message from a remote system to another remote system.

Configuring /etc/syslog.conf

The most important aspect of configuring the /etc/syslog.conf file is thinking through what you want to get out of it. In other words, what messages do you want, how do you want them processed, and how quickly do you want them? As you read through the remainder of this book, exactly what you want will become clearer. As you work with syslog and the information it generates, you will evolve to a zen state, wherein you begin to visualize the output of syslog before you have implemented it!

Let's begin by taking a look at a representative /etc/syslog.conf file in Example 8-1. This happens to be the /etc/syslog.conf file as it ships with Red Hat 5.2 (well, almost, anyway—the line containing @central is not there by default). Notice that the record beginning with kern.* is commented out. If you uncomment this line, then all kernel messages at all levels will be written to the system console.

Most of the log messages, based on the entries in Example 8-1, will end up in /var/log/messages. This is due to the line beginning with *.info; mail.none;authpriv.none, which means that messages from all facilities at level info and higher except mail and authpriv messages will be written to

Example 8-1 Sample `/etc/syslog.conf` File

```
# Log all kernel messages to the console.
# Logging much else clutters up the screen.
#kern.*                                              /dev/console
# Log anything (except mail) of level info or higher.
# Don't log private authentication messages!
*.info;mail.none;authpriv.none                       /var/log/messages
# The authpriv file has restricted access.
authpriv.*                                           /var/log/secure
# Log all the mail messages in one place.
mail.*                                               /var/log/maillog
# Everybody gets emergency messages, plus log them on another
# machine.
*.emerg                                              *
*.emerg                                              @central
# Save mail and news errors of level err and higher in a
# special file.
uucp,news.crit                                       /var/log/spooler
```

`/var/log/messages`. Note that this file will include kernel messages at level `info` and higher. If you uncomment the line containing `/dev/console`, the same messages will be duplicated to the console. You may specify many actions for one selector in this way.

All `authpriv` messages end up in `/var/log/secure`. As previously mentioned, the distinction between `auth` and `authpriv` is quite vague. You will find that most (if not all) PAM authentication messages are logged to facility `auth` instead of `authpriv`. Over time, this will probably be rectified. In the meantime, you may wish to have all of your authentication messages go to a single file. The following modification to Example 8-1 would do the trick:

```
*.info;mail.none;authpriv.none;auth.none             /var/log/messages
authpriv.*, auth.*                                   /var/log/secure
```

This will place all authentication messages in one file and should make searching for authentication-related entries easier, whether done manually or with a program or script.

OH, BY THE WAY...

Both `/var/log/messages` and `/var/log/secure` ship with permissions set to read-write by root only. Contrary to the comments in `/etc/syslog.conf`, therefore, neither is more secure than the other. In general, you probably want all of your log file permissions set as restrictively as possible. You may also wish to set the append-only attribute on your log files. See *File Attributes* on page 75 in Chapter 4 for details on configuring file attributes.

Continuing with the entries in Example 8-1, all `mail` messages will be written to `/var/log/maillog`. It is probably a good idea to keep `mail` log entries separate from other messages generally, and particularly on systems which act as mail servers.

All facilities log emergency messages to all logged-in users via the `write` utility, and `syslogd` will forward these messages to a host called `central`. It is important to note that the host `central` must have its `/etc/syslog.conf` file configured to handle the `emerg` messages or they will be lost.

The last entry in Example 8-1 causes all `uucp` and `news` messages at `crit` level and above to be logged to `/var/log/spooler`. For convenience and consistency, you may also want all such printer messages to be logged there, too. You will cause this to occur by modifying the last line of Example 8-1 as follows:

```
uucp,news,lpr.crit                      /var/log/spooler
```

NOTE

> After you have modified the `/etc/syslog.conf` file, you must inform `syslogd` about the changes by sending it the HUP signal. The simplest way to accomplish this is to issue the command `killall -HUP syslogd`. This causes `syslogd` to reread the configuration file. If you specify a new log file in `/etc/syslog.conf`, sending a HUP signal will cause the file to be created. Many versions (Red Hat 5.2/6.0 are not among them) of UNIX require that a file must exist before `syslogd` will write to it. In such cases, you will need to create the file first.

Configuration Tips   You probably won't configure `/etc/syslog.conf` the same way on every system. That is largely because different systems will have different functions. The mail servers, for example, will generate a lot of e-mail-related logs. An `ftp` server will generate a lot of authentication logs and a lot of transfer information (maintained in the separate file, `/var/log/xferlog`). In short, take into consideration the function of the system for which you are configuring `/etc/syslog.conf`. Also take the system's functionality into consideration when you are reviewing the log files.

There are two schools of thought regarding how to build log files. The first suggests that you dump most or all of the log messages into one file and then process that file with other utilities such as `swatch` and `logcheck` (see Chapter 17). The second suggests that it may be simplest to configure your system's logs so that they are of separate functionality—that is, one log file for authentication information, another for internal `syslog` messages (facility `syslog`), another for `mail`, one for facility `user`, and so on. This latter approach is organizationally simpler for human processing and for building specialized scripts or programs to postprocess the specific logs. The `swatch` and `logcheck` utilities easily adapt to this approach as well.

Generally speaking, from a security perspective, you want to configure `/etc/syslog.conf` so that it captures enough information to alert you in the event of a compromise or attempted compromise. Given this era of cheap disks, err on the side of too much information and let tools like `logcheck` and `swatch` filter it for you. Don't become complacent, though! You must still determine which entries are significant and which may be ignored. Unfortunately it

OH, BY THE WAY...

The kill and killall commands are really misnamed. They should be called signal and signalall because they cause signals to be sent to processes. We'll discuss only kill since these two commands operate identically (except for the fact that kill requires a process identifier to which it will send the signal, while killall requires a process name and will send the signal to all processes of that name).

When you issue the kill command, you are causing the specified process to be sent a signal. If you do not specify the signal, such as HUP, on the command line, the default signal TERM will be sent. These signals are not sent directly to the process, however. Rather, the kernel looks up the given process and interrupts it, passing it the specified signal. If the process's interrupt handler accommodates the received signal, then it will execute the appropriate code; for example, if it receives a HUP signal and has been programmed to deal with that signal, it will reread its configuration file. If it is not programmed to deal with a given signal, or it receives the default signal TERM, it will release all of its allocated resources, terminate all subprocesses (called *children*), and then terminate itself. Many of you may be in the habit of issuing kill -KILL or, equivalently, kill -9 for every process you wish to terminate. This is a bad habit. Stop it! Always try kill -TERM (or just kill, since the default signal is TERM) first! Here's why. When you issue kill -9, the kernel does not interrupt the process. Instead it releases all of the process's resources and then terminates the specified process. If the process had any children, they become zombie processes, which appear as defunct when you look at the output of ps. The good news is that an internal kernel mechanism, known as *the reaper* (hey, *I* didn't make these names up!) will eventually release the resources of any zombie processes it finds and reassign them to be children of the process init (process id = 1), thus minimizing the impact of zombie processes. The bad news is that zombie processes are not removed until the next reboot.

This isn't to say that you should never use kill -9. Just use it as a last resort.

takes time and the reading of many log files to reach a point where you will be confident about the distinction. In fact, if you ascribe to the rules in Chapter 2, you will *never* reach a point of confidence. So get used to it, and spend time each day reading the log files.

NOTE

After you have created a new entry in /etc/syslog.conf, you can test the entry with the /usr/bin/logger program. For example, if you create a new entry that specifies the selector local2.debug, you may test it with logger -p local2.debug -t TEST "This is a test". You can also execute the logger program from a script.

Logging to a Central Server   Centralizing the log files for an environment to a specific server can both ease administration and increase security. The key to increasing security when using a centralized log server is securing the server itself. The log server must be as secure as possible and tightly controlled. We discuss an overall approach to building secure limited-purposes systems in Chapter 18.

From an administrative perspective, there are two things you must do to properly configure a central log server. First, you must appropriately configure the `syslog` utility in your environment. Second, you must utilize some time synchronization mechanism so that all of the hosts in your environment will have coincident clocks.

Configuring `syslog` in the Centralized Logging Environment.   You will need to make sure that all the systems in your environment have appropriate entries in their `/etc/syslog.conf` file. For example, let's suppose that our central log server is called `central` (imaginative, aren't we?). Then for all of the systems that use the host `central` as their log server, except `central` itself, we could use an `/etc/syslog.conf` file similar to Example 8-2.

Example 8-2 Sample `/etc/syslog.conf` File for Remote Logging

```
*.info;mail.none;authpriv.none          /var/log/messages
authpriv.*                              /var/log/secure
mail.*                                  /var/log/maillog
*.info                                  @central
```

The host `central` would need to have all the entries listed in Example 8-2 (or something similar), but must **not** have the last entry, namely:

```
*.info                                  @central
```

Note that this configuration file will cause all messages to selector `*.info` to be logged both locally and remotely on `central` (except, of course, for `central` itself).

Once the systems in the environment are taken care of, you will need to run `syslogd` with the `-r` flag on the host `central` as described in *Invoking the `syslogd` Daemon* on page 164. This completes the setup for sending log messages to a centralized server.

Synchronizing System Clocks.   You will want to make sure that the entries in the centralized log files have the correct timestamps. In order to do this, you will need to synchronize the clocks on the various systems throughout your environment. There are three basic ways to do this. You can use `rdate` (remote date), `timed` (time server daemon), or `xntp` (the Network Time Protocol). The `rdate` and `timed` utilities are included with the Red Hat distribution, while `xntp` is on the Power Tools CD. Each of these utilities has its own set of vulnerabilities and levels of implementation complexity, so check out their associated documentation to determine which one works best for you.

Output Examples   You may also want to write your own scripts or programs or use other (besides `logcheck` and `swatch`) existing ones to capture certain types of activity. Example 8-3 shows a sequence of failed login attempts as reported by `login` and PAM to `syslogd` (line wraps are due to formatting constraints), which may represent an attempted break-in.

Example 8-3 Failed `login` Attempts Using the Same Username

```
Mar  2 17:54:15 topcat login[14435]: FAILED LOGIN 1 FROM roadrunner FOR guest,
Authentication failure
Mar  2 17:54:23 topcat login[14435]: FAILED LOGIN 2 FROM roadrunner FOR guest,
Authentication failure
Mar  2 17:54:28 topcat login[14435]: TOO MANY LOGIN TRIES (3) FROM roadrunner FOR
guest, Have exhausted maximum number of retries for service.
Mar  2 17:54:28 topcat PAM_pwdb[14435]: 3 authentication failures; (uid=0) ->
guest for login service
```

Be aware, however, that different attacks will generate different log entries (often called *signatures*). Unfortunately, collecting a thorough list (it will never be complete!) of attack patterns is difficult due to the dynamic nature of attacks. The process of identifying attacks is known as *intrusion detection*. The section *Intrusion Detection* on page 172 provides some resources related to that topic. In the meantime, Example 8-4 shows us a different set of failed login attempts (line wraps!).

Example 8-4 Failed `login` Attempts Using Different Usernames

```
Mar  2 18:00:10 topcat login[14478]: FAILED LOGIN 1 FROM roadrunner FOR guest,
Authentication failure
Mar  2 18:00:16 topcat login[14478]: FAILED LOGIN 2 FROM roadrunner FOR joe,
Authentication failure
Mar  2 18:00:20 topcat login[14478]: FAILED LOGIN 3 FROM roadrunner FOR mary,
Authentication failure
Mar  2 18:00:24 topcat login[14478]: FAILED LOGIN SESSION FROM roadrunner FOR
sdm, Authentication failure
Mar  2 18:00:24 topcat PAM_pwdb[14478]: 1 authentication failure; (uid=0) -> sdm
for login service
Mar  2 18:00:24 topcat PAM_pwdb[14478]: 1 authentication failure; (uid=0) -> mary
for login service
Mar  2 18:00:24 topcat PAM_pwdb[14478]: 1 authentication failure; (uid=0) -> joe
for login service
Mar  2 18:00:24 topcat PAM_pwdb[14478]: 1 authentication failure; (uid=0) ->
guest for login service
```

The important thing about Examples 8-3 and 8-4 is to notice any similar key words or phrases that could be used in writing a script to capture these break-in attempts. In this case, notice that, although these two examples show different log entries for the two attacks, the process identifier (the number in brackets after either the keyword `login` or `PAM_pwdb`) is identical for each sequence of attacks. That, together with the fact that the key phrase `authentication failure` appears in almost every entry associated with these attacks, makes writing a script to capture this information fairly straightforward (of course, in Example 8-3 it could simply be a user who forgot his or her password, representing a false alarm). If you do decide to write your own scripts and/or programs, take advantage of the ones that already exist. Read through them and benefit from the experience—and mistakes—of others.

The `klogd` Daemon

The `klogd` daemon captures and logs Linux kernel messages. Normally, it submits all messages to `syslogd` for logging. However, if invoked with the `-f` `filename` argument, it will log all of its messages to `filename` instead of passing them to `syslogd`. When an alternate file is specified for logging, `klogd` reports all levels or priorities to the file. There is no configuration file for `klogd` equivalent to `/etc/syslogd.conf`. The advantage of having `klogd` avoid `syslogd` is largely for debugging. However, if someone has hacked your kernel, it may be that using this facility will assist in determining the modifications. If you are familiar with the kernel and its source code, this may be valuable. If not, once you've determined that your kernel has been modified in an unauthorized way, it is probably best to recover from pristine backups (discussed in Chapter 3).

NOTE

Both `syslogd` and `klogd` are started when the system enters run level 2. They are killed when the system goes down to run level 1. The controlling script on Red Hat 5.2/6.0 is `/etc/rc.d/init.d/syslog`.

OTHER LOGS

You will find a number of other log files in `/var/log` and potentially elsewhere on your system depending on the distribution you have and the applications you have configured. Of course `/etc/syslog.conf` will list the names and locations of all log files managed by `syslogd`. Others will be managed by other applications. For example, on Red Hat 5.2/6.0, the Apache Web Server generates the `/var/log/htmlaccess.log` file to record client access, as well as `/var/log/httpd/error.log` to capture error conditions outside of `syslog`.

The `cron` utility maintains its own informational log file, `/var/log/cron`. The `linuxconf` utility will generate log files such as `/var/log/netconf.log` whenever it records system reconfiguration information. Samba (a Server Message Block [SMB] based utility similar to NFS in functionality) maintains its log files in the `/var/log/samba` directory.

You will find another set of files in `/var/log` related to connection and process accounting. These files include `wtmp`, `pacct`, and `lastlog`, each of which is discussed in Chapter 7.

Many of these files contain security-related information and therefore require your attention. The standard log files are discussed at various points within this text; others will be application and site dependent.

ALTERNATIVES TO `syslog`

It is possible on very busy systems for `syslogd` to lose messages. On such systems you may want to take a look at `cyclog`. It is a `syslogd` replacement that buffers log messages and makes sure that the log files are synchronized. It also automatically rotates the log files it manages. It is a part of the `daemon-tools` collection of utilities and is available from

```
ftp://koobera.math.uic.edu/www/daemontools.html
```

THE `auditd` UTILITY

One publicly available tool that is quite useful for capturing system activity beyond that of `syslogd` or system accounting (discussed in Chapter 7) is `auditd`. This utility is available from

```
ftp://ftp.hert.org/pub/linux/auditd/
```

This utility allows for the capturing of various system events, such as e-mail, inbound and outbound network connections, logins, `su` usage, file access, and kernel module changes. Unlike `syslogd`, which depends on other processes to generate messages, `auditd` captures system calls in the kernel based on a configuration file. It is similar to the Basic Security Module (BSM) found in Solaris 2.x or the Security Audit Trail (SAT) found in IRIX 6.5.x.

The `auditd` utility can generate a reasonably complete audit trail of the system it runs on. This level of detail is useful for systems that are exposed to the Internet, such as firewalls, web servers, and `ftp` servers. It is also advantageous to run this utility on internal systems that contain sensitive data.

Installing this tool will require a rebuild of the kernel, so make sure that you read the on-line documents `/usr/src/linux/README` and `/usr/doc/HOWTO/Kernel-HOWTO` before proceeding with building a Linux kernel for the first time. *Rebuilding and Recompiling the Kernel* on page 420 in Chapter 15 describes the process of rebuilding the kernel for the Transparent Cryptographic File System (TCFS) and offers a good example.

SUMMARY

This chapter provides an overview of the `syslog` utility. We described the operation of `syslogd` and the configuration file `/etc/syslog.conf`.

FOR FURTHER READING

General System Logging

1. Frisch, Aeleen, *Essential System Administration*, 2d ed., Sebastopol, California, O'Reilly & Associates, Inc., 1995.
2. Hein, Jochen, *Linux Companion for System Administrators*, Harlow, England, Addison-Wesley, 1999.
3. Nemeth, Evi, et al., *UNIX System Administration Handbook*, Englewood Cliffs, New Jersey, Prentice Hall PTR, 1995.

Intrusion Detection

There is an intrusion detection systems (IDS) mailing list. You may subscribe to it by sending e-mail to `majordomo@uow.edu.au` with `subscribe ids` in the body of the message.

The IDS frequently asked questions (FAQ) are available at

`http://www.ticm.com/kb/faq/idsfaq.html`

A survey of IDS and log management tools may be found at

`http://www-rnks.informatik.tu-cottbus.de/~sobirey/ids.html`

For a good overview of intrusion detection, read the book

1. Escamilla, Terry, *Intrusion Detection: Network Security beyond the Firewall*, New York, New York, John Wiley & Sons, Inc., 1998.

## CHAPTER 9

Want to Be root?

Superuser Do (sudo)

Whenever system maintenance requires more than one administrator on a system, either the root password is disclosed to those who are involved or each administrator will have their own root account (see *Multiple root Users* on page 67). In *PAM and su* on page 103, we explored the use of pam_wheel which limits su to root activities to those users in the wheel group. That method has the advantage of restricting root access to a subset of the users on a given system. Such an approach is very valuable, but it does nothing to restrict or limit root privileges, once obtained, and it provides minimal additional logging.

For many systems and computing environments, the simple restrictions imposed by pam_wheel are sufficient. In many other cases, however, there is a need to improve the audit trail for root. That way, when things go awry (whether due to a security compromise or not), the details are available and remedies may be determined. In yet other situations, the need for granting limited privileges to certain users is essential. Perhaps, for example, certain users have the need to change the run level on their systems regularly. There is a utility that can provide this functionality—it is called sudo.

WHAT IS sudo?

Superuser do or sudo (officially pronounced sue-dew) is a utility designed to compartmentalize root privileges, provide copious logging through syslogd (see Chapter 8) of each privileged command executed, and provide these capabilities either on a per system basis or throughout a network. As with most UNIX/Linux-based utilities, sudo is not without its vulnerabilities. In particular, due to the nature of UNIX/Linux in general, there are many ways to obtain full root privilege after initially being granted certain privileges normally exclusively ascribed to root.

In this chapter, we will explore the configuration and use of sudo in a variety of contexts. We will also identify some of the potential security vulnerabilities associated with its use.

OBTAINING AND IMPLEMENTING sudo

The sudo utility originated in the early 1980s at the State University of New York, Buffalo. Subsequently, a lot of work has been done to sudo at the University of Colorado, Boulder. Numerous authors have contributed to it over the years, including Garth Snyder, Bob Coggeshall, Bob Manchek, Trent Hein, Jeff Nieusma, David Hieb, Chris Jepeway, and Todd Miller. It is currently maintained by Todd Miller. It is distributed under the GPL.

You may obtain the most recent version of sudo—as of this writing, that is Version 1.5.9p4—from

```
http://www.courtesan.com/sudo/
```

at which site you will find the file cu-sudo.v1.5.9p4.tar.gz. This version does not include a digital signature, but it does include the MD5 checksums. It also contains a patch for a recently identified buffer overflow problem. We strongly encourage its use over the RPMs that come with the Red Hat PowerTools CD since they are at version 1.5.9p1. By the time you read this, the RPMs may have been updated. Check out

```
http://www.redhat.com/download/mirror.html
```

for a list of ftp mirrors of the Red Hat distribution; then look for the contribs mirror.

One of the benefits of obtaining software in RPM format is that it often includes a PGP digital signature (PGP is discussed in Chapter 3) and can be verified by using RPM. You can also build binaries such as sudo from the source RPM using the spec file. For complete details on the use of the rpm command, see *Maximum RPM* as listed in the section *For Further Reading* on page 191.

Features of Version 1.5.9p4

Among the features available in version 1.5.9p4:

☞ PAM-aware

☞ Kerberos 5 support (see *Kerberos Resources* on page 192)

☞ FWTK authsrv support (see *FWTK Resources* on page 192)

☞ Numerous bug fixes

Implementing Version 1.5.9p4

After you have obtained the distribution file, cu-sudo.v1.5.9p4.tar.gz, gunzip and untar it into a directory such as /usr/src (we will use this in our examples). The tar extraction will create a sudo.v1.5.9p4 subdirectory that will contain the source code and the configure files necessary to build and install sudo. On the Red Hat 5.2/6.0 distribution, compilation and installation should proceed very smoothly.

This sudo distribution uses the GNU configure utility. Recall from our discussion of OPIE in *Execute configure in /usr/src/opie-2.32* on page 134 that you may view the available options to configure by executing configure --help. In addition to obtaining information about configure that way, there is more detail about configure in the two files INSTALL and INSTALL.configure in /usr/src/sudo.v1.5.9p4. Be sure to review these two files as well as the README, COPYING, and TROUBLESHOOTING files before beginning.

There are numerous options to configure that you may wish to use when you build sudo. A few of the more important options are listed in Table 9.1. As

Table 9.1 Some configure Options for sudo

Option	Description
--with-pam	Enables PAM support. Use of this option requires a valid /etc/pam.d/sudo file.
--with-AuthSRV=*dir*	Enables TIS FWTK* authsrv support (see *FWTK Resources* on page 192). If enabled, *dir* is the base directory containing the FWTK package.
--with-skey	Enables S/Key OTP support.
--with-opie	Enables OPIE OTP support (not necessary if using PAM).
--with-otp-only	Checks only the OTP; does not check Linux password.
--with-SecurID=*dir*	Enables SecurID OTP support.
--with-logging=*type*	Specifies *type* to be one of syslog, file, or both. Default is syslog. If file is chosen, then all logging will be done to /var/log/sudo.log (by default), without using syslogd. This option exists largely for systems with old versions of syslogd. If both is set, then logging will occur to both syslogd and the file.
--with-logfac=*facility*	Specifies the log facility to use. Default is local2, which makes separation of sudo log entries from others simple. Some prefer to set this to auth or authpriv.

Table 9.1 Some `configure` Options for `sudo` (Continued)

Option	Description
`--with-alertmail=`*`user`*	Username for `sudo` to send e-mail messages to. Default is root.
`--with-mail-if-noperms`	If a user attempts to execute a command through `sudo` for which that user is not authorized, then e-mail will be sent to the user specified with the `--with-alertmail` option.
`--with-fqdn`	Use fully qualified domain names. This option allows for both DNS fully qualified domain names (FQDN) like good-guy.ok.com and short names like livfreeordie. However, be warned that, if DNS is not operational, the use of FQDN will break `sudo`.
`--with-umask=`*`mask`*	When sudo executes a command, if that command causes a file or directory to be created it will use the umask specified by *mask*. Default is 0022.
`--without-umask`	Uses the umask associated with the user invoking `sudo`.
`--with-passwd-tries=`*`tries`*	Allows *tries* many attempts at the password. Default is 3.
`--with-tty-tickets`	Normally, when a user invokes `sudo` and successfully authenticates himself or herself, then a ticket file, named after the user, is created in /var/run/sudo. The ticket file specifies the time remaining before the user must reauthenticate with `sudo`. This option causes the files to be named user:tty* instead of just user. This allows the separation of tickets for shared accounts, like admin.
`--with-badpass-message=` `"bad password"`	Specifies the message displayed when a user incorrectly types his or her password at the `sudo` password prompt. Default is "Sorry, try again."
`--with-insults`	Makes the bad password messages interesting.
`--disable-root-sudo`	Disallows root from using `sudo`. This prevents chaining of sudo commands—for example, $ `sudo sudo /bin/sh`.
`--with-exempt=`*`group`*	Members of the *group* specified do not need to specify a password (does not apply when PAM is enabled).
`--with-secure-path=[`*`path`*`]`	Specifies the search path to be used. If this option is used without specifying *path*, then /bin:/usr/ucb:/usr/bin:/usr/sbin:/sbin:/usr/etc:/etc is used.

*TIS=Trusted Information Systems; FWTK = Firewall Toolkit.

you can see, there are a great many options to `sudo configure` (and these aren't all of them). Make sure that you review them carefully and decide which ones are right for your environment. You may also wish to choose different options for different systems (just don't rush; do them one at a time).

Example 9-1 displays the partial output of the configure command. Even though we show this example with PAM enabled, we will look at sudo with and without the use of PAM. Notice that we have specified a more restrictive umask (0027), so that when commands that create files are executed via sudo, they will have no world permissions. The --with-ignore-dot option is incorporated to exclude "." from root's PATH when sudo is invoked. And, we include insults for fun!

Example 9-1 Configuring sudo

```
# ./configure --with-pam --with-insults --with-umask=0027 --with-ignore-dot
creating cache ./config.cache
Configuring CU Sudo version 1.5.9
checking whether to use PAM authentication... yes
...
<lost of output snipped>
...
creating Makefile
creating config.h
creating pathnames.h
You will need to customize sample.pam and install it as /etc/pam.d/sudo
#
```

Now that configure has built the Makefile, among other files, we are ready to compile. Example 9-2 shows the execution of make.

Example 9-2 Compiling and Linking sudo with make

```
# make
gcc -c -I. -I.  -g -O2 -D_PATH_SUDO_SUDOERS='/etc/sudoers' -D_PATH_SUDO_STMP='/
etc/stmp' -DSUDOERS_UID=0 -DSUDOERS_GID=0 -DSUDOERS_MODE=0440  sudo.tab.c
gcc -c -I. -I.  -g -O2 -D_PATH_SUDO_SUDOERS='/etc/sudoers' -D_PATH_SUDO_STMP='/
etc/stmp' -DSUDOERS_UID=0 -DSUDOERS_GID=0 -DSUDOERS_MODE=0440  lex.yy.c
...
<lots of output snipped.
...
gcc -c -I. -I.  -g -O2 -D_PATH_SUDO_SUDOERS='/etc/sudoers' -D_PATH_SUDO_STMP='/
etc/stmp' -DSUDOERS_UID=0 -DSUDOERS_GID=0 -DSUDOERS_MODE=0440  visudo.c
gcc -o visudo sudo.tab.o lex.yy.o visudo.o
#
```

Once compiled and linked, we can install. Example 9-3 shows the output of a successful sudo install.

Example 9-3 Installing sudo

```
# make install
./mkinstalldirs /usr/local/bin /usr/local/sbin /etc /usr/local/man/man8 /usr/
local/man/man5
./install-sh -c -o 0 -g 0 -m 4111 -s sudo /usr/local/bin/sudo
./install-sh -c -o 0 -g 0 -m 0111 -s visudo /usr/local/sbin/visudo
./install-sh -c -o 0 -g 0 -m 0444 ./sudo.man /usr/local/man/man8/sudo.8
./install-sh -c -o 0 -g 0 -m 0444 ./visudo.man /usr/local/man/man8/visudo.8
./install-sh -c -o 0 -g 0 -m 0444 ./sudoers.man /usr/local/man/man5/sudoers.5
#
```

Now we're ready to use it!

USING sudo

Before we can take a look at some sudo examples, we need to explore how sudo works and how we configure sudo with the /etc/sudoers file.

The Functionality of sudo

The sudo command allows an authenticated user to execute an authorized command as root. Both the effective and the real UID and GID are set to 0 (yes, you *really* are root). It determines which users are authorized and which commands they are authorized to use through its configuration file /etc/sudoers. When a user executes sudo, that user will be required to enter his or her password (by default, with PAM or other compile time options, this can change). Once the user is successfully authenticated, then sudo will execute the requested authorized command and exit. The user may request other commands using sudo, including a root shell, and not be required to reauthenticate himself or herself for 5 minutes (default; this is a compile time option; see the INSTALL.configure file in the sudo source distribution).

When executed, the sudo utility attempts to safely run commands by eliminating certain potentially dangerous environment variables, including IFS, ENV, BASH_ENV, and all LD_* and RLD_* variables (used for dynamic loading).

If a user executes sudo and that user does not appear in the /etc/sudoers file, then mail is sent from that user to root (by default, see Table 9.1 on page 175), informing the administrator of an access violation. This event is also logged through syslogd.

Each time sudo is executed, the entire command, including flags and arguments, is logged via syslogd. Included in the log entry are date and time-stamp, username, terminal name, current working directory, and an error message, if any.

The /etc/sudoers File

The /etc/sudoers file is very feature rich. For that reason, it is often overwhelming when all the available bells and whistles are described up front. So we will start with a few simple examples and work our way toward more complex ones.

Let's suppose that you need to set up /etc/sudoers for a single system, called foghorn. On this system, the users bill and mary share the administrative responsibilities. There are two intern users, jane and paul, who are responsible for maintaining the database and making sure that the printer functions properly. In Example 9-4, we see a simple /etc/sudoers file that allows for bill and mary to execute any command as any user. On the other hand, jane and paul have privileges limited to the execution of the database commands and the printer maintenance commands. We'll break down this file

Example 9-4 Simple `/etc/sudoers` File

```
# Simple sudoers file
# Modify with visudo only!
#
# Aliases Section
# User aliases
User_Alias          ADMINS=bill,mary
User_Alias          INTERNS=jane,paul
#
# Runas alias
Runas_Alias         MAINT=root,dbmgr
#
# Command aliases
Cmnd_Alias          LP=/usr/sbin/lpc,/usr/bin/lprm
Cmnd_Alias          SHUT=/sbin/shutdown -r *
#
# Privilege Specifications
ADMINS              foghorn=(ALL) ALL
INTERNS             foghorn=(MAINT) LP,SHUT,/usr/local/db/bin/
```

into the components specified, namely User Aliases, Runas Aliases, Command Aliases, and Privilege Specifications.

User Aliases.   This section simply sets up alias names for the users who will be granted privileges. User aliases require the `User_Alias` keyword. In Example 9-4, `bill` and `mary` belong to the `ADMINS` alias while `jane` and `paul` belong to the `INTERNS` alias. Alias names may be anything except `ALL` which is a reserved keyword.

Runas Aliases.   In Example 9-4, there is one example of a runas alias that requires the `Runas_Alias` keyword. It specifies the list of users—`root` and `dbmgr` in this case—who may be specified with the `sudo -u` invocation (described in *Options to the `sudo` Command* on page 184).

Command Aliases.   These aliases are used to specify lists of commands and require the `Cmnd_Alias` keyword. In this case, the `LP` alias expands to the two commands, `/usr/sbin/lpc` and `/usr/bin/lprm`. The `SHUT` alias expands the very specific command, `/sbin/shutdown -r *` (reboot).

Privilege Specifications.   This section of the file indicates who gets what privileges on which hosts. In Example 9-4, the `ADMINS` may run any command as any user on the host `foghorn`. The `INTERNS` may run only the commands `/usr/sbin/lpc`, `/usr/bin/lprm` (expansion of `LP`), `/sbin/shutdown -r *` (expansion of `SHUT`), and any command in the directory `/usr/local/db/bin/` (these being the database commands). Furthermore, the `INTERNS` may execute these commands on the host `foghorn` only as either the user `root` or `dbmgr` (expansion of `MAINT`). Note that the `*` in the specification of `/sbin/ shutdown -r`; `*` expands to match 0 or more characters (same metacharacter definition in the shell). It is required because the `shutdown` command requires a time argument such as `now` or `+60` (60 minutes from now). See the `shutdown` man page for details.

Examples for the Users in INTERNS   Let's first see what happens when the user `paul` tries to restart the printer daemons **without** using `sudo`. Example 9-5 displays the output of this attempt. Paul does not have the necessary permissions to kill and restart the `lpd` daemon, because it is owned by root. Since Paul has been granted permissions to do this in the `/etc/sudoers` file, he can accomplish his task by using `sudo`. Example 9-6 shows the user `paul` restarting the printer daemons using `sudo`. When `sudo` is executed for the first time, it displays the lecture message and then prompts `paul` for his password. At this point, `paul` may execute additional `sudo` commands without the lecture and password prompt for up to 5 minutes. Paul may extend this time limitation by using `sudo -v`. Even this command will require a password if the 5-minute limitation has elapsed.

Example 9-5 Insufficient Permissions to Restart `lpd`

```
[paul@foghorn]$ /usr/sbin/lpc restart all
lp:
/usr/sbin/lpc: connect: Permission denied
[paul@foghorn]$
```

Example 9-6 Successful `lpd` Restart Using `sudo`

```
[paul@foghorn]$ sudo /usr/sbin/lpc restart all
We trust you have received the usual lecture from the local System
Administrator. It usually boils down to these two things:

        #1) Respect the privacy of others.
        #2) Think before you type.
Password: paul's password
lp:
        daemon aborted
lp:
        daemon started
[paul@foghorn]$
```

Suppose that Paul needs to reboot the system. Based on the `/etc/sudoers` file, he is allowed to execute `/sbin/shutdown -r`. Let's see what happens in Example 9-7 if he executes the `shutdown` command without the `-r` flag. At this point, Paul is uncertain about why he can't reboot the system. After all, Mary told him that he had the permission to do that. So Paul decides to see what privileges he actually has by executing `sudo -l`, as shown in Example 9-8. The output of this command informs Paul that he may execute only `shutdown -r` (just like Mary said). Notice that it also informs him that he may run all commands in `/usr/local/db/bin/`, as well as the commands `/usr/sbin/lpc` and `/usr/bin/lprm` as either the root or dbmgr users. However, he cannot

Example 9-7 Failed `sudo` Execution Due to Incorrect Command

```
[paul@foghorn]$ sudo /sbin/shutdown now
Password:
Sorry, user paul is not allowed to execute "/sbin/shutdown now" as root on foghorn.
[paul@foghorn]$
```

Example 9-8 Using sudo -1

```
[paul@foghorn]$ sudo -1
You may run the following commands on this host:
    (root, dbmgr) /usr/sbin/lpc,/usr/bin/lprm
    (root) /sbin/shutdown -r *
    (root, dbmgr) /usr/local/db/bin/
[paul@foghorn]$
```

execute /sbin/shutdown -r as dbmgr. This is simply due to the fact that running the shutdown command as a user other than root will always result in permission denied.

Now that he knows which command it is, he executes it successfully, as indicated, in Example 9-9. The moral of this story is that the command executed through sudo must match *exactly* that given in /etc/sudoers or as displayed by sudo -1.

Example 9-9 Successful sudo /usr/sbin/shutdown -r Invocation

```
[paul@foghorn]$ sudo /sbin/shutdown -r now
Broadcast message from root (ttyp0) Wed Mar 10 06:55:39 1999...

The system is going down for reboot NOW !!
```

OH, BY THE WAY...

Since we compiled sudo with insults (see Example 9-1 on page 177), let's have a look at what that means. In Example 9-10, we show the user paul mistyping his password twice.

Without the --with-insults compile-time option, whenever you enter an incorrect password, you would simply see the message, Sorry, try again. The UNIX operating system used to be full of humorous, insulting, and sometimes offensive error messages. As it has become more commercialized, most of these messages have been sanitized. So, hearken back to the days of yore, and compile with insults!

Example 9-10 Insulting Error Messages

```
[paul@foghorn]$ sudo /sbin/shutdown
Password:
Listen, burrito brains, I don't have time to listen to this trash.
Password:
Your mind just hasn't been the same since the electro-shock, has it?
Password:
Sorry, user paul is not allowed to execute "/sbin/shutdown" as root on foghorn.

[paul@foghorn]$
```

General Syntax of /etc/sudoers

Now that we have explored some relatively simple examples associated with the /etc/sudoers file, let's take a look at the full suite of capabilities. The file is broken into two major sections, the alias section and the privilege section. The alias section in the file is largely for convenience. It is the privilege section

Table 9.2 Alias Syntax for `/etc/sudoers`

Alias Type Required Keyword	Alias Syntax	Description
`Host_Alias`	`HOSTALIAS=`	Comma-separated list of hostnames, IP addresses, network/netmask, and/or netgroups.[*]
`Runas_Alias`	`RUNASALIAS=`	Comma-separated list of users, groups, and/or netgroups. Specifies UIDs that will be accepted by `sudo -u`.
`Cmnd_Alias`	`CMNDALIAS=`	Comma-separated list of commands or directories. Must be absolutely qualified. When a command is specified, flags and arguments may also be specified. The special characters, `""`, when given as a command argument means that no arguments are allowed. Thus, do not quote commands! When a directory is specified, it includes all commands in that directory.
`User_Alias`	`USERALIAS=`	Comma-separated list of users, groups, and/or netgroups.

[*]Netgroups are groups of (host, user, domain) triples often used for permission checking over the network. See the references noted in *NFS, Samba, NIS, and DNS Resources* on page 40.

of the file that actually avails a particular user of root permissions. Table 9.2 describes the alias options available to this file.

In our earlier examples, we did not look at the `Host_Alias` capability. By using this alias type, we can configure an `/etc/sudoers` file for all the systems in a given environment. It may even be shared via NFS or distributed to multiple systems through the `rdist` or `rsync` utilities.[1]

We also did not explore the `Runas_Alias` capability. This alias, as described in Table 9.2, simplifies the process of specifying the users for which `sudo` will run as, that is assume the real and effective UID of the indicated user.

The privilege specification takes the syntax shown in Example 9-11. While this syntax appears to be very complex at first glance, it is actually quite straightforward. We have already seen some simple examples of this syntax in use in Example 9-4 on page 179. This representation points out the full capabilities of the entries in `/etc/sudoers`. Table 9.3 helps to illustrate the various types shown in Example 9-11. We will look at the further implementation of this syntax in *A More Sophisticated Example* on page 185.

Example 9-11 Syntax of Privilege Entries in `/etc/sudoers`

```
access_group host_type=[(runas_type,runas_type,...)] [NOPASSWD:] \
[!]cmnd_type[(runas_type,runas_type,...)][,[NOPASSWD:] \
[!]cmnd_type[(runas_type,runas_type,...)]] [,... ]\
[:host_type=[...]]
```

---

1. These utilities allow for automated distribution of file(s) to various hosts. See your system documentation for the proper use of `rdist` and `rsync`.

Table 9.3 User Privilege Specification in /etc/sudoers

Parameter	Description
access_group	A *user*, %*group*, +*netgroup*, or USERALIAS.
host_type=	A *host*, IP address, +*netgroup*, *network/netmask*, or HOSTALIAS. The = must follow with no white space.
(runas_type)	A *user*, %*group*, +*netgroup*, or RUNASALIAS. The parentheses are required.
cmnd_type	A command or CMDNALIAS.
NOPASSWD:	No password is required for the command following this keyword. A space is required after the NOPASSWD:.
!	The logical NOT operator. Only applied to cmnd_type.
:	This separator follows a cmnd_type and precedes a host_type= with no intervening white space.
ALL	Special keyword that expands to all of the given type.

There are also metacharacters that may be used in this file. The wildcard and escape characters are defined identically to their shell counterparts. They are described in Table 9.4.

As you might imagine, the /etc/sudoers file can get quite complex. A modestly complex example is given in Example 9-12 on page 185. Also in the section *Vulnerabilities of sudo* on page 191, some of the vulnerabilities associated with misconfiguring the /etc/sudoers file are described. It turns out that,

Table 9.4 Metacharacters in /etc/sudoers

Metacharacter	Description
*	Matches 0 or more characters.
?	Matches exactly 1 character.
[*range*, *range*,...]	Matches any character in the *range*.
[!*range*,!*range*,...]	Matches any character not in the *range*.
\	Escapes the next character.
" "	The null string. Used to indicate that **no** arguments or flags may be passed to a command.
#	Comment character. Any text after this character is ignored.
%	Specifies a UNIX group such as %wheel.
+	Specifies a netgroup such as +admins.

if an `/etc/sudoers` file has a syntax error in it, `sudo` won't work at all. For this reason, the `visudo` command is included with `sudo` distribution.

The `visudo` Command

Only root can execute `visudo`. However, this also means that any user with the appropriate permissions can execute `sudo visudo` (remember, `sudo` sets both the real and effective UID to 0). By default, `visudo` invokes the `vi` editor (this may be changed with the `--with-editor` option to `configure`) and when editing is complete (that is, a save operation is effected, such as ":wq"), `visudo` does a syntax check before saving the file. If there are syntax errors in the file, `visudo` will give you the option to reedit the file, quit without saving the changes, or quit and save the changes. Be warned that if you save syntax errors, `sudo` will not work.

Options to the `sudo` Command

Table 9.5 explains the available options to `sudo`. Remember that use of `sudo` is completely controlled by the `/etc/sudoers` file.

Table 9.5 Options to `sudo`

Option	Description
-V	Prints the version and quits.
-h	Prints the usage message and quits.
-l	Lists the allowed and forbidden commands for the invoking user.
-v	Validates the user. This command will reset the timestamp for the invoking user in `/var/run/sudo`. If the time-out has already occurred, it will prompt the user for a password.
-k	Removes the user's timestamp file, forcing the user to respond to the password prompt at the next invocation of `sudo`. This option never requires a password and may be put in the user's `.logout` file.
-s	Executes the shell specified by the SHELL environment variable or, if not set, the user's default shell as found in `/etc/passwd`. Beware! Any commands executed after the successful invocation of `sudo -s` are not logged! This command is similar to `sudo /path/to/shell`.
-H	Sets the HOME environment variable to that of the target user, which is root by default, but will assume $HOME of target user if -u option is specified.
-b	Puts the command in the background. Using this option disables shell job control. You may wish to specify & at the end of the command instead.

Table 9.5 Options to sudo (Continued)

Option	Description
-r *realm*	Specifies the Kerberos Version 5 *realm*, if not the default. Must have used the --with-kerb5 configure option.
-p *prompt*	Sets the sudo password prompt to *prompt*. Normally, *prompt* is a quoted string. You may also use the special strings %u, which expands to the login username, and %h, which expands to the hostname.
-u *username* | #*UID*	Specifies the *username* or *UID* of the user to run the specified command as if the user is other than root. In the case of specifying a UID, it must be preceded by #.
--	Informs sudo to ignore the arguments following.
command	The *command* that sudo will execute. Required except when using -s, -V, or -H.

A More Sophisticated Example

The /etc/sudoers file provided in Example 9-12 presents a modestly complex illustration. Let's go through each of the components of this file.

Example 9-12 A More Complex /etc/sudoers File

```
#The /etc/sudoers file
# Only edit this file with visudo!
#
# Host Aliases
Host_Alias SERVERS=+majsvrs
Host_Alias DBSERVERS=sidney,topper
Host_Alias DNET=48.6.16.0/255.255.248.0,48.6.32.0/255.255.248.0
Host_Alias AHOSTS=matty,nordike,wilkins
Host_Alias RESTICT=+securehosts
#
# Command Aliases
Cmnd_Alias REBOOT=/sbin/reboot,/sbin/shutdown -r *,/sbin/init 6
Cmnd_Alias SHELLS=/bin/bash,/bin/ash,/bin/tcsh,/bin/csh,/bin/ksh,\
           /bin/zsh,/bin/sh
Cmnd_Alias SU=/bin/su
Cmnd_Alias NIS=/usr/bin/make -f /var/yp/Makefile,/bin/vi /etc/yp/*
Cmnd_Alias UMGT=/usr/sbin/useradd,/usr/sbin/usermod,\
           /usr/sbin/groupadd,/usr/sbin/groupmod,\
           /usr/bin/passwd -u *,/usr/bin/chage -m ? -W [3-7] * ?*
Cmnd_Alias ROOTPW=/usr/bin/passwd -u root,\
           /usr/bin/chage -m ? -W [3-7] * root,\
           /usr/sbin/useradd *-r*,/usr/sbin/useradd *-o*,\
           /usr/sbin/usermod *-o*,/usr/sbin/groupmod *-o*,\
           /usr/sbin/groupadd *-r*,/usr/sbin/groupadd *-o*
Cmnd_Alias SPLOITS=*cp * */*bin* *,*mv * */*bin* *,*ln,*mkfile,*mknod,\
           *chmod,*chown
#
# Runas Aliases
#
Runas_Alias DB=root,dbmgr,sitemgr
#
# User Aliases
```

Example 9-12 A More Complex `/etc/sudoers` File (Continued)

```
#
User_Alias  SRADMINS=mary,bill
User_Alias  DBADMINS=sue,billa,mfruh,rob
User_Alias  JRADMINS=paul,tchase
User_Alias  DEVADMINS=wills,casper,tsu,rhines
#
# User Privilege Specification
#
SRADMINS ALL=(ALL) ALL
#%wheel AHOSTS=ALL This is a bad idea...
JRADMINS SERVERS=NIS,UMGT,!ROOTPW,REBOOT:AHOSTS=REBOOT
DBADMINS DBSERVERS=(DB) ALL,!ROOTPW,!SPLOITS,!SU,!SHELLS
DEVADMINS DNET=ALL:RESTRICT=ALL,!ROOTPW,!SPLOITS,!SU,!SHELLS
```

Host Aliases. This example shows both the use of netgroups—for example, SERVERS=+majsvrs—and the collection of subnetworks through the DNET alias. The other aliases are straightforward lists of hosts.

Command Aliases. This section defines the various commands that will later be used in the User Privilege Specification section. There are a number of commands listed that use metacharacters, and we will review a representative sample.

The REBOOT command alias incorporates a few different ways to reboot the system. Notice that commands that would otherwise allow for effects other than a reboot are restricted to execute a reboot only—for example, the explicit inclusion of /sbin/init 6, which sudo will allow only if it is identically requested.

In the NIS alias, we note that command execution is restricted to the bare essentials for maintaining NIS. A user granted these privileges would be allowed to edit any of the files in /etc/yp (hopefully, and normally, passwd is not in that directory), the directory that contains the text version of the NIS maps (this is not the default location, but it is a common choice). This alias also allows for the execution of the Makefile found in /var/yp, which will cause the updated text versions of the maps to be converted to the appropriate database format and propagated to other NIS servers.

Now look at the entries for the chage command. It appears in both the UMGT and ROOTPW aliases. The only difference between the two is the appearance of ?* in the former alias and root in the latter. Let's examine the chage command as given in UMGT,

```
/usr/bin/chage -m ? -W [3-7] * ?*
```

Given this entry, sudo will require exactly one character after the -m flag (minimum number of days before a password may be changed), followed by exactly one of the characters 3, 4, 5, 6, or 7 after the -w flag (number of days prior to expiration that a user is warned), followed by 0 or more characters (perhaps more flags and arguments), ending with at least 1 character. This last specification requires the use of a username; otherwise the username field to chage could be left blank and default to the current user, which is normally root when using sudo. Of course, the syntax ?* will match root. Hence the second form of the command in the ROOTPW alias. Later on in the file, UMGT is allowed but ROOTPW is negated, having the effect of allowing the use of chage to modify all users' password aging parameters, except root. The other entries that are similar in these two command aliases perform the same function.

The SPLOITS command alias contains commands that may be used for the purpose of exploiting the system. For example, *cp * */*bin* * is intended to match any attempts to copy anything with bin in the directory or file name. Of course, if someone obtains his or her own version of the cp command and renames it to, say, copy, this won't match.

Runas Aliases. There is one very simple alias—DB—that expands to the users root, dbmgr, and sitemgr.

User Aliases. This section should be very clear because it simply assigns specific lists of users to different aliases. Notice that neither netgroups nor groups are used here. This should be the preferred way of configuring this file to avoid the possible exploits of a netgroup or group.

User Privilege Specification. The use of aliases makes this section look quite simple. Yet there is a lot of detail here. We'll go through each one.

The members of the SRADMINS alias may execute any command as any user on any host.

The entry with %wheel at the beginning is commented out, with the comment, "This is a bad idea..." The comment refers to the fact that the privileges afforded the wheel group are compromisable simply by exploiting the wheel group on any one of the systems listed in the AHOST alias. This entry means, if it were to be uncommented, that any member of the wheel group is permitted to execute any command on any of the hosts in the AHOST alias as the user root. Notice that there are no parentheses anywhere, therefore implying that sudo cannot be used to run as any user except root.

The users in the JRADMINS group are allowed to run the commands specified in the NIS, UMGT, and REBOOT aliases, but not those in the ROOTPW alias. They may do this on the hosts in the SERVERS alias as the root user. JRADMINS may also reboot the hosts in AHOSTS.

The members of the DBADMINS alias may execute all commands except those listed in the ROOTPW, SPLOITS, SU, and SHELLS aliases. They may do so as any of the users, root, dbmgr, or sitemgr, but only on the hosts found in the DBSERVERS alias.

Finally, members of the DEVADMINS alias may execute all commands as root on any system in the DNET networks. They may also execute any command as root except for those listed in ROOTPW, SPLOITS, SU, and SHELLS on the hosts in the RESTRICT alias.

As you can see with Example 9-12 on page 185, it is possible to write an /etc/sudoers file that may be used on many hosts. This file may easily be used across different platforms and UNIX operating systems.

WARNING!

Example 9-12 on page 185 has a number of vulnerabilities. For example, while the SPLOITS commands are set up to prevent certain actions by certain users, there is nothing to prevent the use of the cp and mv commands, if those commands are renamed. Also, if a user has the ability to edit a file such as cp or mv, then that user will be able to save it to another location with a different name. The purpose of providing this example is to show the extraordinary flexibility of sudo.

Your rule of thumb with respect to sudo configuration is to simply be very careful about allowing users to have root privileges. Keep things as simple as possible. Ultimately, it comes down to the trust you place in the individual to whom you are granting access. Once you grant a user certain privileges, their account becomes a potential vulnerability and you will want to ensure that the person to whom you are granting these privileges is well aware of the responsibilities incumbent with the privileges.

Setting Up sudo Logging

One of the major advantages of using sudo is the logging it provides. By default, all sudo log messages are processed by syslogd (see Chapter 8 for more information about the syslog utility) via the local2 facility (see Table 9.1 on page 175 for options that can change this behavior). The standard Red Hat 5.2/6.0 /etc/syslog.conf (see Example 8-1 on page 165 in Chapter 8) entry puts all messages at level info and above into the /var/log/messages file. You may wish to isolate all sudo logs to a particular location, in which case the /etc/syslog.conf might look like that shown in Example 9-13. The entries shown will cause all sudo messages to be written to /var/log/sudo.log on the local system; they will also be sent to the syslogd running on the host central.

Example 9-13 Isolating sudo Log Entries in /etc/syslog.conf

```
# cat /etc/syslog.conf
*.info;mail.none;authpriv.none;local2.none          /var/log/messages
...
<output snipped>
...
local2.debug                                        /var/log/sudo.log
local2.debug                                        @central
#
```

Reading sudo Logs

Example 9-14 shows us some sample log entries from sudo (line wraps due to formatting constraints). Each log entry contains the date, timestamp, hostname of execution, username, terminal name, current working directory, user command was executed as, and the command itself. In the first entry in Example 9-14, notice that COMMAND=/bin/bash. This entry could have been generated by either sudo -s or sudo /bin/bash. In particular, note that there are

Example 9-14 Sample sudo Log Entries

```
Mar  9 15:01:55 foghorn sudo:      mary : TTY=ttyp0 ; PWD=/home/mary ;
USER=root ; COMMAND=/bin/bash
Mar 10 05:06:30 foghorn sudo:      paul : TTY=ttyp0 ; PWD=/home/paul ;
USER=root ; COMMAND=/usr/sbin/lpc restart all
Mar 10 05:36:13 foghorn sudo:      paul : TTY=ttyp0 ; PWD=/home/paul ;
USER=root ; COMMAND=validate
Mar 10 05:57:33 foghorn sudo:      paul : command not allowed ; TTY=ttyp0
; PWD=/home/paul ; USER=root ; COMMAND=/sbin/shutdown now
Mar 10 06:49:17 foghorn sudo:      paul : TTY=ttyp0 ; PWD=/home/paul ;
USER=root ; COMMAND=list
```

no log entries after the first one for mary. Anything she did after sudo invoked the shell will not be logged. The same is true for commands like vi; none of the commands entered in a vi session would be logged, including a shell escape.[2]

In the next entry, we see paul executing lpc. Subsequent to that entry, we see COMMAND=validate. This means that paul executed sudo -v to reinitialize his ticket. After that, we see the entry for paul's abortive attempt to run shutdown; sudo generated the error message, command not allowed, in this entry. Finally, we see the entry containing COMMAND=list. This means that paul executed sudo -l.

The sudo utility generates substantial log entries—significantly more information than what you would normally see from pam_wheel and su. The copious logging of sudo, in and of itself, is often motivation enough to use sudo. Both from a security and an administrative perspective, these logs are extremely valuable.

Unfortunately, copious logging also means that more time must be spent analyzing the logs. Fret not! Chapter 17 discusses many ways to automate the analysis of your log files.

PAM and sudo

PAM, PAM, PAM,...Wonderful PAM! For more information about PAM, see Chapter 5.

Since sudo is PAM-aware (and we compiled it that way—see Example 9-1 on page 177), we can create an /etc/pam.d/sudo file. Example 9-15 shows using pam_if and pam_opie (see *OPIE and PAM* on page 143) to force the use of OPIE unless we are at the console or one of the directly connected terminals.

Example 9-15 Example /etc/pam.d/sudo File Using pam_if and pam_opie

```
auth        sufficient      /lib/security/pam_if.so tty=tty[0-2]\
                                    -- pam_pwdb.so shadow
auth        required        /lib/security/pam_opie.so
```

---

2. In vi, the command :shell will invoke a shell, which in this case would be a root shell.

You do not need to use PAM to implement OPIE or S/Key support because that support may be implemented through a `configure` option independent of PAM (see Table 9.1 on page 175).

If you are using OPIE or S/Key generally for network connections (in other words, you've implemented `pam_opie` in other files such as `/etc/pam.d/login` and `/etc/pam.d/ftp`, or you are using OPIE or S/Key replacement programs), then you should do the same for `sudo` as in or similar to Example 9-15. If you implement this example, all will proceed as before except that `sudo` will prompt you for your OPIE OTP whenever you are executing `sudo` from sources other than the console or one of the other acceptable devices.

It should be noted that, as of this writing, `sudo` pays attention only to `auth`-type modules. Therefore, unfortunately, you cannot take advantage of modules like `pam_time`, which is a `session`-only module.

DISABLING ROOT ACCESS

You may want to partially or completely disable the use of `su`. You should minimally disable `su` to root and force all root access through `sudo`. The simplest way to accomplish this is provided in the explanation surrounding Example 5-19 on page 102 in Chapter 5. In short, you may configure your `/etc/pam.d/su` file as shown in Example 9-16. The pertinent entry is shown in **bold**. Note that the file `/etc/security/sudeny` must contain root and any other username for which you want to eliminate `su` access. If you wish to disable the use of `su` altogether, Example 9-17 provides a simple mechanism for this purpose. Here we see that the `pam_deny` entry (shown in **bold**) is added to the top of the `/etc/pam.d/su` file. This will have the effect of denying all `su` attempts.

Example 9-16 Denying `su` with `pam_listfile`

```
auth       required    /lib/security/pam_listfile.so onerr=fail \
           item=user sense=deny file=/etc/security/sudeny
auth       required    /lib/security/pam_pwdb.so
account    required    /lib/security/pam_pwdb.so
password   required    /lib/security/pam_cracklib.so minlen=20 retry=3
password   required    /lib/security/pam_pwdb.so md5 use_authtok
session    required    /lib/security/pam_pwdb.so
```

Example 9-17 Completely Disabling `su`

```
auth       requisite   /lib/security/pam_deny.so
auth       required    /lib/security/pam_pwdb.so
account    required    /lib/security/pam_pwdb.so
password   required    /lib/security/pam_cracklib.so minlen=20 retry=3
password   required    /lib/security/pam_pwdb.so md5 use_authtok
session    required    /lib/security/pam_pwdb.so
```

To ensure that access as root is completely disabled except through `sudo`, you will also want to ensure that the file `/etc/securetty` is empty (described in *Configuring `/etc/securetty`* on page 68) as this completely prohibits a direct login by root.

By minimally disabling access to the root account through the use of su, and by disabling native root access as described in the previous paragraph, you ensure that all root activity will require an initial invocation through sudo. This will provide better logging and greater control over who is allowed to do what as root.

VULNERABILITIES OF sudo

Do not think of sudo as a panacea to limiting root access. It is unfortunately fairly simple to extend the privileges granted to sudo. Suppose that you set up the user paul in the /etc/sudoers file so that he can execute any command as root except for all of the shells (/bin/bash, /bin/ash, /bin/ksh, etc.). Now all the user paul has to do is use vi to edit any file and then execute :shell, to break out into a root shell and circumvent the limitation. He might also decide to copy one of the shells to another location—/tmp/bash for example—and then execute sudo /tmp/bash, which would not be restricted. The moral of this story is to be very careful about whom you grant permissions to; grant them only the commands which they absolutely need. Even then, it is possible that a way will be found to circumvent the limitations imposed by sudo.

Also, be careful about using groups and netgroups in the /etc/sudoers file. If a bad-guy finds a way to get included in a privileged group or netgroup, then it may be a simple matter to exploit full root privileges from there. For this reason, it is recommended that all users in /etc/sudoers be enumerated, as in Example 9-12 on page 185.

Fortunately, you have those wonderful log files! If a user does take advantage of the privileges granted through sudo, you may well be able to determine that such an event has occurred through regular review of the sudo log files. These log files are the biggest security benefit of sudo. So read them! The postprocessing of these log files is discussed in Chapter 17.

SUMMARY

The sudo command allows for substantial controls over which users are allowed to execute commands as root. We looked at installing, configuring, and using sudo as well as the log messages it generates. We also noted that sudo could be the source of vulnerabilities because it executes commands by setting the real UID and GID to root when invoked to run as root. Thus, its configuration file needs careful consideration and testing prior to implementation.

FOR FURTHER READING

Reference Books

1. Bailey, Edward C., *Maximum RPM*, Indianapolis, Indiana, redhat press, 1997.

E-Mail Lists

You may subscribe to the `sudo` mailing list by placing `subscribe sudo-announce` in the body of an e-mail message to `majordomo@cs.colorado.edu`.

Web Sites

The following web site is the `sudo` home page.

    http://www.courtesan.com/sudo/

On-Line Documentation

After extracting `sudo`, you will find the files

    INSTALL
    INSTALL.configure
    README

which contain a lot of information about `sudo`. Be sure to read them.

Kerberos Resources

You will find extensive Kerberos documentation and links to other Kerberos sites at

    http://web.mit.edu/kerberos/www/

FWTK Resources

You will find information about FWTK at

    http://www.tis.com/research/software/

Which Doors Are Open?

Securing Network Services: TCP_wrappers, `portmap`, and `xinetd`

Which network services should be made available? That depends upon many aspects of your computing environment. The best place to begin is with your organization's Security Policy (see Chapter 2), which should establish the philosophy of either generally permitting services (everything is allowed except that which is expressly forbidden) or generally forbidding services (that which is not expressly permitted is denied). Which philosophy you implement will dictate your default behavior. For the balance of our discussion, we will assume the latter policy of denial by default, because it reflects a more secure perspective.

Once you have established the default policy, the next step depends upon individual system requirements. Some systems, for example, will act as network install servers and therefore will need to make available services such as `bootpd`, `rarpd`, and `in.tftpd`. Other systems may only need to provide typical services such as `in.ftpd`, `in.telnetd`, and `sshd`. Still other systems may need to provide NFS, NIS, electronic mail, and/or DNS services. In every case, once you have determined that a particular system needs to provide a specific service, you must determine which systems and users require the services and then configure those services so that only the required systems and users are allowed to access the service. But that's not all! You must then configure the services in such a way that they generate an appropriate amount of log detail. And then you have to read those log files! There is some help with the reading of the log files—we discuss that topic in Chapter 17.

We provide an overview of and references to the topic of network services in *TCP/IP Networking Overview* on page 28. In this chapter, we will consider ways to improve the security of those services we decide to use through the use of the access control lists and additional logging provided by TCP_wrappers. Additionally, we will look at configuring the `portmap` daemon in a more secure way. Finally, we will consider `xinetd`, a replacement for `inetd`, which offers greater flexibility for securing the network services to be made available as well as protection against certain types of DoS attacks.

TCP_WRAPPERS

Almost all of the services provided through `inetd` are invoked through TCP_wrappers by way of the TCP_wrappers daemon, `tcpd`. TCP_wrappers was written and continues to be maintained by Wietse Venema. It is included with many Linux distributions including Red Hat 5.2/6.0 and it runs on most flavors of UNIX. If you don't already have a copy, you can obtain one from `ftp://ftp.cert.org/pub/tools/tcp_wrappers/` as well as various other sites throughout the Internet. Make sure that you pull it down from a site, like this one, that includes a digital signature. Then check the signature!

The TCP_wrappers software is distributable under the terms displayed in Example 10-1. In other words, it is publicly available! This notice is found in the DISCLAIMER file in the top directory of the source tree.

Example 10-1 TCP_Wrappers Copyright Notice

```
* Copyright 1995 by Wietse Venema.  All rights reserved.  Some individual
* files may be covered by other copyrights.
*
* This material was originally written and compiled by Wietse Venema at
* Eindhoven University of Technology, The Netherlands, in 1990, 1991,
* 1992, 1993, 1994 and 1995.
*
* Redistribution and use in source and binary forms are permitted
* provided that this entire copyright notice is duplicated in all such
* copies.
*
* This software is provided "as is" and without any expressed or implied
* warranties, including, without limitation, the implied warranties of
* merchantibility and fitness for any particular purpose.
```

The TCP_wrappers mechanism provides access control list restrictions and logging for all service requests to the service it wraps. It may be used for either UDP or TCP services as long as the services are invoked through a central daemon process such as `inetd`. This requirement is based on the nature of `tcpd`, the TCP_wrappers daemon, which is invoked by `inetd` instead of the service being requested. This is due to appropriate entries in `/etc/inetd.conf`, as shown in Example 10-2.

Notice that, for many of the services (some of which are commented out and therefore not available), the sixth field is `/usr/sbin/tcpd` instead of the

Example 10-2 Default `/etc/inetd.conf` File in Red Hat Distributions

```
# inetd.conf    This file describes the services that will be available
#              through the INETD TCP/IP super server.  To re-configure
#              the running INETD process, edit this file, then send the
#              INETD process a SIGHUP signal.
#
# Version:     @(#)/etc/inetd.conf    3.10     05/27/93
#
# Authors:     Original taken from BSD UNIX 4.3/TAHOE.
#              Fred N. van Kempen, <waltje@uwalt.nl.mugnet.org>
#
# Modified for Debian Linux by Ian A. Murdock <imurdock@shell.portal.com>
#
# Modified for RHS Linux by Marc Ewing <marc@redhat.com>
#
# <service_name> <sock_type> <proto> <flags> <user> <server_path> <args>
#
# Echo, discard, daytime, and chargen are used primarily for testing.
#
# To re-read this file after changes, just do a 'killall -HUP inetd'
#
#echo   stream  tcp     nowait  root    internal
#echo   dgram   udp     wait    root    internal
#discard        stream  tcp     nowait  root    internal
#discard        dgram   udp     wait    root    internal
#daytime        stream  tcp     nowait  root    internal
#daytime        dgram   udp     wait    root    internal
#chargen        stream  tcp     nowait  root    internal
#chargen        dgram   udp     wait    root    internal
#time   stream  tcp     nowait  root    internal
#time   dgram   udp     wait    root    internal
#
# These are standard services.
#
ftp     stream  tcp     nowait  root    /usr/sbin/tcpd  in.ftpd -l -a
telnet  stream  tcp     nowait  root    /usr/sbin/tcpd  in.telnetd
#
# Shell, login, exec, comsat and talk are BSD protocols.
#
#shell  stream  tcp     nowait  root    /usr/sbin/tcpd  in.rshd
#login  stream  tcp     nowait  root    /usr/sbin/tcpd  in.rlogind
#exec   stream  tcp     nowait  root    /usr/sbin/tcpd  in.rexecd
#comsat dgram   udp     wait    root    /usr/sbin/tcpd  in.comsat
#talk   dgram   udp     wait    root    /usr/sbin/tcpd  in.talkd
#ntalk  dgram   udp     wait    root    /usr/sbin/tcpd  in.ntalkd
#dtalk  stream  tcp     waut    nobody  /usr/sbin/tcpd  in.dtalkd
#
# Pop and imap mail services et al
#
#pop-2  stream  tcp     nowait  root    /usr/sbin/tcpd ipop2d
 pop-3  stream  tcp     nowait  root    /usr/sbin/tcpd  ipop3d
#imap   stream  tcp     nowait  root    /usr/sbin/tcpd imapd
#
# The Internet UUCP service.
#
#uucp   stream  tcp     nowait  uucp    /usr/sbin/tcpd  /usr/lib/uucp/uucico  -l
#
# Tftp service is provided primarily for booting.  Most sites
# run this only on machines acting as "boot servers." Do not uncomment
# this unless you *need* it.
#
#tftp   dgram   udp     wait    root    /usr/sbin/tcpd  in.tftpd
#bootps dgram   udp     wait    root    /usr/sbin/tcpd  bootpd
#
# Finger, systat and netstat give out user information which may be
# valuable to potential "system crackers."  Many sites choose to disable
```

Example 10-2 Default `/etc/inetd.conf` File in Red Hat Distributions (Continued)

```
# some or all of these services to improve security.
#
#finger stream  tcp     nowait  root    /usr/sbin/tcpd  in.fingerd
#cfinger stream tcp     nowait  root    /usr/sbin/tcpd  in.cfingerd
#systat stream  tcp     nowait  guest   /usr/sbin/tcpd  /bin/ps -auwwx
#netstat    stream  tcp     nowait  guest    /usr/sbin/tcpd  /bin/netstat    -f inet
#
# Authentication
#
auth    stream  tcp     nowait    nobody    /usr/sbin/in.identd in.identd -l -e -o
#
# End of inetd.conf

linuxconf stream tcp wait root /bin/linuxconf linuxconf --http
#swat       stream  tcp     nowait.400      root /usr/sbin/swat swat
```

daemon. Therefore, when a service with such an entry—like `telnet`—is requested by a client, `inetd` will invoke `tcpd` instead.

Basically, whenever a client requests a service, it will be invoked either through `inetd` or through the `portmap` daemon (RPC services only), or a server daemon will already be running. Server daemons that are run all the time (such as `rpc.mountd`) will be invoked at boot time through a start-up script (`/etc/rc.d/init.d/nfs` in the case of `rpc.mountd`) or started manually. Otherwise, in order for a service to be available on a server, you will find an entry in `/etc/inetd.conf` for management by `inetd` or in `/etc/rpc` for RPC services managed by `portmap`. For a thorough treatment of TCP/IP services in general, see the references cited in *General TCP/IP Networking Resources* on page 39 in Chapter 3.

This means that the functionality provided by `tcpd` is separate from any service being requested. Therefore, to get similar functionality into a daemon that is always bound to a port, such as `syslogd -r` (discussed in Chapter 8), the bound daemon would have to be rewritten for that purpose (Wietse Venema did exactly that for the `portmap` daemon which is discussed in *The Portmapper* on page 218). Figure 10.1 provides an overview of the flow of an initial request to a server in the presence of TCP_wrappers.

As is shown in the figure, TCP_wrappers performs a few simple but very important tasks. It checks the access control list to determine whether a connection should be allowed and submits a log entry to `syslogd`. If the access list allows the service, `tcpd` invokes the appropriate daemon, which then proceeds with its own authentication mechanism (if applicable) and may write its own message to `syslogd`.

Building TCP_Wrappers

If you are using a version of Linux (or UNIX, for that matter) that does not include TCP_wrappers as part of the distribution (unlike Red Hat 5.2/6.0), you will need to compile and link the various programs. Even if you are using Red Hat 5.2/6.0, you may decide that you need to recompile TCP-wrappers with

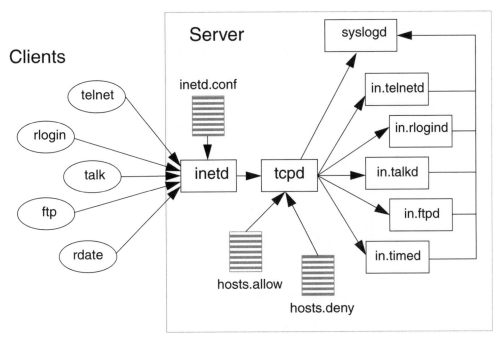

Fig. 10.1 TCP_Wrappers Intercepts and Filters Requests

different options. This section will describe the build options and point out the options used in the Red Hat 5.2/6.0 distribution.

For purposes of the examples in this directory, we will assume that the TCP_wrappers source tree has been loaded in /usr/src/tcp_wrappers. TCP_wrappers compile-time options are all controlled through the Makefile. This is where you will make all the necessary changes prior to executing make. Table 10.1 lists the options (called macros) found in the Makefile, their meaning, and whether or not the option was used to compile the binaries found in Red Hat 5.2/6.0.

Table 10.1 TCP_Wrappers Compile-Time Options

Option	Description	Red Hat Use
REAL_DAEMON_DIR	Fully qualified directory where the network daemons, such as in.telnetd and in.ftpd are located.	/usr/sbin
TLI	Used to turn on System V.4 style Transport Layer Interface (TLI) support.	No
RANLIB	Sets up an index for faster library linking.	Default
ARFLAGS	Specifies the flags to be used with ar, described next.	Default
AR	Creates, modifies, and extracts archives or libraries.	Default

Table 10.1 TCP_Wrappers Compile-Time Options (Continued)

Option	Description	Red Hat Use
AUX_OBJ	Specifies additional object files for linking.	None
STRINGS	Specifies various character string compare and manipulation routines. Used if C library doesn't contain them.	No
LIBS	Specifies object libraries to include at linktime.	None
SYSTYPE	Specifies system-specific compiler options.	None
BUGS	Specifies macros which provide workarounds to known system bugs.	Default
NETGROUP	Specifies the use of NIS netgroups. If you are using netgroups, turn this on.	No
VSYSLOG	Use if the system supports the vsyslog function call. This is turned on by default and will not cause problems even if your system doesn't use this function.	Yes
STYLE	Turns on language extensions as described in the hosts_options(5) man page. It incorporates the macro PROCESS_OPTIONS. It is off by default.	Yes
FACILITY	Specifies the syslog facility used for logging. The default is LOG_MAIL (specified as mail in /etc/syslog.conf). This may be changed dynamically with the SEVERITY option; see Table 10.3 on page 203.	LOG_AUTHPRIV
SEVERITY	The syslog level. The default is LOG_INFO (specified as info in /etc/syslog.conf). This may be changed dynamically with the SEVERITY option; see Table 10.3 on page 203.	Default
DOT	Causes a "." to be appended to all hostnames to reduce DNS search time. If you are not using DNS you probably want to turn this off, which is the default. Note that Red Hat 5.2/6.0 enables this feature, which means that if you are not using DNS, you should turn it off and recompile.	Yes
AUTH	Always attempt to look up the remote username with an RFC931 call. Default is off. When off, RFC931 calls will be made when required by the access control files.	No
RFC931_TIMEOUT	Sets the default time-out period for RFC931 queries to 10 seconds. This may be changed dynamically with the rfc931 option; see Table 10.3 on page 203.	Default
UMASK	Sets the umask for processes run under tcpd. The default is 022.	Default
ACCESS	Enables host access control. Default is on.	Yes
TABLES	Specifies the location of the access control files. By default, they are /etc/hosts.allow and /etc/hosts.deny.	Default

Table 10.1 TCP_Wrappers Compile-Time Options (Continued)

Option	Description	Red Hat Use
PARANOID	This option causes a reverse (IP address to hostname) lookup. When the reverse lookup provides conflicting information with respect to the forward lookup, this option automatically drops the connection. Turning this off merely disables the automated nature of this mechanism; paranoid mode may still be invoked with the PARANOID option; see Table 10.3 on page 203	No
HOSTNAME	Selects automated client hostname lookups. On, by default. Turning this off simply allows for control of hostname lookups through the access control files.	No
KILL_OPT	If on, refuse any connection request that has source routing turned on in the IP header. The default is off.	Yes

A few notes are warranted on Table 10.1. In the "Red Hat Use" column, "No" means that the indicated option was not used or was turned off (commented out with a # character in the Makefile). "Yes" means that the option was used or was turned on (uncommented). "Default" means that the Makefile includes more than one choice for this option, and the one that was originally uncommented was used. Make sure that you read through the README file and the man pages, hosts_access, hosts_options, tcpd, tcpdchk, and tcpdmatch. All of these files are originally found in the /usr/src/tcp_wrappers top-level build directory.

OH, BY THE WAY...

If you are wondering how to determine which compile-time options were used by the folks at Red Hat for their distribution, it turns out that they maintain this information in an appropriately named file with a .spec suffix. This file is part of the source RPM, so that when you install it, it will end up in the directory /usr/src/redhat/SPECS by default. For TCP_wrappers, the file is called, tcp_wrappers-7.6.spec. To determine the compile-time options, search this file for the Patch keyword, which will specify the name of the patch file; in this case it is tcpw7.2-config.patch, which is in the directory /usr/src/redhat/SOURCES (use locate or find to determine the location). The file is in simple diff output and may be applied to the TCP_wrappers Makefile with patch or read to determine which options were used. Note that this file will report a – in front of lines that were removed and a + in front of lines which were added. Although not the case for TCP_wrappers, you will often find additional compile-time options specified by the make invocation recorded in the .spec file. This file may also be used to build its program. See *Maximum RPM* as cited in *RPM Resources* on page 28 for further details.

Running make linux for TCP_Wrappers   Once you have determined which options you want to use, implement them by modifying the TCP_wrappers Makefile accordingly. Even if you are going to use the defaults, as described in

Table 10.1, you *must* still edit the `Makefile` and uncomment the appropriate single instance of `REAL_DAEMON_DIR` or make an appropriate modified entry. In addition, you will subsequently need to make the following changes before you run `make`.

Edit the `Makefile` in `/usr/src/tcp_wrappers` (or wherever you put the source tree) and change the entry

```
CFLAGS  = -O -DFACILITY=$(FACILITY) $(ACCESS) $(PARANOID) $(NETGROUP) \
```

to

```
CFLAGS  = -DFACILITY=$(FACILITY) $(ACCESS) $(PARANOID) $(NETGROUP) \
```

that is, remove `-O`. Continue editing the `Makefile` and change the entry

```
linux:
        @make REAL_DAEMON_DIR=$(REAL_DAEMON_DIR) STYLE=$(STYLE) \
        LIBS= RANLIB=ranlib ARFLAGS=rv AUX_OBJ=setenv.o \
        NETGROUP= TLI= EXTRA_CFLAGS="-DBROKEN_SO_LINGER" all
```

to

```
linux:
        @make REAL_DAEMON_DIR=$(REAL_DAEMON_DIR) STYLE=$(STYLE) \
        LIBS= RANLIB=ranlib ARFLAGS=rv AUX_OBJ= \
        NETGROUP= TLI= \
        EXTRA_CFLAGS="-DBROKEN_SO_LINGER -DSYS_ERRLIST_DEFINED" all
```

The changes shown here remove `setenv.o` and add `-DSYS_ERRLIST_DEFINED`.

Now you are ready to run `make linux`. Example 10-3 displays some of the output. The compilation is complete!

Example 10-3 Sample `make linux` Output

```
# make linux
make[1]: Entering directory '/usr/src/tcp_wrappers'
cc -DFACILITY=LOG_MAIL    -DHOSTS_ACCESS -DPARANOID  -DGETPEERNAME_BUG -
DBROKEN_FGETS -DLIBC_CALLS_STRTOK    -DDAEMON_UMASK=022 -DREAL_DAEMON_DIR='/usr/
sbin'   -DSEVERITY=LOG_INFO  -DRFC931_TIMEOUT=10  -DHOSTS_DENY='/etc/hosts.deny'
-DHOSTS_ALLOW='/etc/hosts.allow'    -DBROKEN_SO_LINGER -DSYS_ERRLIST_DEFINED   -
Dvsyslog=myvsyslog -DALWAYS_HOSTNAME -c tcpd.c
cc -DFACILITY=LOG_MAIL    -DHOSTS_ACCESS -DPARANOID  -DGETPEERNAME_BUG -
DBROKEN_FGETS -DLIBC_CALLS_STRTOK    -DDAEMON_UMASK=022 -DREAL_DAEMON_DIR='/usr/
sbin'   -DSEVERITY=LOG_INFO  -DRFC931_TIMEOUT=10  -DHOSTS_DENY='/etc/hosts.deny'
-DHOSTS_ALLOW='/etc/hosts.allow'    -DBROKEN_SO_LINGER -DSYS_ERRLIST_DEFINED   -
Dvsyslog=myvsyslog -DALWAYS_HOSTNAME -c hosts_access.c
...
<lots of ouput snipped>
...
cc -DFACILITY=LOG_MAIL    -DHOSTS_ACCESS -DPARANOID  -DGETPEERNAME_BUG -
DBROKEN_FGETS -DLIBC_CALLS_STRTOK    -DDAEMON_UMASK=022 -DREAL_DAEMON_DIR='/usr/
sbin'   -DSEVERITY=LOG_INFO  -DRFC931_TIMEOUT=10  -DHOSTS_DENY='/etc/hosts.deny'
-DHOSTS_ALLOW='/etc/hosts.allow'    -DBROKEN_SO_LINGER -DSYS_ERRLIST_DEFINED   -
Dvsyslog=myvsyslog -DALWAYS_HOSTNAME -c tcpdchk.c
```

Example 10-3 Sample `make linux` Output (Continued)

```
cc -DFACILITY=LOG_MAIL   -DHOSTS_ACCESS -DPARANOID  -DGETPEERNAME_BUG -
DBROKEN_FGETS -DLIBC_CALLS_STRTOK   -DDAEMON_UMASK=022 -DREAL_DAEMON_DIR='/usr/
sbin'   -DSEVERITY=LOG_INFO  -DRFC931_TIMEOUT=10  -DHOSTS_DENY='/etc/hosts.deny'
-DHOSTS_ALLOW='/etc/hosts.allow'   -DBROKEN_SO_LINGER -DSYS_ERRLIST_DEFINED  -
Dvsyslog=myvsyslog -DALWAYS_HOSTNAME -o tcpdchk tcpdchk.o fakelog.o inetcf.o
scaffold.o libwrap.a
make[1]: Leaving directory '/usr/src/tcp_wrappers'
#
```

Now, to install the software, follow the steps outlined in Example 10-4. If you wish to use alternate directories (such as /usr/local/sbin instead of /usr/ sbin, for example) or different permission settings, feel free to modify these steps accordingly. Also, note that the first step incorporates mkdir -p, which will not be necessary if the indicated directories already exist. If you execute it anyway, it will benignly report its inability to create directories that already exist. Note that the strip operation on the executable images removes the symbols therefrom, providing modest performance and security enhancements.

Example 10-4 Installing TCP_Wrappers

```
#mkdir -p /usr/{include,lib,man/man3,man/man5,man/man8,sbin}
#cp hosts_access.3 /usr/man/man3
#cp hosts_access.5 hosts_options.5 /usr/man/man5
#cp tcpd.8 tcpdchk.8 tcpdmatch.8 /usr/man/man8
#ln -sf hosts_access.5 /usr/man/man5/hosts.allow.5
#ln -sf hosts_access.5 /usr/man/man5/hosts.deny.5
#cp libwrap.a /usr/lib
#cp tcpd.h /usr/include
#install -m755 safe_finger /usr/sbin
#install -m755 tcpd /usr/sbin
#install -m755 tcpdchk /usr/sbin
#install -m755 tcpdmatch /usr/sbin
#install -m755 try-from /usr/sbin
#strip /usr/sbin/tcpd /usr/sbin/tcpdchk
#strip /usr/sbin/tcpdmatch /usr/sbin/safe_finger
#strip /usr/sbin/try-from
```

Optionally, you may also wish to copy the additional files

```
BLURB CHANGES README DISCLAIMER Banners.Makefile
```

to a standard resource directory. On Red Hat 5.2/6.0, this is normally /usr/ doc/tcp_wrappers-7.6.

Finally, you may clean the source tree (remove all generated object and binary files) by executing make clean, as displayed in Example 10-5.

Example 10-5 Cleaning Up after Installation

```
# make clean
rm -f tcpd miscd safe_finger tcpdmatch tcpdchk try-from *.[oa] core \
cflags
#
```

This completes the compilation and installation! Let's go on and see how TCP_wrappers works.

Access Control with TCP_Wrappers

TCP_wrappers implements access control through the use of two files—/etc/
hosts.allow and /etc/hosts.deny. As you might have guessed, the /etc/
hosts.allow file is an allow list, while the /etc/hosts.deny file is a deny list.
They share the same syntax, and both offer features that make them considerably more utilitarian than simple allow and deny lists. Let's have a look.

A very simple /etc/hosts.allow file is shown in Example 10-6. In this
example, we are allowing access to in.ftpd from any system in the 172.17.0.0
network and any system from the 139.6.77.0 subnetwork. For telnet access,
we are accepting any host in the eng.sprocket.com subdomain. Last, we will
respond to finger requests only from the list of hosts shown. In Example 10-7,
we show a trivial companion /etc/hosts.deny file to the allow file shown in
Example 10-6. The file in Example 10-7 has the effect of denying everything
that is not explicitly allowed in Example 10-6.

Example 10-6 Simple /etc/hosts.allow File

```
# wrapper allow list
in.ftpd: 172.17.,139.6.77.0/255.255.255.0
in.telnetd: .eng.sprocket.com
in.fingerd: nomad,topcat,otter,foghorn,\
            c58608-a,underdog
```

Example 10-7 Simple /etc/hosts.deny File

```
# wrapper deny list
# deny everything
ALL: ALL
```

These two files taken together constitute the complete set of restrictions
imposed on all services that are invoked through tcpd.

Note that blank lines and lines beginning with #, appearing in either
the deny or allow file, are ignored by tcpd. Also, as displayed in the last two
lines of Example 10-6, a \ character acts to continue a line by escaping the
newline. The general syntax of an entry (also called a *rule*) in either file is of
the form

```
daemon[,daemon,...] : client[,client,...] [: option : option ...]
```

NOTE

The availability of the options requires the use of the compile time flag -DPROCESS_
OPTIONS (see *Building TCP_Wrappers* on page 196). If this option is not chosen,
then the syntax of the entries becomes

```
daemon[,daemon,...] : client[,client,...] [: shell_command]
```

where shell_command may be any single shell command.

Table 10.2 Specifying the Clients in Allow and Deny Files

Client Syntax	Description
hostname	Specifies the hostname or IP address of the client system. If using the hostname, it must be resolvable to an IP address through /etc/hosts, NIS, or DNS.
.*domain*	Use of this syntax assumes DNS. Any hostname that resolves to *hostname.domain* is granted access. For example, if .*domain* is .acme.com, then any host in the DNS domain acme.com is a match.
net_number.	This syntax matches the portions of the IP address shown. For example, if *net_number.* is 87.3., then any system whose IP address begins with 87.3. will match regardless of the netmask being used.
@*netgroup*	The leading @ indicates that a netgroup is specified causing a match for every host in the netgroup. Netgroups can be used only to match clients.
net_number/netmask	This syntax provides for specifying subnetworks. For example, 144.20.16.0/255.255.240.0 will match all of the addresses from 144.20.16.0 through and including 144.20.31.255.

In this case, daemon must match a daemon name exactly as it appears in /etc/inetd.conf, and that daemon must be invoked through tcpd. Multiple daemons may be listed on the same line and separated by commas. After the daemon list, a colon must appear followed by a client or optionally a comma-separated list of clients. The clients may be specified in a variety of forms as described in Table 10.2.

After the client list, if a colon appears, it indicates that one or more optional keywords follow each, delimited by a colon. These options are available only if PROCESS_OPTIONS are turned on at compile-time (see STYLE in Table 10.1 on page 197). The options are listed in Table 10.3.

Table 10.3 Extending Capabilities in Allow and Deny Files

Optional Keyword	Description
nice *value*	Sets the nice *value* for the process.
keepalive	Causes the server to periodically send a message to the client. If the client does not respond, the connection is considered broken and will be terminated. For use only with TCP services.
linger *seconds*	Specifies the number of *seconds* after the termination of a connection during which the server will attempt to send undelivered data.

Table 10.3 Extending Capabilities in Allow and Deny Files (Continued)

Optional Keyword	Description
severity *facility.level*	Allows for the relocation of log messages through syslogd. Normally, the Red Hat 5.2/6.0 implementation will log to auth-priv.info. By using this option, you may change both the facility and level, such as with severity local0.warn. If you change the facility, then you may also need to make an appropriate entry in /etc/syslog.conf for this change to have an effect. Use of this option does not require the facility, but it does require the level.
allow deny	These options permit maintaining both allow and deny rules in the same file. If used, one of these two mutually exclusive options must appear last in the rule. See *Condensing TCP_Wrappers Rules into One File* on page 213 for examples.
spawn *shell_command*	Executes the specified *shell_command* as a child process. See *Using spawn* on page 210 for examples.
twist *shell_command*	Executes the specified *shell_command* as a replacement process to the process specified as the last field in the /etc/inetd.conf file. See *Using twist* on page 211, for examples.
rfc931 *seconds*	Causes the server to execute a call to the client in order to obtain the username invoking the request. The client must be running identd or similar RFC931 or RFC1413 compliant daemon. A time-out for the call may be specified in *seconds*; the default is 10 seconds. This option does not apply to UDP services.
banners *dir*	Specifies the fully qualified directory, *dir*, in which tcpd will search for a file of the same name as the wrapped daemon, the contents of which will be displayed prior to the login prompt. See *Using banners* on page 206, for example. This option is available only for certain TCP services. Services such as in.rshd in remote execution mode will not work with banners.
setenv *var value*	Allows for the establishment or modification of a shell environment variable (*var*); usually this option is followed by a spawn or twist option.
umask *value*	Sets the umask for any operations in a rule; *value* must be in octal.
user *username.group*	Causes the privileges within the rule to be set to the specified *username* and optionally the specified *group*.

It turns out that many of the options described in Table 10.3 may utilize information collected by tcpd. This is accomplished through a defined set of variables, listed in Table 10.4. The information is carried in letters and may be expanded with a preceding %, such as %a for client IP address and %d for the daemon name.

Table 10.4 Variable Expansions in Allow and Deny Files

Variable	Expansion
`%a`	Client IP address.
`%A`	Server IP address.
`%c`	Becomes `user@host`, `user@IPaddress`, `hostname`, or `IPaddress`, depending upon what is available.
`%d`	The name of the daemon.
`%h`	The client hostname or IP address if hostname unavailable.
`%H`	The server hostname or IP address if hostname unavailable.
`%n`	The client hostname. Resolves to unknown if host is `unknown` and to `paranoid` if a reverse DNS lookup was performed and the hostname provided by DNS does not match the hostname claimed by the client.
`%N`	The server hostname.
`%p`	The process identifier (PID) of the daemon.
`%s`	Becomes daemon name, `daemon@host`, or `daemon@IPaddress`, depending upon available information. See *Distinguishing Source Interfaces for Multihomed Servers* on page 213, for example use of the `daemon@host` pattern.
`%u`	The client username. Resolves to `unknown` if not known. Use of this variable will cause `tcpd` to attempt an RFC931 call.
`%%`	Resolves to `%`.

There are also a number of wildcard characters available for use in these files, such as ALL (see the last line of Example 10-7). These are described in Table 10.5.

NOTE

> The `tcpd` stops when it finds the first daemon/client match. In short, it will grant access when it finds a matching pair in `/etc/hosts.allow`; access will be denied if a matching pair is found in `/etc/hosts.deny`. Otherwise access will be *allowed*. Therefore, make sure that you configure the deny file appropriately because the default behavior is to allow unless directed to the contrary. On the other hand, if neither file exists, then all wrapped daemons will deny access. Thus, you can turn off access to all wrapped services simply by renaming the allow and deny files. The only exception to these rules is that the `localhost` is always granted access.

As we can see, the TCP-wrappers access control files syntax gives us a lot of flexibility. Let's take a look at what we can do with this syntax in some more complex examples.

Table 10.5 Wildcards in Allow and Deny Files

Wildcard	Description
ALL	Matches everything.
LOCAL	Matches any hostname that does not contain a "." character.
KNOWN	Matches any user whose username is known. Matches any host whose hostname and IP address are known. Examples are given in *Using twist* on page 211 and in subsequent sections.
UNKNOWN	Matches any user whose username is unknown. Matches any host whose hostname or IP address is not known. Examples are given in *Using twist* on page 211 and in subsequent sections.
PARANOID	Matches any host for which there is a hostname/IP address mismatch based on a reverse DNS lookup of the IP address. If the compile-time option -DPARANOID is used, all such connection attempts are automatically dropped and this option does not control access. The Red Hat 5.2/6.0 implementation does **not** compile with DPARANOID. See *Building TCP_Wrappers* on page 196 for more information regarding compile-time options.
EXCEPT	This keyword is actually an operator that may appear in either daemon lists or client lists. Examples are given in *Using spawn* on page 210 and in following sections.

Using banners   Suppose that you want to display a message to anyone connecting to your system *before* they attempt to log in. You can accomplish this very simply using the banners option in either the allow or deny file or both. Example 10-8 provides an example entry for in.telnetd in the /etc/hosts.allow file.

Example 10-8 banners Entry for in.telnetd

```
# wrapper allow file
in.ftpd: 172.17.,139.6.77.0/255.255.255.0
in.telnetd: .eng.sprocket.com: banners /etc/security/banners/allow
in.fingerd: nomad,topcat,otter,foghorn,\
            c58608-a,underdog
```

The in.telnetd entry with the banners option, in this case, will cause tcpd to look for the file

      /etc/security/banners/allow/in.telnetd

and display its contents prior to posting the login prompt. You will need to create this file—which you may do manually or use the Banners.Makefile as described in *Using Banners.Makefile* on page 208. If the contents of this file appears as shown in Example 10-9 then when Mary logs in from underdog.eng.sprocket.com, she sees the message displayed in Example 10-10.

Example 10-9 Sample Allow Banner File

```
# in.telnetd allow message
Welcome to %H.
You are logging in from %c.
Remember all activity on this system is recorded.
If you don't like this policy leave now!
```

Example 10-10 Banner Displayed upon Connection

```
underdog$ telnet topcat
Trying 172.17.33.111...
Connected to topcat.
Escape character is '^]'.
Welcome to topcat.eng.sprocket.com.
You are logging in from underdog.eng.sprocket.com.
Remember all activity on this system is recorded.
If you don't like this policy leave now!

Red Hat Linux release 5.2 (Apollo)
Kernel 2.0.36 on an i686
login:
```

Notice that the message appears prior to the `login` prompt. Notice also that `%c`, in `/etc/security/banners/allow/in.telnetd`, as shown in Example 10-9, expands to `underdog.eng.sprocket.com`, and `%H` expands to `topcat.eng.sprocket.com`, as defined in Table 10.4 on page 205. Recall that `%c` expands to the information available to the server—`topcat` in this case—and note in particular that no user name appears. Let's modify Example 10-8 on page 206 as given in Example 10-11.

Example 10-11 Modified `banners` Entry for `in.telnetd`

```
# wrapper allow file
in.ftpd: 172.17.,139.6.77.0/255.255.255.0
in.telnetd: .eng.sprocket.com: rfc931: \
          banners /etc/security/banners/allow
in.fingerd: nomad,topcat,otter,foghorn,\
          c58608-a,underdog
```

Then the line from Example 10-10

```
You are logging in from underdog.eng.sprocket.com.
```

becomes

```
You are logging in from mary@underdog.eng.sprocket.com.
```

because the option `rfc931` caused `tcpd` to issue a call to `identd` on the client `underdog` and to obtain the username `mary`. If `identd` were not running on `underdog`, or if it were running but declined to supply the username information, the `rfc931` call would simply add no new information. It is important to note that, if a rule references `%u`, it will implicitly make the `rfc931` call.

The log entry generated by the successful `telnet` connection by Mary would appear as follows in `/var/log/secure` (default location on Red Hat 5.2/6.0):

```
Apr 11 09:23:24 topcat in.telnetd[3632]: connect from under-
dog.eng.sprocket.com
```

The information contained in this line includes the following from left to right:
date and time (`Apr 11 09:23:24`), server hostname (`topcat`), daemon name
(`in.telnetd`), PID in brackets (`3632`), success (`connect`) or failure (`refused
connect`), and the client hostname (`underdog.eng.sprocket.com`).

Using deny `banners` works identically except that the option would
appear in the `/etc/hosts.deny` file. Also make sure that you specify a different
directory for the deny message. An example deny banner is given in the following section.

Using `Banners.Makefile`.   It turns out that there is a handy `Makefile` that
you may use to create these banner files. If you are using Red Hat 5.2/6.0, you
will find it in `/usr/doc/tcp_wrappers-7.6/Banners.Makefile`. Otherwise, if you
pulled down TCP_wrappers from one of the Internet sites, you will find it in
`tcp_wrappers-7.6` subdirectory of the build directory. In either case, copy `Ban-
ners.Makefile` to your `banners` directory. We'll use `/etc/security/banners/
allow` for the allow messages and `/etc/security/banners/deny` for the deny
messages in our examples. Example 10-12 depicts the necessary steps to effect
this copy. Note that we changed the name of the file from `Banners.Makefile` to
`Makefile`. This will save typing when we execute `make`, since `make` expects its
`Makefile` to be named `Makefile`, `makefile`—or `GNUmakefile`. If it's not one of
those names—for example, if it were `Banners.Makefile`—you would need to
execute `make -f Banners.Makefile`.

Example 10-12 Copying `Banners.Makefile`

```
# cd /usr/doc/tcp_wrappers-7.6/
# cp Banners.Makefile /etc/security/banners/allow/Makefile
# cp Banners.Makefile /etc/security/banners/deny/Makefile
```

All you have to do is create a file called `prototype` in each of the two
directories which contain the desired message. For example, in the directory `/
etc/security/banners/deny`, we might create a `prototype` file that looks like
the one shown in Example 10-13.

Example 10-13 Sample Deny `prototype` File

```
# Deny Prototype
Hello, %u@%h trying to connect to %d.
What are you doing here? You aren't authorized and
I'm afraid I've logged this attempt. Do it again and
I'll have to tell your mother.
```

Once you have written the prototype, you can execute `make` in the appropriate directory as exhibited in Example 10-14. Note that the `ls` output
shows that the `Makefile` caused three banner files—`in.ftpd`, `in.rlogind`, and
`in.telnetd`—to be generated. The `Makefile` is also set up to create messages
for `finger` and `rsh` (however, the banner will not be displayed if `rsh` is used

for remote execution). Example 10-15 shows how to make the message for in.fingerd.

Example 10-14 Output of make and ls in /etc/security/banners/deny

```
# make
cp prototype in.telnetd
chmod 644 in.telnetd
sed 's/^/220-/' prototype > in.ftpd
chmod 644 in.ftpd
echo 'main() { write(1,"",1); return(0); }' >nul.c
cc  -s -o nul nul.c
rm -f nul.c
( ./nul ; cat prototype ) > in.rlogind
chmod 644 in.rlogind
# ls
Makefile     in.ftpd       in.rlogind  in.telnetd  nul          prototype
```

Example 10-15 Creating the Deny Message for in.fingerd

```
# make in.fingerd
cp prototype in.fingerd
chmod 644 in.fingerd
#
```

If we add an appropriate entry to the /etc/hosts.deny file—for example

```
in.fingerd: ALL: banners /etc/security/banners/deny
```

then whenever an unauthorized (not found in the /etc/hosts.allow file) finger attempt is made, the message will be displayed.

Now let's see what happens when Joe attempts to finger the user mary on topcat. The outcome is shown in Example 10-16.

Example 10-16 Unauthorized finger Attempt

```
$ finger mary@topcat.eng.sprocket.com
[topcat.eng.sprocket.com]
Hello joe@sly.no.good.org trying to connect to in.fingerd.
What are you doing here? You are not authorized and
I'm afraid I've logged this attempt. Do it again and
I'll have to tell your mother.
```

The log generated by this failed attempt would appear as,

```
Apr 11 13:56:04 topcat in.fingerd[3907]: refused connect from
sly.no.good.org
```

in the /var/log/secure file.

If you wish to have distinct messages for each daemon, you will need to either manually modify each file or create a customized script or Makefile to do it for you. You may also create additional directories as needed utilizing different messages for different circumstances. For example, you may wish to create special messages for clients that resolve to UNKNOWN (see Table 10.5 on page 206). One way to accomplish this is to place the following entry in your /etc/hosts.deny file

```
ALL: UNKNOWN: banners /etc/security/banners/unknown
```

Then any client who connects to this server and for whom the server cannot determine either the hostname or the IP address (either of which may be due to network problems, such as the DNS server not responding) will be denied access and a suitable message may be displayed.

As noted in Table 10.3 on page 203, you cannot use `banners` with UDP services nor with certain TCP services such as `in.rshd` and `in.talkd`.

Using spawn   The `spawn` option allows you to specify any shell command within a given rule. This includes any custom shell script or program. Let's take a look at some examples.

The TCP_wrappers package includes a special finger program—`safe_finger`—that implements numerous safety mechanisms to protect against finger servers including: limiting the amount of data it will accept, limiting the line length it will accept, and implementing a hard time-out limit. The `safe_finger` program accepts the same arguments as `finger`. The purpose of using finger from TCP_wrappers is to obtain more information about whoever is trying to establish a connection to your system. If the connecting client provides a response to the `safe_finger` probe, then you can use this information in many ways. Example 10-17 displays a sample entry in the `/etc/hosts.deny` file. It uses `safe_finger` and then pipes the result to a mail message that gets sent to root. This procedure of querying the client based on an incoming request from that client is called a *booby trap* in the TCP_wrappers documentation.

Example 10-17 Sample Use of EXCEPT and safe_finger

```
# hosts.deny
ALL EXCEPT in.fingerd: ALL: spawn (/usr/sbin/safe_finger  -lp @%h | \
    /bin/mail -s "Connect attempt from %h using %d" root) &: \
    banners /etc/security/banners/deny
```

WARNING!

Be careful about using ALL in conjunction with shell commands such as `/usr/sbin/safe_finger`. In addition to the potential `finger` loop problem described in the next paragraph, it may be that the invocation of a shell command may not work as expected with certain services. For example, the ALL entry in Example 10-17 will capture incoming `portmap` requests (see *The Portmapper* on page 218), by default, on Red Hat 5.2/6.0 systems. Given this rule, a `portmap` request that is denied will cause the generation of the e-mail, but will benignly fail the `safe_finger`. Other commands may not be so friendly, so make sure that you test things out before you go live!

The `-l` flag used with `safe_finger` forces formatting of the response to one user per line, making it easier to subsequently parse; the `-p` flag suppresses plan and project information. Notice that we will not respond to incoming `finger` attempts (EXCEPT `in.fingerd`) with our `safe_finger`; this avoids potential infinite `finger` loops in the case that the client system responds to `finger` queries with a `finger` of its own! Now that we have this file set up, when Joe attempts unauthorized access, say, via `rlogin` or `ftp` or `telnet`, then he will get the same deny message as shown in Example 10-16 on page 209, and additionally root on the server (`topcat` in this case) will get an e-mail message similar to that shown in Example 10-18.

Example 10-18 E-Mail Generated by Example 10-17 Entry

```
From root   Sun Apr 11 05:16:31 1999
Date: Sun, 11 Apr 1999 05:16:31 -0600
From: root <root@topcat>
To: root@topcat
Subject: Connect attempt from sly.no.good.org using in.telnetd

 [sly.no.good.org]
 Login: root                          Name: root
 Directory: /root                     Shell: /bin/bash
 On since Sat Apr 10 20:51 (MDT) on tty1    18 hours 57 minutes idle
    (messages off)
 On since Sat Apr 10 20:52 (MDT) on ttyp0 from :0.0
    17 hours idle
 On since Sat Apr 10 21:47 (MDT) on ttyp1 from :0.0
    13 minutes 30 seconds idle
 Mail last read Sun Apr 11 04:04 1999 (MDT)

 Login: joe                           Name: Joseph James
 Directory: /home/joe                 Shell: /bin/bash
 On since Sun Apr 11 15:47 (MDT) on ttyp2 from topcat
    1 second idle
 No mail.
```

As you can see, a lot of information can be obtained through `finger` (which is one reason why it is suggested that `in.fingerd` be turned off). Since `spawn` allows for any shell command, there are a variety of actions that can be taken based on the rules provided. For example, we might replace the invocation of `/bin/mail` in Example 10-17 with a different command, such as a script that keeps count of the number of times a particular user makes unauthorized connection attempts, and, when it reaches a threshold (like three such attempts), an action is performed, such as generating a page to the administrator or shutting down a particular service. In fact, such a script does exist in the public domain—it is called `swatch`—and we will explore its capabilities in Chapter 17.

Using `twist` The `twist` option causes a specified daemon or command to be invoked instead of the daemon indicated in `/etc/inetd.conf`. For example, if `/etc/inetd.conf` has an entry such as

```
    ftp stream tcp     nowait root     /usr/sbin/tcpd in.ftpd -a -l
```

then, normally, whenever a successful request for `ftp` is encountered, `/usr/sbin/in.ftpd -l -a` will be invoked. Suppose that you have configured an anonymous `ftp` environment (see the resources cited in *Internet Services*

Resources on page 255 for more information about anonymous ftp servers) for internal use. Further suppose that your internal Security Policy requires all systems to run identd, but that it also specifies that internal access to ftp servers, like the one in the example above, is critical to productivity. To satisfy this criteria, you can implement TCP_wrappers to take different actions based on whether a given user is identifiable; you can also, as we see in Example 10-19, invoke different daemons based on the availability of a particular user identity. As indicated in Table 10.5 on page 206, tcpd will report KNOWN if a user's identity is known and UNKNOWN if it is not. Notice the use of @KNOWN in both in.ftpd rules in Example 10-19. Recall from Table 10.5 on page 206 that, in the case of client lists, this will match only if both the hostname and IP address are known. Therefore, a result of UNKNOWN for a hostname may mean that hostname resolution services are not working properly. The presence of this option forces a reverse lookup (regardless of compile-time options; see *Building TCP_Wrappers* on page 196). Further, in Example 10-19 we see entries in an /etc/hosts.allow file that distinguish between known and unknown users in the following way. By virtue of the fact that the entry KNOWN@KNOWN appears, whenever an incoming ftp request occurs tcpd will generate an RFC931 call (regardless of compile-time options) to get the incoming username. If it is successful, then the rule matches and in.ftpd -a -l is invoked from the compile-time daemon source directory (/usr/sbin in the case of Red Hat 5.2/6.0). Note that the -l flag to in.ftpd causes in.ftpd to log the connection, and the -a flag causes in.ftpd to check the /etc/ftpaccess file. See the references cited in *Internet Services Resources* on page 255 and the ftpd(8) man page for more information.

Example 10-19 Sample /etc/hosts.allow Using twist

```
# hosts.allow
in.ftpd: KNOWN@KNOWN

in.ftpd: UNKNOWN@KNOWN: banners \
   /etc/security/banners/unknown: spawn (/bin/echo "Policy Violation!" \
   | /bin/mail -s "%h isn't running identd!" root@%H,root@%h)&: \
   twist PATH=/usr/sbin/extra;exec in.ftpd -i -o -l
in.ftpd: PARANOID: banners /etc/security/banners/paranoid: \
   spawn (/bin/echo "%n reported when %u@%h connected using %d" | \
   /bin/mail -s "Alert! Hostname Lookup Failure!" root@%H)& :deny
in.ftpd: ALL: deny
```

On the other hand, if the request to the client for the username fails, the username will resolve to UNKNOWN. In such a case, the connection is still allowed, but a special banner is displayed (presumably notifying the user that identd is not running on the client), and e-mail is sent to both root on the server (root@%H) and root on the client (root@%h) notifying the administrator that a Security Policy violation has occurred. Finally, we see the use of the twist option, which causes /usr/sbin/extra/in.ftpd -i -o -l to be invoked instead of /usr/sbin/in.ftpd -a -l. The use of PATH=/usr/sbin/extra (it is used in this example simply to illustrate the capability) causes the change in the directory path and is required only if the daemon you wish to invoke is not in /usr/sbin (Red Hat 5.2/6.0 default). Note that the -i and -o flags to in.ftpd cause the logging of uploaded and downloaded files, respectively, to /var/log/xferlog, by default.

Next, in Example 10-19, if the client resolves to PARANOID (reverse lookup of IP address to hostname disagrees with forward lookup of hostname to IP address) on the server, tcpd displays a special message to the client, sends e-mail to root notifying the administrator of the problem, and then denies access with the deny keyword. In an internal environment, as is the case with this example, it is quite likely that PARANOID reports are indicative of networking troubles, nonetheless, such reports should always be thoroughly investigated. The use of PARANOID in these files assumes that the -DPARANOID option was **not** chosen at compile time (as is the case with Red Hat 5.2/6.0). Finally, the last line of the example denies ftp access under any other circumstance.

Condensing TCP_Wrappers Rules into One File   In the previous section, we saw the use of the deny option in an /etc/hosts.allow file. Use of this option, along with the allow option, will permit you to build a single file for access control. This approach may well be a convenience under circumstances in which the rules are relatively straightforward. More lengthy rule sets, such as those configured for a major server system, may be organized more easily in a typical two-file system.

Example 10-20 presents a simple example of a one file access control list. In this case, /etc/hosts.allow is used. Note the use of the keyword LOCAL. This will match any host that does not have a "." in its name. Since this is an allow file, the behavior is to allow matched entries. The last entry overrides this behavior with the deny keyword. You could accomplish the same thing in a deny file, using the allow keyword as appropriate. Whether you use the deny or allow keyword, it must appear last in the rule.

Example 10-20 A Single File Access Control List

```
# hosts.allow file
# Internal systems only allow telnet and ftp
in.ftpd: KNOWN@LOCAL: banners /etc/security/banners/allow
in.telnetd: KNOWN@LOCAL: banners /etc/security/banners/allow
ALL: ALL: banners /etc/security/banners/deny: deny
```

Another use of these keywords is to keep complex rule sets in one file as in Example 10-19 on page 212. In that case, all of the rules regarding in.ftpd are maintained in one location making it easier to understand and troubleshoot.

Distinguishing Source Interfaces for Multihomed Servers   It may be that you are putting together a single ftp server with multiple network interfaces. In such a case, you can use TCP_wrappers to direct daemon invocation based on the destination IP address (described as server endpoint patterns in the TCP_wrappers documentation) used in the requesting packets. Example 10-21 gives us a very simple example. In this example, we use the form `dae-mon@IPaddress`; however, any client form, as described in Table 10.2 on page 203, may be used instead of the IP address. This is one way to cause an incoming `ftp` request to be serviced based on destination IP addresses.

Example 10-21 Sample Allow Entries Using Server Endpoint Patterns

```
# hosts.allow
# ftp server entries
in.ftpd@24.1.11.113: ALL EXCEPT .evil.com:twist in.ftpd
in.ftpd@24.2.8.118: ALL EXCEPT .evil.com:twist in.wuftpd
```

NOTE

You cannot use EXCEPT with network numbers in client lists. For example, `172.17. EXCEPT 172.17.1.3` will not have the desired behavior.

Putting It All Together   Building the `hosts.allow` and `hosts.deny` files takes some consideration. You will probably end up with a variety of configurations depending upon the use of a given system—typical desktop systems will likely have very simple access control lists; server systems will have somewhat more complex lists; systems exposed to untrusted networks, such as the Internet, may have highly specialized lists.

Perhaps the best approach to determining the prototypical list for a given type of system is to consider what that system does. Make a list of services that the system needs to provide and, very important, an associated list of clients. If you aren't sure whether a service is to be provided, deny it (unless your Security Policy indicates otherwise). You can always go back and add it later.

As an example, let's suppose we have an internal server that provides `ftp`, time, and POP3 services to the internal networks. All POP3 services are localized on two networks—172.17.0.0 and 172.18.0.0; all other networks use `sendmail`. Further assume that in this environment there are engineering test networks—172.19.0.0 through and including 172.19.15.255—that do not utilize the time services but do utilize `ftp`. For simplicity, suppose that all networks in this environment begin with 172 in the first octet of the IP address. Every system runs `identd`, except the PC and MAC clients that live on either the 172.17.0.0 or 172.18.0.0 network. Example 10-22 provides an allow file matching these criteria. Remember that `tcpd` stops when it reaches the first match, so order is important in this file. Also notice that we do not use the form KNOWN@KNOWN for `in.timed`. This is because a username query to the client will not work with `in.timed`. The remaining entries are quite similar to those previously discussed. We provide more activity around `ftp` because it is more likely to be used to compromise the system.

Example 10-22 Working Allow File

```
# hosts.allow
in.ftpd: KNOWN@KNOWN, UNKNOWN@172.17., UNKNOWN@172.18.

in.ftpd: UNKNOWN@KNOWN: banners \
    /etc/security/banners/unknown: spawn (/bin/echo "Policy Violation!" \
    | /bin/mail -s "%h isn't running identd!" root@%H,root@%h)&

in.ftpd: PARANOID: banners /etc/security/banners/unknown: \
    spawn (/bin/echo "%n reported when %u@%h connected using %d" | \
    /bin/mail -s "Alert! Hostname Lookup Failure!" root@%H)& :deny

in.timed: 172.19.0.0/255.255.240.0; deny

in.timed: KNOWN

ALL: ALL: deny
```

In addition you may wish to create an /etc/hosts.deny file that contains
the single line

```
ALL: ALL
```

for clarity, although it is not necessary because of the final line in Example 10-22.

In Example 10-23, we view three log entries generated by attempted
access to the server topcat using the /etc/hosts.allow file shown in Example
10-22. The first two lines reflect granted access to ftp; however, notice that in
the second case there is no username. This means that the line containing
mary@underdog matched the first in.ftpd rule in Example 10-22, while the line
containing roadrunner matched the second in.ftpd rule. The last line in
Example 10-23 occurs because of the first in.timed rule in Example 10-22. A
more useful way to check the rules is discussed in the next section.

Example 10-23 Sample Log Entries

```
Apr 11 14:03:57 topcat in.ftpd[3947]: connect from mary@underdog
Apr 11 14:04:29 topcat in.ftpd[3948]: connect from roadrunner
Apr 12 12:38:04 topcat in.timed[819]: refused connect from 172.19.1.3
```

While there is certainly tremendous value in building access control lists
for the purpose of controlling access, it is not the only thing that can be done
with TCP_wrappers. Consider the case of a DMZ or firewall system (discussed
further in Chapter 16). One approach to establishing an early warning system on such systems is to leave many of the ports most likely to be attacked
open in /etc/inetd.conf and booby-trap them. For example, you might not
comment out references to in.rlogind and in.ftpd in /etc/inetd.conf; then
you could create an /etc/hosts.deny file that looks something like the one in
Example 10-24. Notice that we do not use the standard facility and level for
these entries; instead we use local5 (arbitrarily chosen, but it should not be
used for anything else). This way, you can configure /etc/syslog.conf (see
Chapter 8) to cause log messages generated by activity associated with this
deny file to a separate file and then process it with a utility such as logcheck
or swatch (discussed in Chapter 17). You must watch these files carefully,
however. If someone perpetrates a DoS attack against a system configured in

this way and the perpetrator uses spoofed but valid IP addresses, this system will `finger` a lot of innocent sites! You may decide, therefore, not to use the `safe_finger` request as shown in Example 10-24. However, the log files alone may prove their value in identifying a potential attack.

Example 10-24 Use of Deny File as an Early Warning Mechanism

```
# hosts.deny
# Nobody should ever try to connect via these services
# So let's find out as much as we can and log, log, log

in.rlogind: ALL: severity local5.warn: spawn (/usr/sbin/safe_finger \
    -lp @%h | logger -p local5.warn; /bin/echo "%u attempted %d from \
    %h" | /bin/mail -s "Someone's Knocking!" root)&

in.ftpd: ALL: severity local5.warn: spawn (/usr/sbin/safe_finger \
    -lp @%h | logger -p local5.warn; /bin/echo "%u attempted %d from \
    %h" | /bin/mail -s "Someone's Knocking!" root)&
```

OH, BY THE WAY...

If you don't know what daemon name to specify in an allow or deny list, you can put an allow ALL daemons rule in the file temporarily (and in a contained, trusted environment), and then issue a request from a client to the server. TCP_wrappers will generate a log entry that will include the name of the daemon it expects to see in the access control rules. Use this information to modify your rules accordingly.

TCP_Wrappers Utility Programs

The TCP_wrappers distribution includes three utility programs. They are `tcpdchk`, `tcpdmatch`, and `try-from`. These utilities exist for the purpose of testing your TCP_wrappers configuration.

Using `tcpdchk`   The `tcpdchk` utility provides syntax checking of the /etc/hosts.allow and /etc/hosts.deny files against the /etc/inetd.conf file. This is a good utility to run when you first implement /etc/hosts.allow and /etc/hosts.deny and subsequently when you make changes to those files.

There are four flags associated with this utility. They are described in Table 10.6.

Table 10.6 Flags of `tcpdchk`

Flag	Description
-a	Displays additional information whenever access is granted without an explicit `allow` keyword.
-v	Verbose. Normally `tcpdchk` outputs only warnings and errors.
-d	Uses the `hosts.allow` and `hosts.deny` files in the current working directory. Useful for debugging.
-i *filename*	Uses the specified *filename* instead of /etc/inetd.conf.

Example 10-25 illustrates the use of `tcpdchk`.

Example 10-25 Sample `tcpdchk` Output

```
# tcpdchk -av
>>> Rule /etc/hosts.allow line 10:
daemons:  in.ftpd
clients:  KNOWN@.eng.sprocket.com
warning: /etc/hosts.allow, line 10: implicit "allow" at end of rule
access:   granted
>>> Rule /etc/hosts.allow line 11:
daemons:  in.ftpd
clients:  UNKNOWN@.eng.sprocket.com
warning: /etc/hosts.allow, line 11: implicit "allow" at end of rule
access:   granted
>>> Rule /etc/hosts.allow line 12:
daemons:  in.ftpd
clients:  PARANOID
option:   deny
access:   denied
...
<lots of output snipped>
...
>>> Rule /etc/hosts.allow line 15:
daemons:  ALL
clients:  LOCAL
option:   banners /etc/security/banners/allow
warning: /etc/hosts.allow, line 15: implicit "allow" at end of rule
access:   granted
>>> Rule /etc/hosts.deny line 9:
daemons:  ALL
clients:  ALL
option:   banners /etc/security/banners/deny
access:   denied
#
```

Using `tcpdmatch` The `tcpdmatch` utility takes a daemon/client pair as input and checks the rules for a match. It then provides a resolution, either denying or granting access. Example 10-26 exhibits its typical use.

Example 10-26 Sample `tcpdmatch` Output

```
# tcpdmatch in.ftpd underdog
client:   hostname underdog.eng.sprocket.com
client:   address  172.17.55.124
server:   process  in.ftpd
matched:  /etc/hosts.allow line 11
access:   granted
#
```

As you add rules, `tcpdmatch` is a very useful tool for checking anything you add. It is also an excellent utility for determining the behavior of the various keywords and options described in this text.

Using `try-from` The `try-from` utility tests the hostname and username lookup mechanism. You may use `rsh` to test it, which requires running `in.rshd`, setting up the appropriate allow entry in `/etc/hosts.allow` (or `/etc/hosts.deny` with the `allow` option), and creating an entry in `/etc/hosts.equiv` or in the appropriate `$HOME/.rhosts` file on the server. Just be sure to close that hole after your tests! Once done, you may execute `try-from` as in Example 10-27. Notice that the values of the variables captured by `tcpd` are listed. See Table 10.4 on page 205 for a description of these variables.

Example 10-27 Using `try-from`

```
$ rsh topcat /usr/sbin/try-from
client address   (%a): 172.17.55.124
client hostname  (%n): underdog.eng.sprocket.com
client username  (%u): mary
client info      (%c): mary@underdog.eng.sprocket.com
server address   (%A): 172.17.33.111
server hostname  (%N): topcat.eng.sprocket.com
server process   (%d): try-from
server info      (%s): try-from@topcat.eng.sprocket.com
$
```

TCP_Wrappers Vulnerabilities

The TCP_wrappers program itself is very mature and, thanks to the continuing attention of its author and many users throughout the world, bugs are identified and fixed quickly. The vulnerabilities associated with its use usually come from the other programs it depends on, such as DNS and `identd`.

There are all sorts of things that can occur that will cause a breach of the security provided by TCP_wrappers. If a system granted access by the wrappers is compromised, for example, then there are no defenses. If DNS names and IP addresses are spoofed, it will be impossible for TCP_wrappers to detect a PARANOID condition. DoS attacks can fill up the log files. The `identd` daemon on a remote system may be configured to provide false information. In short, there are no guarantees.

The TCP_wrappers package does provide a fair amount of logging of connection activity and it also forces would-be bad-guys to do a lot more work to compromise a system using the wrappers. In any event, this should not be your only tool or your only line of defense. In particular, any system exposed to an untrusted external network such as the Internet should be additionally configured with `ipchains`. Critical internal systems should take advantage of `ipchains` as well. See Chapter 16 for a detailed look at the use of `ipchains`.

THE PORTMAPPER

For a complete discussion of the purpose and general functionality of the `portmap` daemon, check out the references listed in *General TCP/IP Networking Resources* on page 39 in Chapter 10. The purpose of this section is to describe the enhanced Portmapper Version 4[1] (default in Red Hat 5.2/6.0)

---

1. Some System V.4-based UNIX systems, such as Solaris 2.x, use `rpcbind` instead of `portmap`. Wietse Venema also maintains an enhanced version of `rpcbind` for those systems.

access control and logging capabilities. Like TCP_wrappers, this version of the portmapper was written and continues to be maintained by Wietse Venema.

If you are running Red Hat 5.2/6.0, this version of the portmapper is already installed and running on your system. The source code is available in RPM format either from the CD or from `ftp://ftp.redhat.com/`. You may also obtain the source in `tar` format from

> `ftp://coast.cs.purdue.edu/pub/tools/unix/portmap/`

Once again, whatever the source, obtain and check the signatures.

Building the Portmapper

In all likelihood, if you already have a compiled `portmap` Version 4, you won't need to recompile because there aren't many functional options (unlike TCP_wrappers). For the purposes of our discussion, we assume that the source tree is installed under `/usr/src/portmap`. The preparatory steps for compiling and linking `portmap` are quite similar to those for TCP_wrappers. All options are contained in the `Makefile`. Table 10.7 lists the configurable

Table 10.7 Portmapper Version 4 Compile-Time Options

Option	Description	Red Hat Use
FACILITY	Specifies the `syslog` facility to be used for logging. Default is `LOG_MAIL`.	`LOG_AUTH`
HOSTS_ACCESS	Enables the use of `/etc/hosts.allow` and `/etc/hosts.deny` access control files. Default is on.	Yes
CHECK_PORT	Causes requests to register/unregister services on a privileged port to be allowed only if the request itself comes from a privileged port. Default is on. Turn this off if your system disallows the use of privileged ports by the portmapper.	Yes
SA_LEN	Turn this on if your system uses variable length socket address structures. Default is off.	No
ZOMBIES	When the portmapper is configured for verbose logging (a run-time option discussed in subsequent sections), zombie processes may be left. Default is off.	Yes and -Dlint
ULONG	If the operating system does not support the `u_long` definition, turn this on. Default is off.	No
WRAP_DIR	Specifies the directory location for `libwrap.a`. Default is `../tcp_wrappers`.	`/usr/lib`
AUX	Additional object files for linking. Default includes `daemon.o` and `strerror.o`.	Default
LIBS	Additional libraries for linking. Default includes `-lrpc`.	Default

`Makefile` options, along with the Red Hat 5.2/6.0 choices (as defined in Table 10.1 on page 197). Notice that the compilation options have the `portmap` log output to the `auth` facility instead of the `authpriv` facility. Therefore, all `portmap` log entries will appear in `/var/log/messages` instead of `/var/log/secure` by default. Also, the `ZOMBIE` compilation option is modified for use with Red Hat 5.2/6.0 in a *required* way. It is noted below.

After you have determined which options you want to use, you will need to modify the `Makefile` accordingly for them to take effect. You will also need to modify the `Makefile` as follows (for Red Hat 5.2/6.0).

Edit the `Makefile` and change

```
COPT    = -Dconst= -Dperror=xperror $(HOSTS_ACCESS) $(CHECK_PORT) \
```

to

```
COPT    = -Dconst= $(HOSTS_ACCESS) $(CHECK_PORT) \
```

removing `-Dperror=xperror` from the line. Also, change the line

```
CFLAGS  = $(COPT) -O $(NSARCHS) $(SETPGRP)
```

to

```
CFLAGS  = $(COPT) $(NSARCHS) $(SETPGRP)
```

removing `-O` from the line. Finally, change the line

```
# ZOMBIES = -DIGNORE_SIGCHLD     # AIX 4.x, HP-UX 9.x
```

to

```
ZOMBIES = -DIGNORE_SIGCHLD -Dlint
```

by uncommenting the line and adding `-Dlint`.

Once you have made all the necessary changes, you can execute `make` as shown in Example 10-28. This will generate three binaries: `portmap`, `pmap_dump`, and `pmap_set`, each of which is discussed in the following sections.

Example 10-28 Output of `make` for Portmapper

```
# make
cc -Dconst= -DHOSTS_ACCESS -DCHECK_PORT  -DFACILITY=LOG_AUTH   -
DIGNORE_SIGCHLD -Dlint            -c portmap.c -o portmap.o
...
<lots of output snipped>
...
cc -Dconst= -DHOSTS_ACCESS -DCHECK_PORT  -DFACILITY=LOG_AUTH   -
DIGNORE_SIGCHLD -Dlint            -o pmap_set pmap_set.c
#
```

Next you will need to install what you've compiled. Initially, you merely need to copy the appropriate files to the appropriate system directories as shown in Example 10-29. Feel free to change the destination directories to suit your needs.

Example 10-29 Installing the Portmapper Binaries

```
# install -m 755 -s portmap /sbin
# install -m 755 -s pmap_set /usr/sbin
# install -m 755 -s pmap_dump /usr/sbin
```

Since the portmapper runs all the time and is not invoked through inetd, we need to set up the appropriate run control scripts so that it is started and terminated at the appropriate run levels. If you are using Red Hat 5.2/6.0, this is already done (so you can go on to the next section); otherwise you will need to write or obtain a start-up script for the portmapper. You will find a copy of the start/stop script portmap.init in the Red Hat source RPM for portmap. A portmapper stop/start script similar to portmap.init is provided in Example 10-30. The differences between this script and the default portmap.init script are described throughout the following subsections of this section. Modify this as necessary for your system.

Example 10-30 Portmapper Start/Stop Script

```
#! /bin/sh
#
# portmap        Start/Stop RPC portmapper
# chkconfig: 345 11 89
# description: The portmapper manages RPC connections, which are used by
#              protocols such as NFS and NIS. The portmap server must be
\
#              running on machines which act as servers for protocols \
#              which make use of the RPC mechanism.
# processname: portmap

# Source function library.
. /etc/rc.d/init.d/functions

# Get config.
. /etc/sysconfig/network

# Check that networking is up.
if [ ${NETWORKING} = "no" ]
then
        exit 0
fi

[ -f /sbin/portmap ] || exit 0

# See how we were called.
case "$1" in
  start)
        echo -n "Starting portmapper: "
        daemon portmap -v

        echo
        touch /var/lock/subsys/portmap
        ;;
  stop)
        echo -n "Stopping portmap services: "
        killproc portmap

        echo
        rm -f /var/lock/subsys/portmap
        ;;
  status)
        status portmap
```

Example 10-30 Portmapper Start/Stop Script (Continued)

```
        ;;
  restart|reload)
        /usr/sbin/pmap_dump > /root/pmaptable
        $0 stop
        $0 start
        /usr/sbin/pmap_set < /root/pmaptable
        rm -f /root/pmaptable
        ;;
  *)
        echo "Usage: portmap {start|stop|status|restart|reload}"
        exit 1
esac
exit 0
```

Once you have obtained a script of this form, you simply need to place it in the appropriate directories. We'll assume that the name of the script is `portmap.init` for the purpose of the following examples. Example 10-31 illustrates the steps necessary first to copy the script to the `/etc/rc.d/init.d` directory (standard start/stop script location for Red Hat and other Linux distributions) and then to create links to the appropriate run-level directories. Your system's run-level S (start) and K (stop) script numbers may vary.

Example 10-31 Establishing the Portmapper Start/Stop Script for Run-Level Changes

```
# cp portmap.init /etc/rc.d/init.d/portmap
# ln -s /etc/rc.d/init.d/portmap /etc/rc.d/rc0.d/K89portmap
# ln -s /etc/rc.d/init.d/portmap /etc/rc.d/rc1.d/K89portmap
# ln -s /etc/rc.d/init.d/portmap /etc/rc.d/rc2.d/K89portmap
# ln -s /etc/rc.d/init.d/portmap /etc/rc.d/rc6.d/K89portmap
# ln -s /etc/rc.d/init.d/portmap /etc/rc.d/rc3.d/S11portmap
# ln -s /etc/rc.d/init.d/portmap /etc/rc.d/rc4.d/S11portmap
# ln -s /etc/rc.d/init.d/portmap /etc/rc.d/rc5.d/S11portmap
```

Finally, if your system uses the `chkconfig` utility, you will need to add the appropriate entry for `portmap`. If you included the entry `chkconfig: 345 11 89` or similar appropriate entry in the start/stop script (Example 10-30), then simply execute

```
# chkconfig --add portmap
```

and you are done!

NOTE

If you are unfamiliar with run levels and `chkconfig`, check out the references given in *System Administration* on page 80 in Chapter 4 and the `chkconfig` man page.

It is important to note that, when this version of the portmapper starts, it drops root privilege as soon as it binds to port 111. This limits exploitation of `portmap` or one of the RPC programs it calls. However, it also means that the access control files must be minimally readable for the group `bin`.

Implementing Portmapper Access Control

Implementing access control for the `portmap` daemon is similar to that of TCP_wrappers. The capabilities described here assume that TCP_wrappers is installed and, in particular, depend upon the `libwrap.a` library, which is a part of TCP_wrappers.

The portmapper uses the same `/etc/hosts.allow` and `/etc/hosts.deny` files for access control as TCP_wrappers uses. It also automatically authorizes the `localhost`. The options for the `portmap` daemon, however, reflect a subset of those available to TCP_wrappers. In Table 10.8 we list the type of option followed by a list of available capabilities for that option when used in conjunction with the portmapper. It may be useful to cross-reference the information contained in this table with the information in Tables 10.2 through 10.5. While this list clearly represents a reduction in functionality, it does preserve the ability to use the important `spawn` option and, of course, to limit access based on IP addressing. Other than these restrictions, the syntax for the portmapper is identical to TCP_wrappers.

In Example 10-32, we see a representative sample of the use of a `portmap` entry in `/etc/hosts.allow`. In this instance, we deny `portmap` services to the subnetwork of addresses from 172.19.0.0 through and including 172.19.15.255. We allow the (illegal) broadcast addresses used by many PCs for NFS and other `portmap`-based services, but we make a special log entry for such requests so that we can detect when a potential attack occurs from those addresses. Next, all other IP addresses beginning with 172.17 are allowed. Everything else is denied. Now let's take a look at the log entries.

Example 10-32 Sample Entries for the Portmapper

```
# hosts.allow
portmap: 172.19.0.0/255.255.240.0: deny

# Many PC's still don't broadcast properly
portmap: 255.255.255.255, 0.0.0.0: spawn (/usr/sbin/safe_finger \
    -lp @%a | logger -p local5.warn)&

# Allow the rest of our internal network
portmap: 172.17.

# Deny everybody else
portmap: ALL: deny
```

Table 10.8 Available Syntax and Options for the Portmapper

Syntax Type	Availability for `portmap`
Client specification	`IP address`, `net_number.`, or `net_number/netmask`. Note that hostnames **cannot** be used.
Extended options	`allow`, `deny`, `spawn`, `setenv`, and `umask`.
Variable expansion	`%a`, `%c`, `%d`, `%p`, and `%s`. Note that the server IP address is **not** available and that `%d` and `%s` expand identically.
Wildcard	`ALL`

The `portmap` Log Entries

It turns out that the `portmap` daemon is ordinarily silent about its activity. Only failed requests will generate a log message, by default. In some cases, this may be sufficient; however, ordinarily more detail is desired. In order to increase logging to incorporate both unsuccessful and successful connections, you simply need to invoke `portmap -v` instead of `portmap`. The script in Example 10-30 on page 221 does exactly that. In Example 10-33, we see a series of log entries generated by `portmap -v` (line wraps are due to formatting constraints). There is only one unsuccessful attempt shown in Example 10-33—the last line; all of the other entries exist because of the `-v` flag to `portmap`. The fields in each record of the log file are given in Table 10.9.

Example 10-33 Sample Log Output from `portmap -v`

```
Apr 12 10:50:24 topcat portmap[6112]: connect from 172.17.55.124 to get-
port(mountd)
Apr 12 10:51:03 topcat portmap[6113]: connect from 172.17.1.3 to getport(mountd)
Apr 12 11:01:15 topcat portmap[6193]: connect from 172.17.1.3 to
getport(nlockmgr)
Apr 12 11:01:15 topcat portmap[6194]: connect from 172.17.1.3 to getport(nfs)
Apr 12 11:02:08 topcat portmap[6199]: connect from 172.17.1.3 to getport(mountd)
Apr 12 11:06:12 topcat portmap[6214]: connect from 172.17.1.3 to getport(mountd)
Apr 12 14:55:53 topcat portmap[6624]: connect from 172.17.1.3 to dump()
Apr 12 14:58:15 topcat portmap[6640]: connect from 172.17.1.3 to dump()
Apr 12 14:59:27 topcat portmap[6657]: connect from 172.17.1.3 to getport(sprayd)
Apr 12 14:59:27 topcat portmap[6662]: connect from 172.17.1.3 to getport(sprayd)
Apr 12 15:13:38 topcat portmap[6724]: connect from 172.17.55.124 to
callit(rstatd)
Apr 12 21:28:24 topcat portmap[7089]: connect from 172.19.7.38 to dump(): request
from unauthorized host
```

It should be noted that, when a host is denied by rule in `/etc/hosts.allow` or `/etc/hosts.deny`, or generally when an error condition occurs, the client will see only an error message of the type `Program Not Registered` because the portmapper does not pass back the specific error condition. However, more specific error messages will be logged on the server by both the portmapper and the requested service (if the error condition was not caused by a deny rule). Normal error messages will be generated by daemons after a client request has been passed to it by the portmapper.

Gracefully Terminating and Recovering the Portmapper

Since the portmapper is very dynamic in terms of allocating ports and invoking services, it is important to gracefully terminate and restart it whenever it becomes necessary to do so. The two programs, `pmap_dump` and `pmap_set`, which come with Portmapper Version 4, provide this functionality.

Whenever you need to terminate the portmapper, do so by executing the steps outlined in Example 10-34 to ensure that the state of processes under its control are maintained. The use of the file `/root/pmaptable` in this example is

Table 10.9 Log Records Generated by the Portmapper

Record	Description
Date and time	Date and timestamp, such as `Apr 12 15:13:38`.
Server	Hostname of the server, such as `topcat`.
Daemon name	Name of the daemon, as with other TCP_wrappers entries. For the portmapper, it will always be `portmap`.
[PID]	Process identifier used for this session, such as `[6724]`.
`connect from` *IP Address*	The IP address of the client.
`to` Type of call	The type of call may be one of the following: `null`: a null call. `set`: register a program, usually effected by `killall -HUP inetd` after `/etc/rpc` has been modified. `unset`: unregister a program, such as with `rpcinfo -d`. `getport`: get the port number for the RPC program. `dump`: get all registered RPC programs, normally the result of `rpcinfo -p`.
(Program name)	The name of the RPC program, such as `(mountd)` for the NFS mount daemon.
Message	A message explaining the reason for rejection. No messages are generated for successful calls.

somewhat arbitrary. The choice of the `/root` directory is based largely on the fact that its permissions prohibit world access, providing some protection against unauthorized modification of the table. The name of the table itself is completely arbitrary.

Example 10-34 Gracefully Terminating and Restarting `portmap`

```
# pmap_dump > /root/pmaptable
# killall portmap
# /sbin/portmap
# pmap_set < /root/pmaptable
# rm -f /root/pmaptable
```

If you use the script given in Example 10-30 on page 221, you may simply execute

```
# /etc/rc.d/init.d/portmap reload
```

to accomplish the same steps as given in Example 10-34. Note that the `/etc/rc.d/init.d/portmap` script that ships with Red Hat 5.2/6.0 will **not** properly execute the steps in Example 10-34 when given the `reload` or `restart` options and should not be used for that purpose. If you do not terminate and restart the `portmap` daemon in this way, your system will probably need to be rebooted to recover properly.

Portmapper Vulnerabilities

As outlined in *TCP_Wrappers Vulnerabilities* on page 218, the principal vulnerabilities associated with the portmapper have to do with its dependencies. Since the portmapper relies mainly upon IP addresses for its access control, there is no protection against spoofed addresses (which need to be taken care of by `ipchains`; see Chapter 16). Furthermore, the portmapper cannot protect against services that it does not control after the initial invocation, such as `rpc.mountd`.

Of course, there is always the possibility that a vulnerability in the portmapper itself will be identified, so be sure to regularly read the appropriate newsgroups, such as `comp.unix.security`, and subscribe to the pertinent e-mail lists, like `bugtraq` (for more information about resources, see Appendix A).

UNWRAPPED SERVICES

In spite of the fact that you may have implemented TCP_wrappers and Wietse Venema's Portmapper Version 4, there are still networking daemons that remain unwrapped. Among such services are `named` (the DNS daemon), `rpc.mountd`, and NIS daemons. There is a package called `securelib` that can assist in securing some of these services. The general topic of securing these and other related services is discussed in the references provided in *General TCP/IP Networking Resources* on page 39. You may also secure some of these services through `xinetd` in the next section.

Still other services, such as custom applications like databases, may not be invoked through `inetd` and therefore are not covered by TCP_wrappers. In such a case, thoroughly investigate your security options for each such service and implement restrictions according to your Security Policy.

Be careful about using `syslogd -r` (discussed in Chapter 8) because it has many potential vulnerabilities and does not offer any access control. In particular, it is subject to a DoS attack in which the filesystem containing the logs is deliberately filled.

REPLACING `inetd` WITH `xinetd`

Up to this point, we have discussed using the existing `inetd` and portmapper utilities with wrappers to provide some protection against unauthorized access and to provide additional logging. The latter is a reasonably effective early warning mechanism. There is an alternative to this approach. You can implement `xinetd`, a complete replacement for `inetd`.

The extended Internet services daemon—`xinetd`—provides many of the capabilities seen with TCP_wrappers and the portmapper and adds some capabilities not incorporated into those utilities. There are some disadvantages, however, that make for an additional bit of work. Let's examine this daemon.

WARNING!

> The configuration of `xinetd` is quite different than that of `inetd`. Also, the additional features of `xinetd` make for more complex configuration entries. This means that, at least initially, you may make mistakes in configuring `xinetd`. These mistakes could have severe security ramifications. Therefore, take the necessary time to learn about and extensively test `xinetd` configurations.

Advantages of `xinetd`

`xinetd` provides access control in a way that is quite similar to TCP_wrappers or the portmapper. It additionally affords the following functionality:

- ☞ Access control for TCP, UDP, and RPC services.
- ☞ Access limitations based on time.
- ☞ Extensive logging capabilities for both successful and unsuccessful connections.
- ☞ Implements RFC 1413 username retrievals.
- ☞ Provides for hard reconfiguration by killing services that are no longer allowed.
- ☞ Provides numerous mechanisms to prevent DoS attacks.
  - ✗ Limit on the number of daemons of a given type that can run concurrently.
  - ✗ An overall limit of processes forked by `xinetd`.
  - ✗ Limits on log file sizes.
- ☞ Provides a compile-time option to include `libwrap`, the TCP_wrappers library.
  - ✗ Causes `/etc/hosts.allow` and `/etc/hosts.deny` access control checks in addition to `xinetd` access control checks.
- ☞ Provides for the invocation of `tcpd`.
  - ✗ All TCP_wrappers functionality is available.
- ☞ Services may be bound to specific interfaces.
- ☞ Services may be forwarded (proxied) to another system.

We discuss all these features in detail in the following sections.

Disadvantages of `xinetd`

In spite of `xinetd`'s capabilities, there is a downside.

☞ The configuration file, `/etc/xinetd.conf`, is incompatible with `/etc/inetd.conf`.

  ✗ However, a conversion utility, `xtoa`, is included with the distribution.

☞ Time-outs and other problems occur for RPC services, especially on busy systems.

  ✗ However, `xinetd` and `portmap` may coexist, allowing RPC through the portmapper.

☞ `xinetd` is not currently shipping as a part of most Linux distributions.

Each of these issues will be discussed below.

  We should note that `xinetd` does not consult the `/etc/services` file for service configuration. `xinetd` only uses it to determine which services are listed.

Obtaining `xinetd`

The `xinetd` daemon was originally written by Panagiotis Tsirigotis. Rob Braun has made numerous enhancements and currently maintains it. The latest version, as of this writing, is 2.1.8.6b5. You can obtain either a `gzipped`, `tar` archive of the source or RPM packages of both the source and i386 executables from

```
http://synack.net/xinetd/
```

The RPMs contain PGP signatures, but the `gzipped`, `tar` archive does not. If you choose to use the RPM binaries, check the signatures and then, if you wish, skip the section *Building `xinetd`* on page 229.

  Next we will cover compiling, linking, and installing `xinetd`. Then we will go on to discuss the syntax of the `xinetd` configuration file and the flags associated with the `xinetd` daemon. After that, we will look at some examples and log messages.

NOTE

xinetd Version 2.2.1 is available which is **not** newer than nor does it incorporate the additional functionality described for `xinetd` Version 2.1.8.6b5. The last update for `xinetd` 2.2.1—found at `ftp://coast.cs.purdue.edu/pub/tools/unix/xinetd/`—was April 1997, and it does not appear as if anyone is actively working on that version. The folks who put together `xinetd` 2.2.1 used version numbering that conflicts with the copyright (see the `COPYRIGHT` file in the distribution). Rob Braun has adhered to the version numbering described in the copyright, hence the discrepancy in version numbers. Version 2.1.8.6b5 of `xinetd` described herein continued to be actively worked on at the time of this publication. Check `http://synack.net/xinetd/` regularly for new releases.

Building xinetd

After you have downloaded and built the source tree for xinetd, you will find a configure script for the purpose of building the Makefile and related files for compilation and linking (see *Implementing Version 1.5.9p4* on page 175 in Chapter 9 for a more detailed discussion of the configure utility). This implementation of configure utilizes only a few options. You may view the available options with configure --help.

By default, the xinetd configure utility uses /usr/local as its destination root directory. If you wish to use a different root directory, you may do so with the --prefix option. Example 10-35 uses --prefix=/usr and the --with-libwrap (the latter for incorporating libwrap access control) options. Also, this example uses /usr/src/xinetd as the build directory.

Example 10-35 Using configure for xinetd

```
# ./configure --prefix=/usr --with-libwrap
creating cache ./config.cache
checking host system type... i686-pc-linux-gnu
checking target system type... i686-pc-linux-gnu
checking build system type... i686-pc-linux-gnu
checking for gcc... gcc
checking whether the C compiler (gcc  ) works... yes
...
<lots of output snipped>
...
checking for netdb.h... yes
updating cache ./config.cache
creating ./config.status
creating Makefile
#
```

Now that the Makefile is built, we can proceed with creating the binaries. The output of the make execution is displayed in Example 10-36.

Example 10-36 Compiling and Linking xinetd

```
# make
for lib in sio str misc xlog pset ; do \
        ( cd libs/src/$lib ; make install LIBDIR=/usr/src/xinetd/libs/lib
INCLUDEDIR=/usr/src/xinetd/libs/include MANDIR=/usr/src/xinetd/libs/man
"INSTALL=/usr/bin/install -c" "DEFS=-DHAVE_LIBCRYPT=1 -DHAVE_UNISTD_H=1 -
DHAVE_GETPAGESIZE=1 -DHAVE_MMAP=1 -DHAVE_ISATTY=1 -DHAVE_MEMCPY=1 -
DHAVE_WAITPID=1 -DHAVE_SIGVEC=1 -DHAVE_SETSID=1 -DHAVE_STRFTIME=1 -
DSTDC_HEADERS=1 -DR_OK=4 -DHAVE_SYS_FILE_H=1 -DHAVE_FTW_H=1 -DHAVE_LINUX_TIME_H=1
" RANLIB=true "CC=gcc" DEBUG=-O ) \
; done
...
<lots of output snipped>
...
gcc -O -o xinetd access.o addr.o builtins.o child.o conf.o confparse.o
connection.o env.o flags.o ident.o init.o int.o intcommon.o internals.o log.o
logctl.o main.o msg.o nvlists.o parse.o parsesup.o parsers.o reconfig.o retry.o
sconf.o server.o service.o shutdown.o signals.o special.o tcpint.o time.o
udpint.o util.o redirect.o options.o -L/usr/src/xinetd/xinetd-2.1.8.5/libs/lib -
lsio -lstr -lmisc -lxlog -lpset -lcrypt  || rm -f xinetd
make[1]: Leaving directory '/usr/src/xinetd/xinetd'
#
```

Now that we have created the binaries, let's install them. Example 10-37 shows the results of `make install`. The installation causes the `man` pages for `xinetd`, `xinetd.conf`, and `xinetd.log` to be copied to subdirectories of `/usr/man`. Be sure to review them. The `xinetd` daemon is copied to `/usr/sbin`. These directories were chosen based on our use of the `--prefix` option to configure. Notice the reference in the last line of Example 10-37 to `itox`. This very valuable utility (discussed below) can be used to convert our existing `/etc/inetd.conf` to an `/etc/xinetd.conf` file.

Example 10-37 Output of `make install` for `xinetd`

```
# make install
/usr/bin/install -c -m 755 xinetd/xinetd /usr/sbin
/usr/bin/install -c -m 644 xinetd/xinetd.conf.man /usr/man/man5/xinetd.conf.5
/usr/bin/install -c -m 644 xinetd/xinetd.log.man /usr/man/man8/xinetd.log.8
/usr/bin/install -c -m 644 xinetd/xinetd.man /usr/man/man8/xinetd.8
You must put your xinetd.conf in /etc/xinetd.conf
There is a sample config file in xinetd/sample.conf and you can
use xinetd/itox to convert your old inetd.conf file to an xinetd format
#
```

Once you've built and installed the software, you will need to set up the appropriate start/stop scripts so that `xinetd` is invoked at boottime. A start/stop script, called `xinetd`, is provided with the RPM source distribution, and after installing, can be found in the directory `/usr/src/redhat/SOURCES`. You will need to modify that script in order to make it useful. Example 10-38 displays a modified version of that script and incorporates the necessary signals for proper use of the `restart` and `reload` options. Notice that the additional options, `hard` and `soft`, have been added to the script. For an explanation of the signals, see Table 10.16 on page 251. Other aspects of this script will be discussed throughout the remainder of this chapter.

Example 10-38 Sample `xinetd` Start/Stop Script

```
#! /bin/sh
#
# chkconfig: 345 50 50
# description: xinetd is a powerful replacement for inetd.
#              xinetd has access control machanisms, extensive logging
#              capabilities, the ability to make services available based
#              on time, and can place limits on the number of servers
#              that can be started, among other things.
# processname: xinetd
# pidfile: /var/run/xinetd.pid
# config: /etc/sysconfig/network
# config: /etc/xinetd.conf

# Source function library.
. /etc/rc.d/init.d/functions

# Get config.
. /etc/sysconfig/network

# Check that networking is up.
if [ ${NETWORKING} = "no" ]
then
        exit 0
fi

[ -f /usr/sbin/xinetd ] || exit 0
```

Example 10-38 Sample `xinetd` Start/Stop Script (Continued)

```
[ -f /etc/xinetd.conf ] || exit 0
# See how we were called.
case "$1" in
  start)
        echo -n "Starting xinetd: "
        [ -f /var/run/xinetd.pid ] && rm -f /var/run/xinetd.pid
        daemon xinetd -pid 2> /var/run/xinetd.pid

        echo
        touch /var/lock/subsys/xinetd
        ;;
  stop)
        echo -n "Stopping xinetd: "
        rm -f /var/run/xinetd.pid 2> /dev/null
        killproc xinetd

        echo
        rm -f /var/lock/subsys/xinetd
        ;;
  status)
        status xinetd
        ;;
  restart|reload)
        $0 stop
            sleep 3
        $0 start
        ;;
  soft)
        killall -USR1 xinetd
        ;;
  hard)
        killall -USR2 xinetd
        ;;
  *)
        echo "Usage: xinetd {start|stop|status|restart|soft|hard}"
        exit 1
esac
exit 0
```

With this script in place, you may easily cause `xinetd` to reread its configuration table, using either the `soft` or `hard` option for a soft or hard reconfiguration, respectively. See *Signals Available for Use with `xinetd`* on page 250 for a discussion of soft and hard reconfiguration options.

WARNING!

While it is entirely possible to simultaneously run `inetd`, `xinetd`, and `portmap`, they must not have equivalent service configurations. For example, if both `inetd` and `xinetd` have configuration entries for `telnet`, then only one of the two daemons will service the request. Normally, this behavior is benign and will simply generate log messages that indicate that `inetd` or `xinetd` (whichever one started at the last boot) could not bind to a particular port (23 for `telnet`) because it was already in use. Problems can occur, however, especially if the `flags = REUSE` (see Table 10.10 on page 232) option is specified for `xinetd`. This will make the socket available for binding even if `inetd` is already bound to it, which may in turn allow usually unauthorized connections. In short, if you are using a combination of two or all three daemons—`inetd`, `xinetd`, and `portmap`—make sure that they serve daemons exclusively.

You may generally follow the steps outlined in *Building the Portmapper* on page 219, and particularly in Example 10-31 on page 222, to set up the necessary scripts. Don't forget to run `chkconfig` as shown after Example 10-31.

The `xinetd` Configuration File

The `xinetd` configuration file is, by default, `/etc/xinetd.conf`. Its syntax is quite different than, and incompatible with, `/etc/inetd.conf`. Essentially, it combines the functionality of `/etc/inetd.conf`, `/etc/hosts.allow` and `/etc/hosts.deny` into one file. Each entry in `/etc/xinetd.conf` is of the form

```
service service_name
{
        attribute operator value value ...
        ...
}
```

where `service` is a required keyword and the braces must surround the list of attributes.

The *service_name* is arbitrary, but is normally chosen to conform to the standard network services. Additional and completely nonstandard services may be added, as long as they are invoked through a network request, including network requests from the `localhost` itself.

There are a number of *attributes* available, which are described in Table 10.10 on page 232. We will also describe the required attributes and rules of attribute usage later in this section.

The *operator* may be one of =, +=, or -=. All attributes may use = which has the effect of assigning one or more values. Some attributes may use the forms, += and/or -= which have the effect of adding to an existing list of values or removing from an existing list of values, respectively. The attributes that can use these latter forms are noted in Table 10.10.

The *values* are the parameters set to the given attribute.

Table 10.10 Extended Internet Services Daemon Attributes

Attribute	Description and Allowed Value
socket_type	The type of TCP/IP socket used. Acceptable values are `stream` (TCP), `dgram` (UDP), `raw`, and `seqpacket` (reliable, sequential datagrams).
protocol	Specifies the protocol used by the service. Must be an entry in `/etc/protocols`. If not specified, the default protocol for the service is used.
server	Daemon to invoke. Must be absolutely qualified.
server_args	Specifies the flags to be passed to the daemon.
port	Port number associated with the service. If listed in `/etc/services`, it must match.

Table 10.10 Extended Internet Services Daemon Attributes (Continued)

Attribute	Description and Allowed Value
wait	There are two possible values for this attribute. If `yes`, then `xinetd` will start the requested daemon and cease to handle requests for this service until the daemon terminates. This is a single-threaded service. If `no`, then `xinetd` will start a daemon for each request, regardless of the state of previously started daemons. This is a multithreaded service.
user	Sets the UID for the daemon. This attribute is ineffective if the effective UID of `xinetd` is not 0.
group	Sets the GID for the daemon. This attribute is ineffective if the effective UID of `xinetd` is not 0.
nice	Specifies the `nice` value for the daemon.
id	Used to uniquely identify a service when redundancy exists. For example, `echo` provides both `dgram` and `streams` services. Setting `id=echo_dgram` and `id=echo_streams` would uniquely identify the `dgram` and `streams` services, respectively. If not specified, `id` assumes the value specified by the `service` keyword.
type	May take one or more of the following values: RPC (for RPC services), INTERNAL (for services handled by `xinetd`, like `echo`), UNLISTED (a service not listed in a standard system file, such as `/etc/rpc` or `/etc/services`).
access_times	Sets the time intervals for when the service is available. Format is `hh:mm-hh:mm`; for example, `08:00-18:00` means the service is available from 8 A.M. through 6 P.M.
banner file	Accepts an absolutely qualified file, the contents of which are displayed to the client whenever a failed connection occurs.
flags	One or more of the following options may be specified: REUSE: Sets the TCP/IP socket to be reusable. This is particularly valuable when `xinetd` is terminated and restarted. See *Signals Available for Use with `xinetd`* on page 250 for further details. INTERCEPT: Intercepts packets destined to single-threaded daemons and performs an access check. Cannot be used with INTERNAL services. NORETRY: Do not retry `fork` if it fails. IDONLY: Accept connections only if the client returns the UID to an RFC1413 call. The USERID value must be set for `log_on_success` and/or `log_on_failure` attributes for this value to take effect. Only available for multithreaded, stream services. NAMEINARGS: Allows for the first argument in the `server_args` attribute to be a fully qualified path to a daemon, allowing for the use of TCP_wrappers (very cool!).
rpc_version	Specifies the RPC version number or numbers for the service. Multiple version numbers are specified in a range; for example, `2-3`.

Table 10.10 Extended Internet Services Daemon Attributes (Continued)

Attribute	Description and Allowed Value
rpc_number	Specifies the RPC program number if it does not exist in /etc/rpc.
env	A space-separated list of VAR=VALUE, where VAR is a shell environment variable and VALUE is its setting. These values will be passed to the service daemon upon invocation, together with xinetd's environment. This attribute supports the += operator in addition to =.
passenv	A space-separated list of environment variables from xinetd's environment that are passed to the service daemon upon invocation. Setting no value causes no variables to be passed. This attribute supports all operators.
only_from	Space-separated list of allowed clients. The syntax for clients is given in Table 10.11. If this attribute is specified without a value, it acts to deny access to the service. This attribute supports all operators.
no_access	Space separated list of denied clients. The syntax for clients is given in Table 10.11. This attribute supports all operators.
instances	Accepts an integer greater than or equal to 1 or UNLIMITED. Sets the maximum number of concurrent running daemons. UNLIMITED means no limit is imposed by xinetd.
log_type	By default, xinetd logs to syslogd using the selector daemon.info. There are two available values: SYSLOG facility [level]: Sets the facility to one of daemon, auth, user, or local0-7. Setting the level is optional. All levels are accepted. FILE file [soft [hard]]: Specifies the indicated file for logging instead of syslog. The limits, soft and hard, are optionally specified in KB. Once the soft limit is reached, xinetd logs a message to that effect. Once the hard limit is reached, xinetd stops logging all services that use this file. If no hard limit is specified, it becomes soft plus 1%, but cannot exceed 20 KB by default. The default soft limit is 5 KB.
redirect	This attribute assumes the syntax, redirect = IPaddress port. It has the effect of redirecting a TCP service to another system. The server attribute is ignored if this attribute is used.
bind	Binds a service to a specific interface. Syntax is bind = IPaddress. This allows hosts with multiple interfaces (physical or logical), for example, to permit specific services (or ports) on one interface but not the other.
log_on_success	Specifies the information to be logged on success. Possible values are PID: PID of the daemon. If a new daemon is not forked, PID is set to 0. HOST: Client host IP address. USERID: Captures UID of the client user through an RFC1413 call. Available only for multithreaded, streams services. EXIT: Logs daemon termination and status. DURATION: Logs duration of session. By default, nothing is logged. This attribute supports all operators.

Table 10.10 Extended Internet Services Daemon Attributes (Continued)

Attribute	Description and Allowed Value
`log_on_failure`	Specifies the information to be logged on failure. A message indicating the nature of the error is always logged. Possible values are ATTEMPT: Records a failed attempt. All other values imply this one. HOST: Client host IP address. USERID: Captures UID of the client user through an RFC1413 call. Only available for multithreaded, streams services. RECORD: Records additional client information such as local user, remote user, and terminal type. By default, nothing is logged. This attribute supports all operators.
`disabled`	Available for use only with the special `defaults` entry (see *The defaults Entry* on page 237). Accepts a space-separated list of services that are unavailable. It has the same effect as commenting out the service entry in the `/etc/xinetd.conf` file.

Before we examine Table 10.10, let's consider a simple example. In Example 10-39, we see a partial `/etc/xinetd.conf` file. Notice that, in spite of the formatting differences, the information contained in these records is identical to what is found in `/etc/inetd.conf` (see Example 10-2 on page 195). The reason that these two entries look so similar to `/etc/inetd.conf` is because they were generated from `/etc/inetd.conf` with the `itox` utility, which simply converts `/etc/inetd.conf` entries to the proper syntax for `xinetd`. In this case, the attributes (everything inside the braces and to the left of the = symbol) are very straightforward in their meaning as are the associated values (everything inside the braces and to the right of the = symbol).

Example 10-39 Partial `/etc/xinetd.conf` File

```
service ftp
{
        socket_type     = stream
        protocol        = tcp
        wait            = no
        user            = root
        server          = /usr/sbin/in.ftpd
        server_args     = -l -a
}
service telnet
{
        socket_type     = stream
        protocol        = tcp
        wait            = no
        user            = root
        server          = /usr/sbin/in.telnetd
}
```

The easiest way initially to create the `/etc/xinetd.conf` file is with the `itox` utility. The syntax for its use is simply (this example assumes that the current working directory is the `xinetd` build directory)

```
# xinetd/itox -daemon_dir /usr/sbin </etc/inetd.conf >/etc/
xinetd.conf
```

The option -daemon_dir /usr/sbin to itox specifies the actual location of the daemons, which we would not be able to determine from /etc/inetd.conf if TCP_wrappers is implemented. Once done, you may start adding attributes and values that restrict access and increase logging. Be sure to modify the /etc/xinetd.conf to take advantage of the features of xinetd; otherwise, if you just convert /etc/inetd.conf to /etc/xinetd.conf, xinetd will behave identically to inetd.

Table 10.10 details the attributes and values that may be used in /etc/xinetd.conf. There are certainly a large number of attributes. We will take a look at some examples in the section *Configuration Examples* on page 243, which will clarify many of these attributes.

The syntax for only_from and no_access lists is given in Table 10.11. We provide the syntax for specifying hostnames, IP addresses, and networks. Notice that the syntax for netmask in the last entry of Table 10.11 differs from what we've seen before. Instead of taking a traditional decimal or hexadecimal representation of the netmask, it takes an integer that represents the number of highest-order (left-most) bits which are set to binary 1 in the netmask. So, in the example given, the value of netmask is set to 20, which means that the left-most 20 bits are set to 1, the remaining 12 bits are set to 0, or

```
11111111 11111111 11110000 00000000
```

Table 10.11 Access Control List Syntax for /etc/xinetd.conf

Syntax	Description
hostname	A resolvable hostname. All IP addresses associated with the hostname will be used.
IPaddress	The standard IP address in dot decimal form.
net_name	A network name from /etc/networks.
x.x.x.0 x.x.0.0 x.0.0.0 0.0.0.0	The 0 is treated as a wildcard. For example, an entry like 88.3.92.0 would match all addresses beginning with 88.3.92.0 through and including 88.3.92.255. The 0.0.0.0 entry matches all addresses.
x.x.x.{a, b, ...} x.x.{a, b, ...} x.{a, b, ...}	Specifies lists of hosts. For example, 172.19.32.{1, 56, 59} means the list of IP addresses, 172.19.32.1, 172.19.32.56, and 172.19.32.59.
IPaddress/netmask	Defines the network or subnetwork to match. For example, 172.19.16.0/20 matches all addresses in the range 172.19.16.0 through and including 172.19.31.255.

which is the binary representation of the decimal netmask `255.255.240.0`.

Now that we've seen the basic attributes, let's have a look at the ones that are required, the special services, and some configuration examples.

Required Attributes   Certain attributes must be specified for every service. Some services need more attributes than others because they are unlisted (not in `/etc/services` nor `/etc/rpc`). Table 10.12 lists the required attributes.

Special `xinetd` Services   There are four special entries that may be specified in the `/etc/xinetd.conf` file. They are `defaults`, `servers`, `services`, and `xadmin`. The `defaults` entry is not a service and must not have a preceding `service` keyword (otherwise, it will be treated as a service called `defaults`). Each of these special entries is described in the following four sections.

The `defaults` Entry.   The purpose of the `defaults` entry in the `/etc/xinetd.conf` file is to specify default values for all services in the file. These default values may be overridden or modified by each service entry. The attributes that may be specified in the `defaults` entry are listed in Table 10.13. This table also indicates the acceptable modification behavior in subsequent service entries.

Example 10-40 provides an example defaults entry as it might appear in `/etc/xinetd.conf`. Here we see that, for all services, log messages will be sent to the `syslogd` daemon via the `local4.info` selector. Successful connections to services will cause the PID, client IP address, termination status, and time of connection to be logged. Unsuccessful connection attempts will have the client IP address logged. The maximum number of instances for any one service is set to eight. Two services—`in.tftpd` and `in.rexecd`—are disabled.

Table 10.12 Required Attributes

Attribute	Required By
`socket_type`	all services
`wait`	all services
`user`	services listed in `/etc/services` or `/etc/rpc`
`server`	noninternal services
`port`	non-RPC services that are not in `/etc/services`
`protocol`	all RPC services and all other services not in `/etc/services`
`rpc_version`	all RPC services
`rpc_number`	any RPC service not listed in `/etc/rpc`

Table 10.13 Attributes Available to `defaults`

Attribute	Service Modification*
log_on_success log_on_failure only_from no_access passenv	May be overridden with = operator or modified with either the += or -= operators.
instances log_type	May be overridden with = operator.
disabled	Service may be commented out, but the `disabled` attribute may not be used within a service entry.

*The modification behaviors are clarified in *Configuration Examples* on page 243.

Example 10-40 Sample `defaults` Entry in `/etc/xinetd.conf`

```
defaults
{
        log_type          = SYSLOG local4 info
        log_on_success    = PID HOST EXIT DURATION
        log_on_failure    = HOST
        instances         = 8
        disabled = in.tftpd in.rexecd
}
```

The use of the `defaults` entry essentially offers a shortcut for establishing certain attributes throughout the file, being applied to all services that do not set these attributes otherwise.

NOTE

If you do not have a `defaults` entry in your `/etc/xinetd.conf` file and subsequently decide to add one, you must terminate and restart `xinetd` in order for the `defaults` to take effect. This is also true for any new service you may add to `/etc/xinetd.conf`. This can be accomplished by

```
# killall -TERM xinetd
# /usr/sbin/xinetd
```

or, if you are using the modified script shown in Example 10-38 on page 230, simply execute

```
# /etc/rc.d/init.d/xinetd restart
```

However, this execution will not behave properly if you use the default script provided with the RPM package.

The servers Entry. The purpose of the `servers` special service is to provide a list of daemons currently running on the server, together with pertinent information about those daemons. In other words, it provides a list of active connections. This is a useful mechanism for troubleshooting as well as for

examining the state of `xinetd`. Example 10-41 displays a sample `servers` entry
in the `/etc/xinetd.conf` file. Notice that this service is of the INTERNAL,
UNLISTED type, which means that it is an internal function of `xinetd` and that
it is not listed in `/etc/services`. The port number used is completely arbitrary.

Example 10-41 Sample `servers` Entry

```
service servers
{
        type                = INTERNAL UNLISTED
        socket_type         = stream
        protocol            = tcp
        port                = 9997
        wait                = no
        only_from           = 172.17.33.111
        wait                = no
}
```

Note that this service is available only from the specific IP address
`172.17.33.111`, which should be the IP address of the server itself. This disallows any other host from obtaining this information from this server. The
security ramification here is very simple—if this information were available to
be read by others on other systems, it could well lead to an exploit based on
the knowledge of which daemons are currently running. It is perhaps ill
advised to run this server at all except for debugging purposes, since any user
on `172.17.33.111` is able to obtain this information by executing `telnet`
`172.17.33.111 9997` as shown in Example 10-42 (line numbers added for clarity). Note that `xinetd` simply provides the information and exits, providing no
interactive connection. The output shown in Example 10-42 tells us that there
are two running `telnet` daemons (lines 5 and 31), one with the PID of 5931
and the other with the PID of 5961 (lines 6 and 32, respectively). There is one
`ftp` daemon (line 18) running with the PID of 5960 (line 19). Some connection
information and logging information is provided for each running daemon.
Probably not the sort of information you want floating around, and, in general,
for security reasons you may want this turned off, except perhaps on tightly
secured systems. To turn it off, make sure that no entry of the type shown in
Example 10-41 is present in your `/etc/xinetd.conf` file.

Example 10-42 Example Output of `servers` Service

```
 1    $ telnet topcat 9997
 2    Trying 172.17.33.111...
 3    Connected to topcat.
 4    Escape character is '^]'.
 5    telnet server
 6    pid = 5931
 7    start_time = Sat Apr 17 10:32:15 1999
 8    Connection info:
 9            state = CLOSED
10            service = telnet
11            descriptor = 20
12            flags = 9
```

Example 10-42 Example Output of `servers` Service (Continued)

```
13              remote_address = 10.48.3.2,39958
14              Alternative services =
15      log_remote_user = YES
16      writes_to_log = YES
17
18      ftp server
19      pid = 5960
20      start_time = Sat Apr 17 10:49:06 1999
21      Connection info:
22              state = CLOSED
23              service = ftp
24              descriptor = 20
25              flags = 9
26              remote_address = 172.17.55.124,2320
27              Alternative services =
28      log_remote_user = YES
29      writes_to_log = YES
30
31      telnet server
32      pid = 5961
33      start_time = Sat Apr 17 10:49:20 1999
34      Connection info:
35              state = CLOSED
36              service = telnet
37              descriptor = 20
38              flags = 9
39              remote_address = 172.17.1.3,35461
40              Alternative services =
41      log_remote_user = YES
42      writes_to_log = YES
43
44      Connection closed by foreign host.
45      $
```

The services Entry.   The purpose of the `services` special entry is to provide a list of available services. As with the `servers` special entry, this is a useful troubleshooting utility, but, for the same security reasons as cited above, it
should probably be left off. Nonetheless, let's see how it works.

Example 10-43 illustrates a sample `services` entry in the `/etc/`
`xinetd.conf` file. Once again, the choice of port numbers is arbitrary. Also, notice
that access is limited to `topcat`, which is the hostname of the server itself.

Example 10-43 Sample `services` Entry in `/etc/xinetd.conf`

```
service services
{
        type            = INTERNAL UNLISTED
        socket_type     = stream
        protocol        = tcp
        port            = 8099
        wait            = no
        only_from       = topcat
}
```

As with the `servers` service, any user may execute `telnet topcat 8099` and obtain the output from the `services` service, as long as that user is logged in to `topcat`. Example 10-44 provides the details. Note that `xinetd` simply provides the information and exits, providing no interactive connection.

Example 10-44 Output from a Query to the `services` Internal Service

```
$ telnet topcat 8099
Trying 172.17.33.111...
Connected to topcat.
Escape character is '^]'.
servers tcp 9997
services tcp 8099
ftp tcp 21
telnet tcp 23
shell tcp 514
login tcp 513
talk udp 517
ntalk udp 518
pop-2 tcp 109
pop-3 tcp 110
imap tcp 143
linuxconf tcp 98
Connection closed by foreign host.
$
```

The xadmin Entry. This special service entry provides an interactive way of obtaining the information provided by the `servers` and `services` special services. An example `/etc/xinetd.conf` entry is given in Example 10-45 (again the choice of port numbers is arbitrary). Much like the `services` and `servers` services, there is no password or other protection for this service, so make sure that you use an `only_from` entry of the type shown here, allowing requests from only the server itself.

Example 10-45 The `xadmin` Entry

```
service xadmin
{
        type             = INTERNAL UNLISTED
        socket_type      = stream
        protocol         = tcp
        port             = 9967
        wait             = no
        only_from        = topcat
}
```

As with the previous two special service types, you merely need to `telnet` to the port listed—in this case, `telnet topcat 9967`. Unlike the previous two services, `xadmin` provides an interactive environment. As of this writing, there are five commands that you may execute once you have connected to the `xadmin` server. They are `help`, `show run`, `show avail`, `bye`, and `exit`. The `help` command displays the other commands together with a brief usage message. The `bye` and `exit` commands both close the connection. The `show run` and `show avail` commands provide the information provided by `servers` and `services`, respectively. Example 10-46 shows the use of each of these commands.

Example 10-46 Using the `xadmin` Service

```
$ telnet topcat 9967
Trying 172.17.33.111...
Connected to topcat.
Escape character is '^]'.
> help
xinetd admin help:
show run  :    shows information about running services
show avail:    shows what services are currently available
bye, exit :    exits the admin shell
> show run
Running services:
service  run retry attempts descriptor
telnet server
pid = 5931
start_time = Sat Apr 17 10:32:15 1999
Connection info:
        state = CLOSED
        service = telnet
        descriptor = 20
        flags = 9
        remote_address = 10.48.3.2,39958
        Alternative services =
log_remote_user = YES
writes_to_log = YES

telnet server
pid = 5961
start_time = Sat Apr 17 10:49:20 1999
Connection info:
        state = CLOSED
        service = telnet
        descriptor = 20
        flags = 9
        remote_address = 172.17.1.3,35461
        Alternative services =
log_remote_user = YES
writes_to_log = YES

xadmin server
pid = 0
start_time = Wed Dec 31 17:00:00 1969
Connection info:
        state = OPEN
        service = xadmin
        descriptor = 20
        flags = 9
        remote_address = 172.17.33.111,17165
        Alternative services =
log_remote_user = NO
writes_to_log = NO

> show avail
Available services:
servers
xadmin
services
ftp
telnet
telnet
shell
login
talk
ntalk
pop-2
pop-3
imap
```

Example 10-46 Using the `xadmin` Service (Continued)

```
finger
auth
linuxconf
> bye
bye bye
Connection closed by foreign host.
$
```

Once again, notice that a nonroot user can access this service; therefore, exercise caution in making this special service available for the reasons outlined at the end of the section *The `servers` Entry* on page 238.

WARNING!

> As pointed out in the previous three sections, the special services—`servers`, `services`, and `xadmin`—produce information which may be used to compromise your system. You probably don't need these services running all the time, perhaps just when you are debugging. In any event, if you *do* run these services, make sure that you configure access control using either `access_from`, `no_access`, or both. Also, use the `bind` attribute for these services to further restrict access. Using `bind` is discussed in *Using the `bind` Attribute* on page 246.

Configuration Examples   In this section, we will take a look at a number of different examples, the behavior associated with them, and the log messages that get generated from them.

Access Control.   We'll begin with a simple access control example. In Example 10-47, we see a `login` service entry for the server `topcat` that allows access from any system whose IP address begins with 172 except for those whose address begins with 172.19. We include the `defaults` section in this example

Example 10-47 Sample `login` Service Entry in `/etc/xinetd.conf`

```
defaults
{
        log_type        = SYSLOG local4 info
        log_on_success  = PID HOST EXIT DURATION
        log_on_failure  = HOST
        instances       = 8
}
service login
{
        socket_type     = stream
        protocol        = tcp
        wait            = no
        user            = root
        flags           = REUSE
        only_from       = 172.0.0.0
        no_access       = 172.19.0.0
        log_on_success  += USERID
        log_on_failure  += USERID
        server          = /usr/sbin/in.ftpd
        server_args     = -l -a
}
```

for clarity. Given this entry for the login service, which is invoked through an rlogin command from the client, let's examine a successful and unsuccessful attempt and the logs they generate.

Suppose that the host underdog has the IP address 172.18.5.9. Then, when Mary executes rlogin to topcat, she would be granted access. The successful login is shown in Example 10-48. While Example 10-48 is not terribly exciting, let's look at the log entries generated by Mary's action. These are shown in Example 10-49. The last entry in Example 10-49 reflects the exit condition when Mary logs out. You can always trace the exit of a session by PID so long as you specify that the PID is to be logged in /etc/xinetd.conf, as in Example 10-47. The log entries are as follows: Every xinetd log entry records the date and timestamp, followed by the server hostname, then xinetd, followed by the PID of xinetd in brackets. The first record of Example 10-49 begins with the START keyword indicating the initiation of the session; next the daemon invoked is identified (login), then the PID of the invoked daemon, and last the client address.

Example 10-48 Successful rlogin Attempt

```
[mary@underdog]$ rlogin topcat
Password:
Last login: Wed Apr 14 17:45:02 from roadrunner
[mary@topcat]$
```

Example 10-49 Log Entries Associated with Example 10-48

```
Apr 15 11:01:46 topcat xinetd[1402]: START: login pid=1439
from=172.18.5.9
Apr 15 11:01:46 topcat xinetd[1439]: USERID: login OTHER :mary
...
<lots of unrelated output snipped>
...
Apr 15 11:39:31 topcat xinetd[1402]: EXIT: login status=1 pid=1439 dura-
tion=2265(sec)
```

The second entry begins with the USERID keyword indicating that an RFC1413 call was issued successfully. It is followed by the service name (login), the remote system's response to the RFC1413 call (OTHER in this case), and then finally the remote username (mary).

These log entries are relatively straightforward, but Table 10.14 provides a list of explanations regarding the keywords (such as START, USERID, and EXIT) and the information following that keyword.

Now let's suppose that joe attempts to use rlogin from the host sly.no.good.org (IP address, 19.152.1.5). Example 10-50 displays the result of his attempt. It seems that Joe is getting a little frustrated. Or maybe he's trying to break in (nah, couldn't be!). Let's take a look at the log entries generated by these three attempts in Example 10-51. Notice that the log entries do not include the remote username, even though we have specifically requested that information by virtue of the log_on_failure attribute in Example 10-47

Table 10.14 Description of `xinetd` Log Entries

Log Keyword	Format and Description
START	START: service_id [pid=PID] [from=IPaddress]
	This entry is recorded whenever a service has started. The service_id is the name of the service as specified by the id attribute (recall that if this attribute is not explicitly set, it assumes the value of the service argument; see Table 10.10 on page 232); the PID is the process identifier of the invoked daemon, or 0 if no daemon is invoked (only recorded if PID is specified to log_on_success); and the IPaddress is the client's IP address (only recorded if HOST is log_on_success).
EXIT	EXIT: service_id [type=s] [pid=PID] [duration=#(sec)]
	This entry is recorded when a daemon terminates, only if EXIT is specified to log_on_success. The service_id and PID entries are as before. The type entry will record the exit status or signal that caused termination. The duration captures the duration of the session in seconds and requires the DURATION option to log_on_success.
FAIL	FAIL: service_id reason [from=IPaddress]
	This entry is generated whenever a failed attempt occurs and at least one value is specified to the log_on_failure attribute. The service_id is as before. The reason is a simple word or phrase explaining the cause of failure. The IPaddress is the client's and the HOST value to log_on_failure must be set for this to appear.
DATA	DATA: service_id data
	Recorded only when the RECORD value to log_on_failure occurs. The service_id is as before. The data recorded depends upon the service, but normally includes the remote username if available and status information.
USERID	USERID: service-id text
	This information is recorded only when the USERID value is specified to log_on_success or log_on_failure or both. The service_id is as before. The text includes the client's response to the RFC1413 call and, in particular, the remote username.
NOID	NOID: service_id IPaddress reason
	This entry will appear only if the IDONLY value is set to the flags attribute and the USERID value is set to at least one of log_on_success or log_on_failure. The service_id is as before. The IPaddress given is the client's. The reason is a failure status.

Example 10-50 Failed `rlogin` Attempts from Unauthorized Host

```
sly.no.good.org$ rlogin topcat
topcat: Connection reset by peer
sly.no.good.org$ rlogin -l paul topcat
topcat: Connection reset by peer
sly.no.good.org$ rlogin -l mary topcat
topcat: Connection reset by peer
sly.no.good.org$
```

Example 10-51 Log Entries Associated with Example 10-50

```
Apr 15 12:08:40 topcat xinetd[1402]: FAIL: login address from=19.152.1.5
Apr 15 12:08:52 topcat xinetd[1402]: FAIL: login address from=19.152.1.5
Apr 15 12:12:49 topcat xinetd[1402]: FAIL: login address from=19.152.1.5
```

on page 243. This is because the remote host, `sly.no.good.org`, is not running the `identd` or similar daemon (maybe Joe is up to something!). Because the host `sly.no.good.org` is not in the `only_from` list in Example 10-47, even if we added the entry `flags = IDONLY` to the `login` service entry, it would not record the fact that `sly.no.good.org` is not running `identd`. Such a log record will occur only if the host is allowed.

There is one last log entry to examine. Note that the attribute `instances` is set to `8` in Example 10-47. What happens to the ninth login session? When the ninth user attempts to `rlogin` to `topcat`, that user will see the following error message:

```
rcmd: topcat: Address already in use
```

and the log entry recorded on `topcat` for this event will be

```
Apr 15 13:37:33 topcat xinetd[1402]: FAIL: login service_limit
from=172.17.55.124
```

Comparing this record to the description given in Table 10.14, the `FAIL` keyword is followed by the service, then an explanation for the failure (`service_limit` in this case), and finally the client address.

Using the bind Attribute. The `bind` attribute allows for associating a particular service with a specific interface's IP address. Suppose we have an internal `ftp` server that supplies read-only resources for company employees via anonymous `ftp` (see *Internet Services Resources* on page 255 for more details regarding services such as `ftp`). Further suppose that this `ftp` server has two interfaces—one that attaches to the corporate environment and the other that connects to a private internal network that is generally accessible only to employees who work in that particular group. While there are a number of things that need to be done to secure this server (`ipchains` being one; see Chapter 16), we will consider only the requirement to provide two different `ftp` services based on interfaces in this example. Example 10-52 shows two `ftp` service entries in `/etc/xinetd.conf` that would implement the desired functionality. Again, the `defaults` section is provided for completeness.

Notice that each of the two `ftp` service entries has a unique `id` attribute (see Table 10.10 on page 232). There is no limit to the number of services with the same name as long as each has a unique identifier. In this case, we set the `id` attribute to `ftp` for the internal `ftp` server and `ftp_chroot` for the external anonymous server. Note that in the latter case the daemon invoked is `/usr/sbin/anon/in.aftpd` (this is the effective equivalent to `twist` for TCP_wrappers), which is different than the former service.

Example 10-52 Binding Services to Specific Addresses

```
defaults
{
        log_type            = SYSLOG local4 info
        log_on_success      = PID HOST EXIT DURATION
        log_on_failure      = HOST
        instances           = 8
}
service ftp
{
        id                  = ftp
        socket_type         = stream
        protocol            = tcp
        wait                = no
        user                = root
        only_from           = 172.17.0.0 172.19.0.0/20
        bind                = 172.17.1.1 # widget
        log_on_success     += USERID
        log_on_failure     += USERID
        server              = /usr/sbin/in.ftpd
        server_args         = -l -a
}

service ftp
{
        id                  = ftp_chroot
        socket_type         = stream
        protocol            = tcp
        wait                = no
        user                = root
        bind                = 24.170.1.218 # widget-srvr
        log_on_success     += USERID
        log_on_failure     += USERID
        access_times        = 8:30-11:30 13:00-18:00
        log_on_success     += USERID
        log_on_failure     += USERID
        server              = /usr/sbin/anon/in.aftpd
}
```

The use of `bind` in each case will allow packets destined only to that interface to invoke the indicated daemon. Thus, we can reach the anonymous server by executing `ftp widget-srvr`. Since there are no access controls for that service, everyone has access. However, access is granted only between 8:30 A.M. through 11:30 A.M. and 1 P.M. through 6 P.M. due to the `access_times` attribute.

On the other hand, executing `ftp widget` will be successful only if the first two octets of the client IP address begin with 172.17 or the request comes from an address in the range 172.19.0.0 through 172.19.15.255 because of the `only_from` attribute.

Using the redirect Attribute. The `redirect` attribute provides a method for proxying a service through a server. In other words, the user may `telnet` to a particular server running `xinetd`, and that server would open another connection to a different system. We can accomplish this with the entries in `/etc/xinetd.conf` shown in Example 10-53. Here we are using `telnet` as the example, but it could be used with any TCP service. The REUSE value to the flag

attribute is essential. Notice the use of the `bind` attribute. It has the following
effect. If the command `telnet 172.17.33.111` (or `topcat`, in this case) is used,
then the connection will be made to the server itself (`topcat`). If, on the other
hand, the command `telnet 201.171.99.99` is used, then the connection will be
forwarded to the host `172.17.1.1` (`foghorn`) at port `23` (the `telnet` port). Example 10-54 shows the effect of the latter command. Hey—`foghorn` isn't running
Linux! That's OK, these other UNIX variants will be around only for a little
while longer!

Example 10-53 Use of `redirect` and `bind` in `/etc/xinetd.conf`

```
service telnet
{
        socket_type       = stream
        wait              = no
        flags             = REUSE
        user              = root
        bind              = 172.17.33.111
        server            = /usr/sbin/in.telnetd
        log_on_success    = PID HOST EXIT DURATION USERID
        log_on_failure    = RECORD HOST
}
service telnet
{
        socket_type       = stream
        protocol          = tcp
        wait              = no
        flags             = REUSE
        user              = root
        bind              = 201.171.99.99
        redirect          = 172.17.1.1 23
        log_on_success    = PID HOST EXIT DURATION USERID
        log_on_failure    = RECORD HOST
}
```

Example 10-54 The Effect of `redirect`

```
$ telnet 201.171.99.99
Trying 201.171.99.99...
Connected to 201.171.99.99.
Escape character is '^]'.

UNIX(r) System V Release 4.0 (foghorn)

login:
```

Since Linux supports up to 256 logical interfaces per physical interface,
you could theoretically proxy up to 256 distinct addresses for each physical
address on the system.

While the `redirect` mechanism may be quite useful, be cautious about
implementing it. Make sure that logging occurs both at the proxy server and
at the end system. Other arguably more secure approaches to implementing
proxies are discussed in the references cited in *General Firewall References*
and *DMZ Resources* on page 488 in Chapter 16. However, this implementation
may be convenient in tightly controlled internal networks.

Incorporating TCP_wrappers. Including TCP_wrappers functionality in `/etc/xinetd.conf` is so simple that, except for the significant functionality it represents, it is anticlimactic. All of the capabilities of TCP_wrappers can be incorporated through `xinetd`, just as they were through `inetd`. Example 10-55 displays a sample `/etc/xinetd.conf` file that uses TCP_wrappers for many of its services. Wherever `/usr/sbin/tcpd` is set as the value for the attribute server, that service will be wrapped. Notice also that such entries *always* have the `server_args` attribute set to the daemon to be invoked (fully qualified path). This is required! Recall from *Building `xinetd`* on page 229 that we compiled `xinetd` with `libwrap`. Whether you compile with `libwrap` or not, the configuration file in Example 10-55 will behave as expected. Compiling with `libwrap` has the effect of incorporating only the access restrictions (not the options) found in `/etc/hosts.allow` and `/etc/hosts.deny`. What is shown in Example 10-55 provides the entire set of features—banners, `spawn`, `twist`, etc.—of TCP_wrappers. Everything we said about TCP_wrappers, beginning with the section *TCP_Wrappers* on page 194, now applies here.

Example 10-55 Using TCP_wrappers in `/etc/xinetd.conf`

```
defaults
{
        log_type           = SYSLOG local4 info
        log_on_success     = PID HOST EXIT DURATION
        log_on_failure     = HOST
        instances          = 8
}
defaults
{
        log_type           = SYSLOG local4 info
        log_on_success     = PID HOST EXIT DURATION
        log_on_failure     = HOST
        instances          = 8
}
service xadmin
{
        type               = INTERNAL UNLISTED
        flags              = REUSE
        socket_type        = stream
        protocol           = tcp
        port               = 9967
        wait               = no
        only_from          = topcat
}
service ftp
{
        id                 = ftp
        socket_type        = stream
        protocol           = tcp
        wait               = no
        user               = root
        only_from          = 172.17.0.0
        log_on_success     += USERID
        log_on_failure     += USERID
        access_times       = 8:00-16:30
        server             = /usr/sbin/tcpd
        server_args        = /usr/sbin/in.ftpd -l -a
}
```

Example 10-55 Using TCP_wrappers in `/etc/xinetd.conf` (Continued)

```
service telnet
{
        socket_type     = stream
        wait            = no
        flags           = NAMEINARGS REUSE
        user            = root
        bind            = 172.17.33.111
        server          = /usr/sbin/tcpd
        server_args     = /usr/sbin/in.telnetd
        log_on_success  = PID HOST EXIT DURATION USERID
        log_on_failure  = RECORD HOST
}
service telnet
{
        socket_type     = stream
        protocol        = tcp
        wait            = no
        flags           = REUSE
        user            = root
        bind            = 201.171.99.99
        redirect        = 172.17.1.1 23
        log_on_success  = PID HOST EXIT DURATION USERID
        log_on_failure  = RECORD HOST
}
...
<remainder of file snipped>
...
```

The `xinetd` Daemon

The `xinetd` daemon accepts a number of arguments. These arguments may be overridden by attributes in the special service `default`, or by individual attribute entries in one or more services. However, all parameters given here or their defaults control the behavior of `xinetd` itself. For example, if the `filelog` flag is specified to `xinetd`, then it will log all state transformation messages there, even though the `/etc/xinetd.conf` file specifies other log locations for service-related messages. The available arguments are listed in Table 10.15.

It should be noted that all status information reported by `xinetd`, such as reconfiguration notices, always appears in the log file specified by the `-syslog` or `-filelog` flags (`syslog` selector `daemon.info`, by default), regardless of the settings, through `defaults` or otherwise, in `/etc/xinetd.conf`. Also, if you want to capture the PID of `xinetd` in a file, you may do so with

```
xinetd -pid 2> /var/run/xinetd.pid
```

as shown in the script given in Example 10-38 on page 230.

Signals Available for Use with `xinetd`   The `xinetd` daemon also takes special actions based upon certain signals being sent. Table 10.16 describes the functionality of each of the signals it accepts. Note that you must terminate `xinetd` with the SIGTERM (or more simply TERM) signal whenever you add new services or a `defaults` entry, or whenever one of the following attributes is

Table 10.15 Flags of `xinetd`

Flag	Description
-d	Debug mode. Output may be used with a debugger such as `gdb`.
-syslog *facility*	Specifies the `syslogd` facility. One of `daemon`, `auth`, `user`, `local0-7`.
-filelog *file*	Specifies the *file* to which logs are written instead of `syslog`. Must be absolutely qualified.
-f *config_file*	Specifies the configuration file. Must be absolutely qualified. Default is `/etc/xinetd.conf`.
-pid	Causes the PID to be written to standard error.
-loop *rate*	Specifies the number of daemons forked per second. Default is 10. You may wish to change this for faster machines.
-reuse	Sets the TCP socket to be reusable, which means that other daemons may be started while previous instances are running. You have more specific control over services when using this with the `flags` attribute (see Table 10.10 on page 232).
-limit *numproc*	Limits the total number of concurrently running processes started by `xinetd` to *numprocs*.
-logprocs *limit*	Limits the number of concurrent RFC1413 requests to *limit*.
-shutdownprocs *limit*	When the RECORD value to the `log_on_failure` attribute is used, `xinetd` forks a service called shutdown to collect information when the service terminates. This option limits the total number of concurrently running shutdown processes to `limit`.
-cc *interval*	Forces `xinetd` to run a consistency check on its internal state every *interval* seconds. May manually be accomplished with `killall -IOT xinetd`.

Table 10.16 The `xinetd` Signals

Signal	Action
SIGUSR1	Soft reconfiguration. Rereads `/etc/xinetd.conf` and adjusts accordingly.
SIGUSR2	Hard reconfiguration. Rereads `/etc/xinetd.conf` and kills all daemons that no longer match the criteria set forth in the configuration file. For example, if a client is connected to the server and that client is added to the `no_access` list, then this signal will terminate the client's session.
SIGQUIT	Terminates `xinetd` **without** terminating any of the daemons it forked.
SIGTERM	Terminates all of the daemons forked by `xinetd`; then terminates `xinetd`.
SIGHUP	Dumps `xinetd` state information to `/tmp/xinetd.dump`.
SIGIOT	Checks for corruption of internal databases and reports the result.

changed on any service—protocol, socket_type, type, or wait. Whenever you issue a soft or hard reconfiguration signal to xinetd, a log entry of the type shown in Example 10-56 will be written. This particular example is the result of a hard reconfiguration. Note that one service was terminated as a result of this hard reconfiguration (identified by dropped=1).

Example 10-56 Log Record for a Hard Reconfiguration of xinetd

```
Apr 15 14:42:31 topcat xinetd[1402]: Starting hard reconfiguration
Apr 15 14:42:31 topcat xinetd[1402]: readjusting service servers
Apr 15 14:42:31 topcat xinetd[1402]: readjusting service services
Apr 15 14:42:31 topcat xinetd[1402]: readjusting service telnet
Apr 15 14:42:31 topcat xinetd[1402]: readjusting service shell
Apr 15 14:42:31 topcat xinetd[1402]: readjusting service login
Apr 15 14:42:31 topcat xinetd[1402]: readjusting service talk
Apr 15 14:42:31 topcat xinetd[1402]: readjusting service ntalk
Apr 15 14:42:31 topcat xinetd[1402]: readjusting service pop-2
Apr 15 14:42:31 topcat xinetd[1402]: readjusting service pop-3
Apr 15 14:42:31 topcat xinetd[1402]: readjusting service imap
Apr 15 14:42:31 topcat xinetd[1402]: readjusting service linuxconf
Apr 15 14:42:31 topcat xinetd[1402]: readjusting service ftp
Apr 15 14:42:31 topcat xinetd[1402]: Reconfigured: new=1 old=12 dropped=1 (services)
```

NOTE

As of this writing, the most reliable way to ensure that a modified /etc/ xinetd.conf file is read is to stop and restart the xinetd daemon. It is best to terminate xinetd with a SIGTERM signal (or by using a script similar to that given in Example 10-38 on page 230). As described in this section, sending xinetd a SIGTERM causes it to terminate (with a SIGKILL or signal number 9) every daemon under its control. Sometimes there is a delay before xinetd's children terminate which means that, if you kill and immediately restart xinetd, it may not be able to bind to all ports (an error message to this effect will be entered in the log file for xinetd, **not** the log file[s] specified for the services). This is why the sleep 3 command appears in the script in Example 10-38 between the stop and start commands. You may completely obviate this problem by using the flags = REUSE attribute and value for TCP services, such as telnet and ftp, or by specifying the -reuse option to xinetd itself.

WHICH ONE SHOULD I USE?

The principal disadvantages to xinetd were identified in *Disadvantages of xinetd* on page 228. Perhaps the most significant of them is that xinetd is not currently part of any major Linux distribution. This fundamentally means that additional administrative effort is required to install it on each system where it is desired. And, of course, this has an additional impact every time you upgrade. This type of issue, while significant, may be mitigated somewhat if you employ the suggestions outlined in Chapter 18.

One of the significant benefits of xinetd for any systems exposed to an untrusted network, such as the Internet, is its ability to limit the number of daemons running and the amounts of log data it accepts. This can make the perpetration of a DoS attack against such a protected system much more difficult. Additionally, its ability to bind services to a particular interface and proxy services to another host is a useful feature for some systems exposed to the Internet. Generally, its ability to invoke `tcpd` and logging make it useful for all systems. Maybe someday it will replace `inetd`.

On the other hand, TCP_wrappers and `inetd` are distributed as part of Linux from most vendors. Administrative effort is therefore lower. Also, TCP_wrappers is commonly used and is quite mature. Both TCP_wrappers and `inetd` have been and continue to be extensively exposed to critical review. Do not underestimate this aspect of any tool as it may well have significant ramifications with respect to the security of your computing environment. As always, check `bugtraq`, `comp.unix.security`, and other similar resources (see Appendix A) as a regular part of your administrative activity.

Since `xinetd`, `inetd`, and `portmap` can coexist peacefully (so long as they don't try to simultaneously provide the same services—see the Warning on page 231), there may be some cases where it is advantageous to use a combination of these tools. In any event, the tool or combination of tools you implement should be part of your overall security strategy (see Chapter 2).

In general, it probably makes sense to run `xinetd` on those systems that are most likely to come under attack as well as any systems that are mission critical. Whether or not you should install `xinetd` everywhere depends on your Security Policy and how much time you have.

SUMMARY

We covered a lot of stuff in this chapter! We looked at `inetd` and TCP_wrappers as well as the portmapper and its access control mechanism. We finished with a discussion of `xinetd`. While `xinetd` offers many features and benefits, we noted that it is more complex to configure and maintain and that it lacks the maturity of `inetd`.

We also pointed out that, whichever mechanism you use, it is important to eliminate all services that are not expressly allowed by your Security Policy. Make sure to wrap all allowed services and take full advantage of access control. Use `ipchains` and/or other utilities that provide additional protection. Finally, make sure that you regularly read the log files generated by the various utilities.

FOR FURTHER READING

Resources for TCP_Wrappers

All files are in the top-level directory of the source tree:

```
DISCLAIMER
Makefile
README
README.NIS
```

There is one paper in the distribution.

1. Venema, Wietse, *TCP WRAPPER: Network Monitoring, Access Control, and Booby Traps*, Mathematics and Computing Science, Eindhoven University of Technology, The Netherlands, no date.

The UNIX manual pages:

```
hosts_access(3,5)
hosts_options(5)
tcpd(8)
tcpdchk(8)
tcpdmatch(8)
```

Resources for the Portmapper

All files are in the top-level directory of the source tree, except where noted:

```
/usr/src/redhat/SPECS/portmap-4.0.spec
Makefile
README
```

The UNIX manual pages:

There are no manual pages for the portmapper!

Resources for xinetd

All files are in the top-level directory of the source tree. The INSTALL document is somewhat misleading as it does not mention the configure utility:

```
COPYRIGHT
INSTALL
Makefile
README
xinetd/sample.conf
```

The UNIX manual pages:

```
xinetd(1)
xinetd.conf(5)
xinetd.log(5)
```

Web resource:

```
http://synack.net/xinetd/faq.html
```

You may subscribe to the `xinetd` e-mail list by sending e-mail with `sub-scribe xinetd` in the body of the message to `majordomo@synack.net`. The subject line is irrelevant.

Internet Services Resources

These two books provide good background and security information related to Internet servers:

1. Garfinkel, Simson, and Gene Spafford, *Web Security & Commerce*, Sebastopol, California, O'Reilly & Associates, Inc., 1997.
2. Liu, Cricket, et al., *Managing Internet Information Services*, Sebastopol, California, O'Reilly & Associates, Inc., 1994.

The following web sites contain valuable information about securely configuring Internet servers:

```
http://www.cert.org/ftp/tech_tips/
http://ciac.llnl.gov/ciac/documents/ciac2308.html
```

## CHAPTER 11

Let 'Em Sniff the Net!

The Secure Shell

One of the most important utilities in the public domain is the Secure Shell (SSH) written by Tatu Ylonen. This client-server utility provides the capability to build an encrypted tunnel between two or more hosts, protecting all aspects—including passwords—of the communication from eavesdroppers. This is particularly useful for accessing systems over the network as root. This chapter covers obtaining, installing, and implementing this utility.

OVERVIEW OF SSH

The Secure Shell is a client-server application that provides secure communications through encryption, host authentication through an RSA-based mechanism, and a variety of options for user authentication. It provides replacement programs for rlogin, rsh, and rcp. It also provides for encrypted X Window System connections and encrypted sessions for any TCP connection.

Before we get on to the business of installing, configuring, and using SSH, we will explore the authentication processes of SSH.

Host-Based Authentication Using RSA

The authentication processes described in this section use symmetric and asymmetric encryption schemes. Please refer to *Cryptography* on page 41 in Chapter 3 for further details related to encryption.

When a user invokes `ssh`, the client-side program, it requests a connection with a remote host (the server). The server must be running the SSH daemon (`sshd`). When the server receives the client's `ssh` request, it responds by sending the client its *Public Host Key* (we'll call it *H*) and its *Public Server Key* (we'll call it *S*). The term *Host Keys* refers to the RSA private/public key pair generated by `sshd` at install time; by default the Host Keys utilize a modulus of 1024 bits. Thus, *H* is the Public Host Key and is stored in the file `/etc/ssh/ssh_host_key.pub` (the default location for the version we will use in this chapter; see *Compiling SSH* on page 265, for compile-time options relating to the location of the various files). The *Private Host Key* is stored in the file `/etc/ssh/ssh_host_key` and must **not** be encrypted (*Private User Keys*, described in *RSA Authentication* on page 261, on the other hand are normally encrypted for additional security). Consequently, it is critical to properly protect this file with appropriate permissions, and it is a good idea to set the immutable bit (see *File Attributes* on page 75 in Chapter 4) as well. Additionally, the `/etc/ssh/ssh_host_key` file should be fingerprinted by Tripwire (see Chapter 14). These keys may be changed manually by the root user with the `ssh-keygen` program (`ssh-keygen` is discussed in *Using* `ssh-keygen` and *Using* `ssh-keygen` *for root* on page 297).

The term *Server Keys* refers to the RSA private/public key pair that is generated at run time by `sshd` and regenerated every hour (by default) after its first use. These keys use a 768-bit modulus, by default. Neither the Public Server Key, *S*, nor its companion *Private Server Key* is stored on disk.

Once the client has received the *H* and *S* keys, it attempts to verify the server's Public Host Key *H* by checking the two files—`/etc/ssh_known_hosts` and the client user's `$HOME/.ssh/known_hosts`. By default, if the server's Public Host Key *H* is not found in one of these two files, `ssh` will warn the user and ask if the user would like to add the key to `$HOME/.ssh/known_hosts`. While this automatic addition of keys to the file is convenient, it leaves open the possibility of someone spoofing the server. The automated updating of Public Host Keys can be disabled by setting `StrictHostKeyChecking` to `yes` at the command line in the user's `$HOME/.ssh/config` file, or in the systemwide `/etc/ssh/ssh_config` file (discussed in *Configuring the Client Side* on page 275). However, if you disable the automatic updating of Public Host Keys, then you must distribute them manually. The manual process may be enscripted for convenience, at which point any security gains made by enabling `StrictHostKeyChecking` are lost.

After the client successfully validates the server's Public Host Key *H*, the client generates a 256-bit random number, *N*, and encrypts *N* with both *H* and *S* (first with *H*, then with *S*). It then sends the encrypted *N* to the server. *N* is used by both client and server to derive the secret key for symmetric encryption (the U.S. version uses Blowfish, while the international version uses IDEA, by default). This secret key is often called the *Session Key*. All subsequent communications for the duration of the connection are encrypted using the agreed-upon symmetric cipher and the Session Key. This completes the

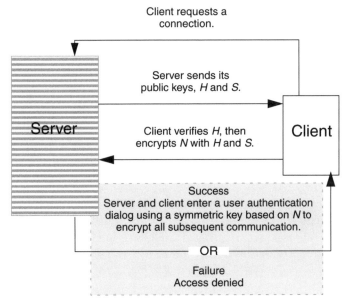

Fig. 11.1 RSA Host-Based Authentication

host authentication component to establishing the SSH session. This process is called *RSA Host-Based Authentication*. Figure 11.1 depicts the flow of events for RSA Host-Based Authentication.

If this process fails for any reason, then access is denied. Once host authentication completes successfully, sshd moves on to authenticate the user.

Authenticating the User

Throughout this chapter we will collectively refer to the client-side programs ssh, slogin, and scp as simply ssh with respect to our description of authentication. In other words, the authentication processes apply equivalently to ssh, slogin, and scp except where noted.

The server and client authentication dialog proceeds based on the configuration of the sshd configuration file /etc/ssh/sshd_config and compile-time options. This process is described in the following sections. The first three sections deal with authentication by sshd without requiring a password from the user. We will call these methods *nonpassword authentication schemes*.

NOTE

As with rlogin, rsh, and rcp, ssh passes the username of the user invoking ssh to the server. You may specify a different user by supplying the username to the -1 argument of ssh (see *Configuring the Client Side* on page 275).

Trusted Host Authentication.   The behavior of `sshd` in the presence of the `$HOME/.rhosts` and `/etc/hosts.equiv` or `$HOME/.shosts` and `/etc/shosts.equiv` files is quite similar to that of `rsh`, but only when `RhostsAuthentication` is set to yes in the `/etc/ssh/sshd_config` file (the default is `no`, and changing the setting to `yes` is strongly discouraged). The latter two files, namely `$HOME/.shosts` and `/etc/shosts.equiv`, are functionally identical to the former two files but are unique to `ssh`. In this way, if you are using both the r-commands (`rsh`, `rlogin`, `rcp`, etc.) and `ssh`, trusted hosts and users may be distinguished. The details of the `/etc/hosts.equiv` and `.rhosts` files are provided in *Trusted Host Files and Related Commands* on page 36 in Chapter 3.

If `RhostsAuthentication` is set to yes in the `/etc/ssh/sshd_config` file and an entry exists in `/etc/hosts.equiv` or `/etc/shosts.equiv` containing the client hostname (except for the root user) matching the incoming request, then the user is authenticated and access is granted. As an alternative to the `/etc/hosts.equiv` or `/etc/shosts.equiv` entry, if the client hostname exists in either the `.rhosts` or `.shosts` file in the user's home directory, then the user will be granted access. This latter scheme supports the root user as well.

If this scheme is turned on and fails for any reason, then the `sshd` will proceed to the next authentication scheme as shown in Figure 11.4 on page 284.

We will collectively refer to the `$HOME/.rhosts` and `/etc/hosts.equiv` or `$HOME/.shosts` and `/etc/shosts.equiv` files as *trusted host files*.

WARNING!

> The use of the `$HOME/.rhosts` and `/etc/hosts.equiv` or `$HOME/.shosts` and `/etc/shosts.equiv` files exclusively for authentication affords no additional authentication security over the procedure described in *Host-Based Authentication Using RSA* on page 257 and is *not* recommended.
>
> Furthermore, while it is possible to configure a server to support `sshd` together with `in.rshd`, `in.rlogind`, `in.rexecd`, and `rexd`, it is strongly discouraged. If each of these r-daemons is not disabled, then all of the security and authentication benefits of `ssh` may be completely circumvented.

Rhosts and RSA Authentication.   This scheme adds a bit of protection over simple trusted hosts checks. It is controlled by the `RhostsRSAAuthentication` keyword. If that keyword is set to yes (the default) in `/etc/ssh/sshd_config`, if the client/user pair matches an entry in one of the trusted hosts files as described in the previous section, and if the server is able to validate the client's Public Host Key in `/etc/ssh/ssh_known_hosts` or the `known_hosts` file in the user's `$HOME/.ssh` directory, then the user is granted access. Figure 11.2 diagrams this process.

If this scheme is turned on and fails for any reason, then the `sshd` will proceed to the next authentication scheme as shown in Figure 11.4 on page 284.

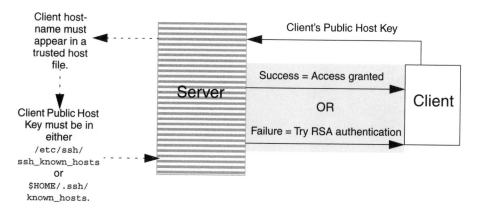

Fig. 11.2 Rhosts and RSA Authentication

RSA Authentication.   This scheme represents the strongest nonpassword authentication mechanism. It is controlled by the RSAAuthentication keyword in /etc/ssh/sshd_config, which is set to yes by default. In this case, the client sends the server the identifier of its *Public User Key*—we'll call it P_i. *User Keys* are identical to Host Keys (1024-bit RSA private/public key pair), except that they are stored in the user's $HOME/.ssh/identity (*Private User Key*) and $HOME/.ssh/identity.pub (Public User Key) files. These keys are generated using ssh-keygen on a per-user basis. Additionally, ssh-keygen will afford the user the opportunity to encrypt $HOME/.ssh/identity, which contains the Private User Key. This is described in *An Initial Example* on page 293 and *Using ssh-keygen* on page 297.

The server looks up the client's Public User Key in the $HOME/.ssh/ authorized_key (discussed in the sections, *An Initial Example* on page 293 and *Options in $HOME/.ssh/authorized_keys* on page 299) file of the user based on the identifier sent by the client. Upon finding the Public User Key *P*, the server encrypts a 256-bit random number *N*, with the Public User Key and sends it to the client. This is called the *challenge*. The client decrypts it with the related Private User Key *T*. The client then computes a 128-bit MD5 hash[1] of the random number and sends it back to the server (only the hash is sent to the server to avoid a particular type of cryptanalytic attack known as a chosen plaintext attack). The server also computes the 128-bit MD5 hash of the random number and compares its computed hash with that sent by the client. If they match, then the user is authenticated and access is granted. Figure 11.3 depicts this process.

This approach requires that each user wishing to use RSA authentication must place his or her User Keys on each system involved. The user will

---

1. Cryptographic hash functions are discussed in *Hash Functions and Digital Signatures* on page 44 in Chapter 3.

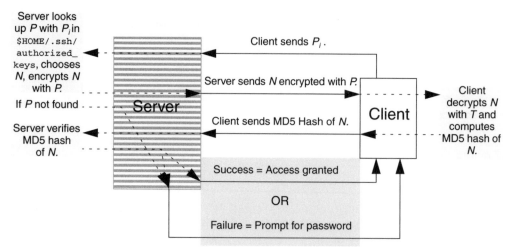

Server looks up *P* with P_i in $HOME/.ssh/authorized_keys, chooses *N*, encrypts *N* with *P*.

If *P* not found

Server verifies MD5 hash of *N*.

Client sends P_i.

Server sends *N* encrypted with *P*.

Client sends MD5 Hash of *N*.

Success = Access granted

OR

Failure = Prompt for password

Server

Client

Client decrypts *N* with *T* and computes MD5 hash of *N*.

Fig. 11.3 RSA Authentication

also be required to enter his or her passphrase each time this authentication procedure is utilized. The submission of passphrases can be accomplished automatically by using the ssh-agent program, discussed in *Managing RSA Authentication with* ssh-agent *and* ssh-add on page 301.

If this scheme is turned on and fails for any reason, then the sshd will prompt the user for an appropriate password based on compile-time options.

NOTE

The RhostsAuthentication, RhostsRSAAuthentication, and RSAAuthentication keywords discussed in the preceding sections were based on the values set in /etc/ssh/sshd_config. These keywords control the behavior of the server. However, they must be set to yes either by option to ssh at the command line, in $HOME/.ssh/config, or in /etc/ssh/ssh_config on the client system in order for the client to attempt to negotiate that particular authentication scheme. In other words, if any of the aforementioned keywords is set to no on the client side, then the associated authentication scheme will never be attempted; whereas, if any of the aforementioned keywords is set to no on the server side, then the authentication scheme is not allowed.

What Are All Those Keys, Again?   Keeping track of all the keys used by SSH is a bit difficult. Table 11.1 lists the keys associated with SSH, details about how they are generated and how long they last, and their purpose. This table provides a handy quick reference of the SSH keys.

Compiled Authentication Scheme.   If you have compiled ssh (see *Compiling SSH* on page 265) with a special authentication mechanism, such as TIS or SecureID, then that scheme may be invoked whenever the appropriate keywords are set in /etc/ssh/sshd_config and /etc/ssh/ssh_config files. If so

Table 11.1 SSH Keys and Their Use

Key Type	Generation and Duration	Purpose and Encryption Type
Server Keys	First generated when `sshd` starts and regenerated every hour after first use.	Used for RSA Host-Based Authentication. Public and Private Server Keys are never stored on disk. RSA asymmetric encryption.
Host Keys	Generated at compile time. Not regenerated automatically. May be regenerated manually. See *Using ssh-keygen for root* on page 297.	Used for RSA Host-Based Authentication and for Rhosts and RSA Authentication. RSA asymmetric encryption.
User Keys	Must be generated manually by the user. May be regenerated manually. See the section, *Using ssh-keygen* on page 297.	Used exclusively for RSA Authentication. RSA asymmetric encryption.
Session Key	Derived from a random number chosen by the client during RSA Host-Based Authentication. Used for the duration of an SSH session for symmetric encryption. Cannot be generated manually.	Used for the SSH encrypted tunnel. All data between client and server is encrypted using this key and a symmetric algorithm upon successful completion of RSA Host-Based Authentication. Algorithm used is Blowfish for U.S., IDEA for international, or as specified by client and supported by server.

configured, then the special authentication scheme will be checked *before* password-based authentication.

Password-Based Authentication. If none of the three nonpassword authentication schemes we discussed succeeds, and if no special authentication compile-time options are chosen, then the user is prompted for his or her password. The version of SSH we are discussing implements PAM as `account`, `password`, and `session` modules only and does not support authentication.

AVAILABLE VERSIONS OF SSH

There are two major releases of SSH—versions 1.2.x and 2.x. The version 1.2.x releases are distributed under a very liberal license that permits use of the product, as long as it is not used for revenue-generating purposes. Reference the file COPYING in the `ssh` 1.2.x distribution for further details. As of this writing, the latest release under these terms is 1.2.27, and its home site is `ftp://ftp.cs.hut.fi/pub/ssh/`. Obtaining and installing this release is discussed in the next section.

Version 2.x of SSH is available under a much more restrictive license. It may be used without charge only for personal purposes. For further information and pricing details of this version, reference `http://www.datafellows.com/`.

There are a number of additional features with the 2.x release such as secure `ftp` and `telnet` replacements. However, due to the licensing restrictions on the 2.x release, we will discuss version 1.2.27.

OBTAINING AND INSTALLING SSH

You can obtain SSH in `tar` format from `ftp://ftp.cs.hut.fi/pub/ssh`. However, an RPM format distribution is also available. It makes installation much easier and incorporates PAM support. Consequently, we will discuss the RPM distribution. The 1.2.27 release of SSH, in RPM format, can be obtained from

    http://www.replay.com/redhat/ssh.html

where you will find both U.S. and international versions. Each of the two versions contains RPMs that are quite similar; the major difference is that the U.S. version is configured and compiled so as to avoid licensing and patent issues with RSA and IDEA in the United States. The U.S. version includes the following RPMs

    ssh-1.2.27-5us.i386.rpm
    ssh-1.2.27-5us.src.rpm
    ssh-clients-1.2.27-5us.i386.rpm
    ssh-extras-1.2.27-5us.i386.rpm
    ssh-server-1.2.27-5us.i386.rpm

Each of the five packages contains separate elements of the SSH utility. Throughout this chapter, we will refer to the collection of these five packages as the RPMs. The package `ssh-1.2.27-5us.src.rpm` contains the source files together with the Linux patches and the RPM `spec` file (see *MAXIMUM RPM* as cited in *RPM Resources* on page 28 for further details of `spec` files). We will look at compiling SSH in the next section.

The `ssh-clients-1.2.27-5us.i386.rpm` package contains the client-side programs `ssh` and `slogin` (for replacing `rsh` and `rlogin`), as well as utilities that provide an X Window System–based network authentication mechanism. This client package also contains the associated `man` pages and the client configuration file, `ssh_config`. It includes everything necessary to set up an SSH client on Red Hat Linux. Note that `slogin` is a symbolic link to `ssh` and is therefore identical to `ssh`.

The `ssh-server-1.2.27-5us.i386.rpm` package contains the server-side daemon, `sshd`, the associated `man` page, an example `/etc/pam.d/ssh` file, and the server configuration file `sshd_config`. These files are used to set up an SSH server.

The `ssh-1.2.27-5us.i386.rpm` package contains the `scp` program (to replace `rcp`), the key generator `ssh-keygen`, `man` pages, and additional documentation. This package is a base package required by any system which will utilize SSH.

The `ssh-extras-1.2.27-5us.i386.rpm` package contains the `make-ssh-known-hosts` perl script, the `ssh-askpass` program, and related `man` pages. These are in a separate package so that these utilities can be left off hosts without Perl or the X Window System (`ssh-askpass` uses the X11 library). The installation of this package is optional.

Compiling SSH

The source tree found in the `ssh-1.2.27-5us.src.rpm` package is derived from the original found at `ftp://ftp.cs.hut.fi/pub/ssh`. Consequently, both utilize the `configure` utility (see *Implementing Version 1.5.9p4* on page 175 of Chapter 9 for a discussion of `configure`) to prepare SSH for compilation. Table 11.2 describes a few of the configuration options available.

There are many other `configure` options; you may view a brief description of each with `configure --help`.

After choosing the appropriate `configure` options, you may run `configure` and then `make` and `make install`. Upon the successful completion of `make`, SSH will generate the initial RSA Host Keys. This is also accomplished if SSH is installed using the RPMs as shown in Example 11-1. Here we show the installation of all RPMs except the `ssh-1.2.27-5us.src.rpm` package. The installation of the base package, `ssh-1.2.27-5us.i386.rpm`, causes the generation of the Host Keys.

The `ssh-1.2.27-5us.i386.rpm` package is required on all systems that will use SSH. The `ssh-server-1.2.27-5us.i386.rpm` package is required on systems that will accept incoming requests from `ssh`. The `ssh-clients-1.2.27-5us.i386.rpm` package is required on all systems that will generate SSH requests using `ssh`. The `ssh-extras-1.2.27-5us.i386.rpm` package is entirely optional.

Example 11-1 Installing SSH Using `rpm`

```
# rpm -ivh *.rpm
ssh ##################################################
Initializing random number generator...
Generating p:  ...........................++ (distance 488)
Generating q:  ..............++ (distance 232)
Computing the keys...
Key generation complete.
Your identification has been saved in /etc/ssh/ssh_host_key.
Your public key is:
1024 33
15426054557127211249788476024775524981701047568925039044494757968188820013
87179674139205166261648174562963556772303711386376494805508598937319957340
81697635844600961829446935388719685474415237238150938233352331363282270968
26946572429678379757705714695037513688623556522818862767365834913776101007
16471677449194123 root@underdog
Your public key has been saved in /etc/ssh/ssh_host_key.pub
ssh-clients ##################################################
ssh-extras ##################################################
ssh-server ##################################################
```

Table 11.2 Options to `configure` for `ssh`

Option	Default	Description
`--prefix=`*path*	Default path is `/usr/local`. Set to `/usr` in RPMs.	Specifies the top-level directory for the `ssh` installation. All binaries, scripts, and `man` pages will be located in subdirectories of this directory.
`--with-none`	No	Allows `ssh` sessions to be established without encryption. This option is not recommended.
`--without-none`	Yes	Disallows `ssh` sessions without encryption.
`--with-rsh[=`*path*`]`	No	Specifies the path to the `rsh` binary. By default the directories in PATH are searched.
`--without-rsh`	No	Disallows the use of `rsh` altogether. This option may be set later in the `sshd_config` file.
`--with-etcdir=`*path*	Default is `/etc`. Set to `/etc/ssh` in RPMs.	Specifies the path to the configuration files, such as `sshd_config` and `ssh_config`.
`--with-securid[=`*path*`]`	No	Enables support for the Security Dynamics, Inc., SecureID one-time password server. *path* is the location of the SecureID daemon.
`--with-tis[=`*dir*`]`	No	Enables support for the TIS authentication server. For use with FWTK or Gauntlet. *dir* indicates the top-level directory tree for the TIS software. See *Additional Firewall Software* on page 486 for further information about FWTK.
`--with-kerberos5[=`*dir*`]`	No	Enable support for Kerberos 5. *dir* is the location of the top-level directory containing the Kerberos 5 software.
`--with-libwrap[=`*path*`]`	No. Turned on in RPMs.	Incorporates TCP_wrappers access control. This option enables the use of `/etc/hosts.allow` and `/etc/hosts.deny` by `sshd`.
`--disable-asm`	No	Normally, when `ssh` compiles, it attempts to use hardware-specific assembler routines for performance benefits. If you are having problems generating keys, try recompiling with this option.
`--enable-group-writeability`	No	Allows for group writeability on files checked via the `strictMode` option. See *A Common Problem* on page 296 for more details.

CONFIGURING THE SECURE SHELL

Now that we've got `ssh` installed, let's take a look at the configuration and key management files. Table 11.3 lists the files, their locations (in accordance with the compile-time options used in building the RPMs), their functions, and whether they are used by the client or server.

In the following two sections, we will look at the server-side and client-side configuration files. Examples and usage for the various configuration options are also provided later in the chapter.

Table 11.3 Configuration and Key Management Files for SSH

File	Client or Server	Description
`/etc/ssh/sshd_config`	Server	Contains the server-side options. Discussed in *Configuring the Server Side* on page 269.
`/etc/ssh/ssh_config`	Client	Contains the client-side options. Discussed in *Configuring the Client Side* on page 275.
`$HOME/.ssh/config`	Client	Client-side options on a per-user basis. These options do not override those in `/etc/ssh/ssh_config`.
`/etc/ssh/ssh_known_hosts`	Both	Contains a list of Public Host Keys of hosts with which `ssh` connections are made. This file is not generated automatically, but can be created and maintained manually.
`$HOME/.ssh/known_hosts`	Both	Contains a list of Public Host Keys of hosts with which `ssh` connections are made. This file can be updated automatically if the `StrictHostKeyChecking` keyword is set to `no` or `ask`. See *Initial RSA Host-Based Authentication Configuration* on page 285.
`$HOME/.ssh/authorized_keys`	Server	Contains a list of Public User Keys of hosts with which `ssh` connections are made using RSA Authentication.
`/etc/ssh/ssh_host_key`	Both, but used only locally.	Contains the Private Host Key. This file is very sensitive and may not be encrypted. It should be root owned and read/write by root (default). Set the immutable bit on this file and make sure that Tripwire checks it. Normally generated at installtime, but may be regenerated with `ssh-keygen` (see *Using ssh-keygen for root* on page 297).

Table 11.3 Configuration and Key Management Files for SSH (Continued)

File	Client or Server	Description
/etc/ssh/ssh_host_key.pub	Both	Contains the Public Host Key. This file should be world readable, owned by root, and writeable by root (default). It contains no sensitive information. Normally generated at install-time, but may be regenerated with ssh-keygen (see *Using ssh-keygen for root* on page 297).
$HOME/.ssh/identity	Client, but only used locally.	Contains the Private User Key. Used only for RSA Authentication. Generated when the user executes ssh-keygen. By default, this file is read/write by the user only and should remain that way. This file will be encrypted if a non-empty passphrase is supplied to ssh-keygen (see *Using ssh-keygen for root* on page 297).
$HOME/.ssh/identity.pub	Both	Contains the Public User Key. Used only for RSA Authentication. This file should be world readable, owned and writeable by the user (default). It is not encrypted.
/etc/ssh/ssh_random_seed	Neither	An encrypted file that contains the seed used for generating random numbers. Used for generating Host Keys and RSA Authentication random numbers. This file is, and should remain, read/write, owned by root.
$HOME/.ssh/random_seed	Neither	Contains the seed used for generated User Keys. This file will be encrypted if a nonempty passphrase is supplied to ssh-keygen (see *Using ssh-keygen* on page 297). This file is, and should remain, read/write, owned by the user in whose home directory the file appears.
/etc/ssh/sshd.pid	Server	Contains the PID of the process currently listening for connections. There may be many sshd processes running.
/etc/environment $HOME/.ssh/environment	Client	These files set shell environment variables for the ssh client.
/etc/ssh/sshrc $HOME/.ssh/rc	Server	Commands in these files are executed after reading the environment files, but before starting the user's shell or executing the user's command.
/etc/hosts.equiv /etc/shosts.equiv $HOME/.rhosts $HOME/.shosts	Server	Trusted hosts files. Described in *Trusted Host Authentication* on page 260. The /etc/shosts.equiv and $HOME/.shosts are unique to ssh.

Configuring the Server Side

In this section we will document the command line options to sshd, the server-side daemon, and its configuration files.

Normally, sshd is invoked at boottime by a start-up script. The RPMs we've used creates the /etc/rc.d/init.d/sshd script and links it to appropriate kill and start scripts (see *Start-Up Scripts* on page 24 in Chapter 3 for an overview of the system scripts). By default, sshd listens to port 22. When a connection request comes in, sshd forks a child sshd that will handle all key exchanges, authentication, encryption, and data transfers for the specific connection. While it is possible to invoke sshd through inetd or xinetd (see *Replacing inetd with xinetd* on page 226 of Chapter 10 for a discussion of xinetd), it is not recommended because of the potential initial delays incurred by the RSA Host-Based Authentication mechanism (described in *Host-Based Authentication Using RSA* on page 257), which may cause premature connection refusals.

The sshd gets its configuration information first from the command line and then from the /etc/ssh/sshd_config configuration file. Command line options take precedence over settings in /etc/ssh/sshd_config. Table 11.4 describes the available command line options to sshd.

The keywords or parameters and their meanings in the /etc/ssh/sshd_config file are described in Table 11.5. All blank lines and lines beginning with # in this file are ignored. All keywords are case insensitive, and a space separates the keyword from its arguments.

Table 11.4 Command Line Options to sshd

Option	Description
-b bits	Specifies the number of bits in the Server Keys. Default is 768 bits.
-d	Debug mode. The daemon generates debug output to syslog. In this mode sshd will not fork subprocesses and will terminate itself upon disconnection.
-f config_file	Specifies the absolutely qualified name of the sshd configuration file. The compiled default for the RPMs discussed herein is /etc/ssh/sshd_config; ordinarily it is /etc/sshd_config.
-g grace_time	Sets the time, in seconds, for clients to authenticate the user. If the user authentication process does not complete prior to this time, then the server will disconnect and exit. The default is 600 seconds (normally, more than sufficient). A value of 0 indicates no limit.
-h host_key_file	Specifies the absolutely qualified name of the file containing the Private Host Key. The compiled default for the RPMs discussed herein is /etc/ssh/ssh_host_key; ordinarily it is /etc/ssh_host_key.
-i	Indicates that sshd is invoked through inetd (or xinetd). Due to authentication delays, particularly if sshd needs to generate new Server Keys, this is not recommended as it may cause premature disconnects.

Table 11.4 Command Line Options to `sshd` (Continued)

Option	Description
`-k key_gen_time`	Specifies in seconds how frequently `sshd` regenerates the Server Keys after its first use. Default is `3600` seconds. A value of `0` causes these keys to never be regenerated and cannot be recommended. Since these keys are never stored anywhere, it is nearly impossible to recover the key after the specified time period. This makes cryptanalytic attacks much more difficult as long as the keys are changed frequently.
`-p port`	Specifies the port that `sshd` listens to for incoming requests. The default is 22.
`-q`	Quiet mode. This suppresses all logging except fatal errors. Normally, the initial connection request, authentication information, and connection termination are logged through the `syslog` facility DAEMON. See the `SyslogFacility` keyword in Table 11.5 for configuration options.
`-V`	Specifies SSH Version 2 compatibility mode. This option should be used in environments where both versions 1.x.x and 2.x.x are running.

Table 11.5 Keywords in `/etc/ssh/sshd_config`

Keyword	Description
`AllowGroups`	This keyword may be followed by a space-separated list of group names. If so specified, only users whose primary group appears in this list will be allowed to log in. This specification is in addition to all other authentication requirements. By default, no group checking is done. Group names may include the `*` and `?` wildcards, which have the same behavior as in the shell.
`DenyGroups`	Same as `AllowGroups`, except that users whose primary groups are listed will be denied access. By default, no groups are denied.
`AllowHosts`	This keyword may be followed by a space-separated list of hostnames or IP addresses. If specified, logins are allowed only from the indicated hosts. The `*` and `?` wildcards may be used. Aliased hostnames will not match, so be sure to use canonical hostnames. Note that, if TCP_wrappers support is compiled in, the intersection of this list and the rules in `/etc/hosts.allow` applies. See *TCP_Wrappers* on page 194 in Chapter 10 for a discussion of TCP_wrappers.
`DenyHosts`	Same as `AllowHosts`, except that it denies access requests from the listed hosts. If TCP_wrappers support is compiled in, the intersection of this list and the rules in `/etc/hosts.deny` applies.

Table 11.5 Keywords in `/etc/ssh/sshd_config` (Continued)

Keyword	Description
AllowSHosts	This keyword may be followed by a space-separated list of hostnames or IP addresses. The * and ? wildcards may be used. If specified, trusted hosts ($HOME/.rhosts, /etc/hosts.equiv, $HOME/.shosts, and /etc/shosts.equiv) entries are honored only for the indicated hosts. By default, all hosts may be in a trusted host file. For this to have any effect one or both of the keywords, RhostsAuthentication and RhostsRSAAuthentication must be set to yes.
DenySHosts	Same as AllowSHosts, except that the indicated hosts will not be afforded trusted host status.
AllowUsers	This keyword may be followed by a space-separated list of usernames or username@hostname patterns. The hostname may be either the hostname or IP address. The * and ? wildcards may be used. If specified, only the indicated users (from the indicated hosts, if specified) will gain access. This specification is in addition to all other authentication requirements. By default, all users are allowed.
DenyUsers	Same as AllowUsers except that any entries in the list are denied access.
AccountExpireWarningDays	Specifies the number of days prior to the expiration of a user account that sshd will display a warning to the user. The default is 14; if set to 0, warning messages are disabled. Note that these messages are in addition to any generated by PAM or other mechanisms.
AllowTCPForwarding	If yes, port forwarding requests by the client are honored. If no, they are not.
CheckMail	If yes, sshd will print a message about mail. If no, it will not. The default is yes. This will duplicate messages generated by pam_mail, if that PAM module is used.
FascistLogging	If yes, sshd logs verbosely and includes detailed information about the authentication dialog that is useful for debugging (and may also give an interloper some additional information about the configuration of the environment). The default is no, which should be the setting except for debugging.
ForcedEmptyPasswdChange	If yes, sshd will force a password change. By default this parameter is no, letting PAM take care of these issues.
ForcedPasswdChange	If yes, sshd will force the user to change his or her password if it has expired. By default this parameter is no, letting PAM take care of these issues.
HostKey	Specifies the file containing the Private Host Key. Default is /etc/ssh_host_key. Set to /etc/ssh/ssh_host_key in the RPMs.

Table 11.5 Keywords in `/etc/ssh/sshd_config` (Continued)

Keyword	Description
IdleTimeout	If the connection has been idle for the indicated amount of time, the connection is closed. The time may be specified in *seconds*, *minutes*m, *hours*h, *days*d, or *weeks*w, where *seconds*, *minutes*, *hours*, *days*, and *weeks* are positive integers.
IgnoreRhosts	If yes, all $HOME/.rhosts and $HOME/.shosts are ignored. The /etc/hosts.equiv and /etc/shosts.equiv files are unaffected by this keyword. The default is no.
IgnoreRootRhosts	Same as IgnoreRhosts except that it applies only to root. It defaults to the value of IgnoreRhosts.
KeepAlive	If yes (the default), sshd will check connectivity to the client periodically. If connectivity cannot be verified, sshd closes the connection. This is true even if the verification fails due to a temporary routing problem. To disable this mechanism, you must set this keyword to no in both /etc/ssh/sshd_config and /etc/ssh/ssh_config or $HOME/.ssh/config.
KeyRegenerationInterval	Specifies the time in seconds to regenerate the Server Keys after their first use. The default is 3600. The value 0 means that the key will never be regenerated. The -k command line option overrides this keyword; see Table 11.4 on page 269.
ListenAddress	Specifies the interface to which sshd binds. Normally, this is set to 0.0.0.0, meaning any interface. This is useful on systems with multiple interfaces where you wish to limit incoming ssh connections to a specific interface. The value of this keyword must be an IP address of a local interface.
LoginGraceTime	Sets the time, in seconds, for clients to authenticate the user. If the user authentication process does not complete prior to this time, then the server will disconnect and exit. The default is 600 seconds (normally, more than sufficient). A value of 0 indicates no limit. This value is overridden by the -g command line option; see Table 11.4 on page 269.
PasswordAuthentication	If yes (the default), then, if other nonpassword authentication mechanisms fail, the user is prompted for a password which is verified internally by sshd. Setting this keyword to no disables password authentication altogether.
PasswordExpireWarningDays	Specifies the number of days prior to the expiration of a password that sshd will display a warning to the user. The default is 14; if set to 0, warning messages are disabled. Note that these messages are in addition to any generated by PAM or other mechanisms.

Table 11.5 Keywords in `/etc/ssh/sshd_config` (Continued)

Keyword	Description
PermitEmptyPasswords	If yes (the default), users with no passwords are allowed to be authenticated by sshd. If no, empty passwords are not allowed by sshd.
PermitRootLogin	If yes (the default), then root is allowed to log in. If nopwd, then root does not need to supply root's password, but in this case must be authenticatable through one of the three non-password authentication schemes. Otherwise nopwd behaves like no, disallowing root logins altogether. The exception is that root may execute a command through ssh if RSA Authentication is enabled and configured.
PidFile	Location of the file containing the PID of the master sshd process. The default is /var/run/sshd.pid.
Port	Specifies the port number to which sshd binds. Default is 22.
PrintMotd	If yes (the default), the /etc/motd file is displayed after login.
QuietMode	If no, suppresses all logging except fatal errors. Normally, the initial connection request, authentication information, and connection termination are logged through the syslog facility DAEMON. See the SyslogFacility keyword in this table for configuration options. The default is yes. This keyword is overridden by the -q command line option, if specified.
RandomSeed	Specifies the file containing the random seed for the server. The default is /etc/ssh_random_seed; the default in the RPMs is /etc/ssh/ssh_random_seed.
RhostsAuthentication	If yes, Rhosts Authentication is allowed. The default is no. In order to enable this scheme, this keyword must be set to yes both here and in the appropriate configuration file on the client. See *Trusted Host Authentication* on page 260 for a detailed discussion of this scheme.
RhostsRSAAuthentication	If yes (the default), then Rhosts and RSA Authentication is allowed. In order to enable this scheme, this keyword must be set to yes both here and in the appropriate configuration file on the client. See *Rhosts and RSA Authentication* on page 260 for a detailed discussion of this scheme.
RSAAuthentication	If yes (the default), then RSA Authentication is allowed. In order to enable this scheme, this keyword must be set to yes both here and in the appropriate configuration file on the client. See *RSA Authentication* on page 261 or a detailed discussion of this scheme.

Table 11.5 Keywords in `/etc/ssh/sshd_config` (Continued)

Keyword	Description
ServerKeyBits	Sets the number of bits for the Server Keys. Default is 768. This value is overridden by the -b command line option if set.
SilentDeny	Suppresses error messages to the client and logging on the server if yes. Default is no.
StrictModes	If yes (the default), sshd will not grant access to a user whose home directory and/or .rhosts file are owned by another user or are world writeable.
Umask	Sets the umask for sshd and its subprocesses. Must be specified in octal with a leading 0. Not set, by default.
X11Forwarding	If yes (the default), then X Window System forwarding is allowed.
X11DisplayOffset	Specifies the first display number available to sshd for X Window System forwarding. By default it is set to 1. It may need to be set to a higher value in the presence of other X Window System applications.
XAuthLocation	Specifies the path to the xauth program.

Example 11-2 shows us a sample `/etc/ssh/sshd_config` file. We will discuss the options shown in bold. The remainder are straightforward and can be found in Table 11.5.

Example 11-2 Representative `/etc/ssh/sshd_config` File

```
# sshd config file
Port 22
ListenAddress 0.0.0.0
HostKey /etc/ssh/ssh_host_key
RandomSeed /etc/ssh/ssh_random_seed
ServerKeyBits 768
LoginGraceTime 600
KeyRegenerationInterval 3600
PermitRootLogin yes
IgnoreRhosts yes
StrictModes yes
QuietMode no
X11Forwarding yes
X11DisplayOffset 10
FascistLogging yes
PrintMotd yes
KeepAlive yes
SyslogFacility DAEMON
RhostsAuthentication no
RhostsRSAAuthentication yes
RSAAuthentication yes
PasswordAuthentication yes
AllowUsers mary paul bill
DenyHosts otter *.evil.com
```

The `ListenAddress 0.0.0.0` entry in Example 11-2 has the effect of allowing `ssh` requests to any interface on the system. You may specify a single address instead, at which point `sshd` will accept requests only on that address. This is useful for systems with multiple interfaces, but where you wish to allow connections to only one of them. You cannot specify more than one address.

The `IgnoreRhosts yes` entry will cause `sshd` to ignore all `.rhosts` and `.shosts` files. Be aware, however, that this entry does **not** cause `sshd` to ignore `/etc/hosts.equiv` or `/etc/shosts.equiv`.

The `StrictModes yes` entry forces `sshd` to ignore `$HOME/.rhosts`, `$HOME/.shosts`, `$HOME/.ssh/authorized_keys`, and/or `$HOME/.ssh/identity` files if they are owned and/or writeable by anyone other than the user in whose home directory they exist. This will have the effect of causing nonpassword authentication failures.

The `AllowUsers mary paul bill` entry restricts connections to this server's `sshd` to only the users `mary`, `paul`, and `bill`. All other users making `ssh` requests will be refused.

The `DenyHosts otter *.evil.com` causes `sshd` to refuse any connection attempts from the host `otter` as well as from any host from the domain `evil.com`. Note that `sshd` will only use canonical hostnames, so, if you resolve hostnames first through `/etc/hosts` and then through DNS, for example, you would need to specify the hostname as it ordinarily resolves.[2] Here, `otter` is used without a domain name as it resolves through `/etc/hosts`, whereas `evil.com` is an external domain and will always resolve through DNS.

Configuring the Client Side

Now let's describe the command line arguments to `ssh`, the client-side program, and its configuration files. The `ssh` command takes the following syntax:

```
ssh [-flags] hostname [command]
```

where optional flags are as described in Table 11.6, `hostname` is the hostname or IP address of the remote server, and optionally a command may be specified.

When `ssh` is invoked it obtains configuration information first from the command line, then from the user's `$HOME/.ssh/config`, and finally from the systemwide `/etc/ssh/ssh_config`. If identical parameters are set differently, then the first setting takes precedence. Table 11.6 documents the command line options to `ssh`.

Table 11.7 lists the available keywords or parameters that can be specified in either the `$HOME/.ssh/config` or `/etc/ssh/ssh_config` configuration files. All blank lines and lines beginning with # in these files are ignored. All keywords are case insensitive, and either a space or = separates the keyword

---

2. The control of hostname resolution is through the two files `/etc/host.conf` and `/etc/nsswitch.conf`.

from its arguments. All keywords accept either a `yes` or `no` value except when noted otherwise.

Table 11.6 Command Line Options to `ssh`

Flag	Description
`-a`	Disables forwarding of the authentication agent. See *Disabling X and Agent Forwarding* on page 303.
`-c cipher`	Specifies the symmetric cipher. Available options are `idea`, `des`, `3des`, `blowfish`, `arcfour`, and `none`. The default for the U.S. version is `blowfish`; otherwise it is `idea`. The `none` option turns off encryption and all data transfers via `ssh` will be in the clear. The `none` option is for debugging only.
`-e escape`	Sets the escape character for sessions with a pseudoterminal (`pty`). It is ~ by default. Setting the value to `none` disables escapes.
`-f`	Put `ssh` in the background after authentication and forwarding (if any). See *Exploring ssh Functionality* on page 304 for examples.
`-g`	Allows remote hosts to connect to locally forwarded ports. This dangerous option is discussed in *Port Forwarding and Application Proxying* on page 307.
`-i file`	Specifies the file containing the Private User Key. By default it is held in `$HOME/.ssh/identity`.
`-l username`	Specifies the username to login as on the remote machine.
`-n`	Prevents reading from `stdin`. This option is described in the section, *Exploring ssh Functionality* on page 304.
`-o option`	*option* may be replaced with any `keyword=value` that could be placed in an `ssh` configuration file. You must precede each `keyword=value` with a `-o` flag.
`-p port`	Specifies the remote port number; the default is 22.
`-q`	Quiet mode. Suppresses all messages except fatal error messages.
`-P`	Specifies the use of a nonprivileged local port. Use of this option will disable Rhosts Authentication and Rhosts and RSA Authentication. It is normally used to connect to systems that do not allow connections with privileged source ports.
`-t`	Forces pseudoterminal allocation. Useful for running `curses` or other screen-based applications.
`-v`	Verbose mode. Very useful for debugging all aspects of `ssh`. Additional debugging information can be generated simultaneously by running `sshd -d` (see Table 11.4 on page 269).
`-V`	Prints version number and exits.
`-x`	Disables X Window System forwarding.

Table 11.6 Command Line Options to `ssh` (Continued)

Flag	Description
-C	Compresses all data using `gzip`. For performance purposes, useful only over slow connections such as modem lines. Does enhance security. The level of compression may be controlled by the `CompressionLevel` option (see Table 11.7).
-L *port:host:hostport*	Specifies that *port* is to be forwarded to *hostport* on the remote *host*. Only root can forward privileged ports. Details are given in *Local Forwarding* on page 308.
-R *port:host:hostport*	Specifies that the remote *port* is to be forwarded to *hostport* on the *host*. Only after attaining root privilege on the remote system can privileged ports be forwarded. A further description is provided in *Remote Forwarding* on page 310.

Table 11.7 Keywords in `$HOME/.ssh/config` or `/etc/ssh/ssh_config`

Keyword	Description
Host	Takes a hostname or IP address as a value. The wildcards * or ? may be used. This keyword causes all subsequent keywords, up to the next `Host` keyword, to apply only to the indicated host. In this way, one configuration file may be used to apply to many hosts. The entry `Host *` causes the settings to apply to all hosts. The hostname to match this keyword is the *hostname* given on the command line, as in `ssh hostname`.
BatchMode	If `yes`, password prompting will be disabled. Useful for scripting, but requires that an agent (see *Managing RSA Authentication with ssh-agent and ssh-add* on page 301) be running or passphrases must be provided in the script. The default is `no`.
Cipher	Specifies the symmetric cipher. Available options are `idea`, `des`, `3des`, `blowfish`, `arcfour`, and `none`. The default for the U.S. version is `blowfish`; otherwise it is `idea`. The `none` option turns off encryption, and all data transfers via `ssh` will be in the clear. The `none` option is for debugging only. This setting may be overridden by the `-c` command line option to `ssh`; see Table 11.6 on page 276.
ClearAllForwardings	If `yes`, causes all forwarding in the configuration files and at the command line to be cleared. The default is `no`; however, `scp` will set this option to `yes` to avoid failures.
Compression	If `yes`, `gzip` compression will be used. The default is `no`. This setting may be overridden by the `-c` command line option to `ssh`; see Table 11.6 on page 276.
CompressionLevel	Specifies the `gzip` compression level (see the `gzip(1)` man page). Acceptable values are integers between 1 and 9, inclusive—1 indicates fast but reduced compression; 9 is slow but optimal compression. The default is 6.

Table 11.7 Keywords in `$HOME/.ssh/config` or `/etc/ssh/ssh_config` (Continued)

Keyword	Description
ConnectionAttempts	Specifies the number of tries per second before trying rsh or (if rsh is disabled) failing. The default is 1. Increasing this value may be useful for scripting.
EscapeChar	Sets the escape character for sessions with a pseudoterminal (pty). It is ~ by default. Setting the value to none disables escapes. This setting may be overridden by the -e command line option to ssh; see Table 11.6 on page 276.
FallBackToRsh	If yes (the default), whenever the connection with sshd on the server fails, in.rshd is tried. In such a case, a warning message regarding the failure is displayed to the client.
ForwardAgent	Specifies whether or not the connection to ssh-agent will be forwarded to the remote server. The default is yes. This is further described in *Disabling X and Agent Forwarding* on page 303.
ForwardX11	Specifies whether X Window Systems will automatically be redirected through the SSH-encrypted tunnel and automatically set the DISPLAY environment variable. The default is yes. Further details regarding this option are provided in *Managing RSA Authentication with ssh-agent and ssh-add* on page 301.
GatewayPorts	If yes (the default), then remote hosts may connect to locally forwarded ports.
GlobalKnownHostsFile	Defaults to `/etc/ssh_known_hosts`, but to `/etc/ssh/ssh_known_hosts` in the RPMs. Requires an absolutely qualified path to filename.
HostName	Takes a hostname or IP address as its value. Sets the host to login to. This option is not set by default, and the destination host (server) must be specified on the command line.
IdentityFile	Specifies the file containing the Private User Key. The default is `$HOME/.ssh/identity`.
KeepAlive	If yes (the default), ssh will check connectivity to the server periodically. If connectivity cannot be verified, ssh closes the connection. This is true even if the verification fails due to a temporary routing problem. To disable this mechanism, you must set this keyword to no in both `/etc/ssh/sshd_config` and `/etc/ssh/ssh_config` or `$HOME/.ssh/config`.
LocalForward	Requires a value of the form port host:hostport. Specifies that port is to be forwarded to hostport on the remote host. Only root can forward privileged ports. Details are given in *Local Forwarding* on page 308. This entry may be overridden by the -L command line option to ssh; see Table 11.6 on page 276.
NumberOfPasswordPrompts	Specifies the number of password prompts before giving up. The default is 1. The server sets a hard limit of 5 attempts, so setting this value greater than 5 will have the effect of setting it to 5.

Table 11.7 Keywords in `$HOME/.ssh/config` or `/etc/ssh/ssh_config` (Continued)

Keyword	Description
PasswordAuthentication	If yes (the default), ssh will attempt password authentication when necessary.
PasswordPromptHost	If yes (the default), the remote hostname will be included in the password prompt.
PasswordPromptLogin	If yes (the default), the remote username will be included in the password prompt.
Port	Specifies the destination port number to connect to on the server. The default is 22.
ProxyCommand	Specifies the command to use to connect to the server instead of ssh. The command string extends to the end of the line and is invoked by /bin/sh. Note that %p expands to the port number and %h expands to the remote host.
RemoteForward	Requires a value of the form port host:hostport. Specifies that the remote port is to be forwarded to hostport on the host. Only after attaining root privilege on the remote system can privileged ports be forwarded. A further description is provided in *Remote Forwarding* on page 310. This entry may be overridden by the -R command line option to ssh; see Table 11.6 on page 276.
RhostsAuthentication	If yes, Rhosts Authentication is attempted. The default is no. In order to enable this scheme, this keyword must be set to yes here and in the /etc/ssh/sshd_config on the server. See *Trusted Host Authentication* on page 260 for a detailed discussion of this scheme.
RhostsRSAAuthentication	If yes (the default), then Rhosts and RSA Authentication is attempted. In order to enable this scheme, this keyword must be set to yes here and in /etc/ssh/sshd_config on the server. See *Rhosts and RSA Authentication* on page 260 for a detailed discussion of this scheme.
RSAAuthentication	If yes (the default), then RSA Authentication is attempted. In order to enable this scheme, this keyword must be set to yes here and in /etc/ssh/sshd_config on the server. See *RSA Authentication* on page 261 for a detailed discussion of this scheme.
StrictHostKeyChecking	This option takes one of three arguments—yes, no, or ask. If yes, then the client will never accept unverifiable Public Host Keys from the server (verifiable keys are found in either $HOME/.ssh/known_hosts or /etc/ssh/ssh_known_hosts on the client). If no, then the client will always add unverifiable server Host Keys into the file $HOME/.ssh/known_hosts. If ask (the default), then the client will always prompt the user as to whether or not the unverifiable server Public Host Key should be added to the file $HOME/.ssh/known_hosts.

Table 11.7 Keywords in `$HOME/.ssh/config` or `/etc/ssh/ssh_config` (Continued)

Keyword	Description
UsePrivilegedPort	Specifies whether to use a privileged source (client) port. The default is `yes` whenever Rhosts Authentication or Rhosts and RSA Authentication is attempted; otherwise it is `no`.
User	Takes a username as an argument. If set, all logins will be attempted as this user unless the `-l` command line option (see Table 11.6 on page 276) is used. By default the username of the effective UID is used.
UserKnownHostsFile	Specifies a file to use for automatic updating of Public Host Keys instead of `$HOME/.ssh/known_hosts`.
UseRsh	If `yes`, then the connection will use `rsh` instead of `ssh` and all other options (except `HostName`) are ignored. This option, if set, will obviate all of the security features of `ssh`. To entirely disable the use of this option, make sure that the `in.rshd` and `in.rlogind` are not available on the server. The default is `no`.
XAuthLocation	Takes a fully qualified filename to the `xauth` program.

Since all of these options may appear in any user's `$HOME/.ssh/config` file and such entries take precedence over the `/etc/ssh/ssh_config` file, the user has complete control of the ssh client-side configuration. In particular, this means that the sshd configuration must be made secure to disable unsecure keywords such as `RhostsAuthentication` and `UseRsh` on the client-side. We will explore these and other configuration issues beginning with *Using SSH* on page 282.

An Example Client-Side Configuration File   We provide Example 11-3 to illustrate the contents of either an `/etc/ssh/ssh_config` or a `$HOME/.ssh/config` file. We see that this file will cause the client to attempt all forms of

Example 11-3 Sample Client-Side Configuration File

```
# Example /etc/ssh/ssh_config or $HOME/.shh/config file
Host *
RhostsAuthentication yes
RhostsRSAAuthentication yes
RSAAuthentication yes
TISAuthentication no
PasswordAuthentication yes
PasswordPromptHost yes
PasswordPromptLogin no
FallBackToRsh no
UseRsh no
StrictHostKeyChecking yes
Port 22
EscapeChar ~
Cipher blowfish
```

authentication supported by SSH (except for TIS). Notice that `rsh` will never be tried (due to the entries `FallBackToRsh no` and `UseRsh no`). The setting of `StrictHostKeyChecking yes` is discussed in detail in *Initial RSA Host-Based Authentication Configuration* on page 285. The entry `Host *` means that these configuration settings apply to any host.

The `scp` Program   For completeness, we provide the options to the secure copy (`scp`) program in Table 11.8. The general syntax for `scp` is

```
scp [-flags] [[user@]host1:]filename1 [[user@]host2:]filename2
```

The optional `flags` for `scp` are defined in Table 11.8. The syntax `[[user@]host1:]` `filename1` indicates the source file, whereas `[[user@]host2:]filename2` indicates the destination file. The filenames (or directories, in the case of a recursive `scp`) are required. Optionally, hostnames may be given (`host1` and `host2` may be distinct or identical). Usernames (indicated by `user`) may also optionally be specified; however, the invoking user will be required to authenticate as the given `user`.

    `scp` reads the same configuration files as `ssh` and prioritizes settings in the same way. We will look at `scp` examples in *scp Examples* on page 306.

Table 11.8 Options to `scp`

Flag	Description[*]
-Q	Turns on statistics display for each file transferred. This is the default.
-q	Turns off statistics display for each file transferred.
-c *cipher*	Specifies the symmetric encryption cipher to be used. Identical to `ssh`.
-i *file*	Specifies the location of the Private User Key. Identical to `ssh`.
-L	Uses a nonprivileged port. Same as the -P option to `ssh`.
-o *options*	Identical to `ssh`.
-p	Preserves file modes, access times, and modification times on transfer. Otherwise local `umask` and timestamps apply.
-r	Recursively copies all subdirectories and files in the target directory.
-v	Verbose. Identical to `ssh`.
-B	Batch mode. Identical to the `BatchMode` keyword described in Table 11.7 on page 277.
-C	Enables compression. Identical to `ssh`.
-P *port*	Identical to -p for `ssh`.
-S *path*	Specifies the path to the `ssh` program.

[*]Where an option is indicated as identical to that for `ssh`, see Table 11.6 on page 276.

Using SSH

At this point, if you are eager to test out SSH, you may do so by starting the sshd daemon on a system that will act as a server. You may start the daemon by invoking it

```
# /usr/sbin/sshd
```

or by using the start-up script

```
# /etc/rc.d/init.d/sshd start
```

Both of these invocations assume the use of the previously described RPMs. After sshd is running on the server, you may connect to it from a client (with ssh installed, of course!) by executing

```
$ ssh server
```

where *server* is the hostname or IP address of the server. You may also want to run a network sniffer such as sniffit (see *Network Monitoring* on page 38 for more information about sniffit) to verify that the session is in fact encrypted.

Prior to implementing SSH in your production environment, however, you will need to decide upon the authentication scheme you wish to use as well as which, if any, other TCP services you wish to forward through the SSH-encrypted tunnel. Additionally, you will need to manage your SSH environment by monitoring the log files and properly maintaining the necessary keys. We will first explore the authentication configuration options and the necessary key management, and then we will move on to application proxying and port forwarding. Along the way we will examine the log messages generated by SSH as well as the debugging capabilities of SSH.

Configuring SSH Authentication Behavior

In *Overview of SSH* on page 257, we conceptually explored the authentication mechanism implemented by SSH. In this section, we will examine the configuration of the different schemes. First, however, let's note the behavior of ssh when it attempts to connect to a server that is not running sshd.

sshd Missing in Action

If you execute ssh and sshd is not running on the server system, then, by default, ssh will try to communicate with in.rshd on the server. Example 11-4 shows the results of the case in which mary connects to underdog from topcat via ssh, but sshd is not running on underdog.

This behavior does add the convenience of allowing connectivity whenever you connect to a system that does not run sshd and also to those systems

Example 11-4 `sshd` Not Running on the Server

```
[mary@topcat mary]$ ssh underdog
Secure connection to underdog refused; reverting to insecure method.
Using rsh.   WARNING: Connection will not be encrypted.
Password:
Last login: Thu Jul  1 21:10:38 from pluto
[mary@underdog mary]$
```

which, for whatever reason, are not currently running `sshd`. But it is certainly not secure since it bypasses the enhanced authentication of `ssh` and since all communications pass over the network in the clear. In general, because of the many vulnerabilities associated with `in.rshd`, it should *never* be running. You can disable this behavior in three ways.

1. Set the `UseRsh` keyword to `no` in `/etc/ssh/ssh_config`. This is a very weak solution because any user can override this either at the command line or in his or her `$HOME/.ssh/config` file.

2. Comment out `in.rshd` and `in.rlogind` in `/etc/inetd.conf` (or `/etc/xinetd.conf`). This is strongly recommended and is the preferred approach.

3. Compile `ssh` with the compile-time `--without-rsh` option (see *Compiling SSH* on page 265).

If `sshd` is running on the server, then the authentication process proceeds as described in the following sections.

Authentication Flow of Events

The flowchart in Figure 11.4 illustrates the order in which the various schemes will be checked and what will occur upon success or failure of each. It should be pointed out that, once the initial RSA Host-Based Authentication succeeds, all subsequent communications are encrypted. In particular, all non-password authentication and all password authentication steps are passed through the encrypted tunnel protecting the data from eavesdroppers.

The configuration of each of the authentication mechanisms shown in Figure 11.4 are detailed in the following sections. The title of each mechanism shown in Figure 11.4 corresponds to the title of the section describing its configuration.

TCP_Wrappers Configuration If SSH is compiled with `libwrap` (TCP_wrappers support, which is compiled in the RPMs), then the first check that is done is against the `/etc/hosts.allow` and `/etc/hosts.deny` files. Example 11-5 provides a representative set of entries in `/etc/hosts.allow` for `sshd` access control. There is actually a good deal more flexibility available in this file for `sshd`. We can also utilize the keywords `sshdfwd-`*portname*, `sshdfwd-`*portnumber*, and `sshdfwd-X11` to control client forwarding requests. We will look

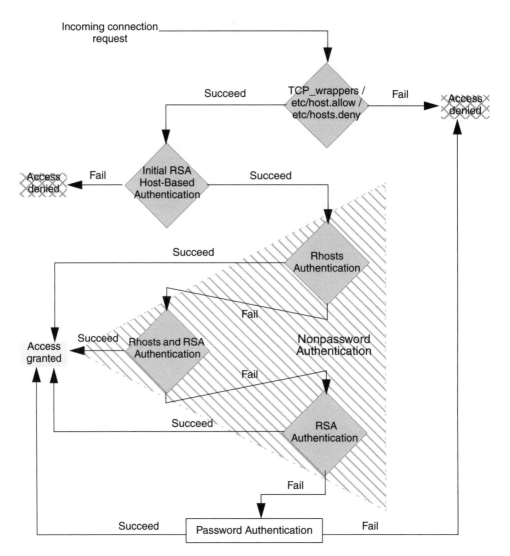

Fig. 11.4 SSH Authentication Flowchart

at these additional keywords in *Disabling X and Agent Forwarding* on page 303
and in *Limiting and Disabling Forwarding* on page 310. TCP_wrappers is
described in Chapter 10. Note that sshd does not support the options described
in the TCP_wrappers host_options man page.

Example 11-5 /etc/hosts.allow sshd Entry

```
# hosts.allow
# Secure Shell
sshd: nomad,topcat,otter,foghorn
```

Initial RSA Host-Based Authentication Configuration The initial RSA Host-Based Authentication mechanism is discussed conceptually in *Host-Based Authentication Using RSA* on page 257. This component of the authentication process **must** complete successfully in order to proceed. The configuration of this mechanism is controlled by the StrictHostKeyChecking keyword either, in order of priority, at the command line, in the user's $HOME/.ssh/config file, or in the /etc/ssh/ssh_config file. The first instance of the keyword is used.

As described in Table 11.7 on page 277, the default value of StrictHost-KeyChecking is ask. Example 11-6 shows the dialog that ensues the first time a client connects to a server. By answering yes to the question, Are you sure you want to continue connecting (yes/no)?, the client (underdog) will cause the server's (pluto) Public Host Key, found in /etc/ssh/ssh_host_key.pub on the server (pluto), to be added to the user's (mary) $HOME/.ssh/known_hosts file. The Public Host Key is automatically added (no prompt) if StrictHostKey-Checking is set to no.

Example 11-6 Default Behavior for First Connection

```
[mary@underdog]$ ssh pluto
Host key not found from the list of known hosts.
Are you sure you want to continue connecting (yes/no)? yes
Host 'pluto' added to the list of known hosts.
Last login: Tue Jun 29 19:02:42 1999 from underdog
[mary@pluto]$
```

The entry shown in Example 11-7 shows the entry found in the user's $HOME/.ssh/known_hosts file. The syntax of this file is the hostname (pluto) followed by the number of bits in the modulus (1024), then the exponent (37), and finally the modulus itself (the really long number that wraps across five lines). The entry represents one line, or record.

Example 11-7 $HOME/.ssh/known_hosts Entry for pluto

```
pluto 1024 37 139857661663910338159911735939483004080805907574078193160
0228711709119552923912117155152003073833763193126259315433111496327932866
9768555950269099939845165060226742862620575327118146476002916650482867126
3643216843142971283973520980501107110407308518030847171864168782555972232
754873432099524150772854588750069
```

This same record looks somewhat different in the /etc/ssh/ssh_host_key.pub file on the server as shown in Example 11-8. The syntax of this file is the number of bits in the modulus (1024), then the exponent (37), followed by the modulus itself (the long number that wraps across five lines), and finally the user@hostname (root@pluto, this is a comment field). Note that the user is always root for the server's Public Host Key.

Example 11-8 /etc/ssh/ssh_host_key.pub Entry for pluto on pluto

```
1024 37 1398576616639103381599117359394830040808059075740781931602022871
1709119552923912117155152003073833763193126259315433111496327932869768552
5950269099939845165060226742862620575327118146476002916650482867126364322
1684314297128397352098050110711040730851803084717186416878255597223275482
754873432099524150772854588750069 root@pluto
```

From these two examples, it should be apparent that one way to incorporate the Public Host Keys to other hosts is to manually copy the entry from the server's file and add it to the client's `/etc/ssh/ssh_known_hosts` file. You could instead add it to a particular user's `$HOME/.ssh/known_hosts` file, but then only that user would have access to the key. The purpose of the system-wide file `/etc/ssh/ssh_known_hosts` is to include all of the commonly connected to servers, whereas the user's `$HOME/.ssh/known_hosts` file should contain servers that the user connects to but that other users typically don't.

If the user had answered `no` to the question `Are you sure you want to continue connecting (yes/no)?` shown in Example 11-6, then the connection would simply have been terminated. Similarly the connection will fail if `StrictHostKeyChecking` is set to `yes` either at the `ssh` command line in `$HOME/.ssh/config` of the invoking user or in `/etc/ssh/ssh_config` of the client system. In this latter case, you will get the error message

```
No host key is known for pluto and you have requested strict checking.
```

This setting will increase security because the automated updating of keys could be compromised by spoofing or a man-in-the-middle attack. Unfortunately, this may mean too much manual effort in large environments where risking such attacks may be necessary. However, since this is the initial authentication step, the risk can be substantially mitigated by other enforced authentication steps such as RSA Authentication (discussed in *RSA Authentication Configuration* on page 293).

Coping with Changing Host Keys.   Another aspect of Host-Based RSA Authentication is that periodically it may be necessary to change a server's Host Keys.[3] This may be the result of compromised keys or it may be that your site policy dictates a periodic change. Whatever the reason, when a server Public Host Key is different than the one stored in either the `/etc/ssh/ssh_known_hosts` or `$HOME/.ssh/known_hosts` file, then a warning will appear such as that shown in Example 11-9. Note that agent forwarding (discussed in *Managing RSA Authentication with `ssh-agent` and `ssh-add`* on page 301) and X Window System forwarding (discussed in *Managing RSA Authentication with `ssh-agent` and `ssh-add`* on page 301 and *`ssh` Examples* on page 304) are disabled. Once again, the question `Are you sure you want to continue connecting (yes/no)?` occurs because `StrictHostKeyChecking` is set to `ask`. Answering yes to this question will not update the key in Mary's `$HOME/.ssh/known_hosts` file, and the message will repeat at each subsequent connection until the discrepancy has been remedied. Mary may accomplish this manually or by removing the appropriate entry from her `$HOME/.ssh/known_hosts` file, which will cause the dialog shown in Example 11-6 on page 285 to reoccur the next time she invokes `ssh` to `underdog`.

---

3. All keys are changed using the `ssh-keygen` utility. Specifically, changing Host Keys is discussed in *Using `ssh-keygen` for root* on page 297.

Example 11-9 Warning Message Due to Changed Server Host Keys

```
$ ssh underdog
@@@@@@@@@@@@@@@@@@@@@@@@@@@@@@@@@@@@@@@@@@@@@@@@@@@@@@@@@@@@@
@        WARNING: HOST IDENTIFICATION HAS CHANGED!         @
@@@@@@@@@@@@@@@@@@@@@@@@@@@@@@@@@@@@@@@@@@@@@@@@@@@@@@@@@@@@@
IT IS POSSIBLE THAT SOMEONE IS DOING SOMETHING NASTY!
Someone could be eavesdropping on you right now (man-in-the-middle attack)!
It is also possible that the host key has just been changed.
Please contact your system administrator.
Add correct host key in /home/mary/.ssh/known_hosts to get rid of this message.
Agent forwarding is disabled to avoid attacks by corrupted servers.
X11 forwarding is disabled to avoid attacks by corrupted servers.
Are you sure you want to continue connecting (yes/no)? yes
mary@underdog's password:
```

You may automate the updating of server Host Keys with the Perl script `make-ssh-known-hosts`, which is included in the distribution and RPMs. It is usually used by root to create and maintain the systemwide `/etc/ssh/ssh_known_hosts` file, but it could be used by any user to maintain his or her local `$HOME/.ssh/known_hosts` file (although this would be necessary only if `StrictHostKeyChecking` were set to yes). This script requires the use of the DNS. The vulnerabilities with this script are the same as with automatic updating via `StrictHostKeyChecking` set to no or ask, then, when asked, `Are you sure you want to continue connecting (yes/no)?` answering yes.

The `make-ssh-known-hosts` script requires a DNS domain name as an argument. It attempts to contact the primary server for the given DNS domain name and to obtain the list of hosts associated with that domain. By default, it will obtain a list of all hosts in subdomains of the given domain as well (use the `-nor` option to prevent recursively searching all subdomains). Once it obtains a list of hosts, it connects to each host via ssh. Once connected to a host, it tries `cat /etc/ssh/ssh_host_key.pub` to get the system's Public Host Key.

By default, `make-ssh-known-hosts` suppresses all password/passphrase prompting. Thus, either the hosts it connects to must be configured with a nonpassword/nonpassphrase authentication scheme or you must use the `-pa seconds` option, where `seconds` is the number of seconds that `make-ssh-known-hosts` will wait for a password. If you use `-pa 0`, `make-ssh-known-hosts` will not time-out after prompting. If it cannot connect to a host, it will attempt to find the key in `$HOME/.ssh/known_hosts`.

Before we can use the `make-ssh-known-hosts` script, we need to make one modification. The script has the location of the Public Host Key hard coded as `/etc/ssh_host_key.pub`. But the RPMs we are using put the Public Host Key in `/etc/ssh/ssh_host_key.pub`. So edit `/usr/bin/make-ssh-known-hosts` and find the line

```
$public_key = '/etc/ssh_host_key.pub';
```

and change it to

```
$public_key = '/etc/ssh/ssh_host_key.pub';
```

Once complete, you are ready to run `make-ssh-known-hosts`.

Example 11-10 displays the output of running `make-ssh-known-hosts` on the host `topcat` as root. In this command, we are specifying the DNS domain name of `toon.com` with the primary server being `roadrunner.toon.com`. The `-pa 60` argument gives us 60 seconds to respond to `ssh` password queries. Note that `make-ssh-known-hosts` in Example 11-10 found four hosts—`pluto`, `topcat`, `underdog`, and `roadrunner`—in the domain `toon.com`. It successfully connected to all hosts but `roadrunner`. The keys have been redirected to `/etc/ssh/ssh_known_hosts`, resulting in that shown in Example 11-11.

See the `make-ssh-known-hosts` man page for further details.

Example 11-10 Running `make-ssh-known-hosts`

```
[root@topcat]# make-ssh-known-hosts -se roadrunner.toon.com toon.com -pa 60 > /
etc/ssh/ssh_known_hosts
/usr/bin/make-ssh-known-hosts:debug[1]: Getting DNS database for toon.com from
server roadrunner.toon.com
/usr/bin/make-ssh-known-hosts:debug[1]: Found 4 hosts, 0 CNAMEs (total 25 lines)
/usr/bin/make-ssh-known-hosts:debug[2]: Trying host pluto.toon.com
Password:
/usr/bin/make-ssh-known-hosts:debug[2]: Ssh to pluto.toon.com succeded
/usr/bin/make-ssh-known-hosts:debug[4]: adding entries :
pluto,pluto.toon.com,10.13.33.111
/usr/bin/make-ssh-known-hosts:debug[2]: Trying host roadrunner.toon.com
/usr/bin/make-ssh-known-hosts:debug[2]: ping failed
/usr/bin/make-ssh-known-hosts:debug[2]: Trying host topcat.toon.com
Password:
/usr/bin/make-ssh-known-hosts:debug[2]: Ssh to topcat.toon.com succeded
/usr/bin/make-ssh-known-hosts:debug[4]: adding entries :
topcat,topcat.toon.com,172.17.33.111
/usr/bin/make-ssh-known-hosts:debug[2]: Trying host underdog.toon.com
Password:
/usr/bin/make-ssh-known-hosts:debug[2]: Ssh to underdog.toon.com succeded
/usr/bin/make-ssh-known-hosts:debug[4]: adding entries : underdog,under-
dog.toon.com,10.13.1.9
[root@topcat]#
```

Example 11-11 `/etc/ssh/ssh_known_hosts` Generated by `make-ssh-known-hosts`

```
[root@topcat]# cat /etc/ssh/ssh_known_hosts
# This file is generated with make-ssh-known-hosts.pl
# $Id: make-ssh-known-hosts.pl,v 1.6 1998/07/08 00:44:23 kivinen Exp $
# with command line :
# /usr/bin/make-ssh-known-hosts -se roadrunner.toon.com toon.com -pa 60
#
# The script was run by  (root) at Sun Jul  4 17:30:26 1999
# using perl (perl) version 5.00404.
#
# Domain = toon.com, server = roadrunner.toon.com
# Found 4 hosts, 0 CNAMEs (total 25 lines)
# SOA = roadrunner root.roadrunner ( 1 3h 1h 5d 1d )
#
pluto,pluto.toon.com,10.13.33.111 1024 35 16585207326350456440664928
86463527052362741552039541006012572870886527908116571625510293904734
43225967939007124014526561307753705189937232139911018982080497980016
84403836830380567376975574158693816811247494237429855845683763057688
69707633671082473013407735342047177997419057918892277753261431097894
942206248626312 pluto
topcat,topcat.toon.com,172.17.33.111 1024 35 1616914172264014628092
```

Example 11-11 `/etc/ssh/ssh_known_hosts` Generated by `make-ssh-known-hosts` (Continued)

```
8254763186304301221509571556760435999044155357179460608285625713782
8939141213273076831876251925433169047609196164173710423934872204479
7532070242221818307554158737907640045150331919829990769072663492777
3098538955881590690352967565733557078929969783267933404332138067692
752398533067165852073263504564066492831561278 topcat
underdog,underdog.toon.com,10.13.1.9 1024 33 1542605455712721124978
4775524981701047568925039044494757968188200138717967413920516626164
8174562963556772303711386376494805508598937319573408169763584460096
1829446935388719685474415237238150938233352331363282709682694657242
9678379757705714695037513688623556522818862767365834913776101071647
1677449194123847602 underdog
[root@topcat /root]#
```

Nonpassword Authentication

After `sshd` has successfully passed the TCP_wrappers and Host-Based RSA Authentication, it moves on to checking the three nonpassword authentication schemes in the order shown in Figure 11.4 on page 284. Each of these schemes will be tried if appropriately configured. We describe the configuration of each in the following three sections.

Rhosts Authentication Configuration   As conceptually described in *Rhosts and RSA Authentication* on page 260, this is the least secure authentication scheme offered by `ssh` and should not be used in a production environment. Nonetheless, it may be useful for debugging or testing purposes.

To configure the server for this scheme make sure that the entry

```
RhostsAuthentication yes
```

appears in the server's `/etc/ssh/sshd_config` file to allow the scheme. Also, the client hostname must appear on the server in one of the trusted hosts files.

To configure the client, you may do one of the following three things (given in order of priority)

1. Invoke `ssh` on the client with, for example

   ```
   $ ssh -o RhostsAuthentication=yes server_hostname
   ```

   to force `ssh` to attempt Rhosts Authentication. Here, *server_hostname* is the actual hostname or IP address of the server.
2. Place the `RhostsAuthentication yes` entry in the user's `$HOME/.ssh/config` file.
3. Place the `RhostsAuthentication yes` entry in the client's `/etc/ssh/ssh_config` file.

By default, Rhosts Authentication is completely disabled on all servers by virtue of the entry,

```
RhostsAuthentication no
```

in `/etc/ssh/sshd_config`. Once again, this scheme is best left turned off.

Rhosts and RSA Authentication Configuration   This authentication scheme is conceptually described in *Rhosts and RSA Authentication* on page 260. To configure authentication using this method, you will need to set the Rhosts-RSAAuthentication keyword appropriately. For the server, make sure that the entry

```
RhostsRSAAuthentication yes
```

appears in /etc/ssh/sshd_config. For the client, you may use the same record as a command line option in the user's $HOME/.ssh/config file or in the /etc/ssh/ssh_config file. You will also need to make sure that the client hostname appears in at least one of the trusted host files on the server.

Let's consider an example. Suppose that we want to allow two trusted hosts access to the server pluto using this authentication scheme. We configure /etc/ssh/sshd_config as shown in Example 11-12. The entries associated with this authentication scheme (those that will be discussed) are in **bold**. Note that the last entry, AllowSHosts topcat underdog, limits the use of this scheme (and Rhosts Authentication, if it were turned on) to users from the two hosts, topcat and underdog. We must also put the hostnames, topcat and underdog, in an appropriate trusted host file on the server pluto. Example 11-13 shows the .shosts file on pluto in the home directory of the user mary.

Example 11-12 Limiting Rhosts Authentication Access with AllowSHosts

```
# sshd config file for host pluto
Port 22
ListenAddress 0.0.0.0
HostKey /etc/ssh/ssh_host_key
RandomSeed /etc/ssh/ssh_random_seed
ServerKeyBits 768
LoginGraceTime 600
KeyRegenerationInterval 3600
PermitRootLogin yes
IgnoreRhosts no
IgnoreRootRhosts yes
StrictModes yes
QuietMode no
X11Forwarding yes
X11DisplayOffset 10
FascistLogging yes
PrintMotd yes
KeepAlive yes
SyslogFacility LOCAL5
RhostsAuthentication no
RhostsRSAAuthentication yes
RSAAuthentication yes
PasswordAuthentication yes
PermitEmptyPasswords no
AllowSHosts topcat underdog
```

Example 11-13 /home/mary/.shosts File

```
# .shosts for ssh
underdog
topcat
```

Now that Rhosts and RSA Authentication is configured, Example 11-14 presents the `ssh` connection request by the user `mary` from `topcat` to `pluto`. This successful connection is encrypted.

Example 11-14 Using Rhosts and RSA Authentication

```
[mary@topcat]$ ssh -o RhostsRSAAuthentication=yes topcat
Last login: Wed Mar 10 12:05:11 1999 from roadrunner
Environment:
  HOME=/home/mary
  USER=mary
  LOGNAME=mary
  PATH=/usr/bin:/bin:/usr/bin
  MAIL=/var/spool/mail/mary
  SHELL=/bin/bash
  SSH_CLIENT=10.13.1.9 1022 22
  SSH_TTY=/dev/ttyp5
  TERM=dtterm
  REMOTEUSER=mary

No mail.
[mary@pluto]$
```

Since we have `FascistLogging` turned on (see Example 11-12 on page 290), let's see what the log files tell us about this connection. We set up logging to go to the facility LOCAL5 (see Example 11-12 on page 290) so that we could isolate the messages from `sshd`. Example 11-15 shows the log entries that were generated by the activity shown in Example 11-14. The entries with the keyword `debug` are a result of using `FascistLogging`. All other entries are standard and will appear in the log file unless `QuietMode` is set to `yes` in `/etc/ssh/sshd_config`.

Example 11-15 Log Messages Generated by the Connection Shown in Example 11-14

```
Jul  1 16:14:11 topcat sshd[14918]: debug: Forked child 14920.
Jul  1 15:47:19 pluto sshd[14920]: connect from underdog
Jul  1 15:47:19 pluto sshd[14920]: log: Connection from 10.13.1.9 port 1022
Jul  1 15:47:19 pluto sshd[14920]: debug: Client protocol version 1.5; client
software version 1.2.27
Jul  1 15:47:19 pluto sshd[14920]: debug: Sent 768 bit public key and 1024 bit
host key.
Jul  1 15:47:19 pluto sshd[14920]: debug: Encryption type: blowfish
Jul  1 15:47:19 pluto sshd[14920]: debug: Received session key; encryption turned
on.
Jul  1 15:47:19 pluto sshd[14920]: debug: Installing crc compensation attack
detector.
Jul  1 15:47:19 pluto sshd[14920]: debug: Attempting authentication for mary.
Jul  1 15:55:00 topcat sshd[14920]: log: Rhosts with RSA host authentication
accepted for mary, mary on underdog.
Jul  1 15:47:26 pluto sshd[14920]: debug: Setting controlling tty using
TIOCSCTTY.
```

Notice, however, that `IgnoreRootRhosts` is set to `yes` in Example 11-14 on page 291. This has the effect of disabling Rhosts and RSA Authentication for root (`/etc/hosts.equiv` and `/etc/shosts.equiv` do not apply to the root user). Nonetheless, let's see what happens when we create `/root/.rhosts` with underdog in it on `pluto`. Example 11-16 displays the results.

Example 11-16 Failed Authentication Due to `IgnoreRootRhosts`

```
[root@underdog /root]#ssh -o RhostsRSAAuthentication=yes pluto
root@pluto's password:
Last login: Thu Jul  1 16:12:49 1999 from underdog
No mail.
[root@pluto /root]#
```

Notice that `sshd` on `pluto` prompts for the root password on `pluto`. There is no indication that Rhosts and RSA Authentication failed, nor why. Let's see if the log file tells us anything. Example 11-17 shows the log file entries that correspond to Example 11-16.

Example 11-17 Log Messages Corresponding to Example 11-16

```
Jul  1 16:14:11 topcat sshd[15022]: debug: Forked child 15025.
Jul  1 16:14:11 topcat sshd[15025]: connect from underdog
Jul  1 16:14:11 topcat sshd[15025]: log: Connection from 10.13.1.9 port 1022
Jul  1 16:14:11 topcat sshd[15025]: debug: Client protocol version 1.5; client
software version 1.2.27
Jul  1 16:14:11 topcat sshd[15025]: debug: Sent 768 bit public key and 1024 bit
host key.
Jul  1 16:14:11 topcat sshd[15025]: debug: Encryption type: blowfish
Jul  1 16:14:11 topcat sshd[15025]: debug: Received session key; encryption
turned on.
Jul  1 16:14:11 topcat sshd[15025]: debug: Installing crc compensation attack
detector.
Jul  1 16:14:11 topcat sshd[15025]: debug: Attempting authentication for root.
Jul  1 16:14:16 topcat sshd[15025]: log: Password authentication for root
accepted.
Jul  1 16:14:16 topcat sshd[15025]: log: ROOT LOGIN as 'root' from underdog
```

While the log file tells us that root successfully passed password authentication, it doesn't tell us that Rhosts and RSA Authentication failed. At this point, we don't even know if Rhosts and RSA Authentication was attempted. In order to get more information, we need to run `sshd` in debug mode on the server. Example 11-18 provides a way to accomplish this. Note that `sshd` is killed prior to running `sshd -d`. If this is not done, you will get an error message indicating that `sshd` is already running. The entries in **bold** represent the information we seek. They tell us that Rhosts and RSA Authentication was attempted, but failed. So, if we were really debugging, we could concentrate our investigation on the server configuration (and hopefully find the `Ignore-RootRhosts` entry). Note that `sshd -d` may be used to debug SSH connections generally and not just specifically with Rhosts and RSA Authentication.

Example 11-18 Using `sshd -d`

```
[root@topcat]# /etc/rc.d/init.d/sshd stop
Stopping sshd: sshd
[root@topcat]# sshd -d
debug: sshd version 1.2.27 [i686-unknown-linux]
debug: Initializing random number generator; seed file /etc/ssh/ssh_random_seed
log: Server listening on port 22.
log: Generating 768 bit RSA key.
Generating p:  ...........................................++ (distance 1214)
Generating q:  ............................++ (distance 430)
Computing the keys...
```

Example 11-18 Using `sshd -d` (Continued)

```
Testing the keys...
Key generation complete.
log: RSA key generation complete.
debug: Server will not fork when running in debugging mode.
log: Connection from 10.13.1.9 port 1022
debug: Client protocol version 1.5; client software version 1.2.27
debug: Sent 768 bit public key and 1024 bit host key.
debug: Encryption type: blowfish
debug: Received session key; encryption turned on.
debug: Installing crc compensation attack detector.
debug: Attempting authentication for root.
debug: Trying rhosts with RSA host authentication for root
debug: RhostsRSA authentication failed for 'root', remote 'root', host 'underdog'.
log: Password authentication for root accepted.
log: ROOT LOGIN as 'root' from underdog
debug: Allocating pty.
debug: Ignoring unsupported tty mode opcode 11 (0xb)
debug: Forking shell.
debug: Entering interactive session.
debug: Setting controlling tty using TIOCSCTTY.
```

Rhosts and RSA Authentication represents a more secure form of authentication than simply authenticating via Rhosts. For an even more secure method, let's look at RSA Authentication.

RSA Authentication Configuration   RSA Authentication is described conceptually in *RSA Authentication* on page 261. It requires considerably more configuration and administration than the other two nonpassword authentication schemes. Such additional effort is commonly the case for better security. In addition to providing better security, it provides greater flexibility by allowing for encrypted X Window sessions (discussed in *Managing RSA Authentication with* `ssh-agent` *and* `ssh-add` *on page 301*). In this section, we will detail the `$HOME/.ssh/authorized_keys` file, which may be thought of as an `ssh` replacement to trusted hosts files; it also generates and manages the required keys stored in that file.

An Initial Example.   Let's suppose that the user `paul` wants to configure RSA Authentication for communication from `underdog` to `topcat`. In this case, `underdog` is the client and `topcat` is the server. Therefore, we will need to generate User Keys on `underdog` and configure `$HOME/.ssh/authorized_keys` on `topcat`. Since we need the Public User Key for the `$HOME/.ssh/authorized_keys` on `topcat`, we'll generate those first.

In order to create User Keys, we need to use the `ssh-keygen` command (detailed in *Using* `ssh-keygen` *on page 297*). Example 11-19 displays the output associated with the execution of `ssh-keygen` by the user `paul` on `underdog`. Notice that `paul` is prompted for a passphrase. If it is supplied, then the Private User Key, stored in `$HOME/.ssh/identity`, will be encrypted. This is a really good idea because anyone who gets the Private User Key can decrypt anything that has been encrypted with the Public User Key (stored in `$HOME/.ssh/identity.pub`, the syntax of this file is identical to that of `/etc/ssh/ssh_host_key.pub` as shown in Example 11-8 on page 285) and can pretend to be the owner of the Public User Key. So, make sure and enter a passphrase! A good range of characters for the passphrase is 10 to 20; the passphrase should not be simple English (or other language) prose as this might be guessed easily. Be sure to remember it because, if you forget it, you will have to regenerate and redistribute your keys. If you do not enter a passphrase, the Private User Key will not be encrypted. Note that the passphrase typed in at the `Enter pass-phrase:` and `Enter the same passphrase again:` prompts are not echoed back to the screen. After the passphrase is entered, `ssh-keygen` displays the Public User Key and reports that it has been stored in `$HOME/.ssh/identity.pub`.

Example 11-19 Generating User Keys with `ssh-keygen`

```
[paul@underdog paul]$ ssh-keygen
Initializing random number generator...
Generating p:  ........................++ (distance 290)
Generating q:  ...............................++ (distance 476)
Computing the keys...
Key generation complete.
Enter file in which to save the key (/home/paul/.ssh/identity):
Enter passphrase:
Enter the same passphrase again:
Your identification has been saved in /home/paul/.ssh/identity.
Your public key is:
1024 35 13352077311307068462507042445063951104287449844411
864065669868257318053040432749349424442561641144284941524
606188211711327052620862857500182874979351902924442794305
995827227108920987905175983827361650684240273956226900399
454133777809835352038374995530819601603340060597525776712
7348572567198546669546491518388 9 paul@underdog
Your public key has been saved in /home/paul/.ssh/identity.pub
[paul@underdog paul]$
```

Now that `paul` has a set of User Keys, he needs to copy the Public User Key, exactly as it appears in `/home/paul/.ssh/identity.pub` on `underdog`, into the file `/home/paul/.ssh/authorized_keys` on the host `topcat`. Thus, the `/home/paul/.ssh/authorized_keys` file must minimally contain the entry as shown in Example 11-20 on `topcat`.[4]

Example 11-20 `/home/paul/.ssh/authorized_keys` File

```
1024 35 13352077311307068462507042445063951104287449844411
864065669868257318053040432749349424442561641144284941524
606188211711327052620862857500182874979351902924442794305
995827227108920987905175983827361650684240273956226900399
454133777809835352038374995530819601603340060597525776712
7348572567198546669546491518388 9 paul@underdog
```

NOTE

Blank lines and lines beginning with # in the `$HOME/authorized_keys` file are treated as comments.

---

4. Example 11-20 shows an entry without options. Options can be specified at the beginning of each record in this file and are discussed in *Options in `$HOME/.ssh/authorized_keys`* on page 299.

Everything necessary for `paul` to use SSH RSA Authentication from `underdog` to `topcat` is now configured. Example 11-21 shows us the result. Notice that `paul` is prompted for the passphrase associated with the User Keys belonging to `paul@underdog`. The passphrase does not traverse the network; it is used locally to decrypt the Private User Key, which in turn is used to decrypt the challenge sent by the server (`topcat` in this case).

Example 11-21 RSA Authentication in Action

```
[paul@underdog paul]$ ssh topcat
Enter passphrase for RSA key 'paul@underdog':
Last login: Thu Mar 11 06:48:24 1999 from roadrunner
You have new mail.
[paul@topcat paul]$
```

The log entries, with `FascistLogging` set to `no`, for the entire session appear in Example 11-22.

Example 11-22 Log Entries Corresponding to Example 11-21

```
Jul  2 12:28:18 topcat sshd[1882]: connect from 10.13.33.111
Jul  2 12:28:18 topcat sshd[1882]: log: Connection from 10.13.33.111 port 1022
Jul  2 12:28:41 topcat sshd[1882]: log: RSA authentication for paul accepted.
Jul  2 12:39:33 topcat sshd[1882]: log: Closing connection to 10.13.33.111
```

If `paul` wishes to authenticate himself in this way on other servers from `underdog`, he must configure `/home/paul/.ssh/authorized_keys` on each server. Similarly, if he wishes to authenticate himself from clients other than `underdog`, he will need to do one of two things: he can generate the necessary keys on each client and subsequently incorporate the Public User Key from each client into the appropriate server's `/home/paul/.ssh/authorized_keys` file, or he can generate the keys once and subsequently copy the `$HOME/.ssh/identity` and `$HOME/.ssh/identity.pub` files to each client. This latter approach is more common and is trivial if home directories are mounted via NFS.

In computing environments of even modest size, managing this process manually is burdensome. There are no utilities within SSH that automate the propagation of appropriate entries in the necessary server-side `$HOME/.ssh/authorized_keys` file (there are other utilities that can provide that functionality—see *Synchronizing Files with `rdist` or `rsync`* on page 301). However, the `ssh-agent` and `ssh-add` utilities provide a mechanism to automate the process of supplying the passphrase automatically, which is useful for scripting. These utilities also allow for the automatic forwarding of X Window System sessions through the encrypted tunnel. Those two utilities are described in *Managing RSA Authentication with `ssh-agent` and `ssh-add`* on page 301.

NOTE

Configuring RSA Authentication as described in this section applies to all users including the root user. See *Using `ssh-keygen` for root* on page 297 for further information relating to the use of `ssh-keygen` by the root user.

A Common Problem.   Let's suppose that you go through the configuration process just described and the results are as shown in Example 11-23. Instead of being prompted for a passphrase, `paul` is prompted for his password on `top-cat`. This is not what we expected. So let's run `sshd` in debug mode on `topcat` to find out what's going on. This is shown in Example 11-24.

Example 11-23 RSA Authentication Not Working?

```
[paul@underdog paul]$ ssh topcat
paul@topcat's password:
```

Example 11-24 Bad Modes Due to `StrictModes`

```
[root@topcat]# /etc/rc.d/init.d/sshd stop
Stopping sshd: sshd
[root@topcat /root]# sshd -d
debug: sshd version 1.2.27 [sparc-unknown-linux]
debug: Initializing random number generator; seed file /etc/ssh/
ssh_random_seed
log: Server listening on port 22.
log: Generating 768 bit RSA key.
Generating p:  ...........................++ (distance 532)
Generating q:  ...........................++ (distance 462)
Computing the keys...
Key generation complete.
log: RSA key generation complete.
debug: Server will not fork when running in debugging mode.
log: Connection from 10.13.33.111 port 1022
debug: Client protocol version 1.5; client software version 1.2.27
debug: Sent 768 bit public key and 1024 bit host key.
debug: Encryption type: blowfish
debug: Received session key; encryption turned on.
debug: Installing crc compensation attack detector.
debug: Attempting authentication for paul.
debug: Trying rhosts with RSA host authentication for paul
debug: RhostsRSA authentication failed for 'paul', remote 'paul', host
'underdog'.
log: Rsa authentication refused for paul: bad modes for /home/paul/.ssh/
authorized_keys
debug: RSA authentication for paul failed.
log: Password authentication for paul accepted.
debug: Allocating pty.
debug: Forking shell.
debug: Entering interactive session.
debug: Setting controlling tty using TIOCSCTTY.
debug: Received SIGCHLD.
debug: End of interactive session; stdin 1, stdout (read 311, sent 311),
stderr 0 bytes.
debug: pty_cleanup_proc called
debug: Command exited with status 0.
debug: Received exit confirmation.
log: Closing connection to 10.13.1.9
[root@topcat /root]#
```

The pertinent entry is shown in **bold**. This entry tells us that the modes (permission bits) are bad—that is because, by default, `StrictModes` is set to yes in `/etc/ssh/sshd_config`, which means that `sshd` will not read any user file whose permissions are less restrictive than `644` (`rw-r--r--`). By default, Red Hat Linux sets every user's `umask` to `002` because of its use of UPG (see *Group Account Management* on page 69). Thus, in this case when Paul created the /home/paul/.ssh/authorized_keys file on topcat, its permissions were set to 664 (rw-rw-r--). To correct this, execute

```
[paul@topcat]$ chmod 644 /home/paul/.ssh/authorized_keys
```

and then the connection will proceed as in Example 11-21 on page 295. Another way to disable this problem is to use the --enable-group-writeability compile-time option (see Table 11.2 on page 266). This latter approach is not recommended because it allows relaxed file permissions across the board, not just for UPG.

Using ssh-keygen. We used ssh-keygen in Example 11-19 on page 294 to generate a set of User Keys for paul. This utility may be used to generate User Keys for any user, including root. The options to ssh-keygen are given in Table 11.9. As noted in the table, the use of the -N and -P options is not recommended, although they add convenience for scripting.

Using ssh-keygen for root. The ssh-keygen program may be used to generate new Host Keys as well as new User Keys. The Host Keys must be generated

Table 11.9 Options to ssh-keygen

Option	Description
-b bits	Specifies the number of bits for the modulus of the keys. Minimum is 512, the default is 1024, and the maximum is 32768. Larger values will significantly impact the performance of your systems.
-f file	Specifies the name of the file containing the Private User Key. The default is $HOME/.ssh/identity.
-p	Requests changing the passphrase used to encrypt the Private User Key without changing the keys themselves.
-u	Requests changing the cipher used to encrypt the key to the current default cipher. The default in the U.S. version is Blowfish; in the international version it is IDEA.
-c	Requests that the comment field in the $HOME/.ssh/identity.pub be changed.
-C 'comment'	Allows for the specification of the comment on the command line rather than having ssh-keygen prompt for it. Be sure to escape any string containing shell-interpreted characters.
-N 'passphrase'	Allows for the specification of the new passphrase on the command line instead of having ssh-keygen prompt for it. Be sure to escape any string containing shell-interpreted characters. Caution: the passphrase in this case will be readable by anyone looking over your shoulder! It is better to allow ssh-keygen to prompt you so that the passphrase will not echo back to the screen.
-P 'old passphrase'	Same as for -N, except that it contains the old passphrase. The same caution applies.

by root. The default behavior of ssh-keygen when executed by root, however, is to generate User Keys for root. So, in order to generate new Host Keys, simply use the -f option as shown in Example 11-25. Make sure that you do **not** specify a passphrase for Private Host Key! When ssh-keygen prompts you for a passphrase, press return.

Example 11-25 Generating New Host Keys

```
roadrunner# ssh-keygen -f /etc/ssh/ssh_host_key
Initializing random number generator...
Generating p:  ....++ (distance 116)
Generating q:  .....................++ (distance 386)
Computing the keys...
Testing the keys...
Key generation complete.
/etc/ssh/ssh_host_key already exists.
Overwrite (y/n)? y
Enter passphrase: <carriage return>
Enter the same passphrase again: <carriage return>
Your identification has been saved in /etc/ssh/ssh_host_key.
Your public key is:
1024331616914172264014628092156127882547631863043012215095713
5567604359990441553571794606082856257137828939141213273076831
8762519254331690476091961641737104239348722044797532070242221
8183075541587379076400451503319198299907690726634927773098538
9558815906903529675657335570789299697832679334043321380676927
5239853307 root@roadrunner
Your public key has been saved in /etc/ssh/ssh_host_key.pub
roadrunner#
```

Once you have generated new Host Keys, don't forget to remove the old Public Host Key entries from the /etc/ssh/ssh_known_hosts and $HOME/.ssh/known_hosts files throughout your computing environment. Otherwise you will get the error message as displayed in Example 11-9 on page 287 and be unable to use X Window System and agent forwarding capabilities.

WARNING!

You must not specify a passphrase for the Private Host Key! If you do, the system will **not** be able to utilize its Private Host Key, which is necessary for the initial RSA Host-Based Authentication. One way to avoid supplying a passphrase for the Private Host Key is to use the command

```
# ssh-keygen -f /etc/ssh/ssh_host_key -N ""
```

You may then alias this command to something like host-keygen. This should help avoid mistakes.

On the other hand, you should utilize a passphrase for root's Private User Key.

Disabling Direct root Access.   We noted in Table 11.5 on page 270 that root access via ssh can be disabled by setting the PermitRootLogin option in /etc/ssh/sshd_config to no. The benefit of this approach is that no one, especially the bad-guys, will be able to connect as root via SSH. If you eliminate root access in this way, you will need to permit su (see *Access Control with* *pam_listfile* on page 100, *PAM and su* on page 103, and *Using pam_access* on page 104) or sudo (see *Disabling root Access* on page 190) to allow for remote administration (unless your Security Policy disallows root access over the network altogether).

Your Security Policy (Chapter 2) ought to tell you when this type implementation is warranted, but generally root access should minimally be eliminated on all systems connected to untrusted networks.

Options in $HOME/.ssh/authorized_keys. We looked at an example $HOME/.ssh/authorized_keys file in Example 11-20 on page 294. That example shows the simplest form of a record for this file. The full syntax for each record (line) in the file is

```
options bits exponent modulus comment
```

where options is an optional field containing one or more of the options described in Table 11.10 (multiple options are separated by commas). The options field need not be present. The bits, exponent, modulus, and comment fields are the same as previously described on page 285 in relation to Example 11-8.

The options field provides a way of adding functionality and restricting use through RSA Authentication. Table 11.10 lists the available options.

As an example of using options in $HOME/.ssh/authorized_keys, let's suppose we want to allow only root on topcat to access underdog using this key. Example 11-26 shows how to accomplish this in the $HOME/.ssh/ authorized_keys file. Note that root on topcat is also not allowed to request forwarded ports or X11 sessions.

Example 11-26 Using Options in $HOME/.ssh/authorized_keys

```
from="topcat",no-port-forwarding,no-X11-forwarding 1024 33 16592797608
9255816651814515035742431797413595850007900570553178645911586962313184
2289618136246086455760642073230687618029978695636444007166223480988249
1206058714399182650275664018867176205554871947749434075180031329995375
7140737301808903571262747513723998968744274802471011579129424946728045
507570134455219729 root@topcat
```

The benefit of using the from option is that only the connections from the IP address that resolve to the canonical hostname (topcat in this case) can use the key in that record. Thus, if someone steals the Private User Key associated with this Public User Key, they will also have to spoof the IP address associated with topcat or poison the host resolution database. Without the from="topcat" entry, anyone who has gotten the Private User Key associated with the Public User Key shown in Example 11-26 will be granted access to underdog through RSA Authentication.

This is why it is so important to choose good passphrases for the encryption of your Private User Key. Doing so will make it exceedingly difficult for anyone to obtain your Private User Key. However, it is possible, with a concerted effort, to get a Private User Key without actually stealing it (see the

Table 11.10 Available `options` in `$HOME/.ssh/authorized_keys`

Option	Description
`from="host-list"`	Specifies a list of space-separated hostnames from which this key will be accepted for RSA Authentication. The wildcards * and ? may be used as well as the negation operator !. This adds access control capabilities so that someone cannot simply steal the User Keys (they would have to steal the keys and spoof the host). TCP_wrappers support provides this functionality prior to this check.
`command="command"`	Causes the specified command to be executed and any command specified by the user to be ignored. Quotes may be used in the command if they are escaped with \.This option is very useful for allowing specific operations such as backups, clock synchronization, and the like. This option does not disable port or X Window System forwarding.
`environment="VAR=value"`	Allows the setting of a shell environment variable, `VAR`, to `value`. This option overrides all other settings of this environment variable (such as through `/etc/environment`; see Table 11.3 on page 267). You may not specify multiple variables inside the quotes, but you may specify multiple `environment="VAR=value"` options.
`idle-timeout=time`	Sets the idle time-out in `seconds`, `minutes`m, `hours`h, `days`d, or `weeks`w, where `seconds`, `minutes`, `hours`, `days`, and `weeks` must be positive integers. This setting overrides any other settings, such as `IdleTimeout` as described in Table 11.5 on page 270.
`no-port-forwarding`	Prohibits TCP port forwarding for this key. This option should be used with the `command` option to ensure the restriction imposed by the `command` option. Port forwarding is described in *Port Forwarding and Application Proxying* on page 307.
`no-X11-forwarding`	Prohibits X Window System forwarding for this key. This option should be used with the `command` option to ensure the restriction imposed by the `command` option. X Window System forwarding is described in *Managing RSA Authentication with* `ssh-agent` *and* `ssh-add` on page 301.
`no-agent-forwarding`	Prohibits agent forwarding by `ssh-agent` for this key. See *Disabling X and Agent Forwarding* on page 303 for more details.
`no-pty`	Prohibits the allocation of a `pty`.

resources in *Cryptography References* on page 47 for information about cryptanalysis). Consequently, it is a good idea to change User Keys on a regular basis. The frequency of changing the keys depends upon the risk associated with your environment (see Chapter 2). For example, extended use over the Internet warrants perhaps monthly changes (again, see *Cryptography References* on page 47), whereas internal use may warrant only quarterly changes.

On the other hand, the fact that one Public User Key in `$HOME/.ssh/` `authorized_keys` can be used to authenticate the user from many hosts is a significant convenience. Only you can decide if the convenience is worth the risk.

Synchronizing Files with `rdist` or `rsync`. While on the topic of convenience, you can automate the management of the `authorized_keys` files (as well as other files) with either the `rdist` (remote distribution) or `rsync` (remote synchronization) utilities.

While `rdist-6.1.0` is included with Red Hat 5.2, it is incompatible with SSH. On the other hand, you may obtain `rdist-6.1.5` from `http://www.magni-comp.com/rdist/`, which is compatible as long as you apply the patch given in the SSH FAQ, found at `http://www.employees.org/~satch/ssh/faq/ssh-faq-4.html` under section 4.4. This latter version of `rdist` is included in the Red Hat 6.0 release. The `rdist` utility is a file distribution program that can be used to maintain identical copies of files over many hosts.

The `rsync` utility is fully compatible with SSH. It is a general-purpose file-copying program that can verify whether or not files on multiple hosts are different and, if so, updates those files requiring updating by simply propagating the differences. This makes `rsync` more efficient. Version 2.1.1 of `rsync` is included in Red Hat 5.2, and version 2.3.1 is in Red Hat 6.0. Its official home page is `http://samba.anu.edu.au/rsync/`.

Either of these programs could be used to synchronize User Keys and Host Keys (among other things). If you implement one or both of them, make sure that they use SSH to secure the transfers.

Managing RSA Authentication with `ssh-agent` and `ssh-add`. The `ssh-agent` utility is a program that holds the User Keys for purposes of authentication and the establishment of the necessary `.Xauthority` entries (Massachusetts Institute of Technology [MIT] magic-cookies, which are used to allow X applications display permissions) to establish encrypted X Window System applications. See *Exploring `ssh` Functionality* on page 304 for an alternative method of encrypting X Window System sessions.

In order for `ssh-agent` (we will often refer to `ssh-agent` as simply the *agent*) to work, it must be the parent of all the processes that will subsequently depend upon it. As such, `ssh-agent` takes a command as its argument. So, for example, to cause all processes in an X session to be able to utilize the agent's capabilities, you could execute

```
$ ssh-agent startx
```

at the command line or put it into a start-up script. Similarly, `ssh-agent` could be used to invoke a shell, in the absence of the X Window System, such as

```
$ ssh-agent /bin/bash
```

In either case, invoking your session through `ssh-agent` will give you the ability to use its features.

Initially the agent holds no keys. In order to add User Keys to the agent, you will need to use the `ssh-add` command. With no arguments, executing `ssh-add` will prompt for the passphrase associated with the invoking user. It then passes the passphrase, Private User Key (stored in `$HOME/.ssh/identity`), and Public User Key to `ssh-agent`. Example 11-27 illustrates the execution of `ssh-add`.

Example 11-27 Using `ssh-add`

```
$ ssh-add
Need passphrase for /home/mary/.ssh/identity (mary@roadrunner).
Enter passphrase:
Identity added: /home/mary/.ssh/identity (mary@roadrunner)
```

To verify that the `Identity` (actually, the User Keys) has been added, we may list all identities maintained by `ssh-agent` with `ssh-add -l` as shown in Example 11-28. Only one entry is listed because it is the only one which has been added thus far. Note that only the Public User Key is displayed.

Example 11-28 Using `ssh-add -l` to List Public User Keys

```
$ ssh-add -l
1024 35 155971740030589148116564771700556225351261296812046254408
6117198857854043287801482186061813199942506918333657756468023152147
386333574733382241382028492393695598668112247267929970885559669087
204543581160063802030469682999381178989220034468062506418833671363
0151162806686650625258186487512130263282836944758784 mary@roadrun
ner
$
```

The agent can hold many keys. Although it expects the keys to be in `$HOME/.ssh/identity` and `$HOME/.ssh/identity.pub`, this is easily overridden by specifying the filename as an argument to `ssh-add`. The options to `ssh-add` are given in Table 11.11.

The agent holds the keys until it terminates or is told to delete them by `ssh-add -d` or `ssh-add -D`. Once the agent has the User Keys, it will manage the

Table 11.11 Options of `ssh-add`

Option	Description
`file`	Specifies the name of the file holding the Private User Key instead of `$HOME/.ssh/identity`.
`-p`	Causes the passphrase to be read from `stdin` or a pipe. Useful in scripts, but be careful about storing passphrases in files.
`-l`	Lists all keys stored by the agent.
`-d`	Deletes the User Keys from the agent matching those keys in `$HOME/.ssh/identity*` or `file` if specified.
`-D`	Deletes all keys from the agent.

RSA Authentication dialog on behalf of the user so that the user is not prompted for the Private User Key passphrase. This is known as *agent forwarding*. It also establishes the necessary X authentication information and sets the DISPLAY environment variable. This process is invoked by ssh as shown in Example 11-29. Note that it informs you that it is generating the MIT-MAGIC-COOKIE for the session. The cookies are good for both underdog and its IP address (in case of hostname resolution failures). At this point, any X Window System application you invoke will be forwarded through the SSH-encrypted tunnel.

Example 11-29 Using ssh with Agent Forwarding

```
[root@topcat .ssh]# ssh underdog
Last login: Fri Jul  2 15:04:57 1999 from pluto
Environment:
  HOME=/root
  USER=root
  LOGNAME=root
  PATH=/usr/bin:/bin:/usr/bin
  MAIL=/var/spool/mail/root
  SHELL=/bin/bash
  SSH_CLIENT=10.13.33.111 1023 22
  SSH_TTY=/dev/pts/5
  TERM=xterm
  DISPLAY=underdog:10.0
  SSH_AUTH_SOCK=/tmp/ssh-root/ssh-2598-agent
Running /usr/X11R6/bin/xauth add underdog:10.0 MIT-MAGIC-COOKIE-1
57cb55807403833150eb32e37c85ddd9
Running /usr/X11R6/bin/xauth add 10.13.1.9:10.0 MIT-MAGIC-COOKIE-1
57cb55807403833150eb32e37c85ddd9
No mail.
[root@underdog]#
```

WARNING!

If you manually set the DISPLAY environment variable to another value, any X applications subsequently invoked will **not** be encrypted.

The MIT-MAGIC-COOKIES are stored in the user's home directory in the .Xauthority file. If someone else obtains the contents of this file, they will be able to utilize that system's display device which could result in the further capturing of sensitive information. Thus, the .Xauthority file permissions should be set to 600 (rw-------) and owned by the user in whose home directory the .Xauthority file appears.

Disabling X and Agent Forwarding. If X11Forwarding is set to no in /etc/ssh/sshd_config on the server and/or no-X11-forwarding is specified in $HOME/.ssh/authorized_keys for the keys being used, then this functionality will be prohibited. X Window System forwarding can also be disabled on the server by setting an appropriate entry in /etc/hosts.deny (if compiled --with-libwrap as is true for the RPMs). The following sshdfwd-X11 entry in /etc/hosts.deny will prohibit pluto and topcat from utilizing X Window System forwarding:

```
sshdfwd-X11: pluto,topcat
```

Agent forwarding—that is, the use of `ssh-agent`—may be turned off on the client by setting `ForwardAgent` to `no` at the `ssh` command line in the `$HOME/.ssh/config` file or in the `/etc/ssh/ssh_config` file. The `-a` flag to `ssh` may also be used.

Password-Based Authentication

If the three nonpassword authentication schemes fail, then `sshd` prompts the user for his or her password. The password is passed through the encrypted tunnel and, if it is entered successfully, then `sshd` will provide the user a shell or execute the command specified by the user. By default, the username and server hostname appear in the password prompt. You may disable these with the `PasswordPromptLogin` and `PasswordPromptHost` keywords set to `no` at the `ssh` command line in the `$HOME/.ssh/config` file or in the `/etc/ssh/ssh_config` file. You may disable password authentication altogether by setting `Password-Authentication` to `no` in `/etc/ssh/sshd_config` on the server.

Further Restricting Access with PAM   If you configure the server-side of SSH to authenticate passed on passwords, you can use `pam_access` to restrict logins further based on `/etc/security/access.conf`. This is due to the fact that `pam_access` is an `account` module type and SSH supports that module type. Since SSH does not support module type `auth`, `auth`-only access control modules like `pam_listfile` are unavailable. The details of using `pam_access` are given in *Using pam_access* on page 104.

Note that, if nonpassword authentication succeeds, any limitations imposed through `pam_access` are ignored.

EXPLORING ssh FUNCTIONALITY

In this section we will take a look at a variety of examples using `ssh` and `scp`. We begin with examples that are similar to `rsh` and `rcp` usage and then move on to port forwarding. In all of our examples, we assume that all servers are running `sshd`. Authentication will proceed as previously described and all sessions are encrypted.

ssh Examples

The simplest use of `ssh` is to log in to a remote system. This can be done very simply with

```
$ ssh remote_host
```

and upon authentication a shell will be opened on the *remote_host* for the invoking user. To log in as a different user, execute the command

```
$ ssh -l username remote_host
```

and, again, upon authentication a shell will be opened on the *remote_host* for *username*.

One of the more common uses of `rsh` is to access a remote tape device for backups and restores. We can accomplish the same thing with `ssh` as shown in Example 11-30. In this case, we use the `-n` option to redirect `stdin` to `/dev/null` so that `ssh` won't block the `tar` command waiting for input. We are asking `ssh` to connect from `topcat` to `underdog` and execute the command `dd if=/dev/st0 bs=20b`. RSA Authentication, in this case, succeeds when Mary correctly submits her passphrase. The `dd` command will read data from the device file `/dev/st0` on `underdog` in blocks of 10,240 bytes (`bs=20b`) and send it back through the SSH-encrypted tunnel to `topcat` where it is piped to the `tar` command on `topcat`. When the `dd` command finishes on `underdog`, `sshd` on `underdog` terminates the SSH connection.

Example 11-30 `tar` Extraction Using `ssh`

```
[mary@topcat]$ ssh -n underdog dd if=/dev/st0 bs=20b|tar xvBpfb - 2000
Enter passphrase for RSA key 'mary@topcat':
drwx------ cmetz/staff        0 1998-01-01 16:54 opie-2.32/
-rw------- cmetz/staff     3590 1998-01-01 16:53 opie-2.32/BUG-REPORT
-rw------- cmetz/staff     3377 1996-08-22 07:50 opie-2.32/COPYRIGHT.NRL
-rw------- cmetz/staff     2606 1998-01-01 16:53 opie-2.32/INSTALL
-rw------- cmetz/staff     2395 1996-09-14 11:06 opie-2.32/License.TIN
-rw------- cmetz/staff    20735 1998-01-01 16:54 opie-2.32/README
-rw------- cmetz/staff    12397 1998-01-01 16:53 opie-2.32/Makefile.in
...
<tar extraction proceeds>
...
[mary@topcat]$
```

In *Managing RSA Authentication with* `ssh-agent` *and* `ssh-add` on page 301, we looked at setting up encrypted X Window System connections automatically. Example 11-31 shows another approach. In this example, Mary executes the given command in an X window. By using the `-f` option to `ssh`, after authentication (which proceeds via password authentication in this case), the process is put in the background, returning control to the invoking window. Shortly after successful authentication, the `nxterm` window from `underdog` will appear on `topcat`.

Example 11-31 Backgrounding `ssh` with `-f` and Starting `nxterm`

```
[mary@topcat]$ ssh -f underdog /usr/bin/X11/nxterm
mary@topcat's password:
[mary@topcat]$
```

WARNING!

If you set the `DISPLAY` environment variable or, for example, if you use `/usr/bin/X11/nxterm -display topcat:0` as the command to `ssh` instead of that shown in Example 11-31, your `nxterm` will not be encrypted. As long as you allow `ssh` to set the display, your X sessions invoked through `ssh` will be encrypted.

scp **Examples**

The scp utility is a secure remote copy utility. It uses the same authentication processes as ssh. Its purpose is to copy files between two hosts through the SSH-encrypted tunnel. Its syntax is described in Table 11.8 on page 281. Example 11-32 shows a user copying the /etc/hosts file from the remote host topcat to the /tmp/hosts file on the local host roadrunner. The user then uses more to verify that the file was in fact transferred.

Example 11-32 Copying a File from a Remote Host Using scp

```
roadrunner$ scp topcat:/etc/hosts /tmp/hosts
mary@topcat's password:
hosts   |   0 KB |   0.6 kB/s | ETA: 00:00:00 | 100%
roadrunner$ more /tmp/hosts
#
# Internet host table
#
127.0.0.1         localhost          loghost
172.17.1.1        foghorn
# local net
...
<contents snipped>
...
roadrunner$
```

As you can see, the user is authenticated by password. Notice that scp produces statistics about the transfer in the line

```
hosts   |         0 KB |    0.6 kB/s | ETA: 00:00:00 | 100%
```

which indicates the local name of the file transferred (hosts), the size of the file (0KB, indicating less than 1 KB), the transfer rate (0.6 kB/s), the time for the transfer (ETA: 00:00:00, indicating less than 1 second), and the percentage of the file transferred (100%). You may disable statistical reporting with the -q option to scp.

Our next illustration, Example 11-33, shows the user mary recursively copying the entire contents of Paul's home directory from the host underdog to the directory /tmp on roadrunner. In this example, Mary is using the -r option to scp for recursion and the p option to preserve file modes, access times, and modification times. The q option suppresses statistical output by scp, and v generates verbose output on the client side (the v option has the same meaning when used with ssh). Note that, while the p option preserves file modes, access times, and modification times, the files copied to roadrunner in /tmp/paul will be owned by mary. Also, the syntax paul@underdog causes scp to authenticate the user paul on underdog; hence the password prompt, paul@underdog's password:(shown in **bold**). The only way Mary can get these files is if she knows Paul's password (which apparently she does).

Note that all of the verbose output prior to the password prompt in Example 11-33 deals with the authentication process. Everything after the password prompt is output related to the request (a recursive copy, in this

Example 11-33 Recursive Copy with scp

```
roadrunner$ scp -rpqv paul@underdog:/home/paul /tmp
Executing: host underdog, user paul, command scp -v -r -p -f /home/paul
SSH Version 1.2.27 [i686-unknown-linux], protocol version 1.5.
Standard version.  Does not use RSAREF.
roadrunner: Reading configuration data /etc/ssh/ssh_config
roadrunner: ssh_connect: getuid 101 geteuid 0 anon 0
roadrunner: Connecting to underdog [10.13.1.9] port 22.
roadrunner: Allocated local port 1020.
roadrunner: Connection established.
roadrunner: Remote protocol version 1.5, remote software version 1.2.27
roadrunner: Waiting for server public key.
roadrunner: Received server public key (768 bits) and host key (1024 bits).
roadrunner: Host 'underdog' is known and matches the host key.
roadrunner: Initializing random; seed file /home/mary/.ssh/random_seed
roadrunner: Encryption type: idea
roadrunner: Sent encrypted session key.
roadrunner: Installing crc compensation attack detector.
roadrunner: Received encrypted confirmation.
roadrunner: Trying rhosts or /etc/hosts.equiv with RSA host authentication.
roadrunner: Server refused our rhosts authentication or host key.
roadrunner: No agent.
roadrunner: Trying RSA authentication with key 'mary@roadrunner'
roadrunner: Server refused our key.
roadrunner: Doing password authentication.
paul@underdog's password:
roadrunner: Sending command: scp -v -r -p -f /home/paul
roadrunner: Entering interactive session.
Entering directory: D0700 0 paul
Sending file modes: C0644 1422 .Xdefaults
Sending file modes: C0644 24 .bash_logout
Sending file modes: C0644 230 .bash_profile
Sending file modes: C0644 124 .bashrc
Entering directory: D0700 0 .xauth
Entering directory: D0755 0 .ssh
Sending file modes: C0600 512 random_seed
Sending file modes: C0600 528 identity
Sending file modes: C0664 332 identity.pub
Sending file modes: C0600 325 known_hosts
Sending file modes: C0600 105 .bash_history
roadrunner: Transferred: stdin 37, stdout 4631, stderr 0 bytes in 2.2 seconds
roadrunner: Bytes per second: stdin 17.0, stdout 2127.6, stderr 0.0
roadrunner: Exit status 0
roadrunner$
```

case). The statistics produced are from the -v option and not through scp—those statistics were turned off with -q. The -v option is very useful for debugging both scp and ssh.

Port Forwarding and Application Proxying

SSH provides the capability of configuring an unused port on a server to be forwarded to another system and port number. In effect, it provides a proxy capability in which an encrypted tunnel is built between two systems and the connection is then forwarded, in the clear, to a third system. Any user may take advantage of this feature; however, the forwarding of privileged ports (port numbers less than or equal to 1023) requires root access. This functionality is provided for in two different ways: local forwarding and remote forwarding. Let's look at examples of each.

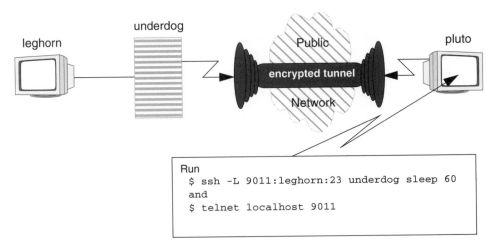

Fig. 11.5 Using SSH Local Forwarding

Local Forwarding   Let's suppose that we have three hosts—leghorn, under-dog, and pluto. Further suppose that we would like to connect from pluto to leghorn and that in order to do that we must go through underdog (a multi-homed host). The network between pluto and underdog is unsecure, but the network between underdog and leghorn is internal and considered secure. What we would like to do is build an encrypted tunnel from pluto to underdog and then let the traffic pass in the clear between underdog and leghorn as depicted in Figure 11.5.

In order to accomplish this, we first execute ssh -L 9011:leghorn:23 sleep 60 on pluto in one shell or window as shown in Example 11-34. This command initiates the encrypted tunnel between pluto and underdog. The first port number, 9011, is relatively arbitrary (for nonroot use it must be greater than 1023 and must not be in use by another process). The leghorn:23 argument tells ssh that we want to forward port 9011 on the local system to port 23 on leghorn. The purpose of the sleep 60 command is to keep underdog busy so that Mary can open the connection to leghorn. Once Mary has sup-plied the passphrase here, then, in another shell or window on pluto, she can execute telnet localhost 9011 as given in Example 11-35.

Example 11-34 Establish Local Port Forwarding

```
[mary@pluto]$ ssh -L 9011:leghorn:23 underdog sleep 60
Enter passphrase for RSA key 'mary@topcat':
```

Example 11-35 Use the Forwarded Port from Example 11-34

```
[mary@pluto]$ telnet localhost 9011
Trying 127.0.0.1...
Connected to localhost.
Escape character is '^]'.

UNIX(r) System V Release 4.0 (leghorn)

login: mary
```

Example 11-35 Use the Forwarded Port from Example 11-34 (Continued)

```
Password:
Last login: Sat Jul  3 14:46:01 from roadrunner
Sun Microsystems Inc.   SunOS 5.5        Generic November 1995
mary@leghorn$
```

This opens the session to leghorn (hey, leghorn is another Solaris system—how did *they* get into a Linux book?). The connection between pluto and underdog will be encrypted, whereas from underdog to leghorn data will pass in the clear (run sniffit to check). Note that, once Mary has successfully logged in to leghorn, the messages shown in **bold** in Example 11-36 will appear in the shell or window that was used to execute ssh -L 9011:leghorn:23 sleep 60 (as shown in Example 11-34). Notice in particular that the forwarded connection will control termination of the SSH session shown in Example 11-36.

Example 11-36 Messages Displayed after Successful Forwarded Connection

```
[mary@pluto]$ ssh -L 9011:leghorn:23 underdog sleep 60
Enter passphrase for RSA key 'mary@pluto':
fwd connect from 127.0.0.1 to local port sshdfwd-9011
Waiting for forwarded connections to terminate...
The following connections are open:
  port 9011, connection from localhost port 1695
```

NOTE

If the port number specified by sshdfwd is listed in /etc/services, then you **must** use the name and not the number. For example, if you wanted to forward http requests, you would have to specify sshdfwd-www and could not specify sshdfwd-80.

In our examples, we used two interactive shells or windows on pluto. We could have implemented RSA Authentication and used scripts to fully automate the building of the forwarded port.

It turns out that, once the command shown in Example 11-34 is executed, any user on pluto can execute the telnet command as shown in Example 11-35. If we don't trust all the users on pluto, this could be a problem. On the other hand, it also means that we can create a user specifically to handle forwarding and automate the process by configuring that user's $HOME/.ssh/.config file with the BatchMode and LocalForward keywords (see Table 11.7 on page 277) set appropriately and then enscripting the process.

WARNING!

If you add the -g option to the command given in Example 11-34 and Example 11-36, then any user on any system will be able to utilize the configured forwarded port with the command

```
$ telnet pluto 9011
```

Therefore, the -g option cannot be recommended as it creates a significant vulnerability. To limit or disable port forwarding, see *Limiting and Disabling Forwarding* below.

Remote Forwarding   Remote forwarding is quite similar to local forwarding. The major difference is that we would execute the forwarding command on underdog in Figure 11.5. For example

```
[mary@underdog]$ ssh -R 9345:leghorn:23 pluto
```

would cause port 9345 to be forwarded to leghorn port 23. Once the connection is established, Mary would then execute

```
[mary@pluto]$ telnet localhost 9345
```

on pluto. All other aspects to this mechanism are as described in *Local Forwarding* on page 308.

Limiting and Disabling Forwarding   The most flexible approach to controlling port forwarding through SSH is to use /etc/hosts.allow and /etc/hosts.deny. For example, if we wish to allow only the host pluto to establish forwarded ports on underdog, we would place the entry

```
sshdfwd-9011: pluto
```

in the /etc/hosts.allow file. Then the entry

```
ALL: ALL
```

in /etc/hosts.deny would produce the desired result.

You may disable port forwarding by setting the AllowTcpForwarding keyword to no in the /etc/ssh/sshd_config file on the server. This disables all port forwarding by the server. It does not disable the invocation of port forwarding attempts. For example, if we disabled port forwarding on pluto in Figure 11.5, we would still be able to use the -R flag to ssh from pluto to set up a forwarded port on underdog.

The only way to completely eliminate port forwarding is to use the compile-time options --disable-client-port-forwardings and --disable-client-server-forwardings for the client-side and server-side, respectively.

WARNING!

> While it is possible to completely disable port forwarding through SSH, port forwarding and proxying can be accomplished in other ways. For example, *Using the redirect Attribute* on page 247 describes how to accomplish proxying with xinetd.

SECURE SHELL ALTERNATIVES

SSH is free under a limited set of circumstances (see *Available Versions of SSH* on page 263). There is a GNU project to produce a completely unrestricted SSH distributed under the GPL. Currently a beta release, you can get more information about this product at

```
http://www.net.lut.ac.uk/psst/
```

As useful and powerful as SSH is, there are many things that it cannot do. For example, it cannot forward UDP-based communications, such as NIS and DNS queries, through the SSH-encrypted tunnel. In order to encrypt arbitrary communications ubiquitously, we must do something else. The easiest alternative is to encrypt at lower layers of the TCP/IP stack. SSH operates at the Application layer of the TCP/IP stack; the principal alternatives operate at the Transport and Internet layers.

For example, the `stelnet` program (available from `http://www.quick.com.au/ftp/pub/sjg/`) requires the Secure Socket Layer (SSL) for encryption; SSL operates at the Transport layer. A publicly available version of SSL, written by Eric A. Young (SSLeay), is available from

```
http://www.psy.uq.edu.au:8080/~ftp/Crypto/
```

SSLeay and associated applications have the advantage of being distributed freely for both commercial and noncommercial use, thereby offering fewer restrictions than SSH. You will also find a listing of other programs that take advantage of SSL at that site.

Another alternative is Internet Protocol Security (IPsec) standardized by a number of Internet RFCs (see *Request for Comment* on page 40 for further information about RFCs). It implements encryption at the Internet layer of the TCP/IP stack, which enhances performance and makes it transparent to the users. The major Linux IPsec implementation project is the Linux free secure wide area network (FreeSwan).[5] You can find more information about Linux FreeSwan at

```
http://www.xs4all.nl/~freeswan/index.html
```

As its name implies, the software is free and may be downloaded from that site. As with many cryptography projects, it is being developed outside of the United States so that it can be available worldwide.

Another ongoing project is Crypto IP Encapsulation (CIPE). This purpose of CIPE is to provide a simple alternative to IPsec. It provides for encrypting connections between IP routers, including Linux. To find out more about CIPE visit

```
http://sites.inka.de/sites/bigred/devel/cipe.html
```

Eventually, SSH will be eclipsed by FreeSwan or CIPE or something similar, but until then it provides a powerful way to encrypt remote logins, remote execution, X Windows, and file copying.

---

5. RSA Data Security, Inc., has a similar commercial project called S/WAN. FreeSwan is also referred to as FreeS/WAN.

SUMMARY

In this chapter we detailed the implementation and configuration of SSH. We showed that it can be used to build an encrypted tunnel for a variety of remote connections including remote logins, remote execution and copying, and X Window System sessions. It also incorporates a variety of authentication mechanisms, including strong RSA Authentication. We emphasized the use of SSH for *all* remote root access.

FOR FURTHER READING

There is a fair amount of documentation available for SSH. In the SSH distribution, you will find the following documents (we assume `/usr/src/ssh` as the top of the source tree):

```
/usr/src/ssh/INSTALL
/usr/src/ssh/OVERVIEW
/usr/src/ssh/README
/usr/src/ssh/README.CIPHERS
/usr/src/ssh/README.DEATTACK
/usr/src/ssh/README.SECURERPC
/usr/src/ssh/README.SECURID
/usr/src/ssh/README.TIS
```

There are also the following `man` pages:

```
make-ssh-known-hosts(1)
scp(1)
ssh-add(1)
ssh-agent(1)
ssh-keygen(1)
ssh(1)
sshd(8)
```

For further information, check out the following web resources:

```
http://www.employees.org/~satch/ssh/faq/
http://www.datafellows.com/
http://www.ssh.fi/
ftp://ftp.cs.hut.fi/pub/ssh/
```

Finally, you can subscribe to the SSH mailing list by putting `subscribe ssh` in the body of an e-mail message to `majordomo@clinet.fi`.

So You *Think* You've Got a Good Password!

Crack

So, you're probably wondering why a white hat[1] would ever want to run Crack. After all, why would the good-guys want to guess passwords? Unfortunately, the answer is: because the bad-guys are doing it. So, ya gotta run Crack to find out if your users are choosing easy to crack passwords.

Crack is a very flexible program that attempts to guess passwords by first taking a large list of possible passwords (called dictionaries), hashing them (see *Passwords Aren't Encrypted, They're Hashed!* on page 45) and comparing the resulting hash to a list of known hashed passwords. A match indicates a guessed password.[2] Crack can also generate variations of the dictionaries by manipulating them based on a set of rules.

The flexibility of Crack comes in various forms. It has a highly configurable rule base for manipulating Crack dictionaries. It can be compiled to crack Linux (DES[3]), MD5, or bigcrypt-hashed passwords. Furthermore, Crack is structured in such a way that it is a simple matter to provide additional code to support other hashing schemes. It can be run effectively on multiprocessor

---

1. In the security biz, *white hat* refers to the good-guys, while *black hat* refers to the bad-guys.
2. It isn't quite this simple due to the "salt." See Bruce Schneier, *Applied Cryptography*, 2d ed., New York, New York, John Wiley & Sons, Inc., 1996, pp. 52–53.
3. Strictly speaking, the standard Linux password-hashing algorithm is a derivative of DES. For simplicity, we will refer to the programmatic interface, `crypt(3)`, when referring to the standard Linux password-hashing mechanism.

systems, and it is capable of being run on many systems in a network with one invocation. And, finally, in the Crack source tree you will find the `Crack7` script, which is capable of executing a brute-force attack against any input ciphertext. In short, given enough time, it can crack *any* static password.

For all its flexibility and improvements over the years, it still requires copious amounts of CPU time. Currently at version 5.0, it operates much more efficiently than previous versions; nonetheless, it takes lots of time to do what it does. Crack was written and continues to be maintained by Alec Muffett. He distributes it under the Artistic License (see the LICENSE file in the Crack distribution) which is quite similar to the GPL.

OBTAINING CRACK

There are many sites on the Internet from which Crack may be obtained. One of them is

```
ftp://info.cert.org/pub/tools/crack/
```

There you will find the following files:

```
alec_muffet.asc
crack5.0.README
crack5.0.tar.gz
crack5.0.tar.gz.asc
```

Pull them all down and add Alec Muffett's key to your PGP keyring.

```
# pgp alec_muffet.asc
```

Then check the signature.

```
# pgp crack5.0.tar.gz.asc
```

If you are using PGP Version 5.0, replace pgp in the above examples with pgpv. After you have read crack5.0.README (of course, you wouldn't skip that, would you?), you can gunzip and untar crack5.0.tar.gz. For the purpose of our discussion, we'll assume that all of the files associated with Crack are in the directory /usr/src/c50a.

MAJOR COMPONENTS OF CRACK

In Figure 12.1, we see an overview of the /usr/src/c50a directory tree. Let's highlight some of the directories and scripts.

Crack Main Scripts. The files within the /usr/src/c50a are mostly self-explanatory (and not shown in Figure 12.1). The two files of significance are Crack and Reporter. The Crack Bourne-shell script is the interface to compil-

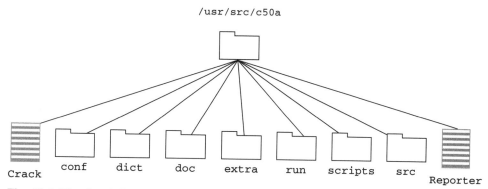

Fig. 12.1 The Crack Directory Tree

ing and running Crack. When run, it starts the `cracker` process, which is the main password-guessing program. The `Reporter` Bourne-shell script is used to convert and display Crack output in human-readable form. Let's look at each script.

Table 12.1 summarizes the options to `Crack`. From this table, we see that the Crack script is a very flexible interface to the `cracker` program.

Table 12.2 summarizes the options to `Reporter`. Note that any other arguments submitted to `Reporter` will be silently ignored.

Crack Directories. The `conf` directory contains dictionary configuration and rules files. These will be discussed in *Crack Dictionaries* on page 321 and *Crack Rules* on page 330. The `dict` subdirectory contains dictionary group directories that in turn contain the dictionaries being used. The `doc` subdirectory contains documentation (read it!). The `extra` subdirectory contains additional scripts and programs, including the brute-force cracking program and its invoking script `Crack7`. The `src` subdirectory contains the source code in three subdirectories—`src/util`, `src/lib`, and `src/libdes`.

Other Crack Scripts. The `scripts` subdirectory contains a number of different utilities, many of which are invoked directly by Crack. Table 12.3 lists the scripts and files found in this directory that will be of use in managing your Crack runs. Each of these files is discussed in this chapter.

But first, let's get an overview of how Crack functions.

CRACK OVERVIEW

When Crack is invoked and provided with a list of passwords to crack, it begins by compiling dictionaries for its source of guesses. The file `conf/dictgrps.conf` tells Crack what sources to use for dictionary building and in what order to search them. Additionally, Crack builds two dictionaries from the information

Table 12.1 Crack Options

Option	Description
-debug	Verbose mode.
-fgnd	Runs cracker in the foreground.
-fmt *format*	Specifies the input file *format*. Crack requires all input password lists be in the Standard Password Format (SPF). The format argument specifies the format from which to convert to SPF. There are two possible arguments—bsd for BSD-style password files, and trad (the default is trad) for System V-style password files.
-from *n*	Begins cracking from rule number *n*.
-keep	Prevents the deletion of temporary files.
-mail	E-mails scripts/nastygram to the user(s) whose password(s) has(have) been cracked.
-network	Runs cracker in network mode.
-nice *n*	Sets the nice level so that cracker will reduce its priority in favor of other jobs.
-makeonly	Compiles and links only.
-makedict	Builds the Crack dictionaries.
-recover	For use in recovering badly terminated Crack runs.
-kill *filename*	Specifies the name of the file that contains a terminate script. Normally, this option is passed to cracker internally by Crack and need not be specified. By default, the filename will be run/K*hostname*.*pid*.
-remote	Used internally by Crack for networking support.

Table 12.2 Reporter Options

Option	Description
-html	Generates output in HTML format. The default format is ASCII text.
-quiet	Suppresses error and warning messages.

Table 12.3 Important Files in the `scripts` Subdirectory

File	Description
`nastygram`	Contains the body of the e-mail message that is sent when Crack is invoked with the `-mail` option.
`pauser`	This Bourne-shell script can be used to conditionally suspend `cracker`.
`plaster`	This Bourne-shell script is used to gracefully terminate `cracker`.
`shadmrg.aix` `shadmrg.sv`	These Bourne-shell scripts are used to merge `passwd` and `shadow` files into one file. The `shadmrg.sv` script is for System V-style files (such as Red Hat) and is for `shadmrg.aix` IBM AIX systems.

found in the password file provided as input; these two dictionaries contain words directly derived from the input file (the gecos dictionary) as well as variations on the information collected (the gcperm dictionary). Once Crack has identified the dictionaries, it uses the instructions contained in the file `conf/dictrun.conf` to proceed with its guessing activities. To do this the `dictrun.conf` file invokes other rules files found in the `conf` subdirectory. It is entirely possible to write a rule that tells Crack to try every permutation of a given-sized password. As Crack goes through the process of obtaining words from the dictionaries and modifies them based on the rules, it hashes each one and compares it to the input list of hashed passwords. Figure 12.2 illustrates this overview. It is, perhaps, readily apparent from this description that Crack requires a considerable amount of CPU resources. Lots of memory won't hurt either.

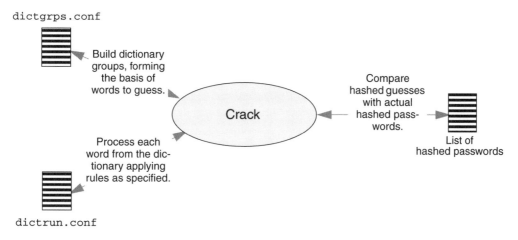

Fig. 12.2 General Flow of the Guessing Process in Crack

BUILDING CRACK

There are a lot of different ways to build Crack. For example, if you are using MD5 or bigcrypt for your password-hashing scheme, you will need to make modifications to the source tree before you compile the program. There is no configure utility for Crack, so you'll have to read the documentation (imagine that) if you have something other than standard UNIX passwords in the standard /etc/passwd and /etc/shadow configuration. We will take a look at building Crack for standard UNIX-hashed passwords, for MD5-hashed passwords, and for bigcrypt-hashed passwords.

If you are going to be running Crack against these different password schemes, you will want to create a build directory for each one. For example, use /usr/src/c50a for UNIX, /usr/src/c50aMD5 for MD5, and so on. If you are further going to be running Crack on different operating systems and/or architectures, it is advisable to build Crack on each one manually (at least the first time) so that you can troubleshoot any problems that might arise. Once compiled, you may place the complete source tree plus executables on a single server (such as a security server) in appropriate subdirectories and then make the entire distribution accessible via NFS. This is particularly convenient when you are running Crack in network mode (see *Running Crack over the Network* on page 328).

Modifying Crack for Linux

Before we look at special cases such as MD5, there are changes that must be made to the crack script itself. When you edit crack, you will find the lines shown in Example 12-1 (line wraps are due to formatting constraints). Simply change the lines in Example 12-1 to those shown in Example 12-2 (line wraps are due to formatting constraints). The modifications in Example 12-2 reflect selecting gcc instead of cc as the compiler, selecting the CFLAGS for gcc instead of for cc, and uncommenting the line with -lcrypt to incorporate that library in the compilation process.

Now you are ready to compile for Linux password guessing. If you are going to build Crack for either MD5 or bigcrypt, follow the steps in *Modifying Crack for MD5* on page 319 and *Modifying Crack for Bigcrypt* on page 319 before you run Crack for the first time; otherwise move on to the section *Compiling Crack Itself* on page 320.

Example 12-1 Default Compiler and Library Specifications in crack

```
# vanilla unix cc
CC=cc
CFLAGS="-g -O $C5FLAGS"
#LIBS=-lcrypt # uncomment only if necessary to use stdlib crypt(), e.g.: NetBSD MD5

# gcc 2.7.2
#CC=gcc
#CFLAGS="-g -O2 -Wall $C5FLAGS"
#LIBS=-lcrypt # uncomment only if necessary to use stdlib crypt(), eg: NetBSD MD5
```

Example 12-2 Modified Compiler and Library Specifications for Linux

```
# vanilla unix cc
#CC=cc
#CFLAGS="-g -O $C5FLAGS"
#LIBS=-lcrypt # uncomment only if necessary to use stdlib crypt(), eg: NetBSD MD5

# gcc 2.7.2
CC=gcc
CFLAGS="-g -O2 -Wall $C5FLAGS"
LIBS=-lcrypt # uncomment only if necessary to use stdlib crypt(), eg: NetBSD MD5
```

Modifying Crack for MD5

In order to prepare Crack for MD5 guessing, you will need to make some simple changes to the source tree. The steps are outlined in Example 12-3.

Example 12-3 Steps Required to Prepare for MD5 Cracking

```
# cd /usr/src/c50aMD5/src
# mv libdes libdes.orig
# cd util
# cp elcid.c elcid.c.orig
# cp elcid.c,bsd elcid.c
```

That's it! You are now ready to compile.

NOTE

The variable PLAINTEXTSIZE is defined in the elcid.c file. For MD5 (in the file elcid.c,bsd), it is set to 16. This means that the largest cleartext password that will be guessed is 16 characters in length. You may increase this to 32 at a significant expense in performance. What is significant? Consider just the alphanumeric characters (a–z, A–Z, 0–9)—this represents 26 lowercase characters plus 26 uppercase characters plus 10 numeric characters, for a total of 62 characters. Thus, the total number of possible 16-character alphanumeric passwords is 62**16 or 4.77×10^{28}, whereas the total number of possible 32-character passwords is 62**32 or 2.27×10^{57}, a considerably larger number of possibilities.

To increase variable PLAINTEXTSIZE further requires additional modification to the source code.

Modifying Crack for Bigcrypt

If you have systems that use bigcrypt, you will need to do a bit more work. To begin with, you must have libc-crypt loaded on your system. If you are running Red Hat 5.2 or later, it is already there. Otherwise you will need to obtain a copy from one of the following sites

```
ftp://prep.ai.mit.edu/gnu/
http://www.redhat.com/
```

and install it. We'll assume that the source directory for the bigcrypt version is `/usr/src/c50aBC/src`. Once you have installed `libc-crypt`, you will need to edit `/usr/src/c50aBC/src/util/eclid.c` and change the two lines (they are close to each other, but not next to each other)

```
#define PLAINTEXTSIZE    8
...
#undef CRYPT16
```

to

```
#define PLAINTEXTSIZE    16
...
#define CRYPT16
```

and now you are ready to compile.

Preparing Crack for `crypt(3)`

You actually need to do nothing for standard `crypt(3)`-hashed passwords; however, the Crack distribution includes `libdes`, a highly optimized hashing engine written by Eric Young. Your Linux system will likely come with `lib-crypt` from the folks at GNU (this is the case with Red Hat 5.2/6.0). If you wish to use `libdes`, simply change directories to the `src/libdes` subdirectory and execute `make`. This step is required if you are going to use `Crack7` (see *Crack7* on page 330).

COMPILING AND LINKING CRACK

Once you have completed the necessary preliminary steps given in the section *Modifying Crack for Linux* on page 318 and the steps outlined for MD5 and/or Bigcrypt, you are ready to compile and link the programs comprising Crack.

      Crack can be invoked with a number of different options. It turns out that if you invoke Crack to start work on a password file, it will compile and link all necessary programs that aren't already built. This may be useful once you know that it will build properly on a given platform; however, the first time through, you probably want to take a stepwise approach. The discrete steps to compile and link the cracking engine and then the dictionaries are outlined in the next two sections.

Compiling Crack Itself

You've basically done all the work. To compile and link the various programs comprising Crack, simply execute `Crack -makeonly`. Example 12-4 provides an illustration. That's all there is to it! Next you'll want to build the dictionaries.

Example 12-4 Execution of `Crack -makeonly`

```
# ./Crack -makeonly
Crack 5.0a: The Password Cracker.
(c) Alec Muffett, 1991, 1992, 1993, 1994, 1995, 1996
System: Linux underdog 2.0.35 #1 Wed Oct 14 10:16:12 EDT 1998 i686 unknown
Home: /tc/custom/crack/c50a
Invoked: ./Crack -makeonly
Option: -makeonly enabled
Stamp: linux-2-unknown

Crack: making utilities in run/bin/linux-2-unknown
...
<lots of output snipped>
...
gcc -g -O2 -Wall -DUSE_STRING_H -DUSE_STDLIB_H -DUSE_SIGNAL_H -DUSE_SYS_TYPES_H -
DUSE_UNISTD_H -DUSE_PWD_H -I../lib -o ../../run/bin/linux-2-unknown/kickdict
kickdict.c ../../run/bin/linux-2-unknown/libc5.a -lcrypt
all made in util
make[1]: Leaving directory '/tc/custom/crack/c50a/src/util'
Crack: makeonly done
```

WARNING!

> If you run `Crack -makeonly` (or otherwise invoke `Crack` to cause compilation) and it terminates on error, you would then correct whatever problems and attempt to recompile. The problem is that, when you rerun `Crack -makeonly`, its first step is to remove all object files (among other things) that were left by the previous compilation attempt. Unfortunately the `Crack` script does not remove the subdirectory `run` (in `/usr/src/c50a`), which causes the script to later assume the existence of object files such as `elcid.o` that it previously removed! To correct this problem, execute `make spotless` or `make clobber` before you rerun `Crack -makeonly`.

CRACK DICTIONARIES

A Crack dictionary very simply is a file consisting of one word per line. The contents don't actually have to be words—they can be any string of characters (or non-English words), including nonalphanumeric characters.

You can easily add your own lists—perhaps words associated with the hobbies, interests, or relatives of your users. You need not worry about adding redundant entries because Crack will make sure that it compiles only a unique dictionary. Variations such as case changes and substitution of numbers for letters (1 for i, 3 for e, etc.) are handled by the rules (which are discussed in *Crack Rules* on page 330). Thus, increasing the dictionary is quite simple.

The Crack distribution expects to find `/usr/dict/*words*` (if your system dictionaries are somewhere else, you will need to modify `conf/dictgrps.conf` as discussed below), and it also comes with its own collection of dictionaries in the subdirectories `dict/1/`, `dict/2/`, and `dict/3/`. So, by default, this collection comprises the Crack dictionaries.

When Crack starts, it generates its dictionaries based on `conf/dict-grps.conf`. This file contains an ordered list of *dictionary groups*. The dictionary group is a collection of word lists, but the ordering is significant in that it reflects the order in which Crack will guess passwords. It will attempt to guess passwords by going through the first group, then the second group, and so on. Example 12-5 shows the default `conf/dictgrps.conf` file. The number to the left of the colon (`:`) is the *dictionary tag* and reflects the priority (the lower the number the earlier it is processed). To the right of the colon is a space-separated list of files to include as part of the dictionary group. Standard shell metacharacters may be used. Relative pathnames (such as `dict/2`) will resolve under the directory from which Crack is invoked (and held by the run-time environment variable `CRACK_HOME`).

Example 12-5 Default `conf/dictgrps.conf` File

```
1:/usr/dict/*words* dict/1/*
2:dict/2/*
3:dict/3/*
```

You can use any filename convention for word lists (dictionaries) that you create or obtain. However, in the `dict/*` subdirectories, the suffix `.dwg` is used. You may also add more dictionary tags to this file and create more dictionary groups. Bear in mind the significance of the ordering in this file and try to arrange your dictionary groups so that the most likely passwords occur earliest in the list. The next section provides resources for additional dictionaries.

After you have added any additional dictionaries, you may build them for Crack by executing `Crack -makedict` as shown in Example 12-6.

Example 12-6 `Crack -makedict`

```
# ./Crack -makedict
Crack 5.0a: The Password Cracker.
(c) Alec Muffett, 1991, 1992, 1993, 1994, 1995, 1996
System: Linux underdog 2.0.35 #1 Wed Oct 14 10:16:12 EDT 1998 i686 unknown
Home: /tc/custom/crack/c50a
Invoked: ./Crack -makedict
Option: -makedict enabled
Stamp: linux-2-unknown

Crack: making utilities in run/bin/linux-2-unknown
...
<lots of ouput snipped>
...
Crack: making dictionary groups, please be patient...
doing group 1...
doing group 2...
doing group 3...
mkdictgrps: uniq'ing dictionary groups...
group 1 and 2...
group 1 and 3...
group 2 and 3...
mkdictgrps: compressing dictionary groups...
Crack: Created new dictionaries...
Crack: makedict done
```

If you add new dictionaries at some future point, you will need to reexecute the `Crack -makedict` command to rebuild the Crack dictionary. Otherwise, you will not need to perform this step again.

Obtaining Other Crack Dictionaries

You may certainly create your own additional Crack dictionaries, but you can also obtain many from the web. Here are two sites from which you can get more Crack dictionaries.

```
ftp://coast.cs.purdue.edu/pub/dict/
ftp://ftp.ox.ac.uk/pub/wordlists/
```

You will also find interesting notes about some of the dictionaries in

```
ftp://coast.cs.purdue.edu/pub/dict/wordlists/README.gz
```

USING CRACK

If you aren't using the shadow file (see *Password Aging and the Shadow File* on page 61 for why you should use the shadow file), then you are ready to run Crack. Otherwise, you need to merge the hashed passwords back into a single file. This is accomplished by executing, for example

```
# shadmrg.sv > /root/passwords
```

where `/root/passwords` could be any filename. We will use this filename in subsequent examples.

If you are running NIS, you could simply use the source password file on the NIS master or execute

```
# ypcat passwd > /root/passwords
```

Now, at last, we are ready to run Crack.

WARNING!

After you have created a merged password file, make sure that it is in a protected directory such as /root (which should have no world permissions at all) and that its permissions are set to read-only by root (`chmod 400 /root/passwords`). You may accomplish this by setting root's umask to 077. The reason you want to do this is because it is entirely possible that someone might execute the ps command, notice the location of this file, and try to copy it. Then he or she would be able to run Crack against it also.

Running Crack

To initiate a Crack run, execute `Crack` as shown in Example 12-7. This will start the `cracker` program. It will run for a long time. Since you probably don't want to wait a few weeks for the results, you can check Crack's progress with the `Reporter` script.

Example 12-7 Initiating a Crack run.

```
# ./Crack /root/passwords
Crack 5.0a: The Password Cracker.
(c) Alec Muffett, 1991, 1992, 1993, 1994, 1995, 1996
System: Linux underdog 2.0.35 #1 Wed Oct 14 10:16:12 EDT 1998 i686 unknown
Home: /tc/custom/crack/c50a
Invoked: ./Crack /root/passwords
Stamp: linux-2-unknown

Crack: making utilities in run/bin/linux-2-unknown
...
<lots of output snipped>
...
Crack: The dictionaries seem up to date...
Crack: Sorting out and merging feedback, please be patient...
Crack: Merging password files...
cat: run/F-merged: No such file or directory
Crack: Creating gecos-derived dictionaries
mkgecosd: making non-permuted words dictionary
mkgecosd: making permuted words dictionary
Crack: launching: cracker -kill run/Kunderdog.1584
Done
```

Note in Example 12-7 that `run/F-merged` does not exist. This file contains previously guessed passwords and therefore will not exist the first time you run Crack.

As Crack guesses passwords, it writes them out to the file `run/Dhost-name.pid`, where *hostname* is the name of the host on which Crack is running and *pid* is the PID. You could read this file, but it is easier on the eyes to use `Reporter` as illustrated in Example 12-8. As the Crack run progresses, you may continue to check its progress in this way.

Example 12-8 Output of `Reporter`

```
# ./Reporter -quiet
---- passwords cracked as of Thu Apr  1 22:02:46 MST 1999 ----
Guessed paul [s1mple]    [/root/passwords /bin/bash]
Guessed jhess [f00bar]   [/root/passwords /bin/ksh]
---- done ----
```

Since Crack runs take so long, let's examine some ways to manage them.

Putting Crack to Sleep   There is a very convenient mechanism that allows for suspending a Crack run. This mechanism is controlled through the `pauser` script that lives in the `scripts` subdirectory. Every minute or so, `cracker` will execute `pauser`. The `pauser` script, by default, is an infinitely looping script that checks for the existence of the file GOTO-SLEEP in the CRACK_HOME directory. If it finds that file, the `pauser` script sleeps for 60 seconds and then checks for it again. If the GOTO-SLEEP file still exists, `pauser` goes back to sleep. If GOTO-SLEEP doesn't exist, the script exits, returning control to the invoking `cracker` program. Thus, to suspend a `cracker` run, all you need to do is create the GOTO-SLEEP file in `/usr/src/c50a`.

But there is much more that can be done with the `pauser` script. Since it is a Bourne-shell script, you can modify it to do anything that a Bourne-shell script can do. For example, perhaps you'd like to suspend Crack based on the number of runable processes. One way to do this is described in Example 12-9. Here, we simply add the steps in bold to the existing `pauser` script. These steps cause Crack to go to sleep whenever there are at least 20 runable processes (one of which may be Crack itself). The use of 20 here is a rather arbitrary upper limit on the number of processes—you may choose a different value, and it may be more appropriate to base the decision on paging and/or swapping activity. Be sure not to suspend Crack based on memory consumption, idle CPU time, or the like because Crack will consume as much of those available resources as it can.

Example 12-9 Sample Script to Suspend Crack

```
<beginning of the pauser script deleted>
...
# this script can be arbitrarily hacked in order to put Crack to
# sleep; the logic is a bit inverted so that it can be hacked to use a
# variety of poll times.
exec </dev/null >/dev/null 2>&1
POLL=60
LOCKFILE="GOTO-SLEEP"
...
<more of the pauser script deleted>
...
while :
do
###
# Sleep infinitely, whilst there exists a lockfile in $CRACK_HOME
###
        if [ -f $LOCKFILE ]
        then
                sleep $POLL
                continue
        fi
...
<more of the pauser script deleted>
...
# wc -l counts newlines & there's always one extra, also need
# to account for the fact that ps reports itself...so the actual
# number of processes is 20 even though we check for 22.
        numprocs=`ps axr|wc -l`
        if [ $numprocs -ge 22 ]
        then
                sleep $POLL
                numprocs=0
                continue
        fi
...
<more of the pauser script deleted>
...
        break           # like, y'know, totally gross, man...
done
exit 0
```

You may want to run Crack only at night and on weekends. If so, the code is already provided for you; simply uncomment `pauser` script lines number 6 through 12 inclusive in Example 12-10 (line numbers added for clarity). Of course, you may modify these lines as needed for your environment.

Example 12-10 Code Causing Crack to Run at Night and on Weekends

```
 1.    <beginning of the pauser script deleted>
 2.    ...
 3.    ###
 4.    # Go to sleep between 0800 and 1759 inclusive, except weekends
 5.    ###
 6.    #        set 'date '+%H %w'' # $1=hour(00..23) $2=day(0..6)
 7.    #
 8.    #        if [ "$1" -ge 8 -a "$1" -le 17 -a "$2" -ge 1 -a "$2" -le 5 ]
 9.    #        then
10.    #                sleep $POLL
11.    #                continue
12.    #        fi
13.
14.             break          # like, y'know, totally gross, man...
15.    done
16.
17.    exit 0
```

Remember, anything you can do on the command line can be enscripted in the pauser script to control Crack runs. Be careful about how much of your system's resources you are using to execute the script, however, as that may have an impact on the decision made by the pauser script.

Gracefully Terminating Crack   If you do find that you need to terminate a Crack run, the best way to do so is by using the plaster script. Example 12-11 illustrates the steps necessary to gracefully terminate Crack. By executing the plaster script, you cause the execution of the script run/Ktopcat.10714, which was generated when Crack was initially invoked. The discrepancies in process identifiers is as a result of one belonging to the Crack script and the other

Example 12-11 Terminating a Crack Run

```
# cd /usr/src/c50a
# scripts/plaster
+ kill -TERM 11146
+ rm -f run/Ktopcat.10714
+ exit 0
# make tidy
find . -name "*~" -print | xargs -n50 rm -f
( cd src; for dir in * ; do ( cd $dir ; make clean ) ; done )
make[1]: Entering directory '/usr/src/custom/crack/c50aMD5/src/lib'
rm -f dawglib.o debug.o rules.o stringlib.o *~
make[1]: Leaving directory '/usr/src/custom/crack/c50aMD5/src/lib'
make[1]: Entering directory '/usr/src/custom/crack/c50aMD5/src/libdes.orig'
/bin/rm -f *.o tags core rpw destest des speed libdes.a .nfs* *.old \
*.bak destest rpw des speed
make[1]: Leaving directory '/usr/src/custom/crack/c50aMD5/src/libdes.orig'
make[1]: Entering directory '/usr/src/custom/crack/c50aMD5/src/util'
rm -f *.o *~
make[1]: Leaving directory '/usr/src/custom/crack/c50aMD5/src/util'
scripts/plaster
scripts/fbmerge
rm -f run/[DIEGTKM]*
rm -f run/dict/gecos.*
rm -f run/dict/gcperm.*
#
```

belonging to the cracker program. In this example, 10714 is the PID associated with Crack, while 11146 is the PID associated with cracker.

The make tidy command, which you need to invoke after scripts/plaster, cleans up various files from the Crack run. You may wish to examine the files before you execute make tidy; these files are found in the run subdirectory. They include the files listed (hostname in this case is topcat) in Example 12-12.

Example 12-12 Files in the run Subdirectory

```
D.boot.8322
Dtopcat.8322
Etopcat.8322
F-merged
Ktopcat.8322
```

The file D.boot.8322 contains error information related to entries found in the submitted password file. These are mostly related to locked accounts and the like. The file Dtopcat.8322 essentially contains state information for Crack. It also provides, among other things, the raw data for Reporter. The Etopcat.8322 file contains errors generated by Crack. The F-merged file contains guessed ciphertext/cleartext passwords; it is used in each subsequent Crack run to determine if the same passwords are still in use. And the Ktopcat.8322 file contains a script that gracefully terminates cracker and is invoked by plaster.

Resuming Crack after Termination   Suppose that for some reason your system reboots during a Crack run, or that Crack is terminated without using plaster. You can resume the run by executing the commands shown in Example 12-13. Since the file Dtopcat.30212 (renamed topcat.recover) contains a record of Crack's activity, the cracker program is able to pick up where it left off.

Example 12-13 Resuming an Abnormally Terminated Crack Run

```
# cd /usr/src/c50a/run
# mv Dtopcat.30212 ./topcat.recover
# cd ..
# ./Crack -recover -fmt spf run/topcat.recover
(c) Alec Muffett, 1991, 1992, 1993, 1994, 1995, 1996
System: Linux topcat 2.0.36 #1 Tue Oct 13 22:17:11 EDT 1998 i686 unknown
Home: /usr/src/custom/crack/c50aMD5
Invoked: ./Crack -recover -fmt spf run/topcat.recover
Option: -recover enabled
Stamp: linux-2-unknown

Crack: making utilities in run/bin/linux-2-unknown
...
<lots of output snipped>
...
Crack: Sorting out and merging feedback, please be patient...
Crack: Merging password files...
Crack: -recover: using existing gecos-derived dictionaries
Crack: launching: cracker -kill run/Ktopcat.8322
Done
```

NOTE

When invoking any of the scripts associated with Crack, you must either specify the fully qualified pathname to the script, or execute the script from the CRACK_HOME directory (CRACK_HOME is /usr/src/c50a in our examples) with a relatively qualified name. For example, to invoke plaster, you could execute

```
# cd /usr/src/c50a
# scripts/plaster
```

or

```
# /usr/src/c50a/scripts/plaster
```

Running Crack over the Network

In Table 12.3 on page 317, we looked at a file called conf/network.conf. This is the file that controls running crack on various systems over the network. It is quite flexible and allows for the specification of any hostname (as long as it is resolvable) to run Crack using either NFS-mounted resources or locally mounted resources. Example 12-14 provides a sample conf/network.conf file. Each record in this file consists of five fields, described in Table 12.4. Each entry reflects a host that can be used to run Crack. When Crack is invoked on the master system (topcat in our example), Crack will divide up the work based upon the relative power (second field) of each system and spawn Crack to each system via rsh (although ssh could and should be used instead; see Chapter 11). This mechanism could dramatically increase the performance of Crack.

Example 12-14 The network.conf File

```
# File Format
# hostname:relative power:nfs [y/n]:rsh username [option]:crack directory
# sparcy - LX
sparcy:1200:y:cracker:/tc/c50aSPARC
# foghorn - P75
foghorn:2750:y::/tc/c50ax86
# underdog - PII333
underdog:5400:y::/tc/c50ax86
```

Once the conf/network.conf file is ready, you simply need to use the -network option with Crack, as shown in Example 12-15. Any Crack runs invoked in this way are entirely controllable from the master system—that is, the system from which Crack was invoked. In particular, Reporter and plaster work as before and are now able to control all remote Crack runs.

Using Crack in network mode works best when resources are shared via NFS or similar mechanism. This is due to the fact that you want each system to use the same dictionaries. So if you are not using NFS, make sure to set the

Table 12.4 The `network.conf` File Record

Field	Description
hostname	The hostname of the remote system.
relative power	A weight assigned to the host reflecting both its CPU capability and availability. Availability is determined by the limitations placed upon the system in the `pauser` script. The higher this value, the more work Crack will assign.
nfs	Use y for NFS-mounted (or similar shared filesystems) Crack directories. Use n otherwise.
rsh username	The username to use for `rsh` purposes if other than the user invoking Crack locally.
crack directory	The top-level directory of the Crack source tree. This becomes CRACK_HOME.

Example 12-15 Invoke Crack in Network Mode

```
# ./Crack -network -mail /root/passwords
Crack 5.0a: The Password Cracker.
(c) Alec Muffett, 1991, 1992, 1993, 1994, 1995, 1996
System: Linux topcat 2.0.36 #1 Tue Oct 13 22:17:11 EDT 1998 i686 unknown
Home: /usr/src/c50aMD5
Invoked: ./Crack -network -mail /root/passwords
Option: -network enabled
Option: -mail enabled
Stamp: linux-2-unknown
...
<lots of output snipped>
...
Crack: launching: netcrack    -mail
netcrack: power: 1200
netcrack: sortkeys: 3
netcrack: users: 8
netcrack: underdog: power=1200 sortkeys=3 (100.0%)
netcrack: crack-rsh  underdog /tc/custom/crack/c50aSPARC/Crack -remote -kill run/
RK1-underdog -mail
Crack 5.0a: The Password Cracker.
(c) Alec Muffett, 1991, 1992, 1993, 1994, 1995, 1996
System: Linux underdog 2.0.35 #1 Wed Oct 14 10:16:12 EDT 1998 sparc unknown
Home: /tc/custom/crack/c50aSPARC
Invoked: /tc/custom/crack/c50aSPARC/Crack -remote -kill run/RK1-underdog -mail
Option: -remote enabled
Option: -kill enabled
Option: -mail enabled
Stamp: linux-2-unknown
...
<lots of output snipped>
...
Crack: launching: cracker -kill run/RK1-underdog    -mail
Done
netcrack: sent 3 sortkeys, 674 bytes
Done
```

NFS flag to n so that Crack knows to rcp (or scp, in the case of ssh usage) the dictionaries to the remote system. Also, the report output will be distributed and not centrally available unless a manual merge is performed.

Crack7

Crack7 is a brute-force password guesser. It takes a single hashed password and attempts to guess it by checking every possible permutation of alphanumeric characters up to 8 characters in length. Since Crack7 is a Bourne-shell script it can easily be modified to guess passwords that include nonalphanumeric characters and greater than 8 characters in length (at the expense of time). By default, the checks for 6-, 7-, and 8-character passwords are commented out.

　　Crack7 is written to use libdes. So, if you are going to use this utility you might want to first compile libdes as described in *Preparing Crack for crypt(3)* on page 320. If you do not wish to use libdes, modify the Makefile in the extra subdirectory by commenting out the reference to libdes and uncommenting the reference to crypt. Once you've modified the Makefile to suit, change directories to the extra subdirectory and execute make to build the brute-force program. Then run Crack7 as illustrated in Example 12-16. How many times do you see guest1 as a password for a guest account?

Example 12-16 Running Crack7

```
# cd /usr/src/c50a/extra
# ./Crack7 S2v0SqZOxX1U2
make: Nothing to be done for 'all'.
brute: ciphertext: S2v0SqZOxX1U2
brute: set 0: a-z0-9 -> '0123456789abcdefghijklmnopqrstuvwxyz'
brute: ciphertext: S2v0SqZOxX1U2
brute: set 0: a-z0-9 -> '0123456789abcdefghijklmnopqrstuvwxyz'
brute: set 1: a-z0-9 -> '0123456789abcdefghijklmnopqrstuvwxyz'
...
<lots of output snipped>
...
brute: guessed S2v0SqZOxX1U2 == 'guest1'
```

Crack Rules

The rules that Crack uses to vary (or, as Alec Muffett fondly refers to it in his documentation, "mangle") the words in the Crack dictionaries are controlled by the dict/dictrun.conf file. We referred to this file previously in Table 12.3 on page 317.

　　A partial listing of the default dictrun.conf file is provided in Example 12-17. When the cracker program runs, it processes this file in the order given. The entries in this file come in one of three formats:

```
dictionary-tag:rulefile
dictionary-tag:|command
:|command
```

We looked at dictionary tags previously in *Crack Dictionaries* on page 321 and found them to be defined in the file conf/dictgrps.conf. Furthermore, we noted there that Crack builds two internal dictionaries—gecos and gcperm.

Example 12-17 Partial dictrun.conf File

```
###
# First, the 'total feedback' run.
###
:|(awk -F: '{print $NF}' run/F-merged | sort | uniq) 2>/dev/null

###
# apply successive conf/rules.foo files to dictionaries
###
gecos:conf/rules.fast
gecos:conf/rules.basic
gecos:conf/rules.perm1
gecos:conf/rules.perm2
gecos:conf/rules.prefix
...
<portions of the file snipped>
...
gcperm:conf/rules.perm3
gcperm:conf/rules.perm4

1:conf/rules.fast
1:conf/rules.basic
1:conf/rules.perm1
1:conf/rules.perm2
1:conf/rules.prefix
1:conf/rules.suffix

# here's an interesting one:
# use 'sed' to select and hack "two" into "2" from dict '1'
1:| sed -ne 's/two/2/gp'
...
<balance of the file snipped>
...
# Generate an exhaustive dictionary 'a' -> 'zzzzzzzz' -  SLOW !
#:| perl -e '$s="a"; print $s++,"\n" while (length($s) < 9);'
```

The syntax dictionary-tag:rulefile causes each word in the dictionary group identified by the dictionary-tag to be mangled by the rule or rules given in the rulefile (rule files are discussed in the next section). In Example 12-17, we see the representative sample 1:conf/rules.fast, which causes all of the words in the dictionary group tagged as 1 to be varied in accordance with the rules found in $CRACK_HOME/conf/rules.fast.

The syntax dictionary-tag:|command causes each word in the dictionary group identified by the dictionary-tag to be varied in accordance with the command following the |. In Example 12-17, we see the representative sample

```
1:| sed -ne 's/two/2/gp'
```

which causes each word in dictionary group 1 to be mangled by the sed script (which substitutes the word "two" with "2").

Finally, the syntax :|command provides a stream of guesses for the cracker program. In Example 12-17, we see the representative sample

```
:|(awk -F: '{print $NF}' run/F-merged | sort | uniq) 2>/dev/null
```

which causes `cracker` to check previously guessed passwords (see *Gracefully Terminating Crack* on page 326 for a discussion of the `run/F-merged` and other run-time files).

Note that the last two lines in Example 12-17 on page 331 suggest a way to perform a search of every possible alphabetic permutation of up to 8 characters in length using a Perl script.

In general, if you need to perform multiple character substitutions, permutations, or other variations of your dictionary words, use `sed` or `perl` or other similar utility in the `dictrun.conf` file. While this type of variation can be accomplished in a rules file, it is probably simpler to configure those types of variations in the `dictrun.conf` file. If, on the other hand, you wish to perform single character manipulations of dictionary words, you need to use a rules file.

Rules Files   There are a large number of rules files in the standard Crack distribution. You can find them in the `conf` subdirectory, all named with the `rules` prefix (with the notable exception of `globrule.conf` discussed at the end of this section) for convenience. We saw some of these files referenced in Example 12-17.

In Example 12-18, we see a representative instance of a rules file—in this case, `rules.perm1`. In this file we see a series of rules that are similar. For example, the entry `/isill` means, if the character `i` appears in the word, then substitute the character `1` for all instances of `i` and set all other characters in the word to lowercase.

Example 12-18 The `rules.perm1` File

```
/asa2l
/asa4l
/ese3l
/hsh4l
/isill
/ls111
/oso0l
/sss$l
```

In Table 12.5 we show the general syntax of the rules files. The syntax is rather cryptic and it takes a bit of time to get used to it.

Table 12.5 Rules File Syntax

Operator	Description
: or space	The no-operation (no-op) indicator. Used for clarity in the rules files. Where you see the word "space", you actually use the space bar, not the word. The : is equivalent and adds visual clarity.
?c	Specifies a class of characters. See Table 12.7 on page 334.
^x	Prefixes the character x to the word.
$x	Appends the character x to the word.

Table 12.5 Rules File Syntax (Continued)

Operator	Description
r	Reverses the order of characters in the word.
u	Forces all alphabetic characters in the word to uppercase.
l	Forces all alphabetic characters in the word to lowercase.
p	Pluralizes the word according to English grammar rules.
c	Capitalizes the first character in the word and sets all other characters to lowercase.
C	Sets the first character in the word to lowercase and sets the remaining characters to uppercase.
t	Changes the case of each character in the word.
d	Appends a copy of the word to itself.
f	Reverses the word and appends it to itself.
sxy or s?cy	Substitutes every instance of character x with the character y or substitutes every character in class c found in the word with the character y.
/x or /?c	Rejects the word unless the character x appears in the word or one or more of the characters in class c appear in the word.
!x or !?c	Rejects the word if it contains the character x or one or more of the characters in class c.
<n	Rejects the word unless it is less than n characters long.
>n	Rejects the word unless it is greater than n characters long.
xnm	Extracts a substring of the word of length m beginning at character n.
onx	Replaces the character x with the nth character of the word. No bounds checking is performed, so this option should be used only with < or > as appropriate.
inx	Inserts the character x in position n of the word, shifting all other characters one position to the right.
=nx or =n?c	Rejects the word unless the nth character is x or a member of class c.
@x or @?c	Removes all instances of the character x or characters in class c.
[	Deletes the first character from the word.
]	Deletes the last character from the word.
(x or (?c	Rejects the word unless x is the first character or a member of class c is the first character.

Table 12.5 Rules File Syntax (Continued)

Operator	Description
)x or)?c	Rejects the word unless x is the last character or a member of class c is the last character.
*	Resets the word to its original state.
`n	Truncates the word to have n characters.
%nx or %n?c	Rejects the word unless it contains n instances of the character x or of characters in the class c.

A number of the operators specified in Table 12.5 require an integer as an argument. Table 12.6 lists the available numeric arguments.

We complete the syntax description by providing the class definitions in Table 12.7. Notice that class specifiers are case insensitive.

Table 12.6 Rules File Numeric Argument Syntax

Numeric Argument	Meaning
0, 1, 2, ..., 9	The numeric values 0, 1, 2, ..., 9
A, B, C, ..., Z	The numeric values 10, 11, 12, ..., 36, respectively.
*	Resolves to the numeric value (in number of characters) of the largest available cleartext password. This value is 8 for DES, 16 for bigcrypt, and, by default, 16 for MD5 (although this assignment is arbitrary for MD5).
+	Resolves to * + 1, e.g. 9 for DES, 17 for bigcrypt, 17 for MD5.
-	Resolves to * - 1, e.g. 7 for DES, 15 for bigcrypt, 17 for MD5.

Table 12.7 Rules File Class Definitions

Class	Definition	Class	Definition
?a or ?A	Alphabetic characters	?s or ?S	Symbols
?c or ?C	Consonants	?u or ?U	Uppercase
?d or ?D	Digits	?v or ?V	Vowels
?l or ?L	Lowercase	?w or ?W	White space
?p or ?P	Punctuation	?x or ?X	Alphanumeric characters

Table 12.8 Some Examples of Rules and Their Meanings

Example Rule	Meaning
!?A1d	If the word contains no alphabetical characters [class A], lowercase all characters [1] and duplicate and append the word [d].
/1s11/ese3/asa2/sss$1	If the word contains the characters 1, e, a, and s [/1, /e, /a, and /s], then substitute 1 for 1, 3 for e, 2 for a, and $ for s. Then set all remaining characters to lowercase [1].
!?A^ :	If the word contains no alphabetical characters [class A], prefix a space to the word [^ :].
^($)	Prefix the word with a (character [^(] and append a) character [$)] to the end of the word.
<*u$!	If the word is less than PLAINTEXTSIZE characters [<*], uppercase all characters [u] and append a ! [$!] to the end of the word.

Whew! Now that we have established the syntax, let's look at a series of examples. In Table 12.8 we provide a list of examples. The syntax that would be found in the rules file appears in the left-hand column, while the meaning of that syntax is given in the right-hand column.

Before you go off and start adding your own rules, check the existing rules files to see if they already exist. If you do add your own rules, make sure that you test them out using minimally configured dictgrps.conf and dict-run.conf files. In other words, build a dictionary with a few words in it that are pertinent to your tests; then configure dictgrps.conf to load only that dictionary and configure dictrun.conf to apply only the new rules to that dictionary. Then make sure that you feed Crack ciphertext that should be guessed by the dictionary with your new rules.

NOTE

The source files in src/util and src/lib do have a DEBUG option that may be turned on by changing

#undef DEBUG

to

#define DEBUG

You may make this change to appropriate source files (such as src/lib/kick-dict.c and /src/lib/rules.c) to debug your rules.

We do need to examine one more rules file. The `globrule.conf` file is shown in Example 12-19. This is a special file that includes two rules. The first rule is applied to every word before the current rule is applied (as set forth in `dictrun.conf`). By default this is a no-op, meaning the word is processed unchanged. The second rule is applied after each word is processed by the current rule. Another way of seeing this behavior is illustrated in Figure 12.3.

Example 12-19 The `globrule.conf` File

```
...
<portions of the file snipped>
...
# first rule == 'prefix', applied BEFORE current rule
# NO-OP (you'll probably want to leave this alone)
:
# second rule == 'suffix', applied AFTER current rule
# SNIP-AT MAWPWLEN
'*
# - you might wish to extend this latter rule to (say)
#          '*>4
# (SNIP-AT MAXPWLEN GREATER-THAN 4) - if you're *SURE* that
# no-one on your system has short passwords....
...
<balance of the file snipped>
...
```

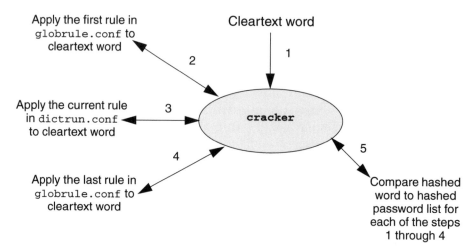

Fig. 12.3 Flow of the Application of Rules to a Dictionary Word

What Do We Do about Cracked Passwords?

That's a good question. There are two basic schools of thought regarding cracked passwords. One is to send the user e-mail (Alec Muffet's `nastygram`). The other is to lock the user's account. Crack does not offer an automated method for user account locking, so you'd have to write a script or program to do that, but it does provide an automated e-mail mechanism.

To cause Crack to send e-mail to a user whose password has been guessed is simply a matter of including the -mail option when Crack is invoked. This will cause the message contained in script/nastygram to be sent to that user. Therefore, you should edit script/nastygram to appropriately reflect your site's policy.

If your site is a large, multinetworked environment, then you may build a database of users based on their mailserver or hostname at which they receive mail. To accomplish this, simply create a directory in CRACK_HOME called, for example, hosts. In this directory you would create a file named after each mailserver or host and in that file place a username, one per line. Next, invoke

```
# ./Crack -mail -fmt tradmail hosts/* /root/passwords
```

Then mail will be sent to username@host based on the file in which the username is found. Note that the option tradmail may be replaced with bsdmail for appropriate environments (FreeBSD, NetBSD, etc.).

THE WHITE HAT USE OF CRACK

Throughout this chapter we have referred to the fact that Crack generally takes a long time to run. A really long time. And that's true if you use Crack just as it is configured by default. So what does this have to do with the moral use of Crack, you ask? (At least, that's what the title of this section *seems* to imply we're talking about.) It turns out that the two go hand in hand and reflect the general issues associated with the use of this utility by system administrators.

OH, BY THE WAY...

In an admittedly statistically insignificant test, it took a PC with a 333-MHz Pentium II processor approximately two hours to crack the password, s1mple, when that password was hashed using MD5. It took only about 10 minutes to crack the same password on the same system when it was hashed with standard Linux crypt(3). Both tests used identical password files as input and identical dictionaries and rules. This result is largely reflective of the effort that has been put forth into optimizing libdes (written by Eric Young) which is the preferred DES hashing engine used by Crack. It is important to point out that while a comparably optimized MD5 algorithm is not included with Crack, that does not imply that one does not exist. It should be equally noted that MD5 is inherently computationally slower than DES. Implementing MD5 for password hashing is discussed in Chapter 5.

Given that Crack can effectively guess any password given enough time, at what point does the system administrator cross the line and go over to the black hat side? Clearly there is no point in guessing every possible password (unless it is your intent to cross the line), but to what level of complexity should Crack be configured? How do we differentiate acceptable and unacceptable passwords?

Unfortunately, there are no easy answers to these questions. In theory, an organization's Security Policy (see Chapter 2) should address this issue, but to address it in sufficient detail to answer these questions thoroughly may well render it inflexible. After all, there's one thing about computing that is an absolute certainty—it will change.

In short, only you and your organization can decide how far to go. And part of that decision must certainly include the time it takes for the Crack runs that are configured on the basis of these decisions.

WARNING!

> You could get in very serious trouble if you use Crack against someone else's password file, even if your intentions are good. The best policy is, don't use Crack against someone else's password file unless you have written permission.

Effectively Using Crack

All comments about Security Policies and moral issues aside, Crack can be a very useful tool in detecting easily guessed passwords. All a bad-guy needs is one. Once unprivileged access to a system is gained, it is simply a matter of time before root is compromised.

Perhaps the most effective way to use Crack is to make it as difficult as possible for Crack to guess passwords in a reasonable amount of time. What's reasonable? An hour, A day, A week? You must decide. We have already described many elements of effecting this approach, such as using pam_cracklib for checking passwords before they are accepted, using MD5 or bigcrypt instead of crypt(3) and enforcing minimum password lengths greater than 8 characters (see Chapter 5), choosing passwords that incorporate alphanumeric and nonalphanumeric characters, enforcing password aging, and protecting your hashed passwords with /etc/shadow or the like.

In spite of all the precautions, bad passwords are out there. So configure Crack dictionaries and rules so that they suit your site's needs. Get to know your users' interests (the bad-guys probably will) and incorporate dictionary entries based on this knowledge.

Make your Crack runs as efficient as possible, using as many CPUs as are available, perhaps even breaking up the collective password file over days or weeks of processing, cycling through different parts at different times.

Security is an endless and fruitless battle. Nowhere is it more clear than with static passwords. If someone is after your site, they'll probably find a way to get in. A big part of this book is to help you identify such an occurrence at the earliest possible time. So, don't sweat it—get a good night's sleep. You won't learn how to set your pager off until Chapter 17.

SUMMARY

In this chapter, we took a detailed look at Crack. We discussed how it works, what it does, and how it can be configured. We also looked at some of the ethical issues surrounding its use.

FOR FURTHER READING

There is a limited amount of documentation that comes with Crack. You will find it in the source tree (assuming /usr/src/c50a is the top level of the source tree) as follows:

```
/usr/src/c50a/manual.txt
/usr/src/c50a/doc/
```

## CHAPTER 13

What's Been Happening?

Auditing Your System with `tiger`

So, your system is up and running. And everything is fine, right? (We hope so.) Nevertheless, it pays to be paranoid and check the security of your system in several different ways. Because philosophies of UNIX vendors differ,[1] some UNIX systems are more vulnerable than others out of the box. Auditing tools can help identify vulnerabilities before someone compromises your machine. You will also want to know, for example, if one of the users (or even you) accidentally changed the ownership or permissions of a file. The `tiger` scripts are a UNIX auditing package you can use to help with this task, and you can set them up to run automatically.

OVERVIEW OF `tiger`

`tiger` is a set of Bourne-shell scripts and C programs designed to help evaluate the security of UNIX systems. It is part of a suite of tools originally written in 1992 at Texas A&M University and is copyrighted by Doug Schales, Dave Safford, and Dave Hess.[2]

---

1. Ease of collaborative work vs. security as a design goal will provide different results out of the box.

2. For more information on the suite of tools, see `ftp://ftp.net.tamu.edu:/pub/security/TAMU/tamu-security-overview.ps.gz`.

tiger was written to be easy to use by a novice administrator, yet easy to modify. One assumption tiger makes is that the root account can be compromised if any other user or group can modify files that root owns or executes. As such, tiger examines fundamental elements from root's environment (cron jobs, PATH, permissions, mail aliases, etc.) to see if they are subject to compromise and generates a report. tiger's goal is to find and report vulnerabilities.

You can configure tiger to run regularly through cron, or you can run parts or all of it as you find the need. Robert Ziegler has contributed some modifications to allow it to run better on Linux. As of this writing, the latest version is tiger-2.2.4p1. Look for another release to be out around the beginning of 2000.

Obtaining tiger

You can obtain the source from the tiger home site (Texas A&M University [TAMU]) or from COAST.

```
ftp://net.tamu.edu/pub/security/TAMU/tiger-2.2.4p1
ftp://coast.cs.purdue.edu/pub/tools/unix/TAMU/
```

You should find the following files:

```
mitchell-pgpkey.asc
tiger-2.2.4p1.README
tiger-2.2.4p1.tar.gz
tiger-2.2.4p1.tar.gz.asc
```

Add the PGP key to your keyring and verify the file's integrity (use pgpv if you are using PGP Version 5.0)

```
# pgp mitchell-pgpkey.asc
# pgp tiger-2.2.4p1.tar.gz.asc
```

Review the README file, and unzip and untar the tiger source files into a build directory. We will use /usr/src/tiger.

Major Components of tiger

In Figure 13.1, we see an overview of some major components of the /usr/src/tiger directory tree. Files and executables are striped, and directories are left unshaded. The cronrc and tigerrc files are used for configuration. The site-sample file can be copied and modified to form your own site file. It is used for configuration purposes. The configuration files are discussed in *The tiger Configuration Files* on page 347. The main script is tiger. It is run from the command line and will run a prescribed set of scripts to generate a security report, reading your configuration files to determine which scripts to call. The tiger-cron script is used as an interface to tiger when run via cron (see *Installing*

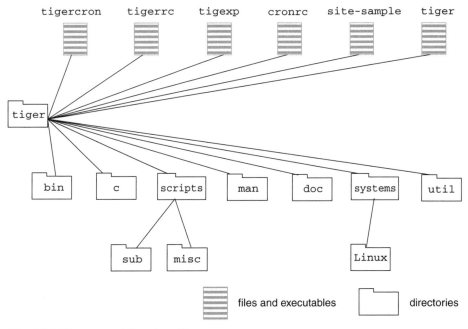

Fig. 13.1 The `tiger` Directory Tree

tiger to Run through `cron` on page 368). The `tigexp` script provides verbose explanations for `tiger` message IDs and is described in *Deciphering `tiger` Output* on page 373.

Moving on to the directories used by `tiger`, the `bin` directory will hold binaries that `tiger` may use during execution. These are described in Table 13.2 on page 347. The `c` directory holds the source code for these binaries. Explanatory messages used by `tiger` security reports are stored in files under the `doc` directory. These are used by scripts discussed in *Deciphering `tiger` Output* on page 373 and are covered in more detail in *Modifying `tiger`* on page 375. The `man` directory contains `man` pages for the `tiger` and `tigexp` scripts. You may view these by installing them in your system `man` directory or by executing the command

```
nroff -man filename | more
```

or

```
man filename
```

where you would replace *filename* with `/usr/src/tiger/man/tiger.8` or `/usr/src/tiger/man/tigexp.8`.

The `scripts` directory contains the meat of the code used by `tiger`. Here you will find Bourne-shell code used to generate the security report. Helper scripts, which are not callable directly, reside in the `sub` and `misc` subdirectories.

The `tiger` scripts are described in the next section. The `systems` directory holds operating-system-specific information such as signature files, SUID files expected to be found, and the utilities required to collect the input from each system type so that `tiger` can use it as data. Contents of the `systems` directory are described in *Modifying `tiger`* on page 375. Somewhat related, the `util` directory contains general utilities used by `tiger` during run time or when porting `tiger` to a new platform. Again, refer to *Modifying `tiger`* on page 375 for more information. Let's review some of the scripts, configuration files, and documentation files.

`tiger` Scripts   The main script in the top-level directory is called `tiger`. This script queries your operating system to determine the environment and reads the `tiger` configuration files to see what parts of `tiger` you want run. The main `tiger` script then calls other executables to do the work. We'll talk more about configuration later, but let's look at Table 13.1 to review the other executables `tiger` may call. Each of these scripts is located in the `scripts` subdirectory. Note that Table 13.1 references keywords associated with `tigerrc`. These keywords are described in Table 13.6 on page 352.

Many of these scripts can be run three ways—individually, on demand from the command line, or automatically. For a few scripts where no `tigerrc` variables exist, the script is not automatically run and can only be run standalone. We'll talk about this more in *Overview of Run-Time Operation* on page 360 and in *Installing `tiger` to Run through `cron`* on page 368.

Table 13.1 `tiger` Scripts

Script Name	Description	Associated `tigerrc` Keywords
check_accounts	Checks accounts for possible problems, such as disabled accounts that have valid shells, .rhosts files, cron jobs, home directory or dot-file permission problems, non-zero .hushlogin files, accounts with no passwords, and attempted comments in the password file.	Tiger_Check_ACCOUNTS USERDOTFILES
check_aliases	Searches for possible misconfigurations in the sendmail aliases file, such as nonroot-owned program aliases and included files, files with extra write permission, and other vulnerabilities.	Tiger_Check_ALIASES
check_anonftp	Checks for a variety of anonymous ftp misconfigurations, such as files owned by the user ftp and presence of .rhosts.	Tiger_Check_ANONFTP

Table 13.1 `tiger` Scripts (Continued)

Script Name	Description	Associated `tigerrc` Keywords
check_cron	Reports `cron` jobs containing group- or world-writeable components, relative pathnames, and references to executables or files not owned by the owner of the `cron` job or by system accounts.	Tiger_Check_CRON
check_embedded	Evaluates components of paths in executables, verifying that ownership and permissions of each component do not introduce vulnerabilities.	Tiger_Check_EMBEDDED Tiger_Embed_Max_Depth Tiger_Embed_Check_Exec_Only Tiger_Embed_Check_SUID Tiger_Embed_Report_Exec_Only Tiger_Embedded_OK_Owners Tiger_Embedded_OK_Group_Write
check_exports	Examines how filesystems are exported and produces INFO, WARN, or FAIL messages based on level of vulnerability.	Tiger_Check_EXPORTS
check_group	Cross-references GIDs found in the passwd and group files, reports misconfigurations and duplicates.	Tiger_Check_GROUP
check_inetd	Cross-references the `services` file and the `inetd.conf` file, reports executable ownership problems and possible misconfigurations; looks for vulnerable `services`.	Tiger_Check_INETD
check_known	Looks for presence of "storage" places commonly used by intruders, e.g., X Windows server and `lost+found` directory.	Tiger_Check_KNOWN
check_netrc	Reports nonplain file `.netrcs` and `.netrc` files containing nonanonymous FTP logins and passwords; reports if these files are world readable.	Tiger_Check_NETRC
check_nisplus	Checks NIS+ password entries for misconfigurations.	(none)
check_passwd	Reports misconfigurations, conflicts, and duplicate names/UIDs in password file sources.	Tiger_Check_PASSWD

Table 13.1 `tiger` Scripts (Continued)

Script Name	Description	Associated `tigerrc` Keywords
check_path	Reports ownership or permission problems with components in the PATH, presence of "." in PATH.	Tiger_Check_PATH Tiger_Check_PATHALL Tiger_ROOT_PATH_OK_Owners Tiger_ROOT_PATH_OK_Group_Write Tiger_PATH_OK_Owners Tiger_PATH_OK_Group_Write
check_perms	Examines system files for problems with owner, group, or permissions; reports vulnerabilities.	Tiger_Check_PERMS
check_printcap	Reports permission or ownership problems with files or executables associated with printer control.	(none)
check_rhosts	Examines .rhosts files and reports misconfigurations or policy violations.	Tiger_Check_RHOSTS RHOST_SITES
check_sendmail	Checks for misconfigurations with sendmail.	(none)
check_signatures	Compares cryptographic hash of binaries found on the system with those in a database. The database is most often generated from the original distribution.	Tiger_Check_SIGNATURES
check_system	Performs system-specific checks (none of which currently exist for Linux).	(none)
crack_run	Runs the Crack utility.	Tiger_Collect_CRACK Tiger_Crack_Local Tiger_Run_CRACK (See also the site file for CRACK and REPORTER)
find_files	Checks for a variety of files, including unowned (no username associated with the UID), SUID, SGID, or unusual device files.	Tiger_Check_FILESYSTEM Tiger_Files_of_Note Tiger_FSScan_Setuid Tiger_FSScan_Seggid Tiger_FSScan_Devs Tiger_FSScan_SymLinks Tiger_FSScan_ofNote Tiger_FSScan_WDIR Tiger_FSScan_Unowned Tiger_FSScan_ReadOnly

You can also get more information about what these scripts do by reviewing the explanation files located in `/usr/src/tiger/doc`. The `tigexp` script uses these files for its explanations. We discuss the use of `tigexp` in more detail in *Deciphering `tiger` Output* on page 373.

tiger Binaries. In addition to scripts, `tiger` uses a small number of binaries when evaluating the system. The source code is located in the `c` directory. As the programs are referenced, they are compiled automatically (if needed), and the object code is placed in the `bin` directory. Table 13.2 lists and describes these files.

The `tiger` Configuration Files   There are several files that `tiger` reads for configuration information. Table 13.3 shows a list of these files. We will cover some of these files in more detail in *Overview of `tiger` Configuration* below. All configuration file locations are relative to the source tree—`/usr/src/tiger` in our case.

The `tiger` Documentation Files   There are several documentation files included in the `tiger` distribution (see Table 13.4). We strongly recommend reading everything listed in Table 13.4 with the exception of the contents of the `doc` subdirectory which is discussed in *Deciphering `tiger` Output* on page 373.

Overview of `tiger` Configuration

There are two parts to configuring `tiger`. The first part involves adding or changing path information about the commands `tiger` will use. The second part of customization involves choosing which parts of `tiger` you would like to run, and when. These are straightforward once you know which files to edit.

Table 13.2 Binaries Used by `tiger`

`tiger` Binary	Use
md5	Source code to implement the MD5 message digest algorithm. Used by several of the `tiger` scripts.
realpath	Small program to resolve a pathname into its real name (removing symbolic links, "." and ".." components; or, with the -d flag, to return the resolved components of the real pathname. Used by many of the `tiger` scripts.
snefru	Source code to implement the `snefru` one-way cryptographic hash algorithm. Used by several of the `tiger` scripts.
testsuid	A small program to check the integrity of the setuid() system call. Used by the check_known script.

Table 13.3 `tiger` Configuration Files

File	Description
cronrc	Similar to a regular `crontab`, but used by `tiger` when run via `tigercron`.
site | site-*hostname*	Contains configuration system environment information specific to your site. Checks for `site-`*hostname* first, then `site`.
tigerrc	Preferences on the checks `tiger` should perform, and policy information needed to determine what your site allows.
systems/Linux/2/embedlist	List of files to evaluate during `check_embedded`.
systems/Linux/2/facl.strict	File access control list permissions. Used to determine permission problems.
systems/Linux/2/file_access_list	More file access control permissions. Used to determine permission problems. This is the default used in the `tiger` configuration.
systems/Linux/2/inetd	Expected contents of the `inetd.conf` file.
systems/Linux/2/rel_file_exp_list	List of scripts containing relative pathnames, which `tiger` will ignore.
systems/Linux/2/services	Expected contents of the `services` file.
systems/Linux/2/sgid_list	List of expected SGID files.
systems/Linux/2/signatures	Database of signatures against which to compare signatures of system binaries.
systems/Linux/2/suid_list	List of expected SUID files.

Table 13.4 Sources of `tiger` Documentation

Files/Directories	Use
BUG.EXTERN	Documents bugs found in other operating systems and what workarounds were made in `tiger` to avoid the bugs.
CHANGES	History of changes to the `tiger` distribution.
COPYING	License information and information about copying.
CREDITS	Contributors and sources.
DESCRIPTION	Brief overview of `tiger`, what it does, and why.
README	Basic description and references to more information.

Table 13.4 Sources of `tiger` Documentation (Continued)

Files/Directories	Use
`README.1st`	Where to start.
`README.linux`	List of changes to the TAMU distribution to support Linux.
`USING`	A short introduction on running `tiger`.
`doc`	Contains the informational messages used by `tiger`. They are utilized by `tigexp` to provide explanations to the codes generated by `tiger`.
`man`	Contains `man` pages for `tiger` and `tigexp`.

The `site` File   You will need to create at least one `site` file for your location. You can have more than one `site` file if you have multiple hosts, although you need to do this only if you want to customize `tiger` to run differently on each host. The `site` file stores information such as whether NFS/NIS should be used when checking user accounts or the name of your automount file (if you have one). You should copy the `site-sample` file in your build directory to `site` and customize it.

```
# cp site-sample site
```

Table 13.5 shows some of the values and descriptions of keywords that may be found in the `site` file. These keywords are actually shell environment variables. Anything after a `#` in the `site` file is interpreted as a comment.

Don't forget to export the variables you've set! Failure to export the variables will make them unavailable to the other `tiger` scripts.

Table 13.5 `site` File Keywords, Values, and Descriptions

Keyword	Value	Description

`GETFSHOST`	`getfs-std`
	`getfs-nfs`
	`getfs-automount`
	`getfs-amd`
		Used to determine if home directory is local or remote:
		`getfs-std`: do everyone, don't check;
		`getfs-nfs`: try to determine if it is NFS;
		`getfs-automount`: try automount tables;
		`getfs-amd`: try amd tables.

`AUTOHOMEMAP`	*mapname*	The name of the NIS automounter map used for users' home directories.
`HOSTNAMESLIST`	one or more hostnames	List of names by which this host is known. Names are separated by "`|`".

Table 13.5 `site` File Keywords, Values, and Descriptions (Continued)

Keyword	Value	Description
FS_DEVDIRS	whitespace-separated list of device directories, or no value	List of directory trees which contain device files. Names should end with "/". This is in addition to those which are standard for the particular system being used. If configured properly, diskless client and /dev directories on a server will be handled automatically.
YP	Y or ""	Indicates whether or not NIS is used. Y means NIS is used; an empty value ("") means NIS is not used.
CRACKDIR	*path_to_Crack_home*	Location of Crack source directory. See Chapter 12.
CRACK	$CRACKDIR/Crack	Location of Crack executable.
REPORTER	$CRACKDIR/Reporter	Location of Reporter executable.
FIND	*path_to_find*	Location of the find program. For Red Hat, replace *path_to_find* with /usr/bin/find.
AWK	*path_to_awk*	Location of the awk program. For Red Hat, replace *path_to_awk* with /bin/gawk.
export	export *VARIABLE1 VARIABLE2*	For each keyword used in this file, an export statement must exist in order to make the shell variable available to the other tiger scripts. For example, export AWK CRACK would make the variables AWK and CRACK globally available. You may have multiple export entries.

Example 13-1 shows a sample `site` file (some lines wrapped due to length). Recall that the "#" indicates a comment, and everything following it will be ignored. In Example 13-1, by specifying GETFSHOST=getfs-std, we have configured tiger to check all home directories, local or remote. This value is used when tiger runs home-directory-related checks, such as check_rhosts. The AUTOHOMEMAP variable, though set, is used only when GETFSHOST is set to getfs-automount or getfs-amd. There are two different export statements, used to make the variables GETFSHOST, AUTOHOMEMAP, CRACKDIR, CRACK, and REPORTER available to other scripts. And last, we set values for the variables CRACKDIR, CRACK, and REPORTER so that, if we are running the Crack program to check passwords, tiger will know where Crack is installed.

When tiger runs, it checks for a site-*hostname* file, where *hostname* is the name of the machine on which tiger is running. If none is found, it then checks for a `site` file.

Example 13-1 Sample `site` File

```
# -*- sh -*-
#
#       tiger - A UN*X security checking system
#       Copyright (C) 1993 Douglas Lee Schales, David K. Hess, David R. Safford
#
#       Please see the file `COPYING' for the complete copyright notice.
#
# site-sample - 04/22/93
#
#-------------------------------------------------------------------------------
#
#
# Sample site configuration file
#
# Rename this to either "site" or "site-`hostname`"
#
#-----------------------------------------------------------------------
#
# How to determine whether user home directory is local or remote?
#
GETFSHOST=getfs-std # Do everybody... don't check
#GETFSHOST=getfs-nfs # Try to guess if it is NFS mount
#GETFSHOST=getfs-automount # SUN automount tables
#GETFSHOST=getfs-amd # BSD 4.4 AMD tables
#
# Name of file or NIS map containing automounter maps for user directories
#
AUTOHOMEMAP=userhome.amd

export GETFSHOST AUTOHOMEMAP
#
# List of '|' separated names this host is known by.
#
# i.e:
#HOSTNAMESLIST="topcat|mydomain.com"
HOSTNAMESLIST="$HOSTNAME"
#
# Any of the utilities can be replaced by placing assignments here
# Most of the variables are the uppercase version of the command
# name, though there are a few exceptions.
#
#FIND=/usr/local/gnu/bin/find
#AWK=/usr/local/bin/mawk
#
#-----------------------------------------------------------------------
#
# Define where Crack is installed (this is the path to the Crack script)
#
CRACKDIR=/usr/local/src/crack
CRACK=$CRACKDIR/Crack
REPORTER=$CRACKDIR/Reporter

export CRACKDIR CRACK REPORTER
```

The `tigerrc` File   The `tigerrc` file stores your choices of what checks to run and allows policy-based customization. To give you an idea of the kind of policy stuff we're talking about, here's one example.

Many people believe that only root or other system accounts should be allowed to own system files. Think of the weakest link in the chain theory. If a less protected account is compromised, then root, trusting these files, is vulnerable. There are similar rules for groups and system files. You are more secure if you do not allow nonsystem groups write permissions to system files and directories. Rik Farrow's book (cited in *For Further Reading* on page 379) discusses this in more detail.

So all vendors are smart and know this, right? Well, not all vendors ship their systems this way, and not all administrators care to make changes. This is a policy decision. Carefully review all the keywords in the `tigerrc` file and configure them to match the policy at your site. Then `tiger`'s output will show you only the policy violations.

The distribution comes with several sample `tigerrc` files. The `tigerrc-all` file is configured to do all checks. You should copy one of the sample `tigerrc` files to `tigerrc` in the top level of your build directory and edit it to your taste. Some of the checks take longer to run than others. A list of keywords and values that you can use in a `tigerrc` file is shown in Table 13.6.

Table 13.6 `tigerrc` Keywords, Values, and Descriptions

Keyword	Value	Description
Tiger_Check_PASSWD	Y or N	Enables or disables check of `passwd` file for problems (`check_passwd` script); usually runs quickly.
Tiger_Check_GROUP	Y or N	Enables or disables check of `groups` file (`check_group` script); usually runs quickly.
Tiger_Check_ACCOUNTS	Y or N	Enables or disables examination of password file and files in users' accounts for oddities (`check_accounts` script); time varies by number of users.
Tiger_Check_RHOSTS	Y or N	Enables or disables examination of users' `.rhosts` files for policy violations (`check_rhosts` script); time varies by number of users.
Tiger_Check_NETRC	Y or N	Enables or disables examination of users' `.netrc` files (`check_netrc` script); time varies by number of users.
Tiger_Check_ALIASES	Y or N	Enables or disables examination of system `aliases` files (`check_aliases` script); usually runs quickly.
Tiger_Check_CRON	Y or N	Enables or disables check of users' cron jobs (`check_cron` script); usually runs quickly.

Table 13.6 `tigerrc` Keywords, Values, and Descriptions (Continued)

Keyword	Value	Description
`Tiger_Check_ANONFTP`	Y or N	Enables or disables examination of anonymous FTP configuration (`check_anonftp` script); usually runs quickly.
`Tiger_Check_EXPORTS`	Y or N	Enables or disables check of exported file systems (`check_exports` script); usually runs quickly.
`Tiger_Check_INETD`	Y or N	Enables or disables examination of system inetd file (`check_inetd` script); usually runs quickly.
`Tiger_Check_KNOWN`	Y or N	Enables or disables search for known vulnerabilities (`check_known` script); usually runs quickly.
`Tiger_Check_PERMS`	Y or N	Enables or disables check of system and home directory permissions (`check_perms` script); fairly quick.
`Tiger_Check_SIGNATURES`	Y or N	Enables or disables comparison of signatures on your system with those in a database of signatures that comes with `tiger` (`check_signatures` script); a few minutes to run.
`Tiger_Check_FILESYSTEM`	Y or N	Enables or disables execution of `find_files` script.
`Tiger_Check_PATH`	Y or N	Enables or disables examination of components in user's PATH for possible weaknesses (`check_path` script); fast for root, varies for all.
`Tiger_Check_EMBEDDED`	Y or N	Enables or disables examination of embedded paths in executables for weaknesses (`check_embedded` script); several minutes.
`Tiger_Check_SYSTEM`	Y or N	Enables or disables execution of operating system–specific checks. Note: this keyword is missing from `tigerrc-all`; add it to your `tigerrc` if you wish to use it.
`Tiger_Show_INFO_Msgs`	Y or N	Configures whether or not to show INFORMATORY messages in `tiger` report.

Table 13.6 `tigerrc` Keywords, Values, and Descriptions (Continued)

Keyword	Value	Description
Tiger_Run_CRACK	Y or N	Enables or disables a call to the Crack program (`run_crack` script); can take a long time to run. (If this is set, you also need to edit the `site` file.)
Tiger_Output_Width	0 or desired line length	Width of lines in report, in number of characters. Defaults to `79`; `0` means an unlimited number.
Tiger_CRON_Output_Width	0 or desired line length	Width of output lines generated by `tiger` when run via `tigercron`. Set this once and do not change it; otherwise the differences of output will show a lot of changes due to the different formatting. `0` means unlimited line length.
Tiger_Embed_Max_Depth	0, 1, 2, 3, ...	This refers to the depth of recursion to use when running the `check_embedded` script. If an embedded path refers to a file, check each referenced file until the recursive depth is met, or until there are no more files to check. Large depths of recursion can sometimes require more memory than is available; if `check_embedded` hangs, try using a smaller `Max_Depth` value.
Tiger_Embed_Check_Exec_Only	Y or N	`Y` means search only executables for embedded paths; `N` means search all regular files including executables for embedded paths.
Tiger_Embed_Check_SUID	Y or N	Enables or disables embedded path check of SUID files. This may take a little longer; the file system must be scanned for SUID files first.
Tiger_Embed_Report_Exec_Only	Y or N	`check_embedded` reports files that are writeable or not owned by root. If `Y` is set, only executables will be reported. Use `N` to report regular files and directories in addition to executables. Currently device files are not reported.
Tiger_Embedded_OK_Owners	one|or| more| usernames	List of usernames you allow to own system files. Names are separated by | with no white space. Files owned by other users will be reported.

Table 13.6 `tigerrc` Keywords, Values, and Descriptions (Continued)

Keyword	Value	Description
Tiger_Embedded_OK_Group_Write	no value or one|or| more| groupnames	List of group names you allow to have write access to system files. Names are separated by | with no white space. If set, files with group write other than allowed are reported. No value means no groups should have write access.
Tiger_Check_PATHALL	Y or N	Enables or disables check of PATHs in all users' start-up files.
Tiger_ROOT_PATH_OK_Owners	one|or| more| usernames	List of usernames allowed to own files in root's path. Names are separated by | with no white space.
Tiger_ROOT_PATH_OK_Group_Write	no value or one|or| more| groupnames	List of groups you allow to have write access to executables in root's PATH. Names are separated by | with no white space. No value means no group is allowed to have write access.
Tiger_PATH_OK_Owners	one|or| more| usernames	List of usernames allowed to own files in other users' PATHs. Names are separated by | with no white space.
Tiger_PATH_OK_Group_Write	no value or one|or| more| groupnames	List of groups allowed to have write access to executables in non-root user PATHs. Names are separated by | with no white space. No value means no group is allowed to have write access.
Tiger_Collect_CRACK	Y or N	Specifies whether or not to wait for the output of Crack if Crack was run. Y means wait for Crack to finish before exiting; if set to N, if Crack is finished, the output will be collected and reported; otherwise, `tiger` will report where the output will be when Crack does finish.
Tiger_Crack_Local	Y or N	If Y, only the local password information is used for Crack. If N, also try to use NIS, NIS+, etc., for Crack source.
Tiger_Mail_RCPT	*username*	User to whom `tigercron` output should be mailed.
Tiger_Files_of_Note	list of / separated files	List of filename globs to look for on the system. These are usually filenames crackers use but try to hide.

Table 13.6 `tigerrc` Keywords, Values, and Descriptions (Continued)

Keyword	Value	Description
`Tiger_FSScan_Setuid`	`Y` or `N`	Enables or disables search for SUID executables.
`Tiger_FSScan_Setgid`	`Y` or `N`	Enables or disables search for SGID executables.
`Tiger_FSScan_Devs`	`Y` or `N`	Enables or disables search for device files.
`Tiger_FSScan_SymLinks`	`Y` or `N`	Enables or disables search for strange symbolic links.
`Tiger_FSScan_ofNote`	`Y` or `N`	Enables or disables search for file-names specified by the `Tiger_Files_of_Note` keyword.
`Tiger_FSScan_WDIR`	`Y` or `N`	Enables or disables search for world-writeable directories.
`Tiger_FSScan_Unowned`	`Y` or `N`	Enables or disables search for unde-fined owners/groups.
`Tiger_FSScan_ReadOnly`	`Y` or `N`	Enables or disables scan of read-only filesystems.
`USERDOTFILES`	space-sep-arated list of dot files	Double-quoted, white space-sepa-rated list of dot-file names, such as `.forward`, `.mailrc`, `.cshrc`, etc.
`RHOST_SITES`	no value or `list｜of｜hosts`	List of hosts you allow to appear in users' `.rhosts` files. Anything not allowed will be reported. Patterns are those which can be used in Bourne-shell 'case' statements.

Example 13-2 shows a sample `tigerrc` file (some lines wrapped due to length). The first part of the file contains variables representing `tigerrc` scripts and a setting of `Y` or `N` that tells whether or not to run that particular script. Note that statements in the `tigerrc` file can be in any order; if the same variable appears more than once, the last value of the variable will be used. For example, at the top of this configuration file, we are specifying 16 scripts to run (the lines `Tiger_Check_PASSWD` through `Tiger_Check_EMBEDDED`). The # on the line is a comment and will be ignored. For testing purposes, you can edit this file and change some of the values to `N` to keep from running certain scripts.

The rest of the file contains mostly script and output customization infor-mation which we'll get to next. Note the directive

```
        Tiger_Run_CRACK=Y
```

that directs `tiger` to run Crack.

Example 13-2 Sample `tigerrc` File

```
#
# 'rc' file for tiger.  This file is preprocessed, and thus
# can *only* contain variable assignments and comments.
#
#-----------------------------------------------------------------------
#
# Select checks to perform.  Specify 'N' (uppercase) for checks
# you don't want performed.
#
Tiger_Check_PASSWD=Y # Fast
Tiger_Check_GROUP=Y# Fast
Tiger_Check_ACCOUNTS=Y# Time varies on # of users
Tiger_Check_RHOSTS=Y# Time varies on # of users
Tiger_Check_NETRC=Y# Time varies on # of users
Tiger_Check_ALIASES=Y# Fast
Tiger_Check_CRON=Y# Fast
Tiger_Check_ANONFTP=Y# Fast
Tiger_Check_EXPORTS=Y# Fast
Tiger_Check_INETD=Y# Could be faster, not bad though
Tiger_Check_KNOWN=Y# Fast
Tiger_Check_PERMS=Y# Could be faster, not bad though
Tiger_Check_SIGNATURES=Y # Several minutes
Tiger_Check_FILESYSTEM=Y# Time varies on disk space... can be hours
Tiger_Check_PATH=Y# Fast for just root... varies for all
Tiger_Check_EMBEDDED=Y# Several minutes
#
# Should messages tagged with INFO be shown?
#
Tiger_Show_INFO_Msgs=N
#
# In order for this to be effective, you should define 'CRACK' in
# a 'site' file.
#
Tiger_Run_CRACK=Y # First time, ages; subsequent fairly quick
#
# Line size (for formatting of output)... default is 79...
# Specifying '0' means unlimited
#
Tiger_Output_Width=79
#
Tiger_CRON_Output_Width=0
#
# On small memory systems, a large search depth can result in out
# of memory situations for 'sort'... :-(...
#
Tiger_Embed_Max_Depth=3
#
#
Tiger_Embed_Check_Exec_Only=Y
#
#
Tiger_Embed_Check_SUID=Y
#
#
# Note that currently, device files are never reported.
#
Tiger_Embed_Report_Exec_Only=Y
#
# Who do you allow to own system files.
```

Example 13-2 Sample `tigerrc` File (Continued)

```
# List of usernames separated by '|'... no whitespace
#
Tiger_Embedded_OK_Owners='root|bin|uucp'
#Tiger_Embedded_OK_Owners=root
#
#
Tiger_Embedded_OK_Group_Write=root
#
#
Tiger_Check_PATHALL=N # Check all user PATHs in startup files.
#
# Who can own executables in 'root's PATH?
# List of usernames separated by '|'... no whitespace
#
Tiger_ROOT_PATH_OK_Owners='root|uucp|bin|news'
#Tiger_ROOT_PATH_OK_Owners='root'
#
#
Tiger_ROOT_PATH_OK_Group_Write=root
#
# Who can own things in other users PATH?
# List of usernames separated by '|'... no whitespace
#
Tiger_PATH_OK_Owners='root|bin|daemon|uucp|sys|adm'
#
#
Tiger_PATH_OK_Group_Write=
#
#
Tiger_Collect_CRACK=Y
#
#
Tiger_Crack_Local=Y
#
# Who gets output from 'tigercron'?
#
Tiger_Mail_RCPT=root
#
# List of '/' separated filename globs (NOT pathnames) to look for
# on the filesystems.
#
Tiger_Files_of_Note="..[!.]*/.* */.* */.[!.]/.log/.FSP*"
#
# File system scan - things to look for
#
Tiger_FSScan_Setuid=Y # Setuid executables
Tiger_FSScan_Devs=Y # device files
Tiger_FSScan_SymLinks=Y # strange symbolic links
Tiger_FSScan_ofNote=Y # weird filenames
Tiger_FSScan_WDIR=Y # world writable directories
Tiger_FSScan_Unowned=Y # files with undefined owners/groups
#
# Should we scan read-only filesystems
#
Tiger_FSScan_ReadOnly=N
#
#
USERDOTFILES=".alias .kshrc .cshrc .profile .login .mailrc .exrc .emacs .forward
.tcshrc .zshenv .zshrc .zlogin .zprofile .rcrc .bashrc .bash_profile .inputrc
.xinitrc .fvwm2rc .Xsession .Xclients"
#
#
RHOST_SITES='topcat|mydomain.com'
```

Many of the scripts have configurable options. They are all listed in Table 13.6 on page 352. In Example 13-2 on page 357, we make several customizations. First, we configure `tiger` to not report messages of level INFO (with `Tiger_Show_INFO_Msgs=N`) and to set the width of reports run both on the command line (79 characters wide) and through `tigercron` (0, which means unlimited line length).

Next, for the `check_embedded` script, we specify to check three levels of recursive depth; to check only executables (in other words, not all regular files), but to check anything that is a SUID file; and, when generating the report, report only the embedded files found that are executable. (There's a difference between checking and reporting; you will probably want to try both settings and see the difference or leave them both set to Y.) Also with `check_embedded`, we have said that we will allow root, bin, and uucp to own embedded system files (`Tiger_Embedded_OK_Owners`), but they can be writeable by only the root group (`Tiger_Embedded_OK_Group_Write`).

For the `check_path` script we configure to not check user PATH variables. Similarly, to `check_embedded`, we specify root, bin, uucp, or news can own executables in root's path and that only root can write to them (`Tiger_ROOT_PATH_OK_Owners` and `Tiger_ROOT_PATH_OK_Group_Write`). There are similar variables that can be used if you check PATHs belonging to the users (`Tiger_PATH_OK_Owners` and `Tiger_PATH_OK_Group_Write`).

We configure `tiger` to wait for the output from Crack before producing the `tiger` report (`Tiger_Collect_CRACK`) and to crack local (`Tiger_Crack_Local`) passwords, rather than those from NIS. We've configured it to send the `tigercron` output to root (`Tiger_Mail_RCPT`).

The `Tiger_Files_of_Note` (other than being cryptic looking) is a list of files of a specific pattern to report. We are using the line that came with the sample `tigerrc` in Example 13-2 on page 357. It will look for files with spaces, three or more dots, `.log`, and `.FSP`, which at one time or another were fairly good signs of intrusion.

Near the end of the file, there are several configuration options for the `find_files` script that allow us to enable or disable certain types of checks or to scan read-only file systems. We've enabled them all (`Tiger_FSScan_*`), except we don't want to check read-only file systems (`Tiger_FSScan_ReadOnly=N`).

We haven't added anything to our USERDOTFILES variable—we are using what came in the sample file. These dot files will be checked for correct permissions and characteristics with the USERDOTFILES variable. And finally, the RHOST_SITES variable defines what hostnames to ignore (if any) in `.rhost` files. We're allowing the users to have topcat or mydomain.com in their `.rhosts` files.

Table 13.7 shows a list of command-line options that may be used with `tiger`.

Table 13.7 `tiger` Command-Line Options

Option	Use
-v	Prints `tiger` version information.
-B	Specifies `tiger` base directory on the command line.
-l	Specifies `tiger` log directory.
-w	Specifies `tiger` work directory.
-b	Specifies `tiger` binary directory.
-c	Specifies `tigerrc` file.
-e	Generates a verbose report (with full explanations inserted where each message ID appears).
-E	Produces a report similar to the default report, but generates a separate report that includes the full text of each message ID referenced in the output.
-S	Server check. Means check the server and the diskless clients configured on it. Probably doesn't work very well on systems other than SunOS 4.
-O	Specifies operating system.
-A	Specifies architecture.
-R	Specifies revision of OS.
-t	Specifies `tiger` test mode.

OVERVIEW OF RUN-TIME OPERATION

`tiger` comes preconfigured for a variety of operating systems. Much of this information is stored in the `systems` directory (and typically needs to be tinkered with only by developers). When you run `tiger` (or a stand-alone `tiger` script), the `scripts/config` executable tries to locate the most appropriate configuration files, but it will use more generic configuration information if it cannot locate exact matches. The configuration that it uses is reported at the beginning of the output. The `config` script also parses command-line options. An example of the output is shown in Example 13-3.

Example 13-3 `tiger` Shows Which Configuration Files Were Used at Run-Time.

```
# scripts/check_perms
Configuring...

Will try to check using config for 'i686' running Linux 2.0.36...
--CONFIG-- [con005c] Using configuration files for Linux 2.0.36. Using
configuration files for generic Linux 2.
Not all checks may be performed.
```

If your particular operating system or version of an operating system isn't found, you can try your hand at adding support. See *Modifying* `tiger` on page 375.

At this point, you should be finished with the configuration and ready to run `tiger` from the command line. You can also run the scripts individually, as shown in Example 13-4. (Now go find Joe and see what he's up to!) We describe the scripts in more detail in the next section.

Example 13-4 Running `check_rhosts` Stand-Alone

```
# scripts/check_rhosts
Configuring...
Will try to check using config for 'i686' running Linux 2.0.36...
--CONFIG-- [con005c] Using configuration files for Linux 2.0.36. Using
configuration files for generic Linux 2.
Not all checks may be performed.
# Performing check of /etc/hosts.equiv and .rhosts files...
# Checking accounts from /etc/passwd...
--WARN-- [rcmd013w] User joe's .rhosts file contains an attempted comment
line
--FAIL-- [rcmd002f] User joe's .rhosts file has a '+' for host field.
#
```

`tiger` Scripts

`tiger` was written to check the fundamental configuration of the system; this includes file and directory permissions checks, ownership checks, cross-reference checks, and so on. The scripts that perform these checks can be run either through the main `tiger` script (if configured in the `tigerrc` file) or by themselves whenever you feel like running a particular check. Some of the scripts have helper utilities that cannot be run by themselves. The scripts that perform these checks are examined in this section.

check_accounts. This script checks for problems with user accounts. It will report disabled accounts that may potentially be used via a `.forward` file containing a command, an `.rhosts` file, or `cron` jobs. It will also check for problems with the password file including passwordless accounts, nonroot accounts with UID `0`, and misconfigurations such as attempted comments in the password file. In addition, `check_accounts` looks for nonzero length `.hush-login` files (sometimes used by intruders to hide information), as well as permission problems on home directories that could allow files to be added or removed by others. Presence of these items may indicate a misconfiguration, allow a disabled account to continue to be used, or reveal signs of a compromise. The `check_accounts` run time depends on the number of accounts on your system. Example 13-5 shows a sample run of `check_accounts`.

check_aliases. The `check_aliases` script examines the aliases used by the `sendmail` program and reports possible vulnerabilities and misconfigurations.

Example 13-5 Running the `check_accounts` Script.

```
# scripts/check_accounts
Configuring...

Will try to check using config for 'i686' running Linux 2.0.36...
--CONFIG-- [con005c] Using configuration files for Linux 2.0.36. Using
configuration files for generic Linux 2.
Not all checks may be performed.

# Performing check of user accounts...
# Checking accounts from /etc/passwd.
--WARN-- [acc001w] Login ID adm is disabled, but still has a valid shell
(/bin/sh).
--WARN-- [acc001w] Login ID bin is disabled, but still has a valid shell
(/bin/sh).
--WARN-- [acc001w] Login ID daemon is disabled, but still has a valid shell
(/bin/sh).
--WARN-- [acc001w] Login ID ftp is disabled, but still has a valid shell
(/bin/sh).
--WARN-- [acc001w] Login ID games is disabled, but still has a valid shell
(/bin/sh).
--WARN-- [acc001w] Login ID gopher is disabled, but still has a valid shell
(/bin/sh).
--WARN-- [acc001w] Login ID lp is disabled, but still has a valid shell
(/bin/sh).
--WARN-- [acc001w] Login ID mail is disabled, but still has a valid shell
(/bin/sh).
--WARN-- [acc001w] Login ID news is disabled, but still has a valid shell
(/bin/sh).
--WARN-- [acc001w] Login ID nobody is disabled, but still has a valid shell
(/bin/sh).
--WARN-- [acc001w] Login ID operator is disabled, but still has a valid shell
(/bin/sh).
--WARN-- [acc001w] Login ID uucp is disabled, but still has a valid shell
(/bin/sh).
--WARN-- [acc006w] Login ID lp's home directory (/var/spool/lpd) has group
`daemon' write access.
--WARN-- [acc006w] Login ID mail's home directory (/var/spool/mail) has group
`mail' write access.
```

The script will report known problems such as presence of the `uudecode` alias, references to `include` files that are owned or writeable by nonroot users or that do not exist, and existence of `program` aliases that do not exist or are owned or writeable by nonroot users. Included aliases or program files that are nonroot owned or writeable may allow nonroot users to execute commands with root privileges.

_check_anonftp._   This script verifies that the setup of anonymous FTP has been done correctly. The home directory field in the password file for the FTP user is checked for errors that could lead to compromise of the machine; the ownership and permissions of files in the FTP directory hierarchy are checked for problems. If FTP is not configured properly, unauthorized access to the system could be obtained.

_check_cron._   The `check_cron` script examines the owner and permissions of the actual `cron` command and the directory components contained in the path to the `cron` command. If a user's `cron` job is owned by a user other than the one running the job or owned by a nonsystem account, or if any of these components are writeable by others, the command is reported as a possible vulnerability to that account. The owner of the `cron` job does not have control over the integrity of the file and execution of the `cron` job could lead to compromise.

check_embedded. The `check_embedded` script searches for embedded pathnames contained in files or binaries referenced by root and/or other users, and reports potential points of weakness. If an embedded name in turn refers to another embedded filename or binary, the check for embedded names is performed again recursively until all names have been checked or the maximum recursive depth is reached (a configurable option). Here a weakness means that the file or binary is owned or writeable by a nonsystem account.

There are many configuration options for this script (see Table 13.6 on page 352). You may choose to examine SUID binaries only, all binaries, or all regular files. You may choose to perform this check for root or for all users, or you might configure which users and groups are allowed to own the files that are being checked (the more restrictive, the more secure), and specify the level of recursive depth.

When run by itself, `check_embedded` refers to the `embedlist` in the `tiger` systems directory and will check for embedded names in the files listed there. When run in conjunction with other `tiger` scripts, a list of files or binaries referenced by root or other users (per your configuration options) is generated and checked in addition to the `embedlist`.

This script can take a few minutes to run. If your system has very little memory it may hang trying to do recursive checks; you may want to limit the depth it can search. Example 13-6 shows output from `check_embedded`.

Example 13-6 Output from `check_embedded`.

```
# Performing check of embedded pathnames...
--WARN-- [embed001w] Path `/usr/lib/uucp/uucico' contains `/usr/sbin/uucico'
which is not owned by root (owned by uucp).
Embedded references in: /bin/linuxconf->/etc/rc.d/init.d/linuxconf
                        /bin/linuxconf->/etc/rc.d/init.d/network
                        /bin/netconf->/etc/rc.d/init.d/linuxconf
--WARN-- [embed002w] Path `/usr/sbin/uucico' is not owned by root (owned by
uucp).
Embedded references in: /bin/linuxconf->/etc/rc.d/init.d/linuxconf
                        /bin/linuxconf->/etc/rc.d/init.d/network
                        /bin/netconf->/etc/rc.d/init.d/linuxconf
```

check_exports. The `check_exports` script examines the way in which filesystems (if any) are exported from your system and reports possible misconfigurations and vulnerabilities that may be present. There are a number of options that can be used when exporting filesystems, and, when used without care, your files could be viewed or modified by unauthorized people. The `check_exports` script will warn you if the anonymous ID is set to 0, which could cause unauthorized access. It reports any vulnerabilities caused by exporting filesystems with root access to other machines or by giving read or write access to all hosts. It will also flag dangerous exporting of the `/` or `/usr` filesystems.

check_group.   Cross-references the group file looking for duplicate GIDs and groupnames, malformed entries, and inconsistencies that are probably the result of misconfiguration but should be investigated and corrected. This should run quickly.

check_inetd.   The `check_inetd` script is designed to cross-reference the `inetd.conf` file with the `services` file, check the ownership and permissions of files referenced therein, verify that the files indicated in `inetd.conf` do exist and that they refer to the path expected. `tiger` tries to verify that the services are running on the expected port and that no vulnerable services are enabled. In order to perform these checks, `tiger` will attempt to compare the files on your system to files in the `tiger systems` subdirectory. The script may not run to the best of its ability if the files for your particular system are not available. Note that you will need to modify this script if you are using `xinetd`.

check_known.   `check_known` searches for known signs of intrusion. It looks for the presence of directories where normally plain files are expected and reports files in directories commonly used by intruders to hide files. It also searches for filenames that have been used by intruders in the past. The run time for this is usually short.

check_netrc.   The `.netrc` file is used by FTP programs to store login and password information. The `check_netrc` script examines `.netrc` files and will report nonanonymous login information if found and if readable by others. It also looks for `.netrc` files that are symbolic links or directories (as both are unexpected). Example 13-7 shows a run of `check_netrc`.

Example 13-7 Running the `check_netrc` Script

```
# scripts/check_netrc
Configuring...

Will try to check using config for 'i686' running Linux 2.0.36...
--CONFIG-- [con005c] Using configuration files for Linux 2.0.36. Using
configuration files for generic Linux 2.
Not all checks may be performed.

# Performing check of .netrc files...

# Checking accounts from /etc/passwd...
--WARN-- [nrc002w] User bob's .netrc file contains passwords for
non-anonymous ftp accounts.
```

check_nisplus.   This script attempts to verify that the permissions are correctly set on NIS+ password entries. It can only be run stand-alone, unless you modify the main `tiger` script to run it.

check_passwd.   The `check_passwd` script looks for possible misconfigurations or signs of compromise by reporting duplicate UIDs and usernames in the password file, as well as malformed password entries and conflicts between files on your system (such as passwd and shadow). This should run fairly quickly. Sample output from `check_passwd` is shown in Example 13-8.

Example 13-8 Running `check_passwd`

```
# scripts/check_passwd
Configuring...
Will try to check using config for 'i686' running Linux 2.0.36...
--CONFIG-- [con005c] Using configuration files for Linux 2.0.36. Using
configuration files for generic Linux 2.
Not all checks may be performed.
# Performing check of passwd files...
--WARN-- [pass002w] UID 0 exists multiple times in /etc/passwd.
```

check_path. This script examines the PATH of root or all users (according to variables set in the `tigerrc` file; see Table 13.6 on page 352) and reports directories that are writeable by others, not owned by system users or the user being checked. It also looks for the presence of ".", in the path, all of which can lead to execution of a Trojan horse program.

check_perms. This script examines the permissions of files and devices and reports any that have more accessibility than they should (world readable, or group writeable, for example). This script depends on availability of a system-specific file (`file_access_list`) in the `systems` subdirectory and may not run if a full port has not been done for your particular type and version of operating system.

check_printcap. The `printcap` file, used for printer control, may contain references to filters that may be run when a job prints. The `check_printcap` script evaluates the ownership and permissions of the files and directories associated with printer control and reports vulnerabilities. Execution of a vulnerable filter could result in unauthorized access.

check_rhosts. This script examines user `.rhosts` files and the `hosts.equiv` file for vulnerabilities and misconfigurations. Presence of + + or an entry containing a host but no user (both of which could lead to unauthorized connections) is reported, as are files with extra permissions which could allow someone to modify the file or gain information useful in compromising an account. The script verifies that there are no unusual characters present in the files and checks for `.rhosts` that are symbolic links or directories (both unexpected under normal circumstances). A policy configuration option enables you to allow certain local hosts to be present in users' `.rhosts` files but to report unapproved hosts (refer to Table 13.6 on page 352). Sample output from `check_rhosts` was shown in Example 13-4 on page 361.

check_sendmail. The `check_sendmail` script is dated, but it was designed to look for versions of sendmail that are old and likely to contain security holes. If it finds you are using the `smrsh` (`sendmail` restricted shell) to control which programs may be executed by sendmail program aliases, it will check to see if your `smrsh` configuration allows potentially dangerous scripts to be run. `smrsh` is part of the `sendmail` distribution; for more information, see the `sendmail` documentation cited in *sendmail Resources* on page 379. Example 13-6 on page 363 shows output from check_sendmail.

check_signatures.   Each of the files or binaries on your system can be fingerprinted with a cryptographic hash, or *signature*. The check_signatures script compares the cryptographic hash of each of the binaries and important files on your system against a set of cryptographic hashes stored in a database used by tiger. The database is created from files in the original OS distribution and may also contain cryptographic hashes of binaries distributed as patches to the operating system or binaries that are known to be compromised. These checks should be considered supplemental to tripwire (see Chapter 14).

Databases of signatures for several OS distributions are distributed with tiger. Updates are made available occasionally at the tiger FTP site, or you can try your hand at generating your own (see *Modifying tiger* on page 375 for more information). By running check_signatures against a good database, you can find out if any of the executables on your system have changed from the distribution, which is usually a sign of an intrusion. When you apply patches or new software to your system, you can add updates to your database of signatures.

check_system.   Occasionally, there may be a check that is specific to a particular OS or flavor of that OS that you don't want to run on every system. check_system executes a prescribed list of scripts written specifically for the host operating system. There is a tigerrc option to enable or disable running of the system-specific scripts (see Table 13.6 on page 352); if enabled, all system-specific checks will be run. For more information on check_system, see *Modifying tiger* on page 375.

crack_run.   If you have configured Crack on your system (discussed in Chapter 12), you can ask tiger to run Crack as part of your regular tiger routines. See *Running Crack from tiger* on page 373 for details on configuration. Sample output from run_crack is shown in Example 13-9.

Example 13-9 Running the run_crack Script.

```
# scripts/crack_run
Configuring...

Will try to check using config for 'i686' running Linux 2.0.36...
--CONFIG-- [con005c] Using configuration files for Linux 2.0.36. Using
configuration files for generic Linux 2.
Not all checks may be performed.

# Running Crack on password files...
(c) Alec Muffett, 1991, 1992, 1993, 1994, 1995, 1996
System: Linux topcat 2.0.36 #1 Tue Oct 13 22:17:11 EDT 1998 i686 unknown
Home: /usr/local/src/crack/c50a
Invoked: /usr/local/src/crack/c50a/Crack /usr/local/src/crack/c50a/run/tmppass
Stamp: linux-2-unknown

Crack: making utilities in run/bin/linux-2-unknown
find . -name "*~" -print | xargs -n50 rm -f
( cd src; for dir in * ; do ( cd $dir ; make clean ) ; done )
make[1]: Entering directory `/usr/local/src/crack/c50a/src/lib'
```

Example 13-9 Running the `run_crack` Script. (Continued)

```
rm -f dawglib.o debug.o rules.o stringlib.o *~
make[1]: Leaving directory `/usr/local/src/crack/c50a/src/lib'
make[1]: Entering directory `/usr/local/src/crack/c50a/src/libdes'
/bin/rm -f *.o tags core rpw destest des speed libdes.a .nfs* *.old \
*.bak destest rpw des speed
make[1]: Leaving directory `/usr/local/src/crack/c50a/src/libdes'
make[1]: Entering directory `/usr/local/src/crack/c50a/src/util'
rm -f *.o *~
make[1]: Leaving directory `/usr/local/src/crack/c50a/src/util'
make[1]: Entering directory `/usr/local/src/crack/c50a/src/lib'
make[1]: `../../run/bin/linux-2-unknown/libc5.a' is up to date.
make[1]: Leaving directory `/usr/local/src/crack/c50a/src/lib'
make[1]: Entering directory `/usr/local/src/crack/c50a/src/util'
all made in util
make[1]: Leaving directory `/usr/local/src/crack/c50a/src/util'
Crack: The dictionaries seem up to date...
Crack: Sorting out and merging feedback, please be patient...
Crack: Merging password files...
Crack: Creating gecos-derived dictionaries
mkgecosd: making non-permuted words dictionary
mkgecosd: making permuted words dictionary
Crack: launching: cracker -kill run/Ktopcat.8746
Done
----passwords cracked as of Sat Jun 5 13:26:45 CDT 1999----

Guessed bob [password] [/usr/local/src/crack/c50a/run/tmppass /bin/tcsh]

----done----

<remainder of output snipped>
#
```

find_files. This script searches for vulnerabilities among SUID or SGID files and reports unusual device files, world writeable directories, unusual filenames, and symbolic links that you may want to know about.

Strange device files lying around your system should be viewed with suspicion. The `find_files` tiger script will report device files found in nonstandard locations. If for some reason you have a need for legitimate device files in nonstandard locations (perhaps for FTP), you may update the FS_DEVDIRS variable in the `tigerrc` file to reflect additional device file locations on your system.

Depending on how your operating system behaves with regard to symbolic links, the outcome to commands involving symbolic links may be surprising. On some systems, for example, ownership of a link may change while, on others, ownership of the *target* of the link may change. `find_files` reports files that are symbolic links to system files.

The `find_files` script also looks for unusual filenames as defined by the `Tiger_Files_of_Note`[3] variable in the `tigerrc` file (see Table 13.6 on page 352). By default, it checks for FSP server control files (often used by crackers for file transfer) and will report files that have no valid owner or group. Check these files and verify that they were installed by you. You may also want to set valid owners and groups.

---

3. The comments in the script `find_files` reference the variable FS_FILES, but actually use `Tiger_Files_of_Note`.

When an SUID or SGID script is discovered, `tiger` tries to determine if these files were part of the original OS distribution. Due to exploitation of race conditions, it is difficult to write safe SUID and SGID programs. For this check, `tiger` needs to have a list of SGID and SUID files in the systems directory. If the list of SUID files for your particular distribution is not present, `tiger` will report all SUID files present on the system.

The presence of relative paths in SUID scripts may lead to compromise if the user can carefully craft a directory hierarchy containing compromised versions of the referenced name; therefore, all such files are reported. Additionally, `find_files` will report any SUID copies of regular binaries that it finds on the system.

Last, `find_files` will report world writeable directories. World-writeable directories can provide intruders a place to store or possibly delete files.

The `tigexp` Script   The `tigexp` script is used to explain individual message IDs, to insert explanations in an existing security report, or to generate a separate list containing the full explanation of all message IDs referenced in a security report. This utility is described in greater detail in *Deciphering `tiger` Output* on page 373.

The `check_symlink` Script   The `check_symlink` script is located in the `scripts/misc` subdirectory of the `tiger` home directory (we've been using `/usr/src/tiger`). This script tests to see whether your system will follow a symbolic link when doing a `chown` or a `chmod`. If it will, then you could inadvertently change the permissions on a security-related file in the course of changing ownership or permissions of a file in a user directory or `/tmp`. This is a stand-alone script; you can run it by itself to test the behavior of your system.

INSTALLING `tiger` TO RUN THROUGH `cron`

If you choose to install `tiger` so it can be run through `cron`, begin by editing `/usr/src/tiger/Makefile`. Verify that the installation directories are configured to reflect your choices. Example 13-10 shows the lines in the `Makefile` you might need to edit, depending on your choice of installation directory.

Example 13-10 Edit the `tiger` Makefile

```
...
TIGERHOME=/usr/local/tiger
...
TIGERWORK=/var/spool/tiger/work
...
TIGERLOGS=/var/spool/tiger/logs
...
TIGERBIN=/var/spool/tiger/bin
...
```

OH, BY THE WAY...

If you are setting up `tiger` on a secure server, the `TIGERHOME` directory can be set read only after the install has been performed. The `TIGERWORK` and `TIGERLOGS` directories will need to be writeable when `tiger` executes, but should be protected from tampering at other times. It is recommended the directories chosen be something private to `tiger` only. Do not use the `/tmp` directory.

Now execute `make` as illustrated in Example 13-11.

Example 13-11 Installing `tiger` with `make`

```
#make
#
#if [ ! -d /usr/local/tiger ]; then \
# mkdir -p /usr/local/tiger; \
# chmod 755 /usr/local/tiger; \
# fi; \
#if [ ! -d /usr/local/tiger/scripts ]; then \
# mkdir /usr/local/tiger/scripts; \
# chmod 755 /usr/local/tiger/scripts; \
#fi; \
...
<lots of output snipped>
...
#chmod 644 /usr/local/tiger/config;
```

Depending on your processor, number of users, and amount of memory, some checks will take longer than others. You will want to run some scripts more frequently than others. For example, you probably will not want to run `Crack` every day (but then again, you're root—you can if you want to).

Now that you have installed `tiger`, you can set up a `cronrc` file to regularly run various parts of `tiger` on your own customized schedule. This involves adding a `cron` job to run `tigercron`, say every hour. `tigercron` will check the `cronrc` file and run only those tasks that you have scheduled, and keep root's `crontab` a little cleaner.

The first time `tiger` runs via `tigercron`, you (or the user configured via the `Tiger_Mail_RCPT` variable in the `tigerrc` file) will receive the full report via e-mail. On subsequent runs, only the changes since the previous run will be reported.

A sample `cronrc` file is shown in Example 13-12.

Example 13-12 Sample `cronrc` File

```
#
# Sample 'tigercron' cronrc file...
#
# By running 'tigercron' from 'cron' say, once an hour:
#
# 0 * * * * .../tigercron >/dev/null 2>&1
#
# You can run the different checks in stages, without having to
# clutter up the crontab for root.
#
#-------------------------------------------------------------------------
```

Example 13-12 Sample `cronrc` File (Continued)

```
#
# Field 1: Comma separated list of hours (0-23) or '*' when this should
# be run.
#
# Field 2: Comma separated list of days of month or '*' when this
# should be run.
#
# Field 3: Comma separated list of days of week or '*' when this should
# be run.  Days of week must be exactly as 'date' prints.
#
# Remaining fields:  Scripts to execute
#
0,8,16 * * check_known
2 * * check_accounts check_rhosts check_netrc check_anonftp
1 * * check_perms check_signatures check_group check_passwd
3 * Mon check_inetd check_exports check_aliases check_path check_cron
2 * Sun find_files
2 1 * crack_run
```

Two sample lines from root's `crontab` are shown in Example 13-13. It is possible to specify a particular `tigerrc` file on the command line.

Example 13-13 Sample `crontab` Entries for `tigercron`

```
0 * * * * /usr/local/tiger/tigercron >/dev/null 2>&1
0 * * * * /usr/local/tiger/tigercron alternate.cronrc >/dev/null 2>&1
```

`tigercron` uses variables in the order specified in Table 13.8 to locate the `tiger` home directory.

Which Scripts Should I Run?

Before we go any farther, let's take a moment to discuss which scripts you might want to run, and how often. If you have multiple machines, you can set up different `cronrc` files for each type of system. You may have machines used for development by users (that's what they tell you they are doing, anyway)

Table 13.8 Preference Order—`tiger` Home Directory Specification

Option	Value
-B	Specify Basedir for `tiger`. If this option is used, it takes priority over the other two methods.
TIGERHOMEDIR	`tiger` will check if your UNIX shell has an environment variable of TIGERHOMEDIR; this value, if present, has priority over TigerInstallDir.
TigerInstallDir	If neither of the other options is set, this value is used. TigerInstallDir is the value assigned to TIGERHOME in the Makefile before installing. This value is copied into all the scripts when `tiger` is installed with make.

and machines that are servers with few or no user home directories. The reason you might not want to run all of the `tiger` scripts all of the time is because some of them can be CPU intensive. `find_files`, `check_embedded`, and `crack_run` usually take the most time. However, we recommend that you run scripts as frequently as practical, as well as running `tripwire`. Start by running everything once a day (with the possible exception of Crack). (Instructions on configuring `tiger` to run Crack are provided in the next section. See *Running Crack from `tiger`* on page 373.) It should not take you too long to decide which scripts should run more or less frequently.

You can set up multiple `tigerrc` files, each with different configurations, and run `tiger` from the command line, using the `-c` option to specify the `tigerrc` file to use. When running `tiger` through `tigercron`, you can specify the `cronrc` file to use with the `-c` option. Recall that, when using `tigercron`, you really should get notification of changes only since the last run, so there should be less output to look at than from the command line. Let's look at some possible differences between system types.

Protected Servers In this scenario, our server has no filesystems exported and no user accounts, but we *are* running anonymous FTP. We may want to run `check_anonftp` several times a day, Crack once a month, and `find_files` once a week. Example 13-14 shows a suggested `cronrc` file for this type of server.

Example 13-14 Possible `cronrc` File for a Protected Server

```
# Field 1: Comma separated list of hours (0-23) or '*' when this should
# be run.
#
# Field 2: Comma separated list of days of month or '*' when this
# should be run.
#
# Field 3: Comma separated list of days of week or '*' when this should
# be run.  Days of week must be exactly as 'date' prints.
#
# Remaining fields:  Scripts to execute
#
0, 17 * * check_known
2 * * check_accounts check_rhosts check_netrc
2, 14 * * check_anonftp
1 * * check_perms check_signatures check_group check_passwd
3 * * check_inetd check_exports check_aliases check_path check_cron
2 * Sun find_files
2 1 * crack_run
```

If running `tiger` from the command line, you could refer to a `tigerrc` that might have a value of `N` for `Tiger_Run_CRACK` and `Tiger_Check_FILESYSTEM`, and values of `Y` for all other checks, as shown in Example 13-15. If you saved this configuration file with the name `tigerrc-server-weekly`, you would execute `tiger` from the command line like so:

```
./tiger -c tigerrc-server-weekly
```

Example 13-15 Sample `tigerrc` File for Weekly Use on a Server

```
Tiger_Check_PASSWD=Y
Tiger_Check_GROUP=Y
Tiger_Check_ACCOUNTS=Y
Tiger_Check_RHOSTS=Y
Tiger_Check_NETRC=Y
Tiger_Check_ALIASES=Y
Tiger_Check_CRON=Y
Tiger_Check_ANONFTP=Y
Tiger_Check_EXPORTS=Y
Tiger_Check_INETD=Y
Tiger_Check_KNOWN=Y
Tiger_Check_PERMS=Y
Tiger_Check_SIGNATURES=Y
Tiger_Check_FILESYSTEM=N # We run this weekly in another tigerrc
Tiger_Check_PATH=Y
Tiger_Check_EMBEDDED=Y
Tiger_Run_CRACK=N # We run this monthly in another tigerrc

<remainder of file not shown>
```

`cronrc` for a Development Machine

On our development machine, we have lots of users. We are exporting files to other machines, and we don't have anonymous FTP set up. We would like to run the scripts that check user accounts every day, check anonymous FTP once a week (just in case), and run `find_files` every day. A `cronrc` file with this configuration is shown in Example 13-16.

Example 13-16 Sample `cronrc` File for a Development Machine

```
# Field 1: Comma separated list of hours (0-23) or '*' when this should
# be run.
#
# Field 2: Comma separated list of days of month or '*' when this
# should be run.
#
# Field 3: Comma separated list of days of week or '*' when this should
# be run.  Days of week must be exactly as 'date' prints.
#
# Remaining fields:  Scripts to execute
#
0,8,16 * * check_known
2 * * check_accounts check_rhosts check_netrc
1 * * check_perms check_signatures check_group check_passwd
3 * * check_inetd check_exports check_aliases check_path check_cron
2 * Sun check_anonftp crack_run
2 * * find_files
```

And as you did for the server, you could create a separate `tigerrc` file for the development machine and run `tiger` from the command line. Example 13-17 shows a sample `tigerrc` file suitable for daily use on a development machine.

If the file were named `tigerrc-devel-daily`, you would use the following command to run `tiger` from the command line:

```
./tiger -c tigerrc-devel-daily
```

Example 13-17 Sample `tigerrc` File for Daily Use on a Development Machine

```
Tiger_Check_PASSWD=Y
Tiger_Check_GROUP=Y
Tiger_Check_ACCOUNTS=Y
Tiger_Check_RHOSTS=Y
Tiger_Check_NETRC=Y
Tiger_Check_ALIASES=Y
Tiger_Check_CRON=Y
Tiger_Check_ANONFTP=N # we check this weekly in another tigerrc
Tiger_Check_EXPORTS=Y
Tiger_Check_INETD=Y
Tiger_Check_KNOWN=Y
Tiger_Check_PERMS=Y
Tiger_Check_SIGNATURES=Y
Tiger_Check_FILESYSTEM=Y
Tiger_Check_PATH=Y
Tiger_Check_EMBEDDED=Y
Tiger_Run_CRACK=N # We check this weekly in another tigerrc

<remainder of file not shown>
```

RUNNING CRACK FROM `tiger`

Once you have installed Crack on your system (see Chapter 12), you can have `tiger` run Crack for you automatically. Example 13-18 shows the variables in the `tigerrc` file that must be edited, and the values required. You also need to edit your `site` (or `site-hostname`) file to specify the paths to the required commands, as shown in Example 13-19.

Example 13-18 Variables in `tigerrc` File Needed for Crack

```
...
Tiger_Run_CRACK=Y
...
Tiger_Collect_CRACK=Y
...
Tiger_Crack_Local=Y
...
Tiger_Mail_RCPT=root
...
```

Example 13-19 Variables in `site` File Needed for Crack

```
...
CRACKDIR=/usr/local/src/crack/c50a

CRACK=$CRACKDIR/Crack

REPORTER=$CRACKDIR/Reporter
...
```

DECIPHERING `tiger` OUTPUT

The output messages that `tiger` generates are labeled with different severities (INFO, WARN, ALERT, FAIL). In most cases, FAIL will indicate a situation where root or another user's data can be compromised. However, the policy tiger uses by default may not match the policies employed at your site. The other levels of severity can be used as a rough guide for a quick analysis of your report, but take a look at the full error message and make sure you take any corrective action that may be necessary.

One of the most useful tools for helping you understand the error messages (which can be cryptic!) is tigexp. You can supply any of the message IDs to tigexp for an explanation, as shown in Example 13-20.

Example 13-20 Using tigexp to Explain an Error Message

```
# ./scripts/tigexp rcmd013w
The /etc/hosts.equiv file and $HOME/.rhosts files do not support comments.
A commented entry is still valid.  It simply indicates a host with the
character '#' as the first letter.  Since an attempt to comment out an
entry indicates that it is no longer needed, it should simply be deleted.
#
```

Or, if you have a security report and would like to add explanations to the entire report, you may run tigexp with the -f or -F against the entire report. The -f option will generate a new report containing only the full text of each unique message ID found in the security report, while the -F option will generate a new report, inserting the full text of each message ID each time a message ID is encountered. With either the -f or -F option, the script expects the filename of a tiger security report, or will read from standard input if no filename is given. Example 13-21 shows a sample of the output that might be generated as a result of executing ./scripts/tigexp -F security.report, while Example 13-22 shows the output that might be obtained from executing ./scripts/tigexp -f security.report.

If you'd like your reports to be more verbose from the start, try one of the explanation command-line options. With the -e command-line option to tiger,

Example 13-21 Report Generated with tigexp -F

```
# Checking accounts from /etc/passwd...
--WARN-- [rcmd006w] User joe's .rhosts file has group `other' and world
read access.

The indicated .rhosts file has permissions other than read and write
for the owner of the file.  Allowing others to read the .rhosts file
provides information about other "trusted" hosts which may allow them
to compromise this host, the trusted hosts, or both.  The permissions
should be at most read and write for the owner of the file.  Note that
on some systems, because of network file systems, it is necessary to
have world read access to the .rhosts file so that client machines can
access the .rhosts file.  Most systems correctly handle this situation
without the need for the world read access.  If yours does not, you
should bring it to the attention of your vendor.

--FAIL-- [rcmd002f] User joe's .rhosts file has a '+' for host field.

A plus sign (+) in the host field of a .rhosts file means that anyone
with the same login ID as the indicated login ID, anywhere on the
Internet, can login as that user, without a password.  Note that all an
intruder has to do is create that login ID on a remote machine that
they have privileged access to.  This should be removed *immediately*
and the system checked for signs of an intrusion.
```

Example 13-22 Report Generated with `tigexp -f`

```
Message ID: rcmd002f

A plus sign (+) in the host field of a .rhosts file means that anyone
with the same login ID as the indicated login ID, anywhere on the
Internet, can login as that user, without a password. Note that all an
intruder has to do is create that login ID on a remote machine that
they have privileged access to. This should be removed *immediately*
and the system checked for signs of an intrusion.

Message ID: rcmd006w

The indicated .rhosts file has permissions other than read and write
for the owner of the file. Allowing others to read the .rhosts file
provides information about other "trusted" hosts which may allow them
to compromise this host, the trusted hosts, or both. The permissions
should be at most read and write for the owner of the file. Note that
on some systems, because of network file systems, it is necessary to
have world read access to the .rhosts file so that client machines can
access the .rhosts file. Most systems correctly handle this situation
without the need for the world read access. If yours does not, you
should bring it to the attention of your vendor.
```

the full explanation of each message ID is printed in the `tiger` report each time a message ID is encountered. This output is similar to that obtained from running `tigexp -f` *reportname*, as shown in Example 13-21. For something not quite as verbose, a command-line option of `-E` will produce the default report, but it will also produce a separate report containing one copy of the text of each message ID referenced in the report. This output is similar to that obtained from executing `tigexp -f` *reportname*, as shown in Example 13-22.

If you prefer running `tiger` manually instead of through `cron`, you may want to take a look at the Merlin tool. This is a Hyper-Text Markup Language (HTML)–based tool that serves as a HTML-based GUI to `tiger` and the reports it generates (see Appendix B).

TROUBLESHOOTING `tiger`

`tiger` is a very complex set of programs. If you're having a problem but aren't sure what is going on, you can try editing the script and changing the `sh` to `sh -x` on the first line. Also review all of your configuration files and verify that the variables are set to what you think they are set to.

If you are still stuck, you might try the `tiger` mailing list. To subscribe, send mail to `tiger-request@net.tamu.edu`, with the subject `subscribe tiger`.

MODIFYING `tiger`

In this section, we try to provide some hints on modifying `tiger`. We will briefly cover modifying scripts, processing files on your system to generate input for `tiger` (we refer to these as `tiger` source files), adding new checks, and generating digital signatures.

Modifying Scripts

If you modify scripts and add your own informational messages for output, you can either update an existing `doc/*.txt` file or create your own text file. Either way, you should update the `doc/explain.idx` (index) file afterward. The easiest way to do this is to create a new one by executing the following commands from the top-level `tiger` directory (we backed up the old index file first) as shown in Example 13-23.

Example 13-23 Regenerating the `tiger` Explanation Database Index

```
# cp doc/explain.idx doc/explain.idx.old
# util/genmsgidx doc/*.txt > doc/explain.idx
```

`tiger` Source Files   There are some utilities in the `systems/Linux/2/` directory that create some of the files used by `tiger`. These are shown in Example 13-24.

Example 13-24 `tiger` Configuration Helper Utilities

```
gen_alias_sets
gen_bootparam_sets
gen_cron
gen_export_sets
gen_group_sets
gen_inetd
gen_mounts
gen_passwd_sets
gen_services
```

The `util/buildconf` script generates the `config` script. If you are porting `tiger`, you may want to pay attention to the files in the lower half of Table 13.3 on page 348. Create a directory structure similar to an existing tree (such as `default`) under the `systems` directory, adding OS and/or release information as appropriate. You can generally get this information from the commands `uname -s` (for the system) and `uname -r` (for the version information). You may have to modify these scripts if the files on your system are in a different location.

Adding New Checks

Scripts may be general—they will be run on every platform—or they may be written to run for a particular operating system, release, revision, or architecture.

To write a new general script, model the new script after an existing `tiger` script and place it in the scripts directory. For the most run-time flexibility, create a new variable for the `tigerrc` file. Edit the main `tiger` script and make it test the value of the variable in the `tigerrc` file (`Y` or `N`). You can now run the script stand-alone, from `tiger`, or via `tigercron`.

For system-specific checks, there are two approaches. The first method involves adding the commands to a script called `check` in the systems directory hierarchy at the appropriate level you wish to check. For example, you could perform a certain check on all Linux machines, or you could check only for kernels of a particular major version or of a specific minor version. If you are porting `tiger`, you can copy the scripts from the default directory into your new hierarchy and then add your commands to the `check` script.

The second approach for running system-specific scripts is to create your new script by modeling an existing one (similar to creating a new general script, including `tigerrc` variables) and then add the name of this script to the file `check.tbl` at the appropriate level in the systems hierarchy.

When the `tigerrc` variable `Tiger_Check_SYSTEMS` is set to `Y`, each `check` script for the host operating system, architecture, release, and/or revision will be run, and each of the scripts referenced in each applicable `check.tbl` file will be executed.

Signatures

There really ought to be an easier way to generate your own `tiger` signatures. It does require some effort to generate a full set. There is a script `util/mksig` that may take you most of the way there, or you can modify it if you are porting to a new system. Example 13-25 shows a portion of a signature file for Linux, as well as some entries from a SunOS file. Normally, they are not found in the same file, but we have shown them together here to provide an illustration of the different entry types, as will be described below. (There is nothing

Example 13-25 Sample Signatures

```
#
# Signature file for Linux 2.0.35 i586, generated Mon Sep 14 04:16:04 EDT 1998
#
Y .        /usr/X11/bin/XConsole b1c052c58959d72361928dd1a1ddffc4 Linux 2.0.35
Y .        /usr/X11/bin/Xwrapper f14994c664e1d150fc849978c1fe6061 Linux 2.0.35
Y .        /usr/bin/at d3c5a2a4f765ff3a476e786d60b618d2 Linux 2.0.35
Y .        /usr/games/atc d44600a27bb7d3be465a945622ab5982 Linux 2.0.35
Y .        /bin/bash a3322c290ef58c0a0fa202af5330a88d Linux 2.0.35
Y .        /usr/games/battlestar e121e5029dd75bd9fdf1d6c8e7abb10b Linux 2.0.35
Y .        /usr/games/canfield 1e0ae1e67e45d4791bd513e9451139db Linux 2.0.35
Y .        /sbin/cardctl d79041f5353e472cb7461e8843959231 Linux 2.0.35
Y .        /usr/bin/chage be61f87ee34a49216c9eebad26af39a1 Linux 2.0.35
Y .        /usr/bin/chfn 8b82be89cbf3911662b98d0a811b480c Linux 2.0.35
Y .        /usr/bin/chsh d2935bf63aa4ebc03f7f98c473e11f12 Linux 2.0.35
Y .        /usr/games/cribbage 1f2f82c7e6a9c2243b5b63cf84348b4f Linux 2.0.35
Y .        /usr/bin/crontab 347fbd2a4f9b3d141a0d77ff30977e76 Linux 2.0.35

<lots of output snipped>

# example of signature with 'O' flag (from SunOS)
O sig008w /usr/etc/portmap d4970849 769874cc 4a45be0f f1639826 00abb3c8 6acc3c52
59698663 630b08bc SunOS 4.1.2 (security patch is 100482)

# examples of signature with 'N' flag (two different hash formats) (Also from
SunOS)
N sig007a /usr/bin/login 1aa8fe34 6a0ef1f7 6fc46ccb 1404cdeb 3a00872e 006dffc2
9e5b070c 31bac62b contains a backdoor (0892).
N sig007a /usr/bin/login 59b3d2647a90f070159393bff6a67dba contains a backdoor
(1293).
```

really *wrong* with having the entries together, but it is pointless; execution of `tiger` will be slower because these signatures will all be compared with those on your system. It is best to give each version of each operating system its own signature file.)

The fields of the signature file are described in Table 13.9.

Typically you would want a cryptographic hash of all binaries, important system files, and any file that can contain executable code. If you add a patch to your system, you can stick the cryptographic hash for it in your signatures file. Say we patched `/bin/login`. We would change the entry for `/bin/login` in our signatures file from this original line with the Y flag

```
Y . /bin/login 35a316e1f53101e682ec149026480224 Linux 2.0.35
```

to these two lines

```
O sig004w /bin/login 35a316e1f53101e682ec149026480224 Linux 2.0.35
Y . /bin/login b16492290ef50a8c0fa202af5592988d Linux 2.0.35
```

In the replacement set, the original entry has the Y replaced with the letter O to indicate that files matching this cryptographic hash are now obsolete. The ".." is changed to the message ID of an appropriate message (see `doc/signatures.txt`), and we have added a new line with a Y flag (latest known binary) and a cryptographic hash for the replacement `/bin/login` binary.

Table 13.9 Fields of the signature file

Field	Represents
Flag	Flag is Y, N, or O.
	Y (Yes) represents a cryptographic hash from the original distribution or a replacement binary. A flag of Y indicates that no known patch for this file exists as of the time these hashes were created. (This flag may be found on the latest version of a patch, if multiple patch releases exist.)
	N (No) represents a binary with a known backdoor. You do not want to have these binaries on your system.
	O (Obsolete) represents a binary for which a patch exists. The second field is the message ID that will be displayed if the file matching this cryptographic hash is found on the system.
Message ID | '.'	If flag is N or O, this field contains the message ID of patch (`sig006w`, for example; see `doc/signature.txt`); if flag is Y, this field contains ".".
Filename	The path to the file.
Cryptographic hash	MD5 or Snefru hash of the file.
System	Output from `uname -s`.
Release	Output from `uname -r`.

RECOMMENDATIONS

We recommend that you run `tiger` on newly installed systems to identify anything that needs to be hardened prior to putting them in a production environment. Also run `tiger` regularly on running systems to look for changes. Tune `tiger` first by running it several times from the command line until your configuration is set as you like it to be and you have made any necessary system changes. Then install and run `tiger` via `tigercron`. Run additional audit tools such as `tripwire`. Protect your log files and use a secure server or read-only media if possible.

SUMMARY

We attempted to cover many configuration options of the `tiger` scripts. `tiger` is a complex set of scripts and programs but can help bring fundamental system vulnerabilities to your attention.

FOR FURTHER READING

1. Farrow, Rik, *UNIX System Security: How to Protect Your Data and Prevent Intruders*, Reading, Massachusetts, Addison-Wesley, 1991.

Mailing List for `tiger`

To subscribe to the `tiger` mailing list, send e-mail to `tiger-request@net.tamu.edu` with the subject `subscribe`.

`sendmail` Resources

For further information regarding `sendmail`, read the excellent book

1. Costales, Bryan, with Eric Allman, *sendmail*, 2d ed., Cambridge, Massachusetts, O'Reilly & Associates, Inc., 1997.

   Also check the related web site

   `http://www.sendmail.org/`

Setting the Trap

Tripwire

Hopefully, you haven't been implementing all the really cool stuff we've been talking about into a production environment yet (testing and playing with stuff is OK), because you really need to do *this* before you do *that. This* is Tripwire.

The Tripwire utility won't do anything to dynamically protect your environment, but it will act as an incredibly valuable alarm system. Its purpose is to capture an image of all the important files and directories on your system, and then, when you run it in compare mode, it will let you know if something has changed. In this way, if an unauthorized user has compromised your system by adding back doors or Trojan horses, you will find out about it the next time you run Tripwire. If there are but a handful of tools you are considering implementing, Tripwire (or equivalent funtionality) *must* be among them. If you are running a firewall on your gateway, or if you are using a Hypertext Transfer Protocol (HTTP) or FTP server or any other system in a perimeter network, you really ought to implement Tripwire on those systems. Additionally, every system considered mission critical, containing important data, acting as a server, or otherwise associated with a significant part of your environment should be serviced by Tripwire.

In particular, after you have installed a system and all of the additional software for that system from pristine sources, you will want to use Tripwire to capture a pristine image of your system. After that, and only after that, is your system ready for the production environment. Subsequent to introducing that system to the production environment, you will want to run Tripwire regularly, but on an unpredictable basis. Such a procedure together with the regular reading of system log files will alert you to the vast majority of system compromises.

TRIPWIRE OVERVIEW

The Tripwire utility is actually quite straightforward in what it does and how it is configured. When invoked, Tripwire reads a configuration file. The configuration file tells it which files and directories to pay attention to and what information to gather about those directories and files. Once the information is gathered by running Tripwire in the *initialize mode*, it is placed in a database, which needs to be securely stored. Whenever Tripwire is run again, it uses the information it finds in the database and compares it to the information that is actually on the system. This is known as *compare mode*. If it finds any discrepancies (changes), it reports them to you. All of these changes should be checked out thoroughly. If unauthorized activity is identified, you will need to recover the system (see Chapter 18 for further details). If the changes are a result of authorized activity, you will have the option of updating the database so that future Tripwire compare runs do not report the same differences. Updating is accomplished through Tripwire's *update mode*.

Figure 14.1 illustrates the overall functionality of Tripwire. We will look at each of the modes and the configuration file in the following sections, but we need to begin with obtaining and installing Tripwire.

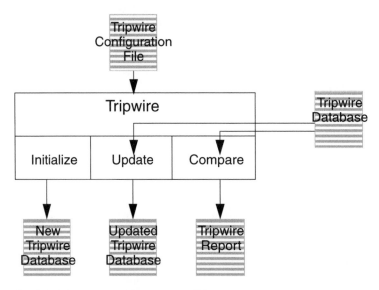

Fig. 14.1 Functional Overview of Tripwire

OBTAINING AND INSTALLING TRIPWIRE

Tripwire was developed by Gene Kim and Eugene H. Spafford at Purdue University. The publicly available version of Tripwire (version 1.2) is available from numerous sources, including

```
http://www.cs.purdue.edu/coast/ (COAST Archive)
http://www.redhat.com/
```

Both of these sites include digitally signed files. The files at the COAST Archive are source only, while both source and Intel precompiled versions are available from the Red Hat site. If you pull down these versions, be sure to check the PGP signatures! You can obtain Tripwire Version 1.3 (officially called Tripwire Academic Source Release 1.3) from Tripwire Security Systems, Inc. (TSS), at

```
http://www.tripwiresecurity.com/
```

This version has a number of bug fixes and enhancements. In particular, it fixes the database consistency problem that required the use of `twdb_check.pl` in version 1.2. Otherwise, it is substantially similar to version 1.2. Consequently, our discussions will be applicable to both versions, the differences being noted where appropriate.

Tripwire Version 2.x was recently released by TSS. TSS offers binary versions of this product for free for noncommercial use. It runs on Red Hat 5.0 or later and is in RPM format.

Unfortunately, none of the files from TSS are digitally signed. This is a particular problem with Version 2.x, since TSS offers only binaries. Therefore, if you are going to use that version, put it on a test system and watch for unusual behavior before you go live with it.

Tripwire Version 1.2

Since Tripwire Version 1.2 ships with Red Hat 5.2/6.0 (on the Power Tools CD, or from `ftp://ftp.redhat.com/`), we will use that version. There are two RPM packages on Red Hat 6.0—`tripwire-1.2-2.src.rpm` contains the source and `tripwire-1.2-2.i386.rpm` contains the binaries. For Red Hat 5.2, these files will be `tripwire-1.2-1.src.rpm` (source) and `tripwire-1.2-1.i386.rpm` (binaries). The RPMs from Red Hat 6.0 contain minor bug fixes (see the file `/usr/doc/tripwire-1.2/Changelog` as noted in Example 14-1 on page 385 for details); thus you should use those packages even if you are running Red Hat 5.2.

Even if you intend to recompile the source, you probably will want to obtain these RPMs since the `Makefile` and some of the source files require modification to run on Linux. Both RPM files contain PGP 2.6 signatures, so be sure to verify them as follows:

```
# rpm -Kv tripwire-1.2-2.src.rpm
# rpm -Kv tripwire-1.2-2.i386.rpm
```

If you don't have the Red Hat PGP public key, it is available either on the CD or at the Red Hat web site.

After downloading and verifying the signatures on these packages, install them as follows:

```
# rpm -ivh tripwire-1.2-2.src.rpm
# rpm -ivh tripwire-1.2-2.i386.rpm
```

All of the source files will end up in /usr/src/redhat/SOURCES in the form of the following three files:

```
tripwire-1.2-rhlinux.patch
tripwire-1.2.tar.Z
tripwire.verify
```

The tripwire-1.2-rhlinux.patch file contains the modifications necessary to compile on Red Hat Linux. The file contains a daily cron entry that is also placed in /etc/cron.daily when you extract tripwire-1.2-2.i386.rpm. The tripwire-1.2.tar.Z contains the actual source code. You will need to uncompress and untar this file. When you do so, you will end up with the following three files:

```
Readme
T1.2.tar
T1.2.tar.asc
```

Read the Readme file. The T1.2.tar.asc file contains a PGP signature and MD5 checksum for the T1.2.tar file which contains the source files. You will need Eugene Spafford's public key (available from http://www.cs.purdue.edu/people/spaf) to verify the digital signature. Once done, extract the files from T1.2.tar. By default, this will put all of the source in the directory /usr/src/redhat/SOURCES/tripwire-1.2. Even if you are not going to recompile the software, you will need the scripts identified in Table 14.1 (their locations are referenced relative to /usr/src/redhat/SOURCES/tripwire-1.2).

The file tripwire-1.2-2.i386.rpm contains the binaries for Tripwire. Extracting the package yields the files shown in Example 14-1. We suggest that you review the files in the directory /usr/doc/tripwire-1.2 because there is a lot of useful information there. Notice that the Tripwire configuration file tw.config is located in /etc by default. As we will discuss in some detail throughout this chapter, this file will need to be relocated to a read-only filesystem. The same is true for /usr/sbin/tripwire, which is the Tripwire engine. The /var/spool/tripwire directory is the default location for the databases, which once again will need to be relocated to a read-only location. The /usr/sbin/siggen utility allows for the generation of the different hash values and takes a file as input. There are occasions where checking one or a few hash values is warranted, justifying the need for this separate utility.

Table 14.1 Necessary Scripts Found in the Tripwire Source Tree

Script	Description
`src/twdb_check.pl`	A Perl script that verifies the integrity of the database against the configuration file. It is discussed in *Tripwire Update Mode* on page 402.
`contrib/CheckConfig`	A Bourne-shell script that checks the syntax of the configuration file against the existence of the files and directories referenced therein. It is discussed in *Tripwire Initialize Mode* on page 396.
`contrib/tw_newinode.pl`	A Perl script that corrects captured inode[*] numbers in the database after `fsirand`,[†] or equivalent, is run.
`contrib/zcatcrypt`	A sample script using FIFO files with the `-cfd` option to `tripwire` and incorporating encryption and compression. We will look at examples similar to this in *Routine Tripwire Runs—Compare Mode* on page 399.

[*]An inode (index node) is maintained by the filesystem for each file. See the references cited in *System Administration* on page 80 for further details about inodes.
[†]The `fsirand` utility is used to randomize the selection of inode numbers, making NFS file handles more difficult to guess. It is available on Solaris platforms.

Example 14-1 Contents of `tripwire-1.2-2.i386.rpm`

```
/etc/cron.daily/tripwire.verify
/etc/tw.config
/usr/doc/tripwire-1.2
/usr/doc/tripwire-1.2/Changelog
/usr/doc/tripwire-1.2/FAQ
/usr/doc/tripwire-1.2/INTERNALS
/usr/doc/tripwire-1.2/README
/usr/doc/tripwire-1.2/README.FIRST
/usr/doc/tripwire-1.2/Readme
/usr/doc/tripwire-1.2/TODO
/usr/doc/tripwire-1.2/WHATSNEW
/usr/doc/tripwire-1.2/docs
/usr/doc/tripwire-1.2/docs/README
/usr/doc/tripwire-1.2/docs/appdev.txt
/usr/doc/tripwire-1.2/docs/designdoc.ps
/usr/doc/tripwire-1.2/docs/sans.txt
/usr/man/man5/tw.config.5
/usr/man/man8/siggen.8
/usr/man/man8/tripwire.8
/usr/sbin/siggen
/usr/sbin/tripwire
/var/spool/tripwire
```

Additionally, the RPM includes an example configuration file `/etc/tw.config`. It also adds the file `/etc/cron.daily/tripwire.verify` to automate Tripwire compare-mode runs (see *Routine Tripwire Runs—Compare Mode* on page 399). You will want to change both of these based on the needs of a particular system as discussed in the following sections.

Finally, notice that the man pages are located in /usr/man. These, together with the information found in /usr/doc/tripwire-1.2, constitute the full collection of documentation for Tripwire.

THE TRIPWIRE CONFIGURATION FILE

The syntax of the Tripwire configuration file is relatively simple. However, the configuration file can become very complex when it is implemented for many different hosts running different operating systems. We will begin with an explanation and a simple example and then move on to a more complex example.

In the Tripwire configuration file, we will find a listing of files and directories that we wish to *fingerprint*. The fingerprint is simply a collection of information about the file or directory, like file size, permission settings, and inode number. It may also include hash values from one or more one-way hash functions (see *Hash Functions and Digital Signatures* on page 44 for further information about one-way hash functions). Associated with each file or directory we will find a collection of *selection masks* that determines the information to be collected for the fingerprint. Table 14.2 describes the available selection masks that, when used in the configuration file, will cause Tripwire to capture the indicated information.

As you can see, all of the lowercase letters in Table 14.2 specify a file attribute. If the attribute is listed as part of the collection of attributes preceded by a + symbol, then Tripwire will incorporate that attribute in the fingerprint. If an attribute is part of the collection of attributes following a - symbol, then Tripwire will ignore that attribute.

The numeric selection masks represent different hash functions. Selecting one or more of these will cause Tripwire to compute and store the hash value(s) of the indicated file or directory using the indicated hash function. Using multiple hash functions dramatically reduces the chances that a file could be compromised and its hash values spoofed.

The uppercase letters in Table 14.2 represent templates. Their definitions are given in the description column of the table. Templates are convenient to use and will be explored further in subsequent examples. The character > may also be incorporated with any selection mask or template combination and is used to indicate that we want to pay attention only to decreases in file size, ignoring increases.

By default, the Tripwire configuration file is called tw.config. If you use the Red Hat RPMs, Tripwire expects this file to be in /etc; however, you may specify an alternate location with the -c option to the tripwire command (the tripwire command is further detailed in *The tripwire Command* on page 395). In Example 14-2 (line numbers added for clarity), we see a simple Tripwire configuration file. This example is only for the purpose of our discussion. For a more realistic example, see Example 14-4 on page 393. Notice that in line 1 the directory / is preceded by =. This informs Tripwire that we want to capture

Table 14.2 Tripwire Selection Masks

Selection Mask	Description
p	permission and file type
i	inode number
n	link count
u	UID
g	GID
s	file size
a	access timestamp
m	modification timestamp
c	inode change timestamp
0	null signature
1	MD5 (RSA Data Security, Inc., MD5 Message-Digest Algorithm)
2	Snefru (Xerox Secure Hash Function)
3	CRC-32 (POSIX1003.2); not useful for security purposes
4	CRC-16; not useful for security purposes
5	MD4 (RSA Data Security, Inc., MD4 Message-Digest Algorithm)
6	MD2 (RSA Data Security, Inc., MD2 Message-Digest Algorithm)
7	SHA-1 (NIST Secure Hash Algorithm)
8	Haval (a 128-bit signature algorithm)
9	reserved for future use (currently null)
+*mask*	includes the *mask* in the fingerprint; for example, +pin means to include permission, inode number, and link count
-*mask*	excludes the *mask* from the fingerprint; for example, -pin means to exclude permission, inode number, and link count
R	+pinugsm12-ac3456789 (read-only template, for read-only files and directories)
L	+pinug-sacm123456789 (log files template, for files that are both read from and written to)
N	+pinusgsamc123456789 (ignore nothing template)
E	-pinusgsamc123456789 (ignore everything template)
>	for files that increase in size (such as log files); generates an alert only when file is smaller than previously recorded

Example 14-2 Sample Tripwire Configuration File

```
 1.    =/                L
 2.    /.rhosts          R          # may not exist
 3.    /.profile         R          # may not exist
 4.    /.cshrc           R          # may not exist
 5.    /.login           R          # may not exist
 6.    /.exrc            R          # may not exist
 7.    /.logout          R          # may not exist
 8.    /.forward         R          # may not exist
 9.    /.netrc           R          # may not exist
10.
11.    # Unix itself
12.    /boot/vmlinuz R
13.
14.    <lots deleted>
15.
16.    # Alert if log file is smaller
17.    /var/adm/SYSLOG +pinug>-samc123456789
18.    # Add 78 to important sec tools
19.    /usr/local/bin R+78
20.    # But ignore the tmp directory
21.    !/usr/local/bin/tmp R+78
22.    # Only capture additions/deletions in the test subdirectory
23.    /usr/local/test E
```

information about the directory /, including any file creation or deletion activity in that directory, but nothing about the contents of the directory. If = is not specified, but a directory is, such as in line 19, Tripwire will capture the specified information for the directory and all of its contents recursively down through any subdirectories.

In line 21, we specify a subdirectory of a previously fingerprinted directory. This subdirectory is preceded by the symbol !. This entry causes Tripwire to ignore the indicated directory and all of its contents completely. Notice that the selection mask is identical in both lines 19 and 21. Contrast this behavior with the entry in line 23, where the ignore everything (E) template is used. The E template will cause Tripwire to monitor the indicated directory for added and deleted files but nothing else, unlike the ! which ignores the directory completely.

Note that Tripwire does not traverse filesystems. This means that if, for example, /usr/local/bin/src is a separate partition, the entry on line 19 will not apply and a separate entry would be required for that filesystem. Additionally, Tripwire does not follow symbolic links, but it will capture information about the link itself.

In Example 14-2, most of the entries use unmodified templates (described in Table 14.2 on page 387). Line 17 is an example of an explicit listing of attributes and signatures to capture, while lines 19 and 21 exhibit modifying a template by adding signatures for those entries. These entries could be expanded to, say, R+78-12, which would tell Tripwire to collect SHA-1 (7) and Haval (8) signatures, but not MD5 (1) or Snefru (2) which would otherwise be collected due to the definition of the template.

Extending the Configuration File

The tw.config file also supports additional preprocessor syntax which allows for the extension of the use of a given configuration file to many platforms, customization of templates, and conditional statements. Table 14.3 describes the available syntax.

     Example 14-3 (line numbers added for clarity) illustrates a tw.config file that incorporates some of the parameters shown in Table 14.3. This example is for illustrative purposes only and is not intended for use. A realistic example is provided in Example 14-4 on page 393. In the first part of Example 14-3, we see the use of @@define to create the new templates READ and ALL (lines 3 and 5). These templates are subsequently used in lines 41, 42, 50, and 51.

Table 14.3 Tripwire Configuration File Preprocessor Syntax

Argument	Description
@@ifhost *hostname*	True if *hostname* must identically match the output of uname -n or hostname. If true, all entries after this entry and before an @@endif or @@else entry are executed.
@@ifnhost *hostname*	Same as above except that it will be true if *hostname* does not identically match the output of uname -n or hostname.
@@else	Provides conditional else semantics for use in conjunction with @@ifhost, @@ifnhost, @@ifdef, or @@ifndef.
@@ifdef *variable*	True if the variable is defined.
@@ifndef *variable*	True if the variable is not defined.
@@endif	Closes out the preceding @@if* statement.
@@define *variable string*	Assigns a *string* to a *variable*. If no string argument is given, the null string is assigned.
@@undef *variable*	Unassigns the *variable*.
@@include *pathname*	Includes the file specified through the *pathname* into this file. The included file must use the same configuration syntax.
@@*variable*	Expand to the *string* stored in *variable*.
@@{*variable*}	Same as above. Normally, this syntax is used in conjunction with other strings as with the shell.
||	Logical OR semantics.
&&	Logical AND semantics.

Example 14-3 Preprocessor Syntax in a Tripwire Configuration File

```
 1.  # Create our own templates
 2.  # Use 7&8 instead of 1&2
 3.  @@define READ R+78-12
 4.  # Sometimes we want almost everything
 5.  @@define ALL N-034569
 6.  #
 7.  # Initial definitions for Operating Systems
 8.  @@ifhost eagles || niners || ravens
 9.  @@define SOLARIS
10.  @@endif
11.  #
12.  @@ifhost peru || egypt || maya || inca
13.  @@define IRIX
14.  @@endif
15.  #
16.  # If not one of the above hosts, then Linux
17.  #
18.  @@ifndef SOLARIS
19.  @@ifndef IRIX
20.  @@define LINUX
21.  @@endif
22.  @@endif
23.  #
24.  # Now start processing fingerprints
25.  #
26.  # Special file for Linux
27.  @@ifdef LINUX
28.  @@include /usr/local/ro/etc/tw.config.linux
29.  @@else
30.  # Stuff common to IRIX and Solaris
31.  =/              L
32.  /.rhosts        R        # may not exist
33.  /.profile       R        # may not exist
34.  /.cshrc         R        # may not exist
35.  ...
36.  <lots of common stuff deleted>
37.  ...
38.  @@endif
39.  # IRIX specific
40.  @@ifdef IRIX
41.  /usr/etc @@ALL
42.  /var/ns @@READ
43.  ...
44.  <lots of stuff deleted>
45.  ...
46.  @@endif
47.  # Solaris specific
48.  #
49.  @@ifdef SOLARIS
50.  /usr/ucb @@ALL
51.  /var/sadm @@READ
52.  ...
53.  <lots of stuff deleted>
54.  ...
55.  @@endif
```

In the next section of the file, we determine on which host Tripwire is running. Lines 8 and 12 use the `@@ifhost` to check for specific hosts, each using the logical OR (`||`) capability. If there is a match in one of these two cases, we set a variable to the null string. The null string is used in these cases because the value of the variable will never be used; we are interested only in whether it has been set or not. This is exhibited initially in lines 18 and 19 where we test to see if either `IRIX` or `SOLARIS` has been set; if not, we set the `LINUX` variable to the null string indicating that the host is running Linux.

Subsequently, the conditionals used in the file—specifically at lines 27, 40, and 49—are all based on which variable has been set. Notice that we use a completely separate file for the Linux case and incorporate that file with an `@@include` in line 28 (notice also the use of the filesystem `/usr/local/ro`, implying read-only; this will be further discussed in *Storing the Database* on page 398). Using the preprocessor syntax, you can configure this file in many ways to run on many different systems.

Effectively Building the Tripwire Configuration File

As you may already have determined, setting up this file properly is critical to your system's security. There are three issues associated with this file.

1. The syntax must be correct.
2. The configuration file or files must be secured.
3. All critical files and directories need to be fingerprinted.

Correct Syntax   There is a bit of help with respect to the syntax. In the Tripwire source directory, you will find a subdirectory called `contrib`. There are a number of `README` files there as well as a few utilities, one of which is `CheckConfig`. You can use the `CheckConfig` script to check the syntax of your Tripwire configuration file or files. Essentially, it makes sure that the files and directories that you have specified exist, and it also alerts you when it encounters a symbolic link. It cannot, of course, tell you how you should use Tripwire! The syntax for its use is, for example:

```
# CheckConfig -v /usr/local/ro/etc/tw.conf.linux
```

The `CheckConfig` script does not understand preprocessor syntax. Fortunately, the `tripwire` command has an option (`-E`) that will cause it to parse the preprocessor information and generate a configuration file (sent to standard output, by default). So, if you are using preprocessor commands, you can check the syntax of your file by executing

```
# tripwire -E -c /usr/local/ro/etc/tw.conf.linux | CheckConfig -v
```

If there are any preprocessor syntax errors, they will be reported by Tripwire.

Secure Storage   We note in *Storing the Database* on page 398 that it is best to store the Tripwire database on removable read-only media, such as a CD. We also discuss the encryption of this database in addition to such storage or in the event that the use of removable media is not possible. Not only should the database(s) be securely stored; the `tripwire` program and the configuration file(s) also need secure storage because they too might be tampered with if they are left writeable. Ideally, they generally ought not to be readable either as it allows an interloper to glean valuable information about your configuration and use of Tripwire.

Once again, the best way to accomplish this is to use a CD in a read-only CD-ROM device. Optimally, the system containing this read-only filesystem would be connected to the network only when Tripwire is run. This is an ideal resource for Tiger (see Chapter 13) and Crack (see Chapter 12) runs as well. The system could be a laptop or other dedicated node used for this specific purpose. We'll refer to such a system as a *security server*. In the absence of such a system, the implementation of a local read-only filesystem (see *Filesystem Restrictions* on page 78 of Chapter 4 for filesystem mounting options) for all Tripwire resources is critical. Once the resources are locally mounted read-only, they may be exported via NFS (with access restrictions, of course—see *Some Major Applications* on page 37 for more information about NFS), and Tripwire runs may be effected throughout the internal network. This approach will effectively secure the `tripwire` binary, all configuration files, and the Tripwire database. When Tripwire runs in compare mode, it will need to write reports, which cannot be written to the read-only filesystem. This issue is addressed in *Routine Tripwire Runs—Compare Mode* on page 399.

Fingerprinting Critical Files   The critical question is, "Which files do I Tripwire?" Rather simply, the goal is to capture information about all files and directories that, if compromised, would cause us grief—a rather daunting task even on moderately complex servers, let alone those servers plus all of the various nodes operating on the network.

So, which files and directories are critical? The answer, in part, is provided in the following list.

☞ System binaries and libraries such as those found in `/sbin` and `/lib`.

☞ System configuration files and directories such as `/etc/syslog.conf`, `/etc/pam.d`, `/etc/passwd`, and `/etc/shadow`.

☞ System log files such as those found in `/var/log`.

☞ System data and spool files such as those in `/var/spool`.

☞ Security tools including their binaries, libraries, configuration files, and data files; for example, SSH, `tiger`, Crack, and CFS.

☞ Application binaries, libraries, configuration files, and data files. These could be system files such as those related to NFS and/or additional software such as a database.

Each system will have its own set of critical files and directories. You will need to assess your environment and determine its needs. We supply an example that should give you a reasonably good starting point in Example 14-4. Make sure that you modify this example to fit the needs of the various systems in your computing environment; do **not** use it as it is.

In addition, here are some tips that might help you organize the Tripwire configuration for your environment.

☞ Identify critical files.

✗ If the file is used for read-only or read-mostly, try R or similar template.

✗ If the file is modified frequently and always increases, try the mask +pinug>-samc0123456789.

✗ If the file is modified frequently, but the size is unpredictable, try the mask +pinug-samc0123456789.

☞ Identify critical directories; apply the same rules as above.

☞ If it is unclear as to how to proceed, try R and modify as needed. In all cases, you will find out where changes are necessary because your Tripwire compare mode output will become voluminous!

Example Configuration File for Red Hat Linux

Example 14-4 provides a more realistic tw.config file for Linux. Remember, this is only an example! You will need to modify this file to suit your site's needs.

Now that we have a good idea about how to set up a Tripwire configuration file, let's take a look at how to use the tripwire command.

Example 14-4 Sample tw.config File for Linux

```
#
# Tripwire configuration file
#
# Define our own templates
#
# Binary files
@@define BIN E+pnugsci17

# Read template
@@define READ E+pinugsm17

# Log files
@@define LOGS E+pugn

# Config files
@@define CONFIG E+pinugc

# Directory
@@define DIR E+pnugi

# Device files
@@define DEV E+pnugsci

# root directory
=/                          @@DIR
```

Example 14-4 Sample `tw.config` File for Linux (Continued)

```
# /proc changes a lot, so we'll grab what we can
=/proc                    E+pugi

# Capture these directories
=/tmp                     @@DIR
=/mnt                     @@DIR
=/mnt/cdrom               @@DIR
=/mnt/floppy              @@DIR
=/mnt/disk                @@DIR
=/net                     @@DIR
=/misc                    @@DIR

# root's home - won't change like /home
/root                     @@READ

# critical boot resources including kernel (/boot/vmlinuz)
/boot                     @@READ

# Critical configuration directories and files
# We capture most things with CONFIG & modify
# the rest.
#
/etc                      @@CONFIG
/etc/inetd.conf           @@READ
/etc/rc.d                 @@READ
/etc/exports              @@READ
/etc/mtab                 @@LOGS
/etc/motd                 @@LOGS
/etc/group                @@READ
/etc/passwd               @@LOGS
/etc/shadow               @@LOGS
/etc/security             @@READ
/etc/pam.d                @@READ
/etc/fstab                @@READ
/etc/cron.d               @@READ
/etc/cron.daily           @@READ
/etc/cron.hourly          @@READ
/etc/cron.monthly         @@READ
/etc/cron.weekly          @@READ
/etc/ftpusers             @@READ
/etc/hosts                @@READ
/etc/hosts.allow          @@READ
/etc/hosts.deny           @@READ
/etc/login.defs           @@READ
/etc/logrotate.conf       @@READ
/etc/logrotate.d          @@READ
/etc/securetty            @@READ
/etc/sendmail.cf          @@READ
/etc/ssh                  @@READ
/etc/sysconfig            @@READ

# truncate home - lots of changes in the directory
=/home                    @@READ

# var tree
=/var/spool               @@LOGS
/var/log                  @@LOGS
/var/spool/cron           @@LOGS
/var/spool/mqueue         @@LOGS
/var/spool/mail           @@LOGS

# critical binaries and /usr
/sbin                     @@READ
/bin                      @@READ
/lib                      @@READ
/usr                      @@READ

# device files
/dev                      @@DEV
```

THE `tripwire` COMMAND

The `tripwire` command may take a number of options. These are enumerated in Table 14.4.

Normally, `tripwire` runs in compare mode. This will not be the case when the `-initialize`, `-update`, `-E` (or `-preprocess`), `-help`, or `-version` options are used. When the `-interactive` option is used, `tripwire` first runs in compare mode and then in interactive update mode.

Next we will take a look at running `tripwire` in its three modes of operation—namely, initialize, compare, and update.

Table 14.4 Flags of the `tripwire` Command

Flag	Description
`-initialize`	Generates the database. This is initialize mode.
`-update pathname` `or entry`	This is update mode. It updates the specified pathname or entry in the database. If `pathname` is used and it is a file, then only that file is updated in the database. If `pathname` is used and it is a directory, then that directory and all files and directories in `pathname` and below are recursively updated. If the argument is an `entry` in the configuration file, then the entire entry is updated.
`-interactive`	This mode offers the opportunity to update the database interactively. It first runs in compare mode and then queries the user as to whether or not the database should be updated for each difference it finds.
`-loosedir`	This option reduces the checks on directories by ignoring size, number of links, modification, and inode change times. This increases performance at the risk of losing significant information.
`-d database`	Reads the `database` specified instead of looking in the default location (`/var/spool/tripwire` on Red Hat 5.2/6.0). You may specify standard input with `-d -`.
`-c config`	Reads configuration information from `config` instead of the default location (`/etc/tw.config` on Red Hat 5.2/6.0). Standard input may be specified with `-c -`.
`-dfd openfd`	Reads the database from the open file descriptor `openfd`. This is very useful for compression and encryption.
`-cfd openfd`	Reads configuration information from the open file descriptor `openfd`. This is very useful for compression and encryption.
`-Dvar=string`	Defines the variable `var` as `string`. Acts as if `@@define` were used in the configuration file.
`-Uvar`	Undefines the variable `var`. Acts as if `@@undef` were used in the configuration file.

Table 14.4 Flags of the `tripwire` Command (Continued)

Flag	Description
-i # or all	Informs Tripwire to ignore the listed signatures (replace # with the signature number). Multiple signatures must be provided in a comma-separated list. The use of all instead of a numeric list suppresses all signatures. The purpose of this flag is to increase performance at the possible risk of lost security information.
-E or -preprocess	Just preprocesses the file. Output to standard output.
-q	Suppresses output detail in compare mode. Prints only one line per identified anomaly. In particular, the compare message is not printed.
-v	Verbose. Prints out filenames as they are scanned.
-help	Prints out inode interpretation help message, then exits.
-version	Prints out version information, then exits.

TRIPWIRE INITIALIZE MODE

As described in *Tripwire Overview* on page 382, the purpose of the initialize mode is to build the database. While this mode is used infrequently, it is important to get it right because the database that is generated now will subsequently be used to compare with what actually exists on your system. The database generated is in ASCII format. Thus, it may be read manually. There may be an occasion or two where this comes in very handy because you can do a manual check at any time.

Example 14-5 shows an example initialization of the Tripwire database. Notice that, at the end of the initialization, Tripwire tells you that it placed

Example 14-5 Initializing the Tripwire Database

```
# tripwire -v -initialize
### Phase 1:   Reading configuration file
### Phase 2:   Generating file list
### Phase 3:   Creating file information database
scanning: /usr/local/bin
scanning: /usr/local/bin/opiekey
scanning: /usr/local/bin/otp-md4
...
<lots of output snipped>
...
###
### Warning:   Database file placed in ./databases/tw.db_topcat.
###
###            Make sure to move this file file and the configuration
###            to secure media!
###
###            (Tripwire expects to find it in '/var/spool/tripwire'.)
```

the database—tw.db_topcat in this case—in the subdirectory databases (this subdirectory will be created if it does not exist) of the directory from which Tripwire was invoked. Tripwire reminds you to secure the database and further informs you that, when you run Tripwire in either update or compare mode, it will look for the database in the directory /var/spool/tripwire; this default location is easily overridden by the -c command line flag (see Table 14.4 on page 395).

Effective Tripwire Initialization

The most important element of initializing your Tripwire database is the state of the system on which it is being run. Ideally, you want to run tripwire -initialize on a pristine system—that is, one that was just installed from a pristine source (CD or verified signatures, etc.) and one on which all applications (including publicly available security tools!) were installed from a trusted source. If that is the case, then make sure that you run Tripwire for the first time before it ever goes into production.

If you initialize Tripwire on a system that has already been compromised, then you will not be able to uncover what's been done to the system using Tripwire. Any system that has been introduced to a production environment should be thoroughly analyzed before Tripwire is initialized. The best way to accomplish this is to remove the system from the production environment and reinstall it entirely from the pristine source (including all applications). Unfortunately, this may also be highly impractical. Therefore, here is an alternative.

The Red Hat 5.2/6.0 distribution incorporates the rpm utility, which is discussed at various points throughout this book, mostly as it relates to verifying PGP signatures or installing software. This utility can also be used to verify the software installed on a system against the package to which it belongs. In particular, you can check your system installation against the packages on the CD with rpm -Vp. This command will inform you if any files associated with an RPM package are different from what is in the package. The bash script in Example 14-6 will do this for your binaries. You will want to do something similar for any source or application RPMs you have installed. Any applications

Example 14-6 Package Verification Script

```
#!/bin/bash
#
DIR=/mnt/cdrom/RedHat/RPMS
touch /tmp/verify_packages
for file in 'ls -1 $DIR'
do
  echo "---Checking $file---" >> /tmp/verify_packages
  rpm -Vp $DIR/$file >> /tmp/verify_packages 2>&1
  echo "---Processing of $file complete ---" >> /tmp/verify_packages
done
exit 0
```

not in RPM form will also need to be verified. Be sure that you perform all of your verifications with the system out of the production environment.

If any verification procedure reports anomalies, follow up on each one. Many will be the result of normal system activity, but some will not. Those that fall into the latter category should be rectified by recovering from a pristine source. Do not run Tripwire until you have a high level of confidence that your system is pristine, or as near to pristine as you can make it.

Whichever course of action you take to ready your system for Tripwire, make sure that, after it is prepared, it does not go into the production environment until the initialization is complete. In particular, it would be safest to have it completely disconnected from the network unless you can verify that no rogue users are logged on and that no errant processes are running.

Storing the Database

After you have built your first database, you will want to store it on secure media. It is best to store it on removable media such as a removable disk, CD-ROM, or backup tape. In the case of removable media, be sure to secure it appropriately against both physical compromises and environmental effects (don't put the tape on top of a monitor, for example). The downside of using removable media is that it requires manual steps to use the database. If you will need to run Tripwire on a daily or more frequent basis, this becomes problematic.

If you must leave the database available on a system, a laptop or dedicated security server is ideal, because access can be restricted. As an alternative to these you could use a read-only filesystem on a very secure system in your production environment, although this has some obvious vulnerabilities—in particular, do you trust everyone who has access to the system? The best form of a read-only filesystem is a CD in a read-only drive.

An additional method of securely storing the database is to encrypt it. Consider this approach particularly if the database is to be stored on a read-only filesystem of a host that is connected to the production environment. Encrypting this file is a good idea no matter where the storage location. Example 14-7 provides an illustration of encrypting the database file (for a host called topcat) using PGP (discussed in *An Overview of PGP* on page 45) Version 2.6. This invocation of PGP uses symmetric encryption (IDEA) by virtue of the c flag and wipes out the original file by virtue of the w flag. As indicated, the encrypted file is now tw.db_topcat.pgp. If you are using PGP Version 5, you may encrypt the file with pgpe -c, but you will need to delete the original text file manually.

Another method for encrypting this file is to use CFS or TCFS as described in Chapter 15. This approach is advantageous when you have a number of these files—and perhaps other sensitive files—to encrypt. These two utilities offer the ability to encrypt the contents of an entire directory.

Example 14-7 Encrypting a Tripwire Database File with PGP

```
# pgp -cw tw.db_topcat
Pretty Good Privacy(tm) 2.6.3a - Public-key encryption for the masses.
(c) 1990-96 Philip Zimmermann, Phil's Pretty Good Software. 1996-03-04
Uses the RSAREF(tm) Toolkit, which is copyright RSA Data Security, Inc.
Distributed by the Massachusetts Institute of Technology.
Export of this software may be restricted by the U.S. government.
Current time: 1999/03/29 02:56 GMT

You need a pass phrase to encrypt the file.
Enter pass phrase:
Enter same pass phrase again: Just a moment....
Ciphertext file: tw.db_topcat.pgp

File tw.db_topcat wiped and deleted.
#
```

Once you have encrypted the database, store it in as secure a read-only location as possible. With the advent of writeable CDs, you may want to consider encrypting the data on CD and then mounting it in a read-only CD-ROM drive whenever you use it.

ROUTINE TRIPWIRE RUNS—COMPARE MODE

Now that you have the initial database, you will need to start checking your system against the database on a regular basis. The first question you'll need to answer is, how often should Tripwire be run? The answer depends largely on system use. Systems under heavy usage from untrusted sources such as the Internet may need Tripwire run hourly or even more frequently. Other important systems might run Tripwire daily, while others will run Tripwire every few days. For most systems that exist on an internal network and are used exclusively by presumably trusted users (recall from Chapter 2 that the majority of data compromises are effected internally), weekly should suffice.

The good news about Tripwire is that, if nothing has changed, you won't have any log files to read. It's only when something is modified that you will have to review the output. Let's begin by manually executing `tripwire` in compare mode; then we'll take a look at automating the process.

Running `tripwire` in compare mode requires no special options as was described in *The* `tripwire` *Command* on page 395. This is exhibited in Example 14-8. This example assumes that both the configuration file and database files are located on a read-only filesystem (`/usr/local/ro`) and are being run on a host called `topcat`. Notice that `imapd` has changed in the `/usr/sbin` directory. Tripwire reports that size, inode change times, and signatures are different. Time to check the log files and see what happened! It may be that this daemon was legitimately replaced, but if not a follow-up investigation must be performed. In all likelihood, if there have been any illegitimate modifications of system daemons, libraries, configuration files, etc., you will need to do a reinstallation from a pristine source. See Chapter 18 for further discussion of this issue.

Example 14-8 Running `tripwire` in Compare Mode

```
# tripwire -c /usr/local/ro/etc/tw.config.linux -d \
/usr/local/ro/bin/tw.db_topcat
### Phase 1:   Reading configuration file
### Phase 2:   Generating file list
### Phase 3:   Creating file information database
### Phase 4:   Searching for inconsistencies
###
###                     Total files scanned:        12512
###                             Files added:        2
###                           Files deleted:        0
###                           Files changed:        10657
###
###                     After applying rules:
###                        Changes discarded:        10656
###                        Changes remaining:        5
###
changed: drwxr-xr-x root           4096 Mar 29 16:03:50 1999 /usr/sbin
changed: -rwxr-xr-x root          44530 Mar 29 16:04:04 1999 /usr/sbin/imapd
### Phase 5:   Generating observed/expected pairs for changed files
###
### Attr          Observed (what it is)          Expected (what it should be)
### ==========  ============================  ==============================
/usr/sbin
      st_ctime: Mon Mar 29 16:03:50 1999     Thu Mar 11 15:43:10 1999
/usr/sbin/imapd
        st_size: 44530                       504580
       st_ctime: Mon Mar 29 16:04:04 1999    Sun Jan 31 05:03:45 1999
   md5 (sig1): 2SEH8A0cEcSuqnhaHpds7T         2FbdACI:R:FRz5PM1jK79y
 snefru (sig2): 3OKGd2JndFj.AX3DAB0z58        2KqGEYgjIk8Re0vDm13hW5
```

Clearly, if you have many systems, the manual execution of Tripwire in compare mode will not do. Perhaps the best way to manage Tripwire runs is to use scripts and `cron`. The `bash` script in Example 14-9 (line numbers added for clarity) illustrates a script that automates Tripwire checks. We assume that the configuration file and database are located on a read-only filesystem that we access locally via NFS. Further, we assume that both the configuration file and database are encrypted with PGP.

Example 14-9 Automating Tripwire Compare Runs

```
 1.  #!/bin/bash
 2.  #
 3.  # Decrypt tw database and run tripwire
 4.  #
 5.  # Call me paranoid
 6.  umask 077
 7.  # Set up PGP file descriptor
 8.  PGPPASSFD=0;export PGPPASSFD
 9.  # Set up pipe for encryption
10.  CPIPE=/root/.cpipe
11.  # Set up pipe for config file
12.  TPIPE=/root/.tpipe
13.  # Make & set restrictive permissions for the pipes
14.  mknod -m u=rw,go= $CPIPE p
15.  mknod -m u=rw,go= $TPIPE p
16.  #
```

Example 14-9 Automating Tripwire Compare Runs (Continued)

```
17.   # Send the config file to the tpipe
18.   cat /usr/local/ro/etc/tw.config.linux > $TPIPE&
19.   # Send the passphrase to the cpipe
20.   (echo "The red f0x juMped o'er the fence";cat \
21.      /usr/local/ro/bin/tw.db_topcat.pgp)|pgp -f > $CPIPE 2>/dev/null &
22.   # Start tripwire
23.   tripwire -dfd 4 -cfd 5 4<$CPIPE 5<$TPIPE > /root/Report 2>&1
24.   #
25.   # Clean up
26.   rm $CPIPE $TPIPE
27.   exit 0
```

There is a lot going on in this script, so it merits a discussion. From an overview perspective, we want to decrypt the database file and then pass it together with the configuration file to `tripwire` for the compare run. In this example we are using PGP, so we first need to use PGP to decrypt the file. PGP requires our passphrase to decrypt and will read it from the file descriptor specified in the environment variable `PGPPASSFD`, hence line 8. As noted in Table 14.4 on page 395, `tripwire` will accept input through open file descriptors; thus we set up FIFO files (first in, first out files, also called *pipes*) to do the job. Lines 9 through 15 handle the setup of these pipes. Once the pipes are built, we send the contents of the Tripwire configuration file to one (line 18) and the contents of the decrypted Tripwire database to the other (line 20). In line 23 it all comes together in the `tripwire` command with the output redirected to the file `/root/Report`. The directory `/root` should have very restrictive permissions (preferably `700`) since it contains the pipes and the final Tripwire output.

Notice that in line 20 the passphrase is echoed to standard output. Standard output uses file descriptor 0, which is why we set `PGPPASSFD` to 0.

Because the script must contain the passphrase for PGP decryption (only you can determine if this security-for-convenience tradeoff is worth the risk), it is a file that must be protected. So make sure that the file is set read-execute by root only and maintained in a root-owned, restricted access directory. To further the security of this operation, you may want to make the NFS resource, which contains the encrypted Tripwire configuration and database files, available only when necessary, mounting and unmounting these resources in the script. This can be accomplished on the NFS server by implementing a `cron` job, which exports the resources at the appropriate time. Or, in the case of a security server, it could be done whenever that system is attached to the production network.

In the case of Tripwire compare runs which occur less frequently than once an hour, you may wish to introduce some unpredictability into the times of your runs. This could be accomplished through the use of a script that randomly (or pseudorandomly) selects the time for the next Tripwire run and modifies `cron` accordingly. Such functionality could be added to the script in Example 14-9.

A Note on Performance

The slowest element of the Tripwire program is the computation of signatures. The README file found in the source directory (/usr/src/redhat/SOURCES/trip-wire-1.2) contains a lot of information about each of the signature algorithms and is well worth the time it takes to read. In short, if you find that your Tripwire compare runs are taking too much time, you may have to adjust which signatures and how many of them you require. MD5 and Haval are probably the fastest one-way hash functions that offer security value.

As an example of improving performance, suppose you are collecting the two signatures, MD5 and Snefru, for a large number of files. You can alternate which signatures you check each time you run Tripwire in compare mode by using the -i option; for example

```
# tripwire -i 2
```

will ignore Snefru signatures. Of course, you will occasionally want to check both signatures.

TRIPWIRE UPDATE MODE

The purpose of the Tripwire update mode is to allow you to make selective modifications to the Tripwire database. For example, if the modification to imapd in Example 14-8 on page 400 proved to be an authorized modification, you would want to update the database so that future Tripwire compare runs do not report the same problem. Example 14-10 shows updating of the database.

Example 14-10 Updating a File in the Tripwire Database

```
# tripwire -update /usr/sbin /usr/sbin/imapd
### Phase 1:    Reading configuration file
### Phase 2:    Generating file list
Updating: update entry: /usr/sbin
Updating: update file: /usr/sbin/imapd
### Phase 3:    Updating file information database
###
### Old database file will be moved to 'tw.db_topcat.old'
###            in ./databases.
###
### Updated database will be stored in './databases/tw.db_topcat'
###            (Tripwire expects it to be moved to '/var/spool/tripwire'.)
###
```

NOTE

If you are currently using read-only filesystems for storing your database files (which you should), you will need to remount them as read/write filesystems for the updating process. Or you may wish to copy the files temporarily to their default locations for the update and then manually copy them back to their secure locations (still requires a remount read/write for the copy operation).

Another useful aspect of the update mode is that there will be times when you would like to add an entry to the configuration file. Instead of completely reinitializing the database, you could execute a command such as that shown in Example 14-11. In this example, assume that we have added an entry to fingerprint the /usr/src directory.

Example 14-11 Updating a Configuration Entry in the Tripwire Database

```
# tripwire -update /usr/src
### Phase 1:   Reading configuration file
### Phase 2:   Generating file list
Updating: add entry: /usr/src
### Phase 3:   Updating file information database
###
### Old database file will be moved to 'tw.db_topcat.old'
###          in ./databases.
###
### Updated database will be stored in './databases/tw.db_topcat'
###          (Tripwire expects it to be moved to '/var/spool/tripwire'.)
###
```

WARNING!

Whenever you run Tripwire in update mode to incorporate additions or modifications to the associated Tripwire configuration file, inconsistencies between the configuration file and the database may occur. The twdb_check.pl Perl script will take care of this problem. After an update such as that shown in Example 14-11 is made, simply run twdb_check.pl (you must have Perl installed!) as shown below. Note that no output will be generated (except for error messages).

perl ./twdb_check.pl /var/spool/tripwire/tw.db_topcat /etc/tw.config

Notice that twdb_check.pl requires the database followed by the configuration file as arguments. It is not necessary to use this script with Tripwire Version 1.3 or later.

Generally speaking, Tripwire updates should be performed manually. The exception might be, for example, when you update a software package throughout a production environment that is currently tripwired. In such a case, the use of scripts to automate the update of each system's Tripwire database is warranted.

SUMMARY

In this chapter, we looked at the very important utility, Tripwire. We explored its installation, configuration, and run-time options. We described its value as a file integrity checker which, when used properly, is capable of alerting you to potential exploits. We emphasized the need for securely storing the Tripwire database(s), configuration file(s), and program.

FOR FURTHER READING

On-Line Documentation

The following list represents the documentation that comes with Tripwire.

```
/usr/doc/tripwire-1.2/Changelog
/usr/doc/tripwire-1.2/FAQ
/usr/doc/tripwire-1.2/INTERNALS
/usr/doc/tripwire-1.2/README
/usr/doc/tripwire-1.2/README.FIRST
/usr/doc/tripwire-1.2/Readme
/usr/doc/tripwire-1.2/TODO
/usr/doc/tripwire-1.2/WHATSNEW
/usr/doc/tripwire-1.2/docs
/usr/doc/tripwire-1.2/docs/README
/usr/doc/tripwire-1.2/docs/appdev.txt
/usr/doc/tripwire-1.2/docs/designdoc.ps
/usr/doc/tripwire-1.2/docs/sans.txt
/usr/man/man5/tw.config.5
/usr/man/man8/siggen.8
/usr/man/man8/tripwire.8
```

Web Site

The following web resource contains additional information about Tripwire.

```
http://www.tripwiresecurity.com/
```

Space, the Cracker Frontier

The Cryptographic and Transparent Cryptographic Filesystems

Encryption is a wonderful thing. In a day and age when you never can be sure who's accessing your system, the ability to protect your data through encryption can help you sleep at night. In this chapter we will explore two publicly available tools—the Cryptographic File System (CFS) and the Transparent Cryptographic File System (TCFS)—that will assist you in securing your data.

Both of these utilities operate based on the NFS client-server model, so you will need to make sure that NFS client and server functionality are available on appropriate systems.

OVERVIEW OF THE CRYPTOGRAPHIC FILE SYSTEM

We will take a look at CFS first as it is at the heart of TCFS. In *CFS and TCFS Comparison* on page 431 we will consider the differences between the two.

Unlike PGP, which is capable of encrypting data on a per-file basis, CFS provides a mechanism to encrypt directories and their contents through the standard UNIX filesystem interface. In this way, CFS allows for the encryption of files and directories through almost any filesystem, including the Linux ext2 filesystem and NFS. CFS never stores any cleartext on disk, nor does it ever forward any cleartext over the network.

Users create and access their encrypted directories through the use of a passphrase, which is used to generate the cryptographic key (or keys) for the user-chosen cryptographic algorithm. Once the CFS directory is created, users may access it with the `cattach` command and their passphrase. Everything created inside the CFS directory will be encrypted transparently to the user.

From a system-administrative perspective, the initial setup of CFS is quite simple and is described in *CFS Administrative Tasks* on page 408. The major impact of CFS is on performance related to active reads and writes to CFS resources that require decryption and encryption (backups and restores; for example, capturing and recovering CFS resources in their encrypted state). In environments in which multiple simultaneous access to CFS is anticipated, systems should be configured with copious amounts of memory and high-speed processors. Alternatively, such environments may well benefit from TCFS instead, which is discussed in *Overview of TCFS* on page 416.

CFS Flow of Events

The CFS implementation is not complicated. Figure 15.1 shows the way in which an application passes read/write requests to the CFS daemon (`cfsd`) for decryption and encryption services.

The application actually knows nothing about CFS as it is dealing with a local directory. That local directory simply happens to be an NFS mount point attached to `cfsd` through the `localhost` (loopback interface) at port 3049 (by default). The `cfsd` acts as both an NFS server, which responds to client requests through the mount point (normally `/crypt`), and the encryption engine. The `cfsd` receives and passes encrypted data to the filesystem (through a system call). The filesystem treats the read/write requests from `cfsd` as it would any other read/write request. Thus, the encryption/decryption mechanism is completely transparent to users and the kernel.

Now let's look at obtaining and installing CFS.

OBTAINING AND INSTALLING CFS

CFS was written by Matt Blaze (copyright AT&T). It is freely available, but is subject to the United States export control laws. See the `README.install` file in your build directory for more details.

At the time of this writing, the latest version of CFS is 1.4.0beta2. It is available in the United States and Canada at

```
http://cryptography.org/
```

where you will have to first certify that you are a citizen or permanent resident of the United States or Canada. Then you will be allowed access to the download page (which changes regularly).

Version 1.3.3 of CFS is available worldwide at

```
http://www.replay.com/redhat/cfs.html
```

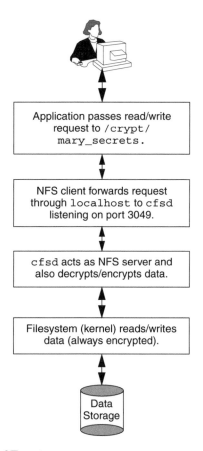

Fig. 15.1 CFS Flow of Events

in RPM format. Both source and ix86 binary RPMs are there. If you wish to simply install the RPM, check the PGP signature and then execute

```
# rpm -ivh cfs-1.3.3-3.i386.rpm
```

You may also install the source RPM similarly.

If you wish to compile the 1.4.0beta2 version, you will need to make a number of changes. These changes will allow for compilation on either Red Hat 5.2 or 6.0. First extract the distribution in a build directory (we will use /usr/src/custom/cfs1.4),

```
# ed/usr/src/custom/cfs1.4
# tar xzvf cfs.1.4.0.beta2_tar.gz
```

In the Makefile, make sure that the flags listed in Example 15-1 are set as shown. Also be sure to comment out the line CC=you_forgot_to_edit_-the_makefile, as shown in Example 15-1.

Example 15-1 Correct CFS Version 1.4.0beta2 `Makefile` Entries

```
<many lines not shown>
BINDIR=/usr/bin    # For our examples
ETCDIR=/usr/sbin   # For our examples
<many lines not shown>
CC=gcc
COPT=-O2 -DPROTOTYPES=1
<many lines not shown>
CFLAGS=$(COPT) -U__STDC__ -D_fileno=d_ino -I$(RINCLUDES)
LIBS=
COMPAT=
RPCOPTS= -k -b
#CC=you_forgot_to_edit_the_makefile
<many lines not shown>
<remainder of file not shown>
```

Next, you will need to apply some corrections to the file `truerand.c` (see `http://www.mit.edu:8008/bloom-picayune/cfs/`). In that file, find

```
longjmp(env,1);
```

and change it to

```
siglongjmp(env, 1);
```

Also find

```
if (setjmp(env))
```

and change it to

```
if (sigsetjmp(env,1))
```

Save the changes and close the file. Now run

```
# make cfs
# make install_cfs
```

and your compilation and installation should proceed without difficulty.

NOTE

> If compilation fails when you run `make cfs`, modify the files `admproto_svr.c` and `nfsproto_svr.c` so that all instances of `xdr_argument` and `xdr_result` are `_xdr_argument` and `_xdr_result`, respectively. Do not globally replace these variables because some instances will already have the leading underscore, `_`. This step must be performed after the failure of `make cfs`.

Now you are ready to set up CFS.

CFS Administrative Tasks

After installing CFS (either version), the root user will need to configure CFS for use. The steps are fairly simple and once done may be automated through start-up scripts. The following two sections cover the details.

Establishing the Bootstrap Mount Point

NOTE

> If you installed CFS by installing `cfs-1.3.3-3.i386.rpm`, you need to execute only the `exportfs -a` step in this section.

CFS requires a bootstrap mount point for the cleartext directories (called *virtual directories*). You may choose whatever name for this mount point you wish. We will use `/.cfsfs`. Create the directory and set the permissions to null.

```
# mkdir /.cfsfs
# chmod 0 /.cfsfs
```

Export this newly created resource by placing the following entry in `/etc/exports`

```
/.cfsfs    localhost
```

and export the resource with

```
# /usr/sbin/exportfs -a
```

At each reboot, this resource will automatically be exported, due to its presence in `/etc/exports`.

Next create the CFS mount point. Again, choose any name. For our examples, we will use `/crypt`.

```
# mkdir /crypt
# chmod 755 /crypt
```

At this point, you are ready to make the resource available.

Running `cfsd` and Mounting the Bootstrap   In order to mount the virtual directory `/crypt` to the bootstrap mount point `/.cfsfs`, you first need to run `cfsd`. By default, `cfsd` runs on port 3049, but, if for some reason you cannot allow `cfsd` to run on that port, you may specify the desired port number as an argument; for example, starting it at the default port 3049

```
# /usr/sbin/cfsd
```

or at a different port, say 9111,

```
# /usr/sbin/cfsd 9111
```

Next, mount the virtual directory to the bootstrap directory.

```
# /bin/mount -o port=3049,intr localhost:/.cfsfs /crypt
```

The option `port=3049` is required since by default the `mount` command attempts to communicate with NFS, which listens to port number 2049. You will probably want to automate this process in a start-up script, such as `/etc/rc.d/rc.local`. The script fragment in Example 15-2 will do the trick.

Example 15-2 Starting `cfsd` and Mounting the Virtual Directory

```
if [ -x /usr/sbin/cfsd ]; then
/usr/sbin/cfsd && \
/bin/mount -o port=3049, intr localhost:/.cfsfs /crypt
fi
```

You may now begin to use CFS!

USING CFS

Once CFS is installed and properly configured, it is available to users on the system. Let's step through the process of setting up and using a CFS directory.

Creating and Attaching CFS Directories

Suppose that Mary, who just found out that the system administrator installed CFS, wants to create an encrypted directory of files on her system. All she needs to do is use the `cmkdir` command to create the CFS directory anywhere she has permissions and then use the `cattach` command to gain access to the directory and its contents in an unencrypted form. Example 15-3 shows the user, `mary`, creating the CFS directory with `cmkdir`. We include the `pwd` command and its output to verify the current working directory. The `ls -ld` command at the end of the example is included to show that the directory was created and appears to be a normal subdirectory of `/home/mary`. After executing `cmkdir secrets`, notice the `Key:` and `Again:` prompts. This is where the passphrase (which is not echoed back to the screen) is entered (`Key:`) and repeated (`Again:`). The passphrase must be at least 16 characters. Don't forget what you decide to use as the passphrase! There is no recovery mechanism for forgotten passphrases outside of cryptanalysis.

Example 15-3 Using `cmkdir` to Create a CFS Directory

```
[mary@topcat]$ pwd
/home/mary
[mary@topcat]$ cmkdir secrets
Key:
Again:
[mary@topcat]$ ls -ld secrets
drwxrwxr-x   2 mary       mary            1024 Jul  9 13:29 secrets
[mary@topcat]$
```

It is also important to choose good passphrases. For example, the non-grammatical phrase

```
Car purple/whiTe: *speed*; rAdaR av0id!
```
[1]

---

1. Since this passphrase is published, don't use it!

is a reasonably good passphrase that is easy to remember (for some people, anyway). Maybe not so easy to type, though.

NOTE

> There will be a noticeable delay after the passphrase is successfully entered twice before control returns to the shell in the form of a command line prompt. Depending on processor speed and available memory, it could take anywhere from 5 to 30 seconds.

Now that the CFS directory exists, Mary needs to attach it to the local /crypt mount point so that she can access it in an unencrypted form. Example 15-4 displays the use of the cattach command for this purpose.

Example 15-4 Attaching a CFS Directory to the cfsd Mount Point

```
[mary@topcat mary]$ cattach /home/mary/secrets mary_secrets
Key:
[mary@topcat mary]$ ls -ld /crypt/mary_secrets
drwx------   2 mary      mary           1024 Jul  9 13:29 /crypt/
mary_secrets
[mary@topcat mary]$
```

Once again, we include the ls -ld command to verify the result. Notice that the attached directory is read/write/execute by mary only. At this point she can start creating secret files in the /crypt/mary_secrets directory (we will refer to this type of attached directory as a *virtual* directory).

WARNING!

> After a CFS directory has been attached to the /crypt mount point, the only security afforded the directory and its contents are the permission settings. In other words, root can easily access the attached resources.

Creating files and or subdirectories in the attached CFS directory is identical to working in normal directories. Example 15-5 shows a simple ASCII file—really_secret—as created by Mary in the virtual directory /crypt/mary_secrets. The contents of the file and the file itself will actually be stored in encrypted form in the CFS directory /home/mary/secrets. This means that every time the data is viewed through a command like cat, it must be decrypted.

Example 15-5 A Simple ASCII File in the Virtual Directory

```
[mary@topcat]$ cat /crypt/mary_secrets/really_secret
        This data is so confidential that we cannot
        print it here.
[mary@topcat]$
```

Let's take a look at the contents of the CFS directory /home/mary/
secrets. Example 15-6 displays the contents of that directory. It shows us that

Example 15-6 The Encrypted File Corresponding to Example 15-5

```
[mary@topcat]$ ls -la /home/mary/secrets
total 7
drwxrwxr-x   2 mary      mary         1024 Jul  9 19:05 .
drwx------   6 mary      mary         1024 Jul  9 16:05 ..
-rw-rw-r--   1 mary      mary            8 Jul  9 14:49 ...
-rw-rw-r--   1 mary      mary            1 Jul  9 14:49 ..c
-rw-rw-r--   1 mary      mary           32 Jul  9 18:25 ..k
-rw-rw-r--   1 mary      mary            7 Jul  9 14:49 ..s
lrwxrwxrwx   1 mary      mary            8 Jul  9 14:55
.pvect_f8104dd80de59f7e9d70ae1786efdbed -> 3498949a
-rw-rw-r--   1 mary      mary           70 Jul  9 14:55
f8104dd80de59f7e9d70ae1786efdbed
[mary@topcat]$
[mary@topcat]$ cat secrets/f8104dd80de59f7e9d70ae1786efdbed
«0ÖJRo8´>f!_hÊÅäSR8óK5Q(îWëÏæ!ØaÆi`üF]«
                                       |úrO
gN{¬N:è4[mary@topcat]$
```

the encrypted file name associated with /crypt/mary_secrets is /home/mary/
secrets/f8104dd80de59f7e9d70ae1786efdbed. And, when Mary cat's that file
out, she sees the encrypted data as shown at the end of Example 15-6.

So what are all those "dot" files? Table 15.1 explains them.

NOTE

You can certainly remove encrypted files with the rm command. However, since the
filenames are encrypted, as your list of files grows it will become difficult to determine which file is which. So it is best to cattach the CFS directory and then delete
files through the virtual directory.

Table 15.1 Dot Files in Encrypted CFS Directory

Dot File	Purpose
...	Contains the cleartext hash of the keys.
..c	Identifies the cipher algorithm used.
..k	The encrypted key file. This encrypted file contains the keys used to encrypt the files in this directory. It is decrypted with the passphrase.
..s	Cipher block size.
.pvect_*	This file is a symbolic link that points to a string containing the initial-ization vector (IV—see the references cited in *Cryptography References* on page 47 for more information about IVs) used for encrypting the file. Each file will have one of these, with the encrypted filename in place of the * as long as the -1 flag is not used with cattach (see Table 15.4 on page 415).

When Mary has finished using the encrypted directory, she can detach it with the cdetach command as shown in Example 15-7. This destroys the vir-

Example 15-7 Detaching the Virtual Directory

```
[mary@topcat]$ cdetach mary_secrets
[mary@topcat]$ ls -l /crypt
total 0
[mary@topcat]$
```

tual directory. Subsequent attachments may be made using the same virtual directory name (mary_secrets, in this case) or an entirely different name. However, any files that were created in the virtual directory will retain their original names because they as well as their contents were encrypted.

WARNING!

Any user can detach any virtual directory regardless of which user issued the original cattach command! For example, the user paul could have executed the cdetach command shown in Example 15-7 successfully. It is almost a foregone conclusion that such action will occur inadvertently on systems with many users. This will most likely lead to data loss if a file is open during the detach operation (and will certainly produce a core file). It is also a potential source of denial-of-service attacks.

Mary may also change her passphrase for a given CFS directory. Example 15-8 illustrates this capability using the cpasswd command. Note that the cpasswd command requires the CFS directory and not the virtual directory as an argument.

Example 15-8 Changing a CFS Directory's Passphrase

```
[mary@topcat]$ cpasswd secrets
Old passphrase:
New passphrase:
Again:
[mary@topcat]$
```

Deleting CFS Directories Deleting directories created with cmkdir is accomplished with rm -r. For example, Mary may delete her secrets directory with the command

```
[mary@topcat]$ rm -r /home/mary/secrets
```

Mary uses rm -r due to the various dot files (as shown in Table 15.1 on page 412) retained in the directory. An alternative approach (and one that is less likely to cause inadvertent removals) is to remove all of the dot files in the CFS directory and then remove the CFS directory with rmdir.

Now that we've seen some examples, let's take a look at the available CFS commands and daemon as well as their options.

The CFS Commands and Daemon Detailed

Table 15.2 lists the commands and daemon associated with CFS and tells which CFS version uses what commands.

The cmkdir and cattach Commands.   While we have seen example uses of the cmkdir and cattach commands, we need to know what their options are. Table 15.3 details the options for cmkdir.

The general syntax of the cmkdir command is

```
cmkdir [ options ] directory
```

where directory may be absolutely or relatively qualified and where it reflects the name of the CFS directory.

The cattach options are given in Table 15.4. The -i option may be quite useful if you walk away from your system or forget to detach the CFS directory.

Table 15.2 CFS Commands

Commands and Daemon	CFS Version	Description
cfsd	All[*]	The CFS encryption engine and NFS server.
cmkdir	All	Used to create CFS directories.
cattach	All	Attaches CFS directories to virtual directories. The virtual directory presents data in cleartext.
cdetach	All	Detaches virtual directories from CFS directories.
cpasswd	All	Used to change CFS directory passphrases.
cmkkey	1.4.0	Allows for multiple passphrases to be associated with one CFS directory.
cname	Prior to 1.3	Lists the actual filenames of a CFS directory.
ccat	Prior to 1.3	Decrypts an encrypted file and displays its contents to standard output.
ssh/cfssh	All	A shell script that cattachs the specified CFS directory to a pseudorandomly chosen virtual directory; then execs a new shell in the virtual directory. This script will not work unmodified with /bin/bash, but will work with /bin/ksh.
esm	All	Encrypted session manager (ESM). A prototype of a session layer (OSI model; see *General TCP/IP Networking Resources* on page 39) encryption mechanism. Has no authentication mechanism and does not encrypt passwords. Use SSH instead (see Chapter 11).

[*]In the context of this table, all means CFS versions 1.3.x and later.

Table 15.3 Options to cmkdir

Option	Description
-1 or -d	Specifies the use of a two-key (112-bit) hybrid DES encryption.
-2	Specifies the use of two-key triple DES encryption. See *Symmetric Encryption* on page 42. This is the default for CFS Versions 1.3.x and later.
-3	Specifies the use of three-key triple DES encryption. Often referred to as "true" triple DES.
-b	Specifies the Blowfish cipher. Not implemented until version 1.4.0.
-m	Specifies the MacGuffin cipher. This cipher is included as an example and is not recommended. It is considered to be a weak encryption mechanism given its key size of 128 bits.
-s	Specifies the SAFER-SK128 cipher.
-o	Old mode. Causes the CFS directories created to be readable by versions prior to 1.3.2 (compatibility mode).
-p	Causes the directories to use less memory when attached. May reduce security somewhat as files created under such a directory may have more information revealed.
--	Causes cmkdir to read the passphrase from standard input.

Table 15.4 Options to cattach

Option	Description
-1	Lower security mode. If used, identical cleartext files will encrypt to identical ciphertext files. In this case .pvect_* (see Table 15.1 on page 412) symbolic links will not exist. In heavy-use situations this mode may need to be used to avoid race conditions.
-t *min*	Sets the time-out of the attach in minutes. After this time, the virtual directory will automatically be detached from the CFS directory. May be specified at compiletime. Default is no time-out.
-i *min*	Sets the idle time-out. If a virtual directory goes unused for min minutes, the virtual directory will be detached from its CFS directory. May be specified at compiletime. Default is no time-out.
--	Specifies that the passphrase is to be read from standard input.

Using CFS over NFS

Using CFS in conjunction with NFS requires no additional configuration. CFS must be installed and configured on the local system. The filesystem in which the encrypted directory resides does not matter. Example 15-3 could just as well have been performed on an NFS-mounted home directory; the results are the same. In particular, all of the data sent over the network to the NFS server containing the physical disk is encrypted.

VULNERABILITIES OF CFS

CFS suffers from a variety of vulnerabilities. It uses NFS internally on the local host and is therefore susceptible to any vulnerabilities associated with the mount daemon. While it never stores cleartext in a filesystem or sends it over the network, it is a user application and thus it is susceptible to paging and swapping activity, which means that passphrases or cleartext may be temporarily stored in swap. Error conditions such as detaching a virtual directory while in use may cause passphrases or other sensitive information to be written into a core file. The fact that any user can detach any virtual filesystem is cause for concern. And, of course, weak or disclosed passphrases probably pose the greatest vulnerability.

Despite its weaknesses, CFS is a very powerful utility for protecting data, especially for one-user systems. Its simplicity and ease of installation make it very attractive.

OVERVIEW OF TCFS

In the sense that TCFS interposes itself between the user and the filesystem, and that it uses NFS to handle the local cleartext communications, it is similar to CFS. Also, as with CFS, TCFS guarantees that no cleartext is ever stored in a filesystem or sent over the network. But the similarities end there; TCFS uses a kernel module to replace the functionality of cfsd. In that kernel module, TCFS introduces a filesystem type—tcfs—with which to establish the TCFS-mounted directory. It uses a daemon xattrd on the server to help associate the keys with particular mounted NFS directories. Instead of associating passphrases (and therefore keys) with each encrypted directory, it associates keys with users based on their user passwords, and all access is determined by this association. The user password is used to encrypt the key that is used for file encryption and decryption.

The fact that TCFS provides a kernel module and incorporates a separate filesystem type does dramatically improve performance. It also means that all keys and cleartext-to-ciphertext (and vice versa) conversions are handled in the kernel. This provides somewhat greater security because keys and cleartext are revealed only in kernel memory or in a virtual filesystem (the local NFS mount) cache for shorter periods of time. However, it also means that there is a significant amount of administrative effort for every system that needs to be a TCFS client.

The additional administrative requirements are nontrivial. Each system participating in TCFS encryption will need to have numerous utilities replaced and the kernel patched and rebuilt. Furthermore, the system administrator will need to mount TCFS resources as necessary whenever a user needs to access his or her encrypted resource.

OBTAINING AND INSTALLING TCFS

TCFS continues to be developed at Universita' Degli Studi Di Salerno in Italy. The current developers include Luigi Catuogno, Andrea Cozzolino, Angelo Celentano, Luigi Della Monica, Aniello Del Sorbo, and Ermelindo Mauriello. This group is led by Giuseppe Cattaneo and Giuseppe Persiano. TCFS is distributed under the GPL. As of this writing, TCFS is supported only on kernel 2.0.x versions. It is available from

```
http://tcfs.dia.unisa.it/
```

where you will find the full distribution, `tcfs-2.2.2-distrib.tar.gz`. After downloading, you may extract the distribution with `tar xvfz tcfs-2.2.2-distrib.tar.gz`. Then the fun will begin!

The distribution contains the TCFS source code for the `tcfs` kernel module; the kernel patch; the TCFS library; modified `mount`, shadow, and `ext2` filesystem utilities; and the encryption kernel module. The distribution packages are described in Table 15.5.

TCFS may be built in the following way. Many of the steps must be executed as root, especially the `make install` steps. It may be easiest to execute all steps as root, as shown in the two lists below. The first, in *The TCFS Client Side* on page 417, is for building the client-side software; the second, in *The TCFS Server Side* on page 424, is for the server side. Any system may act in both client and server capacities. All steps assume that the Linux source tree is located in `/usr/src/linux` (the default for Red Hat). If your source tree is in a different location, you will need to modify the `Makefiles` appropriately.

THE TCFS CLIENT SIDE

The following steps, together with the section *Rebuilding and Recompiling the Kernel* on page 420, constitute the necessary actions to implement TCFS on a client system.

1. Using the command given below, extract the distribution software into a working directory, such as `/usr/src/custom/tcfs` (we will refer to this working directory throughout these steps).

Table 15.5 TCFS Distribution

Distribution File	Contents
`tcfs-2.2.2-distrib.tar.gz`	The distribution GNU-compressed `tar` file. It contains all of the other `tar` and patch files.
`patch-linux-2.0.x`	The patch to the Linux 2.0.x kernel.
`tcfs-2.2.2.tar.gz`	The TCFS source code for the `tcfs` filesystem kernel module and the TCFS encryption module (`3desmodule`).
`tcfslib-0.3.1.tar.gz`	The TCFS library. It contains the source code used to build the key management database libraries.
`tcfsutils-1.2.1.tar.gz`	Contains the utilities used for configuring and managing TCFS users and keys. The utilities are `tcfsgenkey`, `tcfsputkey`, `tcfsrmkey`, `tcfsviewkey`, `tcfsadduser`, `tcfsrmuser`, `tcfsaddgroup`, and `tcfsrmgroup`. These utilities are discussed in subsequent sections.
`mount-2.71-tcfs.tar.gz`	Contains the replacement `mount`, `swapon`, and `losetup` programs.
`e2fsprogs-1.12-tcfs.tar.gz`	The replacement ext2 filesystem programs. Included are `chattr`, `lsattr`, `mke2fs`, `badblocks`, `tune2fs`, `dumpe2fs`, `e2label`, and `fsck`. New attributes are added to `chattr` as described in the section, *Extended Attributes for TCFS* on page 427.
`shadow-980529-tcfs.tar.gz`	Contains replacement `chage`, `pwconv`, `gpconv`, and other programs contained in the `shadow-utils` RPM.
`xattrd-2.1.tar.gz`	Contains the server-side TCFS daemon `xattrd`. This daemon responds to TCFS queries regarding the secure attributes associated with the TCFS resources. It is necessary because NFS cannot handle `ext2` extended file attributes. The `ext2` extended attributes as they relate to TCFS are discussed in *Extended Attributes for TCFS* on page 427.

```
# cd /usr/src/custom/tcfs
# tar xvfz tcfs-2.2.2-distrib.tar.gz
```

The extraction will create the subdirectory `/usr/src/custom/tcfs/tcfs-2.2.2`, yielding the files listed in the *Distribution File* column of Table 15.5.

2. Apply the kernel patch

```
# cd /usr/src
# patch -p0 < /usr/src/custom/tcfs/tcfs-2.2.2/patch-linux-2.0.x
```

3. Extract the source code to the TCFS kernel module into the Linux source tree (the Linux source tree on Red Hat systems is in /usr/src/linux).

```
# cd /usr/src
# tar xzvf /usr/src/custom/tcfs/tcfs-2.2.2/tcfs-2.2.2.tar.gz
```

4. Extract the TCFS library into the working directory.

```
# cd /usr/src/custom/tcfs/tcfs-2.2.2
# tar xzvf tcfslib-0.3.1.tar.gz
```

This will create the subdirectory /usr/src/custom/tcfs/tcfs-2.2.2/tcf-slib-0.3.1. Next you will need to compile and install the libraries and the TCFS PAM module. Execute

```
# cd tcfslib-0.3.1
# make
# make install
# make pam_module
# cp pam_tcfs.so /lib/security
```

to complete this task. Note that the output from these commands has been omitted, as will be the case throughout these steps.

5. You will need to install the user and key management tools. Extract and make as shown below.

```
# cd /usr/src/custom/tcfs/tcfs-2.2.2
# tar xzvf tcfsutils-1.2.1.tar.gz
```

Change the Makefile in /usr/src/custom/tcfs/tcfs-2.2.2/tcfsutils-1.2.1/src so that the lines appear as follows (yes, is instead of if in the comments).

```
# Uncomment line below is you use GLIBC
LOADLIBES=-lcrypt -ltcfs
# Uncomment the line below is you do not have GLIBC
#LOADLIBES=-ltcfs
```

Then

```
# cd /usr/src/custom/tcfs/tcfs-2.2.2/tcfsutils-1.2.1/src
# make
# make install
```

WARNING!

The next three steps involve replacing system utilities. Before proceeding you need to make sure that doing so will not disturb other applications or system utilities on your computer. To do this, verify that the version numbers of the utilities in these next three steps are greater than or equal to those utilities currently installed on your system. To be on the safe side, you may wish to make copies of the programs that will be installed (see Table 15.5 on page 418) prior to proceeding.

6. Extract and make the modified mount, swapon, and losetup programs.

```
# cd /usr/src/custom/tcfs/tcfs-2.2.2/contrib
# tar xzvf mount-2.7l-tcfs.tar.gz
# make
# make install
```

7. Extract, configure, make, and make install the replacement ext2 filesystem programs.

```
# cd /usr/src/custom/tcfs/tcfs-2.2.2/contrib
# tar xzvf e2fsprogs-1.12-tcfs.tar.gz
# cd /usr/src/custom/tcfs/tcfs-2.2.2/contrib/e2fsprogs-1.12-tcfs
# ./configure
# make
# make install
```

8. Create the replacement shadow utilities. Note that one option to configure is --disable-desrpc; you will need to specify this option unless you are using Secure RPC. You must use the --with-libtcfs option and should use the --with-libpam option if you are using PAM.

```
# cd /usr/src/custom/tcfs/tcfs-2.2.2/contrib
# tar xzvf shadow-980529-tcfs.tar.gz
# cd /usr/src/custom/tcfs/tcfs-2.2.2/contrib/shadow-980529-tcfs
# ./configure --disable-desrpc --with-libtcfs --with-libpam
# make
# make install
```

All necessary steps prior to building a new kernel are complete.

Rebuilding and Recompiling the Kernel   The commands outlined in this section are designed to prevent the clobbering of your existing kernel. This way, if the new kernel does not build properly, you will be able to recover by rebooting. In particular, we will use the LILO to accomplish this task.

NOTE

If you are unfamiliar with kernel compilation and building, you should read the /usr/src/linux/README and /usr/doc/HOWTO/Kernel-HOWTO files before proceeding with building a Linux kernel. You will also find additional information related to the kernel in the Red Hat documentation. The steps outlined here assume that you are building the kernel with TCFS support as the only additional component.

For details about LILO, see /usr/doc/lilo-0.20/README and the lilo(8) and lilo.conf(5) man pages.

Since the Linux 2.0.x kernel includes support for loadable kernel modules, there is rarely a need to recompile the kernel. It is necessary only when additional modules, device drivers, or core kernel modifications are desired or required. Such is the case with TCFS. TCFS may be included as a loadable kernel module (preferred approach) or added to the kernel as part of its core (the portion of the kernel that is static and is always resident). Either way, we must rebuild the kernel to include TCFS support.

In order for the following procedure to work, you must have the kernel source tree loaded. The following packages on Red Hat 5.2 (Red Hat 6.0 is identical except for version numbers) represent the minimum necessary. Note that the 2.0.36-0.7 suffix represents the kernel version. Make a note of the version on your system. TCFS requires version 2.0.x.

```
kernel-2.0.36-0.7
kernel-headers-2.0.36-0.7
kernel-source-2.0.36-0.7
kernelcfg-0.5-3
```

If you require Peripheral Component Interconnect (PCI) support, you will also need kernel-pcmcia-cs-2.0.36-0.7. You may determine if these packages are loaded on your system by executing the command

```
# rpm -qa|grep kernel
```

If you are missing anything, install the missing packages before going on.

If you have previously built another kernel and you wish to save configuration information about that kernel, do so now. Executing the next command will remove anything you have done previously.

Start with a clean distribution.

```
# cd /usr/src/linux
# make mrproper
```

Next, create a configuration file to be used for the kernel build. This can be accomplished with one of the commands listed in Table 15.6. The successful

Table 15.6 Kernel Configuration Methods

Configuration Command	Description
make config	An interactive command-line program. For each kernel component, you will have the opportunity to provide a Y (build into the kernel core), M (build a loadable kernel module), or N (do not include in the kernel) answer. Defaults may be accepted with a carriage return.
make menuconfig	A graphic, menu-driven program. Functionally similar to the Red Hat installation program. The menus allow you to navigate through the configuration options at will. Upon selecting Exit, you will be prompted whether or not to save the configuration. Defaults are indicated.
make xconfig	An X Window System program. Similar to menuconfig except that the use of a mouse is required for input. Defaults are preselected.

execution of one of these commands will create the `.config` and `Makefile` files
in `/usr/src/linux`. Choose the one that you prefer, but you will likely find `make
menuconfig` or `make xconfig` to be easier to use. Whichever one you use, you
must ensure that loadable kernel modules are supported. The easiest way to
verify this is to view the `/usr/src/linux/.config` file created by one of the
three commands in Table 15.6 and make sure that the following entries are as
shown below.

```
CONFIG_MODULES=y
CONFIG_MODVERSIONS=y
CONFIG_KERNELD=y
```

These values are the defaults, so unless you inadvertently change one of them,
this is how they will appear. Also, make sure that you select TCFS support.
You will find an entry for TCFS support in the `Filesystems` menu of either
`make menuconfig` or `make xconfig`. Verify by making sure that either

```
HAVE_TCFS=m
```

or

```
HAVE_TCFS=y
```

exists in the `/usr/src/linux/.config` file. If the entry `HAVE_TCFS=m` is used,
then TCFS will be built as a loadable module.

Now we can test the configuration with

```
# make dep
```

which will report any dependency problems with the kernel build. If there are
none, clean up the depend,

```
# make clean
```

If you do run into problems with `make dep`, you will need to correct them and
try the `make dep` and `make clean` again.

There is one header file required by the TCFS kernel module that must
be copied to `/usr/src/linux-2.0.36/include/linux` prior to beginning the
build. Execute the following command to remedy the problem.

```
# cp /usr/src/custom/tcfs/tcfs-2.2.2/modules/3desmodule/kdes.h /usr/
src/linux-2.0.36/include/linux/kdes.h
```

Now, begin the build in `/usr/src/linux`.

```
# make boot
```

This will create the static core kernel and place it in the file `/usr/src/linux-
2.0.36/arch/i386/boot/zImage`. Next build the modules.

```
# make modules
```

This step will take some time. Once complete, you need to install the modules.
First move the original modules to a saved directory; then install them.

```
# mv /lib/modules/2.0.36-0.7 /lib/modules/2.0.36-0.7.old
# make modules_install
```

This last command will create the new /lib/modules/2.0.36 directory. To complete the TCFS additions, you need to build and add the triple DES module (note that, by default, this is the only encryption algorithm supported by TCFS).

```
# cd /usr/src/custom/tcfs/tcfs-2.2.2/modules/3desmodule
# make
# cp tcfs_default_module.o /lib/modules/2.0.36/fs
```

At last we can move the executable static kernel image to the boot directory.

```
# cp /usr/src/linux-2.0.36/arch/i386/boot/zImage /boot/vmlinuz.tcfs
```

Note that we have named the new kernel vmlinuz.tcfs and that we have not removed the original kernel /boot/vmlinuz. This will allow us to boot using our choice of kernels once we modify /etc/lilo.conf.

Suppose that your existing /etc/lilo.conf file appears as shown in Example 15-9.

Example 15-9 Typical /etc/lilo.conf File

```
# cat /etc/lilo.conf
boot=/dev/hda
map=/boot/map
install=/boot/boot.b
prompt
linear
timeout=50
image=/boot/vmlinuz-2.0.36-0.7
    label=linux
    root=/dev/hda1
    read-only
```

To enable booting from either kernel, modify /etc/lilo.conf similarly to that shown in Example 15-10. The changes are in **bold**.

Example 15-10 Adding Another Kernel Instance to /etc/lilo.conf

```
# cat /etc/lilo.conf
boot=/dev/hda
map=/boot/map
install=/boot/boot.b
prompt
linear
timeout=50
image=/boot/vmlinuz-2.0.36-0.7
    label=linux
    root=/dev/hda1
    read-only
image=/boot/vmlinuz.tcfs
    label=tcfs
    root=/dev/hda1
    read-only
```

You must effect the modified `/etc/lilo.conf` by executing

```
# /sbin/lilo
```

Otherwise the changes will not occur at the next reboot.

You may now reboot the system. Shortly, you will see the LILO boot prompt. By pressing the tab key (shown as **<tab>** in Example 15-11) at the LILO boot prompt, the available kernels will be displayed. Choose the one you'd like to boot. Example 15-11 displays choosing `tcfs`. If the `tcfs` kernel does not function properly, you can recover by rebooting. Since `linux` is the default, it will be invoked by the reboot without user intervention. Once you know that `tcfs` is robust, you may modify `/etc/lilo.conf` to automate booting of the `tcfs` kernel.

Example 15-11 Choosing the Kernel

```
LILO boot:  <tab>
linux       tcfs
boot: tcfs
```

After the `tcfs` kernel has booted, you may log in as root and execute

```
# /sbin/modprobe tcfs
```

to verify that the kernel module will load. Upon successful execution of this command, you will see the message

```
TCFS 3.0 loaded
```

in your console. You do not need to execute `modprobe` at every boot. When you first mount a TCFS resource, as described in *TCFS Administrative Tasks* on page 426, the TCFS module will automatically be loaded.

Next we need to set up the server daemon for TCFS.

The TCFS Server Side

Setting up the server side of TCFS is easy compared to the client side. Follow these steps.

1. Create the `xattrd`.

```
# cd /usr/src/custom/tcfs/tcfs-2.2.2
# tar xzvf xattrd-2.1.tar.gz
# cd xattrd-2.1
# make
# make install
```

2. Make sure that `xattrd` runs at each reboot. Place the following lines in a start-up script that runs at run level 2 or 3.

```
if [ -x /usr/local/sbin/xattrd ]; then
        /usr/local/sbin/xattrd
fi
```

Using TCFS

TCFS incorporates a number of utilities for user, group, and key management. These are provided in Table 15.7. We explore these utilities in the following sections.

Configuring TCFS for Use with PAM

If you are using PAM (see Chapter 5), you will need to add `pam_tcfs` entries to the `/etc/pam.d/passwd` file. Since TCFS uses the user's password to encrypt and decrypt the user's file encryption key, it must know when that password changes. Example 15-12 shows the addition of `pam_tcfs` to `/etc/pam.d/passwd`.

Example 15-12 Including `pam_tcfs` in `/etc/pam.d/password`

```
#%PAM-1.0
auth       required     /lib/security/pam_pwdb.so
account    required     /lib/security/pam_pwdb.so
password   required     /lib/security/pam_cracklib.so minlen=13 retry=3
password   required     /lib/security/pam_pwdb.so md5 use_authtok nullok
password   required     /lib/security/pam_tcfs.so
```

Table 15.7 TCFS Utilities

Utility[*]	Used By	Description
sbin/tcfsadduser	Root only	Adds users to the TCFS database. Users must be added prior to using TCFS resources.
sbin/tcfsrmuser	Root only	Removes a user from the TCFS database.
sbin/tcfsaddgroup	Root only	Adds a group to the TCFS database. TCFS groups must exist in /etc/group.
sbin/tcfsrmgroup	Root only	Removes a group from the TCFS database.
bin/tcfsgenkey	All users	Generates a TCFS encryption/decryption key.
bin/tcfsputkey	All users	Pushes the user's key into the kernel. This command must be executed prior to accessing TCFS resources.
bin/tcfsrmkey	All users	Removes the user's key from the kernel module. This command should be executed when work on encrypted resources is complete.
bin/tcfsviewkey	All users	Allows for the viewing of keys and whether or not the key is currently in use.

[*]The paths shown here are relative to `/usr/local`.

You may also wish to include pam_tcfs in other PAM files to automate incorporation of the user's encryption key into the TCFS database. This would allow for the user to access his or her encrypted resources without having to issue the tcfsputkey command (see *Setting up the Encrypted Directory* on page 428 for further details on the tcfsputkey command). Example 15-13 shows the use of pam_tcfs in /etc/pam.d/ftp. This is useful since the tcfsput-key command cannot be issued via ftp. You may also add entries like this to other /etc/pam.d configuration files to suppress the need to use tcfsputkey.

Example 15-13 Using pam_tcfs in /etc/pam.d/ftp

```
#%PAM-1.0
auth       required     /lib/security/pam_listfile.so item=user \
       sense=deny file=/etc/ftpusers onerr=succeed
auth       required     /lib/security/pam_pwdb.so shadow
auth       optional     /lib/security/pam_tcfs.so
auth       required     /lib/security/pam_shells.so
account    required     /lib/security/pam_pwdb.so
session    required     /lib/security/pam_pwdb.so
session    optional     /lib/security/pam_tcfs.so
```

WARNING!

Make sure that, except for /etc/pam.d/passwd, you use the optional flag with pam_tcfs. For example, if you use required with the pam_tcfs entries in /etc/pam.d/ftp, users who have not been added as a TCFS user will not be able to authenticate via ftp! Adding TCFS users is discussed in the next section.

TCFS Administrative Tasks

Before you or other users can take advantage of TCFS, you will need to perform some initial tasks. These are outlined in the following two sections, *Server Side* and *Client Side*.

Server Side   Make sure that xattrd is running. If not, invoke it.

```
# /usr/local/sbin/xattrd
```

You will also need to make a resource available for use. In our examples, we will use /work, which could be a directory or a separate filesystem. We will also assume that the local host is underdog. Add the resource to /etc/exports as shown here.

```
/work   localhost    pluto   topcat
```

In this case, we are exporting /work to the localhost and the remote hosts pluto and topcat. Export the resource as a normal NFS resource with

```
# exportfs -a
```

In this resource, /work in our example, we will need to create directories for users. These directories need to be owned by the users who will be using them as a TCFS directory. If /work is root owned, then root would execute

```
# mkdir /work/mary
# chown mary.mary /work/mary
```

to provide a working directory for the user mary.

Now the root user must add mary to the TCFS user database as shown in Example 15-14. Each user who will utilize TCFS resources must be added in this way, and only root may execute the /usr/local/sbin/tcfsadduser command.

Example 15-14 Adding a User to the TCFS User Database

```
# /usr/local/sbin/tcfsadduser
Username to add to TCFS database: mary
Ok
#
```

Removing a user is similar, as shown in Example 15-15. This is also a root-only command.

Example 15-15 Removing a TCFS User

```
# /usr/local/sbin/tcfsrmuser
Username to remove from TCFS database: bill
Ok
#
```

The user database is maintained in the file /etc/tcfspwdb, which also holds the users' encrypted keys.

Client Side Once the appropriate attributes have been set, you can mount the resource. In this example, we will assume a local mount directory, /mnt/safe. If the resource is to be accessed locally, then the command

```
# mount -t tcfs localhost:/work /mnt/safe
```

would be appropriate. If the resource is remote, then

```
[root@pluto]# mount -t tcfs underdog:/work /mnt/safe
```

provides an example.

Now that the resource is available, TCFS users may utilize it.

Extended Attributes for TCFS

First we need to set the appropriate attributes to ensure encryption of the files in the work directories. There are two attributes, x and G, that are added to the chattr command when the replacement chattr command is installed as described in step 7 on page 420. The x attribute, when applied to a file, indicates that the file is to be encrypted. If the x attribute is applied to a directory, then all files and subdirectories in that directory will be encrypted. The G attribute is used to indicate that the file or directory is to be accessible (encrypted and decrypted) to a TCFS group. TCFS groups are discussed in *TCFS Groups* on page 429.

Mary may set the x attribute on a file or directory owned by the user mary by using the chattr command, as in

```
[mary@underdog]$ chattr +X /mnt/safe/mary
```

which will cause all files and subdirectories created in /mnt/safe/mary to be encrypted **after** /mnt/safe/mary has been mounted as a TCFS resource. Note also that the attribute is set on the mounted directory, not the real directory. This allows TCFS to identify that files are to be encrypted.

Unfortunately, the replacement man page for chattr(1) does not describe either the x or the G attribute.

Setting up the Encrypted Directory

In order for Mary to create encrypted files and directories in the TCFS resource, she must initially create an encryption key and subsequently push that key into the kernel module. The first step is accomplished as shown in Example 15-16. At the password prompt, mary must supply her login password.

Example 15-16 Initially Generating TCFS Encryption Keys

```
[mary@topcat]$ /usr/local/bin/tcfsgenkey
password:
Please, press 10 random keys, so we can create a new key for you:
press 10 keys:**********
Ok.
Key succesfully generated.
[mary@topcat]$
```

Now that mary has a key, she can push it into the kernel module as shown in Example 15-17. Once again, mary must supply her login password at the password prompt.

Example 15-17 Pushing the Key

```
[mary@topcat]$ /usr/local/bin/tcfsputkey
password:
Ok
[mary@topcat]$
```

Now any files and directories created by mary in /mnt/safe/mary will be encrypted on the resource underdog:/work/mary. Only mary will be able to see the cleartext through /mnt/safe/mary. The following examples illustrate this behavior.

The user mary creates a file secret in the cleartext directory /mnt/safe/mary on pluto in Example 15-18.

Example 15-18 Creating a File in the TCFS Directory

```
[mary@pluto] echo "Really secret stuff">/mnt/safe/mary/secret
[mary@pluto] cat /mnt/safe/mary/secret
Really secret stuff
[mary@pluto]$
```

The actual file on `underdog` in `/work/mary` and its contents are encrypted as shown in Example 15-19.

Example 15-19 The Actual File and Its Contents Are Encrypted

```
[mary@underdog]$ ls /work/mary
MWqbLWrg4CsA=
[mary@underdog]$ cat /work/mary/MWqbLWrg4CsA=
",òÖ%EéöæÏÓõ]1¯ù[mary@topcat]$
```

Not even the root user may access Mary's encrypted files as illustrated in Example 15-20.

Example 15-20 Only the User `mary` May Access the File

```
[root@pluto]# cd /mnt/safe/mary
[root@pluto]# ls
ls: .: Permission denied
[root@pluto]#
```

OH, BY THE WAY...

The steps provided here could easily be used by root on sensitive directories such as `/var/log`. While this may be appealing, `/var/log` would need to be TCFS mounted whenever the system is up and running. This means that the root password would have to be supplied at each reboot and also means that no protection is provided if root is compromised. However, it would completely eliminate inspection of the log files by users other than root.

TCFS Groups

In much the same way as described for TCFS users, TCFS groups may be created with the `/usr/local/sbin/tcfsaddgroup` command and removed with the `/usr/local/sbin/tcfsrmgroup` command. TCFS group names must match those in `/etc/group`. TCFS groups may be configured with any number of users and may also be set up to require that a minimum number of users push their keys into the kernel module before access to group files and directories is granted.

TCFS Key Management

TCFS key management is rudimentary at best. The user `mary` may view her key with the `tcfsviewkey -k` command as shown in Example 15-21. She must supply her password in order to view the key.

Example 15-21 Viewing the User's Key

```
[mary@topcat]$ /usr/local/bin/tcfsviewkey -k
password:
TCFS key: Q8aaxA#VeWDAwmDOzwxFBQAA=
[mary@topcat]$
```

She may also determine whether or not her key is pushed into the kernel. Example 15-22 shows the case where the key is in the kernel, indicating that Mary previously executed `tcfsputkey`.

Example 15-22 Verifying that the Key Is in the Kernel

```
[mary@topcat]$ /usr/local/bin/tcfsviewkey -c
TCFS counter: 1
[mary@topcat]$
```

Unfortunately, the key itself cannot readily be changed. There are indications in the source code of `tcfsgenkey` that a `-c` flag is forthcoming, which will allow for the change of keys through that command. As of this writing, however, the only way to change the key is to remove the user with the `tcfsrmuser` command and then add the user back with the `tcfsadduser` command. These commands must be executed by root. Once done, the user may generate a new key with `tcfsgenkey`. Using these steps, numerous keys can be generated by the user. The user must record the TCFS keys generated by using `tcfsviewkey` as in Example 15-21. Each key may be subsequently pushed into the kernel with `tcfsputkey -k` as shown in Example 15-23. The key used to encrypt a file must be pushed into the kernel in this way in order for the file to be decrypted.

Example 15-23 Pushing a Specific Key into the Kernel

```
[mary@topcat]$ /usr/local/bin/tcfsputkey -k Q8aaxA#VeWDAwmDOzwxFBQAA=
password:
Ok
[mary@topcat]$
```

The fundamental problem with the generation and use of keys with respect to TCFS is that the keys are tied to the user's password. Thus, if the user's password is compromised, then so is the current key and only the current key. If other keys have been used, they must be known in order to decrypt any files encrypted with them. This means that the use of multiple keys, while more secure, requires either manual key management or custom software.

VULNERABILITIES OF TCFS

Much like CFS, there will be times when cleartext is stored either in RAM or in a filesystem cache. Unlike CFS, this occurs only in kernel space and for shorter periods of time. In this way, TCFS is more secure than CFS.

Perhaps the greatest vulnerability associated with TCFS is the fact that, by default, all encryption/decryption keys are accessible with the user's password. Disassociating these keys from the user password is possible (as outlined in *TCFS Key Management* on page 429), but it is very cumbersome, making it unlikely that it will be commonly done. As previously noted, future revisions promise improvement. One high note for TCFS is that it is under active development. So join the TCFS mailing list (see *E-Mail Lists* on page 433) and make suggestions!

CFS AND TCFS COMPARISON

TCFS offers a much better-performing implementation than CFS. The implementation is also transparent to users because its resources are accessed through a simple NFS mount (no requirement for a specific mount tied to a special daemon) and could be implemented through the automounter or similar mechanism. On the other hand, TCFS has a significantly weaker method of key generation and, by default, only supports triple DES encryption. TCFS also suffers from very poor documentation.

Perhaps the most significant difference between the two utilities is the administrative burden. CFS is easy to install and once configured is very low maintenance. TCFS is quite difficult to install and requires administrative intervention to manage users and groups and to allow users to create multiple keys.

While both of these utilities have their downsides, they each offer the tremendous benefit of encrypted files and are well worth both putting forth the effort and watching for potential vulnerabilities—consider how vulnerable you are in their absence.

SECURELY DELETING FILES

A topic somewhat related to securing files via encryption is that of securely deleting files. When you delete a file from the `ext2` filesystem, the contents of the file are not removed. Rather the blocks allocated for the file are simply freed for use by the filesystem. Eventually the data will be overwritten when other files require additional disk blocks and the system reuses the blocks from the deleted file. This means that in the interim the data may be available to unscrupulous activity. This includes data that has been temporarily stored in RAM or a disk cache, so this is a pertinent concern regarding CFS and TCFS.

One way to improve upon securely deleting disk files is to use the secure delete attribute on your files as in

```
# chattr +s secret_file
```

which will cause all of the blocks in the file to be set to 0 upon deletion. This attribute and the `chattr` command are discussed in detail in *File Attributes* on page 75 of Chapter 4.

Unfortunately, this technique does not even provide minimal protection against a variety of file recovery techniques. Such techniques are discussed in detail in the article, *Secure Deletion of Data from Magnetic and Solid-State Memory*, by Peter Gutmann (see *Papers* on page 433). This article is available from

    http://www.cs.auckland.ac.nz/~pgut001/pubs/secure_del.html

and is well worth the read. In short, Gutmann suggests that the secure removal of data from disk and RAM requires writing over the data blocks many times with alternating patterns. Moreover, to thoroughly remove data from such media requires specialized equipment and may even require the destruction of the disk or RAM. Whether you need to obtain such specialized equipment to erase your data depends on your Security Policy (see Chapter 2). We will mention two user-level programs that make obtaining erased data expensive and difficult.

One utility that more securely deletes files is `wipe`. It is written and maintained by Berke Durak, copyrighted by the Free Software Foundation (FSF), and distributed under the GPL. You may obtain `wipe` from either `http://gsu.linux.org.tr/wipe/` or `http://altern.org/berke/wipe/`. `wipe` writes 34 patterns, 8 of which are random, over the target file, directory, or filesystem.

Another utility, `secure_delete`, is available from `http://r3wt.base.org/` (then click on "the files"). It is a collection of tools that erase files, filesystems, holes in files or filesystems, swap, and RAM. It uses 38 patterns, 10 of which are random. It is copyrighted by van Hauser. This suite of programs is definitely worth investigating if you are concerned about the CFS and/or TCFS cleartext remnants in swap and RAM.

Both `secure_delete` and `wipe` include Peter Gutmann's paper in their respective distributions.

ALTERNATIVES TO CFS AND TCFS

You may wish to use Pretty Good Privacy (PGP, discussed in *An Overview of PGP* on page 45) for the encryption of files. However, it cannot automatically encrypt all files within a directory as CFS or TCFS can. For a small number of encrypted files, however, PGP offers simpler use and administration.

SSH (discussed in detail in Chapter 11) is strongly recommended over ESM.

SUMMARY

We discussed both the CFS and TCFS utilities for encrypting data on a directorywide basis. We compared the advantages and disadvantages of both tools.

We also briefly discussed some of the tools available to securely delete data files from RAM and disk.

FOR FURTHER READING

Papers

1. Blaze, Matt, *A Cryptographic File System for Unix*, Proceedings of the 1st ACM Conference on Computer and Communications Security, Fairfax, Virginia, November 1993.
2. Gutmann, Peter, *Secure Deletion of Data from Magnetic and Solid-State Memory*, Sixth USENIX Security Symposium Proceedings, San Jose, California, July 1996.

E-Mail Lists

To subscribe to the CFS list, send an e-mail to

```
cfs-users-request@research.att.com
```

with `subscribe cfs-users` in the body of the message.
To subscribe to the TCFS list, send an e-mail message to

```
majordomo@edu-gw.dia.unisa.it
```

with `subscribe tcfslist` in the body of the message.

## CHAPTER 16

We Must Censor!

Packet Filtering with `ipchains`

Until this chapter, we have largely discussed host-based security. Granted, such utilities as SSH, CFS, TCFS, TCP_wrappers, and `xinetd` are network or network-capable applications; however, our discussions of those utilities focus on restricting or securing system and local area networking access. In this chapter, we will discuss the Linux network packet-filtering and masquerading capabilities through the use of `ipchains`. This is a topic that is fundamentally network-centric and generally falls under the auspices of a firewall.

In the context of computing, a firewall is a system that prevents unauthorized network communications to it, from it, and through it. The Linux `ipchains` is capable of establishing rules that provide a reasonably secure firewall under many circumstances. It can also provide a remarkable level of flexibility in terms of selectively restricting traffic flow to, from, and through the system. Additionally, `ipchains` can work in conjunction with other software to provide other options not available in `ipchains` itself. Unfortunately, despite all of its advantages, `ipchains` can't solve every problem.

Linux `ipchains` implements a packet-filtering firewall. This means that each network packet may be filtered against a set of rules. This procedure is performed in the kernel. It specifically causes the kernel to analyze each packet for source and destination IP addresses and port numbers or ICMP types and codes. A more intelligent but similar type of firewall is a stateful packet-filtering firewall. The difference between stateful filtering and `ipchains` is that the stateful filter can keep track of its connections and

435

thereby distinguish packets associated with an established connection and packets that are not. While Linux `ipchains` is incapable of this, there is a wrapper program that can add this functionality on top of `ipchains`. If you need stateful capabilities, check out

```
ftp://ftp.interlinx.bc.ca/pub/spf/
```

where you will find Brian Murrell's stateful packet-filtering project.

Another type of firewall is a proxy-based firewall. This type of firewall operates as a go-between for services. All network connections destined through the proxy-based firewall terminate at the firewall. Then (if the rules allow) the proxy-based firewall will make a connection to the destination system on behalf of the originating host. The proxy-based firewall thereby manages two separate connections. We will touch on proxy firewalls such as Trusted Information System's Firewall Toolkit (FWTK) and NEC's SOCKSv5. It is common to implement FWTK or SOCKS in conjunction with `ipchains`.

Let's begin our detailed look at `ipchains`.

PACKET FILTERING

The concept of packet filtering is a fairly simple one. The contents of the headers (see *TCP/IP Networking Overview* on page 28) of each network packet are checked against a series of rules. Each rule includes an action, so that, when a packet matches a rule, the action component of the rule tells the kernel what to do with the packet. In essence, we can censor network packets. In order to implement the inspection of network packets or to filter the packets, there must be software that provides the capability. The modern Linux kernel includes this capability.

The precise mechanism for packet filtering in Linux depends upon the version of the Linux kernel. The packet-filtering implementation for Linux kernels version 2.1.102 and above is `ipchains`. This includes the Red Hat 6.0 distribution (kernel version 2.2.x). By default, kernel versions prior to 2.1.102 implement `ipfwadm`, including the Red Hat 5.2 distribution (kernel version 2.0.3x). The `ipchains` mechanism provides greater flexibility and capability. Therefore, we will discuss that implementation.

If you are using an earlier kernel implementation that does not include `ipchains` and you need to use `ipfwadm`, visit the site

```
http://www.xos.nl/linux/ipfwadm/
```

for documentation. The syntax and implementation of `ipfwadm` is quite similar to `ipchains` except that `ipchains` includes functionality which is not supported in `ipfwadm`. For kernel version 2.0.34 and later, you may upgrade to `ipchains` with a patch. Visit the site

```
http://www.rustcorp.com/linux/ipchains/
```

and read *IPCHAINS-HOWTO* as noted in `ipchains` *Documentation* on page 487 for further details.

NOTE

> In order to get the most out of this chapter, you ought to be comfortable with the concepts and the administration of TCP/IP networking. *TCP/IP Networking Overview* on page 28 provides an overview and also includes references. Refer to those resources whenever you run across something in this chapter that is not familiar to you.

CONFIGURING THE KERNEL FOR `ipchains`

Normally, when you install Red Hat 6.0 (or Red Hat 5.2 for `ipfwadm`), the initial kernel configuration will include support for `ipchains` (or `ipfwadm`, if Red Hat 5.2) and IP masquerading (see *IP Masquerading* on page 458).

However, if you install with "expert" mode[1] or you rebuilt your kernel (see *Rebuilding and Recompiling the Kernel* on page 420 for a discussion of kernel rebuilding), then you will need to make sure that you select the appropriate kernel configuration parameters to support `ipchains` and IP masquerading. The configuration parameters, the proper choice (either to enable or disable), and descriptions are given in the *Linux IP Masquerade HOWTO*,[2] as cited in *Masquerading Documentation* on page 487. Make sure that you read through that document *before* proceeding!

NOTE

> Red Hat 6.0 includes `ipchains` version 1.3.8. Any version of `ipchains` at or after 1.3.8 is considered stable. As of this writing, `ipchains` is at version 1.3.9. Visit the `ipchains` home page regularly and consider subscribing to the `ipchains` mailing list to keep up to date regarding upgrades and vulnerability reports. The `ipchains` home page and other resources are cited in `ipchains` *Documentation* on page 487.

`ipchains` OVERVIEW

Linux `ipchains` provides for the capability to insert rules into the kernel that will cause all network packets to be filtered against those rules. The rules are

---

1. "Expert" mode is described in the Red Hat Installation Manual, which may be found on-line in the directory, `/usr/doc/rhl-install-guide-en-*/manual`, where you would replace * with your distribution number (5.2, 6.0, etc.). If not on your system go to `http://www.redhat.com/corp/support/manual/index.html`.

2. As of this writing, the *Linux IP Masquerade HOWTO* is a mini-HOWTO; however, it will be a "full" HOWTO in the near future, so we reference it that way.

maintained in a *chain*. There are three permanent chains—they are *input*, *forward*, and *output*. The input chain consists of a list of rules that are applied to all incoming (entering the system) packets. The forward chain consists of a list of rules that apply to all packets that are to be forwarded (see *TCP/IP Networking Overview* on page 28 for a discussion of IP forwarding). The output chain is a list of rules that apply to all packets that are outbound (leaving the system). These three chains always exist and cannot be deleted. Each chain may be configured to invoke custom chains. By default, there are no custom chains and each permanent chain contains an allow-all-packets rule.

Let's explore the general behavior of the chains for inbound, forward, and outbound types of packets as diagrammed in Figure 16.1.

Behavior of a Chain

When a packet is processed against a chain, this means that all of the Internet layer and Transport layer (see *TCP/IP Networking Overview* on page 28 for an overview of RPC) information as well as the network interface involved is compared with each rule in the chain. For the input and output chains, the rules apply to each and every interface (eth0, eth1, ppp0, lo0, etc.) on the system unless the rule specifically identifies a particular interface. If a rule matches, then the action specified by that rule will be taken. Unless the rule's action is DENY or REJECT (meaning destroy the packet—we define all of the actions in Table 16.3 on page 445), the packet passes the chain and moves on to the next step. If no rule matches, then the default rule or last rule, called a *policy*, will apply. Policies are discussed in *Setting Policies (Default Rules)* on page 452.

Malformed Packets

Before a packet is checked against a chain, it is checked for sanity; that is, all of the header information must be valid. If any information contained in any of the headers is invalid—not known to the kernel—then the packet is considered malformed and is destroyed by the kernel with no further processing. This sanity check is indicated in Figure 16.1 by the diamonds containing "Malform?".

Analysis of an Inbound Packet

When a packet arrives, the first thing that is done is a cyclic redundancy check (CRC—see *TCP/IP Networking Overview* on page 28). If the CRC does not match the one carried in the frame, then the packet is destroyed (sent to the "Bit Bucket" in Figure 16.1). Otherwise, the kernel sanity check ("Malform?") is performed; if the packet is malformed, it is destroyed. If the packet is not malformed, it is processed against the input chain. The input chain will destroy the packet if it matches a DENY or REJECT rule. If the rule does not DENY or REJECT

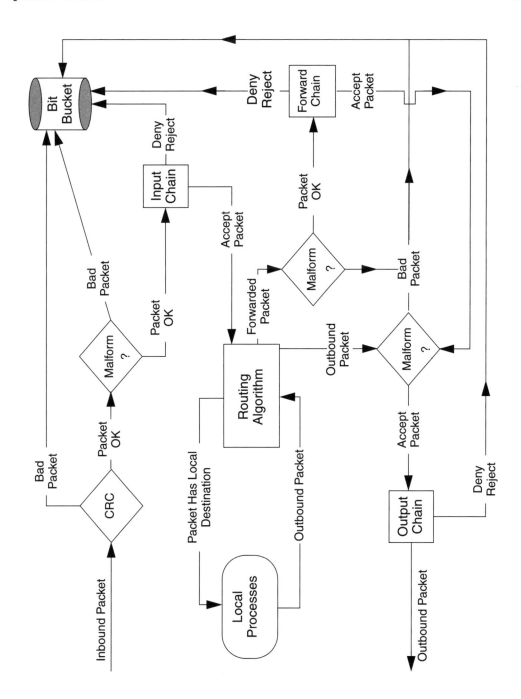

Fig. 16.1 ipchains Flow of Events

the packet, then the packet is passed on to the kernel for destination processing. This is accomplished by invoking the routing algorithm ("Routing Algorithm" in Figure 16.1—see *TCP/IP Networking Overview* on page 28) which determines the next step in processing by determining the destination address.

The routing algorithm determines the destination of the packet. If the destination is the local system, then it is appropriately handled, either internally by the kernel or by passing the packet on to the local process. On the other hand, if the packet is destined to another system, it must be forwarded. All forwarded packets are checked for sanity ("Malform?") and then processed by the forward chain, which either destroys the packet due to a REJECT or DENY, or passes the packet on to the output chain (after the "Malform?" check). Processing by the output chain proceeds as with the other chains—either the packet is destroyed or it is allowed to go on. If the latter, then the packet is sent to the network through the appropriate network interface.

Analysis of an Outbound Packet

If a process on the local system generates a packet that is destined for a remote host, the packet is first processed for the remote destination, then sanity checked, and then processed by the output chain. The output chain will either destroy the packet if the packet matches a DENY or REJECT rule or send it to the network through the appropriate interface.

The Loopback Interface

Packets that arrive at the loopback interface (lo0) or are destined to the loopback are treated as inbound and outbound packets, respectively. The chains may have rules that distinguish particular interfaces as we will see throughout this chapter.

Custom Chains

You can create custom chains, which are simply a list of rules, and invoke them through one of the three permanent chains. Custom chains are discussed in *Adding Custom Chains* on page 461.

INTRODUCTION TO USING `ipchains`

Implementing `ipchains` can be a very complex process. It is best to start simple and then test and verify your configuration before you go on to more complex rules, such as masquerading rules. We will follow this advice by beginning with an initial description of the `ipchains` command, the permanent chains, and some simple examples. We'll move from there to examine some of the more complex features such as custom chains and IP masquerading. In *Building Your Firewall* on page 469, we'll look at some real-world examples.

The `ipchains` Command

There's really no way to simplify the introduction of the flags, options, and actions associated with `ipchains`. So, Table 16.1 lists the flags or commands, Table 16.2 describes the options or parameters, and Table 16.3 notes the actions. We will use examples throughout the remainder of this chapter to clarify the use of many of them.

Each of the flags in Table 16.1 can utilize one or more options, described in Table 16.2. These options are the parameters that comprise a rule.

Table 16.1 Flags of `ipchains`

Flag	Description
`-A` or `--append`	Appends one or more rules to the specified chain.
`-C` or `--check`	Checks a given packet against the selected chain. The `-s`, `-d`, `-p`, and `-i` flags are required (see Table 16.2 on page 442).
`-D` or `--delete`	Deletes one or more rules from the specified chain.
`-F,` or `--flush`	Flushes all the rules in the specified chain.
`-I` or `--insert`	Inserts one or more rules in the specified chain at the specified rule number.
`-L` or `--list`	Lists all the rules in the selected chain. If no chain is specified, then all rules in all chains are listed.
`-M` or `--masquerading`	If used with `-L`, this flag will display all masquerading rules. If used with `-S`, this flag will set one or more masquerading parameters. Masquerading rules are discussed in *IP Masquerading* on page 458.
`-N` or `--new-chain`	Creates a new custom chain. The name of the new chain cannot exceed 8 characters. Custom chains are defined in *Custom Chains* on page 440.
`-P` or `--policy`	Specifies the policy, or default rule, for a permanent chain. Policies cannot be specified for custom chains. This is the last rule in the chain, even though it appears first when listed with `-L`.
`-R` or `--replace`	Replaces a rule in the specified chain.

Table 16.1 Flags of `ipchains` (Continued)

Flag	Description
`-S` or `--set tcp tcpfin udp`	Changes the time-out values used for masquerading. This flag requires three time-out values in seconds—`tcp` for TCP sessions, `tcpfin` for time-outs after receiving a TCP FIN packet, and `udp` for UDP time-outs.
`-X` or `--delete-chain`	Deletes the specified custom chain. There must be no rules that reference the chain you wish to delete. If you do not specify a chain, all custom chains will be deleted. Permanent chains cannot be deleted.
`-Z` or `--zero`	Zero out the packet and byte counters. You may use this flag in conjunction with `-L` which will have the effect of displaying the current accounting information and then resetting the counters to 0.

Table 16.2 Options to `ipchains`

Option	Description
`-b` `--bidirectional` may be used instead of `-b`	Bidirectional. Use of this flag will create a rule that applies to both source and destination IP addresses. It is the same as creating two rules with the source IP address and destination IP address reversed.
`-d [!] address[/mask] [!] [port[:port]` `--destination` may be used instead of `-d`	This option specifies the destination IP address, `address`, for this rule. It may be an IP address, an IP network number, a resolvable hostname, or a resolvable network name (in `/etc/networks` or `/etc/hosts`). Specify the `mask` argument for network addresses. It may be either the actual netmask or the number of leftmost bits set to 1 in the mask. So, setting `mask` to `20` would be the same as setting it to `255.255.240.0`. The optional `!` is the logical NOT operator and reverses the meaning. The address `0.0.0.0/0` means any IP address. You may also use `0/0`. You may also include port number(s) or ICMP codes (described in the section, *ICMP Types and Codes* on page 453) in the optional `port` field(s). If `:` is used, then a range of ports is implied. When using `:` the leftmost port number defaults to 0 and the rightmost to 65535, thus `:1023` means the range of ports 0 through 1023 inclusive.

Table 16.2 Options to `ipchains` (Continued)

Option	Description
`--dport [!] [`*`port:port`*`]` `--destination-port` may be used instead of `-dport`	Allows for the separate specification of ports or ICMP codes.
`[!] -f` or `--fragment`	Specifies that the rule refers to fragments of a packet (see *Packet Fragments* on page 457 for a discussion of IP fragmentation). Such packets will not contain port numbers or ICMP types. The `!` reverses the meaning.
`-h [icmp]`	Help. If used without the optional `icmp` argument, an `ipchains` usage message will be displayed. If used with the `icmp` argument, the ICMP-named types and codes will be displayed. See *ICMP Types and Codes* on page 453 for a cross-reference of names and numbers.
`-i [!]` *`name`* `--interface` may be used instead of `-i`	Specifies the interface to which this rule applies. If this option is omitted, then the rule applies to *all* interfaces. The argument *name* must be the name of the interface, such as `eth0`, `eth1`, `ppp0`, etc. You may use the wildcard `+` to match all interfaces beginning with the specified name; for example, `eth+` will match all interfaces beginning with `eth`, like `eth0`, `eth1`, etc. If `!` precedes `name`, then the rule does not apply to that interface but does apply to all other interfaces. For the input chain, specifying this option causes the rule to inspect packets incoming to that interface. For the output and forward chains, it inspects packets destined to go out the specified interface. Note that the loopback interface must be specified as `lo`.
`--icmp-type [!]` *`type`*	Allows for the specification of an ICMP type. Must be one of the types given by `ipchains -h icmp`. This option is identical to specifying the ICMP type with `-s`.
`-j` *`target`* `--jump` may be used instead of `-j`	Specifies the *target* of the rule, which may be one of the actions described in Table 16.3 on page 445 or the name of a custom chain. If a custom chain, then it cannot be the same as the current custom chain. If this option is not specified, then no action is taken when this rule is matched, but the packet and byte counters will be incremented.

Table 16.2 Options to `ipchains` (Continued)

Option	Description
-l or --log	Causes packets matching the rule to be logged via `klogd` to selector `kern.info`. Very useful option for initial setup and debugging. Be careful with this option, however, as it logs *every* packet that matches.
-n or --numeric	When listing rules, suppresses name translation. Ordinarily, `ipchains` will attempt to convert IP addresses to hostnames, port numbers to services, etc.
-p [!] *protocol* --protocol may be used instead of -p	Specifies the protocol for the rule, which may be any name or number listed in `/etc/protocols`, such as `tcp`, `udp`, or `ip`. The keyword `all`, meaning all protocols, may also be used. It is the default. The `all` protocol may not be used with -c. A preceding ! reverses the meaning.
-s [!] *address*[/*mask*] [!] [*port*[:*port*] --source may be used instead of -s	Identical to -d except that this is the source address. Also, unlike -d, ICMP type numbers may be specified in lieu of ports.
--sport [!] [*port*:[*port*]] --source-port may be used instead of --sport	Allows for the separate specification of a source port or port range.
-v or --verbose	When listing rules, this option adds additional information including, but not limited to, the interface address, rule options, and packet and byte counters.
-x or --exact	Displays the exact packet and byte counts. Ordinarily, `ipchains` rounds to the nearest 1000 (K), 1,000,000 (M), or multiples of 1000M (G).
[!] -y or --syn	Only matches TCP packets that have the SYN bit set and the ACK and FIN bits cleared. Such a TCP packet represents a connection attempt. The ! negates the meaning; that is, it will match return packets for an existing connection. Read through *Rules for Allowing* `ftp` *from the Internal Network to the Internet* on page 474 and, in particular, *FTP Rule 3* on page 476 for more details about this option.
--line-numbers	Available with `ipchains` Version 1.3.9 and later. Lists the number of each rule. Must be used with -L.

Table 16.3 Actions for `ipchains`

Action	Description
ACCEPT	Allows the packet through.
DENY	Drops the packet without generating an ICMP message back to the originator of the packet.
REJECT	Same as DENY except that an ICMP message is sent to the originator. If the rule matches an ICMP packet, then REJECT behaves like DENY and no ICMP message will be sent.
MASQ	Only valid in the forward chain or a custom chain invoked by the forward chain. The matching packet's IP address will be set to the IP address of this host. Masquerading is discussed in *IP Masquerading* on page 458.
REDIRECT	Only valid in the input chain or a custom chain. The matching packet will be redirected to a local port, even if the destination IP address is for a remote host. If the default redirection port of 0 is used, then the packet will be sent to the destination port.
RETURN	If this action is in a custom chain, then the packet is sent to the next rule in the calling chain. If this action is in a permanent chain, then the action in the permanent chain's policy is applied.
custom_chain	The named custom chain is invoked.

In addition to the options described in Table 16.2, there are three other options: The -o option is used for passing matching packets to a device for processing by a user process (as opposed to the kernel), such as a firewall or content inspection[3] application. The -m option marks packets for special handling internally by the kernel (currently, the kernel does nothing with these marked packets). And the -t option is used to modify the type-of-service (TOS) field in the IP header. You can learn more about these options in the `ipchains(8)` man page and the references noted in *ipchains Documentation* on page 487. As of this writing, the -o, -m, and -t options are rarely used.

Most rules will have actions. Those that don't merely act as accounting rules, collecting packet and byte counts. Table 16.3 notes the actions that may be specified for a rule. The actions are case sensitive.

For complete details on the flags, options, and actions, see the `ipchains(8)` man page.

`ipchains` Syntax   The syntax of the `ipchains` command is best understood through examples, which we provide throughout the remainder of this chapter. Generally, `ipchains` takes the form

---

3. Content inspection applications are used to examine the data portion of a network packet or packets.

```
ipchains -[flags] {input|output|forward|custom_chain} [options] [action]
ipchains -M [-L|-S] [options]
```

We will examine many of the ways in which this command can be used.

Some Simple Examples

The first thing that we can do with ipchains is take a look at what rules are established by default. This can be accomplished with the ipchains -L as shown in Example 16-1. The output of this command shows us that there are three chains (the permanent ones)—input, forward, and output. Each of these chains has the same policy, or default action, which is ACCEPT. Thus, at this point, no packets will be rejected by the kernel.

Example 16-1 Listing the Default Rules

```
# /sbin/ipchains -L
Chain input (policy ACCEPT):
Chain forward (policy ACCEPT):
Chain output (policy ACCEPT):
#
```

In following sections, we'll take a look at adding and removing rules from the permanent chains.

Adding a Rule   Let's suppose that we want to completely disable FTP traffic to the host topcat. We could accomplish this by commenting out or removing the ftpd entry in /etc/inetd.conf (or /etc/xinetd.conf, if we're using xinetd—see *Replacing* inetd *with* xinetd on page 226 for a discussion of xinetd). We could also accomplish this using ipchains, as in

```
topcat# ipchains -I input 1 -p tcp --dport ftp -j REJECT
```

This command specifies that rule number 1 be inserted (-I) in the input chain. That rule applies to the protocol (-p) TCP and all packets with the destination port (--dport) of ftp. Any packet matching this rule will be rejected. Now we have a rule that prohibits inbound ftp connection requests. To see that this rule has been added, let's look at a listing in Example 16-2. Notice that, even though we added the rule as rule number 1, there is no rule number associated with the rule. This becomes tedious as your rule sets get large. If you get ipchains Version 1.3.9 or later, you may use the command

```
# ipchains -L --line-numbers
```

to view rule numbers, but the rule numbers will not appear as you add rules. You could also have added this rule with the command

```
# ipchains -A input -p tcp --dport ftp -j REJECT
```

Here we are using append (-A), which means add the rule to the end of the chain, but before the policy (which represents the last rule). In this case, the

Example 16-2 Listing the New Rule

```
[root@topcat]# ipchains -L
Chain input (policy ACCEPT):
target     prot opt    source        destination              ports
REJECT     tcp  ------  anywhere      anywhere                 any -> ftp
Chain forward (policy ACCEPT):
Chain output (policy ACCEPT):
[root@topcat]#
```

two rules are identical, because the only rule in the input chain is the policy. Ordinarily, the behavior of the append and insert are quite different.

There are some additional utilities that make the generation of rules easier. See *The fwconfig GUI* and *Mason* on page 485 for further information.

Let's see what happens when a user on `pluto` attempts to `ftp` to `topcat` after adding the rule shown in Example 16-2. The result is shown in Example 16-3.

Example 16-3 Failed `ftp` Attempt Due to `ipchains`

```
pluto$ ftp topcat
ftp: connect: Connection refused
ftp>
```

Here we see that the error message `Connection refused` is sent to `pluto`. If we had used DENY instead of REJECT in the rule displayed in Example 16-2, `pluto` would never have received any message from `topcat` and the `ftp` would have eventually timed out.

Should I Use DENY or REJECT?   When you use REJECT in a rule and someone from the outside generates a network packet that triggers the rule, then he or she will immediately receive an error message such as `Connection refused`. This makes it appear as if your system is not providing that service. Perhaps this will have the effect of discouraging some crackers.

On the other hand, using DENY will cause the client system to wait for a response from the server that will never arrive. Perhaps this will have the effect of frustrating some crackers. Both DENY and REJECT may also have the effect of fooling some port scanners.

Which of the two actions you use is your call. For most of our examples, we'll use REJECT because it is our preference.

WARNING!

> If you mistakenly use lowercase for the action, you will get a nonintuitive error message. For example, if we execute
>
> `topcat# ipchains -I input 1 -p tcp --dport ftp -j reject`
>
> we would get the error message
>
> `ipchains: No chain by that name`
>
> which does not indicate the problem! So beware.

Removing a Rule   We may either remove or replace a given rule. To delete or remove the rule that we have been working with, we could execute

```
# ipchains -D input 1
```

This syntax has the advantage of being simple to type. Unfortunately, when your chain contains many rules, you first have to list the rules in the chain and then manually count the rules to find out the number of the rule you wish to delete (unless you have a version of ipchains that supports --line-numbers). As noted before, this is tedious and prone to mistakes. Fortunately, another way to delete a rule exists. Simply specify all of the options for the rule exactly as was done to add the rule, but use the -D flag as in

```
# ipchains -D input -p tcp --dport ftp -j REJECT
```

and this will delete the specific rule.

Next let's suppose that we don't want to delete a rule, but we'd like to modify the rule. Suppose that our rule currently appears as in Example 16-2 on page 447. Suppose further that our system topcat has two interfaces. The eth0 interface is connected to the Internet and the eth1 interface is connected to the internal network. In real life, our Internet connection would be identified by a DNS hostname. However, we don't want to use fully qualified DNS names in our rules because, if the DNS resolution is broken, our rules will not work. Therefore we'll use the hostname topcat for the Internet interface. This hostname resolves to 202.7.1.19 or our eth0 interface. So, we'd like to disallow ftp requests from the Internet to topcat, but we want to allow ftp access to topcat internally through the eth1 interface. We can use the -R flag to replace or modify the existing rule. Note that our policy action remains as ACCEPT (which is not recommended, but we'll get to that in *Setting Policies [Default Rules]* on page 452). We can modify our rule to meet the needs outlined in this paragraph, adding -i eth0, with the command

```
# ipchains -R input 1 -p tcp --dport ftp -i eth0 -j REJECT
```

Notice that we have to specify the rule number with the replace (-R) flag. There is no other way to replace a rule. Now that we have replaced the rule, let's see what -L reports in Example 16-4. We will also use -v (verbose) so that we get the ifname (interface name) column displayed. Due to formatting constraints, Example 16-4 contains line wraps for the header and the rule. So

Example 16-4 Displaying the Replaced Rule Using -L and -v

```
[root@topcat]# ipchains -L -v
Chain input (policy ACCEPT: 20083 packets, 1141062 bytes):
 pkts bytes target      prot opt    tosa tosx ifname      mark        outsize
source                  destination              ports
    1    60 REJECT        tcp ------ 0xFF 0x00  eth0
anywhere                anywhere                 any ->    ftp
Chain forward (policy ACCEPT: 0 packets, 0 bytes):
Chain output (policy ACCEPT: 2731 packets, 356485 bytes):
[root@topcat]#
```

let's go through each of the header fields and associate the value in the rule. For the purposes of this discussion, we will refer to the rule as "example rule."

The header for the example rule appears as (line wrapped due to length)

```
pkts bytes target      prot opt    tosa tosx  ifname     mark
outsize  source                    destination           ports
```

Table 16.4 describes each of the fields.

Now that we know what the headers are, let's look at the fields in our example rule (in Example 16-4 on page 448) as

```
   1    60 REJECT     tcp  ------ 0xFF 0x00  eth0
anywhere                  anywhere                any ->    ftp
```

Table 16.4 Header Fields from Example 16-4

Header	Description
pkts	The number of network packets that have matched this rule since the rule was entered, or since the last boot, or since the last time `ipchains -Z` was executed.
bytes	The total number of bytes of all the packets that have matched this rule since the rule was entered, or since the last boot, or since the last time `ipchains -Z` was executed.
target	The action or named custom chain for the rule.
prot	The protocol for the rule.
opt	The options for the rule.
tosa	The TOS bitwise logical AND mask. Set with -t. See the resources cited in `ipchains Documentation` on page 487 for further details regarding this option.
tosx	The TOS bitwise logical XOR (exclusive OR) mask. Set with -t. See the resources cited in `ipchains Documentation` on page 487 for further details regarding this option.
ifname	The interface name to which this rule applies.
mark	The value used to mark this packet. Set with -m. See the resources cited in `ipchains Documentation` on page 487 for further details regarding this option.
outsize	The number of bytes that were copied to a device for handling by a user process. Applies only to rules using the -o option. See the resources cited in `ipchains Documentation` on page 487 for further details regarding this option.
source	The source IP address.
destination	The destination IP address.
ports	The source and destination ports or ICMP code and ICMP type. This field will be displayed as `sourceport -> destport` or `ICMP_code -> ICMP_type`.

Table 16.5 lists the association between each entry and the header from Table 16.4 as well as a brief description for this example rule.

Now that we know how to add, delete, and replace rules, let's go on and look at how to log packets that match a rule.

Logging   For the purpose of capturing log messages generated by ipchains, we will set up an entry in syslogd (see Chapter 8). All ipchains rules that specify logging will be logged with the selector kern.info. So we add the entry

```
kern.info                /var/log/kern.log
```

and then execute

```
killall -HUP syslogd
```

Once again, we will specify REJECT as the action so that the client gets a Connection refused message, and this time we also specify the -l option for logging

```
# ipchains -R input 1 -p tcp --dport ftp -i eth0 -j REJECT -l
```

Table 16.5 Association between the Rule Header and the Example Rule

Matching Header	Value in Example Rule	Description
pkts	1	One packet has been handled by this rule.
bytes	60	A total of 60 octets have been processed by this rule.
target	REJECT	The action of this rule is REJECT.
prot	tcp	The protocol for this rule is TCP.
opt	------	There are no options for this rule.
tosa	0xFF	The TOS logical AND mask.
tosx	0x00	The TOS logical XOR mask.
ifname	eth0	The interface to which this rule applies.
mark	N/A	There is no mark value associated with this rule.
outsize	N/A	This rule does not use -o.
source	anywhere	The source IP address for this rule to match is any address.
destination	anywhere	The destination IP address for this rule to match is any address.
ports	any -> ftp	The source port for this rule to match is any port. The destination port for this rule to match is ftp (port number 21).

Now that we have our new rule, let's suppose that a user from 101.143.3.9 (say, `evil.org`) in the Internet attempts to `ftp` to our site.

```
[evil.org]$ ftp topcat.whatever.the.domain.is.
```

Since our rule utilizes the action REJECT, then `evil.org` will get an immediate `Connection refused`. Since our rule specifies logging, let's take a look at the log file (`/var/log/kern.log`, in our case) in Example 16-5. A log entry will be generated for every packet that matches our rule. As you might imagine, your logs will grow very quickly if you are logging many rules and/or your server is very active.

Example 16-5 Log Entries Generated by Input Chain Rule 1

```
[root@topcat]# tail -f /var/log/kern.log
Aug  6 09:09:53 topcat kernel: Packet log: input REJECT eth0 PROTO=6
101.143.3.9:1025 202.7.1.19:21 L=60 S=0x00 I=181 F=0x4000 T=254
Aug  6 09:09:56 topcat kernel: Packet log: input REJECT eth0 PROTO=6
101.143.3.9:1025 202.7.1.19:21 L=60 S=0x00 I=182 F=0x4000 T=254
Aug  6 09:10:02 topcat kernel: Packet log: input REJECT eth0 PROTO=6
101.143.3.9:1025 202.7.1.19:21 L=60 S=0x00 I=183 F=0x4000 T=254
```

Now, let's describe the entries in the log record. Each record begins with a timestamp followed by the hostname and facility (`Aug 6 09:09:53 topcat kernel:` in the first log entry in Example 16-5). After that, we see `Packet log:`, which tells us that this log entry was generated by `ipchains`. The remaining fields are described in Table 16.6.

All of our log entries will be similar to those defined in Table 16.6. We will look at other examples throughout this chapter.

WARNING!

As noted earlier in this section, log entries are generated for each packet that matches a rule with the `-l` option. This will cause your log files to grow very quickly, and such log files will require special attention. See *Rule Writing and Logging Tips* on page 466 for a further discussion of log file management and tips on which rules to log.

Since we modified our rule to log all matching packets, let's see what the differences are when we list our rule. This is displayed in Example 16-6. Compare this to Example 16-4 on page 448. Note that the only difference between

Example 16-6 Verbose Listing of Our Modified Rule Specifying Logging

```
[root@topcat /root]# ipchains -L -v
Chain input (policy ACCEPT: 27472 packets, 1576415 bytes):
 pkts bytes target     prot opt     tosa tosx ifname      mark       outsize
source              destination          ports
    4   240 REJECT        tcp  ----l- 0xFF 0x00  eth0
anywhere            anywhere             any ->     ftp
Chain forward (policy ACCEPT: 0 packets, 0 bytes):
Chain output (policy ACCEPT: 3012 packets, 373044 bytes):
[root@topcat /root]#
```

Table 16.6 `ipchains` Log Entry Fields

Field	Description
input	In this case, the input chain. The name of the chain in which the matching rule occurred will be listed here.
REJECT	The action (or target) of the matching rule. REJECT in this case.
eth0	The interface at which the packet arrived. In the case of an output or forward chain, this would be the outbound interface.
PROTO=6	The protocol number associated with this packet. In this case 6 means TCP. A list of protocol numbers and names is found in `/etc/protocols`.
101.143.3.9:1025	The source IP address and source port number. In this case, the source IP address is `101.143.3.9` and the source port number is `1025`. If the protocol is ICMP instead of a source port number, you will see an ICMP type.
202.7.1.19:21	The destination IP address and destination port number. In this case, the destination IP address is `202.7.1.19` and the destination port number is `21`. If the protocol is ICMP instead of a destination port number, you will see an ICMP code.
L=60	The length, in octets, of the packet—60 octets in this case.
S=0x00	The TOS. If this value is `0x04` or `0x05`, then the packet must not be fragmented. If the value is `0x02` or `0x03`, then the packet is a fragment. This value of `0x00` indicates that the packet is fragmentable but is not a fragment. See the references cited in *ipchains Documentation* on page 487 for further details regarding TOS.
I=181	The IP identifier. A unique value whose primary purpose is to associate fragmented packets. In this case the identifier is `181`. Note that the other entries in Example 16-5 have different identifiers, meaning they are not fragments of the same packet. See *TCP/IP Networking Overview* on page 28 for further information.
F=0x4000	This is the fragment offset. It is used to reassemble fragmented packets. See *TCP/IP Networking Overview* on page 28 for further details.
T=254	The time to live for this packet in seconds, 254 in this case.
[rule number]	Linux kernel versions 2.2.10 and later will add the rule number, in brackets, of the rule that generated the log message.

Example 16-4 on page 448 and Example 16-6 (besides the packet and byte counts) is that the `opt` column includes the `l` option (`----l-` in Example 16-6).

Setting Policies (Default Rules)   A very important rule in the permanent chains is the default rule. This rule is also called the *policy*. As noted earlier in this chapter, the default policy is ACCEPT. This policy means that if no rules explicitly match a particular packet, then the packet will be allowed through.

While this type of policy may be desirable, and even required (such as at some universities and colleges), you should implement such a default rule only when absolutely necessary.

The preferred policy for all permanent chains is to disallow any packets that survive the rule base. You may accomplish this with the commands shown in Example 16-7.

Example 16-7 Establishing the REJECT Policy for Permanent Chains

```
# ipchains -P input REJECT
# ipchains -P forward REJECT
# ipchains -P output REJECT
```

You may specify any of the actions listed in Table 16.3 on page 445 (adhering to their restrictions)—with the exception of a custom chain—instead of REJECT.

You cannot use the -l (logging) flag with -P. Because of that restriction, it is quite common to add a final catchall REJECT rule in each chain that logs any packets which reach it. We utilize such a rule in *Simple Internal Network* on page 469.

The policy in Example 16-7 implements the philosophy that says, that which is not expressly permitted is forbidden. Once you have established the policy, you may go about the task of determining what you will allow and building the necessary rules. We look at an example of this process in *Simple Internal Network* on page 469.

WARNING!

If you are managing `ipchains` on a system over the network, make sure that you have an allow rule for the type of connection you are using *before* executing the commands in Example 16-7. Otherwise, once you execute those commands, your network connection will drop! Generally, you should always implement new rules at the console so that you do not inadvertently lock yourself out.

In any event, we strongly recommend that the only network connection you use to manage `ipchains` remotely is SSH or something similar (see Chapter 11 for a discussion of SSH and its alternatives).

ICMP Types and Codes   We briefly mentioned the ICMP in *TCP/IP Networking Overview* on page 28. We also provided references that contain further information about ICMP in that chapter. In this section, we provide two reference tables that might come in handy for your rule writing. We also provide some guidelines for choosing which ICMP types and codes to allow and deny in *ICMP Rules in a Custom Chain* on page 461. You will find ICMP references in *ICMP-Related References* on page 488. Please refer there for a more detailed discussion of ICMP types and codes—*TCP/IP Illustrated, Vol. 1* as cited in that section has a particularly good discussion.

You will likely want to disable a large number of ICMP communications relative to your external interface since many of them are used infrequently and have limited applicability to an Internet (or intranet) connection. Some of them, such as ICMP redirects (type 5), have been used for various types of attacks. Others, such as type `destination-unreachable` and code `fragmentation-needed`, are important for overall network functionality.

Table 16.7 lists the association between ICMP type numbers used in the 2.2.x kernel and ICMP type names as output by `ipchains -h icmp`.

Table 16.8 lists the association between ICMP code numbers used in the 2.2.x kernel and ICMP code names as output by `ipchains -h icmp`.

Recall from Table 16.2 on page 442 that you cannot specify ICMP codes with the `-d` and `--dport` options and that you cannot specify ICMP types with the `-s` and `--sport` options.

Sample ICMP Rules   We'll assume the scenario given in *Removing a Rule* on page 448, where our system `topcat` has the external IP address `202.7.1.19` associated with `eth0`. We will also assume the default REJECT policies set in *Setting Policies (Default Rules)* on page 452. Let's suppose that we wish to implement the following rules:

1. Allow `ping` from `topcat` to any external addresses.
2. Disallow external `ping` to `topcat` and log any such attempts.

Perhaps the first question to ask is, does our default REJECT rule really work? The answer is in Example 16-8. Here we are unable to `ping` to the

Table 16.7 ICMP IPv4 Types Supported by `ipchains`

ICMP Type Numbers	ICMP Type Name
0	echo-reply (pong)
3	destination-unreachable
4	source-quench
5	redirect
8	echo-request (ping)
9	router-advertisement
10	router-solicitation
11	time-exceeded (ttl-exceeded)
12	parameter-problem
13	timestamp-request
14	timestamp-reply
17	address-mask-request
18	address-mask-reply

Internet due to our default REJECT rules. If a system on the Internet attempted to ping topcat, it would get no response for the same reason. This latter behavior satisfies the first part of item 2 above. So we need to address item 1 and the logging part of item 2. Let's do it.

Example 16-8 Failed `ping` Attempt Due to Default REJECT Rules

```
[root@topcat]# ping podunk.edu
PING podunk.edu (1.1.1.1): 56 data bytes
ping: sendto: Operation not permitted
ping: wrote podunk.edu 64 chars, ret=-1
^C
[root@topcat]#
```

Table 16.8 ICMP Codes Supported by `ipchains`

ICMP Code Number	ICMP Code Name	Associated ICMP Type Name
0	network-unreachable	destination-unreachable
1	host-unreachable	destination-unreachable
2	protocol-unreachable	destination-unreachable
3	port-unreachable	destination-unreachable
4	fragmentation-needed	destination-unreachable
5	source-route-failed	destination-unreachable
6	network-unknown	destination-unreachable
7	host-unknown	destination-unreachable
9	network-prohibited	destination-unreachable
10	host-prohibited	destination-unreachable
11	TOS-network-unreachable	destination-unreachable
12	TOS-host-unreachable	destination-unreachable
13	communication-prohibited	destination-unreachable
14	host-precedence-violation	destination-unreachable
15	precedence-cutoff	destination-unreachable
0	network-redirect	redirect
1	host-redirect	redirect
2	TOS-network-redirect	redirect
3	TOS-host-redirect	redirect
0	ttl-zero-during-transit	time-exceeded (ttl-exceeded)
1	ttl-zero-during-reassembly	time-exceeded (ttl-exceeded)
0	ip-header-bad	parameter-problem
1	required-option-missing	parameter-problem

First, we'll handle item 1. We need to allow outbound `ping`, which means ICMP `echo-request`. We also need to allow inbound ICMP `echo-reply` in response to the `ping`. We can accomplish this with the commands shown in Example 16-9. The first command in the example appends the rule to the output chain, which allows the ICMP `echo-request` to go out `eth0` (the external interface). The second command appends the rule, which allows the inbound ICMP `echo-reply` through `eth0`.

Example 16-9 Allowing Outbound `ping`

```
[root@topcat]# ipchains -A output -p icmp --icmp-type echo-request -i eth0 -j ACCEPT
[root@topcat]# ipchains -A input  -p icmp --icmp-type echo-reply   -i eth0 -j ACCEPT
```

Example 16-10 shows us a listing to verify the rules.

Example 16-10 Listing the Newly Added ICMP Rules

```
[root@topcat]# ipchains -L
Chain input (policy REJECT):
target     prot opt     source               destination          ports
REJECT       tcp  ----l- anywhere             anywhere             any ->    ftp
ACCEPT       icmp ------ anywhere             anywhere             echo-reply
Chain forward (policy REJECT):
Chain output (policy REJECT):
target     prot opt     source               destination          ports
ACCEPT       icmp ------ anywhere             anywhere             echo-request
[root@topcat]#
```

Let's try to `ping podunk.edu` again. Example 16-11 shows us that the rules work.

Example 16-11 Rules Now Allow Outbound `ping`

```
[root@topcat]# ping podunk.edu
PING podunk.edu (1.1.1.1): 56 data bytes
64 bytes from 1.1.1.1: icmp_seq=0 ttl=255 time=0.5 ms
64 bytes from 1.1.1.1: icmp_seq=1 ttl=255 time=0.5 ms
64 bytes from 1.1.1.1: icmp_seq=2 ttl=255 time=0.5 ms
^C
[root@topcat]#
```

So we have satisfied item 1. Now we need to address the logging part of item 2. The command in Example 16-12 will take care of this. Let's verify. Suppose that a user at `evil.org` (101.143.3.9) tries to `ping topcat`. Example 16-13 shows the logs generated by such activity. Refer to Table 16.6 on page 452 for a description of the fields in each log entry.

An ICMP Type/Code You Should Not Block   Most modern implementations of IPv4 (Linux included) utilize MTU discovery to avoid fragmentation (fragmentation is discussed in the next section). MTU discovery works simply by sending packets out with the don't fragment bit set (see *TCP/IP Networking Overview* on page 28). When such a packet arrives at a system that needs a smaller-sized packet, it responds by sending an ICMP message of

Example 16-12 A Rule that Logs All `ping` Attempts through `eth0` to `topcat`

```
[root@topcat]# ipchains -A input -p icmp --icmp-type echo-request -d top-
cat -j REJECT -l
```

Example 16-13 Log Entries Generated by Packets Matching the Rule in Example 16-12

```
[root@topcat]# tail -f /var/log/kern.log
Aug  6 18:26:17 topcat kernel: Packet log: input REJECT eth0 PROTO=1
101.143.3.9:8 202.7.1.19:0 L=84 S=0x00 I=41410 F=0x4000 T=255
Aug  6 18:26:18 topcat kernel: Packet log: input REJECT eth0 PROTO=1
101.143.3.9:8 202.7.1.19:0 L=84 S=0x00 I=41412 F=0x4000 T=255
Aug  6 18:26:19 topcat kernel: Packet log: input REJECT eth0 PROTO=1
101.143.3.9:8 202.7.1.19:0 L=84 S=0x00 I=41414 F=0x4000 T=255
```

type `destination-unreachable` and code `fragmentation-needed` (see Table 16.7 on page 454 and Table 16.8 on page 455, respectively). If you block this communication, you will be unable to communicate with the system or network that requires the smaller packets.

In *ICMP Rules in a Custom Chain* on page 461, we will look at the most commonly allowed ICMP types.

PACKET FRAGMENTS

Sometimes the data comprising a packet makes the packet too large for transmission over the network. In such a case, the packet will be fragmented into smaller packets. When this occurs, only the first packet will contain the full header information associated with the collection of the packets. Since `ipchains` makes its decisions based on header information, this is a potential problem.

By default, the kernel configuration parameter CONFIG_IP_ALWAYS_DE-FRAGMENT is set to Y. This parameter causes the Linux kernel to reassemble all fragmented packets before processing. As long as this parameter is set, `ipchains` will not have to deal with fragments. Also, configuring the kernel for defragmentation with this parameter is **required** for IP masquerading support.

If you must configure your system so that it does not defragment (that is, fragments must pass through the firewall), then you must patch your kernel or upgrade to at least kernel version 2.2.11 to avoid a vulnerability. See `http://www.rustcorp.com/linux/ipchains/` for the patch and the details. Once you have patched or upgraded your kernel, then you can handle fragmented packets with the `-f` flag. For example, if we have the rule

```
# ipchains -A input -p ftp -s 0/0 ftp-data -d topcat -i eth0 -j ACCEPT
```

and we need to allow second and further fragments associated with this rule through our firewall, we could utilize the rule

```
# ipchains -A input -f -s 0/0 -d topcat -i eth0 -j ACCEPT
```

We cannot be any more specific with the fragment rule because the header will not contain the source and destination ports nor any ICMP types or codes. This rule does leave us vulnerable to exploits that take advantage of the fact that fragments are passed through the firewall. If at all possible, set your firewall up to defragment.

IP Masquerading

Linux IP masquerading gives us a way to hide internal IP addresses from the external network, behind the external interface of the firewall. This is a simple form of network address translation[4] (NAT) in which many internal addresses are mapped to one external address. IP masquerading does this by translating all internal addresses to the address of the external interface associated with the firewall illustrated in Figure 16.2. Thus, internal systems may initiate connections to the external network, but external systems cannot initiate connections to internal systems directly with the use if IP masquerading.

Figure 16.2 depicts the Linux system topcat acting as a firewall using ipchains. It is also masquerading all internal systems as the external address 202.7.1.19. Thus, whenever an internal system, such as the MacOS box (10.1.1.5), sends a packet to the Internet, it translates the outbound packet's source IP address 10.1.1.5 to 202.7.1.19 (*masquerading*). When a packet from the Internet is destined to an internal system, such as the Windows box (10.1.1.2), topcat will translate the destination IP address 202.7.1.19 to 10.1.1.2 (*demasquerading*). Masquerading and demasquerading are implemented through ipchains. Consequently, the procedure described in Figure 16.1 on page 439 still applies with the following exceptions: Masquerading of addresses occurs in the forward chain prior to processing by the output chain. Masquerading rules must be specified in the forward chain. Demasquerading is performed automatically *after* processing by the input chain. Demasqueraded packets are then sent to the output chain directly, skipping the forward chain.

Figure 16.2 purposely shows a variety of operating systems in the internal network. This is to emphasize that the operating system does not matter so long as the networking protocol between topcat and the internal network is TCP/IP.

The rules that implement masquerading are quite straightforward. There are a few issues we must address first, however. In order to properly configure our system for masquerading we must turn on IP forwarding (turn our system into a router—see *TCP/IP Networking Overview* on page 28). We will also want to load kernel modules to provide support for certain applications with respect to masquerading.

---

4. Cisco refers to this as *port address translation*.

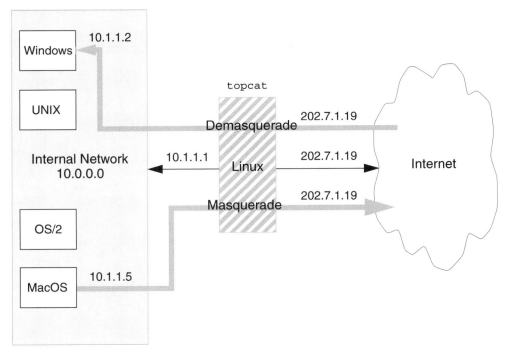

Fig. 16.2 Linux IP Masquerading

NOTE

RFC 1918 (see *Request for Comment* on page 40) specifies the IPv4 addresses that are reserved for internal use and that will never be issued as valid Internet addresses. These addresses are

```
10.0.0.0-10.255.255.255
172.16.0.0-172.31.255.255
192.168.0.0-192.168.255.255
```

If you are building an internal network and someday will be connected to the Internet, we advise you to use these addresses for your internal network. You'll be a good netizen, anyway!

IP Forwarding   There are two ways to turn on IP forwarding in a Red Hat system. The most generic method (that is, the method that will work on all Linux kernels version 2.0.3x and above) is to modify the ip_forward kernel variable. You can do this by executing

```
# echo "1" > /proc/sys/net/ipv4/ip_forward
```

As an alternative on Red Hat, set the FORWARD_IPV4 parameter in the /etc/sysconfig/network script to true. In other words, in /etc/sysconfig/network, change

```
FORWARD_IPV4=false
```

to

```
FORWARD_IPV4=true
```

Either of these approaches will enable IP forwarding and turn your Linux box into a router. This must be done if you wish to enable masquerading.

Kernel Modules that Support Masquerading   There are a number of kernel modules that exist for the purpose of properly handling certain applications in a masquerading environment. Some of the modules are listed in Table 16.9.

If you are going to implement one or more of the applications described in Table 16.9, you will need to add the module(s) with /sbin/modprobe (see the depmod(1) man page). For example, to add the ip_masq_ftp module, execute

```
# /sbin/modprobe ip_masq_ftp
```

This should be done prior to generating the rules.

In *Simple Internal Network Using DHCP* on page 481, we will look at placing the necessary modprobe command(s) into a start-up script. Load only the modules that are absolutely necessary.

Masquerading Rules   Once you have turned on IP forwarding and loaded the appropriate modules, you may add the rules necessary for masquerading. Let's suppose that our network is as depicted in Figure 16.2 on page 459 and that we wish to masquerade all of the internal addresses (network 10.0.0.0). Example 16-14 shows us the necessary masquerading rule.

Example 16-14 Masquerading All Internal Addresses

```
# ipchains -P forward REJECT
# ipchains -A forward -s 10.0.0.0/8 -j MASQ
```

Table 16.9 Masquerading Kernel Modules

Module	Description
ip_masq_ftp	Properly supports ftp masquerading. This module takes care of both active and passive outbound ftp connections.
ip_masq_raudio	Allows for the masquerading of Real Audio over UDP.
ip_masq_irc	Supports the masquerading of Internet relay chat (IRC).
ip_masq_quake	Supports the masquerading of Quake I, II, and III and QuakeWorld.
ip_masq_cuseeme	Supports the masquerading of CuSeeme video conferencing.
ip_masq_vdolive	Supports the masquerading of VDO-live video conferencing.
ip_masq_user	Support for user space access to captured packets (see the -o option in Table 16.2 on page 442).

The first line of this example sets the default rule in the forward chain to REJECT (we actually did this earlier). It is critical that your default forward chain policy is REJECT; otherwise someone could potentially use your system to masquerade his or her activity! The second line is the masquerading rule. It will cause all connections initiated from the internal network destined to the Internet to be masqueraded by topcat.

Masquerading rules in conjunction with other rules will be examined in *Simple Internal Network* on page 469.

ADDING CUSTOM CHAINS

Now that we understand the basics of ipchains, we'll take a look at ways in which we can organize our rules so that management is a little more organized. To this end, we may use custom chains, also known as user-defined chains. A custom chain, much like the permanent chains we've been discussing, is a collection of rules. As with the permanent chains, the rules are checked in order. Unlike permanent chains, however, custom chains cannot have a default rule or policy. In the next section, we'll take a look at example usage of custom chains.

ICMP Rules in a Custom Chain

Let's continue with our example as depicted in Figure 16.2 on page 459. Previously we set up rules that allowed for outbound ping from topcat; disallowed incoming ping requests to topcat and logged all such requests; and disallowed incoming ftp requests. The latter rule is redundant because of our default rule in all chains that denies anything which is not explicitly permitted. This rule base is listed in Example 16-10 on page 456.

Now let's create a custom chain that will accommodate the necessary ICMP rules and allow the most commonly accepted ICMP error messages. We need to worry only about the things we'll allow because of our default REJECT rule.

Recall from Table 16.1 on page 441 that custom chain names must not exceed 8 characters. To create the chain, we execute

```
# ipchains -N icmperr
```

We'll add rules that allow standard ICMP error messages. We'll keep an eye out (see Appendix A) for vulnerabilities associated with these ICMP packets, but so far they're pretty safe. These rules will also help if we need to troubleshoot our connection. Notice that we have not included our earlier ICMP rules (see Example 16-10 on page 456). This is because those rules were specific to the input and output chains. They had to be in order to meet our requirements (see *Sample ICMP Rules* on page 454). The rules in `icmperr` will be invoked by both the input and output chains.

Example 16-15 Adding Rules to a Custom Chain

```
# ipchains -A icmperr -p icmp --icmp-type destination-unreachable -j ACCEPT
# ipchains -A icmperr -p icmp --icmp-type parameter-problem -j ACCEPT
# ipchains -A icmperr -p icmp --icmp-type source-quench -j ACCEPT
# ipchains -A icmperr -p icmp --icmp-type time-exceeded -j ACCEPT
```

Now that we have created the custom chain, we need to invoke the chain through one or more of the permanent chains. Here we will add rules to the input and output chains that will invoke our custom chain. These two commands are shown in Example 16-16. Notice that we invoke the `icmperr` chain only if the protocol is ICMP. While this may be obvious, if we had left off `-p icmp` in the two commands shown in Example 16-16, the rules would still be valid and would inspect every packet against all the rules in `icmperr`. Such a mistake could cause significant performance problems.

Example 16-16 Adding Rules to Invoke the Custom Chain

```
[root@topcat]# ipchains -A input -p icmp -j icmperr
[root@topcat]# ipchains -A output -p icmp -j icmperr
```

Example 16-17 shows us what our rule base looks like now.

Example 16-17 Listing of Rule Base with Custom Chain

```
[root@topcat]# ipchains -L
Chain input (policy REJECT):
target     prot opt    source         destination      ports
ACCEPT     icmp ------ anywhere       anywhere         echo-reply
REJECT     icmp ----1- anywhere       topcat           echo-request
icmperr    icmp ------ anywhere       anywhere         any ->    any
Chain forward (policy REJECT):
Chain output (policy REJECT):
target     prot opt    source         destination      ports
ACCEPT     icmp ------ anywhere       anywhere         echo-request
icmperr    icmp ------ anywhere       anywhere         any ->    any
Chain icmperr (2 references):
target     prot opt    source         destination      ports
ACCEPT     icmp ------ anywhere       anywhere         destination-unreachable
ACCEPT     icmp ------ anywhere       anywhere         parameter-problem
ACCEPT     icmp ------ anywhere       anywhere         source-quench
ACCEPT     icmp ------ anywhere       anywhere         time-exceeded
[root@topcat]#
```

If you wish to delete a custom chain, you may do so with the `-X` flag. The chain must be empty in order to delete it, so you will have to flush it with `-F` first. Example 16-18 shows how we could delete the custom chain `icmperr`.

Example 16-18 Removing a Custom Chain

```
# ipchains -F icmperr
# ipchains -X icmperr
```

ANTISPOOFING RULES

When a host sends packets with the source IP address set to other than its own for the purpose of deception,[5] it's known as IP spoofing. One way to attempt to exploit systems from outside the network is to send packets that have the source IP address of an internal system. It is a good idea to prevent this.

There are two ways to prevent IP spoofing. The first and preferred method is to let the kernel routing code do it for you through source address verification. If the file

```
/proc/sys/net/ipv4/conf/all/rp_filter
```

exists on your system (and it will, by default, on both Red Hat 5.2 and 6.0), then you can turn on source address verification by putting a 1 into each rp_filter file on your system. You will have one of these files in a number of directories. A system with two ethernet interfaces would have the files shown in Example 16-19.

Example 16-19 Listing of All `rp_filter` Files

```
/proc/sys/net/ipv4/conf/all/rp_filter
/proc/sys/net/ipv4/conf/default/rp_filter
/proc/sys/net/ipv4/conf/eth0/rp_filter
/proc/sys/net/ipv4/conf/eth1/rp_filter
/proc/sys/net/ipv4/conf/lo/rp_filter
```

If you were to add another interface to the system, a new directory named after the interface would appear with the rp_filter and other files in it. Consequently, to automate this process, you can write a script. An example of such is provided in Example 16-41 on page 481.

The second way to prohibit IP spoofing is to write specific rules. To see how this might be done, let's consider our continuing example as illustrated in Figure 16.2 on page 459. The 10.0.0.0 internal network is connected to topcat via eth1, while eth0 is the external interface on topcat. The rules in Example 16-20 will do the trick.

Example 16-20 Antispoofing Rules

```
[root@topcat]# ipchains -A input -i ! eth1 -s 10.0.0.0/8 -j REJECT -l
[root@topcat]# ipchains -A input -i eth1 -s ! 10.0.0.0/8 -j REJECT -l
```

The first rule in this example denies any packet with a source IP address beginning with 10 that arrives on an interface other than eth1 (the internal interface). The second rule denies any packet arriving on eth1 (the internal interface) that has a source IP address beginning with anything other than 10. This second rule keeps our internal folks honest!

---

5. Except for the deception part, this is very much like what IP masquerading does.

WARNING!

The Linux kernel versions 2.1.x and 2.2.x automatically detect and deny any packets that arrive on a physical interface but claim a source IP address beginning with
127 (all IPv4 addresses beginning with 127 are reserved for loopback, which is a
software interface called lo0). Unfortunately, the kernel versions prior to 2.1.x and
2.2.x do not do this. So, if you are running Red Hat 5.2 or any other distribution
with a kernel version in the 2.0.x series or earlier, make sure that you add a rule to
prevent spoofing addresses beginning with 127. Such a rule could be implemented
with the command

```
# ipchains -A input -i ! lo -s 127.0.0.0/8 -j REJECT -1
```

This rule will cause any incoming packet arriving at any interface other than the
lo0 interface, with a source IP address beginning with 127, to be denied and logged.
Note: the specification of lo in the command instead of lo0 is **not** a typographical
error. The loopback interface must be specified as lo.

RULE ORDERING IS IMPORTANT!

The order of your rules is critical. Let's suppose that you want to allow the system at IP address 145.3.1.2 SSH access to topcat, but you do not want to allow
any other TCP connections. To disallow the TCP connection attempts, you
could enter the rule given in Example 16-21.

Example 16-21 Rule Rejecting TCP Connection Packets

```
# ipchains -A input -p tcp -d topcat -i eth0 -y -j REJECT
```

This rule rejects all TCP connection initiation packets (-y—see Table 16.2 on
page 442) destined to topcat arriving on the external interface (eth0). Later
on, you decide to add the necessary rules to allow SSH. These rules are given
in Example 16-22.

Example 16-22 Rules Allowing SSH

```
[root@topcat]# ipchains -A input -p tcp -s 145.3.1.2 1023:65535 -d top-
cat 22 -j ACCEPT
[root@topcat]# ipchains -A output -p tcp -d 145.3.1.2 1023:65535 -s top-
cat 22 -j ACCEPT
```

We need two rules. The input rule allows the incoming SSH connection
and the output rule allows the responses.

So, now you try SSH from 145.3.1.2 to topcat and it fails. This is due to
the fact that, when ssh is invoked from 145.3.1.2, the first thing it does is
attempt to establish a connection with topcat. It does this by sending a packet
with the SYN bit set and the ACK and FIN bits cleared (see *TCP/IP Networking Overview* on page 28). To fix the problem, you would simply move the input
rule in Example 16-22 up one, by using first the -D flag and then the -I flag
with the correct rule number.

NOTE

> Notice that we restrict the port numbers that may be used by 145.3.1.2 to 1023
> through and including 65535. In particular, port number 1023 is a privileged port,
> meaning that it requires root privilege to use it. We are allowing this because, by
> default, the SSH client (`ssh`) will try to use source port 1023. This behavior is gener-
> ally considered undesirable because the privileged nature of the port is unique to
> UNIX-like systems (including Linux—for example, an unprivileged user on a Win-
> dows box could run an application using a UNIX privileged source port). You can
> prevent `ssh` from using privileged ports by invoking `ssh -P` on the client and then
> modifying these rules to accept only unprivileged ports. However, the use of `-P` will
> disable both RHosts and RSA and Rhosts Authentication (but still permit RSA
> Authentication) because SSH "trusts" the privileged source port but not an unprivi-
> leged source port. See Chapter 11 for the details of SSH.

While this may seem quite straightforward, as your chains become more
complex, it often becomes difficult to debug them. Often the problem has to do
with the ordering of rules within a chain or rules being in the wrong chain.

Debugging rules can be quite time consuming. Your best bet, when you
are stumped by a problem with your rules, is to turn logging on for the rules
you suspect are causing the problem and to also use a network monitoring
program like `sniffit` (see *Network Monitoring* on page 38). This may give you
enough information to figure things out. As noted in Table 16.6 on page 452,
rule numbers will be logged at kernel version 2.2.10 and later.

The other debugging utility at your disposal is the `-c` flag, but it is of very
limited use. You must specify the parameters of the packet in order for it to
check the packet against the rule base. Example 16-23 gives us two invocations where the only difference is the `-y` flag.

Example 16-23 Using `ipchains -C`

```
[root@topcat]# ipchains -C input -p tcp -s 110.13.1.9 1025 -d topcat 22 -i eth1
accepted
[root@topcat]# ipchains -C input -p tcp -s 110.13.1.9 1025 -d topcat 22 -i eth1 -y
denied
[root@topcat]#
```

In short, if you were trying to debug the problem presented in this section, you
would probably execute the first `ipchains -c` command in Example 16-23. In
all likelihood, this would add to your confusion, because that packet is
accepted. Of course it is! It doesn't have the SYN bit set, the way the packet in
the second `ipchains -c` command does.

SAVING AND RESTORING RULES

You may be wondering how you can capture all these rules you've been playing
with into a file for future use and so you don't have to type them all in again.
There's good news. You can dump your current rule set (all these commands

we've been executing puts them in kernel memory) with the `/sbin/ipchains-save` command. For example

```
/sbin/ipchains-save > /tmp/testrules
```

will put all the rules in a format usable by `ipchains` into the file `/tmp/testrules` in ASCII format. You may use `-v` with this command to view each rule as it is saved.

To put the rules back into memory, execute

```
/sbin/ipchains-restore < /tmp/testrules
```

You can specify the `-v` option here as well to get a listing of each rule as it is added. This command also permits the `-f` option which flushes each chain before the rules are added.

RULE WRITING AND LOGGING TIPS

Your rules should, first and foremost, be based on your organization's Security Policy (see Chapter 2 for a further discussion of security policies). This will tell you what is and is not permitted. From there you will be able to establish a rule set.

Generally speaking, if your Security Policy permits, use DENY or REJECT as your default rule for each permanent chain. Write your ACCEPT rules by specifying as many options as possible. The following list provides some hints.

☞ Specify both source and destination IP addresses and ports.

☞ Do not use DNS names in your rules because they will not resolve if DNS is down and your rule sets will not load.

☞ Whenever possible, specify unprivileged ports (port numbers 1024 through and including 65535).

☞ Set up logging for any new rule or any rule that is still being tested. Also, log anything that should not occur.

This will limit the number of packets that might slip through; it will also make your rules easier to read and understand. We will do this in our examples in *Building Your Firewall* on page 469.

Anything that should not occur, or anything you don't think should occur, should be logged. It is a good idea to implement a catchall rule (see *Finally!* on page 480 for an example) that is the last rule in the chain and denies everything. Such a rule should have the logging option set.

Setting up a lot of logging does have the undesirable side effect of filling up your disks and generally adding to your work load. The utilities, `logrotate`, `logcheck`, and `swatch`, presented in Chapter 17 should help considerably.

Most important, test your rule base as you build it. This will make debugging much simpler and allow for catching problems that are hidden inside a complex rule set.

Changing Rules

If you need to change your rules in any way and for any reason, it is a good idea to use blocking rules while you work on the rule set. You can do this by adding the rules

```
# ipchains -A input 1 -j REJECT
# ipchains -A output 1 -j REJECT
# ipchains -A forward 1 -j REJECT
```

and then add, modify, or delete the necessary rules. When you are done, delete the above three rules.

Alternatively, you could disable your external interface by executing

```
# ifconfig eth0 down
```

where you would replace eth0 with the correct external interface on your system.

Make sure that you test your new rule base as much as possible before going back on-line.

`ipchains` Start-up Scripts

The whole point of using `ipchains` is to set up your firewall and to protect your system and internal network. To this end, once you have a working rule set, you will want to implement a start-up script so that your rules will be reestablished at each reboot.

There are two basic ways to do this. The first utilizes `ipchains-restore` as described in *Saving and Restoring Rules* on page 465. Example 16-24 provides us with an example start-up script, which we will call `fwconfig`. Once we have written this script and placed it in `/etc/rc.d/init.d`, we can set up the symbolic links with

```
# chkconfig --add fwconfig
```

which will then create start-up scripts with priority 9 in run levels 2, 3, 4, and 5 and kill scripts at priority 91 in run levels 0, 1, and 6, due to the

```
# chkconfig: 2345 9 91
```

entry (see the `chkconfig(8)` man page for more details). These run levels were chosen so that the firewall configuration is installed before networking starts (see the `/etc/rc.d/init.d/network` start-up script) and is removed after networking is stopped. This limits your vulnerability.

We could accomplish essentially the same thing by using a script that explicitly sets rules using the `ipchains` command. Example 16-41 on page 481 is one such script. The advantage of utilizing a script such as the one provided by Example 16-41 is that it offers greater flexibility in controlling the rule base. To utilize this approach, copy the script in Example 16-41 (or something similar) to /etc/fw/rules[6] and make it executable. Then simply change the script in Example 16-24 to appear something like that in Example 16-25 (additions noted in **bold**; depmod and modprobe are removed since they are in the script in Example 16-41).

Notice that we store our file in /etc/fw. The /etc/fw directory permissions should be 700 and it should be owned by root. If /etc/fw/rules is a file, its permissions should be 600; if it is a script, then 700. In either case /etc/fw/rules should be owned by root. The point is, only the root user should be able to access the file.

Example 16-24 ipchains Firewall Start-up Script

```
#!/bin/sh
#
# ******Firewall Start-Up Script***********
#
# chkconfig: 2345 9 91
# description: Activates/Deactivates ipchains firewall
#
#
#
case "$1" in
    start)
        # Verify the existence of the rule base
        if [ ! -f /etc/fw/rules ]; then
            echo "The ipchains rules don't exist!"
            echo "Can't start the firewall. Be Afraid!"
            exit 1
        fi
        /sbin/depmod -a
        /sbin/modprobe ip_masq_ftp
        /sbin/ipchains-restore < /etc/fw/rules
        echo "Firewall is up."
        ;;

    stop|open)
        /sbin/ipchains -F
        /sbin/ipchains -P input ACCEPT
        /sbin/ipchains -P output ACCEPT
        /sbin/ipchains -P forward ACCEPT
        echo "Firewall is down."
        ;;

    save)
        /sbin/ipchains-save > /etc/fw/rules
        echo "Rules saved."
        ;;

    *)
        echo "Usage: /etc/rc.d/init.d/fwconfig {start|stop|clear|save}"
        ;;
esac

exit 0
```

---

6. The use of /etc/fw/rules is arbitrary. The advantage of creating a separate directory, /etc/fw in this case, is that the directory permissions in addition to the file permissions can be made very restrictive.

Example 16-25 `ipchains` Firewall Start-up Script

```
#!/bin/sh
#
# ******Firewall Start-Up Script***********
#
# chkconfig: 2345 9 91
# description: Activates/Deactivates ipchains firewall
#
#
#
case "$1" in
    start)
        # Verify the existence of the rule base
        if [ ! -x /etc/fw/rules ]; then
            echo "The ipchains script doesn't exist or isn't"
            echo "executable! Can't start the firewall. Be Afraid!"
            exit 1
        fi
        /etc/fw/rules
        echo "Firewall is up."
        ;;

    stop|open)
        /sbin/ipchains -F
        /sbin/ipchains -P input ACCEPT
        /sbin/ipchains -P output ACCEPT
        /sbin/ipchains -P forward ACCEPT
        echo "Firewall is down."
        ;;

    save)
        /sbin/ipchains-save > /etc/fw/rules
        echo "Rules saved."
        ;;

    *)
        echo "Usage: /etc/rc.d/init.d/fwconfig {start|stop|clear|save}"
        ;;
esac
exit 0
```

BUILDING YOUR FIREWALL

In this section, we will explore a simple firewall scenario and go through a detailed look at building the rules for that scenario. This example is not intended to meet the needs of any particular environment, so use it at your own risk. The primary purpose of this section is to deepen your understanding of the way in which `ipchains` and IP masquerading work.

Simple Internal Network

For our first example, we'll use the scenario described in Figure 16.2 on page 459. We provide a simplified diagram in Figure 16.3 to set the stage.

For simplicity, this example will use a static external IP address. This approach provides a nice example for an internal network that must be firewalled from the rest of an organization's intranet (just change Internet to

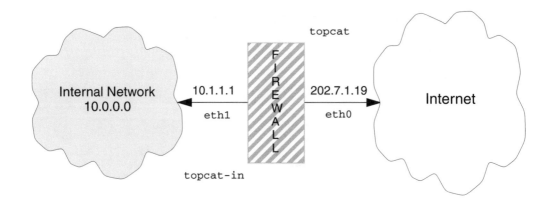

Fig. 16.3 Small Internal Network Example

intranet in Figure 16.3). We will look at dynamically assigned IP addresses, such as Point-to-Point Protocol (PPP), cable modem, and digital subscriber line (DSL) Internet connections in *Simple Internal Network Using DHCP* on page 481.

As before, `topcat` will be our Linux firewall with the external interface `eth0`, configured for the Internet IP address `202.7.1.19`, with a netmask of `255.255.255.240` (this means that our network address is `202.7.1.8`; see *TCP/IP Networking Overview* on page 28 for references that detail subnet masks). The external address resolves to the hostname `topcat`. The internal interface `eth1` is configured for the internal IP address `10.1.1.1`. This internal address resolves to the hostname `topcat-in`.

We'll make the following directives about what to allow and deny. This is based on our Security Policy (see Chapter 2), of course! We will assume that DNS and e-mail services are provided by our independent service provider (ISP). All e-mail is retrieved via a Post Office Protocol Version 3 (POP3) server. E-mail must be sent via SMTP. We'll use the hostname/IP address assignments shown in Table 16.10 for our primary DNS server, secondary DNS server, and mail server.

☞ **Default Policy.** Our default policy is REJECT.
☞ **Internal Network.** We want to allow our internal users to `ping`, `ftp`, and web browse any Internet destination. We must masquerade because we have only the one legal Internet IP address. We also want to allow internal access to `topcat-in` via SSH only.
☞ **External Network.** We do not want to allow any inbound connections from the Internet. So we need to configure our firewall to allow return connections only for our internal users.

Table 16.10 Simple Internal Network Example Server Addresses

Hostname	IP Address	Purpose of Host
dnssvr1	202.7.1.225	The primary DNS server.
dnssvr2	202.7.1.226	The secondary DNS server.
mail	202.7.1.227	The POP3 server. POP3 for retrieving mail, SMTP for sending mail.
rtr-isp	202.7.1.17	The router to the ISP. Our default gateway.

Let's implement the rules to meet these requirements. We take the approach of manually executing each command for the purposes of clarifying the example. The steps are outlined beginning with *Initial Steps and the Default Policy* below, continuing through *Finally!* on page 480. Example 16-41 on page 481 captures the manual commands into a script.

Initial Steps and the Default Policy   In accordance with our discussion in *Changing Rules* on page 467, we take down the interfaces and then flush the chains and start with a REJECT rule. We will remove the first REJECT rule when we are finished (see *Finally!* on page 480). We also set the default policy to REJECT. These steps are shown in Example 16-26. Note that we also added the two rules

```
[root@topcat]# ipchains -A input -i lo -s 0/0 -d 0/0 -j ACCEPT
[root@topcat]# ipchains -A output -i lo -s 0/0 -d 0/0 -j ACCEPT
```

to allow all communications through the loopback interface.

Example 16-26 Initial REJECT Rules

```
[root@topcat]# ifconfig eth1 down
[root@topcat]# ifconfig eth0 down
[root@topcat]# ipchains -F
[root@topcat]# ipchains -I input 1 -j REJECT
[root@topcat]# ipchains -I output 1 -j REJECT
[root@topcat]# ipchains -I forward 1 -j REJECT
[root@topcat]# ipchains -A input -i lo -s 0/0 -d 0/0 -j ACCEPT
[root@topcat]# ipchains -A output -i lo -s 0/0 -d 0/0 -j ACCEPT
[root@topcat]# ipchains -P input REJECT
[root@topcat]# ipchains -P output REJECT
[root@topcat]# ipchains -P forward REJECT
[root@topcat]# ifconfig eth1 up
[root@topcat]# ifconfig eth0 up
```

Now let's set up antispoofing (see *Antispoofing Rules* on page 463). We need to put a 1 in every rp_filter file, so we'll just use a short script as shown in Example 16-27.

For those of you using kernel versions 2.0.x and earlier, be sure to add the last command shown in Example 16-27 to prevent loopback spoofing. This rule won't hurt if you are using kernel version 2.1.x or 2.2.x.

Example 16-27 Antispoofing Script

```
[root@topcat]# for file in /proc/sys/net/ipv4/conf/*/rp_filter
> do
> echo "1" > $file
> done
[root@topcat]# ipchains -A input -i ! lo -s 127.0.0.0/8 -j REJECT -l
[root@topcat]#
```

We must next establish IP forwarding (to allow masquerading) and load the `ftp` masquerading module. Thus we execute the commands shown in Example 16-28. The first command, `/sbin/depmod -a`, performs a dependency check on all kernel modules.

Example 16-28 Initial Steps for Masquerading Support

```
[root@topcat]# depmod -a
[root@topcat]# modprobe ip_masq_ftp
[root@topcat]# echo "1" > /proc/sys/net/ipv4/ip_forward
```

Setting IP Masquerading Time-Outs   By default, the kernel sets time-outs to 15 minutes for masqueraded sessions of all types. There are three time-out parameters that apply to masquerading, TCP time-outs, TCP FIN packet (TCP packets with the finish bit set) time-outs, and UDP time-outs (see Table 16.1 on page 441). TCP FIN time-outs should be short, so we'll use 10 seconds. UDP time-outs are related to the time between the arrival or dispatch of individual UDP packets that belong to the same communication. A good time-out range for this is somewhere between 40 and 60 seconds, so we will use 50 seconds. General TCP time-outs are based on inactivity of a session. So, if you have an established `telnet` connection, for example, and you don't use it for 15 minutes, by default, the connection will be broken. You may find it useful to increase this time-out period; we use 1 hour (3600 seconds). The command is provided in Example 16-29.

Example 16-29 Setting the Masquerading Time-Outs

```
[root@topcat]# ipchains -M -S 3600 10 50
```

Generally Restricting Inbound Requests   We don't allow any inbound connections from the Internet, so we REJECT and log all requests to our internal network (10.0.0.0) and we REJECT all TCP SYN packets (described in *Rule Ordering Is Important!* on page 464) as our first two rules in the input chain as shown in Example 16-30.

Example 16-30 Reject All Inbound Attempts

```
[root@topcat]# ipchains -A input -i eth0 -p tcp -d 10.0.0.0/8 -j REJECT -l
[root@topcat]# ipchains -A input -i eth0 -y -p tcp -d topcat -j REJECT
```

ICMP Rules   At this point, we can deal with our ICMP requirements. We need to allow outbound `ping` and disallow incoming `ping`. We already established these rules in *Sample ICMP Rules* on page 454. But we'll be a little more careful, in accordance with *Rule Writing and Logging Tips* on page 466.

We need four rules to allow `ping` to go from our internal network to the Internet. Here's why. A user on a client in the 10.0.0.0 network executes a `ping` to a system in the Internet. The `ping` generates an ICMP `echo-request`, which goes to `topcat-in (eth1)` and is initially processed by the input chain. So we need a rule for that. The ICMP `echo-request` is then passed on to the forward chain for routing. We'll use the masquerading rule for that. Next the packet is passed on to the output chain to head off to the Internet via `eth0`. We'll need another rule there.

Then the packet leaves `topcat` and reaches the server. The server responds with an ICMP `echo-reply`, which arrives at `topcat (eth0)` to be processed by the input chain. We'll put a rule in there. Because the address is masqueraded, it skips the forward chain and goes straight to the output chain for processing before it heads out `eth1` and back to the internal client.

We also do not want to respond to `ping` requests from the Internet, so we'll add a rule for that—Example 16-31 provides the rules. (The numbering to the left is for illustrative purposes and will not actually appear.)

Example 16-31 Rules to Manage `ping`

```
1.  root@topcat]# ipchains -A input -p icmp --icmp-type echo-request -i eth0 -s
    0/0 -d topcat -j REJECT
2.  [root@topcat]# ipchains -A input -p icmp --icmp-type echo-request -i eth1 -s
    10.0.0.0/8 -d 0/0 -j ACCEPT
3.  [root@topcat]# ipchains -A forward -i eth0 -s 10.0.0.0/8 -d 0/0 -j MASQ
4.  [root@topcat]# ipchains -A output -p icmp --icmp-type echo-request -i eth0 -
    s topcat -d 0/0 -j ACCEPT
5.  [root@topcat]# ipchains -A input -p icmp --icmp-type echo-reply -i eth0 -s
    0/0 -d topcat -j ACCEPT
6.  [root@topcat]# ipchains -A output -p icmp --icmp-type echo-reply -i eth1 -s
    0/0 -d 10.0.0.0/8 -j ACCEPT
```

☞ Rule 1 disallows any `ping` requests from the Internet. Note that we use REJECT. Recall from Table 16.3 on page 445 that DENY and REJECT are identical when the rule matches ICMP.

☞ Rule 2 allows client `ping`s from the internal network to pass through the input chain when they arrive at `eth1`.

☞ Rule 3 is the general masquerading rule. It masquerades all internal 10.0.0.0 addresses as 202.7.1.19. This rule will masquerade all traffic and is required by all subsequent rules that permit external access.

☞ Rule 4 permits the `echo-request` to traverse the output chain with respect to `eth0` and head off to the destination system.

☞ Rule 5 allows the return `echo-reply` to traverse the input chain after it enters `eth0`.

☞ Rule 6 permits the `echo-reply` to pass through the output chain with respect to `eth1` and go off to the internal client.

To better understand the flow of the packet as well as the chains it passes through, it may be useful to take a look at Figure 16.4 on page 475. That diagram is specific to `ftp` and is discussed in *Rules for Allowing* `ftp` *from the Internal Network to the Internet* below, but the flow of packets through the chains is conceptually the same for all traffic through the firewall.

Now that we have taken care of `ping`, we need to set up the rules for ICMP error messages. We'll use the custom chain in Example 16-15 on page 462. Be sure to create the chain before you execute the commands given in Example 16-15. Once accomplished, we can add rules to jump to the `icmperr` chain as shown in Example 16-32.

Example 16-32 Rules that Invoke the ICMP Custom Chain

```
[root@topcat]# ipchains -A input -p icmp -s 0/0 -d topcat -j icmperr
[root@topcat]# ipchains -A output -p icmp -s ! 10.0.0.0/8 -d 0/0 -j icmperr
```

Note that we are specifying both source and destination in these rules. In particular, we will not allow our internal network to generate ICMP messages out to the Internet.

Except for the rules in *Finally!* on page 480, the rules we add after this point are not order dependent as long as they are added *after* the ones we've added up through this section.

Rules for Allowing `ftp` from the Internal Network to the Internet   Based on the requirements provided in *Simple Internal Network* on page 469, we must allow `ftp`. The setup for `ftp` is fairly complex because it utilizes two distinct ports for communication. In active `ftp` mode (executing `ftp` from the command line), the initial packet generated by the client sets the destination port to `ftp` (port number 21). For responses from the server, 21 becomes the source port number. When the client requests data from the server—for example, by executing `ls` at the `ftp` prompt—the client sends the request using the `ftp-data` port (port number 20) as the destination port. Passive `ftp` (usually implemented through web browsers) allows the `ftp` server to choose the data port. Fortunately we don't need to worry about passive `ftp` because `ip_masq_ftp` (see the references cited in the section, *Masquerading Documentation* on page 487) automatically takes care of it for us. But we do need to write the rules. It will help our understanding to refer to the diagram in Figure 16.4.

In order to configure this capability, we will need eight rules for `ftp` and one masquerading rule. The masquerading rule will be general and will apply to all connections originating from the internal network. As we step through this process, the numbers in Figure 16.4 correspond to the FTP rules noted in the following sections. The reference to masquerade in Figure 16.4 corresponds to *Masquerade Rule* on page 476.

FTP Rule 1.   A client in the internal network wants to connect to the Internet via `ftp`. The client will execute a command like `ftp ftp.reallycool.com`.

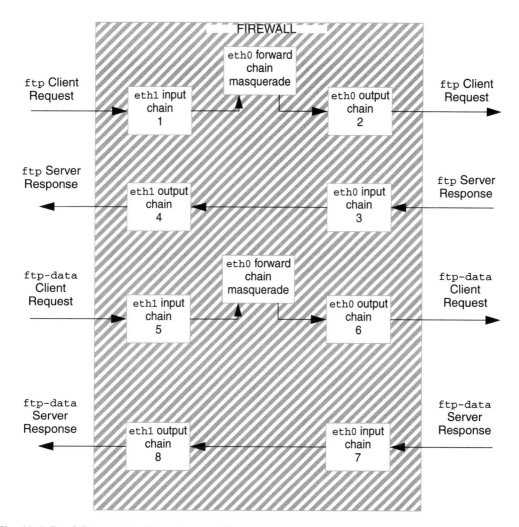

Fig. 16.4 Dual Connection Requirement for `ftp`

This generates a packet with the source IP address from the 10.0.0.0 network and the destination port number set to `ftp`. It will arrive at `topcat-in` (`eth1`). So, write the rule

```
[root@topcat]# ipchains -A input -i eth1 -p tcp -s 10.0.0.0/8
1024:65535 -d 0/0 ftp -j ACCEPT
```

This rule lets the packet through the input chain. Now we need to pass it through the forward chain. Note that we limit the source ports to unprivileged ones. This is a good idea, just to be on the safe side, and we'll do it wherever possible.

Masquerade Rule.   We previously added the masquerading rule in step 2 of Example 16-31 on page 473. This is a nonspecific rule that will masquerade everything from 10.0.0.0 to 202.7.1.19 through `eth0`. The next chain to deal with is the outbound chain.

FTP Rule 2.   We need to allow the packet which was accepted by **FTP Rule 1** through `eth1` through the output chain for `eth0`. Do this with

```
[root@topcat]# ipchains -A output -i eth0 -p tcp -s topcat 1024:65535
-d 0/0 ftp -j ACCEPT
```

Note that we specify the source as `topcat` instead of the 10.0.0.0 network. That is because the packet has been masqueraded. At this point, the `ftp` request from the internal client will be able to pass through the firewall to the server in the Internet.

FTP Rule 3.   Now we need to reverse the process and allow the server to reply to the client. The server will generate a packet with the source port number set to `ftp` (port 21) and the destination IP address to `topcat`. This packet will arrive on `eth0`. Thus the rule

```
[root@topcat]# ipchains -A input -i eth0 -p tcp -s 0/0 21 -d topcat
1024:65535 -j ACCEPT ! -y
```

Since this incoming response is to a masqueraded packet, the address will be demasqueraded, the forward chain will be skipped, and the packet will be sent on to the output chain for processing.

NOTE

> Since **FTP Rule 3** occurs after the TCP SYN REJECT rule (due to -A) entered as the first command in Example 16-30 on page 472, `ftp` connection requests from the Internet will never reach this rule. But we're paranoid, so we've added ! -y to this rule. We will do this for **FTP Rule 7** as well.

FTP Rule 4.   We need to allow the packet to pass back to the internal host that requested the `ftp` service to begin with. Accomplish this with

```
[root@topcat]# ipchains -A output -i eth1 -p tcp -s 0/0 ftp -d
10.0.0.0/8 1024:65535 -j ACCEPT
```

Notice that we may once again specify the real internal network address (as the destination this time). At this point, `ftp` connections will work. You will be able to log in via `ftp`. Try it! Then, try to execute `ls` and watch it fail! Let's fix that next.

FTP Rule 5.   The next thing the client will want to do is establish a data connection. When the client executes an `ls`, `get`, `put`, etc., command, it will generate an `ftp-data` (port number 20) packet. This rule is identical to that in **FTP Rule 1** except for the port.

```
[root@topcat]# ipchains -A input -i eth1 -p tcp -s 10.0.0.0/8
1024:65535 -d 0/0 ftp-data -j ACCEPT
```

Once the packet passes this rule, it will go on to the forward chain. We already set up that rule in **Masquerade Rule** on page 476, so there is nothing further to do. The packet will pass through the forward chain, the source IP address being masqueraded, and then will go to the output chain. So we'll add that rule next.

FTP Rule 6.   This step is identical to **FTP Rule 2** except for the port. The rule is

```
[root@topcat]# ipchains -A output -i eth0 -p tcp -s topcat 1024:65535
-d 0/0 ftp-data -j ACCEPT
```

At this point the Internet `ftp` server can receive `ftp-data` requests from our internal client. Next we need to allow the server to respond to the request.

FTP Rule 7.   This step is identical to **FTP Rule 3** except that the port is `ftp-data`.

```
[root@topcat]# ipchains -A input -i eth0 -p tcp -s 0/0 21 -d topcat
1024:65535 -j ACCEPT ! -y
```

Once again, demasquerading occurs after this chain, the forward chain is skipped, and processing is passed to the output chain.

FTP Rule 8.   This rule is identical to **FTP Rule 4** except for the port.

```
[root@topcat]# ipchains -A output -i eth1 -p tcp -s 0/0 ftp-data -d
10.0.0.0/8 1024:65535 -j ACCEPT
```

We're done! Now users on the internal network can access the Internet via `ftp` (that was a lot of work—ask for a raise).

Allowing DNS, POP3, and Web Access   Conceptually, every rule required for these services is like that for `ftp`. The basic difference is that we won't have two distinct ports to deal with. DNS and POP3 do utilize both TCP and UDP, so we will need to deal with that. We'll cover each of the services in separate subsections.

DNS Rules.   We need to allow DNS queries from internal hosts and from `topcat` to reach the DNS servers in the Internet. The port number for DNS is 53 and its equivalent name from `/etc/services` is `domain`. Example 16-33 provides the necessary rules. Once again, we write the rules following the flow of events shown in Figure 16.4 on page 475. (The numbers to the left are for descriptive purposes.)

Rules 1 through 4 accept DNS queries from the internal network through `eth1` in the input chain. Rules 5 through 8 allow those queries out to the Internet through `eth0`. Rules 9 through 11 allow the DNS responses to return through `eth0`. Note that once again we disallow TCP SYN packets. We

Example 16-33 Rules to Permit DNS Queries

```
 1.  [root@topcat]# ipchains -A input -i eth1 -p tcp -s 10.0.0.0/8 -d dnssvr1
     domain -j ACCEPT
 2.  [root@topcat]# ipchains -A input -i eth1 -p tcp -s 10.0.0.0/8 -d dnssvr2
     domain -j ACCEPT
 3.  [root@topcat]# ipchains -A input -i eth1 -p udp -s 10.0.0.0/8 -d dnssvr1
     domain -j ACCEPT
 4.  [root@topcat]# ipchains -A input -i eth1 -p udp -s 10.0.0.0/8 -d dnssvr2
     domain -j ACCEPT
 5.  [root@topcat]# ipchains -A output -i eth0 -p tcp -s topcat -d dnssvr1 domain
     -j ACCEPT
 6.  [root@topcat]# ipchains -A output -i eth0 -p tcp -s topcat -d dnssvr2 domain
     -j ACCEPT
 7.  [root@topcat]# ipchains -A output -i eth0 -p udp -s topcat -d dnssvr1 domain
     -j ACCEPT
 8.  [root@topcat]# ipchains -A output -i eth0 -p udp -s topcat -d dnssvr2 domain
     -j ACCEPT
 9.  [root@topcat]# ipchains -A input -i eth0 -p tcp -d topcat -s dnssvr1 domain
     -j ACCEPT ! -y
10.  [root@topcat]# ipchains -A input -i eth0 -p tcp -d topcat -s dnssvr2 domain
     -j ACCEPT
11.  [root@topcat]# ipchains -A input -i eth0 -p udp -d topcat -s dnssvr2 domain
     -j ACCEPT
12.  root@topcat]# ipchains -A output -i eth1 -p tcp -d 10.0.0.0/8 -s dnssvr1
     domain -j ACCEPT
13.  [root@topcat]# ipchains -A output -i eth1 -p tcp -d 10.0.0.0/8 -s dnssvr2
     domain -j ACCEPT
14.  [root@topcat]# ipchains -A output -i eth1 -p udp -d 10.0.0.0/8 -s dnssvr1
     domain -j ACCEPT
15.  [root@topcat]# ipchains -A output -i eth1 -p udp -d 10.0.0.0/8 -s dnssvr2
     domain -j ACCEPT
```

cannot do this for UDP. Rules 12 through 15 permit the DNS responses to flow back to the internal clients.

POP3 Rules. Next we'll add the rules for e-mail access. Since POP3 uses SMTP (port 25, also known as smtp) to send mail, we need to include those as well. We list the rules for POP3 in Example 16-34. As with DNS, POP3 uses both UDP and TCP, so our rules allow for that.

Example 16-34 Rules to Permit POP3 Retrieval of E-Mail

```
[root@topcat]# ipchains -A input -i eth1 -p tcp -s 10.0.0.0/8 -d mail
pop-3 -j ACCEPT
[root@topcat]# ipchains -A input -i eth1 -p udp -s 10.0.0.0/8 -d mail
pop-3 -j ACCEPT
[root@topcat]# ipchains -A output -i eth0 -p tcp -s topcat -d mail pop-3
-j ACCEPT
[root@topcat]# ipchains -A output -i eth0 -p udp -s topcat -d mail pop-3
-j ACCEPT
[root@topcat]# ipchains -A input -i eth0 -p tcp -d topcat -s mail pop-3 -
j ACCEPT ! -y
[root@topcat]# ipchains -A input -i eth0 -p udp -d topcat -s mail pop-3 -
j ACCEPT
root@topcat]# ipchains -A output -i eth1 -p tcp -d 10.0.0.0/8 -s mail
pop-3 -j ACCEPT
[root@topcat]# ipchains -A output -i eth1 -p udp -d 10.0.0.0/8 -s mail
pop-3 -j ACCEPT
```

Now let's enter the rules for SMTP to allow e-mail to be sent. These are shown in Example 16-35. Note that SMTP uses TCP only.

Example 16-35 Rules to Permit SMTP Sending of E-Mail

```
[root@topcat]# ipchains -A input -i eth1 -p tcp -s 10.0.0.0/8 -d mail
smtp -j ACCEPT
[root@topcat]# ipchains -A output -i eth0 -p tcp -s topcat -d mail smtp -
j ACCEPT
[root@topcat]# ipchains -A input -i eth0 -p tcp -d topcat -s mail smtp -j
ACCEPT ! -y
root@topcat]# ipchains -A output -i eth1 -p tcp -d 10.0.0.0/8 -s mail
smtp -j ACCEPT
```

Web Access Rules. Similarly, we allow access to the World Wide Web (WWW). The port number for web access is 80 and its name is www. The rules are similar to previous rules and are shown in Example 16-36. Note that in this example we allow web access only to port 80. Many web servers will use other port numbers. If you wish to allow certain port numbers, such as 8080 and 8008, you would need to add rules similar to those shown in Example 16-36 for that purpose. If you wish to allow any port number for web access, you duplicate the rules shown in Example 16-36 with rules that specify 1024:65535 instead of www. Such an approach allows all TCP traffic initiated internally to go through the firewall. Make sure that your Security Policy permits this. For completion, we show such permissive rules in Example 16-37, but note that these are not supportive of the requirements specified in the description of our example (see *Simple Internal Network* on page 469 and following subsections).

The use of the rules outlined in Example 16-37 does make the rule sets simpler but also represents a less restrictive implementation. These rules are not used in the subsequent Example 16-41 on page 481.

Example 16-36 Rules to Permit Web Access

```
[root@topcat]# ipchains -A input -i eth1 -p tcp -s 10.0.0.0/8 -d 0/0 www
-j ACCEPT
[root@topcat]# ipchains -A output -i eth0 -p tcp -s topcat -d 0/0 www -j
ACCEPT
[root@topcat]# ipchains -A input -i eth0 -p tcp -d topcat -s 0/0 www -j
ACCEPT ! -y
[root@topcat]# ipchains -A output -i eth1 -p tcp -d 10.0.0.0/8 -s 0/0 www
-j ACCEPT
```

Example 16-37 Rules to Permit All Internally Initiated Traffic Using Unprivileged Ports

```
[root@topcat]# ipchains -A input -i eth1 -p tcp -s 10.0.0.0/8 -d 0/0
1024:65535 -j ACCEPT
[root@topcat]# ipchains -A output -i eth0 -p tcp -s topcat -d 0/0
1024:65535 -j ACCEPT
[root@topcat]# ipchains -A input -i eth0 -p tcp -d topcat -s 0/0
1024:65535 -j ACCEPT ! -y
[root@topcat]# ipchains -A output -i eth1 -p tcp -d 10.0.0.0/8 -s 0/0
1024:65535 -j ACCEPT
```

This completes the rules necessary for the required services specified at the beginning of *Simple Internal Network* on page 469. It should be noted that these rules allow access to the services specified by any of our internal hosts and from `topcat` itself.

Allowing Internal SSH   The last thing we need to do to meet the requirements set forth for this example (see beginning of *Simple Internal Network* on page 469) is permit SSH connections from the internal network to `topcat-in`. The port number for SSH is 22 and its name is `ssh`. This is much easier than the other rule sets since we do not need to allow the SSH connections to pass through our firewall. The necessary rules are given in Example 16-38.

Example 16-38 Rules Allowing SSH from the Internal Network to `topcat-in`

```
[root@topcat]# ipchains -A input -i eth1 -p tcp -s 10.0.0.0/8 1023:65535
-d topcat-in ssh -j ACCEPT
[root@topcat]# ipchains -A output -i eth1 -p tcp -d 10.0.0.0/8 1023:65535
-s topcat-in ssh -j ACCEPT
```

NOTE

If we also want to allow `topcat-in` to connect to the internal network via SSH we could accomplish this by adding `-b` (bidirectional) to each of the rules in Example 16-38.

Finally!   We're nearly done! We just have a couple more steps. First let's reject everything we haven't explicitly allowed and log such activity. This will make our log files grow rapidly, so we'll need to manage them as described in *Rule Writing and Logging Tips* on page 466. These are the catchall rules. We append them to the end of each chain as shown in Example 16-39.

Example 16-39 Catchall REJECT Rules

```
[root@topcat]# ipchains -A input -l -j REJECT
[root@topcat]# ipchains -A output -l -j REJECT
[root@topcat]# ipchains -A forward -l -j REJECT
```

Now let's remove the initial blocking rules that we input prior to modifying our chains (see *Initial Steps and the Default Policy* on page 471). Execute the commands given in Example 16-40 to accomplish this.

Example 16-40 Removing the Blocking Rules

```
[root@topcat]# ipchains -D input 1
[root@topcat]# ipchains -D output 1
[root@topcat]# ipchains -D forward 1
```

We've now implemented the firewall to meet the requirements set forth at the beginning of *Simple Internal Network* on page 469. At this point, you will want to save your configuration, using `ipchains-save`, and/or write a script to reinstate this rule base at each reboot (see *ipchains Start-up Scripts* on page 467). In the next section we will look at an example set of start-up scripts that incorporates everything discussed in this example.

Simple Internal Network Using DHCP

"But," you say, "I use PPP! How do I do this with PPP?" Or maybe you use DSL, a cable modem, or some other mechanism that requires the Dynamic Host Configuration Protocol (DHCP). No problem.

Let's assume that our example is identical to that given in *Simple Internal Network* on page 469. The main difference between that example and using DHCP or PPP with dynamic addressing is in the way we obtain the IP address for the external interface.

NOTE

> If you are not familiar with the basic configuration of PPP and/or DHCP, please review the resources cited in *ISP Connectivity-Related Resources* on page 487.

The script in Example 16-41 incorporates all of the rules we implemented in *Simple Internal Network* on page 469. It uses shell environment variables to make the script more adaptable to many situations. It also adds the required rules to allow DHCP to work, and it fetches the dynamically assigned IP addresses. The script is commented, but, to make it easier, the additional entries for DHCP (PPP, DSL, cable modems, etc.) are in **bold**. If you are using DHCP, you will not necessarily use all of the entries in **bold** because some of them apply to PPP specifically. So use the entries appropriately.

Use this script, or something similar, as a start-up script to start your firewall at boot time. See *ipchains Start-up Scripts* on page 467 for details on setting up start-up scripts.

Example 16-41 Firewall Start-up Script

```
#!/bin/bash
# Begin with setting some environment variables—first PATH
PATH=/sbin:/usr/sbin:/bin:/usr/bin;export PATH

# External Interface—uncomment the one you use or set appropriately
EXIF="eth0"
# EXIF="ppp0"

# Internal Interface—set appropriately
INIF="eth1"

# DMZ Interface—set appropriately
# DMZIF="eth2"

# If you are using static IP addresses, set it below
EXIP="202.7.1.19"     # topcat
# If you use DHCP, you'll need to fetch the address
# Uncomment the next line if you use DHCP, such as DSL, PPP, etc.
# EXIP="`ifconfig|grep -A 2 $EXTIF|awk '/inet/ { print $2 }'\
#     |sed -e s/addr://`"
```

Example 16-41 Firewall Start-up Script (Continued)

```
#
# DHCP addresses are "leased" for a period of time after which
# the address may change, so make sure that this script is
# re-run each time the IP address changes. See DHCP documentation

# Now set the external broadcast address.
# This script only uses the broadcast for DHCP.
#EXBCAST="202.7.1.31"
#
# To get the broadcast address for DHCP uncomment the next line
# EXBCAST="`ifconfig|grep -A 2 $EXTIF|awk '/inet/ { print $4 }'\
#     |sed -e s/Bcast://'"
# Next set your internal IP address
INIP="10.1.1.1"    # topcat-in
#
# Now set the network variables
INNET="10.0.0.0/8"
# DMZNET="202.7.1.24/30"    # Uncomment this if used
#End of variable section

# Let's be paranoid and enter blocking rules to start
# We'll disable them at the end. Also we'll allow lo here and
# set up the REJECT policy.
ipchains -F
ipchains -I input 1 -j REJECT
ipchains -I output 1 -j REJECT
ipchains -I forward 1 -j REJECT
ipchains -A input -i lo -s 0/0 -d 0/0 -j ACCEPT
ipchains -A output -i lo -s 0/0 -d 0/0 -j ACCEPT
ipchains -P input REJECT
ipchains -P output REJECT
ipchains -P forward REJECT
#

#
# initial masquerading requirements
depmod -a
modprobe ip_masq_ftp
echo "1" > /proc/sys/net/ipv4/ip_forward
ipchains -M -S 3600 10 50
# end initial masquerading requirements

# DHCP support requires this...uncomment if necessary
echo "1" > /proc/sys/net/ipv4/ip_dynaddr
#
# anti-spoofing
for file in /proc/sys/net/ipv4/conf/*/rp_filter
do
    echo "1" > $file
done
ipchains -A input -i ! lo -s 127.0.0.0/8 -j REJECT -l
# end anti-spoof

# Internet input rejects
ipchains -A input -i $EXIF -p tcp -d $INNET -j REJECT -l
ipchains -A input -i $EXIF -y -p tcp -d $EXIP -j REJECT
# end input rejects

# ICMP Custom Chain—catch important ICMP messages
#     our catch-all reject rule will drop the rest.
# First create the chain...no problem if it already exists.
# Real problems if it doesn't.
ipchains -N icmperr 2>/dev/null
# Now add the rules
ipchains -A icmperr -p icmp --icmp-type destination-unreachable -j ACCEPT
ipchains -A icmperr -p icmp --icmp-type parameter-problem -j ACCEPT
ipchains -A icmperr -p icmp --icmp-type source-quench -j ACCEPT
```

Example 16-41 Firewall Start-up Script (Continued)

```
ipchains -A icmperr -p icmp --icmp-type time-exceeded -j ACCEPT
# end ICMP Custom Chain

# ICMP rules—Allow ping out but not in.
ipchains -A input -p icmp --icmp-type echo-request -i $EXIF -s 0/0 -d $EXIP -j
REJECT
ipchains -A input -p icmp --icmp-type echo-request -i $INIF -s $INNET -d 0/0 -j
ACCEPT
ipchains -A output -p icmp --icmp-type echo-request -i $EXIF -s $EXIP -d 0/0 -j
ACCEPT
ipchains -A input -p icmp --icmp-type echo-reply -i $EXIF -s 0/0 -d $EXIP -j
ACCEPT
ipchains -A output -p icmp --icmp-type echo-reply -i $INIF -s 0/0 -d $INNET -j
ACCEPT
ipchains -A input -p icmp -s 0/0 -d $EXIP -j icmperr
ipchains -A output -p icmp -s ! $INNET -d 0/0 -j icmperr
# end ICMP rules

# Masquerading Rule
ipchains -A forward -i $EXIF -s $INNET -d 0/0 -j MASQ
# end masq
# Support for DHCP client
ipchains -A input -i $EXIF -p udp -s 0/0 bootps -d 255.255.255.255 bootpc
ipchains -A input -i $EXIF -p tcp -s 0/0 bootps -d 255.255.255.255 bootpc
ipchains -A output -i $EXIF -p udp -s 0/0 bootpc -d 255.255.255.255 bootps
ipchains -A output -i $EXIF -p tcp -s 0/0 bootpc -d 255.255.255.255 bootps
# end DHCP client rules

# ftp rules
ipchains -A input -i $INIF -p tcp -s $INNET 1024:65535 -d 0/0 ftp -j ACCEPT
ipchains -A output -i $EXIF -p tcp -s $EXIP 1024:65535 -d 0/0 ftp -j ACCEPT
ipchains -A input -i $EXIF -p tcp -s 0/0 ftp -d $EXIP 1024:65535 -j ACCEPT ! -y
ipchains -A output -i $INIF -p tcp -s 0/0 ftp -d $INNET 1024:65535 -j ACCEPT
ipchains -A input -i $INIF -p tcp -s $INNET 1024:65535 -d 0/0 ftp-data -j ACCEPT
ipchains -A output -i $EXIF -p tcp -s $EXIP -d 0/0 ftp-data -j ACCEPT
ipchains -A input -i $EXIF -p tcp -s 0/0 ftp-data -d $EXIP 1024:65535 -j ACCEPT ! -y
ipchains -A output -i $INIF -p tcp -s 0/0 ftp-data -d $INNET 1024:65535 -j ACCEPT
# end ftp rules

# DNS rules
ipchains -A input -i $INIF -p tcp -s $INNET -d dnssvr1 domain -j ACCEPT
ipchains -A input -i $INIF -p tcp -s $INNET -d dnssvr2 domain -j ACCEPT
ipchains -A input -i $INIF -p udp -s $INNET -d dnssvr1 domain -j ACCEPT
ipchains -A input -i $INIF -p udp -s $INNET -d dnssvr2 domain -j ACCEPT
ipchains -A output -i $EXIF -p tcp -s $EXIP -d dnssvr1 domain -j ACCEPT
ipchains -A output -i $EXIF -p tcp -s $EXIP -d dnssvr2 domain -j ACCEPT
ipchains -A output -i $EXIF -p udp -s $EXIP -d dnssvr1 domain -j ACCEPT
ipchains -A output -i $EXIF -p udp -s $EXIP -d dnssvr2 domain -j ACCEPT
ipchains -A input -i $EXIF -p tcp -d $EXIP -s dnssvr1 domain -j ACCEPT ! -y
ipchains -A input -i $EXIF -p tcp -d $EXIP -s dnssvr2 domain -j ACCEPT
ipchains -A input -i $EXIF -p udp -d $EXIP -s dnssvr2 domain -j ACCEPT
ipchains -A output -i $INIF -p tcp -d $INNET -s dnssvr1 domain -j ACCEPT
ipchains -A output -i $INIF -p tcp -d $INNET -s dnssvr2 domain -j ACCEPT
ipchains -A output -i $INIF -p udp -d $INNET -s dnssvr1 domain -j ACCEPT
ipchains -A output -i $INIF -p udp -d $INNET -s dnssvr2 domain -j ACCEPT
# end DNS rules

# POP-3/SMTP Rules
ipchains -A input -i $INIF -p tcp -s $INNET -d mail pop-3 -j ACCEPT
ipchains -A input -i $INIF -p udp -s $INNET -d mail pop-3 -j ACCEPT
ipchains -A output -i $EXIF -p tcp -s $EXIP -d mail pop-3 -j ACCEPT
ipchains -A output -i $EXIF -p udp -s $EXIP -d mail pop-3 -j ACCEPT
ipchains -A input -i $EXIF -p tcp -d $EXIP -s mail pop-3 -j ACCEPT ! -y
ipchains -A input -i $EXIF -p udp -d $EXIP -s mail pop-3 -j ACCEPT
ipchains -A output -i $INIF -p tcp -d $INNET -s mail pop-3 -j ACCEPT
ipchains -A output -i $INIF -p udp -d $INNET -s mail pop-3 -j ACCEPT
ipchains -A input -i $INIF -p tcp -s $INNET -d mail smtp -j ACCEPT
```

Example 16-41 Firewall Start-up Script (Continued)

```
ipchains -A output -i $EXIF -p tcp -s $EXIP -d mail smtp -j ACCEPT
ipchains -A input -i $EXIF -p tcp -d $EXIP -s mail smtp -j ACCEPT ! -y
ipchains -A output -i $INIF -p tcp -d $INNET -s mail smtp -j ACCEPT
# end POP-3/SMTP Rules

# Web Access Rules
ipchains -A input -i $INIF -p tcp -s $INNET -d 0/0 www -j ACCEPT
ipchains -A output -i $EXIF -p tcp -s $EXIP -d 0/0 www -j ACCEPT
ipchains -A input -i $EXIF -p tcp -d $EXIP -s 0/0 www -j ACCEPT ! -y
ipchains -A output -i $INIF -p tcp -d $INNET -s 0/0 www -j ACCEPT
# end Web

# SSH Rules
ipchains -A input -i $INIF -p tcp -s $INNET -d $INIP ssh -j ACCEPT
ipchains -A output -i $INIF -p tcp -d $INNET -s $INIP ssh -j ACCEPT
# end SSH

# Catch-All rules
ipchains -A input -l -j REJECT
ipchains -A output -l -j REJECT
ipchains -A forward -l -j REJECT
# end Catch-All

# Remove blocking rules
ipchains -D input 1
ipchains -D output 1
ipchains -D forward 1
# end remove
```

`ipchains` ISN'T JUST FOR FIREWALLS!

It's not! This very powerful utility can be implemented on a system with a single interface. Much of what we have described in this chapter applies to such a case, and the rules will be simpler when only a single interface is involved. You should implement `ipchains` along with other restrictive utilities such as `xinetd` on all your critical servers.

ONE MORE THING...

Just because you allow a service for a given destination system with an `ipchains` rule doesn't mean it will work. Remember, the service must be running on the server, too! See Chapter 10 for a further discussion of network services.

SUPPLEMENTARY UTILITIES

Other Examples

There are excellent examples of `ipchains` in the *IPCHAINS HOWTO*, TrinityOS, and the *Linux IP Masquerading mini HOWTO* documents. These documents are cited in *ipchains Documentation* on page 487 and *Masquerading Documentation* on page 487.

Port Forwarding

There are a variety of tools that provide for the forwarding of connections from the firewall to an internal, privately addressed system. These tools support the forwarding of SMTP, www, ftp, and other services. The two major tools that support this functionality are IPPORTFW for kernel versions 2.0.x and IPMASQADM for kernel versions 2.2.x. These tools are discussed in *Linux IP Masquerading mini HOWTO* as cited in *Masquerading Documentation* on page 487.

To learn more about IPPORTFW visit

```
http://www.ox.compsoc.org.uk/~steve/portforwarding.html
```

It turns out that IPMASQADM for kernel versions 2.2.x contains a superset of the functionality in IPPORTFW. To learn more about it, visit

```
http://juanjox.kernelnotes.org/
```

The `fwconfig` GUI

The fwconfig utility provides a graphical user interface (GUI) front end to writing ipchains rules. Find out more about it at

```
http://www.mindstorm.com/~sparlin/fwconfig.shtml
```

Mason

Mason is available from

```
http://users.dhp.com/~whisper/mason/
```

It is a utility that generates rules dynamically. You set up and run Mason on the system that will be your firewall. Then you execute the allowable network-based commands to, from, and through the firewall to be. Mason dynamically collects the activity and generates rules. In this way, it is both an incredible learning tool and a rapid rule set developer. Think of the typing time you'll save!

It is not a panacea, however. The rule base Mason generates is only as secure as the quite extensively flexible configuration file it uses (/etc/ masonrc). It is a tool that can save a lot of time and help you learn about ipchains, but the resulting chains require close inspection, editing, and testing before you go live with them.

Mason is well worth obtaining and using, if for nothing other than the learning experience it will provide.

The Network Mapper (nmap)

The Network Mapper (nmap) is a very sophisticated port scanner. It can generate a variety of different types of packets. It can generate all types of normal packets like TCP, UDP, ICMP, ftp, and many others. It can also generate fragments and oversized packets. It is a very good utility to use to test your firewall. The bad-guys will use it against you, so you should use it first. You can obtain it from

```
http://www.insecure.org/
```

Additional Firewall Software

There are two publicly available proxy-based firewall packages that operate well in conjunction with ipchains. They are the Firewall Toolkit (FWTK) and SOCKSv5. Both of these packages offer full-featured proxy services (although they do so in different ways) and user authentication. You can find out more about FWTK at

```
http://www.tis.com/research/software/
```

Also, *Internet Security: A Professional Reference*, cited in *General Firewall References* on page 488, contains configuration details about FWTK. SOCKS can be obtained from

```
http://www.socks5.nec.com/
```

Virtual Private Networks and Encrypted Tunnels

In *Secure Shell Alternatives* on page 310, we pointed out some of the available tools for the purpose of building encrypted tunnels and/or virtual private networks (VPN).

THE NEXT GENERATION...

The good news is that ipchains is much more flexible and capable than ipfwadm. The other bit of good news is that the follow-on replacement to ipchains is in the works—it will provide significant functionality enhancements. There will also be a suit of tools to allow for ipchains (and possibly ipfwadm) syntax to be used. The next-generation replacement for ipchains is called netfilter;

it is currently running in the 2.3.x version of the kernel, and you can learn more about it at

```
http://www.rustcorp.com/linux/netfilter/
```

SUMMARY

In this chapter we took an introductory look at the `ipchains` utility. We discussed how to configure this packet-filtering software to limit connections through a Linux system connected to two different networks. We also note a variety of other resources which further detail the use of `ipchains`.

FOR FURTHER READING

`ipchains` Documentation

The *IPCHAINS-HOWTO* written by Paul Russell can be obtained from

```
http://www.rustcorp.com/linux/ipchains/HOWTO.html
```

Make sure that you read this document!

You will also find the TrinityOS resource, written by David A. Ranch, extremely valuable for this and general security related topics. It can be found at

```
http://www.ecst.csuchico.edu/~dranch/TrinityOS.wri
```

Make sure that you read this, too!

Masquerading Documentation

The *Linux IP Masquerade HOWTO*, written by David A. Ranch and Ambrose Au, is available at

```
http://ipmasq.cjb.net/
```

This document is an absolute **must** read if you are going to use IP masquerading.

ISP Connectivity-Related Resources

You will find HOWTO documents related to ISP connections, cable modems, PPP, DHCP, and DSL at the Linux Documentation Project home site:

```
http://metalab.unc.edu/LDP/
```

We provide a list of many of the pertinent documents below.

```
ADSL (mini HOWTO)
Cable-Modem (mini HOWTO)
DHCP (mini HOWTO)
DHCPcd (mini HOWTO)
ISP-Hookup-HOWTO
ISP-Connectivity (mini HOWTO)
```

General Firewall References

1. Atkins, Derek, et al., *Internet Security: A Professional Reference*, Indianapolis, Indiana, New Riders Publishing, 1996.
2. Chapman, D. Brent, and Elizabeth D. Zwicky, *Building Internet Firewalls*, Sebastopol, California, O'Reilly & Associates, Inc., 1995.
3. Cheswick, William R., and Steven M. Bellovin, *Firewalls and Internet Security*: *Repelling the Wily Hacker*, Reading, Massachusetts, Addison-Wesley Publishing Company, 1994.
4. Kyas, Othmar, *Internet Security Risk Analysis, Strategies and Firewalls*, London, England, International Thomson Computer Press, 1997.
5. Siyan, Karanjit, Ph.D., and Chris Hare, *Internet Firewalls and Network Security*, Indianapolis, Indiana, New Riders Publishing, 1995.

DMZ Resources

These two books provide good background and security information related to Internet servers:

1. Garfinkel, Simson, and Gene Spafford, *Web Security & Commerce*, Sebastopol, California, O'Reilly & Associates, Inc., 1997.
2. Liu, Cricket, et al., *Managing Internet Information Services*, Sebastopol, California, O'Reilly & Associates, Inc., 1994.

The following web site contains an instructive how-to document on securely configuring DMZ systems.

```
http://ciac.llnl.gov/ciac/documents/ciac2308.html
```

ICMP-Related References

The following web site provides a listing of ICMP types and codes for both IPv4 and IPv6.

```
http://www.isi.edu/in-notes/iana/assignments/icmp-parameters/
```

You will find good discussions of ICMP types and codes and their purpose in the following books. *IPv6: The New Internet Protocol* particularly covers the revisions to ICMP for IPv6.

1. Comer, Douglas E., *Internetworking with TCP/IP Vol. I: Principles, Protocols, Architecture*, 3d ed., Englewood Cliffs, New Jersey, Prentice Hall, 1995.

2. Huitema, Christian, *IPv6: The New Internet Protocol*, Upper Saddle River, New Jersey, Prentice Hall PTR, 1996.

3. Perlman, Radia, *Interconnections: Bridges, Routers, Switches, and Internetworking Protocols*, 2d ed., New York, New York, Addison Wesley, 2000.

4. Stevens, W. Richard, *TCP/IP Illustrated, Vol. 1: The Protocols*, Reading, Massachusetts, Addison-Wesley, 1994.

A SPECIAL ACKNOWLEDGMENT

We extend a very special thank you to David A. Ranch who, in spite of an exacting schedule, made time to critique this chapter.

Wiretapping Is Not So Much Fun, After All!

Log File Management

Throughout this book, we've been discussing log files and telling you how important it is to read them. Log files record information that can typically be boring but sometimes is extremely important. For example, you may be experiencing a hardware failure, misconfiguration, or an intrusion. Frequent review of your log files helps you learn information like this the easy way rather than the hard way.

You also need to make sure you reset your logs and cycle out the old ones periodically so that your disk doesn't fill up. Proper management of your log files ensures that they are available when you need them. If you back up your log files regularly with the rest of your system, you extend the availability of this audit information.

All these things may seem like tedious work, but there are a few tools that can help. We'll cover `logrotate`, `swatch`, and `logcheck` in this chapter. Each of these tools does one thing particularly well, and using them all helps to add layers of protection to your system.

GENERAL LOG FILE MANAGEMENT

You should log as much information as you can to your log files. Chapter 8 discusses the configuration of the `syslog` utility. In particular, *Logging to a Central Server* on page 167 describes the configuration and security requirements for centralized logging. Logging to a central, secure server can greatly ease log file administration and reduce the likelihood of log file tampering by an intruder.

Set the permissions on log files so that they are readable only by root. Some packages log sensitive information that could help someone compromise your system should the log entry be seen. Verify your rotation scripts retain secure permissions on the new log files that are started.

Determine a schedule by which log files are rotated. Keep log files long enough to be useful should you need them, but not so long that you fill up your disk and experience problems. You'll have to use trial and error to figure out what is best for your system(s) and amount of activity.

Most important, read your log files! Use these utilities to assist you with separating the important stuff from the entries that can be ignored. Err on the side of showing more entries until you can safely configure your scripts to ignore what you do not need to see. Investigate when you see unusual entries, but remember that log file entries not only can be generated by utilities and programs you expect, but could also be introduced to your log files by someone running the `logger` program or a user-written program using the `syslog` call.

`logrotate`

`logrotate`, written by Erik Troan, is designed to cycle your log files automatically, removing the oldest and starting new ones, and is usually run through `cron`. You can have it cycle your files on a regular schedule, but you can also configure it to cycle when your files pass a certain threshold in size. `logrotate` is flexible; you can tell it how many old files to keep and whether to compress or mail log files when they are rotated. `logrotate` handles the important job of physical file management well.

Obtaining and Installing `logrotate`

The `logrotate` utility is included with the Red Hat 5.2/6.0 distribution. In the event that you do not have `logrotate`, it is available as both source and binary RPMs from

```
ftp://ftp.redhat.com/pub/redhat/
```

Configuring `logrotate`

Your configuration file can incorporate the following parts: default values (they can be overridden later as necessary), configuration parameters for 0 or more log files, optional directives to include configuration information for other log files, and comments, which follow the # sign. Table 17.1 shows the `logrotate` configuration file directives and their uses. We take a look at a number of the configuration directives in the following sections.

Table 17.1 `logrotate` Configuration File Directives

Directive	Action
`compress`	Uses `gzip` to compress the old log file. See also `nocompress`.
`copytruncate`	Copies the active log to create the backup, then truncates the active log file. Use this directive when you have processes appending to open files. `copytruncate` allows the log process to continue writing to the open file.
`create mode owner group`	Rotates out the old file, and creates the new file with (optional) specified *mode*, *owner*, and *group*. If omitted, the *mode*, *owner*, and *group* of the new file will be those of the old file. The `create` is done before the `postrotate` script, if one is present. See also `nocreate`.
`daily`	Rotates logs every day.
`delaycompress`	If used in conjunction with `compress`, doesn't compress the file rotated out until the next time this file is cycled.
`errors address`	Mails any `logrotate` errors to *address*.
`ifempty`	Rotates the log file even if it is empty. This is the default behavior; also see `notifempty`.
`include file|directory`	Reads *file* or files in *directory*, ignoring nonregular files and files ending with a taboo extension (see `tabooext`). Files are processed as if they appeared inline in the file that included them.
`mail address`	Mails files being cycled out of existence to *address*. See also `nomail`.
`monthly`	Cycles log files monthly. They are cycled the first time `logrotate` runs each month, normally the first day of the month.
`nocompress`	Does not compress cycled log files. See also `compress`.
`nocopytruncate`	Creates a copy of the original log, but does not truncate the original file. See also `copytruncate`.
`nocreate`	Overrides the `create` option; no new log files will be created.
`nodelaycompress`	Overrides `delaycompress`. Compression is done at cycle time.
`nomail`	When log files are cycled out of existence, does not mail a copy. See also `mail address`..
`noolddir`	Keeps cycled logs in the same directory as the current log(s). See also `olddir directory`.
`notifempty`	Does not rotate the log if it is empty. See also `ifempty`.
`olddir directory`	Keeps cycled logs in *directory*. *directory* must be on the same file system as the current log(s).

Table 17.1 `logrotate` Configuration File Directives (Continued)

Directive	Action
postrotate/endscript	Commands between this pair of statements will be executed after the log is rotated. The `postrotate` and `endscript` keywords must each appear on lines by themselves, inside of log rotation instructions (they cannot be used as defaults).
prerotate/endscript	Commands between this pair of statements will be executed just prior to cycling of the log. The `prerotate` and `endscript` keywords must each appear on lines by themselves, inside of log rotation instructions (they cannot be used as defaults).
rotate *count*	Number of times to rotate files before they are removed. A 0 (zero) means remove the file rather than keeping an old version of it. A 4 would mean one current and four old copies of a file.
size *size* | *size*k | *size*M	Rotates files when they exceed a threshold of *size* bytes. You can also specify *size*k or *size*M to indicate kilobytes or megabytes, respectively.
tabooext [+] *list*	By default, the list of extensions to ignore contains .rpmorig, .rpmsave, v, and ~. Set a new list of extensions to ignore by using `tabooext` *list* or add to it with `tabooext` + *list*.
weekly	Rotates log files on a weekly basis, usually the first day of the week.

Table 17.2 shows command-line options that can be used with `logrotate`. As you can see from Table 17.2 `logrotate` is quite flexible. By default, `logrotate` expects to find the `/etc/logrotate.conf` configuration file. Example 17-1 shows a sample (with line numbers added for explanation purposes). We discuss the entries in `/etc/logrotate.conf` in the following sections.

Table 17.2 `logrotate` Command-Line Options and Their Uses

Option	Use
-d	Debug mode. Read-only; no changes will be made to the logs or `logrotate` state file.
-f	Forces `logrotate` to run. This option is quite useful after new entries have been made.
-s *statefile*	Uses *statefile* instead of the default `/var/lib/logrotate.status` (allows multiple users to manage files).
--usage	Displays usage, version, and copyright information.

Example 17-1 Default `/etc/logrotate.conf` File

```
 1.   # see "man logrotate" for details
 2.   # rotate log files weekly
 3.   weekly
 4.
 5.   # keep 4 weeks worth of backlogs
 6.   rotate 4
 7.
 8.   # send errors to root
 9.   errors root
10.
11.   # create new (empty) log files after rotating old ones
12.   create
13.
14.   # uncomment this if you want your log files compressed
15.   #compress
16.
17.   # RPM packages drop log rotation information into this directory
18.   include /etc/logrotate.d
19.
20.   # no packages own lastlog or wtmp -- we'll rotate them here
21.   /var/log/wtmp {
22.   monthly
23.   rotate 1
24.   }
25.
26.   # system-specific logs may be configured here
```

Setting Default Values   It is convenient to set default values at the top of your configuration file for those values you will use on most of your log files. For example, you may want all errors mailed to one e-mail address and all files rotated weekly. Lines 1 through 12 in Example 17-1 show the use of default values. Here we specify log files should be rotated weekly (line 3), we want to keep four copies of old log files (line 6), all errors are to be mailed to root (line 9), and new log files should be created automatically (line 12).

Include Directive   RPM packages usually install their log rotation information in the directory `/etc/logrotate.d`. You may choose to install your log rotation information in a different place. When you have rotation information in several places, you can pull all this into your main configuration file with the `include` directive. When `logrotate` sees an `include` directive, it reads in the file specified (or files in the directory specified), just as if it appeared in the main configuration file. The `tabooext` directive can be used to tell `logrotate` to ignore files with certain extensions. Line 18 of Example 17-1 shows the `include` directive in the `/etc/logrotate.conf` file, which incorporates the contents of the `/etc/logrotate.d` directory.

The `/etc/logrotate.d` directory could contain rotation information for a variety of utilities. Example 17-2 shows a few files. The entries in each of these files will be incorporated in `/etc/logrotate.conf`. We look at the `/etc/logrotate.d/syslog` file in the next section.

Example 17-2 List of Rotation Files in `/etc/logrotate.d`

```
# ls -1 /etc/logrotate.d
cron
linuxconf
samba
syslog
uucp
```

Configuration Parameters   Configuration parameters for a particular file follow the format shown in Example 17-3. The first line refers to the name of the log file and contains an opening brace. Zero or more directives appear between the opening brace and a closing brace, which appears on a line by itself.

Example 17-3 Format of Rotation Information for Log File

```
# comments follow pound signs
/path/to/logfile {
}
# another comment
/path/to/another/logfile {
directive
}
```

Lines 20–24 of Example 17-1 on page 495 show configuration parameters for `/var/log/wtmp`. This entry causes the `/var/log/wtmp` file to be rotated on a monthly basis, and we retain one backup.

Let's examine the `/etc/logrotate.d/syslog` file shown in Example 17-4.

Example 17-4 The `/etc/logrotate.d/syslog` File

```
/var/log/messages {
prerotate
/usr/bin/chattr -a /var/log/messages
endscript
postrotate
/usr/bin/killall -HUP syslogd
/usr/bin/chattr +a /var/log/messages
endscript
}

/var/log/secure {
prerotate
/usr/bin/chattr -a /var/log/secure
endscript
postrotate
/usr/bin/killall -HUP syslogd
/usr/bin/chattr +a /var/log/secure
endscript
}

/var/log/maillog {
prerotate
/usr/bin/chattr -a /var/log/maillog
endscript
postrotate
/usr/bin/killall -HUP syslogd
/usr/bin/chattr +a /var/log/maillog
endscript
}
```

Example 17-4 The `/etc/logrotate.d/syslog` File (Continued)

```
/var/log/spooler {
prerotate
/usr/bin/chattr -a /var/log/spooler
endscript
postrotate
/usr/bin/killall -HUP syslogd
/usr/bin/chattr +a /var/log/spooler
endscript
}
```

logrotate will insert the information from the `/etc/logrotate.d/syslog` file into `/etc/logrotate.conf` when it encounters the `include` directive. The defaults we set at the top of the main file will also apply when rotating these files.

The `/etc/logrotate.d/syslog` file also illustrates the `prerotate` and `postrotate` directives. The statements inside the `prerotate/endscript` directives cause logrotate to remove the "append only" (`chattr -a`) attribute from the file before the file is rotated. After rotating the file (using the defaults found in the main file plus any overriding directives), the `postrotate/endscript` directives cause logrotate to send the HUP signal to syslogd to let it know it needs to start writing to the new file and then to reset the "append only" attribute on the file to protect it from tampering. You can place any shell commands inside the `prerotate/endscript` or `postrotate/endscript` directives to include any script or program you write yourself.

logrotate will read in all of the files in the `/etc/logrotate.d` directory before it actually begins to process them.

For an example of an included file that overrides the defaults we set in `/etc/logrotate.conf` (see Example 17-1 on page 495), see Example 17-5. In this case the rotation information for linuxconf stipulates that the `htmlaccess.log` file should not be rotated if empty (`notifempty`), and logrotate-related errors should be mailed to webmaster. The values of nocompress and weekly do not end up overriding those defined in the main file.

Example 17-5 Overriding Default Directives in an Included File

```
# logrotate file for linuxconf RPM
/var/log/htmlaccess.log {
errors webmaster
notifempty
nocompress
weekly
prerotate
/usr/bin/chattr -a /var/log/htmlaccess.log
endscript
postrotate
/usr/bin/chattr +a /var/log/htmlaccess.log
endscript
}

/var/log/netconf.log {
nocompress
monthly
```

Example 17-5 Overriding Default Directives in an Included File (Continued)

```
prerotate
/usr/bin/chattr -a /var/log/netconf.log
endscript
postrotate
/usr/bin/chattr +a /var/log/netconf.log
endscript
}

/var/log/boot.log {
nocompress
monthly
prerotate
/usr/bin/chattr -a /var/log/boot.log
endscript
postrotate
/usr/bin/chattr +a /var/log/boot.log
endscript
}
```

Pulling It All Together

There's not a lot of work required to install and run `logrotate`. Basically, all you have to do is identify your log files, create rotation directives for them, and run `logrotate` through `cron`. By default, Red Hat ships with the `cronjob` shown in Example 17-6 to accomplish this.

Example 17-6 `logrotate cronjob` run from `/etc/cron.daily`

```
# cat /etc/cron.daily/logrotate
#!/bin/sh
/usr/sbin/logrotate /etc/logrotate.conf
```

swatch

`swatch` (the simple watchdog) is a program designed to keep an eye on your log files and to notify you when interesting events occur. You can run `swatch` in batch mode—you examine a log file's contents and exit—or in monitor mode—`swatch` continuously watches the log file, evaluating each new record (*tailing* the file). `swatch` can provide notification in a more real-time fashion than `logcheck`. A drawback, however, is that you need to have a `swatch` process running on each machine you wish to monitor and for each log file, which can be cumbersome if you do not log your files to a central machine.

   `swatch` was written and is maintained by E. Todd Atkins, who distributes `swatch` under the GPL. `swatch-3.0` provides a variety of notification options (seven colors if your terminal provides that support, terminal bell, e-mail, messages to your terminal window, etc.) and offers greater ease of configuration over `swatch` Version 2. If you already have configuration files written for `swatch` Version 2, the Version 3 release has a compatibility mode to read the older-style configuration files and a utility you can use to convert the older-format files to the new format.

Obtaining `swatch`

`swatch` can be found at its official home site or at the COAST archive

```
ftp://ftp.stanford.edu/general/security-tools/swatch/
ftp://coast.cs.purdue.edu/pub/tools/unix/swatch/
```

From the `ftp` site, you will need the following files (or the latest version available):

```
FILES
swatch.tar.asc
swatch-3.0.tar.gz
```

The `FILES` file contains information about retrieving the PGP key used to sign the distribution.

You can retrieve the PGP key from a link off of the `http://www.stan-ford.edu/~security` page. Download the public key (we'll call it `stanford-security-pgp.asc`), add the key to your PGP keyring, and verify that the signature is good (or use `pgpv` if you use PGP version 5),

```
# pgp stanford-security-pgp.asc
# pgp swatch.tar.asc
```

`swatch-3.0` requires Perl 5 or greater and the following Perl modules:

```
Time::HiRes,
Date::Calc,
File::Tail
```

If you don't have the required Perl modules already installed on your system, the `swatch` installation script will attempt to install them for you automatically from one of the Comprehensive Perl Archive Network (CPAN) sites.[1] Failing this, you can install them yourself.

Unzip and untar to reveal files as shown in Example 17-7. As always, read the usual files (COPYING, README, etc.) to learn the details about this program (especially KNOWN_BUGS).

Example 17-7 Contents of `swatch` Distribution

```
CHANGES
COPYING
COPYRIGHT
INSTALL
KNOWN_BUGS
MANIFEST
Makefile.PL
README
README.Y2K
examples/
swatch
swatch_oldrc2newrc
t\
```

---

1. See the home page at `http://www.cpan.org/` for more information.

Since the installation script can attempt to install Perl modules from CPAN, you may want to read the following brief overview of CPAN before starting. If you've already used CPAN, feel free to skip ahead to the next section.

OH, BY THE WAY...

There are hundreds of CPAN sites, but they are all mirrors of one master site. The mirrors exist so you can find a site close to you from which you can retrieve all things Perl. The Perl modules are libraries written for a prescribed purpose, contributed by people on the net. (You can write and contribute your own, if you wish.) One such module is CPAN.pm. This module can be used in Perl programs to help you install other modules your program might need. However, you should read the following statement on security at CPAN.

```
SECURITY
There's no strong security layer in CPAN.pm. CPAN.pm helps you
to install foreign, unmasked, unsigned code on your machine. We
compare to a checksum that comes from the net just as the
distribution file itself. If somebody has managed to tamper with
the distribution file, they may have as well tampered with the
CHECKSUMS file. Future development will go towards strong
authentication.
```

If you do choose to use the CPAN.pm module to automatically install modules, you should at least install the MD5 module at your site so that the CPAN.pm module can verify the signature of the package you are downloading. You can find the MD5 module (and a README file explaining how to install it) at a CPAN site in the directory

```
modules/by-module/MD5/
```

If you can't get the CPAN.pm module to work, you can still FTP the required modules and signatures from a CPAN site, verify them yourself, and place them in your Perl library directory (/usr/lib/perl5 on Red Hat).

When you run the CPAN.pm module, it will ask you questions about your preferences on CPAN sites. Example 17-8 shows a sample of the dialog, snipped for brevity. Since there are many mirrors, you can choose a site close to you. See the CPAN home page for more information.

Installing swatch

swatch is fairly simple to install. Begin by executing perl Makefile.PL, as shown in Example 17-8. There's a lot of dialog from the CPAN.pm module as it attempts to locate the server and as it retrieves the modules. You have to go through the CPAN.pm configuration dialog only one time, and then your preferences are saved for next time.

Example 17-8 Sample CPAN.pm Dialog during perl Makefile.PL

```
# perl Makefile.PL
/usr/lib/perl5/CPAN/Config.pm initialized.
The CPAN module needs a directory of its own to cache important
index files and maybe keep a temporary mirror of CPAN files. This may
be a site-wide directory or a personal directory.
First of all, I'd like to create this directory. Where?
CPAN build and cache directory? [/home/root/.cpan] /root/.cpan
If you want, I can keep the source files after a build in the cpan
home directory. If you choose so then future builds will take the
files from there. If you don't want to keep them, answer 0 to the
next question.
How big should the disk cache be for keeping the build directories
with all the intermediate files?
Cache size for build directory (in MB)? [10]
The CPAN module will need a few external programs to work
properly. Please correct me, if I guess the wrong path for a program.
Don't panic if you do not have some of them, just press ENTER for
those.
Where is your gzip program? [/usr/bin/gzip]
Where is your tar program? [/bin/tar]
Where is your unzip program? [/usr/bin/unzip]
Where is your make program? [/usr/bin/make]
Where is your lynx program? [/usr/bin/lynx]
Where is your ncftp program? [/usr/bin/ncftp]
Where is your ftp program? [/usr/bin/ftp]
What is your favorite pager program? [/usr/bin/less]
What is your favorite shell? [/bin/tcsh]
Every Makefile.PL is run by perl in a separate process. Likewise we
run 'make' and 'make install' in processes. If you have any parameters
(e.g. PREFIX, INSTALLPRIVLIB, UNINST or the like) you want to pass to
the calls, please specify them here.
If you don't understand this question, just press ENTER.
Parameters for the 'perl Makefile.PL' command? []
Parameters for the 'make' command? []
Parameters for the 'make install' command? []
Sometimes you may wish to leave the processes run by CPAN alone
without caring about them. As sometimes the Makefile.PL contains
question you're expected to answer, you can set a timer that will
kill a 'perl Makefile.PL' process after the specified time in seconds.
If you set this value to 0, these processes will wait forever. This is
the default and recommended setting.
Timeout for inacivity during Makefile.PL? [0]
We need to know the URL of your favorite CPAN site.
Please enter it here: ftp://ftp.funet.fi/pub/languages/perl/CPAN
Testing "ftp://ftp.funet.fi/pub/languages/perl/CPAN" ...
Issuing "/usr/bin/ftp -n"
Local directory now /root/.cpan/sources
GOT /root/.cpan/sources/MIRRORED.BY
"ftp://ftp.funet.fi/pub/languages/perl/CPAN" seems to work
WAIT support is available as a Plugin. You need the CPAN::WAIT module
to actually use it. But we need to know your favorite WAIT server. If
you don't know a WAIT server near you, just press ENTER.
Your favorite WAIT server?
[wait://ls6.informatik.uni-dortmund.de:1404]
If you're accessing the net via proxies, you can specify them in the
CPAN configuration or via environment variables. The variable in
the $CPAN::Config takes precedence.
Your ftp_proxy?
Your http_proxy?
Your no_proxy?
commit: wrote /usr/lib/perl5/CPAN/Config.pm
Checking for Date::Calc    ...
You don't have the Date::Calc module installed.
Would you like to install the module now? y
Issuing "/usr/bin/ftp -n"
```

Example 17-8 Sample CPAN.pm Dialog during perl Makefile.PL (Continued)

```
Local directory now /root/.cpan/sources/authors
GOT /root/.cpan/sources/authors/01mailrc.txt.gz
Going to read /root/.cpan/sources/authors/01mailrc.txt.gz
Issuing "/usr/bin/ftp -n"
Local directory now /root/.cpan/sources/modules
GOT /root/.cpan/sources/modules/02packages.details.txt.gz
Going to read /root/.cpan/sources/modules/02packages.details.txt.gz
Issuing "/usr/bin/ftp -n"
Local directory now /root/.cpan/sources/modules
GOT /root/.cpan/sources/modules/03modlist.data.gz
Going to read /root/.cpan/sources/modules/03modlist.data.gz
Running make for STBEY/Date-Calc-4.2.tar.gz
Issuing "/usr/bin/ftp -n"
Local directory now /root/.cpan/sources/authors/id/STBEY
GOT /root/.cpan/sources/authors/id/STBEY/Date-Calc-4.2.tar.gz
Date-Calc-4.2/
Date-Calc-4.2/t/
Date-Calc-4.2/t/f023.t
Date-Calc-4.2/t/f005.t

<lots of output snipped>
```

When you finally have all the required Perl modules (it may take a few iterations of perl Makefile.PL to get them all), you can run perl Makefile.PL one more time to create the Makefile; then execute make, make test; then finally make install to copy swatch and its man pages to the appropriate directories, as shown in Example 17-9 (some lines wrapped due to length).

If you get an error the first time you run swatch (Missing } or core dump), check the few first lines in /usr/bin/swatch. If you have

```
#!/bin/sh -
eval 'exec perl $0 ${1+"$@"}'
```

Example 17-9 Executing perl Makefile.PL and the make Commands

```
# perl Makefile.PL
Checking for Date::Calc    ... ok
Checking for File::Tail    ... ok
Checking for Time::HiRes 1.12  ... ok
Checking if your kit is complete...
Looks good
Writing Makefile for swatch
# make
Manifying ./blib/man1/swatch.1
cp swatch ./blib/script/swatch
/usr/bin/perl -I/usr/lib/perl5/i386-linux/5.00404 -I/usr/lib/perl5 -
MExtUtils::MakeMaker -e "MY->fixin(shift)" ./blib/script/swatch
# make test
PERL_DL_NONLAZY=1 /usr/bin/perl -I./blib/arch -I./blib/lib -I/usr/lib/perl5/
i386-linux/5.00404 -I/usr/lib/perl5 -e 'use Test::Harness qw(&runtests $verbose);
$verbose=0; runtests @ARGV;' t/*.t
t/swatch...........ok
All tests successful.
Files=1,  Tests=1,  0.17 CPU secs ( 0.15 cusr 0.02 csys)
# make install
Writing /usr/man/man1/./swatch.1
Writing /usr/bin/./swatch
Writing /usr/lib/perl5/site_perl/i386-linux/auto/swatch/.packlist
Appending installation info to /usr/lib/perl5/i386-linux/5.00404/perllocal.pod
```

then replace the line containing /bin/sh with a line to call perl, so that the first few lines are

```
#!/usr/bin/perl
eval 'exec perl $0 ${1+"$@"}'
```

The /bin/sh line does work on other systems, but it doesn't work for Linux.

Configuring and Running swatch

swatch reads a configuration file in order to know what events to report and which method(s) to use. There are also command-line options you can use to give additional information to swatch. For example, if you rotate your logs, you can tell swatch to restart just after your logs rotate. The command-line options for swatch are shown in Table 17.3.

With no command-line options, swatch runs as if it were invoked as

```
swatch --config-file=~/.swatchrc --tail-file=/var/log/messages
```

Table 17.3 Command-Line Options to swatch

Option	Use
--config-file=*filename* -c *filename*	Location of swatch configuration file. Defaults to $HOME/.swatchrc
--restart-time=[+]*hh*:*mm*[am|pm] -r [+]*hh*:*mm*[am|pm]	Directs swatch to restart after *hh* hours and *mm* minutes. Assumes a 24-hour clock if am/pm are omitted. Use of a + directs swatch to restart after *hh*:*mm* has elapsed from now (am/pm are ignored if used with +).
--input-record-separator= *regular_expression*	Directs swatch to use the *regular_expression* as the record separator. Defaults to carriage return.
--help	Prints swatch usage information and exits.
--version	Prints swatch release version and exits.
Choose only one of the following command-line options:	
--tail-file=*filename* -t *filename*	Continuously monitors *filename* as new lines are added. swatch does not exit.
--read-pipe=*command* -p *command*	First runs *command*, then pipes its output through swatch.
--examine=*filename* -f *filename*	Runs current contents of *filename* through swatch and exits; does not continue monitoring *filename*.
For debugging purposes:	
--dump-script[=*filename*]	For debugging: prints a copy of the Perl code swatch generated to *filename* or STDOUT instead of actually running it.

If `swatch` cannot locate a configuration file, it will run in a sort of "demo" mode, matching every line in the `messages` file and choosing a random action to display each. You can try this to see how the different methods work on your terminal. We'll describe the configuration file format and notification methods in the next section.

Format of the `swatch` Configuration File   The configuration file will contain patterns along with the actions that should be taken if that pattern is seen. The pattern must be a regular expression that can be parsed by Perl.

Regular expressions to be matched or ignored are defined by keywords and the = sign. The keywords and possible values are listed in Table 17.4.

Table 17.4 Keywords and Values Used by `swatch`

Keyword	Value
`watchfor=`*`regular_expression`*	The regular expression to watch for in the log file.
`ignore=`*`regular_expression`*	A regular expression to ignore.
`waitfor=`*`regular_expression`*	Ignore all other regular expressions until you see this one.
`echo` [=*`mode`*]	Output the line containing the pattern. The default mode is `normal`, but you can also choose `bold`, `underscore`, `blink` (blinking text), `inverse`, `black`, `red`, `green`, `yellow`, `blue`, `magenta`, `cyan`, `white`, or highlighting colors of `black_h`, `red_h`, `green_h`, `yellow_h`, `blue_h`, `magenta_h`, `cyan_h`, or `white_h`. These may not work on all terminals.
`bell` [=*`N`*]	Output the matched line, and ring the terminal bell `N` times. The default is 1.
`exec=`*`command`*	When the pattern is matched, execute *`command`*. You can pass fields from the matched line to *`command`*. `$N` in the *`command`* string will be replaced with the `N`th field from the matched line; `$0` or `$*` in the *`command`* string will be replaced by the entire matched line.
`mail` [=*`address`*:*`address`*:...]	If no address is given, mail the matched line to the person running the program; otherwise, send the matched line to the person(s) specified with the `mail` keyword.
`pipe=`*`command`*	Pipe the matched lines into *`command`*.
`write` [=*`user`*:*`user`*:...]	Use `write(1)` to echo the matched lines to the terminal of user(s) specified with the `write` keyword.
`throttle=`*`options`*	This keyword limits actions on the matched line. The specified actions are taken the first time the pattern is encountered, but *`options`* is a time value to wait before taking additional action. After the time period has passed, a summary of the number of occurrences of the pattern is printed.

swatch is distributed with a few sample configuration files (in the exam-ples directory). Example 17-10 shows a file that can be used to monitor /var/log/messages. We have added a pattern for our printer that uses the throttle keyword to limit the number of error messages we receive (and we removed

Example 17-10 Sample swatch Configuration File

```
#
# Personal swatch configuration file
#
# Watch for bad login attempts
watchfor = /INVALID|REPEATED|INCOMPLETE/
echo=inverse
exec="/usr/local/sbin/badloginfinger.pl $0"
exec="/usr/local/sbin/call_pager.pl 5551234 911"
bell=3

# Important program errors
watchfor = /LOGIN/
echo=inverse
bell=3
watchfor = /passwd/
        echo=bold
        bell=3
watchfor = /ruserok/
echo=bold
bell=3

# cranky printer, throttle messages for 2 hours
watchfor = /printer/
echo
throttle=2:00

# Ignore this stuff
ignore = /sendmail/,/nntp/,/xntp|ntpd/,/faxspooler/

# Report unusual tftp info
ignore = /tftpd.*(ncd|kfps|normal exit)/
watchfor = /tftpd/
echo
bell=3

# Kernel problems
watchfor = /(panic|halt)/
echo=bold
bell
watchfor = /file system full/
echo=bold
bell=3

watchfor = /kernel/
echo
bell

watchfor = /fingerd.*(root|[Tt]ip|guest)/
echo
bell=3

# We want to be notified if anyone executes "su".
# They should be using "sudo."
# Be sure to keep the ":" after "su" to avoid matching "sudo".
watchfor = /su:/
echo=bold
exec="call_pager.pl 5551234 888"
pipe="/usr/bin/lpr"

watchfor = /.*/
echo
```

some of the SunOS stuff). For real-time notification when you are away from your terminal, you can use the exec and pipe keywords. swatch-2.2 came with some utilities that could be used in the configuration file (badloginfinger.pl and call_pager.pl), but they don't seem to be included with version 3.0. If you like, you can grab them out of the older version 2.2 or replace them with similar utilities you may already have. Our example shows a call to badloginfinger.pl, which will safely finger the site from which the bad login came. We also send notification of the bad login attempt to our pager via the call_pager.pl utility, and use the pipe keyword to echo output from su to a printer.

Because swatch reports only what you tell it to, you might want to consider keeping the report all pattern (/.*/) at the end of the file, carefully adding patterns to ignore as you go along. For purposes of this illustration, our configuration file will be saved in /usr/local/etc/swatch/swatchrc.messages. You will need to create configuration files for each log file that you want to monitor with swatch.

If our messages file is rotated every day, we can tell swatch to restart itself just after that happens. The command to continuously monitor this file, restarting every morning, might look something like this:

```
swatch -t /var/log/messages -c /usr/local/etc/swatch/swatchrc.mes-
sages -r 04:01
```

You may also invoke the restart through logrotate. Example 17-11 provides an example entry that may be placed in /etc/logrotate.d for /var/log/messages.

Example 17-11 Restarting swatch on /var/log/messages through logrotate

```
/var/log/messages {
prerotate
/usr/bin/chattr -a /var/log/messages
endscript
postrotate
/usr/bin/killall -HUP syslogd
/usr/bin/chattr +a /var/log/messages
/usr/local/etc/swatch -t /var/tail/messages -c /usr/local/etc/swatch/
swatchrc.messages -r + 0
endscript
}
```

Using the command and configuration file as shown in Example 17-10, we might see output similar to that in Example 17-12 echoed to our monitoring window (lines wrapped due to length).

If you update the configuration file while swatch is running, send the swatch process an ALRM or HUP signal. It will reread its configuration file and restart. swatch terminates gracefully when you send it a QUIT, TERM, or INT signal.

swatch is pretty good at making sure you receive notifications. With a little tuning of the configuration file, it should work well for you, but use additional tools as well.

Example 17-12 Sample of Output Generated from `swatch` Based on Example 17-10

```
Mar 2 17:54:15 topcat login[14435]: FAILED LOGIN 1 FROM roadrunner FOR guest,
Authentication failure
Mar 2 17:54:23 topcat login[14435]: FAILED LOGIN 2 FROM roadrunner FOR guest,
Authentication failure
Mar 2 17:54:28 topcat login[14435]: TOO MANY LOGIN TRIES (3) FROM roadrunner FOR
guest, Have exhausted maximum number of retries for service.
Mar 2 17:54:28 topcat PAM_pwdb[14435]: 3 authentication failures; (uid=0) ->
guest for login service
Mar 2 18:00:10 topcat login[14478]: FAILED LOGIN 1 FROM roadrunner FOR guest,
Authentication failure
Mar 2 18:00:16 topcat login[14478]: FAILED LOGIN 2 FROM roadrunner FOR joe,
Authentication failure
Mar 2 18:00:20 topcat login[14478]: FAILED LOGIN 2 FROM roadrunner FOR mary,
Authentication failure
Mar 2 18:50:38 net-print.mydomain.com printer: paper out
Mar 2 18:50:38 net-print.mydomain.com printer: error cleared
Mar 2 18:50:38 net-print.mydomain.com printer: cover/door open
Mar 2 18:50:38 net-print.mydomain.com printer: error cleared
4 in 0:28:06 net-print.mydomain.com printer: paper out
4 in 0:28:06 net-print.mydomain.com printer: error cleared
4 in 0:28:06 net-print.mydomain.com printer: cover/door open
4 in 0:28:06 net-print.mydomain.com printer: error cleared
```

logcheck

`logcheck` is a utility designed to periodically check the new stuff in your log files for an "unusual" item while ignoring the items you don't care about. It then mails the events of interest (if any) to you in a nice summary. `logcheck`'s philosophy is to report known *bad* events (by matching keywords in a configuration file) and to report everything else it hasn't been told to ignore. While `swatch` can be used in a real-time fashion, you can use `logcheck` to receive notification of all those other log entries that may not be as time sensitive but are just as important.

`logcheck` comes with a helper utility that is smart enough to know when your log files have been rotated by checking the inode numbers and file size. It also keeps track of the portion of the log file that has already been processed so that you get a report only of new events (or no report if there are no events to report). `logcheck` should not overlook any important events, as its default behavior is to report everything you tell it to, along with everything you don't specifically tell it to ignore.

`logcheck` is a free clone of the `frequentcheck.sh` script distributed with the Gauntlet firewall by Trusted Information Systems, Inc. Craig H. Rowland is the author of `logcheck` and obtained permission from TIS to release this clone. See the LICENSE file distributed with `logcheck` for more information.

Obtaining `logcheck`

You can obtain `logcheck` from its home page or COAST:

```
http://www.psionic.com/abacus/logcheck/
ftp://coast.cs.purdue.edu/pub/tools/unix/logcheck/
```

As of this writing, the latest version of `logcheck` is 1.1. To retrieve the latest version of `logcheck`, the author's PGP key, and the signature file for `logcheck`

```
logcheck-1.1.tar.gz
logcheck-1.1.tar.gz.asc
signature-file.asc
```

Add the author's PGP signature to your keyring and verify that the signature of the package is good as shown in

```
# pgp signature-file.asc
# pgp logcheck-1.1.tar.gz.asc
```

or use `pgpv` if you are using PGP Version 5.0.

Major Components of `logcheck`

Major files used by `logcheck`, and their use, are shown in Table 17.5.

Configuring and Installing `logcheck`

Edit `systems/linux/logcheck.sh`. Find the CONFIGURATION SECTION and verify that the SYSADMIN variable is set so that the output will be mailed to the appropriate person (it defaults to root),

```
SYSADMIN=root
```

Review the default installation directory choices and make any changes to suit your taste. We used the defaults shown in Example 17-13. If you choose not to use the default locations for these files, you will have to edit the `Makefile` and modify it appropriately.

Next review the LOGFILE section in the same file. This is the place where you tell `logcheck` which log files you want it to examine. If you have any other files, you can add them to the end of this section. See Example 17-14 for an illustration.

After saving any changes, you are ready to install (unless you need to edit the `Makefile` because you customized the installation directories!). Now execute `make linux`. (The different systems come with different keyword files.) Example 17-15 shows the output generated while installing `logcheck`.

Set up a `crontab` to run `logcheck`, maybe once an hour.

```
0 * * * * /usr/local/etc/logcheck.sh
```

Now let's take a look at the files containing the patterns `logcheck` looks for (or ignores). There are four files and they are read in a specific order. The files come populated with a set of keywords, but you can add your own. Please read Craig's README files before you do this—they do contain a lot of useful informa-

Table 17.5 Major Files Used by logcheck

File	Use
logcheck.sh	This is the main script that logcheck should run via cron. logcheck reads the logcheck configuration files and your log files (with help of the logtail program) to generate a report.
logtail	Tracks information on the log files. Remembers how much of each log file has been processed, and notes log file inode and file size, which it uses to determine if log file has been rotated. The information gathered by logtail is stored in a file named *log_filename*.offset, in the same directory as the log file. logtail is a C program.
logcheck.hacking	This configuration file contains keywords that indicate a system attack. Log entries are searched to match these keywords. The search for these keywords is case insensitive. All matches will be shown at the top of your report to get your attention. This configuration file is checked first.
logcheck.violations	This configuration file contains patterns matching events indicating either a system problem or possible impending threat. This file is consulted after the logcheck.hacking file. The keywords in this file are also searched case insensitively.
logcheck.violations.ignore	The violations.ignore configuration file contains keywords similar to those found in logcheck.violations but which are ignored. logcheck will treat the keywords in this file case sensitively. Use this file carefully and make sure you don't ignore something important.
logcheck.ignore	The last configuration file to be read. Any keywords listed in this file, if matched, will be ignored. The keywords in this file are also treated case sensitively. Again, be careful about specifying the pattern to ignore.

Example 17-13 Default Installation Directories Used by logcheck

```
LOGTAIL=/usr/local/bin/logtail
TMPDIR=/usr/local/etc/tmp
GREP=egrep
MAIL=mail
HACKING_FILE=/usr/local/etc/logcheck.hacking
VIOLATIONS_FILE=/usr/local/etc/logcheck.violations
VIOLATIONS_IGNORE_FILE=/usr/local/etc/logcheck.violations.ignore
IGNORE_FILE=/usr/local/etc/logcheck.ignore
```

Example 17-14 Configuring logcheck to Monitor Specific Files

```
$LOGTAIL /var/log/messages > $TMPDIR/check.$$
$LOGTAIL /var/log/secure >> $TMPDIR/check.$$
$LOGTAIL /var/log/maillog >> $TMPDIR/check.$$
$LOGTAIL /var/log/tcplog >> $TMPDIR/check.$$
```

Example 17-15 Installing `logcheck` with `make`

```
# make linux
make install SYSTYPE=linux
make[1]: Entering directory `/usr/local/src/logcheck/logcheck-1.1'
Making linux
cc -O -o ./src/logtail ./src/logtail.c
Creating temp directory /usr/local/etc/tmp
Setting temp directory permissions
chmod 700 /usr/local/etc/tmp
Copying files
cp ./systems/linux/logcheck.hacking /usr/local/etc
cp ./systems/linux/logcheck.violations /usr/local/etc
cp ./systems/linux/logcheck.violations.ignore /usr/local/etc
cp ./systems/linux/logcheck.ignore /usr/local/etc
cp ./systems/linux/logcheck.sh /usr/local/etc
cp ./src/logtail /usr/local/bin
Setting permissions
chmod 700 /usr/local/etc/logcheck.sh
chmod 700 /usr/local/bin/logtail
chmod 600 /usr/local/etc/logcheck.violations.ignore
chmod 600 /usr/local/etc/logcheck.violations
chmod 600 /usr/local/etc/logcheck.hacking
chmod 600 /usr/local/etc/logcheck.ignore
Done. Don't forget to set your crontab.
make[1]: Leaving directory `/usr/local/src/logcheck/logcheck-1.1'
```

tion. As you will see, you can use the wildcard `.*` to match any pattern in a line, should you choose to modify the distribution `logcheck.*` configuration files.

`logcheck.hacking`   The `logcheck.hacking` file is read first. This file should contain patterns that represent actual hacking activity. Lines in your log files that match any of these patterns will be reported in the first section of your report, and you should investigate if you see them. The `logcheck.hacking` file as originally distributed is shown in Example 17-16. Note that the key words in this file will be searched without respect to case.

`logcheck.violations`   After the patterns for hacking are reported, `logcheck` looks for patterns matching the contents of the `logcheck.violations` file. Patterns in this file tend to represent negative activity, but are not necessarily the signatures of hacking. Log entries (if any) matching these patterns will be reported next in the report with the heading, "Security Violations." The `logcheck.violations` file as distributed is shown in Example 17-17.

Example 17-16 `logcheck.hacking` Pattern File

```
"wiz"
"WIZ"
"debug"
"DEBUG"
ATTACK
nested
VRFY bbs
VRFY decode
VRFY uudecode
VRFY lp
VRFY demo
VRFY guest
VRFY root
```

Example 17-16 `logcheck.hacking` Pattern File (Continued)

```
VRFY uucp
VRFY oracle
VRFY sybase
VRFY games
vrfy bbs
vrfy decode
vrfy uudecode
vrfy lp
vrfy demo
vrfy guest
vrfy root
vrfy uucp
vrfy oracle
vrfy sybase
vrfy games
expn decode
expn uudecode
expn wheel
expn root
EXPN decode
EXPN uudecode
EXPN wheel
EXPN root
LOGIN root REFUSED
rlogind.*: Connection from .* on illegal port
rshd.*: Connection from .* on illegal port
sendmail.*: user .* attempted to run daemon
uucico.*: refused connect from .*
tftpd.*: refused connect from .*
login.*: .*LOGIN FAILURE.* FROM .*root
login.*: .*LOGIN FAILURE.* FROM .*guest
login.*: .*LOGIN FAILURE.* FROM .*bin
login.*: .*LOGIN FAILURE.* FROM .*uucp
login.*: .*LOGIN FAILURE.* FROM .*adm
login.*: .*LOGIN FAILURE.* FROM .*bbs
login.*: .*LOGIN FAILURE.* FROM .*games
login.*: .*LOGIN FAILURE.* FROM .*sync
login.*: .*LOGIN FAILURE.* FROM .*oracle
login.*: .*LOGIN FAILURE.* FROM .*sybase
kernel: Oversized packet received from
attackalert
```

Example 17-17 `logcheck.violations` Pattern File

```
!=
-ERR Password
ATTACK
BAD
CWD etc
DEBUG
EXPN
FAILURE
ILLEGAL
LOGIN FAILURE
LOGIN REFUSED
PERMITTED
REFUSED
RETR group
RETR passwd
RETR pwd.db
ROOT LOGIN
SITE EXEC
VRFY
"WIZ"
admin
```

Example 17-17 `logcheck.violations` Pattern File (Continued)

```
alias database
debug
denied
deny
deny host
expn
failed
illegal
kernel: Oversized packet received from
nested
permitted
reject
rexec
rshd
securityalert
setsender
shutdown
smrsh
su root
su:
sucked
unapproved
vrfy
attackalert
```

As with `logcheck.hacking`, the keywords in this file will be searched without respect to case.

logcheck.violations.ignore   It may be that a pattern found in the violation section will appear in messages you want to see as well as in those you would rather not see. The `logcheck.violations.ignore` pattern file provides the flexibility of ignoring certain patterns that contain a pattern found in `logcheck.violations`.

There is only one entry in the `logcheck.violations.ignore` file as distributed. It is there to ignore messages captured because of `logcheck.violations`. If you modify this file, be sure you are specific about the pattern to ignore so that you do not ignore other entries accidentally.

The `logcheck.violations.ignore` file as distributed contains the following line:

```
stat=Deferred
```

Case is important with respect to the entries in this file.

logcheck.ignore   This is the last pattern file checked. If a log entry has not already been matched by one of the previous pattern files (`logcheck.hacking`, `logcheck.violations`, or `logcheck.violations.ignore`), then the entry will be reported unless it matches a pattern in this file. When adding patterns to ignore, be as specific as you can so that you will not accidentally ignore something you might want to see. Example 17-18 shows the patterns contained in the distribution version of `logcheck.ignore`. Patterns in this file are checked with respect to case.

Example 17-18 `logcheck.ignore` Configuration File

```
authsrv.*AUTHENTICATE
cron.*CMD
cron.*RELOAD
cron.*STARTUP
ftp-gw.*: exit host
ftp-gw.*: permit host
ftpd.*ANONYMOUS FTP LOGIN
ftpd.*FTP LOGIN FROM
ftpd.*retrieved
ftpd.*stored
http-gw.*: exit host
http-gw.*: permit host
mail.local
named.*Lame delegation
named.*Response from
named.*answer queries
named.*points to a CNAME
named.*reloading
named.*starting
netacl.*: exit host
netacl.*: permit host
popper.*Unable
popper: -ERR POP server at
popper: -ERR Unknown command: "uidl".
qmail.*new msg
qmail.*info msg
qmail.*starting delivery
qmail.*delivery
qmail.*end msg
rlogin-gw.*: exit host
rlogin-gw.*: permit host
sendmail.*User Unknown
sendmail.*User Unknown
sendmail.*alias database.*rebuilt
sendmail.*aliases.*longest
sendmail.*from=
sendmail.*lost input channel
sendmail.*message-id=
sendmail.*putoutmsg
sendmail.*return to sender
sendmail.*return to sender
sendmail.*stat=
sendmail.*timeout waiting
smap.*host=
smapd.*daemon running
smapd.*daemon running
smapd.*delivered
smapd.*delivered
telnetd.*ttloop: peer died
tn-gw.*: exit host
tn-gw.*: permit host
x-gw.*: exit host
x-gw.*: permit host
xntpd.*Previous time adjustment didn't complete
xntpd.*time reset
root 1
```

`logcheck` Output

The first time `logcheck` runs, it will read all log files (that it was configured to process) in their entirety. The `logtail` program will create a *logfile.offset* file for each log file, in the same directory as the log file. Each event in each log file will be parsed and compared to patterns in the `logcheck.*` pattern files; all output that is not ignored (if any) will be mailed to the user listed in the SYSADMIN variable in the `logcheck.sh` file.

On subsequent runs, `logcheck` will read the *logfile.offset* files and ignore the part of the log file that has already been processed. All new events will be parsed and a report will be sent if there are any entries that should not be ignored.

A sample of `logcheck` output is shown in Example 17-19.

Example 17-19 Sample `logcheck` Report

```
Active System Attack Alerts
=-=-=-=-=-=-=-=-=-=-=-=-=-=
Mar 2 04:01:45 topcat sendmail[682]: NOQUEUE: "wiz" command from
roadrunner.mydomain.com [123.45.123.45] (123.45.123.45).
Security Violations
=-=-=-=-=-=-=-=-=-=
Mar 2 04:01:08 topcat sshd[7589]: refused connect from 123.45.123.45
Mar 2 04:01:25 topcat sshd[7601]: refused connect from 123.45.123.45
Unusual System Events
=-=-=-=-=-=-=-=-=-=-=
Mar 3 04:02:01 topcat syslogd 1.3-3: restart.
Mar 3 04:02:01 topcat syslogd 1.3-3: restart.
Mar 3 04:02:01 topcat syslogd 1.3-3: restart.
Mar 3 04:02:01 topcat syslogd 1.3-3: restart.
Mar 3 04:06:45 topcat sudo:    joe : TTY=ttyp5 ; PWD=/home/joe ; USER=root
; COMMAND=/usr/bin/chmod 4755 sh

Mar 3 04:08:29 topcat portmap[22220]: connect from 123.45.123.45 to
callit(ypserv)
```

Troubleshooting `logcheck`

If you are not receiving reports, verify that the *filename*.offset files are being created in the same directory as your log file. If they are not, there is something wrong with `logtail`. Make sure it is installed and that the path in `logcheck.sh` points to the right place. Verify that events are actually being logged (try the `logger` program). Run `logcheck` from the command line to verify that it will send mail to the proper person. Verify that you remembered to add a `cronjob` to run `logcheck` automatically.

Summary

Good log file management is an essential part of system security. The tools we have discussed in this chapter will help ensure that your files are complete and available when you need them and that you will be alerted of problems in a timely manner.

This Is an Awful Lot of Work!

Implementing and Managing Security

It is an awful lot of work. And there's a lot of stuff we haven't talked about! To put all the extra work in perspective, though, think about the labor required to recover from a major destructive break-in. From that perspective, the effort involved in securing your systems and networks begins to look like it might be worth it.

The first thing to bear in mind regarding the level of effort you put into securely configuring each system is your organization's Security Policy (discussed in Chapter 2). A well-planned and well-implemented Security Policy will save a lot of time and effort on your part when you are trying to figure out what you need to do for your computing resources. If a Security Policy does not exist, refer to the resources noted in Chapter 2 and create one. While not ideal, you can create a Security Policy as you implement security throughout your computing environment. If that is your case, be sure to reconcile your security implementation with the Security Policy once that policy is complete.

In this chapter, we will review the topics covered throughout this book. We will also discuss ways to simplify the process of implementing, configuring, and utilizing Linux security features and the various publicly available tools previously described. Throughout this chapter, we will assume that your Security Policy requires the adoption of the philosophy, *that which is not expressly permitted is forbidden*. If your policy is different, you will need to adjust accordingly.

SO, WHERE DO I START?

Now, that's a good question! The material covered in this book can be imposing. So much to do, so little time... But, as with anything else related to computers, as you continue to work with the concepts and methods presented in this book, other books, and other reference resources, you will ultimately reach a point where security administration becomes a part of your overall administrative efforts. Indeed, you should consider security administration as an integral part of the care and feeding of your computing environment.

Let's first look at some general tasks and then move on to the specific needs of systems that play specific roles.

Hardening Linux

Each system that you plan to introduce to your production environment, regardless of its role, should be *hardened*. Hardening means configuring your out-of-the-box Linux system in accordance with your Security Policy. Under our assumption of *that which is not expressly permitted is forbidden*, it means that we need to configure the system for only those things that we allow and deny all else.

Let's outline a general procedure. This procedure applies to all systems regardless of what role they ultimately play. It is specifically geared toward freshly installed systems **before** they are attached to the production environment. (For systems that are already installed, see *What if My Systems Are Already in the Production Environment?* on page 524.) We make specific recommendations for the roles various systems play (NFS, NIS, DNS servers, etc.) in subsequent sections. The order given here may be modified to suit your needs except for step 1 and steps 13 through 16.

1. Install your system.
2. Configure LILO.
3. Secure filesystems, important files, and important directories.
4. Restrict the root account.
5. Secure user and group accounts.
6. Configure PAM and OTP.
7. Configure `syslog`, `logrotate`, `logcheck`, and `swatch`.
8. Configure `sudo`.
9. Configure network services.
10. Implement and configure SSH.
11. Set up CFS or TCFS.
12. Configure `ipchains`.
13. Run `tiger`.
14. Run Tripwire.

15. Make a pristine backup.

16. Connect to the production environment.

Each of the items listed has its own section below.

Install Your System   The first step in securing your systems is also the first step in getting them ready for use—installation. We briefly covered this topic in *Linux Installation and LILO* on page 22.

We recommend that you install your system from one of two resources. The best resource from which to install is a CD obtained from a reliable source such as Red Hat. If this is inconvenient—for instance, if you have a large number of systems to install—then consider installing over the network from a secure install server; that server having been installed from a pristine source. The caveat here is that the install server must be very secure. Ideally, the install server will not be part of your production environment and the installation source must be read-only. Network installation can be accomplished with `ftp`, NFS, or KickStart. For details regarding `ftp` or NFS installation, see the *Red Hat Linux 6.0*[1] *Installation Guide* (located in the directory `/usr/doc/rhl-install-guide-en-6.0` or at `http://www.redhat.com/corp/support/manuals/index.html`). For KickStart installation information, see the `KickStart-HOWTO` (located in the file `/usr/doc/HOWTO/KickStart-HOWTO` or at `http://metalab.unc.edu/LDP/`).

If you install from any other source, you will be accepting a certain amount of additional risk. Be very aware of what that risk means to your environment before you proceed. If this is your situation, make sure that you check PGP signatures and MD5 hash values for everything you download.

During the installation process, you will have the opportunity to select the software you want to install and the daemons that get started at each reboot. In both cases, choose only the software and daemons that are required for that particular system. Also, as of Red Hat 6.0, you will be given the opportunity to use MD5 hashing for your passwords instead of the traditional `crypt(3)` hashing. By all means choose MD5 hashing unless you have a particular reason not to (such as software which cannot interpret MD5 hash values). See *PAM and Passwords* on page 86 for more details on using MD5 hashing for passwords.

Once your installation is complete, install and configure any additional software that you need to use on each system. Make sure that any such additional software also comes from a pristine source, if possible. Check PGP signatures and MD5 hash values where appropriate.

Configure LILO   As noted in *Linux Installation and LILO* on page 22, we recommend that you set up a password that will be required for booting into single-user mode.

---

1. Replace with 5.2 or other release as appropriate.

Secure Filesystems, Important Files, and Important Directories   In *Filesystem Restrictions* on page 78, we looked at some of the available options for mounting local filesystems. We noted that, in general, SUID scripts and programs and special character and block device files should not be in users' home directories. Minimally, mount /home (or whatever your users' home directory is called) with the nosuid and nodev options. If your users do not need to use executable programs and scripts, then add the noexec option.

Depending upon your Security Policy and your environment, you may need to set the ro option on some of your system filesystems. Generally, if you are exporting a filesystem via NFS or Samba read-only and it is a filesystem that is used read-only locally, then it should be mounted read-only locally.

Throughout the book we discussed setting file and directory permissions more restrictively on certain sensitive system files—for example, remove all world rights on the directory /etc/pam.d (discussed in Chapter 5); remove all world rights on all log files in /var/log (discussed in Chapter 8). In general, unless there is some functionality that requires it, all system configuration files should minimally have no world rights. Remove group rights as well unless there is a need for them. The same holds true for sensitive user files such as those associated with SSH (discussed in Chapter 11).

Restricting the root Account   The root account is discussed in *The Root Account* on page 66. We recommend the following configuration. Remove all entries from /etc/securetty (discussed in *Configuring /etc/securetty* on page 68). This will disallow native root logins entirely. The only way to access the root account will be through su or sudo. However, we additionally recommend disabling su access to root to force all root access through sudo. Implementing this restriction is described in *Disabling root Access* on page 190. This approach offers the best audit trail for all root use. It also gives you the greatest control over the privileges granted to particular users. In the case of systems requiring multiple administrators, this approach avoids the requirement of creating multiple root accounts or sharing the root password. Since the user who gains access as root through sudo supplies his or her own password, it is imperative that good password choices are made. A more secure, but much less convenient approach is to enforce the use of OPIE (see Chapter 6) passphrases with sudo. The sudo utility is discussed in detail in Chapter 9.

This level of restriction may not be required for all systems. If you wish to avoid installing sudo on certain systems, then you will minimally want to restrict su to root through the use of pam_wheel as described in *PAM and su* on page 103. You will still maintain logging information as captured by the PAM modules in /etc/pam.d/su. You may wish to add pam_warn to the auth stack in /etc/pam.d/su to generate additional log information. See *PAM and the other Configuration File* on page 108 for further details relating to pam_warn. This approach does not allow you to limit the privileged actions granted to users in the way that sudo does.

In spite of these recommendations, if you configure /etc/securetty to allow native root access, keep the list of allowable devices to an absolute minimum. If you have no serial devices attached to the system and you are not using virtual consoles, the only entry in /etc/securetty should be tty1. We discourage this approach generally and particularly on systems that are important (as defined by your Security Policy) because, while native logins are logged, you will neither be able to track the original user who logged in as root nor can you restrict access as root to certain users when they log in on the allowable device(s) specified in /etc/securetty.

Secure User and Group Accounts There are a couple of ways to manage your user and group accounts, manually or through a service such as NIS.

If you are managing them manually, use the shadow file as described in *Password Aging and the Shadow File* on page 61. You can either add the necessary users one at a time or copy, via scp (of course!—see Chapter 11), the /etc/passwd and /etc/shadow files from another system. Be sure to review these files for correctness before going on. The same comments apply for group accounts.

If you use NIS or NIS+ or a similar service, configure your system for that purpose. Note that, as of this writing, NIS cannot use shadow files and opens a variety of other vulnerabilities. See *NFS, Samba, NIS, and DNS Resources* on page 40 for further details. In any event, be thoroughly familiar with the service you are using to maintain your user and group accounts before you implement it.

Configure PAM and OTP PAM is discussed in Chapter 5 and OTP (OPIE and S/Key) are discussed in Chapter 6.

As noted in *Install Your System* on page 517, make sure that you configure PAM with MD5 password hashing. Also, be sure to set minlen reasonably large (see *PAM and Passwords* on page 86). Your Security Policy should dictate the size, but, in the absence of a policy, we recommend a minimum length of 16 characters and encourage the use of passphrases requiring at least one of each different type of character.

There are a great many features with PAM, so take advantage of them in accordance with your Security Policy. In particular, you will probably want to enforce login times (pam_time), resource limits (pam_limits), and access control lists (pam_listfile or pam_access) on critical systems.

It is probably too inconvenient to implement OPIE everywhere, but it is a good idea to minimally implement it on any critical servers in your environment. We strongly recommend the use of OPIE on all systems exposed to the external network (Internet or other untrusted network). In particular, your firewall and DMZ systems (see *Firewalls and the DMZ* on page 525) should be configured to authenticate exclusively with OPIE.

Configure syslog, logrotate, logcheck, and swatch Configuring syslog is discussed in Chapter 8. Implementing and configuring logrotate, logcheck, and swatch are discussed in Chapter 17. We will refer to these tools as *log management tools*. Throughout the book we discussed configuring logging for a variety of circumstances.

You want to configure `syslog` and the log management tools to meet the needs of your environment. Certain systems will need to be configured in different ways; for example, a web server will need to have additional configuration for the log management tools to capture the essential information it generates.

All critical systems in your environment should be configured to write log messages locally **and** to a central log host. The central log host should be treated as a critical system and allow a minimum of services (ideally only SSH). It should also allow only administrator (users who are the administrators) access.

If you are going through the process of log file management for the first time, or you have limited experience with it, take a dynamic approach. Pay close attention to the messages generated and decide which entries need your attention and which do not. Initially, err on the side of too much information. As you become more comfortable with the log entries, you will be able to filter out those that are not important.

The goal is to have your utilities generate as many log entries as are necessary to meet your Security Policy. In some cases, this will mean that you must maintain an audit trail of all activity on some systems. For systems that require it, turn on process accounting and include its logs as well as connection accounting logs in your review process (see Chapter 7). You may also need to run `auditd` (see *The `auditd` Utility* on page 171) on some or all of your systems. The goal for the `logcheck` and `swatch` utilities is to capture critical information and make you aware of it quickly so that you can attend to the problem and deal with it appropriately. Have all of the messages sent to a central e-mail address that gets read regularly.

The rest of the log data is to be maintained by `logrotate`. It is a good idea to archive your log files in their entirety for some period of time (check your Security Policy, but 1 to 3 years is not uncommon). Be sure to add the appropriate and necessary `prerotate` and `postrotate` scripts (see *logrotate* on page 492).

Configure sudo   The sudo utility is covered in Chapter 9. When preparing `sudo` for compilation with the configure utility, choose the appropriate options. We recommend that you minimally use `--with-pam` and `--with-ignore-dot` (and, of course, `--with-insults!`). Once you have compiled `sudo`, you may make it available to other systems employing the same architecture type (for example, x86).

Set up your `/etc/sudoers` file so that it is as simple as possible and grants the minimum necessary privileges. Recall that the configuration file is configurable for many hosts, so depending on your environment you may need only one file. If you prefer, you may configure `/etc/sudoers` for each "class" of host. A class of hosts would be, for example, the collection of all desktops used in an engineering group. Another class might be the collection of NFS servers maintained by the same group of administrators. Either way, keep it simple and limit privileges.

The most secure way of implementing sudo is with OTP (see Chapter 6). The most flexible way of doing this is through PAM (see *PAM and sudo* on page 189) and OPIE (see *OPIE and PAM* on page 143). It is not as inconvenient as it first seems, and after all only the administrators need to do this. So it's not like you are asking all of your users to use OTP. Minimally implement OPIE on your critical servers.

Configure Network Services   Network services, TCP_wrappers, the portmap daemon, and xinetd are discussed in Chapter 10. Minimally, make sure that all of the r-commands (see *Trusted Host Files and Related Commands* on page 36) are disabled. Use SSH (see *Implement and Configure SSH* below) if you require that functionality.

The really great news is that Red Hat 5.2/6.0 incorporates TCP_wrappers for all services invoked through inetd. Take advantage of this. Since we are assuming *that which is not expressly permitted is forbidden*, create /etc/hosts.allow to contain the allowable services and hosts. The /etc/hosts.deny file must minimally contain ALL:ALL (to deny everything that is not explicitly allowed) and, based on your Security Policy, may contain booby traps and additional logging rules (as described in *Access Control with TCP_Wrappers* on page 202) to capture information about unauthorized attempted access. Make sure that you include the necessary portmap restrictions as well (see *Implementing Portmapper Access Control* on page 223). If a service is not permitted and your Security Policy does not require logging of attempted use of those services, then make sure to comment them out in /etc/inetd.conf.

Someday, perhaps, xinetd will be distributed with Linux instead of inetd. Such a distribution would be *fantastic*. For now, however, replacing inetd with xinetd on all of your systems may be too tedious. If you adopt the concepts put forth in *Reducing the Workload* on page 523, you will be able to considerably reduce the effort associated with implementing xinetd everywhere. Unfortunately, there is a fair amount of work up front to reach that point. Thus, we strongly recommend that you minimally implement xinetd on all critical servers and all systems exposed to the external network (see *Firewalls and the DMZ* on page 525). Take full advantage of the process limitations and log file size limitations (see *Replacing inetd with xinetd* on page 226) that may be imposed by xinetd. Also, use TCP_wrappers for all services with xinetd, just as you would for inetd in conjunction with the other access control capabilities, such as bind, access_times, only_from, and no_access (see Table 10.10 on page 232).

Implement and Configure SSH   You **must** use SSH (or something similar, such as SSLeay; see *Secure Shell Alternatives* on page 310) for all remote root access. Period. See Chapter 11 for the details of SSH. We strongly recommend that you implement and use SSH for all X Window System access (see *Exploring ssh Functionality* on page 304). While this will not prevent theft of .Xauthority files from compromised systems, it *will* prevent fruitful network monitoring (see *Network Monitoring* on page 38) of the X Window System authentication data. We also strongly encourage you to use RSA Authentication (see *RSA Authentication Configuration* on page 293), especially on critical servers. Given that secure RSA Authentication requires manual configuration, it can be too time consuming to configure everywhere. In such cases use password authentication and take advantage of the access restrictions that may be imposed by PAM through pam_access (see *Further Restricting Access with PAM* on page 304).

Set up CFS or TCFS   The best defense against a system that is compromised is encrypted data. Only the very best crackers will be able to decrypt encrypted files without the password/passphrase. Set these utilities up wherever necessary, and strongly encourage your users to choose good passphrases (even if they have to write them down and keep them in their wallets or purses).

Consider using these tools to encrypt sensitive system data such as your Tripwire database as well as using the tools described in *Securely Deleting Files* on page 431 to securely delete the most sensitive files.

See Chapter 15 for a complete discussion of CFS and TCFS.

Configure ipchains   The ipchains utility is not just for firewalls. Obviously, if you are building a firewall you will want to utilize this functionality (we strongly recommend the use of additional software as described in Chapter 16). At a minimum, implement ipchains on all critical systems, firewalls, and DMZ systems to allow only those connections permitted by your Security Policy, denying everything else. Do this in addition to imposing restrictions through other utilities as described in *Configure Network Services* on page 521 and *Implement and Configure SSH* on page 521.

We detail the use of ipchains in Chapter 16.

Run tiger   Once you have completed the configuration of a system, you need to configure and run tiger as described in Chapter 13. Thoroughly review the output of the tiger run and correct any vulnerabilities it identifies. Then run tiger again to be sure that you did not miss anything.

Run Tripwire   Configure and run Tripwire. A good Tripwire configuration file for Red Hat Linux is provided in *Effectively Building the Tripwire Configuration File* on page 391. Make sure that you modify this file to capture additional information based on the configuration requirements of each system. Run Tripwire to create the database and then store it securely as described in *Storing the Database* on page 398. This is a very critical element to the overall security of each system and **must** be done prior to putting each system into production use.

The database will be used for future Tripwire runs as outlined in *Internal Maintenance* on page 525 and *External Maintenance* on page 526. Tripwire is described in detail in Chapter 14.

Make a Pristine Backup At this point, you are ready to back up the system. This backup must capture all of the changes made to the system and is to be used for recovery purposes whenever necessary, but particularly when a system has been compromised. You will subsequently need to back up each system immediately after successful `tiger` and Tripwire runs as described in *Internal Maintenance* on page 525 and *External Maintenance* on page 526.

Connect to the Production Environment If the system you are working on serves a special purpose, review *The Internal Network* on page 524 and *Firewalls and the DMZ* on page 525. If what you are trying to do is not covered, thoroughly research the vulnerabilities and security ramifications of whatever you are attempting to configure prior to proceeding.

If the system you are working on does not require any additional configuration, you may connect the system to the production environment now.

Selecting the Right Tools

Neither this outline nor this book should be considered definitive. We cannot possibly cover every conceivable situation nor every available tool. Take advantage of the many references provided in this book and the resources listed in Appendix A and Appendix B. In addition, do your own research to arrive at the best solutions for your environment.

Most important, view security administration as a dynamic and ever changing process. As time goes on, many other tools, vulnerability prevention recommendations, and new operating systems will become available. Stay on top of these issues and adjust accordingly. Use the tools that best suit your needs.

REDUCING THE WORKLOAD

Much of what is described in *Hardening Linux* on page 516 can be automated through programs, scripts, and RPM (see *RPM Resources* on page 28). You can use RPM to package the tools that you will be using and then write your own custom programs and/or scripts to configure your systems as described in steps 2 through 15 on page 516. Initially, this represents a lot of work, but, once accomplished, hardening your systems for production use will require less time and resources. You will need to continue to keep current with vulnerabilities, changes in software, and so on. But once the programmatic or scripted framework is in place, you can focus your attention on more important maintenance issues (see *Internal Maintenance* on page 525 and *External Maintenance* on page 526).

You can fully automate the entire process (except for attaching the system to the production network) by using KickStart as referenced in *Install Your System* on page 517. If you do this, make sure that you use a secure server as your KickStart server.

Throughout this book, we have cited numerous web sites that contain a variety of software packages. Take advantage of these resources when building your own collection of security tools because many of the resources are already in RPM format. Two web sites in particular contain a good collection of RPM packages.

```
http://www.rpmfind.net/linux/RPM/
http://www.replay.com/redhat/
```

WHAT IF MY SYSTEMS ARE ALREADY IN THE PRODUCTION ENVIRONMENT?

Where possible, start over and follow the steps in *Hardening Linux* on page 516. However, where circumstances prohibit you from starting over, there is a limited set of things you can do. To begin with, you can verify all of your system packages against the source (such as the CD) using RPM as described in *Effective Tripwire Initialization* on page 397. As noted in that section, checking the operating system's RPMs is the easy part. It's all the other software that may have been added that may be difficult to verify. And each anomaly uncovered through this process must be checked out manually. Most important, if you uncover any evidence that the system has been tampered with by unauthorized root access, you must reinstall. Evidence of unauthorized root access can come in many forms—for example, service daemons (i.e., `in.telnetd`, `in.ftpd`, etc.) that are not as originally installed or anomalous entries in `/etc/passwd`, unauthorized `.rhosts` files, or other system configuration files. For more details regarding identifying system compromise, see Chapter 24, *Discovering a Break-In*, in *Practical UNIX and Internet Security* as referenced in *System Security* on page 80 and the references in *Intrusion Detection* on page 172.

THE INTERNAL NETWORK

You may think that you don't need to go through the steps outlined in *Hardening Linux* on page 516 for internal systems. Before you draw that conclusion, refer to your Security Policy and don't forget that the majority of system compromises originate internally (see Chapter 2).

Critical Internal Servers

In addition to the steps outlined in *Hardening Linux* on page 516, you will need to securely configure internal server systems based on the service or services that they will provide.

For NIS, NFS, and DNS resources, see *NFS, Samba, NIS, and DNS Resources* on page 40. For these and other server software, thoroughly investigate the configuration from a security perspective and log extensively. In addition, depending on the criticality of the system and your Security Policy, you may need to implement system accounting (see Chapter 7) and system auditing (see *The* `auditd` *Utility* on page 171).

For all server systems, we strongly recommend the use of `xinetd` and `ipchains` in addition to the tools previously discussed. Use redundant access control through `ipchains` and other mechanisms (such as NFS access restrictions). Implement OPIE everywhere and use SSH for all remote connections.

In addition, the critical security servers (log host, KickStart server, security server containing read-only Tripwire databases) should not use NIS or DNS. They may be NFS clients, but you should avoid NFS server services except where absolutely necessary.

Internal Maintenance

Run `tiger`, run Tripwire, run Crack, and read your log files! Or at least the log messages captured by `swatch` and `logcheck`. Really.

Regularly, but unpredictably, run `tiger` and Tripwire on every system. On critical servers, you will want to do this every few days or perhaps daily. On non-critical internal systems, you will need to do this every week or so. Upon the successful completion of these runs and satisfactory review of the log files, you will be able to make a new pristine backup. This backup captures the stable security state of the system from which you may recover in the event of an intrusion.

Pay attention to all of the data that `logcheck` and `swatch` generate. Review that information regularly, especially on critical systems. Occasionally, check the log files themselves to make sure that you aren't missing something with `logcheck` and `swatch`.

Run Crack in accordance with your Security Policy. This usually ends up meaning every two to six weeks. Your Security Policy must tell you what to do about cracked passwords—there are a number of alternatives (see Chapter 12).

FIREWALLS AND THE DMZ

While we looked in depth at the topic of `ipchains` in Chapter 16, we only briefly discussed firewalls. The DMZ (demilitarized zone, also known as the perimeter network) consists of systems that are available to the external network such as the Internet. Examples of DMZ systems include web[2] and ftp

---

2. See Garfinkel, Simson, and Gene Spafford, *Web Security & Commerce*, Sebastopol, California, O'Reilly & Associates, Inc., 1997, for a good source of web security information.

servers. There are a lot of resources that cover these topics, some of which are cited in *Additional Firewall Software* on page 486.

When configuring firewalls and DMZ systems, the steps noted in *Hardening Linux* on page 516 apply to the extreme. These systems must be very tight, allowing absolutely no services except for those that are specifically required (such as `in.ftpd` for the `ftp` server and `httpd` for the web server). For remote administration use only SSH and make sure that `ipchains` is configured to allow the required services exclusively. Have all log entries written locally and to a central log server. All of this is in addition to securely configuring each system for its purpose.

Watch these systems very closely. DMZ systems are considered sacrificial. Have the backups ready. When DMZ systems are compromised, identify the vulnerability (if possible), fix it (if possible), and reinstall.

External Maintenance

The discussion provided in *Internal Maintenance* on page 525 applies here as well, except that you will need to run the tools more frequently and pay closer attention to your log files. Depending on your Security Policy and the activity level on these servers, you may well need to run Tripwire multiple times a day and `tiger` at least daily.

BREAK-IN RECOVERY

Unfortunately, the best way to recover from any break-in is from a pristine backup. The problem is that once a system has been compromised, it is essentially impossible to determine everything that has occurred, especially if the system's root account was compromised. Log files and utilities such as `auditd` help tremendously, but many of the tools available in the cracker community are quite sophisticated. So recover from a pristine backup. However, you may need to do other things before you recover! Only your Security Policy can tell you what those things are. For a good treatment of this topic, see Chapter 24, *Discovering a Break-In*, in *Practical UNIX and Internet Security* as referenced in *System Security* on page 80 and the resources in Appendix A.

ADDING NEW SOFTWARE

Adding software to a production environment is a reality that must be faced. Whenever this necessity occurs, make sure that you understand the security ramifications of the new software—for example, must it run SUID? Does it require a user account, and if so will someone be able to log in as that user? What types of files does it write? Where does it write them? What are the permissions? And so on.

If possible, install the software from a pristine source, like a CD from a reliable vendor (evil.org is probably not reliable). If the software is obtained from an unreliable source such as the Internet, minimally check the PGP signature and hash values. If none exist, or you just feel that the software might be buggy or contain some undesirable side effects, check it out in a safe test environment first. See *Software Testing* on page 48 for further details.

ONLY THROUGH KNOWLEDGE...

Consider this book to be just one element of your overall library of security resources. Take advantage of the many resources cited throughout this text. Join some or all of the e-mail lists noted and make time to read those e-mails. Spend time each week exploring some of the many security web sites. Make it a priority to understand, learn, and know more about Linux security.

No matter how much you know, there's always something you don't know. There's always more to learn. Good luck!

Keeping Up to Date

The Internet can provide you with instantaneous access to information on ways to secure your machine. Unfortunately it also provides access to publicly available scripts or programs that people can use to break into your machine. The following sections identify web sites, e-mail lists, and Internet news groups that provide additional information about both types of information.

WEB PAGES

AFCERT

Lots of security information. The AFCERT exists to provide assistance to U.S. Air Force units and other government agencies.

```
http://afcert.csap.af.mil/
```

AusCERT

Provides a point of contact in Australia for the Internet community to deal with computer security incidents and their prevention.

```
http://www.auscert.org.au/
```

Caldera OpenLinux

```
http://www.calderasystems.com/
http://www.calderasystems.com/news/security/
```

CERT (Computer Emergency Response Team)

A great source of security and vulnerability information.

```
http://www.cert.org/
```

CFS

Cryptographic File System by Matt Blaze.

```
ftp://ftp.research.att.com/dist/mab/
http://www.cryptography.org/
```

CIAC (U.S. Department of Energy's Computer Incident Advisory Capability)

Security bulletins, Internet hoaxes, virus information, chain letters, and other resources.

```
http://ciac.llnl.gov/
```

COAST (Computer Operations, Audit, and Security Technology)

One of the largest dedicated academic computer security research groups in the world. A valuable security archive.

```
http://www.cs.purdue.edu/coast/
```

CSI (Computer Security Institute)

Provides service and training for network, information, and computer security professionals.

```
http://www.gocsi.com/
```

Debian GNU/Linux

```
http://www.debian.org/
http://www.debian.org/security/
```

The DOE Information Security Server (DOE-IS)

A collection of tools, documents, and other resources related to information security that have been made available by sources within and outside of the DOE.

```
http://doe-is.llnl.gov/
```

FAQ.org

Compilations of frequently asked questions.

```
http://www.faq.org/
```

FIRST (Forum of Incident Response and Security Teams)

Aims to foster cooperation and coordination in incident prevention, to prompt rapid reaction to incidents, and to promote information sharing among members and the community at large.

```
http://www.first.org/
```

Global Network Security Systems

A number of references on security-related topics including firewalls, sniffing, and spoofing.

```
http://www.gnss.com/
```

IEEE (Institute of Electrical and Electronics Engineers)

Information about IEEE and services it provides.

```
http://www.ieee.org/
```

IETF (Internet Engineering Task Force) Request for Comments

RFCs largely relating to the Internet.

```
http://www.ietf.org/rfc.html
```

Internet Security Systems

Many UNIX security resources.

```
http://www.iss.net/
```

IPSec Protocol

A source for documents related to the IP security protocol.

```
http://www.ietf.org/html.charters/ipsec-charter.html
```

IPv6 Information Page

```
http://www.ipv6.org/
```

ISC (Internet Software Consortium)

Information related to DNS (Domain Name Service), INN (InterNetNews), and DHCP (Dynamic Host Configuration Protocol).

```
http://www.isc.org/
```

(ISC)^2

Offers professional certification in the field of security.

```
http://www.isc2.org/
```

ISSA (Information Systems Security Association)

Good general security information, links, and references.

```
http://www.issa-intl.org/
```

LASG (Linux Administrators Security Guide)

```
https://www.seifried.org/lasg/
```

Lawrence Berkeley Laboratory

Home of tcpdump and other useful tools.

```
http://ee.lbl.gov/
```

Linux Documentation Project

Documentation on many Linux components.

```
http://metalab.unc.edu/LDP/
```

The Linux Kernel Archives

Kernel source and Linux-related software.

```
http://www.kernel.org/
```

Linux Online

```
http://www.linux.org/
```

Mandrake Linux

```
http://www.linux-mandrake.com/
http://www.linux-mandrake.com/en/fupdates.php3
```

Maximum RPM

The definitive guide to RPM.

```
http://www.redhat.com/knowledgebase/rhlinuxdocs.html
```

NIST Computer Security Resource Clearinghouse

Computer security information and resources to help users, systems administrators, managers, and security professionals better protect their data and
systems.

```
http://csrc.nist.gov/
```

North American Cryptography Archives

```
http://www.cryptography.org/
```

Open Group Request for Comments

RFCs mostly relating to the distributed computing environment.

```
http://www.opengroup.org/rfc/
```

OPIE

One-Time Passwords in Everything by Craig Metz. Replacement UNIX programs that provide one-time password user authentication.

```
http://inner.net/opie/
```

OTP Working Group

Source of OTP-related documents and information.

```
http://www.ietf.org/html.charters/otp-charter.html
```

PAM Information

```
http://linux.kernel.org/pub/linux/libs/pam/
```

PGP Commercial (USA)

```
http://www.pgp.com/
```

PGP Freeware (USA)

```
http://web.mit.edu/network/pgp.html
```

PGP from GNU

```
http://www.gnupg.org/gnupg.html
```

PGP International

```
http://www.pgpi.com/
```

Postfix

Information about the postfix MTA (mail transfer agent).

```
http://www.postfix.org/
```

Psionic

Free security software and advice.

```
http://www.psionic.com/
```

Red Hat Linux

```
http://www.redhat.com/
http://www.redhat.com/support/
http://www.redhat.com/news/lwn/weekly.security.html:
ftp://updates.redhat.com/
```

The Risks Forum

Digest of security and other risks in computing. Also provides information on the Risks mailing list, searching the Risks archives, and the USENET Risks newsgroup.

```
http://catless.ncl.ac.uk/Risks/
```

SAGE

The System Administrators Guild, a technical group of the USENIX Association.

```
http://www.usenix.org/sage/
```

SANS

System Administration, Networking, and Security.

```
http://www.sans.org/
```

SANS Security Roadmap

A list of resources and tips related to site security.

```
http://sans.org/roadmap.htm
```

Secure Linux Projects

```
http://www.bastille-linux.org/
http://www.kha0s.org/
http://www.reseau.nl/securelinux/
```

Secure Programming FAQ

```
http://www.whitefang.com/sup/
```

Security Focus (and `bugtraq` Archive)

Hosts the `bugtraq` archive and mailing list; offers links to vendor security information, vulnerability advisories, and security news.

For the `bugtraq` Archives, choose `forums->bugtraq->archives` from the home page.

```
http://www.SecurityFocus.com/
```

sendmail

Good information about sendmail-related vulnerabilities.

```
http://www.sendmail.org/
```

S/KEY

Developed at Bellcore. One-time password system for UNIX.

```
http://www.ece.nwu.edu/CSEL/skey/skey_eccs.html
```

Slackware

```
ftp://cdrom.com/pub/linux/
```

slashdot

Linux and computing news.

```
http://www.slashdot.org/
```

SSH (Secure Shell)

Originally written by Tatu Ylonen, now maintained by SSH Communications Security and Data Fellows.

Commercial and free versions of software designed to be secure replacements for the r* tools. It can also do port forwarding and file transfers. It can be compiled with support for Wietse Wenema's TCP_wrappers program. The server runs on UNIX, and there are clients available for a growing list of operating systems.

```
http://www.ssh.fi/sshprotocols2/
```

S.u.S.E. Linux

```
http://www.suse.com/
http://www.suse.de/security/index.html
```

TrinityOS

Written and maintained by David A. Ranch, probably the most comprehensive general security resource on the web.

```
http://www.ecst.csuchico.edu/~dranch/TrinityOS.wri
```

UNIXPower

Lots of UNIX resources.

    http://www.unixpower.org/security/

USENET FAQs

An archive of frequently asked questions on many subjects.

    http://www.cis.ohio-state.edu/hypertext/faq/usenet/FAQ-List.html

USENIX

The Advanced Computing Systems Administration.

    http://www.usenix.org/

xinetd

Configurable replacement or enhancement for inetd.

    http://synack.net/xinetd/

FULL DISCLOSURE RESOURCES

The following sites publish details of various vulnerabilities. This is a sample of the kind of information that intruders may already know about breaking into your site.

8lgm

Exploits, references, intrusion database, and suggested defenses.

    http://www.8lgm.org/

COAST

There is also a list of underground sites at

    http://www.cs.purdue.edu/coast/hotlist/

Infilsec

Vulnerabilities and exploits for a variety of operating systems.

    http://www.infilsec.com/

Insecure.org

Port scanners, exploits, and computer security-related publications.

```
http://www.insecure.org/
```

L0pht Heavy Industries

Full disclosure security bulletins, tools, and other resources.

```
http://www.l0pht.com/
```

Phrack

Underground magazine.

```
http://www.phrack.com/
```

Rootshell

Full disclosure exploits, security news, and documentation.

```
http://www.rootshell.com/
```

MAILING LISTS

Mailing lists are usually a great way to keep up to date. Please note addresses to be used for subscription and unsubscription requests, and do not mail the entire list. People will yell at you. When you subscribe, save the directions that are mailed to you—they usually tell you how to unsubscribe.

Digest lists are sometimes available when the regular list has a lot of traffic. A digest usually consists of a collection of messages. With digest lists, the subscriber usually receives a digest either each day or when the collection of accumulated messages reaches a certain threshold in size.

In most cases, you can specify the address to which you wish to subscribe to permit, for example, a *reflector* list at your site. (Reflector lists allow one message to be sent from the list host, cutting down on CPU and network traffic; they also allow local management of list subscribers.)

There is usually a special address to which you can send mail if you are having list-related problems. Try "listname-owner" or check on a related web site.

`bugtraq`

Up-to-date reports on recent vulnerabilities in UNIX and Linux.

To subscribe, mail `listserv@securityfocus.com` with `subscribe bugtraq your_e-mail_address` in the subject of the message.

CERT Advisories Mailing List

Advisories, summaries, and vendor-initiated bulletins.

To subscribe, mail `cert-advisory-request@cert.org` with `subscribe your-email-address` in the subject of the message.

CFS Mailing List

For users of the Cryptographic File System.

To subscribe, mail `cfs-users-request@nsa.research.att.com` with `subscribe` in the subject of the message.

CIAC Advisories Mailing List

CIAC Information Bulletins and Advisory Notices contain important, time-critical computer security information.

To subscribe, mail `majordomo@rumpole.llnl.gov` with `subscribe ciac-bulletin` in the subject of the message.

Debian-Security Mailing List

To subscribe, mail `debian-security-announce-REQUEST@lists.debian.org` with `subscribe` in the subject of the message.

`exploit-dev` Mailing List

Full disclosure list devoted to discussion of potential exploits.

To subscribe, mail `listserv@securityfocus.com` with `subscribe exploit-dev Firstname Lastname` in the subject of the message.

`fwconfig` Mailing List

Sign up for the mailing list on the web page at `http://www.mindstorm.com/~sparlin/fwconfig.shtml`.

Incidents Mailing List

Discussion of security incidents.

To subscribe, mail `listserv@securityfocus.com` with `subscribe incidents Firstname Lastname` in the subject of the message.

Intrusion Detection Systems

Discussions about methods of intrusion or intrusion detection.

To subscribe, mail `majordomo@uow.edu.au` with `subscribe ids` in the subject of the message.

`ipchains` Mailing List

Mailing list for bug reports, discussion, development, and usage.

To subscribe, mail `ipchains-request@rustcorp.com` with `subscribe` in the subject of the message.

ISS Mailing List

ISS hosts several mailing lists. See the information on the ISS alert, secnews, or nsa mailing lists, or see their web page for more choices (`http://xforce.iss.net/maillists/`).

ISS `alert` Mailing List   Product announcements and updates, new vulnerabilities and exploits, etc.

To subscribe, mail `majordomo@iss.net` with `subscribe alert` in the subject of the message.

ISS `secnews` Mailing List   Moderated list for people interested in receiving the latest information on network security events and news announcements including press releases and security conferences.

To subscribe, mail `majordomo@iss.net` with `subscribe secnews` in the subject of the message.

ISS `nsa` Mailing List   Discussion of assessment, vulnerability checks, implementation of policy, etc.

To subscribe, mail `majordomo@iss.net` with `subscribe nsa` in the subject of the message.

`lasg` (Linux Administrators Security Guide) Mailing List

To subscribe, mail `majordomo@lists.seifried.org` with `subscribe lasg-announce` in the subject of the message.

Mandrake Mailing List

See `http://www.linux-mandrake.com/en/flists.php3` for information on several mailing lists.

Redhat Linux Security

To subscribe, mail `linux-security-request@redhat.com` with `subscribe` in the subject of the message.

`rootshell` Mailing List

Announcements and exploits of UNIX vulnerabilities.

     To subscribe, mail `majordomo@rootshell.com` with `subscribe announce` in the subject of the message.

     `rootshell` mailing list archives are at `http://www.rootshell.com/mailinglist-archive`

RPM Mailing List

Excellent list; recommended.

     To subscribe, mail `rpm-list-request@redhat.com` with `subscribe` in the subject of the message.

SANS Network Security Digest

Monthly newsletter highlighting recent vulnerabilities and providing security references for more information.

     To subscribe, mail `digest@sans.org` with `subscribe network security digest` in the subject of the message.

`security-audit` Mailing List

This list is for discussion of the auditing and hardening of the security of the Linux OS in a more systematic way. Not for exploits.

     To subscribe, mail `security-audit-subscribe@ferret.lmh.ox.ac.uk`.

Sneakers Mailing List

Firewalls and general security. Reserved for lawful tests and techniques.

     To subscribe, mail `Sneakers-Request@CS.Yale.EDU` with `subscribe` in the subject of the message.

SSH Users Mailing List

For users of `ssh`.

     To subscribe, mail `majordomo@clinet.fi` with `subscribe ssh` in the subject of the message.

`sudo` Mailing List

Mailing list for users of `sudo`.

To subscribe, mail `majordomo@cs.colorado.edu` with `subscribe sudo-users` in the subject of the message.

SuSE Mailing List

Visit the home page for instructions on subscribing.

```
http://www.suse.com/Mailinglists/index.html
```

TCFS Mailing List

For users of the Transparent Cryptographic File System.

```
tcfslist@mikonos.dia.unisa.it
```

To subscribe, mail `majordomo@edu-gw.dia.unisa.it` with `subscribe` in the subject of the message.

`tiger` Mailing List

Questions, answers, and announcements about the `tiger` auditing tool.

To subscribe, mail `tiger-request@net.tamu.edu` with `subscribe` in the subject of the message.

USENET NEWSGROUPS

```
comp.mail.sendmail
comp.os.linux.networking
comp.os.linux.security
comp.security.ssh
comp.security.unix
```

Tools Not Covered

There are a lot of good tools out there, but we didn't have time to write about everything. Here we provide references to some of the tools we thought you might want to check out on your own.

AAFID (Autonomous Agents for Intrusion Detection)

Eugene Spafford & Diego Zamboni

A set of small tools and an infrastructure that can be used to provide distributed monitoring and intrusion detection on a network of hosts. The code is written in Perl 5.

Home page:

```
http://www.cs.purdue.edu/coast/projects/autonomous-agents.html
```

FTP site:

```
ftp://coast.cs.purdue.edu/pub/COAST/tools/AAFID/
```

FreeSwan

Team Effort.

Free version of Secure Wide Area Networking, provides IPsec and IKE for Linux. FreeSwan provides authentication and encryption services, enabling you to build virtual private networks. This allows you to create secure communications over an insecure network. Learn more at

> `http://www.xs4all.nl/~freeswan/`

fwconfig

Sonny Parlin
> Provides a GUI front-end to writing `ipchains` rules.

> `http://www.mindstorm.com/~sparlin/fwconfig.html`

FWTK (Firewall Toolkit)

Network Associate's commercial firewall designed to run on UNIX systems.

> `http://www.tis.com/research/software/`

Mason

William Stearns wrote this tool that helps you interactively generate firewall rules dynamically.

> `http://users.dhp.com/~whisper/mason/`

Merlin

Created by CIAC. Extensible GUI interface to security tools such as SPI-Net, `tiger`, COPS, Crack, and Tripwire. Written in Perl. Nice interface for reading reports produced by the tools.

> `http://ciac.llnl.gov/ciac/ToolsUnixSysMon.html#Merlin`

nessus

Renaud Deraison
> Modular port scanner for several varieties of UNIX.

> `http://www.nessus.org/`

netfilter

Rusty Russell
> Replacement for `ipchains` in kernel version 2.3.x.

> `http://www.rustcorp.com/linux/netfilter/`

nfsbug

Leendert van Doorn
> C code to locate NFS misconfigurations and bugs that can lead to unauthorized access.

> `ftp://coast.cs.purdue.edu/pub/tools/unix/nfsbug/`

nfstrace

Matt Blaze
> Toolkit for monitoring ethernet traffic and collecting NFS activity information.

> `ftp://coast.cs.purdue.edu/pub/tools/unix/nfstrace/`

nfswatch

David Curry and Jeff Mogul
> Monitors and provides statistics on NFS traffic.

> `ftp://ftp.ers.ibm.com/pub/davy/`

nmap (Network Mapper)

Fyodor
> Port scanner. Generates a variety of different types of packets (ICMP, UDP, TCP, `ftp`, etc.). Can be used to test your firewall.

> `http://www.insecure.org/`

SHADOW (Secondary Heuristic Analysis for Defensive Online Warfare)

Naval Surface Warfare Center
> Intrusion detection software. Allows you to collect and analyze data with the help of `tcpdump`, `libpcap`, and configurable filters. Comes ready to recognize a variety of attack signatures.

> `http://www.nswc.navy.mil/ISSEC/CID/`

SOCKSv5

SOCKSv5 is an industry standard (RFC1828). SOCKSv5 can be used to create a firewall.

> `http://www.socks5.nec.com/`

SSLeay

Eric Young's Secure Socket Layer and supporting libraries.

```
ftp://ftp.psy.uq.oz.au/pub/Crypto/SSL/
```

Glossary

acceptable use policy (AUP)   A policy describing expected behavior of a user who has an account on a system. AUPs may list activities that are specifically not allowed, such as distribution of unsolicited commercial e-mail, unauthorized access, etc., that may result in termination of the account.

bugtraq archive   The collection of messages previously sent to the bugtraq mailing list, a full-disclosure UNIX security list. See Appendix A.

C program   The C language is a popular systems programming language. It was originally developed by Ken Thompson and Dennis Ritchie.

CERT   An organization that can provide help recovering from or preventing computer intrusions.

Computer Security Institute (CSI)   A company that provides service and training for network, information, and computer security professionals.

CPU   Used to stand for central processing unit, now it can refer to one or more processors on a computer. Performs computations and controls other components of the computer.

Crack   A program designed to guess hashed UNIX passwords by iteratively generating a guess, hashing it, and comparing it to the target. If they match, the password has been guessed.

Cryptographic File System (CFS)   A filesystem on which the stored files are encrypted or decrypted once the user authenticates.

D

daemon   A program running in the background on a UNIX system, accepting requests on a port, named pipe, or UNIX domain socket, to provide some service.

DMZ   Demilitarized zone. One or more secured hosts that are logically between an internal network and external network. This is a protected area and an additional buffer to prevent unauthorized access.

DNS   Domain name service. A distributed, hierarchical system that exists to provide mapping between named items and typed data.

DSL   Digital subscriber line. Technology that allows faster transmission rates to be obtained over regular telephone lines.

F

Federal Bureau of Investigation (FBI)   Principal investigative arm of the U.S. Department of Justice. It can also provide services and training to other law enforcement agencies in the United States.

File Transfer Protocol (FTP)   Protocol used to transfer files from one computer to another.

Firewall   Used to restrict or prevent access from one computer system to another.

ftp   *See* File Transfer Protocol.

G

gecos field   A field in the password file containing information about the UID, such as the user's name.

GNU   GNU's Not UNIX. A Free Software Foundation project to produce a complete and freely available version of the UNIX operating system and utilities.

GPL   GNU General Public License. The copyleft, it spells out the licensing details of GNU and other software distributed under the GPL.

graphical user interface (GUI)   Software that accepts input from a program displaying graphics and possibly accepting mouse input rather than from text on the command line.

group identification numbers (GID)   A number representing a particular UNIX group, used by the operating system and in programs. Usually /etc/ group provides a mapping between GIDs and group names.

H

Haval A one-way cryptographic hash function. It produces a variable-length hash.

HTTP HyperText Transfer Protocol. The protocol used to transfer most of the HTML documents around the web.

I

IDEA A block cipher algorithm operating on 64-bit data blocks using a 128-bit key. Originally used by PGP.

inetd A daemon that manages connections for a list of daemons found in inetd.conf. inetd listens for connection requests and will spawn the daemon.

Internet Protocol Security (IPsec) A protocol designed to provide authentication and confidentiality (encryption) for IPv6. While it is required to be supported, it is not required to be used. There is some support for IPv4.

L

LILO Linux loader. Used to boot the Linux kernel or another operating system.

logrotate Highly flexible set of C programs to manage log files.

M

MD5 RSA Data Security, Inc., MD5 message digest algorithm. A cryptographic hash algorithm that produces a 128-bit hash of a message.

N

Naval Research Laboratory (NRL) The Navy's corporate laboratory.

Network File System (NFS) A protocol that provides the ability to share data from one computer to another, transparently.

Network Information Service (NIS) A system that allows central management of services that may be shared by multiple machines, such as hostname information.

O

one-time password (OTP)   A password system in which a supply of passwords are provided to be used only one time each. This prevents unauthorized access should the password be compromised.

One-time passwords in everything (OPIE)   A set of replacement programs for UNIX to support one-time passwords.

Open Group   A group dedicated to promoting integration of technology within and between enterprises. Formed in a merger with OSF and X/Open.

Open Software Foundation (OSF)   Formed in 1988 to promote the development of open (free) software. Now a division of the Open Group.

P

partition   A subsection of a disk.

password database library (pwdb library)   A library of routines that allow configurable access to and management of /etc/passwd, /etc/shadow, and network authentication systems including NIS and Radius.

path   An environment variable used by shells and other programs containing a list of directories to be searched in order when an unqualified command is referenced.

Perl   A powerful, free programming language.

PGP signature   A cryptographic hash of a file, created with PGP.

pluggable authentication modules (PAM)   Authentication modules provide a number of different ways in which a user may be authenticated.

Point-to-Point Protocol (PPP)   Allows you to send protocols such as IP or IPX over a serial connection. Supports authentication and many options.

portmapper   Daemon that provides mapping between the port on which an RPC program is listening and the program number used by that RPC program. A process attempting to communicate with an RPC program contacts the portmapper to get this information.

Pretty Good Privacy (PGP)   A collection of utilities to generate signatures of files, provide encryption, and perform key management. Originally designed by Philip Zimmermann.

process identifier (PID)   A number associated with a process running on the system. Assigned by the kernel and will be reused when the process terminates.

R

RADIUS Remote authentication dial-in user service. Provides authentication and accounting information. Typically used with PPP servers but is also being applied to other services. Described in RFC 2138 and RFC 2139. There are several free implementations available.

RAM Random access memory. Fast memory that holds parts of the operating system and data currently being used.

RFC Request for comments. A proposal for an Internet standard or an informational document, written by a committee and subject to review. After a period of review, a proposal may become an Internet Standard.

risk analysis The process of analyzing a system for weaknesses in data integrity, availability, and confidentiality.

rlogin A command that allows users to gain remote access to a UNIX system. Considered to be an insecure protocol.

RSA Public key cryptosystem developed by Rivest, Shamir, and Adleman. The RSA algorithm keys use numbers that are computationally difficult to factor.

rsh Remote shell. A program that allows execution of a command on a remote UNIX machine. Many people do not allow the r-commands to be used on their systems because of problems with the security model.

S

SAMBA A program that provides Microsoft file sharing service (SMB) on a UNIX machine. It provides both client and server support.

Secure Shell (SSH) A secure replacement for the r-commands.

secure socket layer (SSL) A collection of protocols that implement encryption tunnels at the Transport layer.

server message block (SMB) Also session message block. The Microsoft protocol used for file sharing.

SGID Set group identifier. A SGID program runs with effective group permissions of the group to which the file belongs.

SHA-1 A cryptographic hash algorithm designed by NIST and NSA. Produces a 160-bit hash.

shadow file A non-world-readable file that contains encrypted passwords and information about password expiration.

signature file A file containing the cryptographic hash of another file. Used to verify the authenticity and integrity of the original file. In the case of `tiger`, signature files contain multiple signatures along with the name of the file with which the signature is associated.

Snefru A one-way cryptographic hash function. Messages are hashed into 128- or 256-bit values.

standard password format (SPF) A format used by many UNIX operating systems, wherein each field in order contains the value of a prescribed piece of information.

SUID (Set User Identifier) An SUID program runs with the effective permissions of the owner of the file.

superuser do (`sudo`) A program that provides configurable, controlled root privileges and an audit trail of which commands were executed by whom.

`syslog` A daemon that accepts messages from other processes and logs them to a file or the console window if the level and facility of the message match or exceed those specified in the syslog configuration file.

T

TCP Transmission Control Protocol. A connection-oriented networking protocol.

TCP_wrappers A set of programs that provide extensive logging and authorization control over programs compiled with `libwrap` or those started from `inetd`.

`telnet` A program that allows users to log in from one computer to a remote computer.

Transparent Cryptographic File System (TCFS) Similar to CFS, but implemented as a kernel module.

Tripwire A utility to record fingerprints of UNIX files and to notify you if anything changes.

U

UDP User Datagram Protocol. A connectionless networking protocol.

UNIX A popular operating system developed by Ken Thompson and Dennis Ritchie.

user identification number (UID)   A number representing a particular user name. Used by the kernel and other programs. /etc/password provides mapping between the number and the name.

X

xinetd   A more secure replacement for inetd.

Back | Forward | Home | Reload | Images | Open | Print | Find | Stop

http://www.phptr.com/

What's New? | What's Cool? | Destinations | Net Search | People | Software

PRENTICE HALL

Professional Technical Reference
Tomorrow's Solutions for Today's Professionals.

Keep Up-to-Date with

PH PTR Online!

We strive to stay on the cutting-edge of what's happening in professional computer science and engineering. Here's a bit of what you'll find when you stop by **www.phptr.com**:

@ Special interest areas offering our latest books, book series, software, features of the month, related links and other useful information to help you get the job done.

Deals, deals, deals! Come to our promotions section for the latest bargains offered to you exclusively from our retailers.

$ Need to find a bookstore? Chances are, there's a bookseller near you that carries a broad selection of PTR titles. Locate a Magnet bookstore near you at www.phptr.com.

! What's New at PH PTR? We don't just publish books for the professional community, we're a part of it. Check out our convention schedule, join an author chat, get the latest reviews and press releases on topics of interest to you.

✉ Subscribe Today! Join PH PTR's monthly email newsletter!

Want to be kept up-to-date on your area of interest? Choose a targeted category on our website, and we'll keep you informed of the latest PH PTR products, author events, reviews and conferences in your interest area.

Visit our mailroom to subscribe today! **http://www.phptr.com/mail_lists**